ROAD TO EKATERINBURG

Nicholas and Alexandra's Daughters 1913-1918

ROAD TO
EKATERINBURG

NICHOLAS AND ALEXANDRA'S DAUGHTERS 1913-1918

E C S BANKS

SilverWood

Dedicated to my late father, Owen

Published in 2012 by the author using SilverWood Books Empowered Publishing®
30 Queen Charlotte Street, Bristol BS1 4HJ
www.silverwoodbooks.co.uk

Front cover shows the Grand Duchesses Marie, Tatiana and Olga (seated) 1915
Back cover shows Tatiana and Olga at tea in 1914; the Tsarina with Anastasia and Tatiana
during a carriage ride; and Tatiana dressed as a nurse pictured with her sister Anastasia
All photographs by kind permission of Beinecke Library, Yale University, unless otherwise stated

ISBN 978-1-78132-035-8

British Library Cataloguing in Publication Data
A CIP catalogue record for this book is available from the British Library

Set in Bembo by SilverWood Books
Printed in the UK by The Short Run Press
on paper certified as being from responsible sources

Acknowledgements

With my grateful thanks for the assistance of the British Library at Boston Spa, countless British record offices, libraries and art galleries, and Yale University (for the photographs). The books are based on thirty years of the author's own historical and genealogical research. These books are factual and not in any way fictional. They are part of a series of six books written by ECS Banks for the Grand Duchesses Olga, Tatiana, Marie and Anastasia. This is their own story told by those who knew them and largely by themselves. The words are entirely mine, but it is their story told by myself with full explanations of their personal narratives and commonplace books. This has never been done before and will probably never be done satisfactorily again.

This is a work written as a novel but one that includes the facts. Unlike most academics, I do not intend to throw facts at the unfortunate reader and expect them to work out the story for themselves. I have read extensively the works of Charles Dickens, WM Thackeray, the Bronte sisters, Jane Austen and John Wyndham, and even the works of Florence Barclay – the Grand Duchesses Tatiana's and Marie's favourite author. I have read the books the Grand Duchesses read including Sir Walter Scott, Count Leo Tolstoy and George MacDonald in an effort to understand their characters. I have listened to the music they played and studied their works of art. It is a wholehearted attempt to understand their thoughts and the people that influenced them.

I have also studied the history of the era extensively and, even as a small child, insisted on reading books on Queen Victoria's family, architecture and modern history. I borrowed my mother's library tickets and generally read fourteen books a fortnight – the maximum I could contrive to borrow. My father had to carry this huge load and constantly complained that I always had to borrow the largest books each time. He would have greatly appreciated the new Kindle which has made studying books far easier and lighter. I quickly discovered how to order books from the 1920s as I disliked the more modern works on the whole and always went back to the original source. I also greatly disliked the inaccurate books I often found and the ones that relied heavily on the work of others and liberally repeated the mistakes of others. To me, the Queen was Queen Victoria although I have lived my entire life under the reign of Her Majesty Queen Elizabeth II of course.

The first draft of the six volumes was completed in December 2007; the second draft of the first four books (including these two) was completed in December 2011; and the last two were in their second draft by the spring of 2012. The six books were written in reverse order much like the Tsarina's favourite opera *The Ring Cycle* by Wagner as I feel that it is a far better way to see how each generation was influenced by the actions of the previous. Every action has a reaction. Books five and six no longer exist apart from in the original form.

With special thanks to Colin for all his care and attention in caring for me during my recovery from cancer and eight subsequent operations and countless serious complications; to my dedicated GP and friend Omar; to my excellent surgeon Rick; and my friend, physio and fellow ballet enthusiast Kath. For all those who tried to stop me publishing these books thanks for giving me extra reasons to complete the work. I would like to thank my wonderful Publishing Director Helen for her time and patience, and to my excellent proofreader Carol.

The author would like to thank all those at SilverWood Books for their assistance in the publishing of this book. I would also like to thank Murray Gold for the soundtrack to my work; his music was an excellent accompaniment to my writing. The earlier work (naturally begun in the 1970s) was done to the accompaniment of Sir Edward Elgar's little known *Nursery Suite* written for the young Princesses Elizabeth and Margaret; the famous *1812 Overture* by Tchaikovsky and various other composers including Prokoviev. The music of the Russian ballets was the most common general theme and yet I adore the music of Shirley Manson and Debbie Harry. The words of Shirley's song *Right Between the Eyes* are my comment to all who attempt to bully anyone. My final thanks are naturally to my translator who wished to remain anonymous: the late 'Emma' R. The books are of course respectfully dedicated to His Imperial Majesty Tsar Nicholas II of Russia; the Tsarina Alexandra; the Grand Duchesses Olga, Tatiana, Marie and Anastasia Nicolaevna and the Tsarevich Alexei Nicolaevich; Klementy Nagorny; Countess Anastasia Hendrikova; Mlle Catherine Schneider and all the others who died with the Imperial family including the man 'who was the Doctor' – maybe Time can be re-written!

ECS Banks
April 2nd, 2012

PLATES

All photographs by kind permission of Beinecke Library, Yale University, unless otherwise stated.

First page – The Grand Duchesses Olga and Marie on the balcony of the Alexander Palace, Tsarskoe Selo, 1913

Second page top – The Grand Duchess Olga, the Tsar Nicholas II of Russia, Nicholas Rodionov and Paul Voronov

Second page bottom – The Grand Duchess Tatiana with the Tsarina Alexandra after she had typhoid, 1913

Third page top – The Grand Duchess Tatiana on board the Imperial yacht *Standart*

Third page bottom – The Tsar and Tsarina at tea with Anya Vyrubova (foreground), Tatiana and Olga (far left), Marie (centre), Anastasia (standing), Nicholas Sablin (centre), 1914

Fourth page – The Grand Duchesses Marie, Tatiana, Anastasia and Olga with their cameras, 1914

Fifth page top – The Grand Duchesses Tatiana and Olga, 1914

Fifth page bottom – The Tsar and Tsarina with Anastasia, Olga and at right Tatiana, Marie and Anya Vyrubova at tea, 1914

Sixth page top – The Tsar and Tsarina at tea with Anastasia, Olga, Tatiana, Sablin (foreground) and Anya Vyrubova, 1914

Sixth page bottom –The Grand Duchess Olga with her godchild, niece of Anya Vyrubova

Seventh page – Anya Vyrubova and Grand Duchess Olga, 1915

Eighth page – The Grand Duchesses Anastasia, Tatiana, Marie and Olga (left to right) with the Tsarina Alexandra, 1916

Ninth page –The Grand Duchesses Olga, Tatiana and Marie on the Imperial yacht, *Standart*

Tenth page top – The Tsar and Tsarina with (left to right) Marie (hidden), Olga, Anastasia (front) and Tatiana

Tenth page bottom – The Grand Duchess Olga (back 2nd to right) and Tatiana (seated)

Eleventh page top – The Tsarina and Grand Duchess Olga and Anya Vyrubova, Grand Duchess Tatiana in front as nurses at their infirmary

Eleventh page bottom – The Tsarina (seated) with Olga and Tatiana (near door) and Anya Vyrubova (to right of Tsarina) with patients and staff at their infirmary

Twelfth page – The Grand Duchesses Marie and Anastasia at their infirmary

Thirteenth page – The Tsar at Tobolsk with Olga (left), Anastasia and Tatiana on the roof of the greenhouse at the Governor's house at Tobolsk

Fourteenth page – Marie (left) with Tatiana (back) and Olga (seated), June 1915

Fifteenth page top – Livadia Palace, 1942 (Photo from the author's own collection)

Fifteenth page bottom – Massandra, near Livadia Palace, 1942 (Photo from the author's own collection)

Sixteenth page – 2,000 year-old statue of a nymph from Livadia, which has since vanished (Photo from the author's own collection)

Seventeenth page – Ai-Petri in the Crimea where the Tsar often walked (Photo from the author's own collection)

Eighteenth page top – View of Yalta from Livadia Palace, 1942 (Photo from the author's own collection)

Eighteenth page bottom – Livadia Palace, 1942 (Photo from the author's own collection)

Introduction

This is the real-life story of the four daughters of the last Tsar of Russia. Set in Russia between 1913 and 1918, it is the true story of the Grand Duchess Anastasia and her older sisters Olga, Tatiana and Marie. It shows how their lives were transformed from over-protected teenagers to nurses during the First World War, through revolution, imprisonment and ultimately murder, ending in a finale worthy of the Keystone Kops – when the bodies were moved several times under the most ridiculous circumstances. It has the usual conflict and interplay between four very different teenage sisters and their mother who spent her days *resting* on the sofa continually exhausted from doing very little.

The story starts in early 1913 in the run-up to the Tercentenary (300th anniversary) of Romanov rule and the eighteenth birthday of the Tsar's oldest and favourite daughter Olga. She had a doomed shipboard romance with a sailor on her father's yacht followed swiftly by and his sudden marriage to a suitable young lady.

The outbreak of war in 1914 brings the Tsar into conflict with his own near relatives, and his wife and daughters turned to nursing. The Tsarina was a strict mother but, between nursing wounded soldiers and her own ailments, her elder daughters gradually slipped away to spend more and more time with not only their commoner friends but also with young soldiers.

The revolution in 1917 puts a stop to any newly found freedoms the girls enjoyed. The family were imprisoned within the palace and were only allowed out into their gardens by permission of the officer in charge. They spent their time growing vegetables outside but, by the late summer of 1917, the former Imperial family were transported into exile in Siberia where conditions deteriorated further, on an almost daily basis.

Just when they were starting to get used to the new regime at Tobolsk, they were ordered to move again, but this time the family were split up temporarily when the son became seriously ill and could not be moved.

The conditions of the final place of imprisonment (named the *House of Special Purpose* or Ipatiev House) were worse still, though the daughters attempted to make friends with their soldier guards. They had, all their lives, been surrounded by soldiers but soon the guards were changed into hardened revolutionaries and former factory workers rather than actual soldiers.

Olga's character changed dramatically in the final years and she became quieter and more and more religious. Marie remained the same outgoing, down-to-earth girl she had always been and she eventually influenced the behaviour of Tatiana and Anastasia and she became the leader of the pack of girls rather than the victim of their bullying as she had as a small child.

They were murdered, along with their parents, brother and servants in July 1918 and it is only in recent years (2008) that the body of Anastasia was finally found along with that of her brother Alexis, the others having been found originally in 1979.

Although many books have been written about the Tsar and Tsarina, and Anastasia's story has been made into a cartoon and famous fictional movie (with Ingrid Bergman in 1956), the portraits of the four Grand Duchesses have always been entirely fictional. No one has actually written the story of the Grand Duchesses.

They are of course Grand Duchesses, not Princesses or Grand Princesses. That last word on the subject is given to the late Tsar's sister Olga Alexandrovna (obviously herself the daughter of an Emperor). When asked once by a little girl when she was living in Canada if she really was a princess, the outraged Olga had replied that she certainly was not a princess; she was a grand duchess. These same words were repeated in her excellent biography by Ian Vorres.

Little was really known about the lives of the Tsar of Russia's daughters – there was far more known about the manner of their deaths. It was not until Glasnost that the letters and diaries of the girls began to slowly emerge in print in the West and yet guarded by the archives more assiduously than the girls had been in their own restricted lives.

The Grand Duchesses were seen as angelic, with the possible exception of Anastasia. Even when photographs were published in books clearly showing them smoking cigarettes, it was nearly always ignored as if they could not possibly have smoked! The four Grand Duchesses were no angels, and were much the same as girls of today from a privileged background. They played tennis, rode horses and bicycles, swam in the sea, took photographs, went for long walks and did needlework.

However, they played tennis and rode bicycles within the rooms and corridors of the Alexander Palace itself, with no concern for any damage created. Marie and Anastasia played loud music in their bedroom, when their mother was having a meeting in a room directly below them. Olga deliberately smashed glass in windows and broke a table. She and Anastasia often admitted to cheating at games.

It was often stated that one of the Grand Duchesses would stay behind *on duty* looking after their sick mother, whilst their three sisters went for a walk or visited somewhere else, but it is clear that Olga preferred to stay with her mother to enable her to be near her current favourite male friend. The girls were often ill with minor ailments and, with four teenage daughters it was inevitable that at any time one or more of them would either have a slight cold, sprained ankle or period pains, which meant they would stay behind.

The Grand Duchesses were all very human and this is their story from 1913 to 1918. It shows the usual everyday lives of the Grand Duchesses and their parents, the Tsar and Tsarina of Russia, and their younger brother, the Tsarevich, and how normal life was never the same from the summer of 1914 until their untimely deaths in the summer of 1918.

The Russian calendar was thirteen days behind that of the rest of Europe until 1918. As a result the Christmas seems unusually late in Russia. (The term *versts* for example is an obsolete form of measuring a distance. One *verst* was equal to 500 *sazhen* or 3,500 feet.)

Chapter One

New Year 1913

The Tsar of Russia, Nicholas II, traditionally spent the first day of the year in Russia's capital St Petersburg at the breaking of the Neva ice ceremony but would then return home to the Alexander Palace. The British Ambassador, Sir George Buchanan, felt that Nicholas longed to take part in the social whirl of activities as other members of society and even his own sisters did. When, one year, Nicholas heard from his sisters Xenia and Olga that the Ambassador was holding a party with dancing afterwards, he exclaimed that it would be fun. The Ambassador dearly wanted to invite the Tsar to the party but knew it would be pointless as he knew that the Tsar and his wife rarely attended such events.

Nicholas and Alexandra (known as Alix) lived in a rather isolated world where they saw few people except the aged Minister of the Imperial Court, Count Fredericks, the Tsarina's confidante, the eternally unpopular Anya Vyrubova, and those aides-de-camp and ladies-in-waiting who were currently on duty. Unlike the Tsar's widowed mother the Dowager Empress, they did not attend parties and balls unless it was absolutely necessary and it was a fait accompli that Alexandra would leave early with the excuse of a headache or *feeling tired*. (Alexandra categorised the severity of heart pains she suffered on a scale of 1 to 3 but, despite tests made a few years before, no heart problems had ever been discovered.) It is possible that she was suffering from high blood pressure which would, untreated, give some of the symptoms she continually complained of. She also may well have suffered from a thyroid hormone condition, something her late mother Alice seemed to have suffered as her letters to the Queen show often.

Alix was continually tired; had a high pulse rate (up to 100 on occasions); she complained of swollen feet at times; ate little but never lost weight; she slept badly; was unable to walk any distance, yet if she rested all day by the end of the day she appeared to improve, sometimes quite dramatically. She took *adonis vernalis* a homeopathic remedy in order to regulate her pulse. It could well indicate that she had a rare form of high thyroid that can in some cases lead to 'atrial fibrillation' which would fit with all these symptoms. It can spontaneously occur in patients despite them previously suffering for several years with low levels of the hormone. As it is rarely understood in the 2000s, it is likely it was not discovered during her lifetime but would have confirmed her complaints of heart problems were quite genuine.

By 1913, the Tsarina was almost totally exhausted as the previous autumn her beloved son had almost died and she had given herself up totally in an effort to aid his recovery. She was desperate for rest and longed for peace and quiet but, as the Tercentenary approached, it was inevitable that she would have to go out in public and travel long distances; something that she hated. She preferred to stay at home and had never been outgoing since the death of her mother when she was six. Their daughters, however, longed to attend parties but usually only went to those organised by their aunt Olga Alexandrovna, sister of Nicholas II, on a Sunday afternoon, or the impromptu events organised by Madame Vyrubova.

The Tsar was (unlike his wife Alexandra) extremely social but had few occasions to socialise. He had a remarkable memory and could remember soldiers he had met many years before at military occasions. His daughter Marie appeared to have inherited his gift as her former Irish-born nanny Margaretta Eager later hinted. The young Grand Duchess watched out for people who passed by the palace and appeared to remember where she had seen each of them before, if they looked familiar to her. She termed those she recognised as her friends and, according to Miss Eager, she was always right. Marie had what was known as the royal memory for faces.

It also shows how desperate the child was for friends.

As the New Year of 1913 began, there seemed little hope of changes in the lives of Nicholas, his wife Alexandra, or their five children – Olga (17), Tatiana (15), Marie (13), Anastasia (11) and Alexei (8).

Most days were very much alike for the Imperial family. They routinely removed from one of their palaces to another at set times of the year. The earliest months of the year, any year, were spent at the Alexander Palace, in the village of Tsarskoe Selo, which of course means the Tsar's village. The Alexander Palace was within easy walking distance (for all but Alexandra) of the larger and more ornate Catherine Palace, simply known as the Big Palace to the children of the Tsar. The Catherine Palace was normally only used for official ceremonies and receptions, and was not the home of Nicholas and his family. They preferred the smaller and less formal Alexander Palace. The larger Catherine Palace had been built by the architect Rastelli in the reign of Empress Catherine, but the smaller Alexander Palace had been the work of Quarenghi and had been built on the orders of Empress Catherine the Great for her beloved grandson – Alexander I.

Nicholas and his wife, the former Princess Alix of Hesse, granddaughter of the late Queen Victoria and youngest surviving child of the late Princess Alice, had married in late 1894 and had decided to use the Alexander Palace as their main home. Alix became known as Alexandra Feodorovna. The second name or patronymic name is in the Russian Orthodox Church taken from the father's first name. Girls' names end for example Olga Nicolaevna and boys Alexei Nicolaevich but Alix's patronymic name derived in a different way. In Russia, the Emperor or Tsar usually married a foreign princess as she was given the second name Feodorovna which means something close to *gift of God*. Alexandra's mother-in-law was Marie Feodorovna. It is said that Alix had originally preferred the name Catherine but was talked out of it. Alexandra was the name of her aunt, the Princess of Wales and she had been nicknamed Alix, so the name was more logical than Catherine which had echoes of Catherine the Great.

Nicholas was particularly fond of the Palace as he had been born there and Alix had decorated the family wing of the palace to her own taste. It was not the sort of taste to endear her to society and yet it was lovingly created to form a family home. The furniture came from England and, like her late mother before her, Alix was determined to make her home as cosy as possible. It had sapphire and silver brocade curtains to cut out the inevitable draughts from the Russian winter and they were weighted down with lead. Once the young Tsarevich had the bright idea of cutting out the lead weights and succeeded in doing so.

Alice had married Prince Louis of Hesse in 1862 and she had built her own palace very much in the style of the houses she had known in England. The New Palace as it was known in Darmstadt, before it was destroyed during a bombing raid in the Second World War, had been built in the English style and many thought it reminded them of Buckingham Palace, but it also had aspects of Queen Victoria's seaside home at Osborne House in the Isle of Wight. After Alice's death, her youngest surviving child Alix, then aged six, (her sister Marie, aged four, had died of diphtheria weeks before Princess Alice in 1878) spent a great deal of time in the company of her beloved grandmother Queen Victoria and her late mother's sisters Helena, Louise and Beatrice, and, to a lesser extent, Victoria, the Princess Royal and later Empress of Germany. Alix, as a result of her upbringing, inherited many of the tastes of her grandmother. Although she was devoted to her widower father Louis, the Grand Duke of Hesse, he spent much time travelling between his various homes and Alix and her siblings were left in the company of servants and any of a number of visiting aunts, uncles and cousins.

Alix was determined to make her own home one where she felt *at home*. She wanted somewhere that reminded her of England and of the home her mother had created in Darmstadt. As she had lost her own mother and youngest sister when she was only six years old, Alix was determined to have as normal a family life as possible. Like her grandmother Queen Victoria, Alix was not fond of society and preferred to spend her time within the privacy of her own home with her own children.

Queen Victoria and her husband Prince Albert, the Prince Consort (1819–61), had decided that their nine children were in no need of friends. They felt that any such relationships would lead to trouble. The couple felt that, with five daughters and four sons, the children would be happy enough in their own company. After the death of the Queen's second daughter Alice (1843–78), the mother of Alix, the Queen continued this policy and was determined to keep her Hesse grandchildren away from other children as much as possible. The children had after all a great many cousins. Although Queen Victoria complained that she had too many grandchildren, none had as many children as she did.

To Alix, her cousins Louie and Thora (Princesses 'Marie'-Louise and Helena-Victoria of Schleswig-Holstein), daughters of her Aunt Helena, were as close as sisters. Louise even admitted as such many years later in her own biography. Alix's sisters Victoria, Elisabeth and Irene were all married before she reached the age of sixteen and she was often left in the company of her only surviving brother Ernie. (A second brother, the haemophiliac Frittie, had died in 1873 aged three, only a year after Alix's birth.) Alix was devastated after the death of her beloved father Louis, the Grand Duke of Hesse, in 1892. Before his death, he suffered from heart disease and was said to have an enlarged heart. Alix later convinced herself that she had inherited this illness and, despite various doctors attempting to tell her that she did not have this illness, she convinced herself that she was correct. As a result, she spent much of the day *resting* on a sofa in her famous Mauve Boudoir. On some days, she stayed in bed only to lie on the sofa in the afternoons. On more ambitious days, she sat on her balcony.

Alix sat on her balcony in all weathers. One thing she inherited from Queen Victoria was a dislike of heated rooms and she was quite content to sit on a chair on her balcony wrapped up in furs on a cold day. Alix was determined that her children, her four daughters in particular, would grow up in much the same way she had. She wanted her daughters to behave as perfect English Victorian young ladies but this was something that her daughters found difficult to adhere to. Whilst the Tsarina's second eldest daughter Tatiana was the most dutiful of all her children and the one most likely to remain at home with her adored mother when her sisters went outside into the garden on an afternoon with their father, her sisters were more inclined to rebel against her wishes. Olga was the most likely of all the girls to disagree with her mother. She had always been extremely close to her father. Just as Tatiana was the closest to her mother, Olga was the boon companion of her father Nicholas.

The days for the four Grand Duchesses and their brother were fairly monotonous and Olga in particular found everyday life irksome. According to one of her tutors, it was Olga who of the four girls was the one that always wore her heart on her sleeve. Tatiana on the other hand was determined to keep her feelings to herself and it was impossible to guess what she thought on any subject. Whilst Tatiana kept her mother company and pandered to her every whim, Olga preferred the company of her father.

The Grand Duchesses saw other young people of their own age very rarely. Only on Sundays and holidays did Olga and her younger siblings see much of their cousins and other children of similar social standing. The Tsar's sister the Grand Duchess Olga Alexandrovna was married by 1913 but had no children but her oldest sister the Grand Duchess Xenia, who had married a cousin, the Grand Duke Alexander, known generally as Sandro, had several children, most of whom were boys.

The Grand Duchess Xenia had married Sandro, a close friend of Nicholas II, barely months before Nicholas had married Alix and the two couples became parents in 1895. Xenia's first child had been a daughter – Princess Irina – and a few months later the Tsar's own first child was born. The baby was born in late 1895 and was known as Grand Duchess Olga Nicolaevna to distinguish her from her aunt of the same name. Nicolaevna simply means daughter of Nicholas just as Alexandrovna was daughter of Alexander, Alexander III of Russia being the father of Olga, Xenia and Nicholas.

In the coming years, as Xenia and Alix gradually increased their families, it became more and more difficult for the young Tsarina to cope with the fact that, as she continued to have daughter after daughter, Xenia after her initial daughter went on to have son after son. Their early closeness declined after the birth of Xenia's sons.

As a result, Alix did not wish to see Xenia's children on too regular a basis. When Alix finally did have a son in 1904, the child proved to be a haemophiliac which was naturally devastating for the parents. Alix felt guilty that it had been her who had transmitted the haemophilia to her only son. It could not have been entirely a surprise that he should have this malady as, only months before his birth, Alix's sister Irene (who had married Prince Henry of Prussia, a younger brother of the famous Kaiser William of Germany) had suffered a terrible blow as her youngest son Henry died as a result of an accident at the age of three and a half.

Henry was not the first child to suffer from haemophilia within Alix's family. Her brother Frittie had the same disease and died aged three as a result of a fall. Alix's favourite uncle Leopold whose presence so soothed the widower Louis in the months after Alice's death and who played endless card games with Alix also died as a result of the illness when Alix was almost twelve.

After the birth of Alexei and the discovery of his malady, Alix's main duty was to protect her son at all costs. He fell and bruised himself often as a child and in later years was constantly surrounded by one of two sailor nannies, Andrei Derevenko and his assistant Klementy Nagorny. They were permanently on duty to ensure the safety of Alexei. Luckily Derevenko had two young sons who became the occasional playmates for the child. Unfortunately they were younger than him and obviously not from the gentry so were influential in a way that made Alexei and his sister Anastasia, who spent many hours in the company of her brother, rather mischievous at times. As a result, they both had a habit of misbehaving at times.

Although Alix's sister Elisabeth had married Nicholas's uncle Grand Duke Serge Alexandrovich in 1884 and Nicholas and Alix had met on that day, in later years, despite living in the same country, Alix and Ella, as she was known, rarely met. Ella was a widow when this story begins in 1913. Her husband Serge had been assassinated in 1905 and Ella had started her own religious order working in Moscow with a close friend amongst the poor. She was in some ways continuing the work of her late mother, Princess Alice, who had met Florence Nightingale at Balmoral in the 1850s and was an excellent nurse.

Alix had little in common with her sister Ella who had been a particularly beautiful young woman and had been extremely popular in society. As things were now, Elisabeth was in no position to help Alix or even to see her often. She did sometimes appear at the Alexander Palace and often fell asleep in a chair whilst sitting and chatting to her nieces. It was only at the onset of the war that Alix took a nursing course and finally found her vocation. Tatiana too proved to be a good nurse. Sadly Olga was relegated to the storeroom, but she was happier there.

As 1913 began, life went on much as usual for the Grand Duchesses. The four sisters were known as the Big Pair and the Little Pair. Olga and Tatiana aged seventeen and fifteen at the beginning of 1913 shared a bedroom and a classroom. Marie and Anastasia, thirteen and eleven, did likewise. Alexei as the youngest child and the only son slept alone and worked alone. It was realised that it was a far better idea for Alexei to have a personal tutor with him at all times, keeping an eye on him and encouraging his education. So Pierre Gilliard, who had been the Grand Duchesses' French tutor, was assigned specially to this position. As a result, not only did Alexei's general behaviour improve but his French came on in leaps and bounds.

The sisters' bedrooms were similarly decorated, with camp beds for each of the children, dressing tables and couches with matching green and white cushions. The rooms each had a partition, which was used to give each girl an extra layer of privacy. The girls often moved their beds into the middle of the room in order to get more air in the summer months. The walls of the bedrooms were covered in various religious icons, paintings and photographs. The windows, which were barred for security for the girls, were also fitted with a form of secondary double glazing. The extra layer was taken in and out as the weather changed. They also had heated porcelain stoves in the rooms to add more heat. The windows were also said to contain a novel form of heating. The climate of Tsarskoe Selo could be either incredibly hot or terribly cold.

The Tsarina had decided against employing a French governess for her daughters as she felt that such a person would create a barrier between herself and the girls. As a result, although the girls all read French, they never were as capable as their brother in conversing in the language. He was able to chat to visiting French speakers unprompted during the war, something his sisters would not have had the confidence to do. Of the four sisters, Olga was by far the most intelligent and probably the only one who actually took some enjoyment in her lessons. Marie was inclined to be lazy and Anastasia although actually having some intelligence declined to exhibit it during lessons. Alexei was also fairly intelligent but he was ill too frequently to progress as he should have. Tatiana was not overly intelligent as her letters show. The letters of Tatiana and Marie contain copious spelling mistakes but Marie was probably the best actual writer of letters. She had the skill of entertaining the reader unlike Tatiana or indeed the Tsarina. The Tsarina's letters are enough to make the reader doubt their own sanity at times. She leapt from one subject to another in an almost random manner and had little idea of punctuation. My paragraphs remain short as many readers find long paragraphs impossible to understand, especially dyslexics.

Lessons for the five Imperial children began early in the morning. Each morning before their studies commenced the children were examined by Dr Botkin who took great care of their health. He returned at 6.30 each evening and saw the children after first seeing their mother. The girls were immensely fond of him. In 1913, they restarted their lessons after the Christmas holidays on the first Monday of the new year. Olga and her sister Tatiana studied together and their list of subjects was quite extensive. Unlike most children, they even had lessons on a Saturday morning. The range of subjects included English, mathematics, history, geography, French, Russian and German, music, drawing, dancing, religion, physics and physical exercises. Marie and Anastasia also studied together.

The Grand Duchesses went out into the garden after lunch in all weathers. They went out in sun, rain and even snowstorms. Olga and her two youngest sisters Marie and Anastasia were inclined to complain about the cold in later years but Tatiana never did. She was someone who never complained and did what she saw as her duty and many commentators saw her as rather haughty; something never attributed to any of her sisters. When the sisters went out into the garden, one of them generally remained in the company of the Tsarina who constantly complained of feeling unwell and had headaches frequently. She was prone to bad headaches possibly as a result of high blood pressure or migraines.

Marie appears to have been the second most likely of the sisters to remain with her mother. Olga and Anastasia were almost certain to go outside with the Tsar on an afternoon. If Nicholas visited the capital St Petersburg, he was accompanied not by his wife but by Olga, or Olga and Tatiana. There were many occasions when he went out in the company of all four of his daughters. Although Olga was at seventeen officially 'out', her sister Tatiana was not, but – as she was more confident in social situations than Olga was – the two often accompanied Nicholas.

Whilst the children continued their studies in their classrooms, Alix generally rested in her bedroom or sitting room and Nicholas got to work on an ever-mounting pile of paperwork. As an Absolute Monarch, he was responsible for everything, including dealing with divorce petitions, and spent endless hours at his desk. He did not even have a secretary, preferring to work alone and to seal his own envelopes. His late father had worked equally long hours at his desk and died at the age of forty-nine.

Nicholas attended endless receptions both at home at the Alexander Palace and at various venues in St Petersburg. It was the official capital but Nicholas preferred to live in Tsarskoe Selo away from the confines of the city. The Alexander Palace had an extensive park and plenty of room for exercise, and this is one of the main reasons he liked to stay there. After spending several hours at his desk in a morning, Nicholas liked to walk in the garden. He was accompanied by his dogs, his daughters and, on occasions, his sister Olga Alexandrovna. She visited the palace regularly at the weekend and, on Sunday, held parties for her nieces in her home. She invited people of their own age and must have been a godsend to the teenage girls. She was several years younger than her brother and Alix often stated that she saw Olga as an older sister of her own four daughters.

Nicholas was formerly a colonel in an army regiment and missed his army life after his marriage. He had to stop being a soldier in order to become Tsar. He would have had no time to remain an ordinary soldier. He was at his happiest when under army discipline and disliked giving orders. This was unfortunate as he was the Absolute Monarch of the vast Russian Empire. He delighted in visits to the military and frequently attended military parades and dinners. If it was appropriate, he took his five children along or one or two of them, depending on the circumstances. If there was a parade at the nearby Catherine Palace, Nicholas was often accompanied by his children. Nicholas's young son Alexei at eight years old was as fascinated by the military as his father was. Nicholas always wore a uniform unless he was travelling abroad on holiday. He liked to wear the uniform he thought appropriate for the occasion. Alexei wore a sailor suit as a child and, as war broke out, he went into military uniform.

The Grand Duchesses often accompanied their father to military parades and were friends with many of the soldiers, officers and Cossacks who guarded the Tsar and his family. A church had been built close to the Alexander Palace especially for the soldiers, and the Imperial family attended the regimental church often. The children were constantly surrounded by soldiers of all ages and the younger ones were the nearest in age to them of anyone who the girls saw on a regular basis, so inevitably they became friendly with the men.

Each of the Grand Duchesses was appointed as Colonel-in-Chief to one of the regiments. Olga was in one of the Hussars regiments and Tatiana in one of the Uhlans. The girls had their own uniforms which they wore on the appropriate occasions. Later in the years, Olga and Tatiana would take part in a parade, each on their own horse. In the coming months, the girls would have to train for this occasion. They both rode their horse using a side-saddle which was the vogue for young ladies of the era. As any experienced side-saddle rider knows, although it is more difficult to actually fall off when strapped into a side-saddle, if one does fall badly the injuries are extremely serious.

The two elder Grand Duchesses at the ages of seventeen and fifteen were part girls and part women, as teenagers are. It was often stated that the Grand Duchesses – these two in particular –behaved like little children on occasions. Whilst they were preparing for the parade and the coming Tercentenary celebrations, there was a great deal of pressure in effect on two vulnerable girls who knew little of real life. They did not go to school like other children and rarely even visited shops. As Olga and Tatiana continued their education at home, it must be noted that in England at this time children, unless destined for university and that applied to males almost exclusively, had left school by this age and had embarked on a career or at least an apprenticeship.

Nicholas was invariably joined at lunch by his four daughters and, on occasion, guests. The family priest Father Vassiliev blessed the food before each meal. The man appeared like a figure in a fantasy story with a long black beard, flowing black robes and a large silver cross around his neck. He was a constant presence and a comforting one to the children. They attended church very regularly and Olga's daily writings were liberally sprinkled with religious phrases and prayers for the recovery of her mother and for the safety of her father.

The four Grand Duchesses generally joined their father, Nicholas, in the garden after lunch and all, including Nicholas who could be as child-like as his daughters at times, indulged in wild antics. The delicate Alexei was not permitted to join in the games but was allowed to come out on occasion kitted out in his specially made shoes or even splints on occasions, which must have irked the child. The Tsar and his daughters slid down a small hill in the confines of the park on shovels and appropriately shaped pieces of wood. When the snow fell heavily, they built a huge mountain of snow which was sometimes used for more wild games when they jumped off it into the snow.

The snow mountain melted as the weather heated up the park leaving huge pools of water and often these were deep due to the size of the monument they had constructed. In the afternoons, the children had more lessons on occasions such as music and dancing. The Grand Duchess Olga Nicolaevna was like her mother before her: an excellent pianist and able to play pieces she had heard without resorting to the musical score. Tatiana was also a very gifted pianist but, unlike Olga, failed to play with any real feeling. Olga was unpredictable in her playing. Some days she did nothing and at other times would play for hours at a time. The dancing lessons were an extension of the Victorian obsession for deportment. It was vital for a young lady of the Victorian and Edwardian era to be able to walk correctly and sit down in an elegant manner. There was a correct way to get in and out of carriages and motor cars and of behaving in public. The subject of dancing was important for the girls as they would eventually have to attend many balls and parties and needed to know how to dance and behave on these occasions. Although Olga and Tatiana proved to be especially elegant and sufficiently good dancers, Marie was unfortunately rather ungainly and clumsy and proved much more difficult to teach to dance. When learning to dance, it is vital to know how to stand in the first place and, sadly, the overweight Marie was at a bit of a disadvantage. Nicholas's constant teasing of the girl cannot have encouraged her.

In the cold winter evenings, the Grand Duchesses sat with their mother in her study or sitting room and *worked*. It is an old term that includes sewing, embroidery, knitting and crochet work. The Tsarina's letters of the period confirm that the girls knitted and crocheted. Tatiana and Marie were the two most talented at these skills. In the case of Tatiana and, to a lesser extent, Marie, it was due to their patience; something that Olga did not have.

As the girls *worked*, the Tsarina would sometimes read or *work* herself. She was extremely gifted at all forms of needlework and often made altar covers or items to sell for charity. She disliked her daughters sitting with idle hands. Olga was a committed reader and was widely read. Olga Nicolaevna was fond of poetry and her mother had given her a famous work by Tennyson for a recent birthday. The Grand Duchess also composed poetry, a gift she later shared with Dr Botkin's youngest son Gleb who was also a budding poet.

In the early years of their marriage, Nicholas and, to a slightly lesser extent, Alexandra had visited the opera, ballet and theatre during the first few months of the year. Despite living in the Alexander Palace, the couple regularly moved temporarily to the capital, to the vast Winter Palace which they had used as a base for continued visits to the theatre, opera and ballet. They visited various art exhibitions in the mornings before going out either in the evening or to a matinee performance. Nicholas was never much of an art lover unlike Alix who had grown up with an art-loving family. The Tsar seemed to see the exhibitions as a shop where he was able to buy paintings to decorate the palace.

As her number of children increased and her health declined, Alix was reluctant to travel to St Petersburg and, by 1913, the only opportunities Nicholas and Alexandra had to enjoy music was when it was played by a visiting orchestra or a quartet during special occasions known to the Grand Duchesses as big lunches. It is often translated as breakfast but how many people have breakfast in the early afternoon as the *second* meal of the day?

In the evenings, Alexandra occasionally played a record. She was especially fond of Wagner and was most likely to play a piece by him. In her youth, she had often seen productions by Richard Wagner in the company of her brother Ernie. Alix's close friend Anya Vyrubova lived in a little house nearby and often called in during the course of the evening. Anya was the daughter of a very senior court official but was someone who was almost universally hated. The Tsarina liked her precisely why the others hated her: she was an ordinary, normal person who had no social climbing ambitions. Alix also knew her sister Alya and, after she married, Alya's children were often visited by Alexandra's children. The Grand Duchesses adored children especially Marie and to a lesser extent Olga. Tatiana and Olga were godparents to the first two of Alya's daughters.

As the ladies relaxed on an evening, Nicholas usually remained in the tiny study where he had spent most of the day. He read in the evening from the vast collection of books that were housed in the study. Somehow there were over six hundred books in the tiny study, mostly works on military history and other aspects of history. Nicholas was a soldier first and last; it was his greatest interest and he was at his happiest in the company of the military, if not in the company of his family. On some days when he had nothing to do, he would spend the entire day out shooting. He went to his childhood home of Gatchina often on these occasions where he spent hours shooting anything from bears to hares or pigeon.

On some winter afternoons when *Madame Becker* made an unwelcome call, Olga went for a sedate carriage ride along with one of the ladies-in-waiting. The Tsarina had long ago named her monthly period after someone called Madame Becker. As by the age of sixteen Alix was without a mother or an unmarried sister at home, it is not unlikely that she asked the mother of her dear and only real friend of her childhood, Toni Becker, for advice. Alix liked to give things that she found rather embarrassing, simple nicknames. On other occasions, she used the term *Engineer* Mechanic.

When the Grand Duchesses went out in public, they were always chaperoned either by Olga Butzova, Trina Schneider, Lili Obolenskaya or, even occasionally, Madame Vyrubova or the Grand Duchess Olga Alexandrovna. As young ladies, the Grand Duchesses were always seen out in public wearing hats and gloves. It was *de rigeur*. A lady of that era was never seen out in public dressed inappropriately or without a chaperone if she was unmarried. The Grand Duchesses wore several layers of clothes, as most Victorians had, and wore none of the current brief underwear. They wore long bloomers (long thin knickers), underskirts, brassières and, worse still, corsets made of whalebone. It would have been rather uncomfortable wearing a corset, which all young ladies did at the time from their mid-teens. It had a terribly bad effect on their internal organs after wearing them for many years and must have been a delight to take off at night. In winter, the girls wore leather boots and, in the summer months, shoes which were often lace-up or with a buckle or had two or three straps across the front of the foot. The Grand Duchesses wore either dresses, suits or a simple skirt and blouse. The outfits were made to measure but, after the original owner, dresses were frequently altered and cut down for the next sister. As Tatiana was considerably thinner than Marie, it is more likely that Marie inherited Olga's clothes.

The girls nearly always carried a parasol or an umbrella against the sun or the rain. They each had as they grew older a tiny handbag in which they kept their portable treasures, handkerchiefs, sweets perhaps, and cigarettes. The girls also carried small amounts of cash but this was used for the church collection plate rather than for shopping. They were trained to hold their handkerchief in the left hand so that they could shake the hand of any visitor with the right hand although, as Marie was left-handed, this may have caused her some confusion at times. They also carried their own box brownie cameras if they were going somewhere particularly scenic. They of course would not have had them on *official* occasions.

Each of the girls was said to have a dressing gown in the colours of their own regiment. The dressing gowns of the four Grand Duchesses were actually similar to kimonos and had little in common with the current mass-produced item of the same name. The surviving photographs such as the one of Marie, standing in a doorway wearing her dressing gown, show that they were far more stylish and elegant than normal dressing gowns and were undoubtedly more comfortable as one knows from experience. The girls also wore stockings as opposed to the modern monstrosity known as tights. The stockings were made of wool for the colder months and silk for the summer. Silk is of course far softer and more comfortable than nylon and undoubtedly longer lasting. Nylon was introduced later merely for the means of mass production.

The Tsarina preferred to wear a tea gown whenever possible. The reason why is fairly simple: she had no need to wear a corset under it and, as a result, she was more likely to appear at teatime than at any other time of the day for meals at the palace.

The Grand Duchess Olga at the age of sixteen had reached the age, much to the distress of her mother, when she was supposed to only go out in public with her hair up. She also had to have her skirts and dresses lengthened. Photographs of the Grand Duchesses repeatedly indicate the relative age of each of the girls by the length of their dress; the older the girl, the longer the dress. Olga's hair was put onto her head in a bun for the first time on her sixteenth birthday in 1911. As Tatiana had not yet attained the age of sixteen in the early spring of 1913, she did not have her hair up.

Sundays were the more eagerly awaited day of the week for the four Grand Duchesses. The first duty of the day was to attend a service at one of the nearby churches. The family preferred to attend the regimental church if possible. The Tsar was of course a member of the Russian Orthodox Church and his wife Alix had entered the Church shortly before her marriage. The German Lutheran Princess Alix of Hesse became the Grand Duchess Alexandra Feodorovna, and she naturally became the Tsarina or Empress Alexandra on her marriage. Nicholas preferred to call himself the Tsar rather than the Emperor so I use this term throughout. All the Tsar's children had of course been baptised into the Russian Orthodox Church as babies. When a child is baptised, curiously both parents are banned from the service. Olga was actually one of the junior godparents of her young brother. She was very religious and attended church for the various services on other than just Sunday mornings.

On Sunday afternoons at sometime shortly after lunch, the Grand Duchesses travelled to St Petersburg in the company of their appointed chaperone for the day. The girls, sometimes Olga and Tatiana, or on occasions all four of the girls, visited their paternal grandmother, the Dowager Empress. The Tsar's widowed mother lived at the Anchikov Palace and this is where the girls first went. The Dowager was born a Princess of Denmark and was the younger sister of Queen Alexandra, the consort of the late King Edward VII.

After a brief and fairly stiff and formal hour in the company of their grandmother, the girls left the palace and, with their youthful aunt Olga, returned to her home close by. Olga Alexandrovna once claimed that she and her niece were able to read one another's thoughts. Olga Alexandrovna invited various young people who she thought would amuse her young nieces. The guests would usually include their cousin Irina and one or two of her younger brothers, Zoya de Stoykl the daughter of the lady-in-waiting of the Grand Duchess George (known as Minnie) and the three children of the Leuchtenberg family, namely Sasha (Alexandra), Kolya (Nicholas) and Nadya. The Grand Duchess Olga Alexandrovna often invited young men to her parties including anyone she felt that Olga in particular was fond of. One member of the parties on almost every occasion was Nicholas Sablin, a senior officer from the royal yacht *Standart* and one of the Tsar's many aides-de-camp. He was in his early thirties and constantly in attendance of the Tsarina in particular. He appeared to be especially loyal, sadly as events after proved he was not.

Olga Nicolaeva, like many other girls of her age no matter what station in life or in what era, fell in and out of love frequently. At the beginning of 1913, she was rather attracted to a young man who she named simply by his initials if she ever wrote anything about him. His name was Alexander Konstinovich Shvedov. Olga met the young solider at the various parties she attended at her aunt's and at church. Naturally he attended the regimental church, which may well have been why Olga regularly attended that particular church. She sat next to him as often as she was able at parties and spoke to him whenever she had the opportunity. It was an innocent friendship and in no way a romance as such, but she felt drawn to him. As she went about her everyday life, visiting church, parties, military parades, etc, she always looked out for him. She began to be particularly adept at spotting him in the distance. She must have had good eyesight as she was often able to spot him in the distance.

There were a few occasions when Olga, sometimes accompanied by her sister Tatiana and sometimes without, attended the theatre with her father. The Tsarina had not gone to town with Nicholas for several years, and Olga and her sister gradually replaced their mother at such events. The sisters would have found it extremely exciting to be allowed to attend the theatre. The Tsar did not go very often as it meant that they arrived back home very late at the Alexander Palace and he got up early in order to wade through his endless piles of work so he felt compelled to stay at home whenever possible.

Luckily for the Grand Duchesses, there were occasions when Nicholas did take them to the theatre or to see a ballet or concert. The Tsar was especially fond of a beautiful singer named Nadezhda Plevitskaya and enjoyed her concerts. The lady was actually one of the infrequent visitors to the Sunday afternoon parties where Olga and her sisters went to see their aunt. The girls saw her on occasion and it was probably during these parties that the lady met her future husband – one of the young officers who attended Olga Alexandrovna's parties. (The young lady in question in later years became a communist.) The parties had a rather strange edge to them as Olga Alexandrovna always invited Nicholas Kulikovsky, a man she later married. If Olga Nicolaevna really could read her aunt's mind, as Olga Alexandrovna had claimed of her, she would have known of this relationship.

When Nicholas and his daughters attended the theatre or ballet, they came home on most occasions to find that the Tsarina had already gone to bed. She certainly was not one to stay up late but sometimes she was up as her friend Anya Vyrubova was there keeping her company. Madame Vyrubova did not appear every evening as she sometimes visited her parents or her sister Alya. Another possible reason why the Tsarina would not have attended the ballet is because before his marriage Nicholas was especially close and had a relationship with a ballet dancer by the name of Mathilde Kschessinka. The connection would be one that Alexandra may have found embarrassing and would have connected the ballet with Mathilde and clouded her enjoyment of the occasion. Although Nicholas had always enjoyed the ballet, Alix preferred classical music. Just as Nicholas preferred Russian music, Alix was most fond of German music, which is logical as she spent most of her formative years in Darmstadt. Her father was also, by a coincidence, the cousin of Wagner's patron, the late King of Bavaria. Her favourite work is about the Rhine maidens. She was technically a Princess of Hesse and by the Rhine.

Occasionally the Imperial couple and their children were visited by a native of Tobolsk by the name of Grigory Yefimovich. He went down in history as the infamous Rasputin but was never known by that name by his royal hosts. He sometimes visited the Alexander Palace and, when he did, Nicholas, Alix and the children stopped what they were doing – luckily his visits were late in the day – to listen to him talk. He enchanted all with his stories. He spoke of traditional Russian fairy tales and even the Tsar found the stories riveting. After all, he was passionately proud of his own Russian heritage, even though he was the son of a Danish Princess and the majority of his ancestors had married German princesses. His own grandfather had actually married a Hessian princess as he had done. The children were fascinated by the stories Rasputin told. Tatiana and Marie were probably more impressed by him than Olga, Anastasia and Alexei. In later years, the three children expressed their doubts about him in one way or another. Alexandra was of course the one most impressed by Rasputin and she believed in him to such an extent that she was convinced he was capable of preserving the life of her son Alexei. It was this belief that was the main reason for her friendship with the man. Nicholas, on the other hand, almost certainly merely tolerated Rasputin for the sake of his wife. He always preferred to do just as she wanted and, in later years, when anyone asked about his views on any subject, he merely stated that his wife's views were his own.

There was just one more semi-regular visitor to the Alexander Palace and that was Alix's friend Lili Dehn. Lili, whose real name was actually Julia and her husband occasionally visited the palace, and their son Alexander known bizarrely as Titi was one of the few aristocratic friends of the little Tsarevich. Although Alexander was some four years younger than Alexei, the two boys were devoted but unfortunately did not meet very often. Lili proved to be one of the most loyal friends of the couple and it is interesting to note that the so-called friends of Alix and her daughters were far more loyal long-term than any of Nicholas's acquaintances. He did not really have any friends and the nearest he had to one was the family doctor, Dr Eugene Botkin, who was in attendance on the family to the detriment of his own marriage. His younger children Tatiana and Gleb were occasional visitors to the palace. The children knew most of the stories about the Imperial children via their father, who told them of the latest antics of the legendary Anastasia in particular. Marie, Anastasia and Alexei were closest in age to his children and enjoyed their company. Gleb was a talented artist and drew comic characters for the amusement of the Imperial children. Dr Botkin, of course, died with the Tsar's family.

The month of January was rather confusing as Christmas parties were still being held in the last week of the month. The Dowager Empress had been born in Denmark and was inclined to celebrate Christmas on both dates. The Russian calendar was at the time some thirteen days behind the calendar in Western Europe. When the rest of Europe had adopted the new calendar in the eighteenth century, Russia chose to ignore it and carried on with their own dates, meaning that in the following years Russia got further and further behind the rest of Europe. For example, Olga Nicolaevna was born on the 3rd of November 1895 according to the Russian calendar but in the West her birthday was the 15th of November. In 1901, when Anastasia was born, it meant that her birthday was either the 5th or the 18th of June as the calendar had changed again at the end of the century.

The holiday season, which had been extended due to the conflicting and rather confusing calendars, also saw the showing of motion pictures. The moving camera had only been invented towards the end of the nineteenth century but the Tsar was impressed with the invention enough to have a firm of photographers known as Hahn and Co follow him around all the time when outside the house and film the family. Each of the family had their own camera and own photograph albums, and the cinema was something that Nicholas delighted in. When a film show was given for the children, he was quick to watch it with them. The shows included were to the specification of the ever-strict Tsarina – films taken by Hahn, educational films and comedies. The film shows were one of the few occasions where the Imperial children were joined by their cousins, as these were normally restricted to Sundays and special days. These included not only the actual birthday of each of the Imperial children – four of whom were born in summer and only Olga was born late in the year, but the children's saint's days. Russian Orthodox children were traditionally named after one of the saints so that the child had a second festival day. Olga's saint's day (in the Russian calendar) was the 11th of July yet her birthday was in November.

As the month of January ended, the young Grand Duchesses looked forward to the following month when they would attend various events connected to the Tercentenary (the 300th anniversary) of Romanov rule in Russia. The Tsarina, on the other hand, was undoubtedly dreading it. As Alexei was often ill and frequently suffered some sort of leg injury, the family hoped that he would be well enough to attend the various very public appearances and not give the impression that he was ill. The Imperial couple had chosen to keep his malady a secret but it was known amongst certain of their relatives. The Kaiser, for example, had a nephew in common with Alexandra, little Henry who had died in 1904, and he would have seen the same symptoms in his godson Alexei when they met, although very infrequently of course. Alexandra was not fond of her first cousin and, when the situation demanded that Nicholas and Alix meet him, it was no coincidence that their visits to him or invitations extended to him were of the briefest duration. Nicholas also disliked Alix's cousin but the two had something in common: both had a passionate interest in the army. The two went shooting occasionally but very occasionally. They were due to meet again within a matter of months as Nicholas had been invited to the wedding of the Emperor's only daughter. Nicholas's older daughters had met her many years previously when they made a brief visit to Sans Souci. The Tsarina had no intention of attending though.

The next month began as normal within the Imperial household with the inevitable and interminable lessons for the five children. In the afternoon, the sisters went out into the garden and enjoyed skiing down a small hill in the company of their father. When he was unavailable, the girls were joined by one of the ladies attached to the household such as Catherine Schneider known as Trina or their youthful aunt Olga if she happened to be visiting. The Tsarina, if she ventured out at all, went out in the park that surrounded the palace in a small carriage accompanied by her close friend Anya Vyrubova. Madame Vyrubova had a little house nearby and often called in on the Tsarina. The two ladies generally sat together in the evenings whilst the Tsar read in his room.

When out in the large park, which surrounded the Alexander and Catherine Palaces, the girls often walked to the White Tower and, in the company of their father, they climbed it. The folly had been built many years previously and undoubtedly named after the main building in the Tower of London. Their brother often came out into the park with his sisters but was sometimes taken by carriage or even by sleigh. He was unable to indulge in the wild antics of his sister Anastasia but was nevertheless able to play with them.

On one memorable occasion, the Tsar took his four daughters to St Petersburg where they attended the ballet. The world famous ballerina Anna Pavlova was performing on this occasion and the ballet was an unusual one. *The Pharaoh's Daughter* was first performed in 1862 and begins with an English Lord, with the improbable name of John Bull, and his servant becoming lost during a sandstorm in Africa. The two are on a safari and happen to be close to one of the pyramids. The nobleman is given opium and goes into a dreamlike trance. He imagines that Aspicia, the daughter of the Pharaoh, comes alive. The daughter and John Bull have many adventures before he comes around, and realises it was a drug-induced dream.

On another evening that month, Olga and her sister Tatiana attended an opera in the capital along with their father. Wagner's *Lohengin* was performed and Olga was duly impressed. The Tsarina had attended many Wagner concerts as a young woman and on an evening she would on occasion play a record of one of Wagner's pieces. The Grand Duchesses were surrounded by music. It was played during special festive lunches, and the family attended the regimental church nearby where the Cossacks often sang. The younger Grand Duchesses – Marie and Anastasia – had their own record player and played military marches. There were many opportunities to hear music but it was generally of a military type or classical. Nicholas loved the music of the Russian composers, especially Tchaikovsky, and Olga inherited his taste.

Olga and her sisters often chatted to friends and their aunt Olga on the telephone.

The instrument was an early version of an Ericsson telephone. They spoke to their friends – male and female – who lived in the surrounding area but it was also used internally. The palace was not on the scale of the Winter Palace but nevertheless the Tsarina was inclined to telephone her daughters from downstairs. She rang them in their suite of rooms on the first floor. Although she had a lift installed between the two floors, she found it an easy way to communicate her wishes and instructions to the girls.

One day they had a visit from an old friend of Nicholas, the Emir of Bukhara, Mohammed Alim Khan. He had studied in St Petersburg in the 1890s and was a frequent visitor to Russia. He brought expensive gifts for all concerned. He often gave beautiful and elaborate carpets and impressive jewels. The Tsarina, on the other hand, was not known for giving expensive presents and she was well-known for giving vases. She felt they were the ideal gift for any occasion. As someone who was obsessed with flowers, Alix thought that everyone was always in need of a flower vase.

The Emir was perfectly able to converse in Russian but tradition demanded that he conduct his conversations through an interpreter. Bukhara was an autonomous state within the vast Russian Empire and situated close to the border with Afghanistan.

An English ventriloquist visited Tsarskoe Selo one evening at a party given by the Tsarina's friend Anya at her little house. It was rare that Alexandra stayed up late but on this occasion she did. The Imperial children would have understood the ventriloquist easily enough. They spoke English as an everyday language to their mother, a granddaughter of Queen Victoria, although the children spoke Russian to their father. Alexei, on the other hand, spoke only Russian for quite some time.

Anastasia, in particular, would have loved the act. Watching someone with a wooden doll sat on his knee who was pretending that the doll was talking and not him would have amused the youngest Grand Duchess. As anyone who has ever seen this act would know, the worse the man was at pretending not to be talking the funnier it was to the audience. The Grand Duchesses all had elaborate dolls but Anastasia as a small child had one named Vera that was badly damaged but she loved it all the more for its missing limbs.

The children were taught English by Yorkshire-born Sydney Gibbes. Anastasia was an accurate mimic and it is interesting to speculate whether she ever imitated his accent. Although he had been born in a prosperous family, it is never entirely possible to exclude the last traces of an accent. The older girls had previously been taught by a Scottish teacher, named John Epps, and he was replaced because the girls picked up his accent.

On Sundays, the inevitable visits to the Dowager Empress continued. The young Grand Duchesses visited her at the Anichkov Palace in the capital (St Petersburg) in the early afternoon. On odd occasions, Nicholas visited his mother in the evenings but she rarely visited the Alexander Palace. It is fairly clear that these visits were designed in an effort to include the former Empress in the life of Nicholas and his children but Alexandra very rarely saw her mother-in-law. The two ladies did not get on. The older Empress was a great socialiser and gossip (as her youngest daughter later admitted) but Alix preferred the peace and solitude of the Alexander Palace to the livelier atmosphere of the capital where the Dowager Empress chose to live. She was said to be the only member of the Imperial family who actually enjoyed spending time in the huge Winter Palace. She enjoyed being the centre of attention in society, but Alix did not.

One day, a delegation from Olga's Hussar regiment arrived at the palace to present her with a welcome and surprise bouquet of flowers. She shared her mother's passion for flowers and the four sisters often went outside to pick flowers which they brought back and handed to their delighted mother. The girls tended to pick lily of the valley not only in the Imperial park but when they travelled to Finland on their summer cruise aboard the Imperial yacht *Standart*. There were always plenty of waiting vases for their gifts.

It was generally Anastasia who joined Olga in the snow. Tatiana and, to a lesser extent, Marie were the two most likely to remain indoors with their mother. Tatiana was particularly close to her mother and spent much time in her company but Marie was simply fairly lazy and not inclined to go out as often as her youngest sister Anastasia. Anastasia also spent a lot of time, when she was younger, in the company of her brother Alexei. She was the nearest in age to him. It sometimes left Marie feeling left out – she was not one of the Big Pair – and yet Anastasia split her time between Marie and Alexei. Marie was often reprimanded by her mother in previous years for spending too much time in the company of her cousin Irina and Dmitri who she at one time had a crush on.

Anastasia and her brother were so close that they shared a secret language when they wrote to each other which they named Tarabar. It was merely a simple distortion of some of the words and not too difficult to understand. Anastasia was unofficially given the nickname *Sunshine* on occasions. It had of course been her mother's childhood pet name and she was still known as *Sunny* to her closest friends and family. The name, however, seemed particularly inappropriate to Alexandra who was not known for smiling in public; yet in private she could at times be quite different.

As the 300th anniversary of Romanov rule approached, the Tsarina's sister Ella, the Grand Duchess Elisabeth, arrived from Moscow. The Grand Duchess always wore a habit she had created, which was like that of a nun. Although she spent most of the time seeing to the poor and needy, she did occasionally visit her sister and indeed her brother in Germany and took holidays, unlike most ladies who went into a religious order. Ella made up her own rules and was a firm believer that even nuns needed holidays.

After Ella's arrival, the family got together to watch a film about the very first Romanov Tsar – Michael Feodorovich. It was to get them into the mood for the coming festivities. The film was greatly appreciated by the Tsar's eldest daughter Olga who was especially fond of Russian history.

There was yet another party to attend in the capital before the celebrations began officially. The four Grand Duchesses after briefly visiting their grandmother, the Dowager Empress, went on to their aunts for another party. It was the thing that the girls looked forward most to in the week. It was an opportunity to meet other young people. They played the usual party games of the era including hide and seek. They enjoyed it so much that the games continued when they travelled to Livadia later that year. The atmosphere at Livadia, in the Crimea where a beautiful white palace had been built to the specification of the Tsarina in the Italian style was reminiscent of Osborne House on the Isle of Wight, off the south coast of England where the young Alix had often stayed as a child.

The evening did not end after the girls left the party. Later the Tsar accompanied his two eldest daughters Olga and Tatiana to a concert in aid of the Red Cross. As usual in the circumstances the girls recognised many old friends in the crowd. They seemed to know people wherever they went. It often seemed that Olga and her sisters noticed the same faces wherever they travelled.

Soon after, the Imperial family travelled to St Petersburg for the start of the celebrations. They stayed in the Winter Palace as they usually did when they visited the capital. In the early years of their marriage, Nicholas and Alexandra travelled to the capital at the beginning of each year. The children had rarely seen the Winter Palace in recent years but, with its tiny garden, it was not really that suitable for young and lively children. The boisterous Anastasia, in particular, and the priceless antiques of the Winter Palace seem a frightening combination.

One of the first visits the Imperial family made after their arrival in St Petersburg was to the Cathedral of Christ the Saviour. It was an occasion when Rasputin made a surprise appearance in the cathedral. Although his presence would have delighted the Tsarina, most of the congregation would have been outraged by his sudden appearance. The Tsar's sister the Grand Duchess Olga Alexandrova had also travelled to the Winter Palace with the immediate family, and the young Grand Duchesses sat with their aunt during the evenings. She was a far livelier companion than their mother.

The young Grand Duchesses went out riding in a traditional Russian sleigh the following morning with their chaperone on this occasion, Trina Schneider. The girls were delighted when they sighted their beloved yacht the *Standart* on the waterfront. It was anchored on the river Neva, close to the city. Later the Grand Duchesses Olga and Tatiana visited the Petropavlovskaya Fortress in the company of the Tsar for a memorial service.

The following day, the Tsar and his entire immediate family, including the Tsarina, attended a prayer service at Kazan Cathedral on the Nevsky Prospekt. Nicholas and his son were at the front of the procession to the cathedral in an open carriage. They were followed by the two Empresses, Alix and her mother-in-law the Dowager Empress Marie Feodorovna, in a carriage drawn by magnificent white horses. Finally, the four excited young Grand Duchesses rode together in a barouche. The cathedral had been named after the miracle-making icon of Our Lady of Kazan, which was of course housed within the cathedral.

Anya Vyrubova was amongst those invited to the ceremony and she noticed that Nicholas and Alexei continually looked up at the roof during the service. She was later informed that they had seen a pair of doves overhead and taken this as a good sign.

During the afternoon, the Grand Duchesses Olga and Tatiana, wearing brand new Russian style dresses attended a reception at the Winter Palace along with the Tsar and Tsarina. The reception, which lasted for around an hour and three-quarters, exhausted the Tsarina who had very little strength on a normal day. The following day Alexandra was so worn out that she did not attend the reception held that morning.

That day proved to be a very difficult one for Tatiana as she had drunk a drink made from the notoriously filthy waters of the capital, and she became seriously ill with what proved to be typhoid. The Grand Duchess took no further part in the celebrations. In the evening, Olga attended a showing of the most famous traditional Russian play entitled *A Life for the Tsar*. The story recounted how the truly heroic Ivan Susanin gave his own life so that the young Tsar Michael might live. Amongst the performers were dancers Anna Pavlova, Mathilde Kschessinska and singers Figner and Sobinov.

Later, as Tatiana remained in bed, she was visited by her Aunt Xenia and cousins Irina and some of her many brothers. It was probably unwise for the Grand Duchess to be visited by her relatives. She was constantly visited by her sister Olga, and it was lucky that none of the other family became ill. There would be casualties however later on. Already, Alexei was having problems walking in public. When not driving in a carriage, the boy had to be carried in the arms of a male attendant, a huge Cossack. Once again, fate decreed that the boy was to be seen as a helpless invalid. This had happened before when he appeared in public. He had not sufficiently recovered since the serious attack the previous autumn.

That same Saturday evening, the excited yet nervous Olga Nicolaevna attended a ball at the Assembly of the Nobility. Unfortunately, the Tsarina left early as she normally did on these occasions but Nicholas and his eldest daughter remained until almost midnight. The young Grand Duchess delighted in dancing at every opportunity and she danced the night away whether it was a quadrille or the exciting mazurka. It was her first official ball.

The next day, the Grand Duchess Tatiana remained in bed but her sisters carried on with their usual plans and visited their grandmother the Dowager Empress and, later, their aunt for another party. They saw all the same familiar guests, their cousins and various young officers. The ever present Sablin was amongst the guests as was Olga's current crush Alexander. The games were the usual ones too but still exciting for the young sisters – turkey, rope, slap-on-hands. Olga contrived as usual to sit next to her friend Alexander. The yet more exciting hide and seek was played later – in the dark. It gave the participants ample opportunity to avoid their chaperones and seek the young man of their choice. However, Olga had been sufficiently concerned about her mother and sister as to telephone home to them during the evening and she spoke briefly to the Tsarina. Had she lived in the modern age she would have undoubtedly owned a mobile phone.

The Winter Palace proved to be as restrictive as Nicholas had assumed. Normally on an afternoon, he and his daughters spent their time in the vast park next to the more modest Alexander Palace but the huge Winter Palace built so close to the Neva River had little room for exercise and Nicholas craved the ability to get out into the fresh air each afternoon. Whilst he was able at Tsarskoe Selo to go kayaking, bicycle riding or to build a giant snow mountain, at the Winter Palace he and the children were confined to a tiny garden. In an attempt to get some fresh air, he and his three daughters Olga, Marie and Anastasia climbed onto the roof of the vast palace. It proved to be rather windy but at least the air was fresher and the view would have been outstanding.

Nicholas and his daughters were well used to climbing; not only did they regularly scale the heights of the White Tower in the grounds of the Alexander Palace park but Marie often walked out onto the roof of the palace at their home at Livadia. She was nimble and adventurous enough to climb out of the windows and walk along the ledges. She had probably begun her climbing career after observing the Grand Duke Dmitri do the same. On occasions, she climbed out of the windows and was followed by her siblings, including her brother who occasionally broke the unwritten rule that he should be careful. Marie had inherited her late grandfather's almost super human strength.

Tatiana meanwhile was seriously ill and remained in her room. She was visited regularly in the afternoons by the Tsarina but was attended by the doctor Eugene Botkin and the nurses who had seen the girls grow up and had become almost part of the family. Her youngest sisters Marie and Anastasia, however, made the most of the opportunities for fun and, after being giving permission by their father, indulged in an exciting swim in Nicholas's huge bathtub. It, and two other similar ones in two of the other palaces, was large enough for Nicholas to swim. Olga and her parents watched as the youngsters splashed about in the water.

The next day after a brief visit to the tomb of the Tsar's late father in the Fortress of St Peter and St Paul, the Imperial family returned to Tsarskoe Selo. It was rather risky to move Tatiana at this point but nevertheless she travelled back to the Alexander Palace with the rest of her family. On their return, she was finally isolated from her siblings and moved to another room.

The next day, life returned more or less to normal for the Imperial children, with the obvious exception of Tatiana who remained in bed. The other four children resumed their usual lessons but now Olga was forced to work alone without the companionship of her sister Tatiana. Despite the isolation, Olga still continued to call in on her sister to see how she was. The Tsarina, after the exertions of the past days, was naturally exhausted but managed to get up for meals throughout the day. The children and Nicholas were delighted to get back to their large garden and began building a snow mountain. They were delighted at the help from any of the members of staff. The day was however rather sunny which did not hold out hope for the long-term life of the snow tower. Alexei was brought out into the garden to join the fun but as usual had to take care not to injure himself.

The days now ended in their normal pattern with Nicholas going to his tiny study to read whilst the Tsarina sat in her sitting room in the company of Madame Vyrubova and her daughters. On some evenings, Alexandra played records and on others she played the game of *colorito* with one of her daughters, usually Olga. The board game was one that the Tsarina was particularly fond of. In later years, she played regularly with Marie who invariably let her mother win.

The following month began as quietly as the previous one had, with lessons for the four remaining children of the Tsar. Tatiana slowly began to recover but her temperature was still a little on the high side. Olga, Marie and Anastasia went for a sleigh ride on some mornings, accompanied by a chaperone naturally. In the afternoons, the children continued to build the snow mountain. As Tatiana was unable to attend church, the priest brought the Eucharist to her one morning so she was able to partake in the traditional bread and wine. The snow mountain was under pressure from the weather as the snow began to thaw. Inevitably it would melt as the weather warmed up.

Anya Vyrubova regularly visited the ailing Tsarina in order to give her some company. The Tsar visited the capital for a funeral and attended a military parade and a dinner with the Hussars one evening. He was constantly forced to leave the palace for receptions, ceremonies and meetings. The Tsarina never went out with him and she remained at home resting and attempting to recover from the exertions of the past weeks. She had never really recovered from the endless months of nursing Alexei the previous autumn.

As the snow mountain began to melt and water surrounding it became deeper and deeper, the children had to make other arrangements. Young relatives and friends arrived for the three younger children to play with but Olga, without the regular companionship of Tatiana, was bored. She was missing her friend Alexander. She did not see him every day and felt happier in his company.

When Nicholas attended dinner out one evening, Olga sat with her mother to keep her company. Luckily her Aunt Olga Alexandrovna had arrived for a welcome visit. Her presence was a great boon to her nieces and to Alix. The Tsarina had been rested most of the time since her return from the capital and she appeared to get stronger as each day went on.

Meanwhile Tatiana had had her beautiful long auburn hair cut short. It had begun to fall out and it was drastically trimmed in order to help it grow stronger. The Grand Duchess was unusual in having such short hair, as it was the era of long hair. The fashion of short *bobbed* hair was not until the 1920s. When a young girl had short hair in this era, it was almost certain she had been seriously ill as a lady's hair was always long. As she gradually went out in public, the Grand Duchess felt compelled to wear a wig. Her Aunt Olga who visited that day may well have discussed the time when she had worn a wig. In 1903, the Grand Duchess Olga Alexandrovna had been forced to wear a wig when all her hair fell out. The wig would prove to be hot and itchy. Tatiana naturally felt self-conscious at her short hair and would have been quite traumatised when she saw it fall out. Only someone who has had this happen can understand how distressing it is.

Soon after, there was bad news when word came of the murder in Salonika of the brother of the Dowager Empress. Her brother was the King of Greece and the husband of Olga Nicolaevna's godmother Queen Olga of Greece. On this occasion, the Tsar *and* his wife rushed to St Petersburg in order to comfort the Dowager Empress. Alexandra rarely visited her mother-in-law. After the murder, it was usual for the relatives to go into mourning. It would be Olga Nicolaevna's first experience of wearing black. Alix, on the other hand, virtually grew up in black as photographs show.

As lessons continued for the children and Tatiana remained confined to her room, life carried on much as normal despite the horrific news. One afternoon, Olga indulged in a snowball fight with her male cousins. The Grand Duchesses had no cousins, apart from the children of Xenia that lived in Russia. The Tsar's brother George had died unmarried in 1899; his sister Olga had no children at the time; and his brother Michael, although he had a small son, lived in exile abroad. Michael had, like many of Nicholas's immediate family, married, against the wishes of his brother, a divorcee named Nathalie. She was actually, like Mrs Wallis Simpson many years later, twice divorced. The Tsar's children never met their cousin George and he never met his own grandmother until after the revolution. Unfortunately, George would fall victim to the family curse and died young in the 1930s.

In the afternoon, the three Grand Duchesses Olga and her younger sisters Marie and Anastasia walked to the regimental church but, to their surprise, it was locked so they came back.

In the next few days, the Tsarina remained on her couch feeling ill whilst her daughter Tatiana slowly recovered her strength. Unfortunately Dr Botkin became very seriously ill with typhoid. Another of the family's doctors had to take over from him. The young Grand Duchesses Olga, Marie and Anastasia travelled to St Petersburg on Sunday to see their grandmother. It was a solemn occasion, quite unusual for the three sisters. Their usual visits had been stiff and formal but the atmosphere was now positively dark. The sisters had tea with their grandmother who had been joined by her daughter Olga Alexandrovna. Another visitor was their Aunt Minnie. Known officially as the Grand Duchess George, she was a niece of the Dowager Empress and the daughter of the assassinated King.

The girls went onto their Aunt Olga's as usual but on this occasion there was no party and they quietly leafed through photograph albums. The girls went for a sedate ride along the waterfront and passed by their beloved yacht the *Standart*.

As Tatiana recovered and Alexandra attempted to do so, Anastasia managed to hurt her leg and she too was forced to rest. Luckily by now Tatiana's temperature had returned to normal and the Tsarina appeared to be getting better. As Nicholas returned to the capital once more later, the Grand Duchesses went out in the garden with Trina for a walk or a ride. They had to be chaperoned on every occasion they went out of the house.

On the following Sunday, the Grand Duchesses travelled to the capital to visit their grandmother once more. On this occasion, the visit afterwards to their Aunt Olga was a more normal one and the girls had their usual party that afternoon with the usual party games and guests. Once again, Olga Alexandrova had invited Olga's friend Alexander. It was her only real opportunity to chat to him; normally she only saw him at church or in passing. Luckily for the Grand Duchesses, their aunt and Madame Vyrubova provided opportunities for the girls to be ordinary teenagers and spend time in the company of people of their own age. Usually children met others of their own age at school or perhaps at sports events but Olga and her sisters did none of these things. The only people of their age they saw on a regular basis were the younger soldiers who surrounded them all the time.

The parties were an occasion to eat cakes and sweets, and to listen to records, to play party games and even to dance. It was a rare opportunity to pretend they were normal children and not daughters of the Tsar.

As Tatiana recovered enough to lie on the couch and join the rest of the family at long last, another of the members of the household became ill. Trina, ever loyal to the family, came down with typhoid. It was not uncommon for those in close contact to also become seriously ill. The days continued as usual for the children – lessons, trips to the regimental church occasionally, breaking up the ice in the garden, or sitting with the Tsarina in the evening with the inevitable game of *colorito*. The ice was broken up in the pond and surrounding areas to make sure the water was suitable for kayaking and boating. Olga and her sisters smoked the odd cigarette when they had a quiet moment. None would prove to be heavy smokers; they did not have enough cigarettes to become so. Nicholas, a heavy smoker himself, often gave the girls a gift of one or two.

One Friday morning the three girls Olga, Marie and Anastasia accompanied their father to St Petersburg where the family attended a craft show before heading off for lunch with the Dowager Empress. The Grand Duchess Tatiana had meanwhile progressed enough to be able to eat downstairs with the family. Olga was amused to notice that Tatiana appeared to have grown in height during her illness. The teenager would have been thinner afterwards and this may have indeed made her look even taller than she was. She would indeed be the tallest of the sisters in due course. Anastasia, to her despair, would never grow very tall and never reached more than about 5 feet 2 inches.

On the Monday morning, the Tsar returned to the capital with his daughters. Whilst his two youngest daughters visited the Dowager Empress, Nicholas and Olga visited a military parade. Later, Olga joined her Aunt Olga and travelled to her house for another party. On this occasion, she was joined by her cousin Irina and two of her numerous brothers and, to her delight, yet again by her friend Alexander. She contrived once again to sit next to him as the fun and games continued. She was accompanied home by Anastasia Hendrikova later and found that Nicholas had gone out for the evening and Alexandra was resting with the inevitable Madame Vyrubova in attendance.

As the Grand Duchesses continued breaking up the ice in the garden, one afternoon Marie managed to fall in the water and soak herself. Luckily she came to no harm. The following day, Marie was well enough to join her sisters Olga and Anastasia and the Tsar in a visit to a Dragoon regiment celebration. Marie was of course Colonel-in-Chief of a regiment of the Dragoons although not yet old enough to take part in their parades on horseback as her older sisters would be doing later in the year.

Later, the Tsar and his daughter Olga and his sister of the same name travelled to Manezh near Moscow to attend a prayer service and parade. Once again, not only Tatiana but the Tsarina remained at home. Her daughters were getting quite used to replacing her on these occasions and were happy to accompany their father. The rest of the month was monotonous enough for the young Grand Duchesses with lessons in the mornings and breaking up the ice in the afternoons. The evenings were spent quietly as normal with Olga and occasionally Anya joining the Tsarina.

Luckily the last day of the month was a Sunday and the three young Grand Duchesses Olga and her sisters Marie and Anastasia had the opportunity of travelling to the capital with their chaperone for a visit to their grandmother who they found playing the card game bezique, followed by the excitement of a party at their aunt's. The day proved to be even more interesting than normal when not only did the famous singer Plevitskaya arrive for dinner but Prince Felix Yussopov also arrived and caused consternation amongst the Cossacks for having the audacity to arrive in civilian clothes; he was a civilian. The parties were normally only attended by young officers and other ranks of the armed forces, mainly the army. The poor man had an almost feminine appearance, which unfortunately made him even more of a target for the Cossacks. One of the other male guests named Shangin later married Madame Pleviskaya but sadly died in the early years of the war in 1915.

One of the Tsarina's young ladies-in-waiting Baroness Sophie Buxhoeveden, known as *Isa* to the girls, had become engaged towards the end of the month to a Baron Ungen-Sternberg from the Russian Embassy in Paris. Her engagement was later broken off and the Baroness never married. She would become one of those ladies who were in attendance on the Tsarina and was one of those who was trusted as a chaperone to the young Grand Duchesses. The other chaperones on occasions included Lili Obolenskaya, Trina Schneider, Anastasia Hendrikova and Olga Butzova. Anya Vyrubova and the Grand Duchess Olga occasionally took on the role. The young Tsarevich was constantly in the company of his tutor Pierre Gilliard, and his sailor nannies Derevenko and Nagorny were no longer solely responsible for his safety. The two men were in attendance but Gilliard was moved into his own suite next to that of Alexei. He even had his own servant. Gibbes lived in the capital but later was given a flat in the luxurious Catherine Palace.

Chapter Two

Spring 1913

As the new month began, the Tsar attended a review comprising of new recruits and members of the Infantry regiment and even sailors from the Baltic fleet. Olga, who was also attending, spied an old friend, Paul Voronov, amongst the troops. He was to become very important in her life in the coming months. He had been a constant feature in her life for several years as one of the officers on the Imperial yacht *Standart* but slowly her feelings towards him began to change. She had not however forgotten Alexander and he would remain first in her affections for the foreseeable future.

The following evening proved an exciting one for the Grand Duchess Olga as she was taken to the theatre along with her two youngest sisters Marie and Anastasia. Despite now studying alongside her sister Olga, Tatiana was still not sufficiently recovered to go out in public. That evening, the three sisters and their father, Nicholas II enjoyed a concert at the famous Marinsky Theatre. Once again the singer Plevistskaya was amongst the performers. She was a great favourite of the Tsar. The concert was actually to celebrate the twenty-fifth anniversary of Andreyev and his balalaika orchestra. They were another favourite of Nicholas and Alexandra, and later played private concerts at the Alexander Palace. Unfortunately, Olga became bored by the endless tributes paid to the orchestra leader; patience was not one of her virtues. She had far less tolerance than Tatiana and Marie. Tatiana had been unable to attend the performance and would probably have not looked forward to going out in public in an itchy wig.

After lessons the following morning, Tatiana was finally permitted outside for a sedate carriage ride. Sablin joined Nicholas in the garden to help break up the ice. He returned later to play dice with Nicholas, Alexandra and the ever-present Anya. The two were probably the most regular guests on an evening. The Tsar's cousin Grand Duke Dmitri came on occasions to play billiards with Nicholas in his large study. It was a room rarely used by Nicholas. He much preferred his small study which had been designed exactly to his own taste, but the larger study had been designed with the help of his brother-in-law and Nicholas was never fond of the flamboyant tastes of Ernie. The room had a distinct art nouveau feel. The Grand Duchesses had a frieze in each of the two bedrooms the girls shared in this style.

As the weather improved, the Tsarina began to sit out once more on her balcony. The facilities on the balcony vastly improved in a matter of a few years. It had various lamps and tables and wicker chairs. The balcony was also fitted with a carpet and even curtains. The Tsarina and her daughters used it frequently in the early years of the war. The curtains gave it a sense of privacy.

In the evenings, Alexandra went inside to her famous *mauve boudoir* where she played endless games of *colorito* with her eldest daughter. It is a board game ideally for just two people, although really for children.

Nicholas returned to Manezh soon after but this time with all five of his children. The wooden structure at Manezh had been erected in 1817 to commemorate the fifth anniversary of Russia's victory over Napoleon Bonaparte. It was the first outing for Tatiana for quite some time and the first occasion where she wore her wig. During the afternoon, Nicholas had a meeting with the retiring American Ambassador, Mr Curtis Guild. The meeting took place in the large Corner Sitting Room in the Tsar's private wing of the Alexander Palace. The room was often used for receptions and even parties over the years.

Tsar Nicholas II of Russia was particularly fascinated in the history of his country, as indeed were his children, and on an evening, if he was not playing dice with his companions, he retired to the privacy of his small study where he read one of his many books. He was interested in military history and was especially interested in the military career of Napoleon Bonaparte. His daughter Olga was very interested in the brief life of Bonaparte's son and was sufficiently interested in the subject to take two books on the young man with her to Siberia. Olga was a great lover of reading and the books she took with her into exile, knowing that she would be unlikely to retrieve the other books in her collection in later years, must undoubtedly have been important to her. One book she took was a childhood book, given to her by her Aunt Irene on her eighth birthday by the Scottish author George MacDonald entitled *The Princess and the Goblin*. The book would have reminded her of the time when the book was given to her, which was shortly before the death of her beloved cousin Elisabeth of Hesse. The girl in the book was named Irene by coincidence but, like Elisabeth, was an only child and was eight years old, the age Elisabeth was when she died. The children of Nicholas and Alexandra all had a fascination with goblins and elves. One of the books Tatiana took into exile was *The Country of Elves*.

Meanwhile, soon after, Olga Nicolaevna visited her little godson. The four month-old boy appears to have been a relation of Alexei's sailor nanny Derevenko, possibly his nephew. The child named Yevegeny was the son of Varvara Yuvchenko. She adored small children and had another godchild, one of the daughter's of Anya Vyrubova's sister Alya; the baby had been called Olga.

Later in the day, the Tsar's niece arrived with some of her brothers. Xenia's children often appeared at the palace on Sundays and holidays. On this occasion, the children watched a film show with their Imperial cousins. They were shown colour photographs. Serge Mikhailovich Proskudin-Gorsky travelled throughout Russia taking photographs of fascinating sites and pretty scenes. He had previously visited Nicholas, and the Tsar was impressed enough with the photos to request that the photographer continue his journeys and continue to bring him the wonderful pictures. Nicholas was very interested in photography himself and had many albums full of photographs taken either by himself or the official photographers. He glued the pictures into albums on rainy days usually and, predictably for someone so tidy, he would not tolerate even a spot of glue on the paper. The Tsar's children each had a camera of their own and albums for their work. The younger children decorated the albums with their own paintings, usually of flowers.

At church that morning, Olga had seen her friend Alexander but only from a distance. She was not even able to see his face, just his back. She looked out for him wherever she went but rarely had the opportunity even for a brief chat, apart from on Sundays. Very little happened in the normal everyday lives of the Tsar's daughters. On some mornings, they went for a delightful sleigh ride in the company of a chaperone and the afternoons were spent in the park breaking up the ice or climbing the White Tower. The evenings were equally as boring for Olga, spent playing endless games of *colorito* with her mother. The Tsarina's fear of the evils of society greatly restricted the lives of her daughters.

Some days, Olga was quite content to stay at home. On the days when *Madame Becker* paid a call, the Grand Duchess spent most of the morning in bed. Although the camp beds used by the siblings were not overly comfortable, she was unwell enough to want to stay in bed. She generally spent the first day of *Madame Becker's* unwelcome visit in her room as the pain was at its most intense in the first twenty-four to forty-eight hours. On these days, she basked in the warmth of the sun on her mother's balcony. Alexandra would often join her, and the two sat quietly together.

At the approach of the Russian Orthodox Easter, the Tsarina was desperately hoping that she would be able to take part in the coming festivities. It would need all her strength to participate in all the various ceremonies in the coming week. The congregation stand during the long church services, something that Alexandra found particularly difficult to do. It also meant getting up extra early on one occasion, again not something she was usually able to do. It did not look hopeful that she would be able to cope. The coming months would also mean travelling and the Tsarina was fearful. She was worried how she would manage. The long months spent at the bedside of Alexei the previous year had sapped any little strength she had.

On Holy Thursday or Maundy Thursday as it is known in England, the family attended church. There was the reading of the *Twelve Scriptures* that morning (the original twelve Old Testament readings). Despite feeling distinctly under the weather, Olga participated in the occasion and returned to the palace with candles that had already been lit. She was not quite ill enough not to notice that Alexander was there at the church.

On Good Friday, the Imperial family attended church for the traditional *Lifting of the Shroud* ceremony. It is to re-enact the original day when the shroud covering the body of Jesus Christ was uncovered. The afternoon was spent resting and all retired early in anticipation of an early start the following morning. It was only the Tsar and his daughters Olga, Marie and Anastasia who were intending to rise at 4am to go to the regimental church for the service.

At 4am on Holy Saturday, the Tsar and three of his daughters attended the regimental church for what was known as the *Burial* ceremony. The *Shroud* was carried around the church and afterwards the family returned home for a welcome nap. The morning was already proving to be warm despite the early hour. Easter is far more important than Christmas in the Russian Orthodox Church and a time when the children receive expensive presents.

The family returned to church for the liturgy later in the morning and that afternoon Alexandra and her four daughters visited Anya Vyrubova where they dyed the traditional eggs for Easter. The eggs were supposed to be painted with a mixture of boiled onion peel and scraps of silk. The eggs were believed by many to have magical powers and to be able to ward off evil. The ladies were later joined by Nicholas, in time for tea. Madame Vyrubova had also invited other friends that afternoon including Lili Dehn, Baroness Buxhoeveden, the inevitable Nicholas Sablin and other members of the crew of the Imperial yacht such as Paul Voronov. The family returned to church at 11.30 for matins and only returned to the palace in the early hours of the morning.

On Easter Monday there was the traditional greeting with the members of the court and those from the Joint Command and the Cossacks at the Catherine Palace. Each individual was kissed three times on the face by the enthusiastic Tsar and his exhausted wife. Nicholas and Alexandra stood for up to two hours handing out small coloured china eggs.

In the afternoon, as on the previous day, Olga and her sister Tatiana, now much recovered and sporting a rather fetching yet irritating brown wig, went kayaking on the pond. In the evening the sisters went to visit their grandmother in the capital along with Nicholas for dinner where they met up with Nicholas's sister Xenia and members of her family.

The Tsar and his five children Olga, Tatiana, Marie, Anastasia and Alexei attended a parade late the following morning. The ever-observant Olga Nicolaevna noticed her friend Alexander amongst the men. Nicholas and his sister Olga watched an infantry parade later that day after climbing the White Tower in the park along with the children. Although Tsar of all the Russias, Nicholas II was not averse to behaving like an ordinary though energetic sightseer. The Tsarina meanwhile got no further than the balcony.

After yet another military parade the following morning, the four Grand Duchesses travelled to the capital in order to see their grandmother, the Dowager Empress, but en route to their aunt's house afterwards they made a detour to Mrs Franklin's house. Elizabeth Franklin was the beloved nanny of their aunt and she was seriously ill. She had been very much a mother figure to Olga Alexandrovna. Alix's own nanny Mrs Orchard had died a few years previously but *not*, as most assumed in Russia, nursed with care by the Tsarina, but in England. Her death certificate revealed the truth.

Despite the worry about Mrs Franklin, the party went on as normal. The show went on regardless. Olga and her sisters enjoyed the usual party games of turkey, tag and slap-on-hands. Once again Olga contrived to sit between her friends – on this occasion Sablin and Alexander. She spoke at length with her favourite and found out his birthday and saint's day.

The following morning, the four enthusiastic Grand Duchesses visited the nearby nursery school where they spent almost two hours playing with the little children. It was something the sisters enjoyed thoroughly. They liked to help feed the children and play games with them, and simply cuddle them. Sadly none of them would live to have their own children.

Rasputin arrived that evening and the Imperial family sat humbly as he told them stories that enchanted all concerned. He had a brilliant gift of recounting fairy tales. The children saw him as an old friend, although their individual feelings towards him varied. Olga saw him as someone whose advice she could ask, Tatiana as someone as infallible as her own beloved mother, as did Marie, but the two youngest children, far more intelligent than people generally believed, saw him as ordinary, though well meaning. The Tsarina saw him as something of a saint yet Nicholas merely tolerated him as a necessary evil.

The following afternoon, Nicholas took his children to the Joint Regiments barracks where they watched a succession of games, exercises and exhibitions. The children enjoyed the fun almost as much as the men themselves. Later, Olga and her youngest sister, Anastasia, visited Anya Vyrubova who lived close to the palace. Madame Vyrubova had also invited Countess Kleinmichael and her nieces. The ladies had tea together. In the coming months, Olga's friendship with one of the sisters would be tested to the utmost. Tatiana, however, would remain a lifelong friend of Olga Kleinmichael, which shows how keen Tatiana was to remain friends. She did not have many others unfortunately as her mother did not encourage her daughters to mix with anyone unless absolutely necessary. Interestingly, she did not stop her daughters from staying in contact with Rasputin's two daughters.

The next morning, after a sedate carriage ride accompanied by their appointed chaperone for the day Trina Schnieder, the four sisters returned to the nursery school. They could not resist returning. In the afternoon, they went back to the regimental barracks with their father and brother to watch more fun and games. When they later attended vespers, Rasputin appeared at the altar. Although the Imperial family would not have been at all perturbed, the rest of the congregation, being soldiers, would almost certainly have been surprised, to say the least. He was probably only really popular with certain sections of society but this would not have included the military.

The evening ended as it often did for the Imperial family: with Nicholas reading in his study and the ladies *working*. This probably meant embroidery, crochet or knitting. The Tsarina was averse to seeing her daughters sitting with idle hands. Olga read a great deal, but in the privacy of her own room or away from others.

The next morning began with a rather chilly carriage ride for the Grand Duchesses and, in the afternoon, Olga, accompanied on this occasion only by two of the Tsarina's ladies, Trina Schnieder and Anastasia Hendrikova, made her usual Sunday afternoon visit to the capital. The Grand Duchess called in on her grandmother, the Dowager Empress, and then as usual went on to her aunt's for a party. The crowd was a familiar one with cousins, distant relations and young soldiers. Although predictable, it was nevertheless delightful as far as Olga was concerned; it was her only chance of spending time in the company of her friend Alexander. On this occasion she did not have Anastasia with her as the young Grand Duchess was unwell and suffering from a sore throat. Anastasia was prone to joke and tease and her absence would have made Olga more nervous yet more excited to spend time with her favourite. Despite being a Grand Duchess, she was after all an ordinary teenager in many ways.

That afternoon, the party had been enlivened by music. The Grand Duchess Olga Alexandrovna possessed a record player and the guests listened to a selection of her favourite music including a favourite of her niece Olga Nicolaevna, *In Church*, part of the children's suite by Tchaikovsky. It is one of the least well known of the works of the famous composer but one played easily on the piano by Olga who was a gifted pianist.

On Monday morning, it was a return to the regularity of lessons but Olga was bored. In an effort to dispel her feelings of frustration, Olga rode her bicycle in the garden with her father but it was too cold. She came indoors and joined her sisters in trying on new hats, but she was still bored. In 1913, it was an integral part of a lady's attire and the Grand Duchesses always wore hats when in public. When they rode their bicycles though, they could wear a simple woollen hat to keep out the cold. The Grand Duchesses frequently wore long woollen cardigans in the cold weather rather than coats or fitted jackets. It was a more casual approach to keeping warm and one that they preferred.

The next day was the Tsarina's name's day. It was the day allocated in the Russian Orthodox Church to St Alexandra, the saint after whom the former Princess Alix of Hesse had named herself. Alix was the name she had been given at birth by her own mother, Princess Alice who had used this name for her fourth daughter as it was the nearest to her own name which the Germans had great difficulty in pronouncing. It was also of course the nickname of her aunt and godmother the Princess of Wales, who was by coincidence the older sister of the current Dowager Empress.

There was the usual liturgy and prayer service for the Tsarina at the regimental church. The Tsar's mother came for lunch along with her daughter Xenia. In the afternoon, the Tsarina's daughters rode their bicycles around the park with Nicholas.

On Wednesday, the two eldest Grand Duchesses had lessons, went for a carriage ride along with their chaperone for the day, Trina Schnieder, and rode their bicycles again around the district. Anastasia was kept indoors as she was suffering from tonsillitis.

Anastasia had not recovered sufficiently enough by the next day to get up so spent the day in bed once more. The Tsarina lay out in the warmth on her balcony whilst Nicholas, Olga, Tatiana and Marie took to their bicycles for a ride, followed by a spot of sunbathing by the side of the railway line. Afterwards, the four took to their kayaks. The next day was spent much the same as Anastasia slowly recovered.

On Saturday morning, Nicholas attended a parade along with his son and eldest daughter. The rest of the day followed the recently established pattern – with kayaking but ended with a trip to the regimental church where the Cossacks were singing.

The sad news of the death of Mrs Franklin ensured that Sunday would be quieter than normal. Instead of a party that afternoon, the Tsar took his daughters to pay a call on the grieving Olga Alexandrovna. They had picked a great many flowers earlier for the Grand Duchess. That morning there had been a religious service followed by a big lunch where Olga had been delighted to see her friend Alexander. Unfortunately, as normally on these occasions, she had no opportunity to speak to him and felt shy when confronted by a group of officers and felt tongue-tied as seventeen year-olds often do.

Anastasia had happily recovered enough by Monday to be able to join her father and sisters after lessons on their bicycles and in the kayaks. Nicholas called on his mother that evening whilst the Tsarina as usual remained at home in the company of her daughters and the indispensible Anya Vyrubova. Madame Vyrubova was regularly invited to spend the evening with Alexandra; on the odd occasions she was not asked, she sulked. The Tsarina often described Anya as her fifth daughter and she did indeed feel a sisterly affection for the four Grand Duchesses.

In the evening, Olga telephoned her friend Sablin. He was a constant presence at the palace and, on the occasions he was absent and not on duty, Olga felt the need to chat to him. Like many girls in subsequent decades, the Grand Duchess liked to chat on the phone.

Despite the appearance of snow and hail the following morning, the four Grand Duchesses still ventured outside to walk with their father and to go kayaking on the pond. Anastasia was amongst the party, despite her recent throat problems, which seems a little unwise.

As the next month dawned, the Grand Duchesses knew that in just over a fortnight they would embark on a great adventure. The long-awaited celebration tour for the Tercentenary was about to begin. Before it started, there were more mundane tasks to perform: the usual endless round of lessons each morning. The first day of the new month showed little sign of the change about to come. The Grand Duchesses spent the afternoons in their usual pursuit of kayaking around the pond. The weather did not seem particularly spring-like; during the morning it had snowed. The Tsar's sister Olga Alexandrovna arrived to enliven the party. She sat with the Tsarina and assisted her namesake in some frame embroidery that evening. It still remained pretty domestic on the whole and showed no sign of what was to come.

On Thursday morning, Olga, accompanied by her sister Anastasia went for a quiet walk and decided to call in on her little godson Yevegeny. He was sleeping but the visit had been enough to brighten the spirits of Olga Nicolaevna. She adored babies and must have wondered if she would ever have one of her own. During the afternoon, the sisters rode their bikes and then a double boat. The girls were joined by Andrei Derevenko, and Olga gazed down into the water as the fish came to the surface as it rained. The sisters returned to the same activities the following afternoon.

On Saturday morning, there was the excitement of a parade and one of those big lunches that generally followed. It was one of those increasingly rare occasions where the Tsarina appeared. She was no doubt steeling herself for the coming festivities. The four sisters each sat at one or other of the tables and chatted with the assembled guests. Olga shared a table with her sister Anastasia and Count Eristov amongst others. On these occasions, an extra seat and place was put on each table so that Nicholas was able to chat to all the guests.

Anastasia joined Olga once more that afternoon as the two climbed the White Tower and kayaked in the pond in the company of their father. Tatiana was still remaining inside and her sister Marie appears to have been keeping her company. Marie was said to be fairly lazy and she often stayed inside when her sisters went outside but, on the occasions she did venture out, could be the most lively of all and liable to fall into the water possibly due to her legendary clumsiness. Unfortunately she did not have the grace of her older sisters.

The Grand Duchesses usually travelled to the capital on a Sunday afternoon to visit their grandmother and aunt but, on this occasion, their aunt was staying at the Alexander Palace. After church there was yet another of the big lunches and it gave Olga Nicolaevna a rare opportunity to chat with her friend Alexander on the balcony. She was rarely able to speak with him so close to home.

The Tsar's sister then joined Nicholas and his daughter for a walk, and then the two Olgas went out riding together. Olga Nicolaevna needed to practise as much as possible for the upcoming parade but it was not until the late summer so she had plenty of time to rehearse.

The girls enjoyed the company of their youthful aunt and sat with her in her room. The evening was rounded off nicely when the balalaika orchestra came to play in one of the larger rooms of the palace. As Alexandra rarely went out, it was a welcome break for her. She adored classical music and had grown to love the traditional Russian music over the years. She invited the musicians back in later years after the Tsar had gone to the front during the early years of the war.

Olga sat with Sablin and was content in his familiar company.

Nicholas II celebrated his forty-fifth birthday the following day. It was spent mainly in the company of his four daughters rather than with his wife. Nicholas and his daughters called in on the Dowager Empress and then on his sister Olga Alexandrovna in the capital before returning to Tsarskoe Selo. A special liturgy was celebrated at the church close to the Catherine Palace. The Tsarina remained in her room and did not attend any of the festivities. There was a *baise main* (kissing of hands) followed by another of those big lunches.

The afternoon was spent privately as Nicholas and his daughters went out in the park and rode their bicycles and went kayaking once more. Nicholas had been sent many telegrams during the course of the day and, in the evening he and Alexandra sat down and began to reply to them.

On Tuesday morning, after the children had attended to their usual lessons, the Tsar escorted his five children to the regimental church where a service was held in honour of the Tsar's imminent departure for Berlin. He was about to leave for Germany to attend the wedding of the Kaiser's only daughter. The Grand Duchesses Olga and Tatiana had met the intended bride in 1899 when they had paid a call on the Princess and her youngest brother along with their nanny Miss Eager.

They then went on for a walk and to spend some time in the kayaks once more.

Olga suddenly felt unwell and left to sit on the balcony with her mother. She had been attacked by *Madame Becker* and needed to rest. She recovered enough by the late evening to travel to the railway station with Tatiana to see Nicholas off on his journey to Berlin. He travelled with Count Nirod. As Alexandra was not attending the celebrations in Berlin, she gave Nicholas a letter to give to her sister-in-law Eleanore. She admitted in it that she thought they would see that Nicholas had aged since the illness of his son the previous year.

The following day the Grand Duchesses found themselves in a situation where they had time on their hands. The teachers failed to appear. They sat around reading and doing needlework until Madame Vyrubova appeared. They then tried on some new dresses before deciding to visit the little children at the nearby nursery school. It was their ideal way of spending a few spare hours. As Alix sat quietly in the company of a headache, two telegrams arrived during the evening from Nicholas, assuring her of his safe arrival and that all was going well.

Olga spent a quiet session on the sunny balcony with Tatiana before the sisters went to their lessons. During the afternoon, the Tsar's sister Olga who was visiting escorted the four girls on a ride. They rode past the church and towards the army barracks. They encountered Sablin on their ride and, to Olga Nicolaevna's delight, they saw Alexander too. Olga returned to the sunny balcony later and in the evening Nicholas sent another telegram. He also thoughtfully sent a bouquet of lilac flowers for the Tsarina. It was the type of gift she appreciated; to Alexandra, flowers were more precious than jewels.

The next day, as the Tsarina and her children continued without Nicholas, life went on much as usual. After the inevitable lessons however, the Grand Duchesses were invited to tea at Anya's. She had also invited Countess Kleinmichael who arrived in the company of her two young nieces, Tata and Olga. As the sisters returned to the palace later in the evening, a telegram arrived especially for Olga, much to her delight.

On Friday, the wedding ceremony took place in Berlin. Princess Viktoria-Luise, who the Grand Duchesses had met once when they had visited Germany as little girls, married Prince Ernst August of Hanover. Amongst the guests, apart from Nicholas, was his cousin King George V who had come accompanied by his wife, unlike Nicholas.

Meanwhile, back in Russia, Nicholas's eldest daughters had travelled to the capital to meet their grandmother, chaperoned by Lili Obolenskaya. They were present when the Dowager handed out awards and medals to young ladies who had recently graduated. Olga and Tatiana stayed to attend lunch with the girls and must have found it strange to chat to girls who had attended school, unlike them. It was rare for the Grand Duchesses to meet ordinary yet intelligent girls. Whether it was inspirational or embarrassing is not clear. The Grand Duchesses tended to be shy in company but would have found it fascinating to be able to talk to the girls. Luckily their cousin Irina was amongst the company.

The Tsar arrived back from Berlin soon after.

The eagerly awaited tour began the following Thursday. The Imperial family Nicholas, Alexandra and their five children arrived by train in *Vladimir* in the early afternoon. They were met by a large crowd on their arrival and then the party travelled by motor car to the Uspensky Cathedral. Most of the visits would be to some sort of religious establishment – churches, cathedrals and monasteries. Alexandra remained on the train and was quickly joined by her son who was unable to continue. She was visited by some local women however whilst on the train and was presented with bouquets of flowers.

The voyage was taken along the Volga River intending to retrace the steps of the first Romanov Tsar Michael I from Kostroma to Moscow in 1613 to assume the throne.

The party then boarded the train and set off for *Suzdal*. They arrived mid-afternoon and once again headed for the main cathedral. Afterwards they made calls on two monasteries – the *Rizopolzhensky* and the *Spaso-Yefimovsky*. They made a point of visiting the solid marble tomb of one of Russia's national heroes who had died in 1642.

The Imperial family then travelled on to *Povrovsky monastery* where they had tea with the Mother Superior. Later that evening, they arrived by train at *Bogomolovo* where they visited the monastery and the site of the murder of St Count Andrei Bolgolyubsky. He had died in 1174 and again was one of Russia's national heroes. Nicholas received delegations from the local societies and the group returned to the train.

On Friday morning, the Imperial party arrived by train at *Nizhniy-Novgorod* where they were greeted by a guard of honour made up of the 37th Ekaterinberg regiment. It was ironic as it was in Ekaterinberg that the family were later imprisoned and murdered five years hence.

They then visited the *Spaso-Preobrazhensky* cathedral where they attended a prayer service. At this point, the Tsarina and her son went on to the palace whilst the rest of the family continued their visit. The Tsar and his daughters visited Minin's grave where at litia (a special religious service) took place. They then went to the site where the proposed monument was to be built to the memories of Count Pozharsky and Count Minin, who had helped thwart an attack by Polish troops on the young Tsar Michael in 1613.

The family then assembled at the palace for lunch. The ladies were received by the Mother Superior and the nuns whilst Nicholas then went on to meet local leaders and a new bank. After tea with members of the local nobility, the party went to the pier where they met with local shipbuilding owners and their families. The family then transferred to a steamboat. Several vessels travelled in convoy. The family settled aboard the steamer *Mezhen* but each evening had dinner aboard the *Tsar Michael Feodorovich*.

Late that evening, the convoy of vessels set off for Kostroma.

Saturday proved to be a cold and extremely windy day but luckily it was a rest day for the Imperial travellers. As they settled into their routine, the girls walked on deck and watched the ever changing scenery. The Grand Duchesses were much amused when Alexandra showed them the correct way to curtsy.

On Sunday morning the vessels finally arrived off *Kostroma*. The Imperial family then processed towards the town. The streets were lined by members of the Erivansky regiment, amongst others. Olga was delighted to see an old friend amongst the crowds: Otar Purtseladze. They visited the cathedral only to spot Rasputin amongst the congregation once again. The family then visited the museum dedicated the very first Romanov Tsar and had tea with local members of the nobility. They then returned to the pier and went onto the *Tsar Michael Feodorovich* steamboat for dinner. Olga and Tatiana later joined Nicholas on the riverbank to observe the firework display.

The following morning they returned to the cathedral. The Tsar then visited local leaders at the Governor's House whilst the Tsarina, her sister Ella and the five children visited the Bogoyavlensky monastery. The children were presented with gifts made by the nuns and the local schoolchildren. They then had tea with the Mother Superior. Olga received flowers from her old friend Otar Purtseladze, and the other ladies likewise received bouquets.

In the afternoon, the Imperial family visited an old church, the new Red Cross building and an exhibition before having tea. Later, they returned to the pier and once again went back to the *Tsar Michael Feodorovich* for dinner. The family then returned to their own base, the *Mezhen*. It would be their last night aboard.

The steamer *Mezhen* with the Imperial family onboard left Kostroma for Rostov. Tuesday proved to be a particularly hot and tiring day. The party were met at the pier by an honour guard and then travelled to the *Uspensky Cathedral,* the church of *St John the Baptist* and the *Spassky monastery.* The group then went on to *Iiinskaya* church before returning to the *Tsar Michael Feodorovich* in time for lunch.

In the afternoon, Nicholas and his four daughters visited an orphanage and went on to an exhibition. Despite receiving a tremendous amount of gifts, the day, even for the young Grand Duchesses, proved exhausting. The Tsarina and her son joined the rest of the family before continuing to the *Tolgsky monastery.* After a prayer service, the much-relieved family returned to the *Tsar Michael Feodorevich* in time for dinner. The day ended with a series of heavy downpours and a thunderstorm.

The day had not ended however. After dinner, the Tsar, accompanied by the Tsarina and Olga and Tatiana, left for the Assembly of the Nobility. They were all safely on the train by midnight and rested finally after an exhausting and hot day. The Tsarina had been suffering from tonsillitis, which made the day even harder for her.

The following morning, the train arrived at *Petrovsk.* Once more the Tsarina remained on board as she was still feeling unwell. That afternoon, as Alexandra remained on the train with her son, Tatiana and Marie, the Tsar and his other daughters Olga and Anastasia, together with his sisters Olga and Xenia, travelled to *Pereslavl* by motor car. They visited the *Nititsy, Danilovsky* and *Fedorovsky* monasteries. The party then visited the Vladimir nobility then Nicholas went alone to the *Peresalvinsky* lake where he watched a series of comic turns. On the way back to their base at *Petrovsk* Nicholas and his party called in at the *Church of Life Giving Trinity.*

On Friday morning, the party arrived at the Alexander station in *Moscow* and they headed for the *Troitse-Sergiev* monastery by car to attend liturgy. The Tsar and his family officially arrived at *Moscow* in the mid-afternoon. Nicholas on horseback along with his sister-in-law Grand Duchess Elisabeth, his two sisters and his four daughters travelled by carriage to the *Arkhangelsky Cathedral* where he lit an oil burner placed under the tombs of his illustrious ancestors. Once again Rasputin was amongst the congregation.

The Tsar had tea afterwards in the company of his sisters and daughters whilst the Tsarina rested.

On Saturday morning, Alexandra was greeted by her family on the occasion of her forty-first birthday. Later the Imperial family, including the almost exhausted Alexandra, made an appearance on the *Red Porch* before entering the *Uspensky Cathedral*. They then carried on to the *Chudov monastery*. After lunch, Nicholas and his daughters returned to the monastery and had tea there.

That evening, there was yet another gala dinner where the Grand Duchesses wore their Russian dresses and there was a firework display afterwards. One of the guests that evening was the Tsar's niece Marie Pavlovna, a Princess of Sweden by marriage, who arrived with her son Leonid who was very rarely seen in public with his mother. It was probably his first and indeed last visit to Russia. His parents divorced soon after and the boy remained in Sweden along with his father. Marie returned to the capital.

Nicholas and his daughters visited the *Novospassky monastery* on Sunday morning to attend the liturgy. The young Tsarevich arrived later for the final part of the service. The royal party visited the tombs of the Tsars. Once again, Rasputin made an appearance. The Tsar and his daughters then visited the municipal council where they had tea. They had lunch at the home of Grand Duchess Elisabeth.

One visitor that day in Moscow was the Grand Duchesses' former governess Sophie Ivanovna Tiecheva. The lady, accompanied by her sister and nephew, came to see her former pupils. The Tsarina would have been furious, as she disliked the former governess intensely since she had effectively blown the whistle on Rasputin three years previously. She had complained to Nicholas of Rasputin's presence in the rooms of the two eldest Grand Duchesses. The Tsarina was greatly angered by the accusation that he had assaulted another female member of staff and supported Rasputin, rather than the lady in question, Alexei's Nanny Maria.

That evening, Olga attended a ball at the Assembly of the Nobility along with her parents. The excited young Grand Duchess took part in many of the dances and was partnered by Nicholas Sablin and Otar Purtseladze amongst others. Although she saw Alexander Shvedov she did not dance with him. The Tsarina predictably left early but Olga and her father remained until after midnight.

The next morning the Imperial party rose late. Nicholas and his daughters visited an art exhibition in the Armoury Chamber before attending a quiet lunch in the company of the Tsarina, her sister Ella and Ella's niece Marie Pavlovna. Afterwards, Olga and Tatiana travelled with their older cousin Marie Pavlovna to her childhood home where they met two of the Kleinmichael sisters including Olga. The Tsar and his elder daughters briefly visited the *Voznesensky monastery* before rejoining the train and setting off for home. The exhausted Alexandra complained that the train was shaking her. Olga relaxed with a cigarette.

The family arrived back at the Alexander Palace early on Tuesday morning and visited church soon after for a prayer service. The Tsarina was glad to be home but her daughter Olga had enjoyed the novelty of the tour to such an extent that she would have gladly done it all over again.

In the afternoon, Nicholas went back into his garden and went rowing in one of the double boats along with Vladimir Derevenko and his eldest and youngest daughters Olga and Anastasia. The family had been away for some time and Olga noticed how lovely the garden was looking on their return. The lilac was now in bloom and smelled delightful after a rain shower. Lilac was the favourite scent of Marie who, although she tried various fragrances, always came back to her old favourite. The sisters used *Coty* perfumes. Olga preferred the sweet smelling *Rose The,* Tatiana liked *Jasmine de Corse* and Anastasia favoured the sickly sweet *violette.*

The next day was the sixteenth birthday of the Grand Duchess Tatiana. A prayer service was held in her honour just after noon. A family lunch was attended by the immediate family and the Tsar's sisters Olga and Xenia, who arrived for the celebrations. The afternoon was spent as usual for the Grand Duchesses as they returned to the double boats. They later picked numerous lilies of the valley on one of the small islands in the park. Olga then smoked another cigarette before coming in for tea with her parents, siblings and cousin Irina.

After the tour, life returned to normal.

Marie had become ill by the following day and was moved into a separate room away from Anastasia, with whom she shared a bedroom, as a precaution. She had started with a sore throat and a slightly raised temperature. In view of Tatiana's recent illness, it was probably wise. The other siblings continued with their lessons but then Alexei came down with a sore throat too and a temperature. Alexei's health was always rather delicate due to his haemophilia and Marie seemed to be prone to attacks of tonsillitis. Her tonsils were finally removed in dramatic circumstances at the end of 1914.

On Friday, the two invalids appeared a little better. Olga joined Nicholas at a military parade for retiring Cossacks. Whilst Nicholas handed the men pins, she gave each a card.

Olga tried on her regimental uniform on Saturday afternoon. It was now the beginning of June and, in just over two months' time, the two eldest daughters of the Tsar would take part in a parade on horseback. The two were acclimatising themselves with their uniforms and horses. That afternoon, Olga took the reins as the sisters went for a carriage ride together. Marie and Alexei had both recovered enough to get up. The Tsarevich had spent most of his short lifetime recovering from one illness or another. It had given him the type of patience only really apparent in such children.

On Sunday afternoon, the four young Grand Duchesses were chaperoned by Madame Vyrubova on a visit to their Aunt Olga. On this occasion, Olga was staying at Peterhof, on the Gulf of Finland rather than in the capital. The four excited sisters enjoyed running around the garden and down to the sea. They played tag outside and, at tea, Olga once again managed to sit next to Alexander.

On Monday, a series of photographs were taken of the Tsar and his immediate family. Olga felt bored and this shows in the pictures. The sisters were photographed in pairs, alone, with their parents, etc. The photos are ones that are the most well known of the family. Tatiana appeared wearing her wig.

Olga remained in bed most of the following morning after the arrival of *Madame*

Becker. The family removed to Peterhof for the summer as they usually did at this time of year. It was cooler and fairly windy. The fresh sea breeze was a tonic after the heat of Tsarskoe Selo. The day ending with the Tsar in a holiday mood, he read to Alexandra and the children as he often did when on vacation. He still had to work but the seaside situation gave him more of a holiday feel.

The following morning, Olga stayed in bed a long time again. She found the bed comfortable. The family stayed in one of the smaller houses on the Peterhof estate. The house was fairly small and would have felt cosy if not a little cramped. It had been even smaller but in the early years of his reign Nicholas had added to the little cottage.

A service was held in the early afternoon to celebrate the twelfth birthday of Grand Duchess Anastasia. Later, Olga went for a pleasant ride in the company of Anya Vyrubova. Her parents had a house nearby. The weather was unfortunately not in much of a festive mood as it rained, although the air was undoubtedly fresher than in Tsarskoe Selo or St Petersburg.

The Tsarina's other close friend Lili Dehn arrived in time for tea, along with her young son Alexander known as Titi. The Tsarevich and Alexander enjoyed each other's company despite the four-year age gap. Titi had been born in 1908 and Alexei in 1904. The Grand Duchesses simply enjoyed playing with the boy, as they adored babies and children.

After yet another late start the following morning, Olga was visited by the dentist. The man in question was the family's regular dentist and even visited them in Siberia. Lunch was enlivened by the company of Xenia and her family. The Grand Duchesses' cousins generally arrived for tea on birthdays and other special occasions.

The four sisters and their cousins then travelled to Aunt Olga's by motor car for a party, accompanied by Anya Vyrubova. The Grand Duchess had quite a house full. Amongst the visitors were Olga Nicolaevna's friend Alexander, Victor Zborovsky, Yuzek, Skvortstov and Nicholas Rodionov. The party continued in the garden where the guests ran around playing slap-on-hands, rope, gorelki and the energetic tag.

The party continued inside and the youngsters went upstairs and ten of them managed to climb inside a wardrobe which inevitably broke. Olga and her sisters were amongst the crowd but whether they were in the overstuffed wardrobe or not sadly is not known. If they had have been, it would have been rather a crush and in very close contact with other people – male and female. Whether a chaperone was in the wardrobe or not is not known but had she been there she would have been in no condition to chaperone anyone. The sisters thought the parties were the highlight of their week. They rarely had so much fun or saw so many people of their own age in such close contact – certainly not in a wardrobe.

Meanwhile, back at home, Nicholas and Alexandra chatted with Xenia and Sandro about Irina's suitor Felix. The two would later become engaged.

The evening was rounded off perfectly when Nicholas read a comic story by the writer Teffi on their return. Alexandra had managed to wear herself out on a visit to Countess Hendrikova in Stelna. The Countess was the mother of Alexandra's lady-in-waiting and the Grand Duchesses' chaperone Anastasia Hendrikova.

Late on Friday morning, the four Grand Duchesses travelled by motor car to Stelna to see Grand Duke Konstantin's daughter Tatiana and her baby son. They also called in on Countess Hendrikova. The weather proved to be in a bad mood so the Grand Duchesses remained indoors on their return and Olga amused herself by reading and playing the piano.

As the weather finally improved by the following morning, Olga and Tatiana, accompanied by Trina, took the opportunity to get some horse riding practice in. In the afternoon, the four Grand Duchesses visited Anya for a party whilst their mother returned to Stelna.

Sunday proved to be yet another beautiful day. The day began with a military parade for Nicholas and his daughters followed by one of the big lunches. The afternoon was spent lazily by the sisters sunbathing and picking lily of the valley. Shortly after the Tsar's younger sister Olga arrived, the family left for Kronstadt and for the royal yacht.

After a night spent on the yacht *Standart*, Nicholas and his daughters briefly left to return to Peterhof and attended a service at the cathedral. After the party returned to the yacht, the *Standart* set off. Olga sat in her cabin accompanied by Paul Voronov, Nicholas Rodionov and Nicholas Sablin. The yacht anchored at a familiar spot in the early evening and a prayer service was later held on deck. The yacht inevitably travelled the same route each summer and the site was nicknamed the *Bay of Standart*. The balalaika orchestra, who remained permanently on the yacht when Nicholas was in residence, played during dinner. Later, Olga chose to sit with Paul Voronov again whilst he was on watch.

The young Grand Duchesses loved spending time on the yacht and felt relaxed amongst the ship's company. Nicholas saw more of his family than usual and worked far less than he usually did at the Alexander Palace. The 420 foot long yacht weighed some 5,300 tons and was manned by a crew of 275. It included not only the officers and sailors but stewards, bakers, cabin boys, kitchen boys, engineers, stokers, deckhands and an entire platoon of the Guarde Equipage (Marine Guard) and the ship's brass band and balalaika orchestra.

It would become part of a regular pattern for the young Grand Duchesses in the coming weeks to be in the company of the crew. Olga Nicolaevna grew closer to a young officer named Paul Voronov and delighted in his company. She would forget Alexander once and for all and fall for someone else. It was someone she had known for a few years and was some nine years her senior.

Nicholas was not free from work even at sea. He still had government reports brought to him twice a week and needed to keep up to date with what was happening in the capital and throughout his vast empire. Alexandra and her friend Anya watched as he cut the envelopes and then later threw them into the sea. It was an unusual filing system.

As the annual cruise commenced, the family relaxed and the crew were drawn in to their world and became part of an extended family in a way. Trips were planned ashore most days.

On Tuesday morning, chaperoned by Trina Schneider and Anastasia Hendrikova, the young Grand Duchesses and Paul Voronov went ashore and then travelled by car to *Tukholma Island* which was packed full of large boulders. The party walked along the boulders to the beach. When they arrived, they found that another group from the yacht had arrived before them. The Tsar's sister Olga and a few of the other officers from the yacht were already on the beach.

The group went back to the yacht in time for lunch. The commanders of all the vessels had been invited that day. When the Imperial yacht *Standart* travelled along the coast to Finland, it went in convoy with other ships including the *Polar Star* where Olga Alexandrovna was based. She joined the family during the day but returned to her yacht late in the evening. The ships shadowed the Tsar's yachts in order to protect him from any possible danger.

That afternoon, the family went back ashore but Olga Nicolaevna decided to remain on board with her mother. She sat with Alexandra and they were joined by Sablin, who was always in attendance on the Tsarina, and by Captain Zelenetsey. Tea was served once the rest of the family returned. Olga once again chose to sit with Paul Voronov that evening. The Tsarina had gone down to her cabin; she was already exhausted. It had been a very warm day and she disliked the heat intensely.

On Wednesday morning, the four young Grand Duchesses accompanied by Anastasia Hendrikova and one of the officers from the yacht went ashore once again and headed for the same spot. Once again they were met on the beach by Olga Alexandrovna and her party. The weather on this occasion was not good however as it rained. One of the young officers who had accompanied Olga Alexandrovna amused the party by reading their favourite comic stories by Teffi.

The group returned for lunch once again and all the officers were invited. In the afternoon, Nicholas and his sister returned to dry land. On this occasion, his daughters Olga, Tatiana and Anastasia accompanied him whilst Marie remained on board with her mother. One or other of the Grand Duchesses nearly always remained on board with their mother. The Tsar and his party went for a long walk to the local village. Upon their return they observed Alexei on the beach playing with some other boys.

In the evening, Olga read on deck. She was not alone but accompanied in close proximity by the Tsarina, the Grand Duchess Olga Alexandrovna, Tatiana, Sablin, Anastasia Hendrikova and, of course, Paul Voronov. As the young Olga became more and more fond of the young man, she gradually became surrounded by more and more unofficial chaperones.

The rest of the party were employed in making bead necklaces as they had in the spring. (The Tsarina's brother the Grand Duke of Hesse often sent small items for making necklaces in aid of charity to his sister.)

On Thursday morning, the four Grand Duchesses, accompanied by Trina Schnieder and Anastasia Hendrikova, travelled to one of the nearby small islands. They spent the morning picking the inevitable lily of the valley, which grew profusely on the island. As they arrived, they found that Olga Alexandrovna had already arrived before them with a party of officers.

The Governor-General of Finland, Mr Zein, was invited to lunch on this occasion. They were, after all, holidaying in Finland. After lunch, the Tsar took a party, including his daughters, out in a motorboat and they went to a nearby beach.

That evening, Olga and her sister Tatiana enjoyed a game of forfeits along with Sablin, Anya, Paul Voronov and others. Olga cheated and giggled the night away in pleasant company. It was a warm evening.

On the following morning, Olga chose once again not to go ashore. There was a prayer service at noon for the birthday of Marie. She was fourteen years old. That afternoon, a party went ashore in order to play tennis. The tennis season had now begun for the Imperial family and they would spend many an afternoon indulging in this sport. It was naturally played by the Grand Duchesses in their usual summer clothes. They did not change into special tennis shorts as this would have been quite scandalous at this time. A young lady simply did not show her legs; as a girl grew, her skirts were gradually lowered to ensure that she was dressed correctly. As Anastasia's skirt was obviously a great deal shorter than Olga's by this stage, it would have given her a great advantage.

Olga made a good start to the *season*. She played with the captain of the yacht against Anya and the Tsar's aide Narishkin, and later with the captain against Narishkin and Arseniev.

The younger Grand Duchesses Marie and Anastasia meanwhile waded in the marsh close by.

After the party returned to the yacht, where presumably Tatiana had remained with the Tsarina, Nicholas chose to play a game of dice with the captain and a few of the other men, whilst Olga and her sisters amiably chatted on deck with Voronov and Rodionov. The latter officer was nearly always accompanied by Voronov, and the two grew close to Olga and her sister Tatiana. Rodionov became quite fond of Tatiana; although she liked him, she did not share his affections.

Olga Nicolavna decided against going ashore on Saturday morning. In the afternoon, she had another opportunity to go ashore but decided against it. The Tsarina lay on deck but at one point went downstairs only to return in time for tea. She did not like the heat. Olga meanwhile sat reading but felt she had to go and sit with Voronov.

After dinner that evening, Olga and Tatiana sat with Paul Voronov. Anastasia Hendrikova remained close by as chaperone. Nicholas played dice with some of the men.

On Sunday morning, there was a service on deck. In the afternoon, tennis was resumed. Olga played with Baron Nalde of the *Polar Star*. The couple played against Anya and Semenov. Olga then changed partners but the only thing that remained was her losing streak. She lost each time.

After tea, Olga decided to go rowing with her sister Tatiana in one of the double boats, accompanied by Rodionov. In the evening, Olga and Tatiana played dice on the quarterdeck with the now inevitable Voronov and Rodionov. Hendrikova placed herself close by and acted as chaperone.

On a hot Monday morning, Olga and Tatiana were joined in the double boat by the Tsar. The two sisters resumed the tennis tournament that afternoon. Olga decided to play with Anya against Tatiana and Paul. As usual, Olga lost. After walking on the giant strides (stilts), Olga decided to sunbathe before going back to the yacht and reading. It was too hot for much else.

Olga was very widely read and liked poetry, history and novels, but her sisters Tatiana and Marie's type of reading was rather lighter. They preferred the stories of the British novelist Florence Barclay.

The next days were spent mainly with trips ashore in the mornings and tennis ashore in the afternoons. In the evenings, Olga spent as much time as she could in the company of Paul Voronov whether in the control room or on deck. On each occasion, one or other of the ladies-in-waiting sat close by keeping an eye on the proceedings. Olga Alexandrovna joined the group during the bulk of the day and returned to the *Polar Star* at around 10pm.

Olga's tennis playing skills rapidly declined. It made little difference who she played with: whether it was Anya, her Aunt Olga, or Rodionov, she lost.

Anya developed tonsillitis and remained downstairs in her cabin. She was prone to illness like anyone else but when she became ill Madame Vyrubova took to her bed in order to gain the sympathy of the Tsarina and her family.

On Sunday, there was the usual religious service on deck before a big lunch. Once again, Olga elected to remain on board during the afternoon, ostensibly to read but she soon followed Voronov to the control room. He was not alone, however, and on this occasion had been joined by the ever watchful Sablin and Rodionov.

That evening, Nicholas escorted his four daughters onto the mainland for one of his famous long walks. If there was a longer or more difficult route, he took it. The party were joined by members of the crew from the *Polar Star* and the Tsar's sister. The party walked through the woods and then went for a picnic. They sat around on rocks and a stage was set up for a couple of plays. Afterwards, local people arrived and everyone joined in dancing to an accordion. Olga danced with a young local boy named Matti Mikkola and then with Voronov. The group had dinner on the *Polar Star* and returned to their yacht after midnight.

On Monday afternoon, Olga went ashore in order to play tennis again. She was a little more successful on this occasion. She played a couple of sets with her aunt against her sister Tatiana and Baron Nalde. She won one of the two sets. As the young Grand Duchesses sunbathed in the sunshine, their aunt fell asleep.

Nicholas took up his racquet and, partnered by Pavlov, took on Voronov and Kvoshchinsky. The girls attempted to walk on the stilts once more and then went swimming. They returned to the yacht to find that the Tsarina was complaining of her heart once again. Olga sat on deck before dinner in the company of Voronov, Rodionov and LM Kozhevnikov while the ship was receiving supplies of fuel and food.

Anya did not surface during the day as she was still suffering from tonsillitis. Olga Nicolaevna sat with the Tsarina and Sablin for a while whilst Tatiana was on the upper deck in the company of her Aunt Olga, Rodionov and Zlebov. Olga Alexandrovna left the yacht to return to the *Polar Star* at 10.30 as usual. Alexandra went down to her cabin soon after and Nicholas went to his cabin in order to read, much as he did at home. Olga stayed on deck a little longer to sit with Voronov as he was on duty that night.

Mochalov, a junior mechanic, entertained the remaining guests with his piano skills.

There was a change of members of the Tsar's suite the following morning: Count Grabbe and Alexander Drenteln came aboard the Imperial yacht *Standart* and Arseniev and Naryshkin returned to dry land. Olga went ashore for a game of mixed doubles tennis with her father. The two served against Tatiana and her partner Nicholas Rodionov. The result was a draw as each couple won one game. Afterwards Olga and Rodionov played two games against Nicholas and Captain Rostislav Zelenetsky but with the same result. After a dip in the sea, Olga returned to the yacht.

The Tsarina again went to bed early whilst her eldest daughter joined Paul Voronov in the control room. Olga rejoined Paul after dinner. They were not alone. As Voronov filled out the yacht's log, he and Olga were joined by Olga's aunt and namesake, Nicholas Rodionov, Serge Zlebov and the young Ippolit Mochalov. After a brief official visit by Count Maklakov, moving pictures (films) were shown in the family dining room. It was an account of their Tercentenary visits earlier in the year, including Moscow. The ever-observant Olga spotted her friend Alexander twice.

On Wednesday morning, whilst Nicholas went on the water, Olga remained on deck reading. She spent much of the afternoon ashore indulging in her hobby of tennis. Olga Nicolaevna, in partnering Nicholas Rodionov, finally came up with a winning combination, and the two beat Nicholas and his sister in both sets, but when she played with Nicholas she lost.

After swimming in the sea, Olga returned to the yacht. Alexandra had been lying out on the deck once more and was suffering for it. In the evening, Olga escorted the Grand Duchesses to the *Turkmenets Stavropolya* where films were being shown. Olga sat next to Voronov and later admitted her love for him in her journal. Once again, I M Mochalov entertained with his piano playing abilities. As Olga retired for the evening, Nicholas carried on with his game of dice.

The next day, Olga continued to be *on duty* looking after her mother but in reality she wanted to be near Voronov. Nicholas, his sister and some of the officers went ashore for a long walk and a swim early in the morning. Olga remained on the deck of the *Standart* and quietly read. She was an avid reader and enjoyed reading whenever she had the opportunity. Whilst the family were on board the yacht, she had ample opportunity as lessons were cancelled.

When most of the family went ashore, Olga once again elected to remain on board. The Tsarina was relaxing on the deck where a tent had been erected earlier. Alexandra was joined later by her friend Anya and the ever present Nicholas Sablin. As Olga returned to her book in the early evening, Voronov appeared and she followed him to the control room. He continued writing down the observations in the vessel's logbook whilst Olga dictated. He was unable to stay long as he had to go for his dinner. The Prime Minister Kokovstov appeared on board the *Roksana* with an important governmental report for Nicholas. Afterwards, Olga sat cosily half hidden by the chimney with Voronov and Rodionov. The Tsarina retired early once more to her cabin below and Nicholas read in his.

At noon on Friday, there was a service in memory of the Tsar's brother George.

He had died in the summer of 1899 on this day shortly after the birth of Nicholas's third daughter Marie. He had died as a result of a motorcycle accident but had been suffering for some time with tuberculosis.

Had he lived, George would almost certainly have been of great help to Nicholas. Although the two rarely met in later years due to the severe illness of the Grand Duke, they corresponded and the letters reveal a true friendship, something Nicholas never had with anyone else, with the possible exception of Dr Botkin. George was intelligent enough to talk politics with Nicholas in such a manner that it came naturally. Nicholas never talked on the subject normally. George's death was a real loss, far bigger than anyone realised at the time. George would have been a good influence on the indecisive Nicholas.

Meanwhile, Olga played tennis with Nicholas against Paul Voronov and Pototsky. The Tsar and his daughter managed to win the first set but then lost the next two. As the men went off to swim, the ladies returned to the yacht. Nicholas came back soaking wet later after being splashed whilst kayaking. The high temperatures would have made the water particularly inviting that day.

In the early evening, Olga happened to spot Voronov and she felt compelled to accompany him to the control room where they sat happily together on the sofa chatting. She had to leave Paul later in order to go and dress for dinner. Olga spent a quiet evening after Paul left as he would have to get up early for the watch duty later on. The Tsarina remained in her cabin whilst Nicholas went ashore on the *Tsarevna* to attend a regimental parade at Peterhof the following day. He was away overnight.

As Nicholas was away overnight, on Saturday Olga was forced to take his place and speak to the musicians after lunch in order to extend her appreciation for their playing. The crew took the opportunity of the Tsar's temporary absence to clean the deck. Olga and her sisters went ashore after lunch for tennis. Olga partnered Paul Voronov and Tatiana sided with Rodionov. The latter pair outplayed Olga and her partner. Despite playing seven separate sets, Olga and Paul only won a single set.

Nicholas returned to the *Standart* aboard the *Ukraina* and destabilised his own yacht as the *Ukraina* arrived at great speed accompanied by the *Polar Star*. Alexandra, in the absence of Nicholas, had remained in her cabin all day. Later, Nicholas resumed his game of dice whilst Olga observed Voronov (who was on watch) from the deck below.

The Emperor returned to his tennis on Sunday afternoon. He played in a doubles match against his daughter Olga who on this occasion actually won. She spent the evening once more in the company of Voronov. She sat with her sister Tatiana, Voronov and the young mechanic Ippolit Mochalov on the upper deck bridge.

Chapter Three

Summer 1913

The next day, Monday, was the first day of the next month and it was spent quietly by Olga due to the return of the well known *Madame Becker*, but the Empress was in a worse state. She was suffering from pains in the head, back, arms and legs and was finding it difficult to breathe. The warm weather would not have helped. She was always worse in the heat. After lunch, Olga felt well enough to go up on deck and predictably she decided to visit Voronov.

Olga was bored on Tuesday as she did not see Voronov until late on. That evening she played card games with Voronov, Sablin and Kozhevikov, but Countess Hendrikova was on hand to act as chaperone.

On the next morning, as her sisters went ashore to swim, Olga remained on board. She watched the others play tennis that afternoon before wandering off to pick some wild strawberries. That evening, the yacht finally left for Reval. Yet again, Olga contrived to spend the afternoon with Voronov; she was unable to sit with him later as he was on duty early the next morning and had to go to bed.

Early on Thursday morning, Olga Nicolaevna was awakened by foghorns warning of poor visibility ahead. She could not concentrate on reading when Voronov was nearby but she did not think of moving away.

Olga Nicolaevna was in a happy mood the following morning. She spent the day in the company of Tatiana and their friends Voronov and Rodionov. The Empress was unwell but Countess Hendrikova was on hand as the usual chaperone.

Anastasia was in a bad mood on Saturday. The young Grand Duchess hated to be told that she was short and the sailors enjoyed teasing her about it. Olga had remained on board that morning whilst her sisters went off for a swim. She sat and read. She positioned herself between Alexandra, who she was supposed to be watching, and Voronov.

On Sunday, there was the usual religious service and, in the afternoon, Olga decided to go ashore for once to play tennis. The reason soon became obvious: Paul Voronov also went ashore. The two played tennis together in a doubles game but lost. When she changed partners, she won. That evening, Olga and Tatiana sat in the control room with Voronov. It was a hot day and a tent had been erected in order to give the group some shade.

The following day, the Tsar took Olga and Tatiana on a boat trip. There was the usual tennis during the early afternoon where Olga partnered the Tsar and, for once, she was on the winning side. In the evening, Olga took the opportunity to sit with Voronov during a film show. It was an opportunity to sit next to him without arousing too much attention and had the added attraction for her of being in the dark.

On Tuesday, Nicholas took all four of his daughters on a hair-raising boat trip. They ended up sprayed with not just water but with soot from the engine. The afternoon was spent as usual playing tennis. Once again Olga found a partner capable of winning. It was rare that she beat Tatiana. In the evening, Olga played cards on deck with Voronov, Rodionov, Mochalov and the chaperone for the evening Hendrikova.

Olga played tennis badly the next day and was bored. She was missing the company of Voronov.

She brightened up later, however, when she was able to once more to see her friend.

Olga Nicolaevna received bouquets of roses and many telegrams on her name's day the eleventh, and the annual photograph was taken of all those who took part in the annual summer cruise. She stayed behind during the afternoon when the others went to play tennis. As Alexandra was unwell again, Olga elected to remain with her in the Tsarina's cabin. Sablin was, however, also on duty and sitting with the Tsarina.

The yacht left for Kronstadt on Friday morning. It was the end of the summer cruise. That day, Tatiana had collected the signatures of all the officers and guests aboard the yacht as a memento of the cruise. Olga made the most of her last afternoon on the yacht and sat with Voronov for the final hour. The family left the *Standart* and travelled back to Peterhof aboard the *Alexandria*.

The normal routine was re-established the following morning at Peterhof. The two eldest Grand Duchesses Olga and Tatiana got down to the serious business of training how to make their entrance at the forthcoming regimental parade. In the afternoon, Olga played tennis with her father and Anastasia Hendrikova. There was the consolation of being able to contact some friends from the yacht by telephone later for Olga. She spoke to Sablin and Mochalov.

On Sunday, Olga Nicolaevna spoke to Voronov over the telephone. She also chatted with Rodionov and Sablin. She returned to the tennis court in the afternoon, partnered by Anya. They played and lost to Nicholas and Tatiana. The Tsarina remained indoors complaining of a headache and problems with her heart. Olga meanwhile recalled happy times spent on the Imperial yacht when she overheard a military march in the background when she telephoned Sablin later.

The following morning, Olga rose early in order to catch sight of the yacht – Voronov, of course, was on board. She was wondering what he was doing. He was still on her mind. That morning she and Tatiana again practised for the upcoming regimental parade. In the afternoon, the four sisters played tennis with Anya.

On Tuesday, Olga once again went riding and then played tennis in the afternoon. Unfortunately, the young Tsarevich managed to hurt his arm when waving his arms around whilst playing. It gave him a great deal of pain preventing him from sleeping for quite some time.

That day, Alexandra had sent word to her brother Ernie enclosing some photos that had been taken in the spring. They were expecting Ella to arrive on Thursday, she explained, and their other sister Irene was due to appear on Sunday. The sisters would have to live at the farm because there was no room at the house. Olga was now in the new guest room, Tatiana was in Orchie's old room, and Alexei was housed downstairs with Derevenko.

Olga went out riding again on Wednesday morning and once again played tennis in the afternoon, on this occasion with Nicholas against Hendrikova and Anya Vyrubova. Rasputin arrived in the early evening and spent a short time with Alexei and the Tsarina. He then went to chat to Nicholas and his daughters. Soon after Rasputin's departure, Alexei appeared to improve and fell asleep. Rasputin had probably calmed down both Alexei and his anxious mother, and enabled the boy to relax; when one is more relaxed, the pain tends to ease naturally. Olga still had Voronov on her mind and was more concerned about his whereabouts. The yacht was heading towards Germany.

The next day, Olga and Tatiana had a walk before they returned to their lessons after the long break. A recovering Alexei lay out on the balcony in the afternoon with his mother. The sisters meanwhile played more tennis. The weather was good enough to enable the family to have their tea on the balcony too. Olga heard that the Imperial yacht had reached the German sea.

On Friday, Olga rode once again and resumed the tennis. Olga's former nanny visited in the early evening. She had last seen the children in Moscow and returned once more. She was, according to Alexandra, an enemy of Rasputin having spoken out against him in the past, but the Grand Duchesses had fond memories of her. As the family lapped up the sun on the balcony, Olga was happy to hear that the Imperial yacht *Standart* had safely reached Portsmouth that day.

Olga Nicolaevna spent time with her Aunt Elisabeth the following day. The four sisters dyed scarves together outside on the balcony. Alexandra enjoyed the company of her sisters but she and Ella disagreed on the subject of Rasputin. She was probably closer to Irene who, like Alexandra, had a haemophiliac son and had already lost one to the disease some years earlier. Ella had no children. Olga had once more begun the day with a ride on her horse. Nicholas attended one of his never-ending regimental parades before returning for a game of tennis with his daughters.

On Sunday morning, the Tsarina's sister Irene arrived to see her two sisters.

Irene came from Germany in order to see them (Alix and Ella) – both of whom married Russians. Olga and Tatiana went to meet her. The afternoon was spent by Olga not playing tennis but in riding a boat with her two youngest sisters and a couple of others. Tatiana decided to join Nicholas in kayaking.

Grand Duchess Elisabeth left the following day. Elisabeth spent most of her time visiting various monasteries and working for her own religious order. It was Marie's name's day and a special service was held and one of the big lunches was served. Ella was Marie's godmother. Olga returned to the tennis court in the afternoon with Nicholas and Anya and a couple of the officers from the yacht who had remained in Russia on this occasion. The Tsar accompanied his two eldest daughters on a boat trip later that evening.

Olga and Tatiana went visiting with their Aunt Irene on Monday morning. They visited the Catherine Palace and made a brief excursion to Irene's cousin Miechen. The cosy evening spent out on the Tsarina's balcony was spoilt by the annoying presence of an abundance of flies. Once again the four girls dyed scarves with their mother and, on this occasion, Irene. They were probably making the scarves for a charity bazaar.

Olga and Tatiana visited Kronstadt on the following morning with Nicholas for the unveiling of Admiral Makarov's monument. (He had been the Commander of the Russian fleet during the 1904-1905 war with Japan.) Nicholas met up with his Greek relatives (Queen Olga of Greece was a good friend of the Imperial couple and Olga Nicolaevna's godmother and her son Constantine had been close to Nicholas in the years before his marriage to Alix), and later Olga and Anastasia rode their bicycles to Derevenko's house where they saw Olga's godson Yevgeny. He was almost certainly Derevenko's baby nephew.

On Thursday morning, Olga and Tatiana visited the annual manoeuvres at Krasnoe Selo with their Aunt Irene. Olga spotted an old friend Alexander and recalled that it was actually his birthday. In the evening, as Nicholas went out once more to Krasnoe Selo, the sisters remained at home with their mother and chatted to her and Irene.

On Wednesday after a walk before lunch for Olga and Tatiana, the four sisters spent the afternoon playing tennis again. Nicholas returned to Krasnoe Selo and the ladies, Alexandra and her sister Irene and the four Grand Duchesses spent a pleasant evening together playing cards as they usually did when Irene arrived. Alix had played cards frequently as a child with her late Uncle Leopold after her mother had died. She rarely played after her marriage though. Later, everyone travelled to Stelna to visit Princess Tatiana.

On the following morning, Nicholas left once more for Krasnoe Selo. Irene and her lady-in-waiting escorted Olga and Tatiana on a walk around the district. Rain put a stop to the tennis that afternoon for Olga and her sisters. That evening, Olga was smoking whilst playing cards. It was not an image normally associated with the Grand Duchesses!

On Sunday, Olga and her sisters played tennis and later went visiting with their aunt and met a drunk much to the amusement of young Anastasia who was always liable to see the funny side in any situation. Olga was not amused by her sister's antics. The evening was spent playing cards once again.

The following morning, Olga and her sisters went horse riding whilst Nicholas attended the military manoeuvres. Olga and Tatiana were, of course, training for their part in an important parade. They would be riding with their 'own' regiments. Afterwards, Olga was forced to rest after the probably unwelcome return of *Madame Becker*. In the early evening, Olga and Tatiana were taken on an automobile ride to Sergievka by Irene. The evening ended as it usually did when Irene was around – with a game of cards.

On Tuesday it was the Tsarevich's ninth birthday and it was celebrated in the usual style with a church service and a big lunch. The weather was in no festive mood sadly as it rained heavily all day. He spent part of the day playing with his friends, the sons of Derevenko, on the balcony with some paper lanterns. The sisters played cards once more with their aunt that evening.

The next morning, Olga and Tatiana visited Krasnoe Selo to see their regiments. They were escorted by an ever present chaperone Countess Anastasia Hendrikova. The Grand Duchesses were photographed along with members of their regiments and later visited a military hospital. The three then returned to the military ground and watched as the regiments performed various exercises. The two youngest Grand Duchesses Marie and Anastasia came later. As Alexandra and Irene spent the evening playing cards with the girls, Nicholas went to the theatre for the evening.

The beginning of the next month found Alexei suffering from terrible pain in his arm. In an effort to ease the pain, Olga held a heat pad on his arm. He had hurt his arm recently and was struggling to recover. Olga was relieved to hear that the Imperial yacht (and of course Voronov) had arrived safely in the Dardanelles. She still could not get Paul out of her mind and constantly wondered where he was and what he was doing. In the afternoon, she joined her father and aunt on a tour of a factory. The evening ended in a few games of cards.

On Friday morning, Olga and Tatiana rehearsed entering the parade ground in the company of their Aunt Irene. It was Irene rather than Alexandra who took them in hand and showed them exactly how it was to be done. The Tsarina rarely rode a horse since her marriage, yet in her teens and early twenties she had often ridden when she lived in Darmstadt. A lady-in-waiting of her Aunt Helena had even compared Alix and her cousin Thora as being like the Bennet sisters from Jane Austen's *Pride and Prejudice*. Seeing Alix in 1913, it was impossible to believe how lively she had formerly been. The two Bennet sisters (Kitty and Lydia) were in many ways similar to Alix and her cousin Thora in their younger days. Thora, like Lydia, was the more forward of the two. The two cousins had in former years followed the regiment when Thora's older brother was stationed near to Alix's home at Wolfsgarten.

Nicholas had left for the military manoeuvres early in the morning and arrived back in time for dinner. In the early years of their marriage, Alix, a daughter of a soldier, had attended them with Nicholas. In the evening Olga and Tatiana attended a full dress rehearsal of the parade. Alexei was recovering at last and would after all be able to see his sisters on parade. The Imperial yacht returned to Sevastopol much to the relief of Olga.

On Saturday morning, Olga continued training for the parade. It would be the only time that Olga and Tatiana would take part in such a parade due to the war and ride alongside their father. Afterwards, she observed the military manoeuvres from a convenient vantage point along with their Aunt Irene and younger siblings.

Olga played tennis with her sisters on Sunday afternoon. Once more, Nicholas was away all day at Krasnoe Selo.

The long-awaited ceremony took place on Monday morning with a greatly excited Olga and Tatiana taking centre stage in the parade. The two Grand Duchesses reviewed *their* regiments at a mounted full-dress parade at Peterhof. Olga rode her horse *Regent* and Tatiana *Robino*. Olga was escorted by the experienced Grand Duke Nicholas, known as Nikolasha. She was met by Martynov with a report and then she galloped as she had rehearsed to the sound of the trumpet and formally greeted each squadron before meeting up with the Tsar. She then followed him around once more.

Afterwards tea, photographs were taken of Olga, Nicholas and members of her Hussar regiment. She was then photographed with the ladies. Tatiana had similar photographs taken. As Alexandra had been unable to attend the parade, all those who had attended rode to the garden where Alix was sitting in a carriage with her son. The day had been a great success and all Olga's worries were in vain. Even the weather had cooperated as it had been a suitably hot and sunny day.

On Tuesday morning, there was bad news. The Tsar's aide Count Nirod had died. He had been ill for some time but as recently as May had accompanied Nicholas to Berlin. Later, Olga and Tatiana visited Anastasia Hendrikova's mother at Strelna. After their return, the sisters went for a refreshing boat ride with Nicholas on the *Alexandria* and the *Rabotnik*. Nicholas later attended a memorial service for the Count. Rasputin also made one of his visits in the early evening.

The following morning found Marie Nicolevna ill with a stomach bug but the long train journey to Livadia was not delayed. It cannot have been an easy ride for Marie in the circumstances. The family left Peterhof after a brief prayer service. The Tsarina complained that she had been jolted about on the journey. Nicholas read to the family in the evening aboard the Imperial train. He chose a military topic and read about men who had been awarded the St George Cross.

Thursday was spent travelling south by train. Luckily, Marie had recovered and was feeling much better. Olga amused herself by making up sacks for the coming bazaar. The Tsar's sister joined the train at Kursk. The family briefly got off at Borki to attend a religious service in memory of a train accident in 1888 which had almost killed the entire family.

On Friday, the Imperial family transferred to the yacht at Sevastopol. It had been a hot and dusty journey and the Tsarina had not slept at all. Olga was once more back where she wanted to be: close to her friend Paul Voronov. She had always enjoyed the annual cruise and this year it was a memorable one for her. In the afternoon, Olga and her sister Tatiana joined Voronov in the control room. Olga was happy to be near Paul again and was frustrated when Nicholas took the family for motor boat ride that evening.

On Saturday morning, when Olga, Tatiana and Anastasia accompanied by their Aunt Olga and Sablin and others went ashore to do some shopping, the crowds of people they attracted made it impossible to stay for more than a few minutes. As Marie rested aboard the yacht, her three sisters took a motor boat ride with Nicholas and his sister later in the day to a church that had been ruined during the Crimean war in the 1850s and a naval hospital. The group returned to the yacht before vespers.

The party came on deck later to admire the hydroplanes. Later, Olga and Tatiana sat with Voronov and Rodionov close to the control room but with their aunt acting as chaperone. Nicholas played dice with members of the crew whilst Alexandra and Marie rested.

The next day, the Emperor visited a local monastery with his daughters to attend Mass. Olga would have much preferred to remain on the yacht. Later Olga, Tatiana and Anastasia accompanied Nicholas on a visit to the Harax monastery to see the recent archaeological dig. It was hot and dusty. Nicholas was fascinated with archaeology but had neither the time nor the patience to indulge his passion.

That evening, once more, Olga contrived to sit with Voronov. As usual, however, they were not alone and were accompanied by Rodionov, Mityaev, Tatiana and the

Grand Duchess Olga Alexandrovna. Olga Nicolaevna briefly visited her mother who was complaining that she was having trouble breathing because of the wind. Alexandra was not alone either; she had been joined by the ever-watchful Sablin.

On Monday, Olga and Tatiana, escorted by their aunt, travelled by automobile to Zimonins for a swim and to visit Admiral Malkovsky. After lunch, Olga sat with Voronov on the quarterdeck, chaperoned by her former nurse Shura Tegleva. (Shura later married Pierre Gilliard, the girls' French tutor.)

Nicholas arranged a visit to Balaclava for his daughter Olga but she was eager to return to the yacht. The Tsar and his sister Olga went with Olga Nicolaevna to tea with Count Apraksin and his family. After dinner, Alexandra finally came up on deck. As she sat with Sablin, Olga sat with Voronov in the saloon. Olga and Paul later moved to the kitchen area until late in the evening but again they were not alone. They had been joined by Serge Zlebov, Anatole Mordvinov, Stolitsa and Olga Alexandrovna. Olga admitted in print that evening how much she loved Paul.

The next day, however, Olga Nicolaevna was bored without the company of Voronov, even for a few hours. Olga took her nieces swimming and then came back to the yacht. Yet again, Olga sat with Voronov but also with Rodionov, Tatiana and her aunt. They could never be alone. They were constantly chaperoned and surrounded by others.

Olga found the visit to the site of the battlefields interesting yet was bored without Paul. As the party returned to the yacht once more, Olga went to sit with Voronov. They sat in the saloon listening to a concert but, yet again, not alone. After dinner, Olga sat with Voronov until after midnight but in the company of Olga's aunt, Rodionov and other members of the crew.

As Alexandra lay down quietly in her cabin and rested in the company of Nicholas and Sablin, the three were no doubt aware by now of Olga's close friendship with Voronov which appeared to be getting out of hand. Something had to be done. A Grand Duchess could not be permitted to marry a simple naval officer, especially the eldest daughter of the Tsar.

On Wednesday, the Imperial yacht arrived at Yalta where the party left it for Livadia much to the annoyance of Olga Nicolaevna. She would have much preferred to stay on the yacht rather than move to the 116 room white palace built as recently as 1911. She made the most of her last day on the yacht by sitting with Voronov in the control room whilst she still could. The plan to keep the two apart already appeared to be beginning. The couple were joined by not only Olga Alexandrovna and Rodionov but also Tatiana, Marie and Anastasia and the girls' former childhood nurse Shura.

Even after they had left the yacht, Olga's mind was still on it. She watched its progress through binoculars. She was desperate to see any sign of Paul. This was despite the reappearance of Alexander.

The next day found Olga Nicolaevna still missing her friend. The family attended a religious service in the morning and had lunch with members of the crew, but not Voronov. Again Olga watched for signs of Paul through some binoculars.

In the evening, she and Tatiana played poker with their youthful aunt Olga Alexandrovna. That afternoon, Olga along with Nicholas, his sister and Marie visited the nearby estate of Orianda. It was a favourite place for the Grand Duchesses to walk to for a picnic. It was a few miles west of Livadia and sat perched on the edge of a high cliff above the Black Sea. The beautiful, picturesque, fire-damaged house had walls covered in overgrown honeysuckle and ivy. Tall pine and fir trees grew through the crumbling marble of the walls.

Olga was still missing Voronov on Friday, despite trips along with coast. She walked to Harax along with her now recovered sister Marie, Olga Alexandrovna, Anya and two male companions. They returned by car to the sea and went for a cool swim. It was a hot day. The Tsarina was struggling with the heat as always.

In the afternoon, after a walk to Ai-Danil, the Grand Duchesses had tea on the balcony before playing cards in the evening. Yet again, Olga Nicolaevna looked for Paul through her binoculars but only managed to see Sablin.

On Saturday, the four Grand Duchesses and their father and aunt walked in the nearby vineyards and went down to the sea to swim. They went to the yacht later that morning and Nicholas inspected the crew. They attended a prayer service and lunch aboard the *Standart*. Olga was delighted to be back aboard and sat with Nicholas and Sablin but only saw Voronov in the distance. There was however an impromptu dance afterwards and Olga found herself dancing a mazurka with her beloved Voronov. They left before tea. That evening guests who had fought in the Kulm battle were invited the dinner. The yacht was illuminated in the distance.

Olga Nicolaevna went swimming with her sisters the following afternoon. Despite not seeing Voronov, she was still in a happy mood, recalling the dancing the previous day. The rocky beach at Livadia was covered with runner carpets to the edge of the sea itself.

The next day Monday brought a storm and the return of Voronov for Olga. She was delighted to see him. He arrived in time for lunch along with a couple of other officers from the yacht and the Reverend Father. She managed to sit alone with him on Anya's balcony for a short while. Afterwards she and her sisters went for a walk towards Orianda, followed by a delightful swim. The day ended quietly in a game of cards with the Tsar's sister Olga.

Olga and her sisters went for a walk through the vineyards the next day and went for another swim. In the distance, Olga was able to see signs of boating exercises. The men from the *Standart* were out but she could not see any sign of Voronov. She was desperately longing for his return.

At lunch old friends from the yacht appeared including Nicholas Rodionov but still no Voronov. Nicholas saw more people at Livadia despite never giving formal audiences there.

Olga went out again in the afternoon to the Ai-Petri mountain and on to Uganez and saw eagles flying above. Her friend Darya Hesse arrived in the early evening and the two sat together for a while. Alexei had begun the first of a series of mud baths designed to help ease the pains he suffered continually in his arms and legs, and after dinner on the balcony, Olga had some mud put onto her knees which were aching.

On Wednesday, Olga and her sisters swam without their swimming costumes, in their ordinary clothes. She took the opportunity to look for Voronov with a set of binoculars later. She managed to see him climbing into a barge in the distance. Yet again other members of the yacht arrived for lunch.

The excessive heat resulted in a violent thunderstorm that afternoon. The family observed it from a distance. The four sisters walked to the farm nearby with their Aunt Olga and sampled the milk in all its various forms. The Tsarina was taken down to the sea in her wheelchair by Anya and Sablin.

The three youngest of the Tsar's daughters were unwell by the following morning but all later seemed to have recovered. Olga went without her sisters that morning for a solitary swim with her father. Olga managed to spot Voronov and Sablin through binoculars on the yacht in the distance.

Olga was delighted when Paul Voronov was amongst the guests for lunch that day. One of the other visitors was Rodionov. In the afternoon, the four sisters went for a delightful walk in the company of Anya, Rodionov and Voronov. Olga sat next to him later, whilst the others sat nearby.

On Friday morning, Olga returned to the sea with Tatiana and Nicholas, but only she and Nicholas swam. Once again, she managed to spot Voronov in the distance with her binoculars. After lunch, she sat around and did needlework of some kind on the balcony and in the garden. After tea, Nicholas and his four daughters visited Count Apraksin and his family who lived nearby. The sisters enjoyed playing with their children but later Marie (who had had a runny nose the previous day) became unwell again. Later, Olga took a ride to the sea and also walked in the garden in the company of Anya.

On Saturday, Olga and Tatiana went shopping in Yalta escorted by their Aunt Olga. Olga once more lost at tennis but remained unconcerned. She had partnered Sablin (never much of a tennis player) against Nicholas and Tatiana. Olga later joined with Voronov in a doubles game against Nicholas and Anya. Once more she lost but probably had her mind elsewhere. Marie had spent the day in bed but was improving. She appears to have been rather prone to minor ailments.

Sunday was spent quietly by Olga due to ill health. Marie was still also recovering. As Olga had been visited once more by *Madame Becker*, she chose to stay in the chapel quietly with her brother rather than the main part of the church. She elected to remain at home with her mother in the afternoon when Tatiana and Anastasia went out to Massandra. Marie remained in bed and Olga kept her company later. In the evening, Olga and Tatiana went out for the evening to the theatre.

The next day, Olga rested until lunch when Voronov was amongst the guests. She later went to visit her aunts with Voronov and Serge Zlebov. Her youngest sister Anastasia went for a trip to the coast with her godmother, Grand Duchess Olga Alexandrovna and the Tsar. Olga remained at home again and kept Marie company. In the evening, Olga and Tatiana went to Yalta escorted by Madame Vyrubova where they walked on the waterfront and then bought a scarf for Alexandra. Then they went by horse–drawn taxi cab to the *Standart*. The crew were out taking a stroll. They came back via the vineyards and met an old friend – Alexander. The temperature had dropped so dinner was taken inside rather than on the balcony. The evening ended much as usual with cards for the ladies and with Nicholas reading.

On Tuesday, Olga, Tatiana and Anastasia went shopping in Yalta and once again Olga observed Voronov in the distance with the aid of binoculars. Marie remained in bed.

The next day, Tatiana and Anastasia went for a swim but Olga thought the water was too cold. Unlike her mother Alexandra, Olga disliked the cold intensely. The Tsarina hated the warmth. It was difficult to get the temperature to suit both of them. In the afternoon, Olga, Tatiana and Anastasia played tennis whilst Marie remained in bed once more. Olga lost when partnered by Anya against Nicholas and Tatiana, always a good combination, and she lost once more when she joined with Tatiana against Anya and Anastasia. She then changed to an even more disastrous combination and played with Voronov, who could not help but distract her against Tatiana and Rodionov. Alexandra was watching the proceedings close by with the ever-present Sablin.

The Tsar, Olga, Tatiana, Anastasia and Sablin went to the *Standart* for dinner. Olga sat patiently with Nicholas and Sablin. After dinner, Olga located Voronov on deck and stood with him. Then, as if by magic, everyone began to dance. Olga contrived to dance with Voronov as she happened to be standing next to him. Then the party reassembled downstairs. A string orchestra was playing on deck and Stefanesko played the dulcimer downstairs.

On Thursday, Olga spent a quiet day sunbathing and walking. Once more she was reduced to looking for Voronov with binoculars. In the afternoon, Olga, Tatiana and Anastasia had walked to Harax with their Aunt Olga and the Tsar. Marie was still confined to her room. The Tsar and the four Grand Duchesses had tea with Nicholas's cousin and close friend Grand Duke George and his wife Minnie, known officially as the Grand Duchess George. Nicholas's sister who lived close by was also visiting.

Once more, Anya and Sablin took matters into their own hands and wheeled Alexandra down to the sea in her chair. On this occasion, it wore her out.

The next morning, the three girls (Olga, Tatiana and Anastasia) came close to drowning. They had walked through the vineyards to the sea and they were almost torn away from the safety rope. The sea was very cold. Later, Olga and Nicholas played a doubles tennis match against Tatiana and Rodionov. Unusually on this occasion Olga was on the winning side. She then played with Paul Voronov against Nicholas and her former crush Alexander and lost two out of three games. It was surprising she won anything with the distractions all around.

Alexandra and Marie felt sufficiently recovered to appear at the tea table. They were also joined by Sablin, Rodionov and the commander of the yacht. After tea, Olga along with Tatiana, Anastasia and her Aunt Olga travelled to Yalta where they took a walk along the waterfront and visited Zembinskys store. They met Sablin and Voronov to Olga's immense delight. Olga and her three younger sisters later dined with their parents, Aunt Olga, Sablin and Mordvinov.

The day ended with a ride in a motor car through Orianda and towards the waterfront for Olga, Tatiana, Aunt Olga, Sablin and Rodionov. Olga was disappointed not to see Voronov again.

On the Saturday, the last day of the month, the children took the opportunity to go swimming in the sea for the last time with their Aunt Olga before she left. After a trip to a local monastery for Olga and Tatiana by motor car, they saw her off to wait for her train with her attendants. The girls returned to Livadia later that evening.

The first day of the next month was spent by Olga largely in the company of Voronov playing tennis and tag before an automobile drive in the evening. She and Tatiana played a couple of sets of doubles with Paul Voronov and Alexander Butakov. Olga, who had played with Butakov, managed to lose both sets.

As Nicholas played singles with Nicholas Rodionov, Alexandra looked on. Rain eventually stopped play as Olga changed partners once more, this time teaming up with Paul Voronov against her former partner Butakov and Anya. The group played an impromptu game of tag after tea, with Nicholas joining in the fun along with Voronov.

In the evening, Olga and Tatiana, chaperoned by Nicholas and Madame Vyrubova, travelled to Ai-Danil by motor car. The Tsar was a notoriously fast driver as Anya admitted many years later. They returned via Massandra. The Tsarina unusually had a friend over and was exhausted as a result.

On Monday, Olga played tennis again, after finding it too cold for swimming at Orianda. Her tennis had not improved but her mood did despite the rain. The clay tennis court at Livadia was somewhat hidden by a thick screen of pine and cedar trees which would have given them some shelter on less pleasant days. Olga had played tennis in the company of Tatiana and Voronov. Voronov had appeared at lunch that day and had stayed on for the tennis. She contrived to sit with him again after tea. In the evening, Olga and Tatiana challenged Alexandra to a game of cards. Nicholas had decided to read alone again as he often did.

Olga and her sisters resumed lessons on Tuesday morning. The sisters then went for a swim with Nicholas, and Olga spotted Voronov in the distance through the binoculars. He failed to turn up for lunch but Rodionov was amongst the guests and may have had news of his friend.

Olga continued playing tennis in the afternoon, losing with Sablin on the first occasion against the superior play of Tatiana and Voronov. Olga then partnered Anya against Nicholas and her sister and still lost. She returned to play another game with Sablin but then lost to Rodionov and Tatiana. Invariably they were a winning combination. The family had tea in the garden and Olga sat with Voronov predictably. Olga, Tatiana and Anya went on a drive with Nicholas later in the evening. They drove to Ai-Todor and on to the waterfront where Olga spotted Paul on watch duty. The party returned home straight after.

On Wednesday morning, Nicholas escorted Olga and Tatiana to the sea for a swim. Four of the crew from the yacht arrived for lunch, but Voronov was not amongst the number on this occasion. Afterwards, Olga, Tatiana and Anastasia played tennis. Olga triumphed in a doubles game partnered by Tatiana against Nicholas and Anastasia. Tatiana was clearly a good player. As the games continued, Olga's luck changed again. Although she was buoyed by the appearance of Sablin and Rodionov, she was annoyed that Voronov could not be there. That evening once again Olga, Tatiana, Anya and Nicholas went for a drive in one of the automobiles.

The following day consisted of lessons, swimming and tennis for Olga and her sisters. Finally, with the aid of her younger sister Marie, Olga actually won a set. Marie had the physical strength of Serena Williams but not the skill. However, on this occasion, brute force won the day. Olga was delighted to be able to play tennis with Voronov even if it was for a single set which she naturally lost. She managed to sit with him later. In the evening the usual foursome went for a drive – Olga, Tatiana, Anya and Nicholas. On this occasion, they went to Massandra.

On Friday morning, Olga and Tatiana walked through the vineyards with Nicholas to go for a pleasant swim. In the afternoon, Olga's tennis improved. She partnered the more experienced Anya and beat Nicholas and Tatiana. Voronov arrived and Olga sat with him when she had the opportunity. The Tsar's cousin and close friend Grand Duke George and his wife Minnie arrived from Harax for dinner.

Saturday was spent much the same as usual by Olga and her sister Tatiana. The day began with lessons and a swim. Voronov arrived for lunch along with Butakov, Smirnov and the Reverend Father.

Olga's tennis continued to improve as she was partnered by her beloved Voronov. In the evening, Olga and Tatiana joined Alexandra and Anya on the balcony.

Sunday was spent fairly quietly for Olga and saw the return of an old friend, Alexander, whom she met at church. She enjoyed the sunshine and a trip to Krasny Kamen in the company of Voronov, Rodionov and others. Olga, Tatiana and Anastasia went out for a ride in an automobile in the evening whilst Marie remained on duty with Alexandra.

On Monday morning, Nicholas escorted his daughters Olga and Tatiana for a swim via Orianda. Yet again Olga spotted Voronov with the aid of her binoculars. Tennis resumed after lunch and Olga's winning streak continued. She partnered Rodionov, always an excellent player, against Nicholas and Sablin. She then played with Anya against Voronov and Marie. Alexandra sat close by observing the proceedings. The Tsar and his four daughters returned to the yacht in time for dinner. The evening proved a lively one with dancing and games. Olga contrived as usual to be in Voronov's company all evening. If Nicholas had hoped that Olga would tire of Voronov, he was sadly mistaken.

The next day was quieter for Olga but boring after a brief visit by Voronov. Her moods were certainly influenced by his presence. She began the day with lessons before going off for a swim with Nicholas and her youngest sister. Voronov was amongst those members of the *Standart* crew who arrived for lunch. He did not remain for the tennis.

On Wednesday, Nicholas left for a hunting trip after an early trip to the beach for a swim with his daughters. After a thunderstorm and heavy rain later in the morning, Olga decided to help to sort out items to sell at the forthcoming charity bazaar at Yalta with her mother and others. It was an annual event where all five of the Imperial children sold items off a stall close to the waterfront. Voronov came briefly later in the evening much to Olga's relief.

On the next day, Olga Nicolaevna was missing Voronov and watched for him with binoculars at every opportunity. The day was spent more quietly than usual with lessons and a walk towards Orianda for the family. Alexandra however travelled alongside the walkers in her carriage. Olga had a French reading in the hour before dinner as she often did. She was almost eighteen and coming towards the end of her education. During the evening, she employed her time usefully making items to sell in the bazaar.

Alexandra was an extremely accomplished needlewoman, and her daughters Tatiana and Marie inherited her skill. Marie later made shirts for a friend. They continued dyeing scarves and embroidering items to sell at the annual bazaar. The event was held in aid of charity for the tuberculosis sufferers who lived in the many and varied hospitals throughout the Crimea. The warm air was said to be beneficial for their lungs and, for the same reason, Alexandra and her son were encouraged to stay at Livadia. The house had been completed as recently as 1911 to replace the previous house which was damp.

Olga was in an unusually happy mood on Friday when Voronov returned once more. The four Grand Duchesses spent the afternoon in the company of Voronov (and Anya Vyrubova) and played the piano for him. Olga was an excellent pianist and Paul was obviously fond of music as he was heavily involved with the choir on the yacht.

The following day Olga spent mainly playing tennis with Tatiana, Anya and Nicholas. She saw Voronov but he was in the company of the Kleinmichaels which was particularly irritating for Olga. In the coming weeks, he would be more and more in their company which could only mean one thing: he was interested in one of the nieces of the Countess. It must have been devastating to Olga who knew that in reality she and Paul had no real future.

Nicholas must have been concerned by this time with the amount of time his daughter Olga was spending with Paul Voronov and, although slow to act initially, he realised that something had to be done. During his reign (since 1894) many of his own close relatives had made what Nicholas saw as very unsuitable marriages, including his former sister-in-law Ducky (the first wife of Alix's only brother Ernie) who had married his cousin Grand Duke Kyrill, Nicholas's Uncle Paul to a young divorcee, and, the most painful of all, the Tsar's youngest brother Michael who had married a twice-divorced Nathalie only recently and at a time when Alexei had been seriously ill.

On Sunday, the tennis continued for Olga and her sister. Voronov returned but appeared to be unwell. He must have been told that his close friendship with Olga was a matter of concern by now. He was in a difficult position. If he was in love with Olga as seems likely, he would have felt torn between seeing her and doing what he felt was his duty and marrying someone else. He was nine years older than Olga, who was almost eighteen, and had never shown any inclination to marry previously.

Olga saw Voronov on and off in the coming weeks and noticed that something appeared to have changed but she could not quite understand what had happened.

On Monday, Olga and Tatiana stayed overnight at the hunting lodge with the Emperor and two servants. Nicholas appeared to be making a concerted attempt to distance Olga from Voronov.

The two Grand Duchesses spent a pleasant afternoon picking fruit in the sunshine unaware of any possible ulterior motive. Late that morning, Olga and Tatiana accompanied by Nicholas, Drentlen and Shura Tegleva left by motor car for Zozmodemyansky.

However, en route, Olga spotted Voronov by the sea. Tatiana felt unwell for some reason. The party arrived at their destination early in the afternoon and ate.

Nicholas went hunting whilst Olga and Tatiana amused themselves collecting berries and afterwards made jam out of them. An unsuspecting Olga enjoyed the beautiful scenery. Nicholas, who was fairly addicted to the game of dice, included his daughters and Drentlen in on a game. The girls spoke to Alexandra on the telephone to reassure her that they were fine. The sisters shared a room with Shura. Maybe Nicholas thought the sisters would confide in each other during the night. It seems an innocent enough trip but the timing indicated there was more to it.

The sisters were prone to act up when not on official business. Some old film footage even shows the sisters pushing each other down the stairs outside. The instigator on this occasion was naturally Anastasia. Their Aunt Olga once claimed that the girls very often pushed each other down the stairs in the dark when in the Alexander Palace.

Meanwhile the party returned home the next day. Nicholas went out early deer hunting and was successful. The sisters rose early and attended church. After a pleasant morning soaking up the scenery, the girls chased each other with stinging nettles. They arrived home in the mid-afternoon but once more Olga had managed to spot Voronov, this time on the Imperial yacht as they passed through Yalta again.

Wednesday saw a return to normality for Olga and Tatiana. They had lessons and, after lunch, played tennis again. Olga played with Tatiana but managed to lose every game. Her heart was not in it and she was bored out of the company of Voronov. She sat with a friend before dinner. Ira Bikechevdel was a young lady who appeared infrequently at Livadia.

Olga was still bored the next day and her tennis was barely improving despite playing with Nicholas this time. He was a good tennis player unlike Olga. Earlier she had walked with him and had a quiet smoke as she rested. Nicholas read some amusing comic stories by Teffi aloud in the evening whilst the ladies got on with their needlecraft as usual.

Olga Nicolaevna's mood improved on Friday when Voronov returned. She had no time for tennis as she had to help set up things for the bazaar. Voronov appeared to be unwell but was probably upset at the recent conversations with the Tsar about Olga Nicolaevna. It is likely that Nicholas had warned him about spending too much time in the company of his daughter. Once again, Shura suddenly appeared at dinner. Nicholas had gone out hunting again earlier in the morning and would be away overnight.

The next day Olga was miserable again when Voronov failed to appear. She spent the morning horse riding, side-saddle of course. Nicholas arrived back in time for lunch. After one set of tennis, Olga retired from the court to sit with her mother. *Madame Becker* had returned and it made her mood worse.

In the evening she spent time putting price tags on articles that were due to be sold in the charity bazaar later.

Olga rested on Sunday morning before going out later to the bazaar. The Kleinmichael sisters returned as did Voronov by chance. It must have been frustrating to know that once more they were around.

Olga was intelligent enough to have realised it could not have been a coincidence. She must have suspected something was going on. She began to feel empty inside. Luckily the appearance of other friends helped a little. Alexander reappeared at the sale and again later in the evening. Olga hoped that things would return to normal.

After a late start and a cosy lie-in for Olga, she had the pleasure of Voronov's return at lunchtime. He appeared along with other officers from the yacht. She worked shifts at the bazaar in the afternoon and again in the late evening. Although Voronov was around, he was upstairs and she only saw him from a distance. Alexandra felt unable to go to the bazaar. Rasputin appeared and had tea with Nicholas, Alexandra and Anya. Perhaps he was consulted over Olga's situation. Alexandra usually confided in him.

After a short lie-in, Olga resumed her daily life. After a single lesson, she attended lunch with the assembled guests. Rodionov was amongst the visitors but yet again Voronov failed to appear. The girls returned to the bazaar for a couple of hours during the afternoon where Olga again spotted Voronov but only in the distance. She failed to join in the tennis that afternoon and sat and watched the others with her mother again.

Olga Nicolaevna and her sisters attended a concert in the evening. Amongst the artists performing was Nadezhda Plevitskaya. Many of the performers were amateurs. Olga had to be satisfied with only seeing Voronov from afar.

Tatiana's friend Olga Kleinmichael (Voronov's future wife) took part in the concert. The Grand Duchess Olga had to be restrained from giggling during part of the performance by her father Nicholas. The concert had been arranged by the Tsarina's old friend Princess Bariatinsky in aid of charity. One nervous young performer only managed a squeaking noise whilst endeavouring to sing her very first note. Olga, about to laugh, had to be restrained by Nicholas who gently pressed a warning finger on her knee.

On Wednesday morning, Olga and her siblings resumed their lessons. Olga felt well enough to participate in the tennis that afternoon. Olga and Nicholas managed to beat Tatiana who had partnered the less skilful Sablin on this occasion. Marie and Anastasia joined in later. That evening Olga visited a nearby circus where, to her great delight, she saw Voronov en route. She also saw Rasputin.

The next day, Olga went shopping in Yalta escorted by Sablin and her friend Ira. They saw the boat exercises nearby and Voronov who was taking part. Sablin was later one of the invited guests at lunch.

The tennis was resumed that afternoon and Olga's winning streak continued. She joined Anya in a doubles game against Tatiana and Sablin. Tatiana always played far better when partnered by Rodionov but he was not available. Voronov appeared and Olga played doubles with him against Nicholas and Anya. The game was a draw. Nicholas and Anya were experienced doubles partners. Afterwards, Olga sat in the company of Voronov. He coughed continuously.

Nicholas's sister Xenia and her husband appeared at dinner with their daughter Irina. Xenia and Alix chatted about Irina's prospective fiancé Prince Felix Yussopov. Olga listened as the subject of marriage was discussed and Sandro spoke of his recent American visit.

Paul Voronov was still unwell on Friday and Olga was unable to see him. His ill health may have been 'political' as a way of avoiding the Grand Duchess. Oddly, the Tsarina was also sickly rather than complaining of her usual headaches that day. She may have felt guilty that she and Nicholas had interfered with their daughter's future happiness. Voronov had intended to come but ducked out at the last moment.

That evening, Olga and Tatiana went for a motor car ride with Nicholas and Anya. The ride could have probably been an exciting one as Nicholas liked to drive fast. Later, Olga spotted Sablin and Rasputin in Yalta. Rasputin was suddenly around and possibly observing Olga after speaking about her with her parents recently.

The following day, Olga went out riding once again and met Alexander en route. She was delighted to see him. He was on foot. In the afternoon, Olga joined her parents and Anya in sorting out the photograph album. Nicholas was always determined that the gluing of the photos was done with the utmost neatness and without any glue marks on the pages. Later, Sablin arrived with Voronov and Rodionov. Not long after, Nicholas and his family left to spend the evening with his sister at Ai-Todor. Olga had obviously been reluctant to leave. Once again, Alexandra complained of feeling sick that evening. It was not her usual complaint and a little out of character. Olga sat close by *working* and smoking a cigarette.

Nicholas Rodionov was always close to the Grand Duchess Tatiana, and said to be in love with her, but the Tsar decided against removing him as it would ruin his career.

It may have been safer with Tatiana as there is no clue that she was in love with Rodionov.

On Sunday morning, the family attended church as usual and, in the afternoon, they resumed the tennis tournament. Olga was successful in one set she played partnered by Nicholas against Anya and Tatiana. She repeated the victory with Nicholas later against Tatiana and Rodionov, which was quite an achievement. Olga sat down afterwards and felt the cold. She was frustrated that Voronov had not appeared.

Olga went to an exhibition in Yalta with the Emperor and her sister Tatiana the next day. Yet again there were guests for lunch but Voronov was not amongst the group. Again Olga felt cold when outside playing tennis. She repeated her victory against Tatiana and Rodionov, with Nicholas again.

The party drove back from the tennis court rather than walked that afternoon. The night proved to be a windy one and rather scary at times. Olga spoke on the telephone for the first time with her friend Alexander. She drew comfort from the sound of his voice, in the continued absence of Voronov.

Chapter Four

Winter 1913

Tuesday was the first day of the month and a sign that winter would soon be on its way, even to the warm climate of the Crimea. Olga was already beginning to notice the weather was turning colder and more windy. The day began with a visit to the church and was followed by lunch with members of the crew once again. Although Rodionov was amongst the number, Voronov was again absent.

In the afternoon, the tennis commenced despite an evident turn in the weather. Olga partnered the experienced doubles player Anya and managed to tie against Tatiana and her friend Rodionov. After the game, the group went to look at the waves crashing onto the beach. Olga was still very bored without Voronov. She and Tatiana amused themselves that evening after dinner by trying on Nicholas's jacket. It would have been large on Olga but positively drowned the thin Tatiana. She was unusually thin and quite a contrast to the slightly overweight Marie.

On Wednesday morning after lessons, Olga and Tatiana went shopping in Yalta in the company of Ira. The day progressed in its usual fashion with tennis after lunch with guests from the yacht. Once more, Voronov failed to appear. The afternoon began with tennis once more and, on this occasion Olga's newfound luck appeared to have ended. She played with Nicholas against the formidable team of Tatiana and Rodionov and lost overall. She later teamed up with the powerful forehand of Marie against Anastasia and Kublitsy. In the evening, Marusya and Vera Trepova visited.

The following morning, Olga and Tatiana went riding escorted by Olga Butzova, Victor Zborovsky and an old friend Alexander who was on a borrowed horse. Olga made the most of Alexander's company. She tried to convince herself that she was missing Paul less, but she was deluding herself.

In the afternoon, the sisters returned to the tennis court. Despite teaming up with Marie, the two lost against the superior playing power of Tatiana and Anastasia. It was rare for the sisters to play amongst themselves. A victorious Olga then won a single set against Anya, usually a very confident player. In the evening, Olga read in French with Gilliard who now taught Alexei during the earlier part of the day. Anya returned late on to keep Alix company whilst Nicholas read alone as usual.

On Friday morning after the normal lessons with her sister and companion Tatiana, Olga and her four siblings attended a religious service and a parade in the company of both her parents. It was unusual for Alexandra to appear at these events recently.

In the afternoon, Olga chatted with Alexander and, after tennis where she tied a game with Nicholas against the usually superior team of Tatiana and Rodionov, Olga saw Voronov. He was in a motor car when she first noticed him but she then saw him later with the platoon. He noticed her too to her delight. The parade and service naturally exhausted the Tsarina.

Olga was bored the following day despite a heavy schedule of activities. She only managed to spot Voronov at church that morning and had no other contact with him that day. She played tennis once more with her sisters and had mixed results. Rasputin came once again in the early evening. Later, Nicholas and his daughters travelled to Yalta to the yacht where they watched the illuminations.

Olga was still bored on Sunday and had the added annoyance of the appearance of the Kleinmichael sisters. They seemed to be around a lot recently. The day followed its usual pattern otherwise with church, lunch and tennis.

Olga's mood lightened the next day when her friend reappeared. She enjoyed being able to spend some time with him during tennis matches that afternoon. He had finally been invited to lunch once more. Despite her obvious misgivings of a possible connection with the Kleinmichael sisters, she was nevertheless delighted to see him.

On Tuesday, Olga, together with Tatiana and Ira, went to watch the sea at high tide before lessons. Despite the excessive heat that day, tennis continued as usual. Olga and Anastasia played against Nicholas and Marie and then changed partners and teamed up with Rodionov against Nicholas and Sablin. The outcome was a little mixed but Olga won overall.

At teatime, the Tsar's sister Xenia reappeared along with Sandro and Irina. They informed the family of Irina's betrothal but Olga failed to mention this in her journal that evening. It was not a subject she was happy to mention. The Tsarina announced that she would never let one of her daughters marry Felix. As Felix was a handsome and extremely rich prince, it seems unlikely that she would consider Voronov as a son-in-law. That evening, Alexandra made a visit to Yalta to see Rasputin. Perhaps she wished to talk of marriage again. She brought a gift of a vase for each of her girls afterwards from the glass factory. It may have been that she felt guilty that she and Nicholas were meddling in Olga's future happiness and not even discussing the matter with her.

On Wednesday, Nicholas, escorted by his two eldest daughters and his son, visited the Shirvansky regiment where a service and a parade were held. That afternoon, Olga played tennis again but a new friend appeared. Shurik was her partner in several sets. He would become more important to Olga in the coming months as she began to realise that Voronov would be appearing less frequently.

Olga and Tatiana then went to Ai-Todor with Nicholas for dinner with the Tsar's sister and her family. Irina's fiancé Felix was introduced. Afterwards, Olga and Tatiana indulged in an exciting game of hide and seek in the dark with Irina, Felix, Rodionov and Voronov. Olga kept close to Paul during the evening. Sablin was there however to keep an eye on events. The party returned to Livadia at twelve but Alexandra was still up. Anya had just taken Rasputin back to where he was staying. Once again it looked as though Alexandra was discussing Olga with him. As Nicholas was notorious for not making a decision, it was likely that it was Alexandra with the help of Rasputin, her confidant, who arranged a way out.

The next day was the anniversary of the Tsarina's arrival in Russia as future bride of Nicholas in 1894 and Alix herself seemed to be in unusually robust health. Alexandra presented members of the Crimean regiment with gifts. Olga returned to the tennis court again in the afternoon. She played with Anya against Nicholas and Tatiana. In the evening, the sisters visited the circus where, to her delight, Olga saw Voronov and her new friend Shurik. Alexandra was still up when they returned, having a late-night cup of tea with Anya.

On Friday, the day began as usual with lessons for the Imperial children. Earlier that morning, Nicholas had left for an expedition to Ai-Petri. Olga and her siblings waved to the crew of the *Standart* as they left port. The sisters returned to the tennis court in the afternoon where Olga played with Voronov against Tatiana and Sablin. She then played with Paul against Tatiana and Anya, and later partnered Anya against Tatiana and Paul. She then played with Tatiana against Voronov and Anya. She played consistently badly as she was distracted by Paul. She then went for tea in the company of Tatiana, Anya and Voronov.

Anya Vyrubova had occasion to buy the Tsar tennis socks in the Crimea. He had found it too much of a trial to order his own – with the amount of 'red tape' needed for something seemingly so simple as ordering some socks. He had admired the coloured socks the officers wore. Anya went into Yalta in order to buy him half a dozen pairs. He was delighted. He had disliked playing with simple black socks.

The next day, Olga and Tatiana had an early morning trip to the sea with Anastasia Hendrikova and Ira. The sea was warm. Paul Voronov returned for lunch and stayed to play tennis afterwards with Olga. She played with Anya against Tatiana and Nicholas and then, with Tatiana, played against Voronov and Anastasia. She had mixed results again. Alexandra and Sablin were watching nearby as usual. Olga noticed that Voronov appeared to be more cheerful than he had been of late.

On Sunday, there was the usual religious service, the liturgy, followed by one of the inevitable big lunches. As Nicholas went for a long walk with members of his suite in the afternoon, Olga and Tatiana returned to the tennis court along with Anya and Rodionov. Marie and Anastasia went to Harax in the early evening whilst Olga in sat Countess Hendrikova's room. Later, Olga worked in her mother's room whilst Nicholas read alone.

Olga and Tatiana continued their usual activities the following day – lessons, a walk, lunch with the officers from the yacht, and tennis. In the evening, the two sisters went to a charity ball with Nicholas, Xenia and Irina. Olga danced with various partners including Sablin, Prince Trubestkoi, Vladimir Gantskau and Shurik. She noticed Voronov in the distance but he looked a little upset. She could not work out what had happened to cause this change.

On Tuesday, Olga walked to the sea with Nicholas before lunch. Rodionov was amongst the guests that day. The afternoon followed its usual pattern with tennis and tea. In the evening, Olga and Tatiana went to Harax with Nicholas to dine with

Nicholas's cousin George and his wife Minnie, officially the Grand Duke and Duchess George. Olga was bored without Paul.

When the Tsar went for walks, he was never alone. He was always followed by secret service men. Nicholas nicknamed them 'nature lovers' as they always appeared to be looking at the sky or trees or pretending not to notice him. He liked to give them the slip.

On the following morning, Olga and Tatiana walked to the nearby farm whilst Nicholas left for Krasny Kaem for the majority of the day. In the afternoon, the four sisters played tennis again with Anya, Shurik and Rodionov. Once more Olga's luck was mixed: some games she won and others she lost. She nevertheless enjoyed herself in the company of Shurik to whom she was becoming more attached. She saw Voronov that day but only via the binoculars.

On Thursday morning, Olga went horse riding with Tatiana and met her new favourite – Shurik. He joined the sisters that afternoon for tennis. The Kleinmichael sisters were still in evidence however and she could not avoid them despite probably wanting to in the circumstances.

She must have suspected that they had some connection with Voronov as he was often with them and she frequently mentioned their names and his in the same sentence.

The following morning, Olga went shopping in Yalta with Tatiana and Hendrikova. Olga's friend Ira joined the trip. She was starting to appear more and more often in the absence of Voronov. Rodionov appeared again at lunch and remained for the tennis.

In the early evening, Alexandra again travelled to Yalta to the chapel. She rarely went out in such circumstances and may have gone to meet Rasputin to speak about Olga.

On Saturday morning, Olga walked to the sea with Ira and Anastasia Hendrikova. Ira was appearing more often since Voronov's disappearing act. The sisters played tennis in the afternoon with Nicholas, Rodionov and Sablin. Voronov made an appearance in the early afternoon at Livadia but Olga did not have a chance to speak to him or even see him. She was disappointed yet resigned.

On Sunday, there was a memorial for the late Emperor. Olga was feeling unwell as the situation with Voronov was becoming confusing to her. He kept coming and going, and often seemed distracted when he did come. In the afternoon, the family collected for a service for the departed at the exact place where Olga's late grandfather, who she never met, died in 1894. The sisters then went out briefly for a drive with Nicholas to the sea and returned. The family later attended vespers and had a confession.

There were more services the next day. Olga sat with Alexandra afterwards whilst her sisters went for a walk with their father. She failed to join in with the tennis but sat with Alexandra and the amusing Sablin. She was despairing that she had not seen Voronov for so long.

Olga was pleased to see Shurik again on Tuesday. It helped take away some of the upset at not seeing Voronov. She returned to the tennis court with Nicholas and played a set against Tatiana and Anya Vyrubova. Nicholas managed to damage his finger so went for one of his long walks instead towards Orianda. Alexandra accompanied the group in her carriage. Olga chatted amiably with Shurik.

After dinner, Olga and Tatiana went for an automobile ride towards Yalta. Alexandra went with them unusually as did Anya, Nicholas Sablin, Nicholas Rodionov and Olga's friend Ira. Nicholas was reading alone.

On Wednesday morning, Olga had her very first lesson in art from the architect of Livadia Palace. Meanwhile, Nicholas had gone off hunting for the day to Kozmodemyansk. In the afternoon during a walk towards Massandra with her mother and sisters, Olga saw Paul Voronov who was out walking with a couple of friends. She was delighted to see him despite spending time recently with Shurik.

The next day, Olga went shopping in Yalta with Tatiana and their chaperone Countess Anastasia Hendrikova. Olga looked through the binoculars once more and spotted Voronov.

It was a special day for Alexei. Officers from the sixteenth regiment arrived for lunch and, on the anniversary of the appointment of his grandfather some thirty-five years previously, Alexei took over the post of commander-in-chief of the regiment from Nicholas who had held it for just four years.

In the afternoon, Nicholas, Alexandra and their four daughters went to visit Xenia at Ai-Todor. Whilst Alexandra, Olga and Anastasia drove there, the rest walked. Olga and Tatiana later attended a ball with Nicholas at the new barracks. Olga danced with Shurik amongst others. They came home at eleven.

On Friday, Olga and Tatiana drove to the hunting lodge at Kozmodenyansk with the Emperor and his sister Xenia and others, including the newly engaged Irina and Felix. They ate a meagre lunch in the hut where the sisters had previously stayed with Nicholas overnight with Shura.

A trip to the cinema that evening was cancelled due to the deteriorating condition of Count Dedyulin. Nicholas and Alexandra left to sit with him. That day, Olga had the good fortune to spot Voronov from afar near to the coast.

The ailing Vladimir A Dedyulin (a lieutenant-general attached to the Tsar's court) died during the night. The Imperial family went to his memorial service in the early afternoon. Earlier that day, Olga and Tatiana, along with Anya and Anya's brother Serge, walked the well-trodden horizontal trail.

At lunch Voronov appeared along with Sablin, Butakov and Nevyarovsky. Olga managed to spot Shurik also that day but only in the distance.

On Monday morning, the Imperial children returned once again to their regular studies. In the afternoon, the girls played tennis with Nicholas, Anya and Rodionov. Olga felt distraught without Paul Voronov. In the evening, Olga attended a memorial service for Dedyulin. She was delighted to spot Shurik amongst the crowd.

The next day, Olga attended the funeral of Dedyulin along with her parents and sisters Tatiana and Marie. Afterwards, the family walked behind the coffin towards the military barracks. She spotted Shurik amongst the Cossacks and even Voronov from behind. She was sufficiently enamoured to recognise him from the back amongst so many men.

Afterwards, Nicholas and Marie walked back whilst the others (Alexandra, Olga and Tatiana) remained in the car. In the afternoon, the sisters returned to the tennis court. Alexandra sat and watched the proceedings.

The following day, it was back to the normal routine of lessons and tennis for Olga. She tried to convince herself that she was getting used to Voronov's absence. The Cossack Shurik also failed to appear. In the evening, Alexandra began *colorito* once again with Olga. They had not played the board game for a while.

On Thursday, Olga, Tatiana and Ira went shopping in Yalta escorted by Anastasia Hendrikova. Olga happened to see Shurik on the visit. That afternoon, he returned to the palace to join in the tennis games. Voronov also appeared. Olga delighted in seeing both at the same time and sat next to each of them during tea. Alexandra was getting ready for the cotillion and cut the silk ribbons for it.

The family went to the yacht for dinner that evening, including the Tsarina. As Olga sat next to Voronov, her mother was there to keep an eye on them during the film show. Naturally it would have meant that the lights were dimmed.

Olga was happy when Voronov returned the next day. She sat close to Voronov but her mother was, by coincidence, seated nearby possibly keeping a close eye on her daughter when Voronov was around.

Queen Olga of Greece arrived on the first as the eighteenth birthday of her namesake and godchild Olga Nicolaevna approached. Olga enjoyed playing tennis with her younger sisters and their friends Sablin, Rodionov and Zborovsky. Voronov was amongst the guests at lunch that day but it was with Shurik that Olga played tennis that afternoon. Marie took various photographs of the group. She took her camera to Siberia but it was eventually confiscated.

On Saturday morning, Olga and Tatiana rode their horses in the Livadia area and, in the afternoon, went back to the tennis court. Once again, Olga was partnered by Shurik. Later Olga and the others went to the yacht to set up the room for the coming party. Afterwards, Olga danced on the deck with Sablin and Voronov. The family left after midnight.

Olga's eighteenth birthday was spent at Livadia on Sunday, but it appears she chose later not to recall it in writing.

The day after, life returned to its usual predictable pattern of lessons, long walks, lunch with members of the crew of the *Standart*, and, of course, the tennis matches. Olga continued to sit and chat with Paul Voronov and even played tennis with him but she was still attempting to keep her options open by seeing as much of Shurik as possible. Unbeknown to Olga, she had a secret admirer. That afternoon, one of the guests was a distant relative: Prince Christopher of Greece. He had fallen under her spell and had seen her chatting amiably to Voronov.

Olga was struggling to play tennis at all as she had managed to hurt her leg. She had fallen on some stairs whilst bidding farewell to some of the officers off the previous evening. The embarrassment of the incident may have been partly why she chose to destroy the notes she had written the previous day. That evening, Nicholas took his four daughters to the theatre and cinema where Olga sighted Shurik, the Cossack.

Olga was in a wheelchair by the next day but Voronov came to sit with her. She spent much of the day with him before visiting relatives in Harax that evening. Voronov helped her stick photographs into an album and simply chatted with her. The visit to Harax where the hostess's younger brother Christopher watched Olga would lead to a proposal eventually.

On Wednesday, Olga had her leg treated with mud before the ball that evening! She managed to dance with Voronov briefly but he spent most of his free time with the Kleinmichaels. They managed to keep him away from Olga for most of the evening. Luckily, her other friends Shurik, Zborovsky, Sablin and Mochalev were also there to keep her amused.

Olga had a late start the following morning. She was still unable to play tennis after the accident, and dancing the previous evening would not have helped her recovery. That morning, Nicholas escorted his four daughters to Yalta where they briefly visited the Imperial yacht. Once again, Voronov was on duty and Olga could not fail to notice him. The family returned to Livadia for lunch along with four members of the yacht's crew. Voronov was not amongst the number but he came later for the tennis along with Shurik. At tea, Olga sat between Voronov and her Cossack friend.

Friday was busier than usual for Olga. The day began predictably with lessons but was followed by a trip to Yalta along with Ira. Olga was unable to play tennis that day but sat with her mother and the ever-present Sablin and watched the proceedings. Once again, she managed to sit between Paul Voronov and Shurik during tea. Olga and Tatiana were then escorted to Harax that evening by Nicholas giving the by now smitten Christopher another chance to see Olga. He appears to have made no impression on her.

Saturday was spent more quietly by Olga, sunbathing on the balcony in the morning before lunch. She was still unable to take part in the tennis but was content to watch Shurik and Voronov play. She felt chilly in the autumn air; had she been able to play she would have not noticed the approach of winter.

Yet again, Olga contrived to sit between Voronov and Shurik at tea and later an old friend of Nicholas arrived for dinner: the ever generous and charming Emir of Bukhara. Even Alexandra made an appearance at dinner that evening.

There was a party at Princess Bariatinskaya's on Sunday in honour of Olga and Tatiana. Olga danced a great deal despite being unable to play tennis for days. She took part in the quadrille, waltzes, cotillion and even the mazurka. Nicholas did not take part in the dancing and merely sat nearby playing dice. She enjoyed a waltz with Paul Voronov.

On Monday, after the inevitable lessons, Olga gave her aching foot a soothing soak in some appropriate preparation. The previous night's dancing would have made it worse than ever. In the afternoon, Count Sumarakov, the Russian tennis champion, appeared at the tennis court. Nicholas was delighted to have some real opposition. Olga played again despite an obvious injury. She partnered Shurik against Tatiana and Victor Zborovksy. Olga was not playing well, predictably. She then joined Anastasia in a doubles game against Marie and Shurik. Once again she lost. Then she had a chance of winning as she partnered the champion himself against Nicholas and Rodionov.

Finally, she succeeded but unfortunately such a brilliant player was not usually available on a daily basis. Despite the excitement, she still felt out of sorts without Voronov.

The evening ended once more at Harax where Olga, Tatiana and Nicholas arrived for dinner and Christopher probably gazing at her in admiration, but she failed even to notice him.

Olga was in a better mood the next day but spent it fairly quietly with her sisters playing the inevitable tennis sets on the court. The sisters Tatiana and Marie took on Olga and Anastasia, the latter pair coming off slightly the better.

On Wednesday morning, Olga was still suffering with her foot injury but carried on much as usual despite it. She was cheered by the presence of her new friend Shurik in the continued absence of Voronov. She played tennis with her sisters and Shurik and was charmed by him, but she still wanted Voronov.

Olga was in a good mood the next day after a walk with friends including Shurik and Rodionov. Voronov failed to appear. The family attended the cinema but Alexandra left early as she frequently did.

Olga went to Yalta again on Friday for wool. The young Grand Duchesses spent a lot of time *working* and this needed endless supplies of wool for the knitting and crochet work. Alexandra liked her daughters to be doing something useful in their spare time. All the sisters wore wool cardigans and it is likely that they made them. In Siberia, the former Tsarina and her daughters were forced to make and darn their own clothes. Luckily they had the requisite skills and vast experience.

Voronov was amongst the group of young men from the yacht who arrived for lunch that day. To Olga's delight, he went on a walk later with the family. Nicholas was busy so Sablin escorted Alexandra in her carriage along with Rodionov and Voronov.

In the evening, Nicholas, Alexandra and their two eldest daughters returned to Harax for dinner with Nicholas's cousin and close friend Grand Duke George and his wife Minnie. Minnie's youngest brother had another opportunity to see Olga. She was again unimpressed by the company that evening.

The Emperor and his elder daughters returned to the yacht briefly the next day. Nicholas felt a strong affection for his beloved yacht and all those who served on her. It had been built in Denmark to his instructions and he much preferred it to the other Imperial yacht, the *Polar Star*. The Dowager Empress used the older yacht.

The sisters were taken for a stomach-churning ride in a boat before returning to the palace for lunch. Nicholas took part in the usual sampling of the food ceremony as he did at the palaces on regular occasions. It was something his young son Alexei delighted in joining in when he had the occasion, but not this time.

The afternoon was rainy and there was no attempt at playing any tennis so the family turned to their usual rainy day habit of sticking photographs into albums. Nicholas's children all had their own albums which they liberally mixed with official and candid snaps alike. Voronov arrived to help with the proceedings. He was not alone as he arrived with Stolitsa and, of course, Sablin.

On Sunday, there were family guests. The residents of Harax paid a return visit for Sunday lunch. The guests included George's wife Minnie and her younger brother

Christopher. In the afternoon, the whole family took a walk towards Orianda. Alexandra, as usual, rode in her small carriage. They were joined by Anya, Sablin and Voronov.

That evening, there was a ball at the palace. Olga danced the night away in each of the dances –the quadrille, cotillion and the dizzying mazurka. She danced with Voronov and also Shurik.

Olga spent a quiet Monday after getting up late. It had been a long and exhausting night and, with the onset of *Madame Becker*, she felt like a lie-in, understandably. Pierre Gilliard, a part of the Grand Duchesses' life since 1905, appeared and read to Olga and Tatiana in French.

Voronov was amongst a larger than usual party of guests invited for lunch that day. Olga would have had little opportunity to see him alone. She sat at the edge of the tennis court that afternoon with Alexandra and Sablin whilst the others, including Anya and Shurik, played.

Olga lay in bed until late the next morning but managed to say goodbye to the Emperor before he set off on a hike in the mountains. The Tsarina was feeling unwell and sat in a comfortable chair, but remained dressed and in her night attire. Her children lunched with her whilst Nicholas was away.

In the afternoon, Olga felt sufficiently recovered to go on a walk towards the nearby farm in the company of her sisters, Alexandra in her carriage, Shurik, Rodionov, Kozhevnikov and the chaperones Sablin and Anya. Once more, Voronov failed to appear that day.

On Wednesday, the sisters returned to their studies before attending the usual lunch with guests from the yacht, again not including Paul Voronov, and finally tennis in the afternoon. Olga took the opportunity to side with Shurik after first playing with her sister Anastasia. Alexandra, as usual, watched from close by with Sablin in attendance. Olga was frustrated that Paul had not appeared once more.

Olga was vexed the next day at not seeing either of her close male friends. The day progressed much as usual with tennis in the afternoon but, on this occasion, the sisters were present when Alexandra officially received visitors. They would have had to change of course and one simply could not wear the same clothes for receiving guests and playing an energetic game like tennis.

That evening, Nicholas returned again to Harax for dinner with his relatives. He took his two eldest daughters along. Once again, Olga was not impressed by the usual crowd there.

Voronov returned the following day much to Olga's delight, but she felt unsure of herself. She was almost certainly suspicious that they were being kept apart deliberately. He had been invited to lunch once more along with other officers but not to the tennis matches in the afternoon where she would have had more opportunity to chat alone with him – even if briefly. She had spent the early part of the day (after the usual lessons) in Yalta shopping with Countess Hendrikova. Although it was still the third week in November in Russia, it was already December in the rest of Europe and the Grand Duchesses would have begun to think about Christmas shopping. The sisters had little opportunity to shop at Tsarskoe Selo so this would have been an ideal opportunity.

The Tsar and his wife simply never went shopping apart from some brief occasions in Germany for Nicholas, and had items sent to the palace for inspection. Even when the Grand Duchesses went shopping in Germany in 1910, they brought back jewellery items for the Tsarina to inspect.

The next day progressed with more shopping and tennis for Olga Nicolaevna. In the morning, she visited Yalta along with Tatiana, Ira and Countess Hendrikova. She met Shurik briefly in Yalta.

She lost when playing with Anastasia and then again with Marie and only managed to tie when partnered by Sablin. The tennis champion again returned to play with Nicholas.

Sunday morning began with the usual liturgy and lunch with guests. Afterwards, Nicholas escorted his four daughters on a walk to Massandra. Alexandra rode in her small carriage. Sablin and Rodionov accompanied the group.

The family returned to the yacht that afternoon for tea with some of the officers. The men had so often had lunch with the Imperial family, so this was a return visit. Unfortunately for Olga, Voronov was not on the yacht which was rather unusual and certainly pre-planned. Later, Alexandra, Anya and Olga visited the sanatorium nearby run by the Red Cross. Luckily, Olga spotted Shurik briefly upon their return.

Olga and Tatiana, accompanied by Countess Anastasia Hendrikova, went to see Princess Apraksina the next day. Olga was confused as to what was actually going on with Voronov. He seemed to be happy to come but she was now seeing him in more formal circumstances. She failed to speak to him as she felt unable to.

There was the excitement of a parade in the afternoon. It was a rehearsal for the St George's Day celebrations the following day. Shurik was amongst the men on parade. Later, the four sisters played a thrilling game of hide and seek in the dark in the company of Kublitsky and Kozhevnikov. In the evening, Olga, Tatiana and Nicholas returned to Harax in time for dinner.

Olga attended a memorial service on Tuesday morning and seemed to be glad that she no longer saw much of Voronov. It must have been difficult to see him by now in the circumstances as she could not understand what had changed. The family attended the annual St George's Day parade.

In the afternoon, the Tsar went on one of his long walks in the company of Olga, Anya, Shurik, Rodionov and Babitsyn. They walked through the vineyards and up a hill in the rain. The evening was spent quietly by Olga playing a game of *colorito* with her mother.

The christening the following afternoon of baby Vasily was greatly enjoyed by Olga who adored babies. Afterwards, the sisters returned to the tennis court. Olga enjoyed the company of Shurik, the Cossack, and old friends Nicholas Rodionov and Victor Zborovsky. Nicholas had managed to injure his shin and limped around the court.

On Thursday morning, Olga went Christmas shopping again with Hendrikova but the weather was not exactly festive. It was raining and muddy underfoot. There was no tennis in the afternoon as Nicholas's leg was still giving him trouble after his recent accident. He took Alexandra out for a quiet ride whilst Anya, NP Sablin and LM Kozhevnikov escorted the four sisters on a walk towards Orianda along the horizontal trail.

The afternoon proved exciting for the sisters when they joined in a game of hide and seek in the dark in the pleasant company of Shurik and L M Kozhevnikov. Later, Grand Duke and Duchess George arrived from Harax and Dmitri from nearby Kichkine for dinner.

On the next day, Olga returned to Yalta to continue the Christmas shopping with Trina Schnieder and her younger sister Anastasia. The weather had not improved; it was still damp and muddy underfoot. That afternoon, the sisters again played hide and seek with Shurik, Nicholas Rodionov and Victor Zborovsky.

That evening, Nicholas escorted his four daughters to another charity event organised by Princess Bariatinskaya. Olga finally spotted Voronov, but just briefly. He was at the cinema and Olga saw Shurik there too.

Olga went back to Yalta on Saturday morning for more shopping in the company of Ira and Anastasia Hendrikova. The weather was as wet as on the previous visits.

In the afternoon, Olga's senior godmother Queen Olga of Greece arrived to say her farewells. She had been staying at Harax with her daughter Minnie. Olga and Tatiana, along with Nicholas, escorted the Queen to the pier where she boarded the *Almaz*. They took the opportunity to visit the *Standart* afterwards and observe the *Almaz* disappear into the distance. Olga managed to spot Voronov on the pier.

They briefly called in on Stolitsa who was suffering from water on the knee. Afterwards, Olga and Tatiana played hide and seek in the dark in the delightful company of Paul Voronov, Victor Zborovsky and Nicholas Rodionov.

On Sunday morning, the family attended the liturgy as usual before one of the familiar big lunches. As Sablin arrived later to play dice with Nicholas, Alexandra and Anya, the four sisters went downstairs to play hide and seek once more, this time in the company of Shurik, Rodionov, Kozhevnikov and Zborovsky. Olga had briefly sat with Alexei earlier. He had been unwell recently.

That afternoon, Nicholas and his daughters returned to the *Standart* in time for tea. Olga was delighted to see Voronov but was unsure how to handle the situation. The group arrived back late at Livadia as the car that had been expected to collect them failed to arrive due to some mix-up.

On Monday, Olga and Tatiana accompanied Nicholas on a visit to Ai-Danil to a new children's sanatorium. They returned in time for lunch. Afterwards, Rasputin's wife Praskovya and her daughter Varya arrived for a rare visit.

That afternoon, whilst Nicholas played dice with Sablin, the sisters went down to see Alexei along with their guests Voronov, Rodionov, Zborovsky and, interestingly, Shurik, before going off to play a game of hide and seek. It gave Olga the opportunity to be in the close proximity of both Voronov and Shurik at the same time. Shurik diplomatically chose to play the game with Marie and the two were the seekers. The rest hid rather too successfully and were not found.

In the evening Olga and Tatiana returned to Harax for dinner along with Nicholas. Olga visited the dentist the next morning in Yalta accompanied by her former nurse Shura Tegleva. She briefly saw Voronov as they passed by the *Standart*. In the afternoon, the four sisters and Ira and their chaperone Anya visited the Red Cross sanatorium. After their return, Anya and two of the yacht's officers played dice with Nicholas whilst Alexandra rested, and the sisters played hide and seek with Shurik, Rodionov and Zborovsky. Alexei appeared to be recovering from his latest accident but his leg was still swollen.

A whole pile of potential gifts arrived and the family picked out items of their choice to give to the staff at Christmas. They would be leaving for Tsarskoe Selo shortly.

On Wednesday, after the usual lessons and lunch, the sisters went for a long walk through the vineyards accompanied by Nicholas, Anya, Shurik, Zborovsky and Kublitsky. Alexandra remained at home in the company of Sablin.

On their return, the sisters once again played a game of hide and seek, and Shurik was amongst the crowd. That evening, they called in on Anya who had visitors, Praskoya Feodorovna and her daughter Varya, Rasputin's family. The Tsarina and her daughters later continued sorting out what gifts to give the members of the household for Christmas.

The next day, Olga returned to the dentist in Yalta with Shura. The two ladies walked along the pier and Olga spotted Nicholas Sablin from afar on the *Standart*. For once, Voronov appeared as a guest at lunchtime. There was a rehearsal for the parade due to be held the following day in honour of the Tsar's name's day. Olga observed Paul amongst the marching troops.

That afternoon, Olga enjoyed herself playing hide and seek like a small child on all fours – she was eighteen. Amongst the group were the four sisters, Shurik and Zborovsky. Later the Tsar's ward, the Grand Duke Dmitri, arrived to play dice with Nicholas and others. Alexandra sat close by but was unwell and had been complaining of her heart again. Alexei was continuing to improve.

On Friday morning, there was a parade in honour of the Emperor's name's day. It was celebrated on St Nicholas's Day which is of course an important date in the calendar for children from Scandinavia and parts of Northern Europe. Voronov was amongst those troops who paraded in front of the Tsar that morning. Olga and her sister Tatiana played yet another exciting game of hide and seek later. It is traditionally a children's game but it depends how it is played, of course.

Later, Nicholas, his ward Dmitri and his four daughters had dinner in the saloon of the yacht *Standart* as the celebrations continued. Voronov was somewhat conveniently on duty. A strong wind hurled the yacht around and pushed it towards the pier. The sisters danced downstairs in the green dining room but Olga was disappointed not to have the opportunity of dancing with Paul. They left after midnight and arrived back at Livadia along with Sablin who was, of course, a regular visitor.

Olga returned to the dentist again on Saturday morning with her chaperone Shura. The two rode along the pier and Olga spied Voronov who was on duty aboard the yacht. They collected Tatiana and Anastasia Hendrikova who had been shopping meanwhile.

It was beginning to look like Christmas as it had been snowing all day and the ground was covered in a carpet of white. The girls then got back into the party spirit after lunch and yet again indulged in a game of hide and seek with Rodionov,

Shurik and Zborovsky. The dinner was a formal one with guests including the Spanish Ambassador, Count Veniaza and his wife.

On Sunday, it was unusually windy as Olga went for a walk that afternoon along with her sisters Tatiana and Anastasia, chaperoned by Anya Vyrubova. Marie had remained at home on *duty* as one of the sisters invariably did. Later the fours sisters played charades with Rodionov and Zborovsky. Meanwhile, Nicholas played dice with Alexandra, Dmitri and Sablin.

In the evening, Olga, Tatiana, Nicholas and Dmitri travelled the brief distance to Harax in time for dinner. Olga was bored by the usual company and was missing Voronov desperately by now. It was becoming very cold and the ground was as frosted as a Christmas cake.

Olga returned to Yalta on Monday morning in the company of Tatiana and their chaperone for the day Countess Hendrikova. The weather was bad; it was raining heavily as the girls passed the pier. Olga happened to notice Sablin who did indeed seem to be everywhere.

There were guests at lunch including the Turkish Ambassador to Russia and officers from the *Standart*. They visited the Muzlarsky sanatorium later when the weather was still worse: a blizzard. The sisters played charades after they returned. Olga teamed up with Marie, Anastasia and Shurik, whilst Tatiana played with Zborovsky and Kublitsky. The wind eventually calmed down later in the day.

Olga made a final visit to the dentist in Yalta on Tuesday along with her chaperone Shura. Naturally they stopped briefly by the pier where Olga managed to spot Voronov and, of course, Sablin.

That afternoon Olga, Tatiana and Anastasia went on one of the Tsar's long walks with him and Dmitri. Olga smoked a cigarette on one of the brief stops. Marie remained at home once again to keep her mother company.

In the evening, Nicholas, accompanied by Olga, Tatiana and Dmitri went to the Narodny Dom to see the traditional Russian play *A Life for the Tsar*. Olga spied Sablin, Voronov and Shurik amongst the crowds but, for some reason she could not quite understand why, felt sad.

On Wednesday, Nicholas and his four daughters lunched at Dmitri's nearby estate of Kichkine. They also called in on the Grand Duke and Duchess George at Harax. After their return the family went out for a walk. The weather had luckily improved by now and even Alexandra came out in her small carriage. Olga decided to walk with Shurik who was one of those who accompanied the family despite the fact that Voronov was amongst the number. She felt odd when she later sat next to Paul at tea.

After tea, the girls played charades. Marie and Tatiana partnered Voronov, whilst Olga and Anastasia joined Shurik and Zborovsky. The two eldest sisters then returned to Harax to dine with Nicholas. The party games simply bored Olga once more.

On Thursday, Olga sat with her mother for most of the morning. The rain was unceasing. For once, Voronov was amongst the visitors at lunch. Early in the afternoon, Countess Hendrikova escorted Olga and Tatiana to the Red Cross Sanatorium again. The two sisters later played cards with Zborovsky and Voronov.

The next day, Olga and her friend Ira made a visit to the patients at the nearby Livadia Hospital. That afternoon Olga played charades again with Anastasia and Voronov, which somehow managed to worry Olga. Her sisters Marie and Tatiana sided with Zborovsky. Sadly, Shurik failed to appear as he was unwell.

That evening, Nicholas, accompanied by Dmitri and the four young Grand Duchesses, visited a nearby theatre where they saw some more of the famous colour slides and a film.

On Saturday morning, Olga and Tatiana went shopping once more, escorted on this occasion by Countess Hendrikova. Whilst the ladies were inside Zembinsky's store, Voronov walked by the shop. He was amongst the guests at lunch later that day.

That afternoon the sisters and their attendants went for a walk to the farm despite the terrible muddy conditions. The Grand Duke and Duchess George arrived for dinner as did Dmitri.

Olga was unable to see her friend Shurik on her last day at Livadia. His presence would have been some comfort to her in the absence of Voronov. In the afternoon, the family went to Orianda once more. Early that evening, Olga, Tatiana and Ira visited the Alexander III sanatorium. They passed by the yacht and saw Sablin peeping out at them. He did appear to be everywhere.

On Monday morning, despite the appearance of *Madame Becker*, Olga, Tatiana and their chaperone Hendrikova visited an orphanage for seriously ill children. There was a farewell service at noon. The family were about to leave for Tsarskoe Selo. After lunch, Nicholas reviewed and thanked the troops and the family travelled the brief distance to the yacht by carriage. Olga quickly went to sit with Voronov that evening and chatted away like old times.

The yacht arrived at Sevastopol early on Tuesday morning. Once more, Olga spent time in the company of Voronov although he appeared to be unwell and was probably struggling to cope with his feelings for Olga. The family then travelled home by the Imperial train. The *Standart* was illuminated as they left.

The next day was spent onboard the train. Olga sat with Alexandra for most of the day. Dmitri was accompanying the Tsar and his family back to the north and spent some time playing games with his young cousins. Voronov was also travelling to St Petersburg, but by a different route.

The Imperial family finally arrived back at their main home, the Alexander Palace, in the early evening on Thursday. A service was carried out in Alexei's new rooms. The children's floor had had some alterations in their long absence.

The Tsar and the Tsarina entertained the Dowager Empress, Xenia, Olga, Dmitri and Irina to dinner that evening. After they had left, Madame Vyrubova arrived.

The next day, Olga unpacked her clothes and possessions as the family settled down back in the Alexander Palace for the winter. The family regularly travelled between one home and another at certain times of the year but this visit had been longer than usual.

Olga was happy to hear that Voronov too had just arrived back in the north. The sisters went for a walk to the nearby Znamenie church in the afternoon through the snow. They had tea with Alexandra, Anya and Ira.

Olga Nicolaevna learned the truth on Saturday – she finally understood what had happened to Voronov. His engagement to Olga Kleinmichael was finally announced. He must have known of it for some time and would have found it difficult to deal with his feelings for the Grand Duchess in the changed circumstances. The marriage was probably an arranged one, and Voronov would have not been in a position to argue if this was indeed the case. The Grand Duchess was clearly devastated and Voronov's feelings had not been taken into account. He was clearly very fond of the Grand Duchess but whether he was in love with her remains a mystery to this day – although he probably was but was forced to marry someone else before the situation between him and the Grand Duchess became more serious.

Interestingly, Olga Kleinmichael was the cousin of Countess Vera Kleinmichael who had in 1900 married Prince Dmitri Orbeliani (the brother of the Tsarina's close friend Sonia). Dmitri was a personal assistant to the Tsar's brother-in-law Sandro.

The Tsar's elder daughters attended the Te Deum on Sunday afternoon for Grand Duchess Irina's engagement. Sunday was a difficult day for Olga – attending the engagement party of her cousin when she would have been thinking of the engagement of Voronov. Earlier, the four sisters had attended a parade in honour of the 148th Kaspiysky regiment Anastasia was their Colonel-in-Chief although not officially old enough to be so at twelve years old. It was her name's day.

The day ended with Alexandra and her daughters picking out the inevitable vases for presents for their relatives.

The next morning, Olga and her sister Tatiana visited Anya Vyrubova to see Tatiana's godchild.

Voronov seemed to be in a good mood and Olga tried to make the most of the circumstances. Alya had two young daughters at this time: Tatiana aged four and Olga aged two. She would have a third daughter the following year.

Later, Olga took a very cold walk outside in the garden with Marie, Anastasia and Trina Schnieder. The family decorated their Christmas tree that afternoon. Olga later helped Alexandra sort out the presents. Voronov had arrived at Anya's early with the *good news*.

Christmas Eve was spent as usual at the Alexander Palace. The four sisters went to the regimental church in the morning with their parents and the family lunched together with a single guest, Anya. Later they went to see Trina Schnieder, Lili Obolenskaya and Princess Sonia Orbeliani to hand out gifts and to receive them. Then the family, including Alix, had their own party in the games room.

The Tsar escorted his daughters to his mother's home after tea and they were joined by Xenia and her family. Nicholas and his wife held their own private celebration late that night.

Meanwhile, Olga Nicolaevna listed her presents. The gifts including a sapphire ring and a brooch of aquamarine would have been of little comfort to her in the circumstances but she would continue to maintain a dignified silence over the marriage.

There was yet another liturgy to attend the following morning before lunch. Nicholas and his entire immediate family went to the riding hall to distribute gifts to the Escort regiment. The soldiers entertained their guests with their songs and balalaika playing. Olga was delighted to see Shurik. He was now dearer to her than ever.

On Thursday morning the Grand Duchesses went for another very cold walk along with Trina Schnieder, their chaperone on this occasion. Olga was attempting to keep busy and was reading a great deal. She had always been an enthusiastic reader and threw herself into the new books that she had acquired for Christmas including one called *Perelom* by an author named Markevich.

That afternoon, the five children went to yet another party along with their father and Aunt Olga (in place of Alexandra) and the youngsters took turns to give out the gifts. Shurik was amongst the assembled crowd and Olga managed to chat with him. The Cossacks danced to everyone's delight.

The Empress appeared to be suffering from chest pains. She attended a party the previous day and had been unusually active. Nicholas said farewell to the retiring Austrian Ambassador that day and Olga ended the day with a game of *colorito* with her mother.

Anya Vyrubova later recalled how the Tsarina chose presents carefully, unlike the Tsar. He was far more generous due to having no idea of the real value of things. Nicholas simply chose the gifts he wanted to give from items brought to the palace but Alexandra wanted to know exactly how much each item cost. Nicholas never even carried cash and this caused him an embarrassment on a couple of occasions when the collection plate came around at church. In Siberia, when the family had to surrender their money, Nicholas had none. The one with the most money, and able to lend it to her sister Marie, appears to have been Anastasia who was perhaps a little more careful with her pocket money.

There was a children's party on Friday for Olga and her sisters to attend. She took comfort in the presence of her sisters and young children. She played with them for a long time. The Grand Duchess probably doubted that she would ever have children of her own. The four sisters went for another very cold walk that afternoon. That evening there were guests at teatime – Grand Duke Kyrill and his mother. Dmitri also appeared and stayed for dinner.

That day Alexandra had written to her sister-in-law Onor in order to thank her for the Christmas gifts she had sent from herself and Ernie. The Tsarina admitted that the finest gift that year had been to see Alexei able to walk, despite his evident limp. She also revealed that Marie would soon be taller than Olga. Alexandra stated that Nicholas's sister often visited and she was more like an older sister than an aunt to her daughters. They were very attached to her, she explained.

Ernie had sent his daughters each a sealing-wax heater (for the wax stamp used to seal letters).

On Saturday, Olga remained indoors with her books and, shortly after noon, the Metropolitan and the monks came. The Tsar's sister Olga and her husband appeared later. There was yet another Christmas party that afternoon in the hall for the Cossacks, including of course Shurik and members of the Combined regiment (the Tsar's personal protection squad). Olga was excited and yet embarrassed at talking to the men. The Tsarina once again appeared.

On Sunday, Olga and her sisters visited their grandmother, the Dowager Empress. Olga made the most of the party later by playing charades with Shurik once more. One of the guests, however, was Marie Claire, an older sister of Olga Kleinmichael, but Olga Nicolaevna made the most of the few friends she had.

The Grand Duchesses visited the Dowager Empress again on Monday afternoon. Another party had been arranged helping to lift the spirits of the Grand Duchess. Once again, Olga enjoyed the company of Shurik and the other Cossacks.

On the final day of the year, Olga and her sister attended yet another party. The festivities would have helped to keep Olga's mind occupied although she must have wondered about her future when they played at fortune telling that evening in Trina's room.

Chapter Five

New Year 1914

There was a feeling of festivity on the very first day of 1914 as the sisters played tennis once again but on this occasion it was not outside on the tennis courts but in one of their classrooms. They also branched out into the long corridor in their excitement.

Olga joined in happily with her two youngest sisters' game, probably in an effort to release some of the inbuilt tension. It was only a couple of weeks since she had heard the devastating news that her beloved Paul Voronov, an officer on her father's yacht *Standart*, was about to be married. If that was not hard enough, she found out that she would be amongst the honoured guests at his wedding.

The next day, Rasputin had called on the Tsar and Tsarina, and the three chatted late into the night. It may well have in some way been connected with the Voronov situation. Alexandra had even gone so far as to visit him in Yalta when the family were in Livadia in the autumn. It was so unusual for her to go anywhere without Nicholas, especially in the evening, that it had to be connected in some way with the worry over Olga and Paul's close friendship. As he had come just to see the Imperial couple and not their children, this again was unusual as he normally spoke to them on his irregular visits.

Later, in a more sedate mood, Olga sat quietly indoors with the Tsarina. The Grand Duchesses were always much quieter in the presence of their mother than when alone with their father who liked nothing better than to join in with their wild games. Alexandra suffered from poor health unlike Nicholas.

Since hearing of Paul's imminent marriage, Olga was having difficulty sleeping. It proved to be a very brief engagement. One day in early January, the Tsarina's sister, the Grand Duchess Elisabeth, had arrived from Moscow on a flying visit and told the listeners that Paul and his fiancée had recently visited her. Olga found it impossible to bear. After so many years of observing her mother complaining that her heart had been affected in some way, Olga suddenly felt the same. She was convinced that the emotional pain was damaging her physical heart too.

The everyday routine of the Imperial family would have irked Olga even more than usual. Most days were spent much as any other. The winter months were filled with interminable lessons in various subjects ranging from Russian language to dancing. The lessons themselves were now coming to a close, as Olga was eighteen years old. The afternoons were spent outside in the vast whiteness of the park breaking up the ice on the pond so that the boats could have access, skiing down a hill on some kind of tray or board, or building a huge mountain out of the snow. It inevitably shrank as the weather warmed up.

One brief respite for Olga from her darkest days came with the baptism of her cousin Ioann's baby son Vsevolode. The baby was baptised on the name's day of his paternal aunt and Olga's sister Tatiana, the twelfth. The child's mother was the former Princess Elena of Serbia, a close friend of Olga's since childhood. The baby had been born at Pavlovsk on the seventh so was very young indeed. Although being in the presence of a baby was something Olga dearly loved, it was yet another reminder of the fact that the man she loved was about to marry someone else.

The sisters longed for distraction, which only normally came in the form of parties held by their Aunt Olga on Sundays or the occasional ones held by their mother's friend Anya Vyrubova. Unfortunately the girls, with the possible exception of the youngest Anastasia, had inherited their mother's shyness and were extremely embarrassed when they were the centre of attention. They had so rarely been to the balls that most young ladies of their rank would have gone to as of right. Alexandra had always been determined that they should not mix with girls of their own rank. The few friends they had were drawn from more middle-class backgrounds or even lower. The only real friends they had of any rank were their cousin Irina, who was due to marry very soon, and the daughters of the Duke of Leuchtenberg who they met only at their aunt's parties.

Tatiana was so desperate for friends that she maintained a lifelong friendship with Olga Kleinmichael, the very girl who was about to marry Paul Voronov. Olga Nicolaevna never showed any signs of bitterness towards his intended bride. She appeared to adopt her father's lifelong belief in fate. As one member of the Tsar's entourage noticed at the time, Olga appeared to be happy but only on the surface. Underneath, if you looked hard enough, you could see the signs of some great unhappiness in her past.

Meanwhile, in the run-up to the marriage of Voronov, Olga was still having trouble getting off to sleep and had taken to resting in the Red Room (the Grand Duchesses' personal ante-room) in the afternoons on a sofa. She spent more time than usual in the company of her mother and, on occasions, sang whilst Alexandra played the piano. Olga had always loved music and she drew comfort from it at this most difficult time. She also went back to her books. As an avid lifelong reader, she found solace amongst old familiar works.

Unfortunately for Olga, there was the wedding of her cousin Irina to endure in the coming weeks. Irina was barely months older than Olga and yet her life appeared to have been settled already and Olga was in despair of her own future. A couple of days before Paul Voronov's intended marriage, Olga's Aunt Xenia arrived at Tsarskoe Selo for tea. It seemed an innocuous enough arrival but Xenia had brought with her not only her husband Sandro but the bride-to-be Irina. Alexandra gave her niece a valuable gift of two strings of pearls. Irina was overwhelmed with delight but Olga must have found it hard to look on. The Tsarina was not usually known for her generosity so it was a significant event in itself. Only recently Olga and her sisters had been presented with – glass vases.

Two days later, the Imperial family were present at the marriage of Paul Voronov and Olga Kleinmichael. It would prove a great trial for Olga. Each couple before their marriage in the Russian Orthodox Church are appointed two sponsors and Paul's were the Tsarina and her brother-in-law Grand Duke Alexander, father of Irina. The couple were in effect representatives of their own parents. The two persons could not be husband and wife. Originally the real father and mother were disallowed from attending the ceremony to prove that the couple who intended to marry were doing so without any sign of force. Oddly, baptism is also without the child's parents.

According to the bride-to-be, Nicholas and Alexandra had both expressed a wish to act as sponsor and a greatly embarrassed Paul had chosen the Tsarina. It seemed an extremely generous honour for an officer in the navy.

On the actual morning of the wedding, a gift arrived for the bride, along with a note from Tatiana. The generous present comprised of a golden oil lamp in the shape of three Imperial eagles. It held in place a beautiful pink crystal bowl. The note explained that the gift had come from the Tsarina and requested that it should burn before an icon which she was intending to give to Paul.

As Paul arrived at the Alexander Palace, he was *blessed* by his two sponsors. Later, Nicholas II and his family left for the nearby regimental church where the marriage was to take place. The bride was given away by one of her cousins (her father had died). Paul stood supported by the Tsar, his wife and their four daughters and one son to his right. Nicholas was naturally wearing the uniform of Paul's regiment, the Navy Guards. He always liked to wear the uniform suitable to the place or occasion. He had a vast collection of military uniforms.

The bride's mother was motioned to sit by the Tsarina after she observed the emotional state she was in. The lady initially declined as Alexandra was still standing, but Nicholas brought his wife a chair and the two ladies were seated.

A reception was held afterwards at the home of the Kleinmichaels. Alexandra and Sandro awaited the couple with the traditional welcome of bread and salt. In ancient times, salt was seen as valuable. Nicholas and his children stood watching behind as the couple were *blessed* by their sponsors. Paul was presented with the promised icon. It must have been an emotional moment for Olga.

Two days later, when Prince Felix Yussopov was about to marry the Tsar's niece Irina, he became stuck in a lift and had the indignity of being rescued by the sovereign. Nicholas *gave her away.* The bride's sponsors were Nicholas and the Dowager Empress. Irina's younger brother Vassili acted as an icon boy. As he walked in front of the Tsar, he felt unsure of himself but Nicholas kept him in line by pushing him in the right direction with his knee. Irina also dropped her handkerchief during the ceremony and the ever observant Anastasia retrieved it for her.

The bride wore a lace veil that had previously belonged to the tragic Queen Marie-Antoinette of France. The Austrian-born former monarch was a familiar image to the Tsar's daughters. In the Tsarina's large reception room, there was a portrait of the Queen along with her children presented by the French government.

The day after the wedding of Irina, life continued as normal for her cousins. Olga went back to her singing and spent her time constructively in a little light sewing or embroidery. Tatiana was at her most relaxed with a piece of embroidery in her hands, but Olga was happier in the company of a good book. Tatiana was as practical as Olga was unpractical. Whilst Tatiana would have been content never to read anything other than a light romantic novel, Olga's reading skills were vastly ahead of Tatiana's.

The following evening proved to be far more exciting for the Grand Duchesses. As Tatiana elected to remain at home and keep Alexandra company and continue with her needlework projects, the Tsar escorted his other daughters Olga, Marie and Anastasia into town. They were joined by the Dowager Empress who was far happier in the environment of the city than Alexandra was.

The event was a fascinating one in that it was the twenty-fifth anniversary concert in honour of Nicolas Legat's work with the Imperial theatre. One of the pieces chosen for the special production was the ballet *Esmeralda*. The title part was given to the Tsar's former lover and prima ballerina Mathilde Kschessinka.

The dancer performed the part of *Esmeralda* from Victor Hugo's famous story of the *Hunchback of Notre Dame*. Olga must have enjoyed the performance as in the course of the following months not only did she read the book in French but asked her tutor Pierre Gilliard if she could borrow the follow-up story.

It would have been a great example for Olga to observe her father in the circumstances. He always behaved in an impeccable manner and never let anyone know his true feelings. Whilst the concert was an example of how to behave in a dignified manner in potentially embarrassing circumstances, it may have given her a little sympathy for the position of Mathilde. The lady in question later claimed that she met Olga sometime later and the two got on amiably.

There was great excitement amongst the Tsar's daughters soon after when the Dowager Empress held a ball at the Anchikov Palace in honour of the Grand Duchesses Olga and Tatiana. They were chaperoned by Nicholas and left at 4.30 but the Tsarina left over four hours before. The girls had refused to leave any earlier. Nicholas was loath to take them on many such occasions as he had to get up at seven the following morning in order to work. He complained to a lady-in-waiting that he needed to get up in time to read the reports before he met the appropriate minister.

The girls made a delightful impression on everyone with their beauty and unassuming charm. The two girls wore simple white gowns and found the whole thing rather amusing. At first, no one came up to ask either of the Grand Duchesses to dance. Finally, the Master of Ceremonies approached some of the young officers from Tsarskoe Selo and told them to ask the Grand Duchesses to dance. Afterwards some of the more *fashionable* young men approached the girls for a dance, but in reality they would have been more at ease with the men they were familiar with.

The excitement of the *season* of 1914 continued when the Grand Duchesses Olga and Tatiana were invited to two important social events on the same evening! The Emperor accompanied his mother the Dowager Empress along with his two eldest daughters to the *Folle Journee* held traditionally on the last day before Lent (when the *season* ended due to the onset of Lent) hosted by the Tsar's aunt, Grand Duchess Marie

Pavlovna, and later that evening, in order not to offend the Dowager Empress's friend Countess Betsy Schouvalov, the Dowager Empress along with her granddaughters made a late arrival at her end of season ball.

It was back to reality soon after. It must have been exceedingly boring after the excitement of the previous evening. The Grand Duchesses had tea with their parents in one of the larger rooms in the Alexander Palace, quite a contrast to the previous evening.

The sisters returned to their inevitable unending studies. One evening in the early spring, whilst Olga's sister Marie was having an English lesson with her tutor Sydney Gibbes, the Tsarina made a surprise visit to the classroom. The English man was embarrassed and uncertain of etiquette. He graciously proffered a chair to the lady and continued the lesson whilst standing as he normally did. He had forgotten that he had left the book on the table. The Tsarina asked if this was a temptation for Marie, to see the answers to her questions right in front of her. The flustered Gibbes, who normally held the book in his hands, replied that if Marie ever saw the words by mistake she confessed at once.

Alexandra fairly swiftly turned the conversation from Marie's alleged improvement to her beloved son. She wanted to know how he was getting on with his English lessons. As a small child, Alexei had spoken no English and only Russian. The girls on the other hand had always spoken both English and Russian from early on.

Two days later, Marie used her English skills to compose a comic letter to her missing father, much as her sister Anastasia usually did. She informed Nicholas that she had been using his bathroom and even his personal toilet. She had swum in the large swimming pool-sized bath that had come up to her shoulders but complained that the toilet was very cold and uncomfortable as she had failed to realise that the lid was up.

Marie composed the letter whilst sitting in her room where the open door let in the draught. Her sister Tatiana, she confided, was playing the card game *Halma* with the Tsarina.

A couple of days later, the artist Bobrovsky came to the palace to paint the Tsar. His daughters sat in on the work. That evening, the family looked through some more of the beautiful colour photographs, which they received from time to time from the photographer.

Later in the week, Olga composed her final English composition for Sydney Gibbes, her English tutor. She delivered the dictation on Oscar Wilde's *Selfish Giant* without fault, but a composition she also completed was not so perfect. She was approaching the end of her studies. She was eighteen years of age and normally a girl's education was over well before this age. However, very soon after, Olga was about to become the focus of some very adult speculation. That same evening, the Crown Prince of Rumania (Ferdinand) arrived in Russia along with his wife Marie (a cousin of Alexandra) and their son Prince Carol.

It is remarkable that the end of her studies and the first possible marriage proposal came so close together. It is said that it was the Russian Foreign Minister, Serge Sazonov, who had proposed the potential match as a way of breaking off the alliance between Rumania and Austro-Hungary.

The family had been invited to Russia with a possible match in mind for Olga and Carol. The observant and intelligent Crown Princess Marie noticed straightaway how dull life was for the sisters. She thought Nicholas a little odd. He was very kind and welcoming but was somewhat vague. She found her cousin Alix (some three years her senior in age) as cold and distant as ever. The Tsarina unfortunately had a habit of making her guests feel uncomfortable. The only strangers that she had any real skill with were the elderly, the very young and religious figures. Marie was none of these. The Crown Princess was also the sister of Alix's former sister-in-law Ducky (Victoria-Melita) and the two were never close, even when almost related.

The Crown Princess was both hurt and dismayed by the Tsarina's distant behaviour. As Marie was a mere Crown Princess and not an Empress like Alix was, Marie felt that she was treated as an inferior. Marie could hardly wait to escape from Tsarskoe Selo. She noticed quickly how Alexandra's name was social poison. It was only when the Crown Princess spoke about the possible marriage between Olga and Carol that the Tsarina began to open up. She spoke candidly on the subject.

The two ladies decided that they would do nothing but merely provide suitable occasions for the two to meet and see what happened.

Marie had little hope of her son marrying the Grand Duchess. Neither Carol nor Olga had the slightest interest in each other. She was still in love with Paul Voronov and Carol would have probably found her too unsophisticated. She had had a very sheltered life compared to most young ladies of her age. She had been educated at home and had no real experience of life beyond the palace walls.

Olga Nicolaevna was in an unusually cheerful mood later in the week. The end of her education would have felt to Olga like the start of her adult life, although nothing actually changed and she was still largely treated as a child by her parents.

Chapter Six

Spring 1914

The Imperial family returned to the Crimea soon after. As in the previous autumn, it was decided to travel south for the benefit of the health of the invalids Alexei and Alexandra.

Nicholas had taken the opportunity to go on an overnight trip whilst staying at Livadia in late April but Alexandra found it a great trial to be without him even for a short while. She would soon have to deal with his prolonged absences on a regular basis after the outbreak of war.

The situation between Alexandra and her one time close friend Anya Vyrubova had become unbearable for Alexandra who felt that Anya was constantly demanding more and more attention from her and often seemed to the Empress to be trying to come between Nicholas and Alexandra. She believed that Anya was besotted with the Emperor. Anya did indeed have walls covered with his photos and yet Alexandra's other close friend had photos of the children more prominently displayed at her house.

During the month of May 1914, the Tsar, along with his daughters the Grand Duchesses Olga, Tatiana, Marie and Anastasia, visited the zoological gardens at Kozmodemyansk in the Crimea. Nicholas had of course a small hunters' cottage in the area where he had stayed overnight with his two eldest daughters the previous year. It provided Nicholas with the perfect opportunity for hunting deer. Close to the cottage was a small monastery that contained a source of fresh water, which the local people believed had healing properties. Nicholas and his daughters bathed in the waters but they were not the ones that were ill – it was Alexandra and her son who were constantly unwell.

As usual, the sisters played endless games of tennis with Nicholas and the ever present, although increasingly irritating, Anya. The Tsarina and her daughters embroidered and sewed items to sell at the upcoming charity bazaar and made bead necklaces from beads sent by the Tsarina's brother Ernie from Germany. They were a close family and the four sisters were a solid unit.

It was during one of the Tsar's visits to Kozmodemyansk with his four daughters that Marie decided to climb into the middle of an ornamental lake for some unknown reason. Nicholas helped Marie keep her balance by pushing a chair towards her but her three amused sisters rather hoped she would fall in, but she did not. She had after all the ability to climb walls and was unlikely to be scared easily.

The Tsar and his eldest daughters often returned to spend the evening with the

Grand Duke and Duchess George at Harax on two or even three evenings in each week. Amongst the guests at Harax that year was a friend of Olga, Zoya de Stoeckl. The party dined with all the windows open so the guests were able to capture the view of the landscape outside. On one visit, Nicholas, however, grew bored and, picking up small bits of black bread, rolled them between his fingers and flung them across the table to unsuspecting diners. Several of the bread pellets hit Agnes de Stoeckl's daughter Zoya. (Agnes was a friend and lady-in-waiting to the Grand Duchess George, or Minnie as she was known.)

The young girl grabbed a menu and wrote a hurried message on the back. She then asked the Grand Duchess George to hand it to Nicholas. She requested that he wash his hands in future before he threw any more of the bread as the missiles were quite black.

The greatly amused Nicholas burst into uncontrollable laughter and tears appeared at the side of his face.

The following evening, Nicholas returned to dine at Harax with Alexandra and their daughters Olga and Tatiana. It was a hot night and, according to Agnes de Stoeckl (the mother of Olga's friend), Nicholas seemed tired and somewhat irritated. He found it difficult to relax knowing that he had to return to a mountain of paperwork.

As an autocrat with no personal secretary, he had a great deal to do on a daily basis and he rarely stopped work even when most would have taken the opportunity to rest.

One of the guests that evening was Prince Christopher of Greece and the young prince was suddenly taken with the idea of proposing marriage to the Grand Duchess Olga Nicolaevna. He discussed the situation with his sister and, after a stiff whisky and soda, drove to the White Palace the following afternoon. He later returned to Harax appearing little shaken. His sister pressed him for information and Christopher admitted that he had asked the Tsar for Olga's hand but although Nicholas had been most kind he had declared that Olga was too young to think of such things. This was not strictly true as preparations were being made for a possible marriage to the Rumanian Prince Carol.

The long-awaited bazaar took place soon after on board two of the Tsar's yachts the *Standart* and the *Almaz*. The Tsarina, her daughters and various members of the household (male and female) sold items made especially for the bazaar. The stall also sold souvenir postcards with pictures of the Imperial family on. A series of photographs had been taken the previous year and a new set would be taken in 1914. The event carried over three days and quite a substantial sum was made for the local tuberculosis patients.

During the holiday in the Crimea early that summer, Alexei had taken a walk with a friend one long hot day at Ai-Todor. They had wandered out of the gates to a nearby village but unfortunately the heir was recognised. A crowd soon appeared and surrounded him. They attempted to touch him. He was alarmed but attempted to remain calm. He steadily worked his way back to the gates, smiling, saluting and shaking hands until he was able to return. It was one of the disadvantages of having postcards sold for charity with the photographs of the children on. The five remarkably handsome children were recognised wherever they went.

Pierre Gilliard was concerned that his pupil Alexei was becoming isolated and had an idea but he was not encouraged by the boy's doctor when he suggested giving Alexei more personal freedom. The doctor was worried that the child would come to some harm, which was quite natural under the circumstances. After consultations between the Tsarina and the doctors, it was agreed to give the boy a little more time to himself.

On of the first trips arranged for Alexei, in his new more relaxed regime, was a visit to *Red Rock* in the Crimea. The excited Tsarevich travelled with the Tsar, his tutor Pierre Gilliard, Lieutenant Baron G N Taube of the Imperial yacht *Standart,* the sailor nanny Andrei Derevenko and a Cossack orderly. Alexei immensely enjoyed the outing and even Nicholas was delighted to see how well his son was and how much the outing meant to the boy.

Alexei enjoyed his newfound freedom but predictably an accident happened.

The Tsarevich hurt his leg after falling off a chair he had been standing on. Gilliard felt guilty that it was entirely his fault but the Tsarina refused to blame him in any way. Unfortunately, Alexei continued to have accidents and every time he tried something new and exciting the boy risked life and limb.

As the child's torment continued, Gilliard saw how hard it must have been for the Tsarina; unable to relieve him of the terrible pain he suffered. She felt that, as he had inherited the illness that caused the blood to clot so slowly from her, it was her fault that the child suffered and no one else's.

At this time, the Tsarina spoke of her worries of the marriage prospects of her four daughters. She confided in the Foreign Minister, Serge Sazonov. She knew that her happiness was rare amongst royal marriages and hoped that her daughters would be as lucky as she had been. She stated that the Emperor would ultimately have to decide whether a possible marriage for one of his daughters was suitable or not. Paul Voronov was obviously not suitable, as the Grand Duchess Olga Nicolaevna had found out.

She dreaded the very idea of her daughters marrying and hoped that they would be able to remain in Russia even if they married but knew it was unlikely with four daughters. She spoke of the time when Prince Max of Baden had asked for her hand in marriage. The Tsarina explained that she felt it was her duty to let the sisters make their own choice. She added that they would only intervene if the marriage was unsuitable. This was undoubtedly what had recently happened to Olga.

A series of photographs of the four young Grand Duchesses was taken towards the end of the month for official purposes at the Alexander Palace. They would have been used for handing out at the future visit to Rumania. The series of pictures showed Tatiana without her wig on this occasion and with a rather fetching *bob* which did not actually come into fashion until the 1920s. She also wore a blue silk ribbon around her head in a style very reminiscent of the 1920s. Olga wore a similar ribbon but with her long hair up.

Pierre Gilliard later recalled how the Grand Duchess Olga challenged him as to the real reason for the visit to Rumania. She strongly suspected that an engagement between her and the Rumanian Prince was a possibility and had already made up her mind that she did not want to marry him. The Russian Foreign Minister was amongst those who supported the potential match but Olga was definitely against the idea. She stated that she intended to remain in Russia as she knew she would feel like a foreigner after a marriage to a foreign prince. This is something she may have understood after speaking to Grand Duke Paul's daughter Marie Pavlovna who married a Swedish prince but eventually left him and returned to Russia.

It is alleged that Olga and her sisters purposely sunburned their faces on the voyage to Rumania.

They did enjoy sitting in the sun and had been sunbathing at every opportunity for at least a year.

The Imperial family travelled on the yacht *Standart* from Livadia to Constanza at the end of May. The Rumanian royals greeted the travellers at the landing stage. The group included the aged Queen Elisabeth, her daughter-in-law Marie (Alexandra's cousin) and Marie's various children. Queen Elisabeth appeared in white robes not unlike the ones worn by Alexandra's sister Ella. Alexei was delighted in the young Prince Nicolas who was a year older than the Tsarevich. The two were constantly together during the visit. However, there was a third child included in the party. The youngest daughter of the Crown Princess, Illena found Alexei particularly charming and followed him round too. She was a beautiful little girl and wore a dress that was rather shorter than usual, to say the least, on such occasions.

The Queen was a writer and an eccentric and known as *Carmen Sylva* to her adoring public. She was a charming and generous host and, as she had travelled to Russia in her younger days, an enthusiast about the Empire.

The day's programme proved to be very well packed. The Tsarina, with so little physical strength, struggled to keep up with the constant receptions and visits. The Russian Imperial family drove in state through the town to the cathedral where they attended a religious service. There was a luncheon party afterwards. Nicholas and King Carol then went on to visit the various Russian and Rumanian ships. The exhausted Alexandra rested whilst she had the chance.

A tea party was then hosted aboard the *Standart* and Alexandra worried that there would not be enough food to go around as most hostesses will. After tea, the party, with the exception of Alexandra and the Queen, attended a review. Olga sat beside the Crown Princess and was the centre of attention for all the locals and officials as she was a possible future Rumanian queen.

During the earlier part of the day, an official photograph was taken of the two families. The well-known picture showed Alexei seated on the ground along with his friend Nicolas, Tatiana naturally seated next to her mother, and Olga next to Nicolas. Olga was nursing the youngest member of the family – Prince Mircea. The baby sadly died in a couple of years. After the official photograph was taken, a film shows that, straight after, Olga's sister Marie swiftly rose up from her chair and all but prized the baby off her sister.

There was then a state dinner at the palace where the Tsar gave a speech and impressed all with his clear speaking voice. He spoke French with a better accent than King Carol who sounded particularly German. Luckily, Alexandra did not have to speak as she too had an atrocious French accent. The reception was held in a special hall that had been designed especially for the occasion by the artistic Crown Princess.

The Rumanian Queen had forgotten to put on her official *orders* and an accommodating Alexandra removed hers so that they were equal. She greatly preferred simplicity anyhow. There was the usual *cercle* afterwards. The two granddaughters of the late Queen Victoria (Marie and Alix) were well versed in its intricacies. They simply made a point of speaking to as many of the assembled guests as possible in an appropriate manner, according to their rank and age, whilst the guests stood in a semicircle.

Gilliard claimed that the three youngest sisters had become bored during the dinner and had kept looking at him and winking at their oldest sister.

The Tsarina was almost beside herself with exhaustion by now. The evening ended with a torchlight procession that Nicholas and his daughters watched from the balcony of the palace along with their hosts. Alexandra was too exhausted to attend. The final goodbyes said, the Russians left aboard the *Standart* for Odessa at around midnight.

The family eventually arrived in Odessa but the Tsarina was too exhausted to continue. She only managed to attend a religious service at the cathedral and met some ladies at a reception before she had to retire for the day. The Tsar and his children continued without her. The family then travelled on to Kischinev where the Tsar unveiled a statue to his illustrious ancestor Alexander I who had taken part in the war against Napoleon Bonaparte which so fascinated Nicholas. He had a cousin who married into the Bonaparte family and the children's tutor Pierre Gilliard had previously been employed by the family of a descendant of Napoleon Bonaparte's first wife the Empress Josephine. This connection may well have been why Olga was so fascinated in Bonaparte's son, although of course he was the son of his second wife the Austrian Marie-Louise. Alix's cousin Louise had named herself after this Queen after being baptised with a multitude of names including that of Emperor Franz Joseph her godfather, although in the feminine form.

An interesting observation of the Tsar's four daughters was made by Crown Princess Marie of Rumania at this time. She said that the girls were all very natural and confided in her when their mother was not present, yet when she appeared they always did what they thought she wanted them to.

A few days after the return to Tsarskoe Selo, the King of Saxony arrived on a State visit, and the usual ceremonial of dinners and reviews took place, but as this was a visit of a *Queenless* King, it was far less fatiguing than such visits usually were for the Tsarina. (She did not need to attend any of the ceremonies.) Nicholas and the King presided over a march past of His Majesty's Hussar Guards regiment in the forecourt of the Catherine Palace then attended a lunch in the Great Gallery.

The King, Friedrich August III, was divorced so although he had three sons, all of a similar age to Olga Nicolaevna, as a divorcee since 1903, his sons would not be seen as suitable candidates for the hand of Olga which must have been a great relief. The oldest of the sons, George, later became a priest.

Soon after the departure of the King of Saxony came the British Fleet under the command of the youthful Admiral David Beatty. The Fleet arrived at *Kronstadt* in an impressive show of strength. The Admiral arrived aboard his flagship the *Lion* and was accompanied by the *Queen Mary, Princess Royal* and the *New Zealand*. The Tsar and his family went aboard the *Lion* for lunch. The next day, Nicholas entertained the Admiral, his wife Ethel and members of his party to lunch at Tsarskoe Selo. As the couple were the parents of two young sons, they would have found Alexei and his sisters particularly enchanting as nearly everyone did. Since early childhood, the children were seen in a semi-divine manner by the ordinary Russian people and, everywhere they went, they attracted crowds. In the past, some had merely asked that they be permitted to touch to children for luck.

Nicholas and his family boarded the *Standart* at Peterhof shortly after. Unfortunately, Alexei caught his foot on a rung of a ladder and twisted his ankle. The injury proved to be a rather nasty and painful one and by the evening he was in serious pain. That evening, Pierre Gilliard came upon the Tsarina and Dr Botkin with the child who was weeping and every few minutes, as the pain increased, he screamed. Gilliard went back to his cabin to fetch a book and he attempted to soothe the boy by reading to him as he often did in later years in Siberia. The cruise continued as normal.

Nicholas invariably went ashore when the yacht finally anchored. He and his daughters walked and played endless sets of tennis. The Tsarina of course usually stayed on the yacht in the company of one of her daughters. The previous year it had been Olga who had been on *duty* more than ever as she endeavoured to stay as near to Paul Voronov as possible.

The trip proved to be an eventful one but for all the wrong reasons: whilst Alexei suffered after his fall, the *Standart* crew heard fabulous rumours and stories of terrible deeds. The Tsarina was more concerned about her son but Nicholas could not help but be fascinated when he was informed of the death or, to be more accurate, the assassination of the heir to the Austro-Hungarian Empire, Arch Duke Franz Ferdinand and his morganatic wife Sophie. Nicholas had met the unfortunate victim some years ago when he had visited Russia on behalf of his aged uncle, the Emperor Franz Joseph of Austria. The couple had been murdered in Sarajevo by Gavilo Princip and initially the main concern would have been for their three young orphaned children – Sophie (13), Maximilian (11) and Ernst (10). The murder would have massive ramifications and significance of catastrophic proportions for Nicholas and his immediate family.

However the following day came news of a more personal nature. Rasputin was seriously wounded at his home village of Pokrovskoye by a female agent named Khina Gusseva. She attempted unsuccessfully to commit suicide after she had initially believed she had completed her mission. He was taken to Tyumen and successfully recovered – eventually.

The destiny of Russia and Nicholas himself would have been very different had Rasputin died and Franz Ferdinand survived to see his children grow up, but destiny had other plans. Nicholas was a great believer in *fate* and little did he know what *fate* had in store for him and his immediate family.

Chapter Seven

Summer 1914

Olga Nicolaevna remarked upon the unusual weather conditions at sea that summer when she sent word to her Aunt Xenia shortly after. The summer of 1914 proved to be far more sultry than usual, as if lulling the inhabitants of Europe, into a false sense of security before the storms ahead. However, life carried on as normal and the family returned to their daily habit of taking walks ashore.

Later that day, the Imperial family returned to Peterhof and Alexei was carried ashore – still suffering from a swollen ankle following his fall. Rasputin would not be on hand to assist the boy as he was fighting his own battle after the unsuccessful murder attempt.

The family had returned to Peterhof in time to prepare for the forthcoming French state visit. Maurice Paleologue, the recently appointed French Ambassador, was graciously welcomed by the Tsar, who was dressed in the appropriate naval admiral's uniform. Nicholas was a stickler for wearing the correct attire for each occasion. As the Ambassador lunched aboard the Tsar's yacht the *Standart* the two men chatted of the possibilities for war. Nicholas was convinced that the German Emperor would avoid war at all costs.

Later, the French President, Raymond Poincare, arrived aboard the *France* and was invited to a banquet at Peterhof Palace. Although Nicholas resided in one of the smaller palaces on the estate, the main palace was used for official occasions. The Tsarina appeared in a brocade gown, wearing a diamond tiara in her hair.

Two days later, Nicholas and the French President travelled to Krasnoe Selo for a review of some 60,000 troops. Nicholas rode on horseback whilst Alexandra arrived at the parade-ground in a carriage alongside Raymond Poincare. Olga and Tatiana seated themselves opposite the Tsarina.

The French President entertained the Tsar and Tsarina the following evening aboard the *France*. The Imperial couple arrived in time for dinner accompanied by their two elder daughters. Poincare sat with the excessively shy Tsarina but she found it impossible to remain calm in the circumstances. She complained that the ship's band was making her headache. The President thoughtfully signalled to the band's conductor to refrain from playing. Olga was nearby and observed her mother's dilemma. She spoke quietly to the Tsarina and informed Poincare that her mother was indeed very tired but was nevertheless happy to continue to chat.

Later, Nicholas invited the Ambassador aboard his yacht the *Standart* and the two spoke candidly of the Tsar's conversation with the President. The French Ambassador left after midnight and returned to his home in St Petersburg before dawn.

Once the French President was safely en route home for France, the Austrians duly released the ultimatum they had prepared a few days previously. They had waited until the Russians and French were apart before launching it upon the unsuspecting world. The ultimatum insisted that the Arch-Duke Franz Ferdinand's murder had been plotted in Belgrade and that Serb officials had supplied his weapons and arranged for his secret entry into Sarajevo. Austria demanded *satisfaction*. They demanded that Austrian officers be permitted to enter Serbia in order to carry out their own investigation into the murder. Serbia was given two days to prepare its reply. It had been approved by the Austrian Emperor.

The Serbians immediately appealed to the Russians (their traditional allies) for assistance, but Nicholas was quite determined not to be responsible for beginning a war.

A military council was quickly convened at Krasnoe Selo, and Nicholas summoned the members of the government to a meeting at Tsarskoe Selo the following day. The situation required that a substantial number of Russian troops be put on immediate alert – just in case!

One Wednesday in mid-July, Tsar Nicholas ordered the mobilisation of 1,200,000 Russian troops. He was certain that war was imminent and was presented with an ultimatum by the German Emperor. The Kaiser warned the Tsar of Russia that Germany would mobilize unless Russia ceased to do so within twenty-four hours.

Seemingly unaware of the impending outbreak of war, the lives of the Grand Duchesses carried on much as normal. The Thursday morning was spent as usual for the girls with horse riding for Tatiana and her two youngest sisters Marie and Anastasia. It was fortunate that Olga had remained indoors that morning as the girls met Paul Voronov on their route. The Grand Duchesses also continued with their regular studies.

After lunch, the girls sang and played music accompanied by the ever present Anya Vyrubova and Victor Erastovich Zborovksy who would increasingly feature in the lives of the Imperial family (especially Anastasia) as he would ultimately prove to be a real hero; something few would aspire to. Being a hero is usually a short-term career move in times of real trouble. Tatiana and Anastasia walked towards the sea afterwards for a refreshing swim on an unusually hot day. That evening Olga and Tatiana dined with their father and his youngest sister Olga.

On Friday, Kaiser Wilhelm of Germany issued the formal ultimatum to Russia and asked for assurances concerning the intentions of the French. That morning the four Grand Duchesses went bicycle riding and played on some stilts. The Tsar appeared for lunch but it was clear that he had been attending an important meeting that morning and he appeared to be rather distracted. He had spoken with all the ministers. Things were beginning to get out of hand and although Nicholas was determined to avoid war at all costs, it was beyond his control.

That afternoon, Tatiana made use of one of the telephones already installed within the private apartments of the Tsar. She chatted with a couple of old familiar friends – Nicholas Sablin and Nicholas Rodionov, her old tennis partner. The four sisters later visited a nearby monastery in honour of St Serafim's Day. (It had been Nicholas with the insistence of Alexandra who had made the hermit a saint in the first place in 1903, and the Tsarina had always believed that the action was instrumental in the eventual birth of her only son. It had been Rasputin's predecessor Monsieur Philippe of Lyon who had said that if she prayed to St Serafim she would have a son. There was no such saint at the time so the man with the same name was tracked down and became a saint, despite his body decaying after death. Normally, one of the terms strictly adhered to before canonisation is that the body of the said person should not have decomposed as bodies normally do.) The four sisters were joined by Alix's only two real friends Anya Vyrubova and Lili Dehn. The ladies returned home by car but dropped off Madame Dehn first and the Grand Duchesses remained with her for a while.

The sisters dined with their parents that evening and, once again, Tatiana chatted to Sablin over the telephone. The girls were extremely fond of this new and novel form of communication.

Nicholas, deeply concerned about the potential outcome of the political situation, summoned his more experienced cousin the Grand Duke Nicholas to Peterhof and quickly appointed him as Supreme Commander of the Armed Forces. Nicholas fully intended to take control himself, in due time, as his illustrious ancestor Alexander I had done during the Napoleonic wars. Nicholas was one of the few men able to read about the exploits of his own ancestor in a world-famous novel – *War and Peace*. It was bizarre that the Tsar should once again be staying in the small palace close to Peterhof as he had been in 1905 when he had summoned his uncle after the very first Russian Revolution, which is of course relatively unknown due to the existence of the second one.

After lunch on Saturday, Nicholas walked with his children and attended church. He was in dire need of divine assistance. War appeared to be imminent, and indeed it was. On his return from church, Nicholas was informed that Germany had declared war on Russia. The dinner that evening was disturbed by the appearance of the British Ambassador, Sir George Buchanan, who arrived with a wire from King George V, Nicholas's first cousin. The two men then spent some considerable time composing a reply to their ally. Nicholas was extremely gifted at English but he felt the need for assistance on this vital occasion. He was concerned that a wrong word would lead to trouble. It was unlikely but nevertheless, in such situations, care needed to be taken.

The day had proved to be fairly uneventful for the Tsar's five children. They had had lessons that morning as usual at the villa Alexandria and all five lunched with their parents. Tatiana chatted again on the telephone to her friends Sablin and Rodionov. The girls were continually using the telephones to keep in touch with their friends aboard the yacht. The sisters then went for a walk in the garden with the Tsar. When news came of the declaration of war, the sisters were shocked, outraged and tearful. The Tsarina cried on hearing the news and her daughters swiftly followed suit.

The war against Germany would naturally have been especially difficult for Alexandra. She was particularly close to her brother, who was now on the opposing side to her. Her brother-in-law Louis held a senior position in the British Admiralty and her brother-in-law Henry was the Kaiser's own brother.

The Tsar's mother and sister Xenia were on holiday in England at the outbreak of war and were forced to return via Finland as they had been prevented from travelling via Germany. Alexandra's eldest sister Victoria (and her daughter Louise) left Russia and returned to England via Sweden briefly meeting the Dowager Empress and her daughter on the journey back to Russia.

Late that evening, Alexandra began telephoning everyone concerning the horrific news. One of those called was her lady-in-waiting Baroness Sophie Buxhoeveden. Alexandra announced that war had been declared. Sophie was understandably shocked. The Baroness suspected that it was the Austrians who had started the war but the Tsarina confirmed that it was the Germans. As a German-born Princess, it put Alexandra in an impossible situation: she was now technically the *enemy* to most of her adopted country.

Alexandra insisted on taking a part by reopening the workshops used during the Russo-Japanese war some ten years previously. She wished to reopen the sewing workshops that had been set up in the Winter Palace in the 1904-5 war against Japan.

Nicholas travelled to the capital to officially sign the declaration of war. That morning he had attended church accompanied by his two youngest daughters Marie and Anastasia before attending a peaceful lunch. Meanwhile, Alexandra had travelled to the Ulansky Cathedral with Olga and Tatiana to attend a service. In the early afternoon, Nicholas, his wife and four daughters, and his sister Olga left Peterhof on board the steam launch *Alexandria* for the capital. The family then travelled the rest of the journey by carriage.

Once the Tsar had signed the declaration on Sunday, the family attended a *Te Deum* before he and Alexandra stepped out onto the public balcony where the crowds below were watching in their thousands and loyally singing the National Anthem. Early in the evening, the family left the capital and returned to Peterhof. En route, the sisters had spotted Nicholas Sablin who was accompanied by none other than Paul Voronov.

Pierre Gilliard observed the Tsar that morning when he had come into the schoolroom to kiss his son Alexei *good morning*. He noticed a change in Nicholas's appearance and admitted that the Tsar looked even worse than he had done the previous day. He informed Gilliard that the Germans had just entered Luxembourg, attacked French Customs houses and declared war on France.

The German-born Tsarina took the decision to become a nursing sister and she, along with her eldest daughters plus some other female members of the household including Anya Vyrubova, enrolled in a nursing course under Dr Vera Gedroiz, a rare woman doctor. The student nurses then worked in the wards where the wounded constantly arrived from the battlefield each morning and, in the afternoons, they studied the theory under the same lady doctor.

The unfortunate victims were not only blood stained from their wounds but filthy as they often had to be driven quite a way from the battlefield to the hospital where they were treated. The nurses had to wash their own hands before cleaning up the wounds and bandaging the men. Many were naturally sent straight to the operating theatre, where the Tsarina and her daughters later worked.

On Monday morning, the Tsar along with Alexandra, Olga and Tatiana attended a special prayer service for the members of one of the Tsarina's regiments who were about to depart for the war. Afterwards she blessed each of the men personally and presented them with a small religious icon.

The next day, the eldest sister of the Tsarina arrived in St Petersburg. It was the very day that the British declared war on the Germans. Her timing could not have been worse and it would prove difficult to return to England. Victoria and her daughter Louise were received at the station by the Tsarina and her eldest daughters, the British Ambassador Sir George Buchanan, and Alexandra's lady-in-waiting Baroness Buxhoeveden.

That day, the Tsar received various visitors including his sister Olga, cousin Kyrill and Uncle Paul. They had all come to discuss the current situation. The Grand Duchesses meanwhile cheerfully got down to the serious business of sorting out underwear for the inevitable wounded soldiers who would no doubt arrive soon. Alexandra was intending to open a couple of small hospitals within the grounds of the Catherine Palace. They would need endless supplies of linen and clothes as the wounded would obviously arrive without their own (extra) clothes, undergarments, bedding and suitcases. In former years, Alexandra's mother Alice had done the same during the two wars she lived through whilst living in Germany. Alice had continued nursing on both occasions despite the fact that she was pregnant both times.

The Baroness escorted the guests to the Winter Palace and the following morning the Tsarina, escorted by Olga and Tatiana, arrived at the vast palace to see her sister and niece. The ladies travelled to Peterhof.

On Wednesday, Nicholas received the French Ambassador, Maurice Paleologue, who came officially to discuss recent events. Nicholas was outraged at the Germans' recent attacks on France and their violation of the neutrality of Luxembourg and Belgium. The Ambassador informed Nicholas of his fears that the French army would be crushed by the formidable German army.

It became clear the next day that Austria had also declared war on Russia. It was, of course, exactly what Nicholas had both feared and expected. He held a council of ministers. The Tsarina went into town and returned with her sisters Victoria and Elisabeth who then stayed for lunch and dinner.

Meanwhile, Thursday proved to be a busy day for the Tsar's immediate family. That morning he, along with Alexandra, Olga, Tatiana, Anya Vyrubova and Baroness Buxhoeveden, travelled aboard the *Alexandria* to St Petersburg. They passed by the *Standart* and, once again, the sisters observed Nicholas Rodionov and Paul Voronov. It seems as though Olga would never cease to have opportunities to notice Voronov.

The family then returned to Peterhof in the company of the Tsarina's sisters Victoria and Elisabeth. Whilst the three Hessian sisters spent the day getting reacquainted and chatting of the old days, the next generation of sisters decided to pay a call on Anya. She was entertaining her sister and three small nieces. The Grand Duchesses happily spent the time with the three little girls Tatiana, Olga and baby Alexandra.

On the following Thursday, at the end of the month, Britain and France finally declared war on Austria.

The next day, the four youngest of Nicholas's children resumed their usual lessons whilst Alexandra visited a nearby hospital. The sisters continued their former activities of walking and chatting on the telephone. The Dowager Empress arrived in time for dinner at the Tsar's small house close to Peterhof where his mother also had a small home of her own.

On Monday morning, Nicholas and his family left for Moscow and met up again with Elisabeth. The locals gave the Tsar an enthusiastic welcome which was quite moving according to eyewitnesses.

Unfortunately on Tuesday, it was discovered that Alexei would be unable to walk. The child was utterly distressed; his luck had failed him yet again. It was decided that the only way he could continue with the schedule was for him to be carried in the arms of a huge Cossack. It made it obvious to the assembled crowds who saw him that day that he was a semi-invalid, if not worse.

That day, the Tsar and his family attended a special service at the cathedral. During the ceremony, each of the assembled dignitaries had to kneel at the relics and the tombs of their ancestors. The Tsarina and each of her daughters made two awkward attempts at kissing the figure of the Virgin of Vladimir. The Grand Duchess Elisabeth, on the other hand, executed the task easily. They needed to place their knee on a rather high marble seat in order to reach the figure but only Ella managed first time.

In the afternoon, they inspected one of the Tsarina's new hospital trains and again the children met up with their former governess Sophie I Tiuchieva.

The following day, the Imperial visitors attended Mass at the Church of Our Saviour. The day continued with visits to two more small churches and a *sklad* (a depot for Red Cross supplies).

Later, Pierre Gilliard accompanied the Tsarevich for a trip in a motor car into the hills surrounding the city but, as they returned, the party was suddenly surrounded by a crowd who recognised young Alexei. The chauffeur was forced to stop in one of the narrow streets when he was spotted by the local shoppers. The crowd surged forward and the car was quickly surrounded. The young boy was terrified and sank back as far as he could into the seat. Luckily, they were soon rescued and escaped unharmed. (The Archduke had recently died in similar circumstances when he travelled in an open car.)

The Germans had taken the Belgian capital of Brussels that same day.

Nicholas and his family travelled to the *Troitsko-Sergieveyskaia* monastery the next day in order to collect an important icon that was said to have always accompanied previous Tsars in their campaigns of war.

The family returned home to Tsarskoe Selo the following day. The Tsarina and daughters began their nursing training. The sisters enjoyed the work and felt part of something at long last. Previously they had lived very much on the edge of society, never really being permitted to do anything useful. At last Olga and Tatiana would be able to train for a profession such as they had probably never dreamed of and be around ordinary people of their own age. The Tsarina too found her true vocation and threw herself wholeheartedly into the course and the nursing. Unfortunately, she eventually found that she had not the physical strength to carry on. Tatiana proved to be an excellent nurse but Olga found the work more challenging. After all, the work was very similar to Tatiana's usual role of pandering to the every whim of her mother and looking after her brother, but Olga was not practical-minded and struggled to deal with the brutal realities of war.

On the 10th/23rd of August, Japan declared war on Germany and the humiliating Battle of Tannenberg took place between the 13th (26th) and the 17th (30th) of August 1914. The vast Russian army under General Samsonov was defeated by the Germans. Although Britain and France were Russia's allies, the nations could not even agree on the date. Russia was some thirteen days behind the rest of Europe and it was symbolic of the difference between the east and the west.

A couple of days later, Nicholas inspected a graduation parade for cadets of the Michael and Constantine Artillery Academies and the Nicholas Engineering Academy at the Catherine Palace, Tsarskoe Selo. It was one of the earlier accelerated wartime promotions of young officers who were naturally needed at the front.

That same day, Olga sent word to Nicholas and explained how she was spending her days. She, Tatiana and their mother (the Tsarina) had enjoyed an afternoon at the Catherine Palace where a hospital ward had been set up for the junior soldiers.

After failing to finish what she was writing, Olga began again the following day, something her mother often did. Olga was amused by the young soldiers at the hospital and how they were situated in what was aptly termed the *children's room*.

The following evening, Olga once more put pen to paper. The sisters were now sitting comfortably on the sun kissed balcony drinking tea. Earlier, they had driven to Pavlovsk where they had bought a couple of jars of their favourite strawberry and red bilberry jams. They had called in on Anya where they had met Rasputin's wife and two daughters. Alexei was spending the day outside in the garden whilst Marie was making sure that her friend Nicholas Dmitrievich Demenkov noticed her. He was on duty nearby and she was desperate that he would hear her, so she increased the volume. In later years, he went to the General Headquarters with the Tsar and Marie had a sudden urge to be there too. She increasingly began to sign her letters to her father Nicholas as Mrs Demenkov. She appeared to be completely smitten with the tall Odessa-born soldier.

Meanwhile, the Tsarina and her daughters Olga and Tatiana continued their nursing training. As she sent word to her close friend Olga Voronov, wife of Paul, Tatiana explained on a Friday in early September how she and her sister Olga had gone to the hospital every day to dress the wounds of the soldiers who had been fortunate enough to survive the journey from the front. The Grand Duchesses attended the men of the lower ranks first and then went on to see Alexandra and Anya who were assisting with the soldiers of the officer rank.

Paul had recently departed for the front. Olga Voronov later recalled that the Grand Duchess Olga had presented them both with parting gifts a few days before. Nine months after his marriage, the Grand Duchess contrived to present something to both Paul and his wife when she had the opportunity. The icon was duly given to Paul, as with all Russian soldiers, for luck and hopefully to keep him safe from harm. (He did survive the war and outlived the Grand Duchesses by some fifty years.)

Other members of the household also worked as nurses including Tatiana Botkin and she often met the Grand Duchesses Marie and Anastasia at the Catherine Palace at

Tsarskoe Selo. The Grand Duchesses visited the wounded or worked for the Red Cross (rolling bandages). A hospital was later opened in their names and the two frequently visited the wounded officers. Even Alexei changed his usual attire, according to Sydney Gibbes. He was far too young to join up as a soldier but had his own uniform which he wore on most days until the end of his life (as did Nicholas). The boy wore a simple soldier's outfit and had been presented with a perfect scale model of a rifle.

Gibbes was moved nearer to his pupils. He was now assigned to the Tsarevich as second-in-command of the boy's education, after Gilliard. He became part of the Tsarevich's close inner circle and, like Gilliard, followed the Imperial family into exile in Siberia. He was allocated a magnificent flat in the Catherine Palace, much to his great satisfaction. The son of a Yorkshire banker had finally come up in the world. He was now able to escort Alexei on walks around the palace and grounds.

Meanwhile, the following Wednesday morning, the Tsar travelled to the capital where he visited a military hospital before going on to the *Elagin Palace* along with Alexandra and his two eldest daughters for lunch with his widowed mother. His sister Xenia was also visiting along with her daughter Irina, son-in-law Felix and four of her numerous sons.

On Friday, Olga and Tatiana accompanied the Tsarina to the consecration of a new hospital close to the Alexander Palace. The sisters would soon begin working at one of the newly commissioned infirmaries in the vicinity.

Two days later, Olga and Tatiana accompanied both of their parents to the consecration of an emergency shelter for families.

On the following Monday, Olga and Tatiana began to work on a regular basis at the palace hospitals. The Grand Duchesses began by helping with the dressings (bandages).

The next day, the two elder Grand Duchesses were present during an operation at one of the local palace hospitals. Although Olga had finished the majority of her studies, she still had the occasional lesson and that evening she attended a music lesson.

On Wednesday, Nicholas and Alexandra travelled to the capital to inspect another new hospital. Olga and Tatiana again accompanied their parents and once more attended lunch with the Dowager Empress. The war had necessarily brought Alexandra and her mother-in-law into more contact. Alexandra did not usually accompany Nicholas on his visits to his mother in town.

The following day, as the eldest Grand Duchesses continued assisting at the local hospitals, they began to work later in the day at the warehouse where they spent time in the stores and often stayed behind in order to clean the surgical instruments. Those needed to be thoroughly cleaned each evening.

Olga and Tatiana were amongst those who had their photograph taken on Friday along with some of the wounded soldiers at one of the hospitals. The men would have undoubtedly been those who had sufficiently recovered to face the camera. Many of the patients were still very weak and confined to bed. As they recovered, some men stayed on to act as orderlies until the time that they were sent back to their appropriate regiments. The girls appeared literally as *sisters of mercy* in their new uniforms. They wore simple grey dresses with a pinafore proudly boasting a Red Cross, unless they were working in the operating theatre where they naturally changed into all white uniforms. They had their hair entirely covered by a headdress similar to that worn by a nun but despite this less than flattering form of dress the Grand Duchesses were still not only immediately recognisable but remained quite breathtakingly beautiful.

Meanwhile that day, Tatiana continued to attend her usual lessons, Mass and the infirmary. She was now part schoolgirl and part student nurse.

Marie (short of time) decided to send word to her father Nicholas whilst sitting in the bathroom on Saturday. The four girls shared a large bathroom on the first floor of the Alexander Palace where part of the room was curtained off to use as a dressing room. Their former childhood nurse Shura, who had remained with the family as had many other of their childhood servants, was busy combing Marie's very long, thick, light brown hair. Behind the curtain Tatiana was having a wash. It is a strange place to compose a letter and an odd thing to discuss yet gave an accurate description of the everyday life of the sisters. They were not above sharing a bathroom with each other. Tatiana later left for the infirmary; the work of a hospital naturally carries on no matter what day of the week it is.

That day, in a detailed epistle to Nicholas, Alexandra explained how her daughters replaced her at functions. (Alexandra was only very rarely now attending meetings or receptions in the capital and was replaced by Olga and Tatiana and later also by Marie. The two eldest girls worked in the hospitals' store rooms where the bed linen and towels were kept.) During the afternoon, Tatiana had received Alexei Borisovich Neidhardt in the presence of her mother. (The enterprising Tatiana set up her own relief committee and it was one that continued even after her death. It was a refugee committee had been formed in order to deal with those people displaced as a result of the war. She was never really given the praise she deserved for this innovation.) The very first of the committee meetings that were to be set up at the Winter Palace in the capital would take place within days. Alexandra proudly explained that she would not need to assist Tatiana in the future. She felt that it would be better for them to learn things for themselves. (Unfortunately, this was the only real occasion when the Tsarina actually let her daughters do things for themselves.)

Marie sent a letter of congratulation to Nicholas soon after admitting that she was desperate to join him. (She had always been very close to her father but her favourite Nicholas Demenkov may also have accompanied the Tsar to military headquarters at this time as he did later.) She first began by congratulating Nicholas with the success of a recent but, sadly, rare military victory.

The four sisters had attended a religious service with their mother that morning but had lunched alone. She had been to see some of the wounded arriving by train from the front to be treated at the palace hospital. It had been a long journey for the men. (Some of them had more usual ailments, including appendicitis, but many would naturally be suffering from some degree of shell shock.)

The two youngest sisters then returned to the palace with their mother as she had a reception to attend. (Despite the war, there were still occasions when Alexandra and, to a lesser extent, Olga and Tatiana had to resume their previous existence as a member of the Imperial family. It meant the Tsarina had to remove her nursing outfit and to wear a presentable dress. She had begun to understand that, as a nurse, she had some sort of anonymity, something she found gratifying.) On this occasion, the reception was for sisters of mercy who were about to travel to the Russian front.

The two youngest sisters Marie and Anastasia then went to the larger of the hospitals set up within the grounds of the palace where they looked on as Olga and Tatiana bandaged up even more of the wounded. Marie and Anastasia then wandered off to chat to the officers. (The officers and the *men* would of course have been treated separately. Although the wounded would have been treated initially on the battlefield, the equipment would have been basic to say the least and not very clean. The men then often arrived at the various hospitals scattered throughout the capital with vermin-infested dressings. The orderlies would have done their level best to staunch the bleeding but little else. The scale of their work was at times overwhelming.)

The sisters then dined with their mother and brother who was recovering well from his latest accident when on the yacht. Marie begged Nicholas to take her with him next time he went to headquarters. She added that she might even have to leap onto the train herself.

That day, Olga and Tatiana had returned as usual to their duties at one of the nearby hospitals. The afternoon had been enlivened by a visit to Alexei's new hospital train. At nightfall Olga and Tatiana returned to the hospital where they joined in with a game of dice with one of the patients, Nicholas Karangozov. This young soldier, who appears to have been from an aristocratic family, would play a significant part in Olga's life whilst she was a nurse. He was a constant feature of her life and contrived somehow to appear great many times in the photographs taken at the hospital.

The following day, Marie again sent word to Nicholas detailing Anastasia's amusing antics. The girls had been praying in their brother's room with him when Anastasia managed to hit Marie on the nose. She ended up with a cold sore as a result.

Although the children were supposed to take it in turns to correspond with Nicholas, Marie was undoubtedly the most enthusiastic writer and, to be fair, the most descriptive. Alexei also congratulated Nicholas that day. He remarked that Anastasia was once more playing up by pretending to strangle Pierre Gilliard.

The Tsarina had put pen to paper to Nicholas the day after, but admitted that she had borrowed some writing paper from Anastasia. She had felt unequal to writing the previous day due to a violent headache. Anya Vyrubova, she explained, had been offended after she failed to attend a party she had given the previous evening. The hostess had not been alone however; she had many other guests, including Rasputin.

The work at the hospital had already begun to take its toll on Alexandra's already fragile state of health, but she persisted for as long as she was able. She had sat with her son that evening as he was being read to by one of his doctors, Dr Vladimir N Derevenko and his sisters were attempting to amuse him. (The boy's closest friend was the son of this doctor and named Kolya. It is of course a diminutive of Nicholas.)

Marie revealed to her father that day how his letters were the high point in her mother's day. (Alix's letters were a source of real joy to Nicholas.) Marie explained that Anya Vyubova had dined with them and was now sitting on the sofa alongside the Tsarina.

Anastasia dashed off an amusing letter to Nicholas that day in which she ended by declaring that she would see him in her dreams if he agreed to see her in his. She, like Marie, went into great detail. It was a way of keeping Nicholas grounded and feeling close to home. Anastasia took pen to paper whilst having her hair brushed, as Marie had done in a recent letter. (Alexandra at a similar age had written to her brother Ernie when she having her hair brushed. At this time, the hair brushing was a long process as it was often brushed up to a hundred times in order to make it shine. Shura was the lady in question doing the brushing. The girls had their hair thoroughly brushed before they went to bed each night.)

Olga and Tatiana had not as yet returned home. They had gone to the capital for a committee meeting. Anastasia explained that Marie was also writing to Nicholas at the same time, which meant that Marie's had been added to over quite a period as she had begun it in the Tsarina's sitting room after dinner. She had evidently taken the paper to her bedroom to finish.

Olga and Tatiana were out, and Anastasia felt cheated that she had to go to bed. The youngest sisters had spent the day at their studies before going to work in the hospital stores sorting out the never-ending laundry. A hospital obviously has more need of clean bedding than the average household due to the inevitable blood and iodine stains.

Anastasia cheerfully informed Nicholas that her brother was improving in health which was naturally something that he really wanted to hear. The boy was in good spirits and, after being read to previously by Dr Derevenko, that day he had his tutors read books to him instead. Pierre Gilliard, the child's French tutor, and Peter V Petrov, his Russian tutor, were the men concerned.

On the following day, Alexandra again wrote at length to Nicholas after reading a complimentary British account of the Russian troops and of the imprisonment of the young Grand Duchess Marie Adelaide of Luxembourg – at twenty years old she was barely older than her own daughter Olga. Alexandra remarked that correspondence she had recently received from her German-born friend Gretchen von Fabrice had been severely censored.

She rather wickedly hoped that Anya Vyrubova's leg would not be recovered sufficiently enough for her to sit in on the cosy evenings she had planned for the Tsar's return. Alexandra described Anya as sitting in rooms filled with the Tsar's portrait. She was quite convinced that Madame Vyrubova was obsessed with Nicholas. (Despite her protestations of Anya's selfish behaviour, Alexandra still saw the lady on a regular basis.) That evening she had gone over to Anya's for a brief visit. The Tsar's daughters and the ever present Sablin were already there. Rasputin had been to see Anya earlier that day and Madame Vyrubova felt the urge to inform the Tsarina of what he had said.

Alexandra continued her detailed letter the following morning went on to complain that her late father and brother had struggled to make her former home prosperous and the current war was draining the state. As a former Hessian Princess, she hated the Prussians and hoped that the German troops would behave in a more gentlemanly way. She worried that the German troops would loot and pillage as they made their way through Europe. It was an age-old fear of war. She urged him to instruct the priests to tell the Russian soldiers that property is sacred and that victory should not mean pillage. It was a vain hope as the spoils of war did and still do continue.

That evening Olga and Tatiana returned to the Winter Palace in St Petersburg escorted by their chaperone for the evening Baroness Buxhoeveden.

The King of Rumania, Carol I died at Castle Pelesch, Sinaia on the 27th of September/10th of October 1914 and was succeeded by his nephew Ferdinand I. The new King's wife Marie was a cousin of Alexandra and they had met as recently as a few months ago. It now made Olga's prospective husband Carol a crown prince, not that she cared one jot. That evening, Nicholas and Alexandra visited the Dowager Empress at the *Elagin Palace*. The talk would have inevitably turned towards the Tsar's cousin and close friend Konstantin.

The Grand Duke had lost his soldier son Oleg on this day. Prince Oleg had been wounded in an attack on a German position in East Prussia and, despite being moved to Vilna for an emergency operation, his life could not be saved. He did, however, live long enough to see his parents and to receive the medal of the Order of St George from his heartbroken father. (Oleg was later buried at his own request on the banks of the River Ruza in the Moscow countryside.)

The following day, Olga sent word to Nicholas on behalf of Alexandra who claimed that she felt too unwell even to scribble a brief note. The Tsarina had taken to her bed accompanied by one of her bad headaches. That evening, Olga and Tatiana paid a call on Anya where Rasputin was making yet another appearance. He had made himself at home and was pouring tea for the guests. The lady doctor, Princess Gedriotz, was also at the impromptu party after cancelling the lecture for the evening. Olga explained to her father that the Princess wanted to listen to Rasputin. Rasputin was convinced that the recent heavy rains had helped the troops.

The Tsar returned shortly after and a couple of days later he received the newly appointed American Naval attaché, Captain McCooley, at the Alexander Palace. Life went on as normal for Nicholas once he returned home, but now the chats with the diplomats were less about the state of the weather and more about the war situation. The Americans had, as yet, not joined the war but were nevertheless fascinated to know how things were progressing. It was important to keep in contact with such an important nation as they were a potential future ally and a source of supplies. Unfortunately, a repeated refrain of the Russians during the First World War, or *the Great War* as it was then obviously known, was the constant lack of supplies including, crucially, weapons and arms of all types. They simply had not enough guns to go around, and there were numerous accounts of soldiers picking up rifles from their dead colleagues in order to carry on fighting. (Simply equipping an army the size of Russia was a near impossible task and with the men away from the factories fighting it was inevitable supplies of basic items including food would become scarce. There were naturally less men working on the land and producing food and the transport system in Russia would suffer once the weather worsened. There would be trouble ahead.)

On Tuesday, the Tsar and Tsarina visited Strelna for a memorial service for Konstantin's son. That day, a train full of wounded soldiers had arrived at Tsarskoe Selo. There would be a constant stream of wounded officers and men for the Tsarina, her daughters and the ladies to attend to.

Chapter Eight

Winter 1914

On Wednesday morning the Tsar, his wife and eldest daughters attended the consecration of a new church. That afternoon, Olga and Tatiana travelled the short distance to the capital where they attended a meeting at the Winter Palace, escorted by a chaperone. The sisters would regularly visit the capital once a week, generally on a Wednesday. After they had arrived back, Tatiana chatted on the phone to a couple of the wounded soldiers at the hospital.

The following morning, the two sisters returned to the hospital where they continued dressing the wounds of the patients. The bandages frequently had to be taken off, looked at and redressed. That evening, the Grand Duchesses visited Anya for tea. It was a welcome break from the constant work at the hospital which could be grim at times. Madame Vyrubova was also training to be a nurse, although she would soon end up as a permanent patient after a serious accident.

On Friday morning, Nicholas returned to town with Alexandra and his two eldest daughters to attend a funeral Mass for Oleg. As his body could not be moved due to the fighting, his funeral was held at Ostashero. The family lunched on the train, after which the sisters returned to the hospital.

The next morning was the first anniversary of the death of the Tsar's valet and the family visited his grave in the cemetery. He had served the Imperial family since 1877 until his death in early October 1913.

On Monday, the two eldest Grand Duchesses resumed their new routine. The day began with a brief visit to one of the churches on the estate, on this occasion to the small *Church of the Sign*. They then went to the hospital to deal with the inevitable dressings and they later attended a series of lectures. The Grand Duchesses Olga and Tatiana like all student nurses were doing some menial tasks at the hospital whilst continuing their training part-time.

Nicholas left for Krasnoe Selo the following morning whilst his two eldest daughters returned to the *Church of the Sign* before travelling the short distance to the hospital to continue dressing the men's wounds.

Wednesday morning proved to be very similar for Olga and Tatiana as they returned to the same church before resuming the endless round of wound dressings at the hospital. The Tsarina's sister Ella arrived later for one of her brief visits and Nicholas meanwhile made a brief tour of inspection of the *Petropavlovsk* and the *Poltava* battleships.

The following day, the sisters returned to the *Church of the Sign* before going on to the hospital to wrap more bandages on more wounds. They had the pleasure of chatting with their Aunt Ella at lunch and their Uncle Paul at tea.

On Friday morning, the recently established routine carried on for Olga and Tatiana. They attended a service at the *Church of the Sign* before going to the hospital to resume the bandaging. The day ended with another nursing lecture and a film show.

The Grand Duchesses returned to the hospital where the officers were being treated on Saturday and they were present during two operations at the larger hospital. Olga later sat and chatted with her new friend Nicholas Karangozov at the hospital where she worked on a daily basis. The officers and men were, of course, treated quite separately.

On Sunday, Tatiana was delighted when she was given a gift when she visited Anya. One of the soldiers, Dmitri Malama had left a tiny female puppy for the Grand Duchess. She returned to the Alexander Palace soon after with the little dog in tow. As she was now working regularly at the hospital, the French bulldog inevitably had to be left at the palace during the day and had to settle in with the other two dogs and was reunited with Tatiana at mealtimes. The dog was very lively as most pups are and ran around the rooms and found a convenient lap – Alexandra's. Anastasia and Alexei both already had dogs.

The dog shared Tatiana's room, but Olga had her bed in the same room and soon realised that Ortipo, like many dogs, snored. Olga was less than impressed at this development, especially as she had developed an unfortunate habit of struggling to sleep in the past year.

On Monday morning, Olga and Tatiana travelled the short distance to the railway station to receive more wounded. The number of men was seemingly never-ending and the soldiers had numerous wounds to their legs, arms, stomach, head, etc. The enemy shot at any target, big or small. Later, Tatiana sat with Dmitri Malama who had kindly left the dog for her and Ellis, another of the patients. She had named the dog after Dimitri's horse.

The next morning, the two eldest Grand Duchesses returned briefly to the *Church of the Sign* before attending operations at the hospital. Nicholas and Alexandra went into town that evening where they undoubtedly called in on the Dowager Empress.

On Wednesday, the Grand Duchesses Olga and Tatiana again returned to the *Church of the Sign* before leaving for the hospital. They returned home for lunch where Sablin was a guest. Later, the sisters travelled to the capital where they received charity donations from members of society. It was something neither of the girls enjoyed. It seemed a waste of time as the donations could just as easily have been given to the bank or a suitable court official.

There was more bad news that day as Turkey attacked Russian Black Sea ports. The *Zhemchug* was one of those ships that sank. It was part of an allied squadron and escorted merchant ships in the Indian Ocean.

The same day, the sisters dined with Nicholas, Alexandra and, of course, Sablin. The Tsar was still at home after his recent trip to headquarters. Tatiana's new dog was making herself quite at home by sitting by its delighted new owner.

Two days later, Nicholas received a report on what he saw as the treacherous attack of the Turkish and Germans against the Russian fleet in the Crimean ports. Unfortunately, war is hardly pleasant and the enemy was simply behaving as the *enemy* normally did in attacking the supply route of the opposition. Nicholas was furious; he was someone who rarely if ever showed any emotion in public and on this occasion he had to be calmed down by Rasputin. Finally, he saw some good in the man who was normally the comfort of Alexandra.

The day had gone much as normal for his eldest daughters Olga and Tatiana who had attended a service at the *Church of the Sign* before returning to the infirmary across the snow-covered ground. That day they assisted during operations including one to remove an appendix. Later, Olga sat quietly in the corridor with Baroness Buxhoeveden and the amusing Nicholas Karangozov. The sisters had their own small suite in the hospital including a small bathroom so they had a private place of their own, but they preferred to sit in the corridor with the recovering patients and the other nurses. They had rarely had such a chance to chat freely and thoroughly enjoyed these pleasant interludes.

Olga noted the death of her brother's dog the following day and his replacement. The dog was given the same name as the previous one – Shot. The Tsarevich's dog was buried on the Children's Island. It was a brother of the original. Alexei also had a springer spaniel named Joy.

The day had begun much as usual for the eldest sisters with a brief visit to the *Church of the Sign*. They had then sat chatting amiably in the hallway before attending operations at the larger hospital where the officers were housed. Olga once again sat with Karangozov during her free time. She returned later and sat with him in the ward.

Olga sent word to her beloved father that day, admitting that she felt rather empty after he had departed. She and Tatiana quickly returned to the hospital after he left and continued with the ever mounting dressings. Afterwards, the sisters had simply sat and chatted with the wounded officers.

On Sunday morning, the family attended Mass as usual. The Tsarina along with her four daughters and Anya later paid a call to the Grand Duchesses' hospital. They all sat together cosily in the third ward where the Grand Duchesses generally congregated. It was the same ward where Nicholas Karangozov was. Olga was continually drawn towards this young man but only as a friend. She could not get over Voronov.

On Monday morning, Tatiana returned briefly to her lessons whilst Olga visited an ambulance train with the Tsarina and Marie. Once Tatiana had finished her studies, she joined Nicholas, Alexandra and Olga for a trip to the city. It was not a pleasure jaunt however; they travelled to the Cathedral of St Peter and St Paul for the funeral liturgy to Nicholas's former valet. The party then went on to the *Elagin Palace* for lunch with the Dowager Empress.

On Tuesday, Alexandra informed Nicholas of the progress of her elder daughters. That morning, the sisters had attended the Lower Church to receive Communion. The ceremony was held in the Pestcherny Chapel sited underneath the Old Palace hospital. The small church was sometimes referred to as the cave church due to its unusual setting. It had been dedicated to the saints Constantine and Helen and had been built at the personal expense of the Tsarina and decorated in the Byzantine style.

Olga and Tatiana were attending meetings on behalf of the Tsarina on a regular basis, and each had their own relief committee meetings to attend. That day, Alexandra had visited the newly completed hospital nearby named in honour of Marie and Anastasia. Although the sisters were not nurses, they spent much of their times, apart from their studies, at this hospital amusing the patients. They read aloud to the men and played dominoes and snooker (pool) with the more able. Although Olga had now officially finished her education, Tatiana was currently having lessons, nursing and attending the lectures. She also visited the town for the endless donations. She was probably the busiest of all the Grand Duchesses.

That evening, Olga and Tatiana were both in town. Tatiana had firstly received Alexei Neidhard with a report concerning the charity and then both had attended one of Olga's committee meetings. Alexandra was proud of them and felt it would make them independent, something that in the long term she probably dreaded in truth. After the war, she treated the girls more like she had done when they were children.

The next day, Nicholas sent a telegram (wire) to Alexandra after arriving back safely at headquarters. He had inspected hospitals on the journey back to headquarters and was greatly impressed with all that he had seen.

That day, Tatiana praised her puppy Ortipo as she sent word to her father. The dog was making its presence felt and was a lively addition to the household which already had both Alexei's and Anastasia's dogs. (Later Joy accompanied Alexei to military headquarters.) Ortipo continued to race around the room whilst the family were at tea. Tatiana, in an effort to stay as close as possible to her adored new pet, attempted to compose a letter whilst sitting on the floor of her mother's room. Her handwriting naturally suffered and the dog may have attempted to snatch the pen or paper out of her hands as puppies often do.

Meanwhile, Tatiana and her sister Olga jointly corresponded with their cousin Louise on Wednesday after hearing of the death of their mother's younger cousin Maurice (son of Princess Beatrice). Louise was several years older than Olga but they had formed a close bond on the last occasion they had met in 1910 when the family stayed for some months in Germany.

Olga explained that they had been working in the hospital the entire morning and that they knitted socks for the wounded soldiers in their spare time. She asked if the body of Maurice had been returned to England. Olga then went back to the former topic and explained that she was now at the head of a charity committee and that she had already sat at two meetings. She admitted to feeling embarrassed as she hated the formality of the situation. (Olga was very straightforward and disliked all the fuss that was made of her rank.)

Tatiana's contribution to the letter was brief and she asked Louise to write once more. Tatiana was suffering from an attack of *Madame Becker*. (At least the young officers she saw were spared that indignity.) Olga was forced to complete the short letter and she went on to ask about Louise's youngest brother Dickie who was attending

Osborne Naval College. (He would have found it difficult in the circumstances as he was constantly bullied due to his German ancestry and his royal status – not that bullies usually *need* a good reason to act like the cowards they are. As the Grand Duchesses did not attend school, either as a day boarder or an inmate, they had little idea of the reality other children of their status suffered. He was attending Osborne Naval College which was sited close to his late Great-Grandmother's beloved Osborne House. Dickie Prince Louis of Battenberg, later Lord Mountbatten would have not remembered the old Queen as he was a baby when she died. The Grand Duchesses had visited the Isle of Wight in 1909 and the youngest sisters played on very the same beach where their mother had played in the 1870s.)

That same day, Olga attempted to give Nicholas an idea of life at the Alexander Palace. Her young brother Alexei habitually ate crusts of bread by choice and liked simple soldier's rations and was eating his supper as she wrote whilst sitting on the floor in his blue dressing gown. Marie and Anastasia were evidently making it difficult for Olga to continue as their constant running around chasing each other distracted her. (The sisters, especially Anastasia, were prone to rush about the room and even to push each other down staircases.)

That evening, she continued, Olga and Tatiana had returned to the small hospital where they had sat together with some of the patients in the hallway. They often returned to the infirmary at the end of each day (officially) to clean the surgical implements. Earlier in the day, she and Tatiana had attended a Mass in the cave church.

Anastasia, meanwhile, very briefly mentioned to Nicholas about Rasputin's expected late-night visit. He arrived in the course of her writings. She went on to speak unflatteringly of her sister Olga. The sisters were close but still prone to petty squabbles at times like all sisters. Anastasia claimed that Olga was picking her nose, something Alexandra accused Marie of doing at times.

The following day, Alexandra briefly mentioned her children in her daily epistle to Nicholas. (She rarely mentioned her younger daughters in her correspondence with Nicholas and was generally more detailed in her reports of their brother and older sisters.) That morning, Marie and Anastasia, chaperoned by Baroness Buxhoeveden, had been driven to their own hospital where they spent their time sorting out items of laundry in the stores.

On that day, Olga and Tatiana had returned to the cave church before returning to their hospital. Tatiana's friend Dmitri Malama was finally officially discharged from hospital that day. It had been an important day for the Russians as the Austrians were now on the retreat. The injured men in the hospitals were predictably in a happy mood as a result.

On Friday, Tatiana began the day as usual with lessons before she went on to church and finally to the infirmary where she joined Olga. In the early afternoon, the two sisters joined Alexandra on a trip to the capital.

In a letter on Saturday, Marie complains to Nicholas that she had been unable to see her beloved friend. She was very fond of Nicholas Demenkov and very disappointed when he was not around. Unlike Olga the previous year when she fell for Paul Voronov,

Marie was perfectly open about her affection for the young man. As a third sister, she probably did not feel the pressure her older sisters did to marry a member of the royal family. She would probably have known of her Aunt Olga's affection for a fellow soldier and of her hopes to one day marry him. Like Marie, Olga Alexandrovna was a younger daughter. Marie had always shown a great love for the military ever since she was a small child and was once chastised for admitting that she wanted to kiss every soldier she met.

Meanwhile, Tatiana composed her own version of a visit to her father. She described the unusual apparel of some of the soldiers. Most attempted to wear at least part of their military uniform if they could. Some wore just the tunic and others the trousers, depending on their wounds. Some of the men simply wore nightclothes and a gown over. It must have been humiliating for those who wore their military jacket and cap with thin striped pyjama legs.

Alexei also put pen to paper that day for his beloved father. He was more concerned with his dogs and remaining outside in the snow whilst the weather was fine. He was about to set out for the hospital with his mother and sisters. His (replacement) dog Shot was playing happily with Tatiana's puppy Ortipo.

Meanwhile Tatiana sent word to Nicholas again the next day. Olga was making herself at home that Sunday evening by sitting in the Tsar's favourite chair whilst Marie was content to sit on the floor. Anastasia had already gone up to bed. The Tsarina was making use of the palace telephone facilities to chat to her friend Sonia who was in another part of the palace. (Sonia had become ill in 1903 from a spine wasting disease and was confined to a wheelchair. She died in 1915.) That morning, the sisters attended the (official) consecration of the Crypt Church.

On Monday evening Anastasia described the chaotic scene to Nicholas. Her sisters Olga and Marie were fighting whilst she attempted to dash off a note to him before going to bed. Tatiana was chasing her puppy around the room. Anastasia enclosed a photograph of herself taken in the mirror. She had been having her usual lessons – seven on this particular day which was more than normal – but she had also been helping one of the wounded soldiers to learn to read. (The ability to read was in no way universal in Russia at the time.) Tatiana and Olga had attended a service at the new cave church that morning along with Alexandra and Anya.

On Tuesday, the two eldest sisters visited the church before going onto their usual hospital to work. Later, they travelled to the Alexander Station where yet another ambulance train had arrived.

Tatiana and her siblings were quite naturally patriotic to Russia (especially during the Great War) but on one occasion, unthinkingly, Tatiana had offended her German-born mother. She felt ashamed and on Wednesday had composed a note of apology. Tatiana was especially close to her mother and was mortified to have offended her. She attempted to put things right. The Grand Duchess admitted that she had failed to connect Alexandra and the country of her birth, and explained that she had always seen her mother as a patriotic Russian and nothing else.

Alix replied that same day and admitted that she had not been offended. She quite understood that Tatiana had not meant to say anything hurtful. Tellingly, she hints that others might do so though. She stated that her daughters were unable to hurt her unlike many of their elders. Alexandra admitted that she felt as Russian as they did although she could not but think of her former homeland at times.

Nicholas sent Alix a telegram on Thursday from Ivangorod. He was always delighted to spot old friends in the crowd on visits to the troops and had a remarkable memory for both faces and names. He was intending to drive around the battlefields on Friday and stopping at Dvinsk. Although he had only put the initial letter of the town concerned it was a lapse in security. If one of his enemies, either German or internally, had read the wire, it would have compromised his own personal security.

That day, Marie had sent word once more to Nicholas mentioning those whom she had seen on the previous day when visiting the hospital. She had been nervous at seeing Demenkov with the other men as she was conscious that he would be embarrassed.

Meanwhile back at the Alexander Palace the next day, the young Grand Duchess Marie admits to Nicholas how bored she was at the thought of a lesson with Gibbes. (She was not overly fond of learning. The only really enthusiastic pupils were Olga and on occasions Alexei and Anastasia. There was a whole new exciting life outside and she resented being stuck indoors when her older sisters were nursing and there were so many new people to see.) She dearly hoped that she would see Demenkov at church the following day.

Olga and Tatiana had returned to their usual schedule that morning after the visit the previous day. After attending church, they got down to their nursing duties. Malama arrived again for a brief visit. He clearly could not keep away.

On Friday morning, Olga attended the *Church of the Sign*. She and her sister Tatiana returned to the dressings, on this occasion the one for the officers, before returning to their own hospital where they sat cosily in the corridor with old friend Karangozov and Ledigarov. Later, the two sisters left by train for short tour along with the Tsarina.

On Saturday, the Tsarina, Olga and Tatiana were met at Grodno by Nicholas and Sablin from where they went on to visit a hospital. The Tsar, his wife and two eldest daughters then travelled by train to Pskov where the next day they met German prisoners of war.

Nicholas returned home with his wife and daughters and on Monday he lunched with Alexandra and her sister Ella who was visiting from Moscow.

Tatiana resumed her normal schedule on Monday morning returning to her lessons. Marie and Anastasia carried on with their studies too but frequently visited the hospital named in their honour. After lessons, Tatiana went on a relaxing drive before returning to the hospital with her mother. In the evening, the Grand Duchess attended a meeting with Olga.

On Tuesday evening Marie explained to her father that Olga was not feeling too well and had managed to spill ink all over her hands whilst attempting to write. Marie went on to complain that she was only able to see Demenkov when at church which gave her little chance of speaking to him. Whilst she was writing Lisa Ersberg arrived to light the icon lamps. The sisters were intending to pay a call on Anya Vyrubova later that evening. Rasputin was at Anya's.

The Tsarina and her daughters officially received their nursing certificates on Wednesday. They had trained long hours in the wards and lecture rooms alike. It had been a baptism of fire, training to become a nurse whilst treating wounded soldiers from the battlefield.

The following week, Alexandra sent word to her sister Victoria admitting that wearing the nurse's uniform enabled her to overcome her nervousness. She felt more anonymous in the uniform – just a nurse and not an empress. She explained how she had been to Pskov one day with her daughters Olga and Tatiana and the young Marie Pavlovna and found it so much easier that way. She and her two eldest daughters would soon join Nicholas on his travels.

In a note to Olga that day, the Tsarina recalled her daughter's baptism. She could hardly get to grips with the fact that the following day was the nineteenth anniversary. (It would also be the wedding anniversary of Alexandra and her mother-in-law's birthday.)

Nicholas sent a hurried note to his mother three days later to arrange a meeting on Monday afternoon. He felt the urge to see her the next day before he went away.

Two days later, Alix spoke of her children when she sent word to Nicholas. Once again Olga and Marie were chasing one another around the room but Anastasia had chosen to sit quietly in on one of Tatiana's lessons.

On Wednesday Nicholas found the time to compose a letter to Alexandra and admitted the severe shortage of weapons. It meant that the troops had to observe discretion during battles or the losses would be horrific. He went into great detail about the discrepancies of the army and of the fighting. (It was somewhat dangerous to go into such detail but luckily letters between the couple always went via a trusted courier. However, later that year, at least one letter from Anya to Nicholas did go astray.)

He had seen his cousin Kyrill and his ward Dmitri along with his cousin Kostia's son Ioann. Ioann had asked him if he would appoint his daughter Olga as president of a committee to build a new cathedral in the possibility of his death. (In the event, Olga died a day before he did.) The Tsar's thoughts naturally turned to his own marriage some twenty years previously, in November 1894.

That same day Marie composed yet another of her detailed letters to her father. She explained that after lessons that day she had visited the wounded officers in the larger of the two hospitals, and that one poor man had a large bedsore on his back. (Unfortunately it was and still is a consequence of remaining in bed for long periods.) She informed Nicholas that she intended to sit in his special chair at tea. (There was an ongoing battle for custody of the chair between Olga, Marie and Anya.) She explained that a chair had been broken during a mathematics lesson that day. Her eldest sister Olga and Tatiana had already left for the capital in order to receive donations for charity at the Winter Palace.

Tatiana had also written to Nicholas that day and admitted that she was due to chair a committee meeting the following day, something she found rather boring.

Nicholas sent another wire on Thursday as he continued his journey – on this occasion from Dorogobuzh. He had managed to visit four hospitals that day. When he had arrived in Smolensk, he recalled the visit he had made two years earlier with Alexandra.

(The wounded men were always uplifted after a visit to the hospital by Nicholas, according to his niece Marie Pavlovna. He seemed taller than anyone in the room despite being fairly small. He had a remarkable gift of making the men seem at ease in his company. The Tsarina was generally thought to have the opposite effect, not because she did not care but because she was too nervous and shy. They were frightened by the fear in her eyes and she often mumbled as she spoke, and they could not understand what she said.)

Meanwhile, Alexandra spoke of her work at the hospital. She detailed the amputation of an arm. She had assisted during the operation by handing out the instruments as and when needed. Olga's part in the proceedings had been in threading the thin catgut through the eye of the needles for the doctor to sew up the wounds.

Olga had gone out for a brief walk with Anya and would later take Alexei to see the wounded officers in the Catherine Palace hospitals as they had been desperate to see the heir. (The Tsarevich who had inherited Nicholas's personal charm was eternally popular with the troops as were his beautiful sisters but the Tsarina was not generally popular with the men.)

Nicholas wired Alexandra on Thursday from Toula before she left for her tour. He asked her to visit Kovno and Vilna but for the sake of security only mentioned the place names with an initial. That morning he had visited a munitions factory which employed over 10,000 workers. (It was naturally a thriving industry at the time as it was in most of Europe. In Britain, it was the women who worked in the deadly munitions factories.)

That day, Alexandra wrote briefly yet lovingly to Nicholas before she left for Kovno. She had taken his advice and was intending to go there. She had originally intended to take Baroness Buxhoeveden with her but the Baroness was unwell so she would take Countess Hendrikova. The Tsarina and her party would take letters and parcels from the families of those she would see there.

She was finding it difficult to concentrate with her children all chattering at the proverbial nineteen to the dozen. She asked that he send her greetings to Sablin and Dmitri Sheremetiev who had accompanied him.

She later wrote to Nicholas of Olga and Tatiana's distress at having to face officials at a meeting. (The Grand Duchesses were all shy in public, with the possible exception of Anastasia.) They had no idea that the concert that they were due to attend at the circus was to be attended by the Ambassador and all the governmental ministers.

That Friday evening, the Tsarina, Olga and Tatiana left Tsarskoe Selo by train and arrived at Vilna on Saturday morning. They visited the cathedral at Vilna and then went on to Kovno. They returned back to Tsarskoe Selo on Sunday morning.

Nicholas sent a telegram from Kharkov later revealing that he would shortly be leaving for Ekaterinodor.

That same day Alexandra put pen to paper to explain to Nicholas about her recent visit to Poland. She had just been reunited with Alexei, Marie and Anastasia. She had never left them before. They had arrived back at the Alexander Palace early that morning.

The Tsarina, her eldest daughters, Anya Vyrubova and Countess Hendrikova had left at 9pm and sat up chatting in their train carriage for an hour before retiring to bed. They had called in at Pskov, Vilna and Kovno in the course of the following day. The party had visited sanitary trains and hospitals, the cathedrals at Vilna and had, remarkably, managed to spot Paul Voronov in the street. (He had an uncanny knack of appearing in front of Olga which must have given the girl mixed feelings: delight at his sudden appearance and the pain of knowing he was married to another.)

One officer informed Madame Vyrubova that he recalled seeing the Tsarina when she had travelled to Russia before her marriage. Alexandra clearly remembered the incident. He had followed the carriage on his bicycle and she had reached out and presented him with an apple.

Although Alexandra had requested that the visit to a cathedral was a private one, they had been greeted by on their arrival with electric lights blazing, plants placed into pots and a newly installed carpet on the stairs. The travellers then visited the Red Cross, another two hospitals and a large military hospital where a service was held in the Tsarina's honour. The latter hospital contained a couple of rooms containing German prisoners of war. She was able to converse with some of the men. (How she was received by the German soldiers is not explained but must have been a fascinating meeting, particularly for her daughters after what Tatiana had so recently said about her mother's place of birth: Germany.)

The ladies had then returned to the railway station and left for Landvarovo where the party had inspected the feeding stations and the barracks hospital. They had stopped briefly after spotting a sanitary train. The Tsarina and her daughters gave out small religious images to the wounded at every opportunity.

On Tuesday, Nicholas found sufficient time on the train to compose an unusually lengthy and descriptive letter to Alexandra. He spoke of his delight at being able to sit and breathe in the warm fresh air on the journey. He had received news from her two days previously but it had been difficult to communicate whilst both were moving around.

He was impressed by the beauty of the mountain scenery and the warmth of the air. He kept the carriage door open and was amazed at the sheer number of people who stood at the railway platforms as the train passed by, particularly the immense number of children he saw. (The men would have been away fighting or working elsewhere.)

Nicholas had been delighted with the warmth of the reception he had been given at the hospitals at Ekaterinodor. He apologised for the state of his handwriting as the train was shaking. He had gone to a girl's school and an orphanage. Nicholas teased Alexandra that he and Sablin had been impressed with all the pretty faces they had seen. He wished to explain to Alexandra why his schedule had been altered. He had been asked if he would visit both of the Cossack provinces but had been so busy in recent days he had not been able to even compose a short telegram to Alexandra.

In a letter to Nicholas on Tuesday, Alix explained that her daughters witnessed their first death (although they had both been present when the Prime Minister, Peter Stolypin had been fatally wounded several years before). A soldier had died during one of the operations.

The Tsarina's elder sister Elisabeth had arrived on a brief visit but would only stay overnight.

That day, the elder Grand Duchesses resumed their normal schedule. Tatiana returned to her lessons, attended church and then went back to the small hospital where she worked alongside Olga. The day was brightened by the arrival of Grand Duchess Elisabeth for lunch. (The sisters always ate at the palace rather than at their place of work.)

Nicholas sent Alix a telegram on his safe arrival at Tiflis on Wednesday. He intended to make yet more hospital visits and confessed that he missed his wife greatly.

That day, Tatiana had spent the day as usual, only broken by the brief walk in the park with Anya and Ortipo. She saw the dog less often than she would have liked to as naturally it was not allowed in the hospital.

On Thursday Nicholas telegraphed home from Tiflis. He was exhausted after his long journey but happy with all he had seen. He thanked the Tsarina for her recent letter and those of his son and daughter Marie. (Marie would have had more time to compose letters than her two eldest sisters and was extremely devoted to her father. Olga's devotion to Nicholas is well documented but Marie's is less so.) He asked Alexandra to distribute medals to the wounded on his behalf.

That afternoon, Olga and Tatiana had returned to the capital in the company of their mother. They visited the newly established English hospital on this occasion where the daughter of the British Ambassador, Meriel Buchanan, was also working as a nurse. The Tsarina had known Meriel since she was a little girl, as the family had previously lived in Darmstadt.

Nicholas wired on Friday with an admission of his shyness in front of ladies. He had been escorted around a place where he had seen some two hundred ladies all working for the war effort and then travelled to a tea party with members of the nobility. He rarely saw so many women at one time.

Alexei sent Nicholas a cheerful note that same day. He proudly explained that a special soldier's coat had been made for him and it had been presented by his tutor Petrov along with some useful spades for digging trenches. He felt like a real soldier now. He had stood guard in his new coat. Unfortunately the rain had prevented him from playing outside for the past three days but he was feeling well and studying hard.

The following day, Nicholas (possibly unwisely) wired with his plans. He was intending to leave that evening for Kars.

His daughters meanwhile resumed their usual routine. The four youngest children still had lessons despite it being a Saturday. The eldest sisters went to the hospital later as unfortunately patients cannot have the weekend off.

At the end of November, Nicholas sent another telegram to Alix on his arrival at Kars and he explained that he had attended Mass in the garrison church.

Tatiana proudly sent word of Alexei's bravery that day to her father. The Tsarevich had held a basin for the doctor in order to catch the pus which came out of a wounded soldier during an operation. (It is not surprising that Alexei was unafraid as he himself had spent many an hour in terrible pain and bleeding heavily. He had suffered much and understood the suffering of others.)

During the course of the morning the children had been photographed with the officers at the Catherine Palace hospital. Later they accompanied the Tsarina to the invalid's home where Alexandra distributed St George medals to members of the lower ranks.

Marie and Olga had been thrilled to meet up with friends the previous day. Marie's letter to Nicholas finally confirms the identity of Olga's old friend AKSH. She had seen her beloved Nicholas Demenkov at church and Alexander Shvedov was at a meeting later. She assured Nicholas that both she and Olga were very happy about this.

At the beginning of December, Nicholas sent a brief wire home expressing his delight at finding members of the Kabardinsky regiment lined up on the railway station platform upon his arrival at Sarykamysky. He also thanked Alexandra and Tatiana for their recent letters.

Marie corresponded with Nicholas that day from her mother's room. Anya had elected to sit in Nicholas's chair in his absence. She together with Olga and Marie continually sought the solace and comfort of the Tsar's personal chair when he was away. Marie on this occasion was relegated to sitting on the floor as she often was. Her sisters had all managed to locate a chair each and Alexandra was reclining on her couch as usual.

The following day, Nicholas wired a message home. The weather had improved once they left the mountains. He urged Alexandra not to exhaust herself whilst working at the hospitals. (She had not been used to such physical hard work and naturally it concerned him.)

As lessons continued that day, Marie informed Nicholas of her progress. Once again, the Russian tutor Petrov was reading aloud to Marie and Anastasia. (It was probably Turgenev's *A Hunter's Notes* once again.)

The Tsarina and her daughters Olga and Tatiana returned to Moscow where they were met early on Tuesday morning by Elisabeth, who had lived in the old capital for several years. They travelled by car to the Governor-General's home and afterwards the four ladies lunched together at the Kremlin.

Meanwhile, as he continued his journey, Nicholas telegraphed home from Derbent. He was looking forward to a quiet walk on the seafront and was intending to travel to Vladikaykaz the following day. He sent another wire soon after, in an undated message. He was eager to be reunited with Alexandra.

On Wednesday morning the Tsarina along with her sister and two eldest daughters attended the Assumption Cathedral. The ladies then visited various medical establishments and left Moscow later that evening by train for the next leg of the journey.

That day, Tatiana sent word to her friend Olga Voronova of a young officer from the Life Guards Cossack regiment in her care. She enjoyed listening to him playing the guitar and singing his sad songs. He had been urged to keep the volume down as others were resting.

The Tsarina and her daughters arrived at *Tulu* on Thursday where before noon they attended church and visited three hospitals. They ate on the train and continued on their travels to *Opel*. The sisters chose to stretch their legs when the train stopped at some of the stations but Alexandra remained on board resting. She was exhausted once again.

That day the Grand Duchess Marie was presented with a flower which she pressed and kept in her diary as a keepsake. It had been presented to her by a Colonel Znamenskiy who was a Commander in the 10th Finnish Infantry regiment.

Alexandra and her daughters arrived at *Kursk* on Friday where they attended a service at the cathedral before visiting an infirmary. Once more they left before lunch and ate on the train. Later they took the opportunity to visit an empty hospital train as they passed. Tatiana had taken her little dog along for company. They left the town that evening and went on to the next destination *Belograd* where they visited the cathedral. They later left for *Voronezh*.

Alexandra was reunited with Nicholas at Voronezh on the occasion of his saint's day.

The locals gave the couple an enthusiastic welcome as they arrived in Tambov on Sunday morning and the family then visited the cathedral. Later, Nicholas met an old friend of his father's: the elderly widow Madame Alexandra Nicolaevna Narishkine known as *Aunt Sasha*. His wife and daughters had accompanied him on the visit to her. The party visited three local hospitals before returning to the train for lunch once again.

On Monday morning, the Imperial travellers arrived at *Ryazan* from where they travelled by motor car to the local church, hospital and a warehouse. The family arrived in Moscow that afternoon and were met at the station by Elisabeth.

The three younger children were reunited with their parents at Moscow where the Imperial couple had a less than enthusiastic welcome. The family were then driven to the Kremlin where they visited yet more hospitals and Moscow zemstvo (local council). They were met by Prince Lvov who begged for Alexei's autograph to be written in the visiting book. Alexandra then paid calls on Countess Apraxin and Princess Galatzine, before she and Nicholas visited the Metropolitan Makari.

The family attended the Archangel Cathedral on Tuesday morning and lunched with Elisabeth.

The following morning, after visits to nearby hospitals, the sisters lunched with their former governess Sophie Tiucheva and they spent much of the day quietly in the company of the Tsarina's sister Ella.

Thursday morning was spent quietly but later the family visited a vast hospital nearby which held over 800 wounded and covered five floors. By the end of the visit, all, including the young Olga and Tatiana, were exhausted by the sheer effort of meeting so many men.

On Friday morning, the family attended a couple of the many and varied churches in the vicinity of Moscow including the Church of *Constantine and Helen*. Later, the party visited another palace where wounded officers were being treated. Several of the palaces in Moscow as in St Petersburg had been turned over to use as hospitals. The family returned to the railway station in mid-afternoon.

The Imperial family then travelled back to Tsarskoe Selo with the exception of Nicholas who returned to military headquarters. Before they left Moscow, Alexandra composed a letter for Nicholas.

She reminded Nicholas about organising Christmas trees for the wounded. Both Nicholas and Alix had the habit of writing letters to each other shortly before they were parted. It was their way of leaving a message behind so it could be read later as a comfort to the reader. Alexandra was concerned that Nicholas had to work too hard on his brief returns from headquarters and was convinced that he rested more easily away from the endless round of receptions. (In truth, it may have been that he slept better away from home on his own as he often mentioned that Alix was a restless sleeper and may have kept him awake at times. They would meet again in less than a week.)

The following day, Saturday, Nicholas wired a brief message after meeting up with a group of wounded soldiers. Despite the lack of news, he added that it was frosty yet without any sign of snow. His telegrams were very much the news followed by the local weather report.

Upon their return that day the Grand Duchesses chose to go out in the park for a sleigh ride with Anya. They also visited the wounded officers at the larger of the two hospitals. Marie, however, was suffering from the return of tonsillitis.

The next day, a tired Nicholas sent another wire. He noted that it was quiet along the whole Western front. (It would have been; it was the Christmas 1914 truce when British and German soldiers stopped fighting for a few days and played football in an extraordinary game. Sadly, they were forced by senior officers to carry on the war soon after.)

That evening, Tatiana sat with her mother who was naturally exhausted after the recent journey to Moscow. Alexandra was easily tired and the long train journey and endless receptions had been too much for her. The children had their tea by Alexandra's bedside.

However, it was Marie who had been sufficiently ill with tonsillitis to go to bed. Tatiana had also briefly taken to her bed later after the onset of *Madame Becker*. Alexandra explained to Nicholas that day that Olga liked to walk to work at the hospital as she enjoyed the exercise. (The Grand Duchess probably also enjoyed the freedom and the chance of seeing friends along the way.) Tatiana would follow Olga on to the hospital after a lesson.

Anya had escorted Anastasia out for a turn in the park but both returned complaining of the cold. The following day, Nicholas wired a note of consolation after hearing of the tragic death of Dr Eugene Botkin's son. He was not only the Tsarina's personal physician but he was a good friend of Nicholas. Botkin's two younger children Gleb and Tatiana were close friends of Marie, Anastasia and Alexei. Dr Botkin was one of those who chose to accompany the former Imperial family into exile to Siberia and he paid for his loyalty with his life, leaving behind two teenage children. Luckily, the two children were rescued and later left for exile in America.

Whilst ill with tonsillitis, Marie showed concern for her mother and composed a note asking about her health. It is remarkable that the two should converse on paper when one was simply on the floor above. The Grand Duchess was still suffering from swollen tonsils and a red sore throat, she explained, but the spots had vanished.

Not long after Grand Duchess Marie's tonsils were removed and the teenager lost a great deal of blood as a result. She would possibly have died but for the quick thinking of the Tsarina when the doctor began to panic. It is possible Marie had problems with her blood clotting; although she was unlikely to have inherited haemophilia she would have almost certainly have been a carrier as would her sisters.

On Monday, Nicholas wrote home after hearing of the death of his former tennis partner Alexander Butakov. He had been one of the chosen few who played tennis regularly with Nicholas whilst Olga and Tatiana had regularly paired up with Rodionov and Voronov at Livadia. The young officer left a Swedish-born wife and a young son.

When Tatiana sent word to Nicholas again that evening she was undecided whether to go out. She could have either gone into town with Olga or simply had yet another quiet night in with her mother. The committee meetings were an opportunity for Olga and Tatiana to meet more people but their shyness often made it more of a duty than a pleasure. Alexandra's already fragile health was breaking down after months of working at the hospital and the frequent hospital visits she was making, apart from the recent trip to Moscow.

That day the sisters had returned to their work at the hospital and they had heard of Butakov's demise via the Tsar's cousin Grand Duke Kyrill. Marie was still confined to bed after her most recent bout of tonsillitis. Shura read to her whilst she rested. Olga and Anastasia went out sledging with their chaperone Baroness Buxhoeveden.

Tatiana spent Tuesday fairly quietly with lessons and a rather more sedate sleigh ride accompanied by Countess Hendrikova. She later visited the infirmary but stayed in whilst Olga went out to one of her meetings at the Winter Palace to collect more charity donations.

Nicholas wired home to Alexandra on Thursday as he continued his journey. He inspected the Moskovsky, Pavlovsky and Atamansky regiments and would soon return home for the Christmas holidays.

The following day the Tsar revealed that letters from Anya Vyrubova had mysteriously vanished. It was never satisfactorily explained what happened to them.

He then returned home for Christmas as expected. Nicholas attended the funeral of Alexander Butakov shortly after his return accompanied by Olga and Tatiana, his sisters and Queen Olga of Greece.

The Tsar was suffering from a bad cold at Christmas and was unable to visit his mother as he usually did on Christmas Eve. Unlike Alexandra he was used to working long hours but the added strain of the worry about the war had weakened his usually strong constitution. He had less time to indulge in his passion for long walks and exercise whilst at headquarters.

On Christmas Day (Russian style), the Imperial family attended a festive Mass and enjoyed lunch together. In the afternoon, the family visited the hospital for officers situated in the Catherine Palace. In the evening, they visited the infirmary in order to distribute gifts to the remainder of the wounded. After a family dinner Rasputin paid a call.

Alexandra composed a letter of thanks the day after to her former teacher Miss Jackson in England. She had generously sent gifts of books to both Alexandra and Elisabeth along with a welcome letter with news from England. The Tsarina admitted that she had decided not to send a present to her former teacher as she was not convinced that it would arrive.

· That day the sisters had visited the infirmary. The partially recovered Nicholas attended a family lunch along with Alexandra and Anatole Mordvinov who was on duty that day. The Grand Duchesses then travelled the short distance to the nursery school where they played with the nurses' children.

That afternoon, Olga and Tatiana returned to the two hospitals to visit the wounded. They chatted with Nicholas Karangozov but returned in time for tea. Nicholas and Alexandra had been joined by Dmitri.

On Saturday, the two eldest sisters returned to the church and infirmary. They later distributed gifts to more of the wounded, chaperoned by Countess Anastasia Hendrikova. That evening, they were visited by Nicholas's sister Xenia and by Alexandra's friend Anya.

The family attended Mass on Sunday morning. The Tsar's cousins Boris and Andrei arrived in time for lunch, but the Tsarina remained on the sofa in a separate room with her son. The sisters then visited the Catherine Palace hospital where a well-known gypsy singer Nina Dulkevich was entertaining the troops.

Olga and Tatiana returned to the infirmary on Monday for the operations. That afternoon, Anya's small nieces arrived including Tatiana's godchild of the same name.

On Tuesday, the eldest Grand Duchesses walked to the infirmary accompanied by Madame Vyrubova. The Tsar's cousin George arrived for dinner. He had hosted many such occasions at his home Harax in the Crimea the previous autumn.

On New Year's Eve, Olga and Tatiana went to the *Church of the Sign* before walking to the infirmary. That day, the sisters sat with some of the wounded including Navruzova, (Vladimir) Kiknadze and Yagmina. The second man would in the coming year become a very close friend of Tatiana. He came to the hospital as a wounded soldier but later remained for some time as an orderly.

After Olga had sent the gift of her portrait to her former English tutor John Epps at Christmas, he sent the Grand Duchess a letter of thanks. He was obviously delighted with the gift and spoke hopefully of the war.

Chapter Nine

New Year 1915

The beginning of the New Year began fairly quietly for the Imperial family. They attended Mass together and, after lunch *en famille*, Tatiana supervised her delicate brother on the slide. This specially constructed slide filled a good portion of a room specially allocated for it. It had been the delight of many generations of Imperial children. As Alexei had to be monitored even whilst doing something as simple as playing on a slide, his sister Tatiana obligingly accompanied him. She was that sort of sister.

Later, the sisters went out in the garden where they playfully jumped over a fire. It was these simple games that Nicholas and his daughters had played all their lives. Their brother, the Tsarevich Alexei, naturally was very restricted in his amusements. It had become something of a tradition to jump over the fire at this time of year for the sisters.

Nicholas had the usual reception with the members of the diplomatic corps that day. Naturally Alexandra did not accompany him. She had put a great deal of effort into her nursing but it had sapped the small reserve of energy she had. Nicholas disliked such formal situations; he would have much preferred to spend his precious time with members of his former army regiment. He, like his father before him, worked long hours at his deck, dealing with an ever mounting pile of paperwork and he liked to spend his leisure time outdoors or visiting his old comrades.

The following day, Olga and Tatiana returned to the infirmary where they worked after church in the company of Anya Vyrubova. The Tsarina's friend had been acting as a nurse along with the Tsarina and her elder daughters. Unfortunately, as fate would have it, by the end of the day Anya would be a patient and not a nurse. She was involved in a horrific train crash and initially not expected even to live.

That afternoon, Nicholas had gone with his five children to distribute gifts to some of the wounded. Paul Voronov had made an appearance to the surprise of Olga. The five siblings had then gone on to a concert at the Catherine Palace. Paul had married almost exactly a year previously but Olga was still finding it very awkward when confronted by him in person. If she spoke, the conversation was rather stilted.

In the early evening, General Voyeikov conveyed the news of a horrific train accident to Nicholas. Anya Vyrubova was amongst the wounded and was taken to the palace hospital. She was visited by the Imperial family late that evening. Her parents had already arrived and Rasputin came later to proffer words of comfort. He predicted correctly that she would recover but would always be an invalid. She had been travelling from Tsarskoe Selo to visit her parents. In the circumstances, they came to her.

On Saturday morning, the news concerning Anya appeared favourable and even the Tsarina returned to her duties at the Catherine Palace hospital. Alexandra had begun the day with her daily devotions at the small *Church of the Sign* along with her eldest daughters.

In the afternoon, the family visited the Cossack regiment and the men obliged them with some impromptu Russian dancing – to the delight of all concerned. The Tsar and Tsarina then drove to the infirmary where they remained with Anya for some time. She had broken both of her legs and fractured her skull. (Madame Vyrubova, a divorcee, saw the Imperial family as not only her closest friends but her own family. Alexandra had often jokingly referred to Anya as her fifth daughter and Madame Vyubova sulked if ignored for any length of time by the Tsarina.) Nicholas took the opportunity to see some of the wounded men in the surrounding wards.

On Monday, the eldest Grand Duchesses resumed their usual routine: church, attending to the dressings at the infirmary, lunch at home with their parents, and back to the larger hospital in the afternoon.

As Olga visited Anya on Tuesday, she observed how impatient Anya was compared to the young men she normally treated. She, Tatiana and even Alexandra had spent a great deal of their time treating patients. Although Alexandra had begun to suffer from the work by Christmas, Anya's accident appears to have reinvigorated her.

The sisters went back to the infirmary later that day and spent the evening in the company of some of the patients. Naturally they gravitated towards Ward 3 where Nicholas Karangozov was being treated. Rasputin visited the family that evening after calling in on Anya. Olga was now exhausted from the long hours working in the hospitals and was sleeping badly. Although Tatiana with her placid nature proved to be a perfect nurse, Olga's character was quite different. She was never one for routine, unlike Tatiana. Tatiana had always had the ability to think of others first whereas Olga was rather more of a rebel. If something needed doing, Tatiana would do it, but Olga, like Marie, would want to know why. As a child, she had constantly questioned everything. She was a thinker rather than a doer.

Wednesday began predictably for Tatiana with lessons; on this occasion, religion. She then travelled to the *Church of the Sign* the small church which contained the blessed icon named *Znamenskaya*. Tatiana was more likely to name the church after the icon unlike Olga referred to it as the *Church of the Sign*. The sisters then went to the hospital to call in on Anya, accompanied by their mother. The Tsar's cousin Konstantin came for lunch along with one of his son's. The Grand Duke had still not got over the death of another son Oleg, and his own health was failing. His son had died of his wounds the previous autumn.

That afternoon, Olga and Tatiana made their usual trip to the capital to collect donations. Yet again, the sisters saw Paul Voronov. It was impossible for Olga to avoid him. They had gone into town by train as they usually did accompanied by an ever present chaperone and sat patiently whilst members of society handed over cheques for charity. Tatiana was head of a relief committee. The sisters greatly disliked the formality of the situation and were happier nursing and just being ordinary girls of their age. The uniform gave them some sort of anonymity but it did not prevent them from being shy and nervous in front of strangers.

On one such occasion, Tatiana kicked Baroness Buxhoeveden under the table after she had formally introduced her as Her Imperial Highness. The sisters were usually known as Olga Nicolaevna and Tatiana Nicolaevna at home. The sisters had known the Baroness since childhood and her sudden formal approach came as a shock.

On Thursday morning, Olga and Tatiana returned to the *Church of the Sign* before carrying on to the Catherine Palace hospital. In the afternoon, they called in to check in on Anya before returning to their usual duties. On this occasion, it included cleaning the instruments for the operations to be performed the next day. They happily joined in every activity, however tiresome and boring it would have been to others. To them it was different, therefore exciting, but more to the point it gave them the opportunity of spending time with ordinary girls of their own age. Eventually, they spent more and more time in the company of the wounded men too.

The following morning, Olga and Tatiana assisted on an appendix operation. The operations in the hospital were sometimes more commonplace ones and not all gunshot wounds as one would expect. They walked briefly afterwards. It was an opportunity to get out into the fresh air after the spending the morning concentrating during the long operation. It was a chance for Tatiana to be reunited with her little dog. She could not take her to the hospital so she had to see the dog outside. The ladies-in-waiting and members of the household would be constantly going backwards and forwards to the hospital so one would have dropped the dog off at some point. Some of the ladies of the household also worked at the hospital but some were too old or set in their ways. The Tsar's sister Olga and niece Marie Pavlovna had been quick to enlist as nurses but those with children would have less reason to do so. Marie had left her son behind in Sweden after her separation which was something the Tsarina and her baby-loving daughters could not understand. To her namesake Marie Nicolaevna, marriage and children were the most important things of all.

The Tsar's brother-in-law Sandro appeared in time for lunch and his cousin Andrei at tea. Olga did not return to the infirmary that evening as she had a music lesson. She had the occasional French or music lesson in the early evening. Yet again, Rasputin appeared at nightfall as he had been visiting his friend Anya at the palace hospital. They had been friends for years, although platonic friends despite what everyone thought at the time. (In the coming years Anya *medically* proved her innocence.)

On Saturday, Olga and Tatiana returned to their hospital and in the afternoon called in on patients at another nearby hospital. It was an endless round of hospital visits for the sisters, but mainly they remained in the infirmary. It was becoming as much their home as the Alexander Palace. They had their own little sitting room in the hospital but they much preferred sitting in the hallway or corridor and socialising. It was something they were so rarely able to do and, like all young people of their age, they liked interaction with others. At home they had always assisted the maids when they came to clean the rooms and were even said to have made their own beds.

Whilst her older sisters continued their work at the palace hospitals, Marie dutifully wrote to Nicholas but had little to report. There would be a service later in the day on the occasion of Tatiana's name's day. It would take place in the Tsarina's sitting room. Each child had a special day, like a birthday, where they received gifts. The children were each named after a saint and adopted that saint's day as their saint's day.

After the service Olga and Tatiana returned to their hospital where they spent the early evening sitting in the corridors and chatting. There were of course occasions when there was little to do but the sisters liked the atmosphere of the hospital and the people they met. It was a rare and welcome occasion to meet ordinary people – nurses and patients alike. Later, the four sisters went to the Catherine Palace along with their parents. It would have been much more formal with the Tsar and Tsarina around.

On Tuesday morning, Olga and Tatiana returned to the *Church of the Sign* then went on to the hospital. Afterwards, they visited an ambulance train, a warehouse and a different hospital. It was what is known as a busman's holiday. After lunch, the sisters returned to their own place of work and continued their never-ending round of bandaging soldiers.

The evening was spent quietly at home with a wooden geometric puzzle. It was probably actually Anastasia's but the sisters joined in as a means of *winding down* after the long day. They later took puzzles to the hospital to amuse the men. Such puzzles were in later years used for therapy, so it was a clever move. If a man had a hand or arm injury, attempting to do a puzzle would be a way of using his limbs again, a sort of gentle exercise. It was also, of course, helpful for coordination, something soldiers need.

Wednesday proved to be slightly different for the elder Grand Duchesses: they attended the usual church service and then assisted in a hernia operation. The injury would be a fairly common one as the men moved quickly to avoid serious injury on the battlefront.

In the afternoon, they returned to the capital for the donations before going on to dinner at their Aunt Xenia's. They later called in on Anya to catch up on her progress – or lack of it. She was not the most tolerant of patients.

The following morning there was a great deal of snow on the ground. Sadly, Olga and Tatiana no longer had time to build a snow mountain or ski with their father. In the afternoon, the two sisters visited Anya. They spent all morning at one hospital only to return to another in the latter part of the day.

On Friday, the sisters returned to their hospital duties and Nicholas travelled to St Petersburg for lunch with his mother. The widowed Dowager Empress attended various meetings concerning the Red Cross of which she was head, but remained in the capital. However later she moved to Kiev.

The sisters called in on Anya the following day and took a puzzle to amuse her. They had naturally returned to their duties at the hospital that morning. Later Olga *worked*. She was knitting whilst an obliging patient held the ball of wool for her. Since childhood, she had been taught not to sit with idle hands so brought her knitting along.

On Monday morning, the two sisters returned to their duties at the infirmary.

Again, Olga spent some time knitting whilst one of the patients held the wool ball. At home, when she knitted, Tatiana's dog may well have fought her for the wool ball as puppies often do. The sisters visited the larger hospital in the early evening. They visited the patients, but only worked there if needed in theatre.

The next morning, Olga and Tatiana returned to the hospital. Olga had brought a puzzle again and a couple of the patients decided to join in with the *therapy*. One of the men concerned was of course Karangozanov. Later, Olga returned to the Catherine Palace hospital with her sister Marie. Tatiana sat part of the time with Vladimir Kiknadze who would become a really close friend in the coming months. She was increasingly fond of the young man. He was occasionally pictured in photographs taken at the hospital and appears as a very handsome man with dark hair, an elegant moustache, dark complexion and confident air.

On Wednesday, Olga returned to the infirmary as usual and was joined later by Tatiana. Olga again spent part of the morning knitting and doing a puzzle with the wounded men. She was beginning to find the actual nursing difficult but still felt compelled to visit the hospital. She just began to try and do other things whilst she was there. Eventually, she worked much of the time in the stores. After lunch, the sisters travelled to the capital with Countess Hendrikova acting as chaperone. They then went on to the usual meetings and Tatiana sat in with Olga's donations. After they arrived back at the Alexander Palace, Tatiana resumed her lessons. Olga returned to the hospital and stood around in the corridors chatting before returning home.

The next day, Olga and Tatiana attended a religious service with their parents for the safe return of the Tsar. Nicholas was about to depart once more for military headquarters. The sisters went back to the hospital where they resumed their usual dressings. Olga had returned to her normal duties that day.

Tatiana later returned to the Alexander Palace to sit with her brother who had hurt his leg. As Tatiana resumed her lessons later, Olga returned to the Catherine Palace hospital. The two later visited the infirmary together where Tatiana attempted one of the wooden puzzles with her friend Vladimir Kiknadze. The two were getting closer.

On Friday, Nicholas sent a brief message to his wife from Stavka after his return to headquarters. He had spent a month back at the Alexander Palace and returned back into his usual routine at Stavka (military headquarters) away from his wife and children.

Olga and Tatiana assisted with the hospital operations on Saturday morning. They later went for a walk before Olga returned to work at the warehouse. The four sisters had had tea with Alexei in his playroom. They always sat with him when he was unwell. Tatiana had always spent time with her brother and it was undoubtedly where she developed her nursing skills. He often needed bandages changed and soothing when he was in pain.

In the evening, Olga and Tatiana returned to the hospital to sit with the patients. They were constantly drawn back to the infirmary even when they had nothing to do. They felt happy there.

The next day (Sunday), Nicholas expressed his concerns at leaving his son behind. Alexei was suffering from an injury to his foot. He frequently injured either his foot or his arm. Nicholas warned Alexandra against spending too much time going up and down stairs to him. She often contacted her sick younger children by telephone from the room below in order to save her legs and they often sent each other little notes from the different floors via a servant.

Meanwhile, Alexandra happily reported the improvement in the condition of both Alexei and Anya to Nicholas by post. The Tsarina was lying in semi-darkness in order to rest after spending the morning attending to her son and working at the hospital. She complains that Marie was picking her nose which was something Anastasia had earlier complained that Olga did.

She had spent the earlier part of the day rolling bandages and sitting with the ever complaining Anya. The dogs in the absence of their owners were wandering around the room. (This often led to *puddles* or worse on the carpets, no doubt.) Alexei was playing cards with Dr Derevenko.

Tatiana had written to Nicholas that day with news of an old friend, Otar Purtseladze, an officer of the 13th Grenadier Regiment Erivansky, who had presented Olga with a bouquet the previous year. He was originally believed to have been killed but his wife had just received a letter which explained that he had been captured. He was the father of a small boy whom the sisters later met.

Marie also sent word to Nicholas that day. Alexei had been confined to bed and the Tsarina had been playing games in an attempt to amuse him. (The child had spent much of his brief life in bed. He spent much of his time in his large playroom where his sisters joined him often for tea. He had various toys in the room including an Indian tepee, a small sentry box, board games and other items. He had been given a massive train set as a child, a gift from his diplomatically appointed godfather, the Kaiser of all people, but he preferred to play with more simple toys. His usual daily playmate was Anastasia but she had to attend lessons and visit the hospital so was not always available now. His most usual playfellows were the young sons of his sailor nanny Andrei Derevenko but the boys were quite a few years younger than him.)

On Monday, Nicholas only had time to send a brief message home. He was too busy to write home. He needed to have plenty of time in order to do so as he was a slow writer and found it difficult to compose letters, unlike Alexandra.

That morning Alexandra had joined her elder daughters at the hospital. The three later returned to the palace for lunch. The Tsar's cousin Boris had arrived. (He was one of the three sons of the Tsar's late Uncle Vladimir and his Aunt Marie, known as Miechen. Boris was unmarried and later his mother proposed that he be permitted to marry Olga. Olga's mother was horrified and the refusal caused a further breach in family relations.)

The sisters remained at home in order to keep their brother Alexei company. They had often sat with him in the past as he slowly recovered from one accident or another. Olga and Tatiana attempted to keep him calm and aid his recovery, but the presence of his two younger sisters, especially Anastasia, would no doubt excite the child as they were more lively and prone to argue with him. They later returned to the infirmary where they sat with some of the wounded.

Meanwhile, on Monday, Nicholas visited his sister Olga's hospital at Rovno. She was quite an experienced nurse and enjoyed the ordinary lifestyle away from the court. She had always been bored by court life and much preferred to do something that she considered normal. She had no children of her own and readily took to the idea of nursing. Her nieces were beginning to feel the same. It gave them all a sense of freedom, something none had ever had before.

The following day, Olga and Tatiana returned to the hospital along with Alexandra. The Tsarina helped fill the needles for the injections. Olga once again spoke with Nicholas Karagozanov as she did most days. He was becoming a constant feature in her life.

Later, Nicholas sent a brief message from Kiev. He had been delighted to meet up with his sister Olga and inspect the hospital where she worked. He could see how happy she was.

On Wednesday, the Grand Duchess Tatiana resumed her lessons whilst Olga went ahead of her to the infirmary. Again, she chatted with her friend Karagozanov. The sisters returned to the Alexander Palace for lunch before setting out for the capital. They visited Countess Carlov's hospital on the Fontanka Embankment. It was small unit containing only room for ten officers, but every bed helped. They then went on to collect the usual charity donations at the Winter Palace. Tatiana returned to her lessons later before rejoining Olga at the infirmary where they sat amiably chatting to the patients.

The two sisters continued their usual pre-war routine of walking after lunch, now with Tatiana's dog Ortipo. They spent the greater part of the day away from the Alexander Palace and enjoyed every minute, despite Olga becoming gradually more and more exhausted from the work.

That same day, Olga wrote to Nicholas of her brother's antics. Tatiana was still attending lessons as well as nursing so Olga was forced to spent time on her own whilst her sisters were in the classroom and she usually went to the hospital where she found congenial company.

Marie was amused that day by her brother's mode of transport as she told Nicholas. He was carried upstairs whilst still strapped inside his sledge which must have looked funny. It was like a wheelchair on skates. (Marie always went into greater detail than her sisters.)

That day, the Tsarina proudly wrote of Marie's bravery during a minor operation carried out by Dr Derevenko. She could have only had a local anaesthetic during the procedure which took place in her mother's room. Her finger had become infected and needed treatment but, as a minor operation, the doctor agreed to carry out the procedure at home, within sterile conditions of course.

On his arrival at Sevastopol on Thursday, Nicholas wired that he was preparing to visit the recently returned fleet. It was a return to the Crimea where, in previous years, the family had holidayed, but since the beginning of the war the family would not return to Livadia although they did visit the area.

Meanwhile back at Tsarskoe Selo, the Grand Duchesses continued their usual daily life. Tatiana attended lessons before travelling on to the infirmary. After a delightful sleigh ride in the snow, the sisters had dinner before they returned to the infirmary and spent time sitting with the impatient Anya. Tatiana wrote to Nicholas that day declaring that she really envied him being in the Crimea. It brought back such happy memories of holidays in the area.

However, on Thursday, Alexandra noted that Marie was still suffering. Her finger was clearly still been causing problems after the operation. The two eldest sisters had returned to the hospital where they assisted during operations on the wounded. The four sisters went out during the afternoon in a sledge and complained of being frozen.

The following day, Nicholas sent a telegram from the south of the Empire. He was in his element when amongst his troops whether it was soldiers or sailors.

Anastasia informed Nicholas how she had been skating and teaching Tatiana's dog tricks including giving the paw. (She had always loved dogs and her own little dog was now probably beginning to suffer, unknown to Anastasia. It later died.) She and Marie later went to their own hospital.

That day Olga and Tatiana had as usual returned to the infirmary and, after lunch, had gone to the capital chaperoned by Baroness Buxhoeveden to a ceremony to consecrate an emergency shelter. The two returned to the hospital after tea with Alexandra. They spent the evening with some of the wounded, including the inevitable Karangazonov.

On Saturday, Alix informed Nicholas that two of their daughters Olga and Anastasia were playing with toy pistols. Olga was apt to play wild games with her younger sisters when she had the time but Tatiana never joined in these games. She spent her free time in a more organised way by sewing or writing letters. (Olga had a real pistol later but was discouraged from taking it to Siberia.)

After returning to the infirmary, Olga and Tatiana returned to the palace for lunch with their mother and their guests – Alexandra's sister-in-law Xenia and her estranged cousin (and former sister-in-law) Victoria-Melita. The latter had formerly been married to the Tsarina's brother Ernie which made the relationship somewhat strained. The Grand Duchess (as she now was after marrying Grand Duke Kyrill) had two young daughters. Her first daughter Elisabeth had died in 1903. She had been a close friend of Olga and Tatiana.

The sisters later returned to the hospitals to see Anya and then to stand in the corridor of their infirmary with some of the wounded, including the newly married Seryozha and his young bride plus Tatiana's friend Vladimir Ivanovich Kiknadze. The two Grand Duchesses were now regularly standing in the corridor each time they visited the infirmary. It was the high point of their day.

As he made his way home on Sunday at the beginning of the next month, Nicholas sent a telegram to Alexandra. He was once more eager to return to Alexandra and the children. He was travelling home accompanied by his aides Nicholas Sablin and Anatole Mordvinov.

That morning Alexandra had attended Mass along with her daughters. They lunched *en famille* before Olga and Tatiana left for the infirmary. The sisters sat with the recovering Nicholas Kazangozov and the other patients. Tatiana sat with Vladimir Kiknaze and the two enjoyed playing a puzzle game together. The two sisters later returned home. That afternoon, the four Grand Duchesses along with Alexandra were bundled up and rode in a large double sledge to Pavlovsk. They arrived in time for tea with Alexandra's old friend Princess Marie Baritinskya. She had been Alexandra's lady-in-waiting in the early years of her marriage but had left service in 1898 to nurse an aging parent.

In the evening, Olga and Tatiana returned to the infirmary and sat again with Nicholas Karangozov and the other patients. The men were entertaining the sisters by singing traditional Russian songs. Olga later made a note of several Russian songs in her journal, probably the ones they were singing that evening including *Cossack Lullaby*.

On Monday morning, Olga and Tatiana travelled to the railway station to meet Nicholas and his aide Sablin. Despite his arrival, less than an hour later the sisters returned to the infirmary. Once again they sat with the recovering Nicholas Karangozov. They left to attend a religious service late in the morning and again that evening before dinner. They also called in on Anya before returning to their own hospital.

The following morning was spent at the infirmary by the two eldest Grand Duchesses, but part of the day was spent in the company of their father. They returned to the hospital later when they again played puzzle games with the patients and stood around and chatted in the corridor. Olga naturally visited Karangozov afterwards. Nicholas must have felt that his elder daughters had effectively *left home*.

On Thursday, the sisters attended church before returning to the hospital to continue with the inevitable bandaging. There was an important visitor at lunch: the British Ambassador, Sir George Buchanan, arrived along with General Padzhet. After lunch Olga, Tatiana and Anastasia rode in their sledges to nearby Bablove. They would have normally returned to the hospital but chose on this occasion to rejoin the family as it were.

The two eldest sisters later returned to the Catherine Palace hospital. Nicholas went to St Petersburg to visit his mother. He had seen a great deal less of her since he had been away. Olga and Tatiana called in on Anya before returning to their own hospital where Olga naturally sought out her friend Nicholas Karangozov.

On the following morning, the sisters returned to their hospital. Karangozov had been moved out since he was now able to walk. The sisters visited Anya once more and attended church morning and evening. Alexandra was feeling under the weather and complained of a sore throat.

The Grand Duchesses Olga and Tatiana attended Mass on Saturday morning, the First Saturday in Lent, at the lower church and walked around the White Tower accompanied by Grand Duke Dmitri and the Tsar's aide Anatole Mordvinov. After lunch, they called in on Anya. At tea, the Tsar's Uncle Paul appeared as did Paul Voronov, surprisingly. Rasputin made another appearance later. Yet again he had arrived the same day as Dmitri, one of those who would later become part of the plot to remove him from the Tsarina's life.

On Sunday, Olga attended Mass in the company of her father and sister Marie. She later went on to the Catherine Palace and then to the smaller hospital. She managed to see Karangozov again. The two met often but there was no sign of a romance.

The following morning, after the usual trips to the *Church of the Sign* and to the infirmary, there was an important guest for lunch. Prince Yussopov arrived. He had been abroad and had much to chat about as a result. Later, Olga returned to the Catherine Palace accompanied by Tatiana, Alexandra and Baroness Buxhoeveden. The ladies called in on Anya and the wounded officers in the other wards.

On Tuesday morning, Olga and Tatiana attended a service at the *Church of the Sign* before going on to the infirmary. Later, after news that the Tsar's cousin Kostia was unwell, Nicholas and his daughters travelled to Pavlovsk. Olga and Tatiana sat with his daughter Tatiana and her young children whilst Nicholas saw his cousin. The Grand Duke was not long for this world.

The sisters later returned to the hospital where they sat in the corridor knitting and smoking. They were feeling more and more at home there. At the infirmary they were treated like nurses rather than like children. It was a liberating experience.

Olga and Tatiana returned to the cave church on Friday morning before returning to their hospital with Alexandra. It may well have been a strange feeling to be at the hospital with their mother – the very person who had treated them as children. Later, Alexandra left to join Nicholas and the ailing Kostia at Pavlovsk. That evening Olga had one of her few lessons – music. She was an extremely talented pianist and a good singer. In the days of Jane Austen she would have been said to have been *accomplished*.

The following Tuesday, Olga and Tatiana returned to the *Church of the Sign* before heading back to the hospital. Once again, Olga chatted with Nicholas Karangozov. The Tsarina's old friend Princess Marie Baritinskaya arrived for lunch. In the afternoon, the sisters visited the Toura Muslim hospital which had been specially set up to treat the Muslim patients.

The next morning, Olga and Tatiana drove to the hospital with Alexandra where they called in on the recovering yet ever complaining Anya. In the afternoon, Olga and Tatiana left for the capital to visit the Winter Palace to accept donations as they normally did on a Wednesday afternoon. They arrived home in time for tea and again called in on the impatient patient Anya. (When the sisters were later all suffering from measles in 1917, she contrived to feel worse than they did when she caught the same virus. Marie almost died, but with great dignity.)

On Thursday morning, the two eldest Grand Duchesses returned to the infirmary, after Tatiana's lessons. Olga went on to visit Anya whilst Tatiana assisted with an operation. She was a far more proficient and confident nurse than Olga. After lunch, the sisters returned to the Catherine Palace with Nicholas, Alexandra and Dmitri where the Tsar handed out some military medals to the wounded.

The next morning, the sisters returned to the hospital. As usual, Tatiana had studied first. They then returned for lunch at the palace. They did not eat with their colleagues. It would have been too difficult to deal with the simple yet complicated matter of etiquette. Alexandra handed out diplomas to some fifty nursing sisters who had recently qualified. They later returned to the Catherine Palace hospital to visit the recovering Anya. That evening, after more lessons for Tatiana, the sisters travelled to the capital. They called in on the Dowager Empress but on this occasion were accompanied by Nicholas and Alexandra. The Tsar's sister Xenia was already there with two of her sons.

On Monday morning, Tatiana resumed her usual programme of lessons followed by a shift at the infirmary. She was of course joined by Olga at this point. They returned in time for lunch. They later travelled the short distance to the Catherine Palace (known by the sisters as the Big Palace) and returned to the Alexander Palace in time for tea. That evening, Tatiana had yet another lesson before she and Olga returned to the Big Palace Hospital and called in on Anya.

The following morning, Olga and Alexandra returned to the Catherine Palace hospital with Tatiana after she had attended another lesson or two. The ladies returned in time for lunch. The three later called on Anya and some of the officers. After dinner, the sisters returned to their own infirmary where they spent the evening in the company of the wounded men.

On Friday, Alexei composed a short note to the Tsarina with a request. He was too tired to go to church. He begged Alexandra to let him off. Yet that same day, Nicholas records in his journal that Alexei played in the snow with him. After a lie-in that morning, the Tsarevich appears to have felt well enough to go outside later with his father or he simply wanted to remain in bed on a cold morning as many do.

That evening, Nicholas received the Foreign Secretary, Serge Sazonov, and the British Ambassador, Sir George Buchanan. The family afterwards spent a long while sitting with Anya, in the company of Rasputin. She constantly complained of having no visitors yet she was rarely alone.

On Saturday, Olga heard the sad news that Captain S G Strouve had been killed the previous day. He had been the aide-de-camp of Nicholas's cousin Grand Duke George. Unfortunately he would not be the last to die in such circumstances.

Nicholas sent a telegram to his wife after hearing about Captain Strouve. Many of the young men that they knew would be killed during the war and many more after it during the aftermath of the revolution. Grand Duke George was with the Tsar at the time and Nicholas confirmed that he was keeping busy.

That evening, the Grand Duchesses remained with their mother at the palace. Tatiana had naturally *worked* whilst Olga chose to glue some photographs into her album. The sisters all had their own individual leather-bound albums and each arranged the photographs (often the same ones) to her own taste. Each of the girls had their own box cameras but it was Marie who proved to be the best photographer and even managed to develop her own snaps in Siberia, before her camera was confiscated.

That same day, Alexandra sent word to Nicholas to beg a favour on behalf of her daughters. They desired to use his bath whilst he was away. It was more of an indoor swimming pool than a bath. The little dog of Tatiana's was as usual rushing around and had sat on Alexandra's papers crushing them. Such is the price of owning a dog.

Nicholas found time to reply on Monday. He returned to the vexed subject of supplies. (The Russians suffered from lack of supplies, both arms and ammunition, and it would continue to be a thorn in the side for Nicholas throughout the war. Russia had a vast army and could not keep up with demands. The transport situation in Russia was a disaster, especially during the winter months, and supplies from abroad were naturally at an all-time low. Supplies were constantly lost due to enemy action; submarines sank the supply ships.)

Nicholas confirmed that is was all right for his daughters to use his bath. They had done so before with his permission and it was a great treat for them.

Alexandra wrote that day with bad news: the death of a young soldier in her care by the name of Hrabovo. She was so distressed that she sent Olga, who had accompanied her to the hospital to visit Anya, to join her younger sisters so that she could cry on her own. The young man had greatly impressed all by his quiet dignity. The sisters enjoyed the company at Anya's of her sister-in-law Nina and Olga Voronova.

On Tuesday, Olga and Tatiana returned to their duties at the hospital after Tatiana had completed her studies. They attended at another appendix operation and then sat with Karangozov. The Tsarina and her daughters later attended a memorial service for Hrabovo. Then Alexandra, along with Tatiana, Marie and Anastasia, visited Marie and Anastasia's hospital. Olga and Tatiana later called in on Karangozov and then returned to see Anya.

In a letter that day, Olga informed Nicholas how they were spending their time. Marie was taking her turn in sitting in the Tsar's armchair and imitating him by reading the agents' messages and smoking a cigarette without a holder (ladies would normally have used one). She mentioned Karangozov in the piece, as one of her new friends.

The following day, Nicholas requested more writing paper. It was generally Tatiana who organised such things and would have had it sent on to him. He explained where it was kept.

Alexandra informed Nicholas of the movements of his daughters that day. Olga and Tatiana were in town once more and this time had taken their two younger sisters Marie and Anastasia along for the experience. The Grand Duchesses then elected to see where their former nanny Maria lived.

The following afternoon, Nicholas found time for another letter. He was mildly amused how the members of the suite were continually falling over in the mud. The roads were slippery due to the melting snow and ice. A few days previously, Sazonov (the Foreign Minister) had fallen whilst walking and had bruised his nose and leg; the previous day Drenteln had slipped at the same spot; and today Count Grabbe had fallen, but luckily he was unhurt.

Meanwhile, the Grand Duchess Olga Nicolaevna composed a letter to Nicholas that day from her mother's room. The famous gypsy singer Nadezhda Pleviskaya had arrived to present a donation to the Grand Duchesses' charity, much to Olga's delight. She intended to donate the proceeds of a concert to the charity. Marie had played a game of *colorito* with her mother that evening and Tatiana was knitting stockings for the wounded men.

Olga went on to complain of Felix Yussopov's apparent idleness. She felt that he should have been doing something more useful at a time when most young men were either in the army or navy. He appeared to be wasting his time by doing nothing at all. She and Tatiana had travelled to the capital that afternoon for another committee meeting and later had called in on their Aunt Xenia.

On Saturday morning Marie wrote to Nicholas of her everyday life at the Alexander Palace. There was little to report. Tatiana's dog had already been for a brief visit to her room from Tatiana's room next door. Anastasia was doing some homework.

That same evening, a contented Tatiana found time to correspond with Nicholas after the four girls had been given permission to use the Tsar's bath. Her dog had been as overexcited as ever and caused chaos, (probably anxious to get into the water). The more excited and animated the children were, the more the dog was desperate to join in the fun. Olga and Marie were playing *colorito*.

A delighted Anastasia also put pen to paper that day to thank Nicholas. It was big enough to swim in and all the girls took turns to use it. She was looking forward to a lie-in on Sunday after a week of endless lessons.

On Sunday, the Tsarina informed Nicholas of the birth of a grandchild for his sister Xenia. (It would be her only child.) Alexandra had been convinced it would be a girl. (After so many boys in the family, she may well have secretly thought that they had quite enough already.)

The Tsar sent a telegram in reply after hearing the good news. He was in a happy mood after hearing that things were progressing well in the war and he added that he would be returning by Wednesday morning.

That evening, the girls had gone out for a drive before going on to the Red Cross community and on to Anya. The two eldest sisters then called in on their cousin Tatiana. She had two tiny children of whom Olga was especially fond.

On the same day, Olga informed Nicholas that they had seen Rasputin at Anya's house. (Once more, he appears to have been making himself at home and acting as host by pouring the tea from the samovar.) She also thanked Nicholas for his permission to use his bath. She explained that her mother and Marie were playing *colorito* but neither proved to be a superior player.

Anastasia also wrote to Nicholas in her usual comic style. She spoke of having problems getting rid of *worms* – a way of saying that she was constipated. (Nicholas often had the same problem.) In the next line she had admitted that Olga complained that she was *stinking* which rather confirms the theory. Now Anastasia was in trouble from Olga for picking her nose. Olga, she confided, was rearranging her undergarments.

The following day, Nicholas sent a hurried telegram home exclaiming that the major Austrian fortress of Przemysl had finally been taken after a siege. It was an important moral victory for Russia. They captured some 2,500 officers and 117,000 men.

He had already started a letter after the arrival of two more from Alexandra along with some flowers. He was delighted with the gift as it so reminded him of her.

Tatiana also composed a letter to Nicholas that day. She explained that she had been to see her cousin of the same name the previous day at Pavlovsk. She had been told that Kostia was so confused that he had forgotten about the war altogether.

Tatiana Nicolaevna had heard the news of the recent victory when she was at the hospital, she explained. Tatiana confessed that she found the name of Irina's new baby rather boring. She had called the baby Irina. It did seem a little dull to name the baby after her own mother.

The Grand Duchess Anastasia sent Nicholas a letter that day along with a painting she had done of a small girl. She had done the picture as a thank you for some photographs that he had sent. The picture was of a sweet little girl and done in a style almost cartoon-like.

Anastasia was seen as a comedian by many, as Pierre Gilliard confirmed. She had a remarkable gift for keeping everyone's spirits up; something that would be very much appreciated in the dark days after the revolution.

The following Sunday, the family attended Mass as usual. In the afternoon, Olga and Tatiana walked to the Catherine Palace and called in on Anya. The Tsarevich was unwell and suffering from influenza which could prove dangerous in his condition if he sneezed violently and bled internally.

On Monday, the eldest Grand Duchesses returned to the infirmary to resume their usual duties. Although Alexei was recovering, he chose to remain in bed. The sisters attended church morning and evening. After dinner, Tatiana and Marie were driven to the Catherine Palace hospital where they paid a call on Madame Vyrubova.

The following day, Olga and Tatiana returned to the infirmary but spent much of their time standing in the corridor and chatting. There were not always patients to treat. The wounded came to the hospital all at once so, as the first batch of men recovered, they had little to do until more men arrived. The sisters returned for lunch to discover that the Tsar's cousin Kyrill had arrived. The Tsarina was feeling under the weather and remained on her sofa. As he was the second husband of her former sister-in-law, it may have been a tactical withdrawal. The sisters returned to church in the evening and later chatted on the phone to the hospital patients, two in particular.

On Wednesday, the sisters returned to their hospital duties as usual and went to the church twice during the course of the day. Alexei remained confined to his bed once again.

The next morning, the Imperial family attended Communion at the church but Alexei had Communion at home. He was now suffering from pains in his neck.

On Good Friday, the eldest Grand Duchesses returned to the infirmary and spent much of their time chatting in the corridor with Vladimir Kiknadze, Boris Ravtopolo and others. They returned home for lunch and again for dinner. Again the family attended church in the afternoon. In the evening, the sisters visited Anya. Rasputin had arrived once more to see his friend.

On Saturday, the sisters returned to the infirmary before going back for a festive family lunch. The Tsar's cousin George appeared. Later, the sisters visited Anya and found their mother had already arrived. Although Alexandra constantly complained about Anya, she was in reality devoted to her.

On Easter Sunday, the family attended church and had a family lunch together. In Russia at Easter traditionally everyone is kissed three times on the cheek and greeted with the words *Christ is Risen* and the recipient replies *Indeed He is Risen*.

In the afternoon, Olga and Tatiana, escorted by Baroness Buxhoeveden, went skiing in the garden. It was quite like old times for the sisters. After a brief drive to visit a former maid-of-honour, the eldest sisters returned to the hospital. They felt compelled to return despite the holiday.

The Tsarina had arrived before them once more and was distributing small china Easter eggs. The sisters sat and chatted with their friends including Kiknadze and Karangozov. They then went on to church before calling in on Anya. Nicholas Sablin was also visiting the patient. The two had been acquainted for years and were in constant attendance on Alexandra.

On Easter Monday, the family returned to the church for Mass and the usual procession of the *Shroud* was carried around the church. The family lunched together later with Nicholas's Uncle Paul who had arrived.

In the afternoon, the sisters returned to the Catherine Palace. Alexandra presented Olga and Tatiana with Easter eggs. She then gave eggs to each of the officers at the hospital. The two eldest Grand Duchesses were driven to Pavlovsk to their cousin Tatiana. Whilst Tatiana sat with her cousin, Olga played with the baby girl. They later returned home for a quiet dinner with the Tsarina. Nicholas travelled the short distance to the capital to see his mother. The sisters later chatted on the telephone to their friends Kiknadze and Karangozov.

It was a time when Nicholas traditionally presented both his wife and mother with expensive and elaborate Easter eggs made by Carl Faberge. Each contained a little surprise. Unlike the modern Easter eggs given to children now, they were not made out of chocolate.

Nicholas was delighted to be chosen as godfather to Xenia's new grandchild. The Dowager Empress was another. On the following Saturday, he and his family visited the Yussopov's and attended the christening of their baby daughter Irina.

Chapter Ten

Spring 1915

On the following Thursday, the younger Imperial children resumed their lessons. Tatiana later travelled the short distance to the infirmary where she and Olga chose to stand and chat with the patients in the corridor. They later called in at the Catherine Palace hospital and made a brief visit to a nearby warehouse. After tea with her mother and siblings, Tatiana returned to her studies.

The next day proved to be much the same for Tatiana. She had lessons then returned for a shift at the infirmary. That afternoon, she returned for more lessons before stopping for tea. The Tsarina was suffering from one of her bad headaches so Nicholas dined alone with his daughters as he frequently did.

After Nicholas returned to Mogilev, Alexandra resumed her daily letters, only pausing to briefly mention her children's antics. She was convinced that Tatiana's dog was also missing Nicholas. She informed Nicholas that the little dog was constantly on guard watching and listening for every sound.

The four sisters went to a concert that afternoon at Marie and Anastasia's hospital. It had been arranged by Marie's friend Nicholas Demenkov. Alexei played outside in the park near to the White Tower with the children of Andrei Derevenko (Alexei and Sergei) although their father obviously accompanied the children.

On Sunday, Nicholas wrote at length of his intended trip to the newly captured fortress. He had not decided whether he should go alone or with Grand Duke Nicholas. Although his uncle was technically Commander-in-Chief of the army, he was still the Tsar. It was a tricky situation.

The same day, Olga composed a homely letter for Nicholas. The Grand Duchesses were overwhelmed by the crowds of people who had come to the Catherine Palace to attend a concert arranged by Marie's friend. The sisters had tea together at Anya's with Nicholas Rodionov and LM Kozhevnikov (their former tennis partners). Alexei had arrived later and they all played card games together. Later on, whilst Marie once again played *colorito w*ith her mother, Tatiana sat reading as Olga wrote. Tatiana's puppy slept peacefully by her feet.

Marie mentioned her *friend* Nicholas Demenkov in her next letter to Nicholas. Anastasia's little dog was in trouble for making a mess on the Tsarina's carpet. Anastasia had a shovel ready to clean up any mess her dog was likely to make indoors. Tatiana and Anastasia later visited Anya only to find Rasputin there already.

Nicholas had little to impart on Monday. The weather had improved though as he noted in his wire to Alexandra that day.

Alexandra informed Nicholas how Anya Vyrubova lied to Tatiana about being alone. Rasputin had explained that Anya wanted more visitors and felt that she had not enough people fussing around her.

That evening, in a letter to Nicholas, Tatiana complained of her boredom during the committee meetings. She explained that her mother and Marie were playing *colorito* whilst Olga was chatting to a friend at the hospital on the telephone.

On Wednesday, Nicholas sent a cheerful message home after a drive in the country. He liked to spend as much time as possible in the outdoors and he was more restricted from doing so at headquarters due to lack of time and security issues.

He later found the time to compose a letter. Alexandra felt that Nicholas should visit the newly captured territory without the Grand Duke, but the Tsar disagreed.

Meanwhile, Anastasia enjoyed watching the dogs sleeping on her mother's bed as she revealed to Nicholas in a letter that evening. Tatiana was out that evening at a committee meeting, much to her own annoyance.

The following day, Nicholas sent a special message to Alexandra. He thanked her for the flowers she had sent for their anniversary. It was twenty-one years since their engagement.

The Tsar later composed a long letter in remembrance of their betrothal in 1894. He remarked that no one else had remembered the anniversary. (It seems unlikely that they would in the circumstances. It was a different matter entirely for Nicholas who thought even the weather reminded him of that day in 1894.)

Marie wrote to Nicholas that day and explained that it was the first time that year that they had been able to sit on the balcony. Alexandra had been delighted with the gift of a cross (necklace) she had been sent by Nicholas. Marie remarked that Alexei had asked if he could have permission to sleep in Nicholas's bed.

On Thursday, Tatiana returned to the infirmary and sat with one of the nurses Varvara Vilchkovsky, known to the sisters as *Bibi*. (She would prove to be a lasting friend to the sisters.) The Grand Duchess chose to sit with Kiknadze and Nauruzov before calling in on Anya.

Anastasia noticed a few signs of spring as she mentions in a letter to Nicholas. She and Marie returned to the old familiar task of breaking up the ice on the pond. The water from the pond was not essential for any particular use but after the revolution it was used as a water supply for the palace after the water was cut off by the revolutionaries. It was usually used for boating by Nicholas but he had little time now.

Nicholas sent a message home the following day. He was impressed with both the scenery and the troops he had just inspected and had been reunited with both his sisters on his recent visit.

That day, Tatiana informed Nicholas of Anya's visits to the palace. Anya made herself quite at home and liked to be in the presence of Alexandra as often as possible. Now Anya came to the Alexander Palace each day rather than Alexandra and her daughters calling in on Anya at the hospital. It was certainly more convenient for everyone concerned, except Anya of course. She had to now move around with the aid of two walking sticks or a wheelchair.

Meanwhile, Alexandra informed Nicholas of Marie's visit to the graveyard. Everyone had been moved at the death of the young soldier earlier in the year at their hospital. It was exactly forty days since David Grabovoy had died.

Nicholas sent another message from the same place on Sunday. He was in a cheerful mood and was enjoying the approach of spring.

The same day, Olga joked about a fight between Tatiana and Anastasia's dogs. (Anastasia's dog would not have been in the best of health as it died not long after and may have felt irritable. A very young dog and an elderly sick one are not the ideal combination.) Ortipo was racing around the room and Anastasia's dog Shybzik made a squeaking noise. Marie was once again playing *colorito* against her mother. Anya was escorted to the Alexander Palace by Zhuk and an orderly each day, she added.

After returning to Brody on Monday, Nicholas wrote cheerfully of his visit which he had thoroughly enjoyed. He later found the time during the train journey to compose a long letter home. He had broken the picture frame containing his son's photograph but the high point of the visit was being able to sleep in the enemy's bed. He slept in a bed previously occupied by the Austrian Emperor Franz Joseph. He had, of course, met the Emperor previously in more amiable circumstances.

On Tuesday, Alexandra explained by post to Nicholas how her son was unable to walk but was bravely carrying on and went about in a motor car or carriage instead. It was more dignified than a wheelchair and easier to get about in the snow.

That morning, the four sisters had visited the local church. They later visited a local hospital before going on to Anya's for tea. She had invited various guests including Marie's friend Nicholas Demenkov, Olga's old friend Alexander Shvedov, and Victor Zborovsky, a friend of Anastasia.

The following day, Nicholas informed Alexandra of his movements. Once again, he sent a message to Alexandra announcing where he was about to go when he probably should not have done so due to the security implications, but it never seemed to bother him. He was about to travel to Kamenetz-Podolsk. He later adds that he had unexpectedly seen the Tsarina's Crimean regiment.

On Thursday, Nicholas telegraphs home after inspecting troops at Odessa. He was enjoying the warm weather of the south. It was as pleasant as summer.

That day, Olga and Tatiana had returned as usual to the infirmary, after Tatiana had finished her morning studies. The sisters sat around with their friends including Kiknadze and Barbara Afanaseva, one of the nurses. They seemed in no hurry to return home.

The two sisters travelled to the capital in the company of Baroness Buxhoeveden and ate on the train that afternoon. They made brief visits to another infirmary and to Countess Hendrikova before returning to the Winter Palace. (The Countess was, of course, the mother of the Tsarina's lady-in-waiting Countess Anastasia Hendrikova.) After they arrived back at the Alexander Palace, Tatiana resumed her lessons and later chatted on the telephone with friends at the hospital.

On Friday, Nicholas sent a telegram from Nicolaiev after inspecting the dockyards. He was delighted to be back in the Crimea.

Tatiana admitted, in a letter that day to Nicholas, to smoking a cigarette whilst writing to him. The Grand Duchesses all smoked cigarettes but not on a regular basis. They smoked the odd cigarette and never became heavy smokers. It was like the odd Belgian chocolate to them.

The quiet evening was interrupted by the sound of the dogs, as Anastasia remarks in her letter to Nicholas at nightfall. Several different dishes had been brought for Alexei to sample, possibly the soldiers' rations that Nicholas normally sampled. Anastasia and her sisters and the Russian Professor Petrov forced themselves to help him to eat them.

The following day (Saturday), Nicholas wrote of his visit to the port of Sevastopol on the Black Sea, somewhere he had often visited in previous years joining his regular holiday in the Crimea. He later found time for a long letter, clearly enjoying spending time with the members of the armed forces. He always delighted in their company as it reminded him of his earlier days in the army before he assumed the heavy responsibility of being Tsar.

Olga's letter that day to Nicholas made light of Tatiana's lack of musical skills. Olga was herself an excellent pianist and Tatiana played reasonably well. It was probable that it was the actual tune that Olga found boring.

The children's letters show clearly that it was usually Marie who played with her mother at *colorito* on an evening. The Tsarina later stated that she did not approve of cards, but was probably referring to gambling with cards for money. She had often played cards with her sister Irene in recent years and with her Uncle Leopold as a small child.

That afternoon, Olga and Marie had been out horse riding. Olga rode her usual horse *Regent* but Marie had borrowed Nicholas's horse *Guardemarine*. If she had ridden her father's horse, it meant one of two things: her father's horse was a ladies' horse or, more likely, Marie was sufficiently strong enough to saddle her father's horse with her side-saddle and ride it easily. She was indeed alleged to have a great strength, as her late grandfather Alexander III had.

Meanwhile the Germans invaded Russian Baltic Provinces on the 17th/30th of April 1915.

Despite this, the next day Nicholas wrote enthusiastically after returning from an inspection. He had some important news for his son. He had appointed Alexei as Commander-in-Chief of the 3rd Battalion of the Plastouni. (The Plastouni battalions were normally comprised from Kouban Cossack units consisting of picked marksmen.)

Marie wrote to Nicholas the same day of the antics of Anastasia's dog. The little dog was starting to hide which is a sure sign of *hiding* from pain, as animals often do. Alexei and Anastasia were on Marie's bed playing with the dog. Marie and Anastasia shared a bedroom, but Alexei's room was at the other end of the corridor next to that of Gilliard.

On Monday, Nicholas telegraphed his thanks after receiving a letter from Alexandra. He had stopped at Borki the previous day – the site of a previous serious train accident where Nicholas's father the late Emperor Alexander III saved the lives of his family by holding up the roof of the damaged car enabling his family to escape.

The act of strength may actually had damaged him as he became ill not long after and died at the young age of forty-nine.

Nicholas later sent a message along with some pictures but insisted that he wanted them returned to him later.

Meanwhile, Alexandra informed Nicholas of their children's activities that day. They were presenting medals before meeting up with a group of friends at Anya's house.

Olga mentions the flowers recently sent in her letter to Nicholas the same day. (She later took comfort in spending time amongst the plants in the house in which they were imprisoned in Tobolsk. Alexandra was said to have found flowers her only real friends.) They had earlier visited Anya where they had seen Marie's friend Nicholas Demenkov, Olga's old friend Alexander Shvedov and Anastasia's friend Victor Zborovsky.

On Tuesday, Nicholas sent a message from Orel. He had spent the day visiting a factory and he was expecting to see his sister-in-law Ella the following day.

Nicholas sent a message from Tver the following day after briefly meeting up with the Tsarina's sister Ella who was also an aunt of Nicholas due to her marriage to his late Uncle Serge. They only managed to meet for a matter of ten minutes unfortunately but on the other hand he was looking forward to returning home to Tsarskoe Selo the next day.

The family were reunited once again.

Nicholas sent Alexandra a brief message on his arrival back at headquarters early in May. He was enjoying the warm weather and seemed happy to return.

Olga attended the *Church of the Sign* that same day which was a Tuesday. Tatiana had treated a young soldier earlier in the day at the infirmary. Unfortunately he had to have his tongue cut out. Later Tatiana went to the capital with the Tsarina in order to attend a meeting and visit a warehouse. Olga noted that day not only a telegram had arrived from Nicholas in Vilna but that she had news that Paul Voronov was now on convoy duty. Once again, Voronov had managed to return, even if only on paper. That evening the sisters paid a call on Anya.

Olga sent Nicholas a letter that she hoped would arrive in time for his birthday the next day. She explained that she had remained at home most of the day as she had developed a cough (and *Madame Becker* had paid her a call). Tatiana had helpfully replaced her at the committee.

Nicholas sent a telegram home on Thursday expressing his thanks to Anya who he always referred to as *her*. Although he seemed perfectly happy in her company and often partnered Anya at tennis, he could have merely *put up* with her for his wife's sake, much as he did with Rasputin. He generally let Alexandra have her way on any subject, just to keep the peace. He was by nature a pacifist and disliked arguing.

Tatiana visited the infirmary that day with Alexandra whilst Olga remained at home. She assisted during an operation. That evening the Tsarina, a partially recovered Olga and Tatiana left for a brief visit to Vitebsk. They travelled by train rather than by car or carriage on these long journeys.

That day, Anastasia reassured the Tsarina that she and her sister would behave and not cause trouble. The children often passed little messages to their mother when she was simply on the floor below in the Alexander Palace and the Tsarina replied in the same manner. Alexandra was about to leave her three youngest children alone – apart from the many members of staff and suite who lived in the palace itself.

Alexandra was full of worries and back pains as she wrote to Nicholas during a trip to Vitebsk with a dog on her lap. Tatiana's dog was determined to sit with Alexandra despite being discouraged several times.

Early on Thursday morning she, Olga and Tatiana had arrived at Vitebsk and had first paid a visit to the cathedral. They then inspected four hospitals and ate a hurried lunch on the train. They later visited the Red Cross warehouse where the drugs were manufactured and yet another three hospitals. The ladies made a brief visit to the Governor's House and had tea before leaving for the station.

Grand Duke Konstantin's son-in-law Prince Konstantin Bagration-Muhransky, who was serving as an officer during the war, died on Friday. His young wife Tatiana was naturally heartbroken. He left two small children – Teymuraz and one month-old Natalia. The children were greatly loved by Olga and her sisters and Olga Nicolaevna would often return to play with them as her sister Tatiana sat with her namesake.

The news of his son-in-law coming so swiftly after the death of one of his own sons had a catastrophic effect on the already ailing Konstantin. (He died soon after.) He too was heartbroken. Luckily he did not live to see the murder of the other sons in a few years' time.

On Saturday morning, Alexandra and her two eldest daughters arrived back at the Alexander Palace after their brief trip. They were met at the station by an excited Marie, Anastasia and Alexei, and a chaperone, of course. Olga and Tatiana made a brief visit to the *Church of the Sign* before calling in on Anya. They then returned to the infirmary where they spent much of their time socialising in the corridor and chatting to the patients.

The sisters returned to the palace for lunch with the Tsarina and her friend Princess Sonia Orbeliani. They then went for a char-à-banc ride with their youngest sisters and the chaperone Countess Hendrikova. Olga and Marie returned to visit the patients later at the Catherine Palace hospital and Rasputin arrived afterwards.

That afternoon Olga sent word to Nicholas from the *Mauve Boudoir* and explained that her mother and Tatiana were endeavouring to play some game or other, Anastasia appeared to be writing, and Marie was playing the piano badly. She was attempting to play the *Cherabim Hymn* by Tchaikovsky, a piece well loved by Olga and her siblings. Tatiana's little dog Ortipo was chasing a toy car and had attempted to steal Alexei Trupp's shoe buckle. (Trupp was one of the members of the household who went to Siberia with his employers.)

Nicholas sent a brief message home on Sunday along with a special note from Count Fredericks who had asked to be permitted to send his greetings. The aged Count was a much loved member of the household, but in recent years his memory had begun to fail and he had become confused at times. It had been somewhat of a liability to take him but Nicholas did not have the heart to refuse.

Nicholas finally found the time to compose a long letter to his wife on Whit Monday after a lengthy explanation of why he had not written before. He was concerned that there was a general mood of depression at headquarters.

Meanwhile the Tsarina and her two eldest daughters had attended the service at the new cave church that morning. The three had then done a shift at the infirmary and then went to the Catherine Palace hospital. They continued with the endless round of bandaging and then sat around for a while afterwards chatting. There had been a sudden influx of officers at the Catherine Palace hospital.

Olga later visited the small children at the nurses' school and enjoyed having a cuddle with them, especially a girl named Olechka who was the daughter of one of the emergency nurses. The school was where the children of the nurses played during the time their mothers were on duty.

At nightfall the four sisters dined with their mother before going to Anya's for the remainder of the evening. She had invited several guests including Nicholas Demenkov, Boris Ravtopolo and Alexander Shvedov. Her parties were a welcome end to a hard day at the hospital for Olga, and more especially Tatiana.

Nicholas sent a brief telegram from Stavka to Alexandra on Tuesday morning before he left. He had gone for his last walk and would leave after lunch.

The Tsar arrived home early on Wednesday morning and his grateful family attended a celebration Mass in honour of his safe return. After lunch, the Grand Duchesses gathered cowslips in the park. During the afternoon they attended a concert at Marie and Anastasia's hospital. Olga spotted Paul Voronov amongst the crowd. Yet again, he was there as a constant reminder to Olga of her recent past.

The Tsar's Uncle Paul arrived in time for tea along with his daughter Marie Pavlovna. Later, Alexandra and her daughter Tatiana made a brief visit to Pavlovsk. Princess Tatiana was in great need of comfort after the death of her husband and brother (and the imminent death of her beloved father).

On the Saturday morning, the elder Grand Duchesses attended a service at the *Church of the Sign* before returning to the hospital. They later travelled to the capital for yet another committee meeting. Olga then spent the evening with her mother who complained she had a sore throat. Late that evening, Nicholas presented his daughter Olga with a most welcome gift: the sheet music to the Tchaikovsky Mass which she duly played. He was probably her favourite composer as she shared Nicholas's taste for Russian music.

There was disaster and humiliation again for Russia on the 22nd of May/4th of June 1915; the Austro-German troops recaptured Przemysl in Poland and the Russian front collapsed.

Anastasia was heartbroken at the death of her beloved dog two days later. She had been acting strangely for the past couple of months and had been hiding under the furniture. Shvybzik died of a cerebral inflammation.

As expected, the Tsar's beloved cousin Grand Duke Konstantin died in the first week in June. Nicholas was informed of the news on Tuesday evening by Konstantin's young son George.

That day had begun much as usual for the elder Grand Duchesses. They attended a service together at the *Church of the Sign* and then went to the cemetery with Alexandra. It was where the wounded that failed to recover were buried. That evening Olga and Tatiana went to the capital for a meeting after calling in on their grandmother the Dowager Empress. Yet again Olga spotted Voronov – on this occasion at the committee meeting.

Later that evening, Olga accompanied her family to Pavlovsk. She spent much of the evening comforting the Grand Duke's daughter (Princess) Tatiana and her sister-in-law Elena. Olga and Elena had been close for years. She was a niece of Stana and Militza who had married the Tsar's cousins Nicholas and his brother Peter.

Konstantin's young daughter Vera (aged nine) had been witness to the death of her father and later recalled the traumatic event. She revealed how she had suddenly developed super-human strength when she needed it whilst she was sitting in her father's study and heard him gasping for breath. Vera had then rushed to get her mother but was too late. The child had managed to open the heavy door which had a mirror and a plant in front of it.

Meanwhile the Grand Duchess Tatiana was concerned that the family would not be able to travel to Peterhof that summer as she explained in a letter to Olga Voronova that same day. She also regretted that they would not enjoy their usual cruise.

Olga confided in her journal briefly of her blossoming friendship with a young soldier. She was finally starting to get over the loss of Voronov. He was Dmitri Artemievich Shakh-Bagov who had been wounded in battle close to the village of Zagrody the previous month and had recently arrived at the hospital. On Thursday evening, she had mentioned how she had sat in the corridor with the patients including Shakh-Bagov. A couple of photographs taken of the young man show that he had been awarded the St George Cross, the one that was routinely awarded to members of the lower ranks, ie non-officers. The young man had dark hair and in the pictures taken he appeared quite shy as he often did not directly face the camera but merely looked up as if not wishing to be noticed at all. He was also like Kiknadze – quite dark skinned and handsome but appeared to be much less confident.

Olga wrote of the same young man on Friday. She did his bandaging that day at her hospital so came into close personal contact with him. Later that day, the four sisters joined their mother at church for a special fourteenth birthday service for Anastasia. She was officially made Commander-in-Chief of the 148th Caspian Regiment.

Yet again Olga saw Voronov but now she may have found it less painful as she was developing a close affection for another man. Later the Imperial family returned to Pavlovsk to comfort Kostia's grieving family. Olga sat with her cousin Tatiana and her small son Teymuraz and baby Natalia.

A service for Nicholas's friend Grand Duke Konstantin was held on Saturday and the French Ambassador Maurice Paleologue was shocked at the change in Nicholas as he observed him at close quarters. Nicholas looked older and more troubled than previously. He also noted that Olga appeared to be concerned about the Tsarina and kept a close eye on her throughout the service.

Nicholas and all the other Grand Dukes followed the funeral vehicle on foot. The coffin was carried through the doorway of the church into the heart of it and a liturgy was performed. Paleologue observed that Nicholas's hair was thinner and flecked with grey. Even his face appeared to be more gaunt than normal. The Tsar was escorted by his mother and his wife. The four young Grand Duchesses also accompanied the Tsar.

On Monday morning the Tsar returned without Alexandra or Anastasia to the actual funeral ceremony of the late Grand Duke at the Cathedral of St Peter and St Paul in the capital. The three Grand Duchesses were photographed that day by Anya wearing black and looking very much the adults that their parents failed to see them as. They were particularly beautiful yet Olga, who remained seated unlike her sisters, appeared a little weary. They had not been accompanied by their mother that day but by her sister Elisabeth.

Nicholas and his three daughters lunched with the Dowager Empress and her daughter Xenia before returning to the Alexander Palace. After tea with their parents and Ella, Olga and Tatiana returned to Pavlovsk and to comfort Elena for some time. They returned later and discovered that the Tsar's nephew and niece Dmitri and Marie Pavlovna arrived in time for dinner.

The Ambassador met Nicholas the following morning. The Tsar, it appears, had been deeply affected by the death of his friend and delighted at being so much appreciated by his subjects that morning. Nicholas presided at the launch of the battle cruiser *Ismails*. The French Ambassador congratulated Nicholas with the good reception he had had in the workshops. Nicholas immediately smiled and stated that he was happy to feel himself in touch with his people as he really needed it that day.

There was a great deal of anti-German feeling in Russia and for three days from the 10th/23rd of June 1915, shops, factories and private houses belonging to people with German names were sacked and burned.

Upon his return the next day Nicholas sent a short message to Alix from headquarters. He diplomatically had not mentioned the recent anti-German feeling demonstrated in Moscow.

That day, as she sat close to the tennis court, Olga cheerfully wrote to Nicholas. She was simply enjoying the warmth of the day. Even the wounded men were sitting outside. She explained that she had had a committee meeting in the capital the previous afternoon. Prince Vladimir (Volodya) Volkonsky was the chairman and he had amused Olga by reading his speech at great speed. Later, she said, the sisters were going back to the nurses' school in order to cuddle the babies. She apologised for her letter and confided that she was being eaten up by the mosquitoes.

Tatiana also sent word to Nicholas that same afternoon and admitted that she had regretted not taking cigarettes on a walk as they would have been useful to get rid of the mosquitoes in the garden that summer's day. She was sitting on the grass opposite the Children's Island with her little dog loyally snoozing by her side.

Nicholas sent a note of thanks to Alexandra and Olga on Friday. The weather was oppressive at Stavka, too he confirmed.

Later that day, Nicholas found time to write and took the opportunity to discuss future appointments of Government Ministers with Alexandra. It was something he would not have done before the war.

Alexandra wrote to Nicholas urging him to write to Marie on her birthday. Alexandra praised her favourite Tatiana for going out and riding but complained about the others who she considered as lazy for spending their precious free time playing with babies.

Nicholas sent a message to his wife on Saturday to reassure her that he had written to Marie. He had not forgotten that it was his daughter's sixteenth birthday. (The girl had been so eager to be seen as grown up that she had persuaded her mother to let her have her hair up on her fifteenth birthday, rather than wait for her sixteenth.)

That same day, Marie sat on the balcony to compose one of her long newsy letters to Nicholas. The previous day (Friday), she and her sisters had called in on Anya where an impromptu party was in progress. The guests Anya had invited had included Olga's old friend Alexander. The group had played party games including the ever popular *charades*.

Marie confessed that she had played tennis against Anastasia and had managed to lose all three sets. She fully intended to go back to the nurses' school later to cuddle the little ones.

Earlier she had been to a warehouse with her mother and sister Anastasia, and the two sisters had felt greatly embarrassed having to wear the standard overall and head-scarf. She explained that Tatiana had gone out riding but, as she had a runny nose, she felt unable to accompany her. Earlier she had been at the infirmary in the company of Olga and Anastasia.

That evening, the sisters attended one of Anya's little parties in the company of Nicholas Demenkov, Alexander Shvedov and Victor Zborovsky. There had been a rehearsal for a comic play which the sisters found immensely funny. Earlier they had dined with Alexandra's friend Princess Marie Bariatinskya.

Nicholas sent a telegram to Alexandra with a message to Marie in remembrance of her birthday on Sunday. He was about to attend a ministerial conference.

In a letter to Nicholas, Anastasia tries to keep cheerful, despite still mourning the loss of her dog. She politely thanked the Tsar for a gift of cigarettes that he had left for her. They had attended church that morning where they had played Tchaikovsky's *Lord, have mercy upon us*. Anastasia went on to explain that Ortipo, Tatiana's dog, was rushing around the room looking for Nicholas. The dog had decided the best move was then to jump onto the Tsarina's lap.

Anastasia was grating carrots and radishes and eating them. She was intending to sneak into Alexei's room later and eat all his samples. It was not just her; the teachers did the same, she explained. She finally admitted how much she missed her little dog but cheerfully added that Marie had received many gifts on the occasion of her birthday and had been playing tennis with her (Anastasia).

Nicholas found the time to write more fully on Monday when he mentioned a religious procession which was being planned throughout the land. It was intended as a way of raising the spirits of the people in difficult times.

Marie composed a letter of appreciation to Nicholas the day after her birthday. She had been delighted with her gifts which had naturally included a necklace from her parents. She had attended a special Mass the previous day and Alexandra's friend Anya had managed to attend in her wheelchair. The Grand Duchess had visited Pavlovsk that evening along with Olga, Tatiana and the Tsarina. They had visited Anya's little house for another party in the evening.

Nicholas later wrote at some length concerning the war and general situation on Tuesday. He was not convinced that General Danilov was a spy despite what he had heard. (He was the Quartermaster-General at general headquarters to the Grand Duke Nicholas 1914–15 and later Chief of Staff on the Northern Front. Allegations had been made against the unpopular general.)

Alexandra wrote only briefly of her daughters that day in her daily epistle to Nicholas. Once again she praised Tatiana for spending her free time horse riding. Tatiana had ridden for over an hour whilst the others had been acting at Anya's, she explained.

Olga had also put pen to paper that day to her father that same day but clearly indicates that she was not *acting* as her mother claimed but merely listening to the rehearsal of a play after spending time working hard at the hospital. The sisters had also made items for an exhibition which was being held at Marie and Anastasia's hospital. She praised the dedication of her mother and her youngest two sisters in making items for charity. She went on to explain that, whilst Tatiana had gone for a ride, she had listened to the actors rehearsing for a play at Anya's. Madame Vyrubova's sister, Alya Pistolkors, had praised the acting ability of the men.

That same day, Tatiana also sent word to Nicholas. She informed Nicholas that, on their recent visit to Pavlovsk, her cousin Tatiana's little boy Teymuraz had attempted to get into their car as they were about to leave.

Alexei rather impressively composed a letter in French for Nicholas that day. (Alexei's command of the French language was far superior to that of his sisters and his mother. The Tsar, on the other hand, spoke several languages including French, German, English, obviously Russian and some Danish.) He had been playing with two of his friends in the sand and the heat of the day heated up the temperature of the sand immensely.

On Wednesday, Nicholas attempted to reassure Alexandra about political changes he was considering making. She was concerned about the likely outcome of a change of ministers. He urged her to see old Goremykin who would, he felt certain, calm her down.

That afternoon Olga and Tatiana had gone to the capital to attend a committee meeting. They later had tea with their grandmother at the *Elagin Palace*.

Anastasia wrote to her father on Thursday detailing Anya's movements. She had arrived for lunch with the Tsarina and was about to leave for the capital to see her parents. She and Marie, she explained, had been bicycling the previous day.

On Friday, Nicholas sent Alexandra a letter and an odd parcel. He needed a new bottle of cascara and returned it to Alexandra along with an old candle which was intended for his son who collected them.

Tatiana was greatly impressed when they were presented with two electric lamps for sitting outside on the balcony, as she explains to her father in a letter that day. They were now able to sit out after dinner until late into the evening. That day she had moved her own camp bed into the middle of the room to get more air. (It was something the sisters did each summer.)

Marie confessed to Nicholas that she had lazily watched the soldiers that day. She loved chatting to her friend Demenkov when she had the opportunity. She was not the only one as Olga and Anastasia were content to watch the soldiers too. She and Anastasia had observed Demenkov through the open window the previous day. That day she and Olga had sat on the window sill and watched as the men played draughts. (Marie liked to chat to the soldiers and was interested in their everyday lives. She had always been surrounded by soldiers and loved to talk to them of ordinary life — something she had little understanding of.)

On Sunday, Olga explained to Nicholas that now Baroness Buxhoeden had decided to sit in a chair that she (Olga) had wished to sit in. There seemed to be a permanent scramble over the best seats in the rooms.

That day, Olga had played croquet outside the hospital with her sisters Tatiana, Marie and Anastasia along with their friends Vladimir Kiknadze, Dmitri Shakh-Bagov and others. The sisters visited Anya's little house that evening and played party games with the other guests, including Anastasia's friend Victor Zborovsky.

During tea, the sisters and the other guests sat on the balcony enclosed by curtains. Whilst they sat quietly eating, a lady and a small child passed by. The little child asked that he may be permitted to go to the *bathroom*. The lady and her son had no idea that there were so many people nearby. The sisters and the officers laughed and found it very amusing. Nicholas Demenkov, who had not got the joke at all, was convinced that they were all laughing at him until it was explained.

On Monday, Nicholas sent word from the peaceful surroundings of his Polish hunting lodge where he had not been since 1912.

Olga and Tatiana had as usual returned to their normal weekly routine that morning. They attended a religious service at the *Church of the Sign* before returning for their shifts at their infirmary. The sisters stood around in the corridor chatting with their friends including Olga's friend Dmitri Shakh-Bagov or *Mitya* as she chose to call him.

Later, the sisters resumed their croquet game in the company of Kiknadze and Shakh-Bagov amongst others. The sisters were now becoming very close to their respective male friends and the two young men also appeared to be friends.

Tatiana later returned to the palace for lessons and went out horse riding again. That evening, the four sisters returned once more to console the recently widowed Tatiana. Anastasia described how she and her sister had moved their beds. Anastasia, like her father, preferred to be in the open air if possible. Tatiana had moved her bed a few days previously. (Some days, as contemporary photographs indicate, the sisters did their lessons on the balcony at the Alexander Palace and also when they lived at Livadia.)

Nicholas sent a telegram home after his return from Poland on Tuesday and had a message for Anya. He had not forgotten her birthday and also sent her a wire.

Nicholas composed a very long detailed letter concerning his recent trip to the hunting lodge and had good news of a counter-attack. He had been concerned the night before that the Germans had broken through and were causing chaos.

Meanwhile, Olga was distraught that morning when Shakh-Bagov left the infirmary early on. He had evidently recovered enough to move on. That morning, Olga and Tatiana had walked to the *Church of the Sign* and made their devotions before returning to the infirmary where they continued with the never-ending bandaging.

The sisters played croquet again later. Once more, Tatiana's friend Vladimir Kiknadze was amongst the number. The gentle game was one normally intended for ladies. It was the only one they were really expected to take part in and involved hitting a ball through a series of hoops on the grass.

The sisters then walked the short distance to the Catherine Palace hospital and worked in the warehouse with the other nursing sisters. They later called in on Anya and played with her little nieces – Tatiana, Olga and the baby Alexandra.

On Wednesday evening, Nicholas sent his thanks to Alexandra and Marie for their recent letters. He made a point of explaining that the letters had arrived at 9pm rather than in the morning as they had previously done. He greatly disliked change however minor.

Meanwhile, Tatiana was in a happy summer mood that day. She explained in a letter to Nicholas how she and her sisters sat out on the balcony. She was relaxing after working at the hospital.

The Tsar wrote briefly on Thursday with news of his imminent return on Sunday evening.

Olga informed Nicholas of Anya's continuing difficulties that same day. Her servant was struggling to fit her chair under the legs of the table. She and Tatiana had been working at the Catherine Palace hospital with their brother that afternoon but she had found it very boring. (She was clearly missing Dmitri but failed to mention it.) The sisters had played tennis later. Olga played four sets but (rather predictably) she had managed to lose them all.

She explained that her mother had bought some new furniture for the balcony. The extension to the palace had gained lights and furniture in recent weeks. (The Tsarina enjoyed sitting on her balcony in all weathers. It was kitted out with heavy curtains too, as photographs taken at the time show.)

On Friday Nicholas expressed his delight at the thought of returning home the next day. A heavy downpour of rain had freshened up the hot afternoon. He informed Alexandra that the processions of the cross he had mentioned previously had been planned for the 8th of July.

The following day he sent Alexandra a message before he set off for Tsarskoe Selo. He had been reassured by recent events that it was a good time to go home.

On Monday, all the Erivan officers who were being treated at the Tsarina's hospital were invited to lunch at the Alexander Palace on the occasion of their regimental holiday. Amongst the group was Olga's friend Dmitri Shakh-Bagov. It gave the Tsarina the opportunity to observe the young man and Olga's growing friendship with him.

The following day, Olga and Tatiana once again returned to the *Church of the Sign* before going on to the infirmary. They sat around in the hallway for some time and chatted to friends including Kiknadze. The sisters returned to the palace in good time for lunch which they ate with both of their parents and Grand Duke Dmitri who had just arrived. That evening, the sisters again travelled to Pavlovsk to see Tatiana and her little children. Nicholas briefly called in on Anya later with his daughters.

Chapter Eleven

Summer 1915

As the month changed, life for the Grand Duchesses barely altered. On the first Wednesday of the month, Tatiana resumed her usual classes before attending the *Church of the Sign* and then going on for a shift at the infirmary.

The sisters returned to the palace for lunch where Nicholas's Uncle Paul had arrived with his daughter Marie Pavlovna. After another lesson and a brief boat ride with her brother, Tatiana arrived back at the palace in time for tea. There were yet more guests for tea, which was held on the balcony. The Tsarina's cousin Victoria-Melita arrived with her mother-in-law Grand Duchess Marie. The sisters made yet another visit to Tatiana and her children that evening.

On Saturday morning, Tatiana had a brief lie-in before returning to the infirmary once again. She had lessons on the balcony afterwards as she was feeling unwell; *Madame Becker* had made an unwelcome return visit.

On the following morning, Nicholas planned a day trip back to Peterhof for the day. He and his three youngest children all enjoyed a day by the sea. The older Grand Duchesses had unfortunately been unable to join them as they were working at the infirmary but had attended a wedding of another of the former patients. The sisters then visited Anya before tea and, afterwards, travelled to Pavlovsk to pay a call on Princess Tatiana and her children.

On Monday morning, the elder Grand Duchesses resumed their usual routine – Tatiana attended a class and a service at the *Church of the Sign* with Olga before the two returned to the infirmary. The sisters spent much of the morning outside with some of the patients enjoying a game of croquet. They returned to the palace in time for lunch with their parents.

The family travelled to Krasnoe Selo that afternoon. Nicholas went by car accompanied by Tatiana, Anastasia and Alexei. Olga and Marie arrived in a separate car with a different driver. On a terrifically hot day they observed the troops who were due to leave shortly for the front put through their paces.

There was even more humiliation when, on the 7th/20th of July 1915 Russians retreated as the Austro-Germans closed in on Warsaw.

That day Olga and Tatiana had as usual visited the *Church of the Sign* before going on to the infirmary and playing a few more rounds of croquet with the inmates. As it was a very hot and stuffy day, as Nicholas departed for Kronstadt, Alexandra remained in her room. The sisters returned to the Catherine Palace hospital in the afternoon. There was a refreshing thunderstorm that evening after the oppressive heat of the day.

Olga and Tatiana returned to the hospital on the Wednesday morning to attend to the dressings. The day was brightened in the afternoon by yet another wedding.

On Thursday, the sisters returned to the infirmary where they once again played croquet with some of the wounded. That evening, the Grand Duchesses returned to Pavlovsk to see Tatiana and her little children. Olga enjoyed cuddling the two little ones.

The next day began as usual for Olga and Tatiana, but that evening Olga was presented with gifts from her parents by Nicholas. The following day would be Olga's saint's day but it was a family tradition to be given gifts the night before and she was naturally delighted with the ring and bracelet she received.

The following Wednesday morning, the sisters' routine returned to normal. Whilst Marie, Anastasia and Alexei continued their full-time education, Tatiana had a lesson that morning before departing for the infirmary. She joined Olga for her shift at the hospital where two operations were performed and they naturally returned to the palace for lunch.

Later Nicholas returned to Peterhof with his children and they also visited a battleship. It was the first time the Grand Duchesses had been aboard one. The party then visited Gatchina where they had tea with the Dowager Empress before returning home for dinner. Olga and Tatiana returned to their duties at the infirmary on Friday and later visited a warehouse but returned to the hospital before dinner.

The two eldest Grand Duchesses returned to Peterhof on Saturday in the company of Nicholas. Again they went to see the Admiralty Shipyard which was the wharf where the ships were being constructed. They watched the *Borodino* being launched.

In the afternoon, Olga and Tatiana returned to the Catherine Palace hospital for a brief shift, before returning to the Alexander Palace for tea. That evening, the sisters returned to the infirmary where Tatiana assisted Valentina Cheborariova in boiling the silk (for the bandages). She was a nurse and administrator at the hospital and had grown very fond of the sisters, especially Tatiana. The sisters later visited Elena.

Nicholas returned to Peterhof on Sunday for a few hours with Marie, Anastasia and Alexei. He took Sablin too and proudly showed him where his four youngest children had been born. The Tsarina and her elder daughters meanwhile attended Mass together. After lunch, Olga and Tatiana returned to the infirmary and were present at an operation. They later sat out the hospital garden accompanied by Varvara (*Bibi*, one of the other nurses) and some of the patients before returning to the palace for tea.

Olga and Tatiana returned to the infirmary on Monday morning after a brief visit to the *Church of the Sign*. Alexandra was feeling unwell and only managed to rise by tea time. That evening, the two sisters chose to assist in the cleaning of the infirmary.

On Tuesday morning the Grand Duchesses Olga and Tatiana assisted in a hernia operation. Olga learnt that one of the other soldiers had heard from Dmitri Shakh-Bagov who was in Kursk. The sisters walked to the Grand Palace hospital later but before dinner returned to the infirmary to help clean the medical instruments.

Nicholas attended a tea party on Wednesday in honour of the Dowager Empress's name's day which would be the following day, along with his children, Xenia, Sandro and their children. Alexandra was not present as she was feeling unwell.

Warsaw fell the following day and later Anya remembered how the Tsar reacted to the news. He felt humiliated and took the momentous decision to lead the armies personally. Ultimately it would not be a good move as naturally any losses would be directly attributed to him.

Dmitri Shakh-Bagov returned soon after, just as Olga had hoped, and once again she spent as much time as possible in his company. She and Tatiana returned to the infirmary in the evenings quite often; although officially to help clean the instruments, they began to spend more and more time in the company of Shakh-Bagov and Kiknaze, or *Mitya* and *Volodia* as the girls called them. It soon became a great concern to Valentina who felt responsible for them.

Meanwhile, the following Tuesday, the sisters returned to the infirmary in the late morning. Tatiana and her sister sat with their friends including Shakh-Bagov. They returned to the palace in time for lunch where the Dowager Empress Marie's friend Betsy Shuvalova had arrived on a rare visit. That evening, the sisters called in on Anya where they were rehearsing for a play again. Later that evening Tatiana and Olga chatted on the telephone to Dmitri Shakh-Bagov.

On Wednesday morning, Olga and Tatiana returned to the infirmary where they again spent time in the company of their friends. They later moved outside in order to play croquet but returned to the palace in time for lunch.

Later, Baroness Buxhoeveden chaperoned the two eldest Grand Duchesses to the capital where they went to receive more charity donations. The sisters returned for tea but chose to go back to the infirmary later. Olga and Tatiana stood in the corridor and chatted with their friends. The Grand Duchesses continued their nursing and their romances as August began. Olga and Tatiana were increasingly spending time at the hospital and less time at the Alexander Palace with their mother and younger siblings.

On the first Saturday in the month, Olga and Tatiana returned as usual to the infirmary. Olga spent time again with *Mitya* whilst she could. After lunch, the sisters worked in the warehouse and later Olga spoke to her friend over the telephone.

Olga and Tatiana returned to the infirmary on Monday morning where some of the soldiers chose to sing to the staff. That afternoon, the Tsar's sister Olga returned. She had seen Nicholas recently but the children had not seen her for a year. Again, Olga Nicolaevna chatted to her friend Shakh-Bagov on the telephone during the course of the evening.

On Wednesday, Olga and Tatiana relaxed in the corridor of the hospital in the company of Shakh-Bagov and others. The sisters returned to the capital that afternoon. Olga was becoming bored when she was out of *Mitya's* company. It was a familiar pattern and one that her parents should have noticed as it had happened two years previously with Voronov. There was something new this time though – Tatiana had also become close to someone: Kiknadze. Valentina certainly did notice what was happening and felt concerned. That evening, Olga chatted on the phone to *Mitya*. Luckily, Valentina had felt responsible and attempted to take the sisters under her wing. She managed to get closer to Tatiana than to Olga though.

On one occasion when Tatiana was outside the hospital, she was nervous as a crowd of nurses suddenly appeared. She held onto Valentina's hand and admitted that she felt embarrassed as she had no idea which of the girls she had been *introduced* to. It was a problem only to the highest classes; one simply had to be introduced in order to continue a conversation or friendship. In the way of royalty, one normally could not speak or approach a member of the Imperial family without being introduced first. It was a complex situation. Victorian and Edwardian etiquette was very restricting and often seems baffling if not downright stupid to modern teenagers.

Meanwhile, Tatiana wrote to her mother in her usual childish manner on Thursday. She promised that she would sit up late in order to keep her mother company. She had been spending a lot of time at the infirmary and seeing little of her mother.

The sisters returned to the infirmary on Saturday morning and on this occasion the more expert Tatiana bandaged Dimitri Shakh-Bagov. They visited the Grand Palace hospital that afternoon and then had tea on the balcony. Olga chose to go to bed early as she felt tired. The nursing work was beginning to become too much for her. A letter from Alexandra to her brother revealed that at this time they had many officers who had returned two or three times. Many suffered severely after being hit by explosive bullets which were obviously more effective at seriously injuring the victims.

On Sunday morning, all the family attended church but Olga and Tatiana later returned to the infirmary where they spied Shakh-Bagov sitting out in the garden with the other patients. The sisters chatted to him on the telephone once they returned home. Later, the sisters returned to the cave church to attend Mass.

On Monday, the sisters returned to the infirmary and Olga stood in the corridor chatting with her friend and others, but mainly, of course, with Shakh-Bagov. That afternoon, Alexandra joined her daughters in a visit to the hospital and afterwards there was a prayer service on the hospital balcony to celebrate the anniversary of the opening of the hospital. Olga spoke with *Mitya* once more before returning to the palace in time for tea.

The Dowager Empress had a fraught meeting with her son Nicholas on Tuesday. She strongly opposed his decision to take command of the armed forces. He arrived with his four daughters. Despite the reservations of most, he was unshakeable in his conviction that he would take command of the army just as he had intended to do so all along.

That same day, Olga Nicolaevna had written in a journal of a meeting with her friend *Mitya*. He had clearly replaced Voronov in her affections. She stated that the most important thing was that she had spoken with him that day. The meaning was obvious: she was smitten with him.

The next day, Olga and Tatiana returned to the infirmary where once again Olga contrived to stand in the corridor and chat to her new friend *Mitya*. Later she sat for some time with other patients, including Nicholas Karangozov.

The sisters returned to the hospital early in the evening to clean the instruments again. Yet again, Olga was a short distance from distance *Mitya*. He was sitting nearby.

The sisters returned to the hospital on Friday morning. On this occasion, the Tsarina appeared. Olga and her sister treated various patients with varied injuries including one who had a bone damaged by a bullet. Yet again, Shakh-Bagov was amongst the men to be treated.

In the afternoon, Olga and Tatiana returned to the capital for a meeting. Olga spoke to *Mitya* by telephone later. Nicholas and Alexandra had also visited Petrograd that day to pray at the tomb of the Tsar's illustrious ancestors; then went on to Our Lady of Kazan where they knelt for some time in front of the icon of the Virgin Mary.

On Saturday Nicholas created his Uncle Paul's second wife – Princess Paley. A few days later, Paul's eldest son Grand Duke Vladimir left for the front. Paul was later placed in command of the 1st Corps of the Imperial Guard.

That same day, Tatiana despaired that she was not a man, as she admitted when she put pen to paper to write to the Tsarina. She felt useless. It was, however, clear how little time Olga and Tatiana spent with their mother, if once again Tatiana felt the need to do so. Alexandra and her son had joined Nicholas on a trip to the capital where they attended a meeting at the Winter Palace.

That day, Olga and Tatiana had returned to the infirmary and carried on the endless round of bandaging wounds. They returned for lunch which was again taken on the balcony, but without Nicholas and Alexandra on this occasion. The sisters escorted Nicholas to the station at 10pm. He left with good luck messages from each of his children.

On the next day, en route for headquarters, Nicholas sent a wire to Alexandra. He was confident that he had done the right thing. He had slept well on the train and promised to telegraph that evening.

That day, Alexandra had written to Nicholas explaining how her daughters planned to keep her company whilst he was away. They did not wish her to remain alone on the ground floor at night whilst they slept upstairs. She had discouraged them and explained that she was not exactly alone on that floor. There were, of course, plenty of people around: servants and members of the suite, etc.

Olga, Tatiana and Marie had gone to the church and the two eldest had wished to work at the hospital until lunchtime. Anastasia had been unwell but Alexandra had persuaded Dr Botkin to allow the girl to sit out on the balcony.

Alexandra composed a second epistle later explaining that she and the children had returned to the *Church of the Sign* to light a candle for Nicholas's safe return.

On Monday, Olga composed a long letter for Nicholas. (At headquarters that day the Tsar had signed a mandate concerning the change of command. Grand Duke Nicholas would no longer remain as Supreme Commander of the Russian Army – Nicholas would assume command.)

That morning, Olga had attended a service at the cave church and confided that she had been tempted to hug the small children who were receiving Communion. She then went on to the infirmary but there was little to do. She resumed playing croquet and admitted to Nicholas that she had argued and cheated.

Olga explained to Nicholas that day that she had seen Alexei's friend Irina Tolstoy along with Anya and Rita that day. Anya was lunching with Princess Paley (the wife of Grand Duke Paul and also a relative of Anya) and had read poems by Paul's son talented son Vladimir. Alexei had shown his sisters his magic lantern. (It is a slide show contained in a small unit.) Alexei was resting and being read to by his personal tutor Pierre Gilliard. The Tsarina had been relaxing but had suddenly remembered that she had been due to receive Ordin and Apraxin. Olga complained to Nicholas that the piano tuner who was working upstairs in the girl's crimson reception room was irritating her by playing one single key over and over. It was driving her to distraction. (Her nerves had become a problem in recent months. The work at the hospital was proving to be difficult.)

Meanwhile, Alexandra had been to the cathedral that day to attend Mass, accompanied by Marie. Anastasia was still recovering at home. The Tsarina then travelled the short distance to the hospital to sit with some of the wounded men.

On Tuesday, Nicholas wrote from Mogilev in good spirits. He had been met by Grand Duke Nicholas who had smiled cheerily at him but his own brother-in-law Duke Peter of Oldenburg and his aide-de-camp were quite sullen by contrast. (It was not a popular move as all had been happy with the previous appointment. The Grand Duke was a man of great experience and well liked by all the men.)

Meanwhile, back at the Alexander Palace, Alexandra calmly informed Nicholas of Alexei's bad night. His sisters Olga and Tatiana had attempted to keep up his spirits. Luckily, Anastasia had improved enough that day to be able to accompany Alexandra and Marie to the cathedral and to the hospital later. Tatiana put pen to paper to explain to Nicholas that day how she and Olga had sung their brother to sleep the previous night. The Tsarina had not realised that he was awake, but his sisters luckily had decided to check on him. (He slept on the same floor as his sisters but the Tsarina slept on the lower floor.) They sang songs to him including *From Manglisse to Tiflisse*. Tatiana also confided that Anastasia had recovered from her recent bout of illness.

On Wednesday Nicholas noted a change of luck which he took it as a good sign. He was elated. He had received a wire the previous night from General Ivanov concerning the recent success in Galicia. The Germans had lost over 150 officers and 7,000 men as prisoners and thirty (large) guns.

Meanwhile, Alexandra wrote to Nicholas of Alexei's improvement. Pierre Gilliard's room was next to that of his pupil Alexei and he was reading to the boy on a regular basis. Marie and Anastasia enjoyed playing the gramophone in their room despite the fact that their mother's rooms were directly below. (It must have disturbed her if she was having a meeting or a nap.) She added that Olga and Tatiana had gone to town.

Earlier in the day, Olga and Tatiana had returned to the infirmary to carry on with the inevitable dressings. Olga spent part of the morning simply standing around in the corridor chatting to *Mitya* and Tatiana's friend *Volodia*. Olga and Tatiana later travelled to Petrograd (formerly known as St Petersburg) by train with their appointed chaperone for the day. They had tea with the Dowager Empress as usual at the *Elagin Palace*.

Marie had explained to Nicholas that day that she had attended Mass in the company of her mother and youngest sister Anastasia. She was impressed by the sermon which lasted for almost two hours. She and Anastasia then visited their hospital whilst their elder sisters travelled to the capital.

That day Anastasia was sufficiently recovered to write to Nicholas and admitted that she had caused Marie some embarrassment earlier. When the doctor called, both the girls were in bed. Marie hid under the bedclothes but Anastasia had pulled off the cover so that she could be seen. Marie later had her revenge. When the doctor left, she tipped Anastasia out of her bed and onto the floor.

Meanwhile, a progressive bloc was formed that day in which two thirds of the Duma's members and a large percentage of the state council joined together to demand changes. The bloc's programme included local government reform and Jewish rights. The Duma leaders called for a government enjoying what they termed *public confidence*, ie a Prime Minister acceptable to the progressive bloc. He must then be permitted to chose and control his own ministers. (These were not reforms likely to be popular with the Tsar!)

Nicholas sent a brief message home on Thursday. He had decided to move into the Governor's House due to the damp conditions, and no longer lived aboard the train. Later, he explained how the supplies for the war went one way and the people another. He was not impressed how long letters took to reach him either!

Alexandra wrote that day of the continued improvement in Alexei. He was planning to get out of bed and dress for the first time. His arm was still aching but much less than previously. As Olga and Tatiana had arrived back from town later than she had expected, she had gone to the lower church with Marie the previous evening. She was intending to return to the church later that morning accompanied by Anastasia and Alexei. Olga informed Nicholas of a visit by Rasputin's wife and daughters that day to Anya. She appears to have liked him yet did not venerate him in quite the way her sisters Tatiana and Marie did. He always liked to create a good impression in front of the Grand Duchesses and the Tsarina as an ordinary family man by visiting with his wife and children.

That day, Olga had visited the cave church before going on to the hospital along with Tatiana. Olga's close friend Rita was working alongside Tatiana that day. At noon the sisters attended a prayer service with their mother. Olga and Tatiana were later driven to Pavlovsk where they picked bilberries and cranberries. They also visited Princess Tatiana at Strelna. Grand Duke Paul arrived in time for tea.

The Grand Duchesses were always sent a carriage to collect them each time they went out of the palace along with a chaperone. On one occasion, the lady-in-waiting who was supposed to collect the sisters failed to appear but sent the carriage. Olga and Tatiana jumped at the chance of an impromptu trip. They ordered the driver to stop in the *Gostinny Dvor* as they intended to go shopping. They were not recognised on this occasion due to their uniforms but unfortunately neither sister had any money and had little idea of how to go about shopping. The following day, they asked Valentina how it was done. On the rare occasions they had visited shops in the past in Germany, the Crimea and back in the Isle of Wight in 1909, the sisters always had a lady-in-waiting accompanying them who almost certainly purchased the goods. When alone, their courage had failed them.

On Saturday, Nicholas sent a cheery message home. He was still in a positive frame of mind after the recent victory. Olga and Tatiana returned to the infirmary on Sunday morning after Mass. Olga once again stood in the hallway and chatted with *Mitya*. As Valentina Chebotarieva a senior nurse at the hospital remarked at the time, the sisters seemed to go to the hospital at any excuse. The sisters had both found someone of whom they were especially fond and were determined to see as much of them as possible.

The sisters were normally very shy in company due to the restrictions of their upbringing, and this was the one time when they felt free. Alexandra admitted that she felt less shy when appearing in public with her nurse's uniform on; it was the same for the girls. Olga and Tatiana liked wearing their uniforms as for once they looked just like anyone else. Their hair was covered with the style of headdress and this made them even more invisible – or so they thought. The sisters were far too pretty to go unnoticed. Despite their wishes, everyone knew exactly who they were, and their closeness to Vladimir Kiknadze and Dmitri Shakh-Bagov failed to go unnoticed. Madame Chebotarieva, who felt responsible for them as a chaperone, was more and more concerned at the time they were spending at the infirmary and in whose company.

On Monday, Nicholas sent a short message to Alexandra after the appearance of an old and dear friend Count Keller. Alexandra requested that Nicholas pass on a letter to Sablin from Anastasia. She was concerned that Grand Duke Dmitri would think it wrong that the Grand Duchess write to a member of the court. (Anastasia and her siblings saw Dmitri as an older brother or, more accurately, an older half-brother. He did exactly seem to be one of them.)

Olga mentioned *Mitya* once again in her journal that day. She was concerned that he seemed depressed. That day, she had returned to the infirmary once more in the company of Tatiana and they had continued with the endless round of dressings. They returned to the palace for lunch where the Tsarina's friend Sonia appeared. She had her own room in the palace but, like Anya now, was restricted in her movements and was forced to use a wheelchair.

Marie later sent word to Nicholas. The four sisters were relaxing in the evening and each had contrived to find a chair on which to place their aching feet. Olga was knitting stockings for the wounded men and Tatiana was reading some poetry which was unusual as it was usually Olga who read this. (Perhaps she was in a more romantic mood than normal.) Anastasia was sorting out her old correspondence.

Marie went on to explain that, during the afternoon, they had visited the cemetery where the small church was being erected. The graves were those of the wounded soldiers and officers who had died whilst being treated at the two palace hospitals.

On Monday, Nicholas sent a brief telegram admitting he was too busy to write much. The weather was still oppressive and he was desperately hoping for rain. He later found the time to write a long letter to Alexandra admitting that it was her correspondence that kept his spirits up. He had been visited by his brother-in-law Grand Duke Alexander known as *Sandro* and his cousin Grand Duke Kyrill, amongst others. He spent most days working with General Alexeiev.

Alexandra informed Nicholas how Alexei was eager to see his two female friends at Anya's including Rita. Rita and her numerous siblings were friends with the Grand Duchesses. The other girl was Irina Tolstoy who appeared to be a particular favourite of the young boy.

That day, Tatiana had resumed her lessons before joining Olga at the infirmary. Olga was gradually doing less work at the hospital and spending more of her time chatting with the wounded. Along with Rita, the Grand Duchesses later returned to the hospital to help clean the instruments. Olga, Tatiana and Rita later paid a call on Madame Vyrubova where they met up with Alexei and his friend Irina amongst others.

At the beginning of the next month Olga and Tatiana continued with their work at the hospital. They assisted in an operation on a young officer. Later, as Tatiana returned to her studies, Olga went for a quiet ride in the company of Alexandra and Anya. The two youngest sisters Marie and Anastasia were, according to a letter that day by Olga to her father, tormenting Petrov, their Russian teacher.

On Wednesday, Nicholas sent a brief message to Alexandra. He was sent letters by his children most days. The previous day he had received one from Marie and now, today, he had them from Alexei and Anastasia. He would never have had time to reply to them all. He struggled to keep up with the endless letters from the Tsarina as it was.

Meanwhile that day, Olga and Tatiana had returned once again to the infirmary where they continued with the dressings. Olga naturally chose to stand in the corridor with *Mitya* afterwards. The sisters returned for lunch as usual, on this occasion taken on the balcony. Later, Olga and Tatiana accompanied their mother on a visit to the capital where they called in on one of the many hospitals and met up with Elena, an old friend of Olga. The three then travelled to the *Elagin Palace* for tea with the Dowager Empress and her daughter Xenia. Unlike her younger sister Olga, Xenia did not nurse during the war; she had more than enough children and a new grandchild to keep her busy.

Nicholas sent another short message on Thursday after a letter from his daughter Olga and yet another from the Tsarina. He reported the arrival of another of his cousins, the Grand Duke Boris.

That afternoon, Alexandra and her eldest daughters had tea at her Aunt Miechen's with her cousin (and former sister-in-law) Victoria Melita known as *Ducky*, as she informed Nicholas in a letter. She remarked that her cousin was not looking at her best and even went so far as to say that she looked ugly. The two were not close and Alix's cousin had formerly been her sister-in-law before she divorced the Tsarina's brother Ernie some years previously, so the situation was a complicated one to say the least.

Olga and Tatiana had returned to the infirmary late in the day for over an hour in order to clean the instruments along with Varvara, Valentina and Rita. It appears that Olga's friend *Mitya* assisted the ladies, possibly by lifting the items into the cupboards after they had cleaned them.

That day, Marie was unusually interested in a book her Russian teacher was reading to her and Anastasia – as she writes to Nicholas. She generally did not enjoy reading, unlike her sister Olga. The book was entitled *An Icy House*.

Nicholas sent a brief message regarding the Tsarina's sister Elisabeth on Friday. He had arranged for a car to be made available for her but it would take a week.

He later found time to write a long, detailed letter listing some changes and some of his concerns. He had news for Grand Duke Paul. He intended to send the Grand Duke to the armies, but later. George had been transferred from one army to another after coming under enemy fire. He did not intend to give his brother an appointment. He had never been convinced of his younger brother's ability. He enclosed a small note intended for Anya who constantly wrote to him. (Nicholas struggled to keep up with his work and the correspondence from his wife and daughters without this extra added burden.)

Alexandra explained that day by post to Nicholas how her younger daughters were unenthusiastic at the resumption of lessons, yet their brother had wanted more. She encouraged this by extending the length of his lessons by some ten minutes each.

Anastasia informed Nicholas that day of an amusing man she had seen at a concert. She had evidently enjoyed herself thoroughly. She and Marie had attended the concert with an old friend of Nicholas's named Delazari. There were singers, dancers and a comedian who they had seen once before at Anya's whom she found especially amusing.

Nicholas sent a telegram to Alexandra concerning the Minister of the Interior on Saturday. The man had recently made himself an enemy of the Tsarina and, in a complete change of subject, mentioned that he was sad about Tatiana's dog. (Although it is generally assumed that the dog died and was replaced by another, subsequent letters show that Tatiana's dog later gave birth to *ugly puppies* as she described them. The father was possibly Joy who later went to headquarters with Alexei. The Grand Duchesses all had female dogs but their brother naturally had a male dog, one who was known for wandering off on his own.) Oddly, Tatiana's journal appears not to have mentioned the incident (it was Marie who had done so). She attended classes that morning before returning to the infirmary. That day Olga remained at home with her youngest sisters.

In a letter to Nicholas that day, Olga explains that her brother was managing to see his friend Irina Tolstoy every day. Olga also wrote about an unusual gift she had been offered. She was not impressed with it and had no idea what to do with it. Her cousin Kostia had killed a deer and was intending to present the head to Olga. She was less than impressed. She knew that, as a young deer without horns, it was not really *sporting* and wondered what on earth she would do with such a thing.

Later that evening, Alexandra escorted Tatiana to the capital. Olga was not well enough to go on this occasion. They had also called in on Tatiana at Strelna.

On Sunday, Nicholas sent a brief message home with bad news from the front. Vilna had been evacuated. Nicholas showed his frustration with Foreign Secretary Serge Sazonov's treatment of the aged Goremykin. Alexandra asked for him to be removed from his post the next day (Monday). The Tsar later found the time to write a little more fully. He was delighted to see the return of his friend Grand Duke George. The two had spent many happy hours together at Harax in the past. Olga, on the other hand, had spent many hours being bored.

That day, Alexandra mentioned a party she had attended at her friend Anya's house. Madame Vyrubova had clearly invited the Grand Duchesses' young male friends along. The group included Marie's friend Demenkov and old friends Shurik and Yuzik.

Nicholas sent a brief message in reply to Alexandra's continual requests on Tuesday for the removal of ministers. She wanted Stcherbatov removed.

Nicholas wrote to Alexandra on Wednesday concerning his attitude to the ministerial *strike*. He was amazed that they could do such a thing during a war. He also took the opportunity to send a brief letter to Tatiana after receiving a wire from her. Nicholas admitted that he was amused at Ortipo's *scandal* and was fascinated to see what little monster's pups would be.

That same day, Olga and Tatiana returned to the infirmary as usual but, on this occasion, it was Tatiana rather than Olga who dealt with *Mitya's* dressings. It may have been simply because of Tatiana's superior nursing skills, or Olga's increasing disillusion with the work, or for reasons of propriety.

Later, Olga stood in the hallway and chatted to her friend *Mitya*. After lunch, the two sisters were joined by the Tsarina for a trip to the capital. They visited two hospitals including the Vyborg. Olga had a music lesson later and a night committee, yet she contrived to find time to chat to *Mitya* over the telephone at one point in the evening.

In a telegram to his wife on Friday, Nicholas announced the arrival of his brother Michael to general headquarters. The two brothers had seen little of each other until the recent outbreak of war as the Grand Duke had been banished abroad after marrying against the wishes of his brother Nicholas.

On Saturday, Nicholas sent an affectionate letter home. He had been greatly amused by the rumours that the Germans were nearby. It proved to be a false alarm.

Meanwhile, Olga and Tatiana had returned yet again to the hospital to continue the dressings and for Olga to spend precious time with *Mitya*.

Nicholas sent another cheerful message home on Sunday. He was not exactly sure what was happening. He had asked Boris to inform him of the correct number of losses.

Meanwhile his daughter Olga sent word that day. She revealed that her brother delighted in making bonfires in the open whenever he had the opportunity. He had made a fire close to the sisters' beloved tennis court and was baking potatoes there.

The same day Anastasia joked – in a letter to Nicholas – about a mouse they had found in the bedroom. It did not appear to have been frightened off by the continual presence of several dogs in the household or even the three cats (owned by Marie, Olga and Alexei) who were later rescued from the palace kitchens after the family left for Siberia.

Nicholas wrote to thank Alexandra on Monday for her letters. He continued the story of the German patrol. It turned out to be the tail end of their Russian counterparts!

He later wired after hearing of General DS Arseniev's death but seemed more concerned that his precious papers be returned that had been borrowed from his library. (He had been the tutor to the Tsar's cousins Serge and Paul.)

Nicholas sent a brief and encouraging message home after a telegram from Alexandra. He intended to get the better of the ministers who were coming for a conference the next day.

That same day, Marie sent word to Nicholas. She was about to go for a walk with Olga and Anastasia and hoped they would happen to pass Demenkov who was on duty. The previous day she had gone to the nurses' school to play with the little ones and she had felt sorry for one little girl, an orphan who had called one of the nurses *Mama*.

Whilst Marie was composing her letter, Olga was sitting nearby reading a newspaper and catching up on the latest reports. That evening, Olga and Tatiana travelled to Strelna to see Tatiana and her children.

That day, Varvara had demanded to know who had made such a mess in the cloakroom at the infirmary and had damaged some of the clothing. The young Grand Duchess Olga admitted that it had been her after she had seen a distant relative of hers who had, as on previous occasions, grabbed her by the shoulder. It had greatly distressed her. She named the person concerned merely as K.

On Tuesday, Nicholas was positive that the conference had gone his way. He explained that he had made his opinions clear. That day, Olga had written briefly in her journal of the return of a patient to the hospital. Vladimir Kiknadze had returned with a spinal injury. He had recently been injured during a battle at Meyshagola and was eventually awarded with the St George Sabre for his bravery.

Meanwhile, Tatiana composed a letter to Nicholas explaining that she had attended the General's funeral that morning accompanied by the Tsarina. She also revealed that she had seen Ortipo's puppies but she thought them very small and ugly. (They were probably half spaniel.)

Nicholas wrote on Wednesday to explain why he had so little time for letters. The messenger now left before he had the chance to write.

On Thursday, Nicholas telegraphs his thanks for all his recent letters from home. He was in a positive frame of mind as things appeared to be going well. That same day, Tatiana reported to Nicholas that things were progressing much as usual. She was continuing to have lessons and work in the hospital as before.

Nicholas wrote a long and loving letter home the next day. He discussed the merits of the two Khvostovs – uncle and nephew. Alexandra had been impressed by the younger man and he appeared to be suitable for the post of Minister of the Interior. Unfortunately for Alexandra, he later plotted against her friend Rasputin.

Nicholas sent a telegram later in the day asking Alix to arrange a meeting for him with the younger (AA) Khvstov upon his return to the Alexander Palace.

Marie took pen to paper to write to Nicholas that day after playing card games with Alexei. (She was always one of the most amiable of the Grand Duchesses and spent much of time with the Tsarina, although not as much as her sister Tatiana. Recently Tatiana was often absent due to her hospital work commitments.) Alexei played a card game with the odd title *The slower you go the sooner you reach your destination* in the company of his mother, sister Marie and either Gilliard or Dr Derevenko.

Nicholas was in a happy mood when he sent a telegram on Sunday. He had been able to go out boating on the river with members of his suite much to his evident delight.

That day, the Tsar's children attended another party at Anya's according to their mother. She maintained that her children were playing with their friends. They were no doubt chatting with their friends and may have been playing cards or other parlour games at Anya's. The guests on that occasion included Rita Khitrovo and Irina Tolstoy.

Anastasia wrote to Nicholas that day and she explained that she had spent the previous day quietly in the company of her mother and had stayed up late pasting photographs into an album.

On Tuesday the day before he was due to leave general headquarters, Nicholas wrote briefly to Alix with news of his timetable. He had seen his brother-in-law Sandro that day.

Meanwhile, the four sisters visited the infirmary. Marie spent time with Kiknadze. They worked on a puzzle together. He had recently returned to the hospital after being injured again.

Chapter Twelve

Winter 1915

Nicholas sent a telegram to Alix from Pskov after he had arrived there on Thursday morning. For the first time, he had taken his son Alexei back to headquarters with him. The boy was delighted to be accompanying his father. It was a new month and a new beginning for the eleven year-old.

The Tsarevich and his tutor Pierre Gilliard had been photographed at Pskov station on that same day, along with Alexei's dog Joy. It would become famous as the spot where the Tsar abdicated exactly seventeen months later. Gilliard and Gibbes came along to teach the Tsarevich and the boy enjoyed the change of routine. The dogs were now parted so there would be no more unexpected surprises. The timing was probably no coincidence in the light of recent events.

Alexei shared his father's bedroom and each had his own small bed. The boy studied whilst his father worked. Alexei's schoolroom was situated on the second floor and next to the hall, opposite the main stairs of the Governor's House. It was a small room and, when his mother and sisters visited, the ladies were forced to live on the train. Alexei had lunch with Nicholas but generally ate with his tutors in the evening. (Pierre Gilliard and other members of the suite were housed in the former local courthouse.)

Alexandra found it difficult to part with both her husband and her son. She had never been apart from her son for long and it left a huge gap in her life. It was now twice as difficult as before as she was not only missing Nicholas but also her young son.

That evening, she admitted that she found the separation harder than Alexei seemed to. Like any young child, he was overjoyed at what appeared to be an exciting adventure as far as he was concerned and his first time living in the almost exclusively male military headquarters. He felt quite grown-up. She claimed that she and Tatiana had found it very difficult to part with the child.

Olga, however, was more concerned about her friend *Mitya* who was unwell that day. He had a high pulse rate and a slightly raised temperature. He was complaining about pain in his right shoulder.

On Friday, Nicholas sent a telegram from Rejita to Alexandra explaining his delight at seeing the 21st Corps. He and his son were travelling by train to military headquarters.

Tatiana admits to missing her father and brother too in a letter that same day. It was quiet without Alexei's excited presence in the rooms. That morning, she and Olga had again returned to the infirmary to work and the Tsarina had joined them.

Olga spent much of the day sitting with *Mitya*. The four sisters went for a drive later and attended a service at the church attached to the Catherine Palace hospital. The blessed icon of the Virgin of the Sign was brought from the tiny church and paraded around the hospital wards. Princess Gedroitz who had trained the sisters was seriously ill and it was arranged that Dr Derevenko take over her duties temporarily.

According to a letter Marie composed that evening, Olga and Tatiana returned to the infirmary later in order to clean the instruments. They continued to spend a great deal of time at the hospital. It is clear that they were at the hospital more often in the absence of their father.

The following day, Nicholas sent another telegram to Alexandra. The Tsarevich was clearly feeling quite at home in the company of his father. They had arrived at headquarters late the previous evening and had settled in to their new home by Saturday morning.

Anastasia asked Nicholas to inform Alexei of her musical progress that day. She had been learning to play the Russian balalaika – a guitar-like instrument. The sisters were about to go to Anya's for the evening. Rasputin was already there.

Anastasia went on to explain that she and her sister Marie had met Princess Paley (Grand Duke Paul's second wife) and her little daughters that afternoon. The two families rarely met. Although Anastasia claimed that they were little, Irina was almost twelve and her younger sister Natalia was nearly ten. They had also seen Alexei's young friends Alexei and Sergei Derevenko who were greatly missing his company.

Nicholas sent a note to Alexandra concerning their son's progress. He was fitting into the routine of the military headquarters quite satisfactorily. They had attended a small review, and had a *Te Deum* and were intending to attend church together that evening.

The same day General John Hanbury-Williams recalled how he had been asked to present a gift to the young Tsarevich. The boy was presented with an album of photographs which had been prepared by *The Times* newspaper for him.

Meanwhile, back at Tsarskoe Selo, the Tsarina and her four daughters had attended the consecration service for the small church attached to the military cemetery. That afternoon, the Tsarina returned to the hospital where Dr Derevenko, who had taken over from Dr Gedroitz temporarily, performed an operation.

After the ceremony, Olga and Tatiana returned to their hospital to attend to the dressings and Olga once again sat with *Mitya*. The Tsarina's close friends Anya Vyrubova and Lili Dehn arrived for dinner. As the ladies sat together chatting and talking of Alexei, Olga and Tatiana slipped out to the infirmary to clean the instruments. They were accompanied by Varvara (*Bibi*) and *Mitya* and the recovering Kiknadze. The men helped put the heavier instruments away in the cupboards for them.

Tatiana had written to Alexei that day and asked how comfortable it was to sleep in one room with his father. She also explained that she seemed to spend all day rolling bandages. She sent her best wishes to Gilliard and Nagorny and stated that her dog Ortipo was well. (Alexei had taken his dog with him.)

On Monday, Nicholas thanked Alexandra for Alexei's gifts, one of which hardly seemed suitable. It seems rather odd to give a knife to a haemophiliac and even stranger that he should have been allowed to take it to bed with him. The gifts had been taken by Derevenko and kept until the previous evening, which was of course Alexei's name's day.

Meanwhile, back at the Alexander Palace, the routine of Alexandra and her daughters continued much the same without Alexei. Unfortunately it was inevitable that some of the young wounded soldiers in their care would die and that they would feel obliged to attend the funeral services with the families of the men often unable to travel to the ceremony in time across the vast country. She had just attended a funeral for one young boy, and another one had died in the night at Marie and Anastasia's hospital.

Nicholas sent a telegram on Tuesday after a message had arrived from Rasputin. He had undoubtedly remembered Alexei's name's day too.

He later composed a long overdue letter with details of his son's new routine. Alexei had been eager to be allowed to sit at the table with the others. Nicholas explained that Alexei was the life and soul of the place. He added that the boy said his prayers far too quickly but that he had behaved impeccably during a review.

Nicholas insisted that Alexei and his tutor Gibbes (or Gilliard) sit with him in his room whilst he worked. Gibbes explained that once Alexei had retired to bed the Tsar came in order to say his prayers with the boy. The tutor and the Tsarevich were sometimes forced to amuse themselves quietly when the Tsar was busy.

Alexei's English tutor Gibbes moved to the Hotel France at Mogilev and, each day, walked up the hill to the Governor's House to teach the Tsarevich.

The young Tsarevich enjoyed the new all-male environment, as Gibbes later recalled. It was a great change as he was used to being in a mainly female environment with his mother, four sisters and the ladies-in-waiting at the Alexander Palace. Most of the men had either joined the military services or were away with Nicholas at headquarters by now.

Nicholas made time to write another letter to Alexandra on Wednesday. He was delighted to report that his son had already lost his shyness and was enjoying himself at headquarters. Nicholas's cousin George invariably sat beside Alexei and the boy enjoyed teasing his uncle.

Meanwhile, Olga Nicolaevna still had her friend on her mind. She was still spending her free time with her friend Dmitri. She had been present during an operation earlier in the morning, along with Tatiana of course. She and Tatiana returned to the infirmary that evening to help clean the instruments once more.

Marie explained in a letter that day to her father that she and Anastasia had been rolling bandages at the warehouse. That afternoon, they had travelled to the capital with their mother and had met Countess Hendrikova, the mother of Alexandra's lady-in-waiting. Olga and Tatiana later joined the party in town and they went on together to the Noblemen's Assembly. They had tea on the train.

Tatiana wrote briefly to her brother that day and showed how tactless she could be by informing the Russian tutor that Alexei's letters were better when he did not help him with them. She asked if he was able to play with his friend Kolya (the son of Dr Derevenko) and asked after his dog Joy. She stated that her dog Ortipo greeted him and

Nagorny. She also explained that she had not seen *his* Irina Tolstoy as she had gone to Petrograd. Rita, she explained, was working alongside her and Olga at the infirmary.

Gilliard later recalled how the Tsarina and her daughters spent an evening without the Tsar and Alexei at the Alexander Palace. They wanted to know what he was doing. Alexei was the chief subject of conversation.

The next day, Nicholas sent a brief message to Alexandra with good news. He was too busy for a letter but nonetheless reported that the attack on Baranovitchi the previous day had been successful and they had taken many prisoners.

Alexandra was concerned that her son would injure himself by doing too much. In a letter to Nicholas that day, she urged him to prevent the boy digging too energetically in the sand.

Anastasia noticed the cold that day, as she mentions to Nicholas. (The bedrooms had a form of double glazing that could be put in or out depending upon the weather. Unlike the Tsarina her daughters often complained of feeling cold.)

Nicholas sent another telegram on Friday after post arrived from Alexandra. He had received a letter from his cousin King George V. He had dined with Admiral Sir Richard Fortescue Phillimore that day and it had been he who had brought the letter.

The Tsar had time to write later in the day. It was a constant struggle to manage to compose a letter before the courier left. He left in the early afternoon and this made it difficult for Nicholas to finish in time for the post.

Meanwhile, Alexandra continued to fuss over her son. She repeated that he not be allowed to hurt his arm. She had decided that Marie and Anastasia should be allowed to come on her next visit to headquarters but did not intend to tell the two until Monday. It would be a surprise for them and they would be delighted.

On the same day in an extraordinarily frank letter, Olga admits her bullying ways and rudeness to her father and shows no sense of shame or regret. She and Anastasia locked Mlle Schneider's servant girl in the bathroom and had no intention of letting her out at the moment.

She was sitting near to Gilliard's rooms (next to where Alexei slept) near to the door of his bathroom. She and Anastasia had locked Katya in the room after they dragged her along the dark passage and pushed her in. Olga went on to talk about the weather and the drive the sisters had with Baroness Buxhoeveden earlier. She then says how everyone loves Alexei's letters but ends by stating that she and Anastasia were determined not to let Katya out despite the girl's persistent knocking and crying.

The following day, Nicholas confirmed the date of Alexandra's visit. Thursday would be convenient for him. He also explained that the Grand Duke Paul was too ill to move. (He later died of cancer.)

That day Alexei admitted in his journal to playing tricks on his fellow soldiers. He enjoyed teasing the military attachés stationed at headquarters. (Alexei enjoyed listening to his father's conversations with the officers and ordinary soldiers alike but still preferred to play games with them when possible.)

Meanwhile, Alexandra explained to Nicholas that she and her daughters were about to visit the capital. They were to be present at the opening of a hospital within the Winter Palace itself. She would also be joined by her mother-in-law amongst others. They met up with various old friends including Tatiana's friend Olga Voronova.

That day Tatiana and Olga had a busy day visiting the Winter Palace and working at the hospital. Later Anastasia played the balalaika and Marie the piano as their elder sisters attempted to relax.

Whilst travelling on Sunday Nicholas sent a message to Alexandra to reassure her that all was well.

On Monday, he sent Alexandra another message and assured her that they would soon be reunited. Nicholas and Alexei had visited the hospital at Klevan and the Tsarevich was later awarded the medal of St George, 4th degree, for being close to enemy lines.

Nicholas sent a cheerful message home from Kiev later. He and his son had spent an enjoyable day amongst the troops and he was looking forward to meeting Alexandra and his daughters the next day.

The Tsarina and her four excited daughters arrived at military headquarters for their first visit early on Thursday morning and were met at the station by Nicholas, Alexei and Dmitri. The ladies insisted on visiting the Governor's House to see the living accommodation of Nicholas and his son. The five children then visited a nearby hospital accompanied by the Tsarina. Afterwards they went for a drive and looked over an ambulance train.

General Hanbury-Williams met the Tsarina for the first time at headquarters on Friday. They spoke about Britain, a place where she had spent many happy visits to her late grandmother Queen Victoria. The general sat next to her at dinner that evening.

That day, the Tsarina and her daughters had remained on the train until noon as there was not enough room for them at the house. They later travelled to the nearby village of St Paul before lunch. Nicholas and Alexandra sat alone quietly that evening and chatted whilst their daughters sat together in another room. The conditions were very cramped and the unfortunate ladies-in-waiting were forced to get dressed amongst the cupboards aboard the train.

On Saturday morning, Nicholas rose late and read the papers. He then took Alexei to the reports whilst the Tsarina and her daughters were confined on the train. The family attended church afterwards but Olga chose to remain on the train as she had a headache. They then went for a ride on the train. The ladies left soon after.

Nicholas and his young son left headquarters for a tour of inspection later. Meanwhile, back at Tsarskoe Selo that same day, his daughter Olga candidly admitted in her journal how she sat with her friend *Mitya* whilst Tatiana sat with her friend *Volodia* on hospital beds. It may seem fairly innocent today but it would have not been seen as such by the Tsarina had she known.

Olga noted how she had sat on a bed belonging to another soldier with *Mitya* on Sunday whilst Tatiana had sat on another with *Volodia*.

Tatiana was clearly not quite as shy as she is generally believed to be. Lili Dehn had seen that Tatiana's shyness soon disappeared when she was in congenial company. Once one knew her, the shyness vanished.

By Monday morning, Valentina was becoming greatly concerned about Olga.

The Grand Duchess had become very thin and nervous. (She undoubtedly was struggling inwardly over her feelings for *Mitya* and had found it impossible to come to terms with the sight of the horrific wounds she had seen in the operating theatre.)

Meanwhile Gilliard later recalled the Tsarevich's first visit to the front. General Ivanov had joined the train at Berditchev and General Broussilov at Rovno. The Tsar and Alexei inspected the troops and then paid a surprise visit to a dressing station after nightfall. The tiny building was lit by torches and the wounded soldiers could scarcely believe their eyes at the visitors. Gilliard remembered that Alexei was extremely moved by the sight.

On Tuesday evening, Olga chatted on the telephone with *Mitya* again.

Meanwhile, back at the Governor's House at Mogilev, Nicholas felt secure yet was isolated. He no longer read the newspapers or saw newsreels of the war and preferred to get up late to read his homely letters from Alix. He then took a walk in the afternoons and later played cards or dominoes with his son. They sometimes watched American movies in the evenings.

During the long evenings at the Alexander Palace, Alexandra lay on her couch listening to Olga play the piano or the other children reading aloud or playing cards or puzzles.

Tatiana sold a necklace that had been given to her by the Tsar on her eighteenth birthday and gave the cash to the relief fund. Tatiana was at home less than usual and Marie temporarily accompanied her mother. Tatiana had something else on her mind, or rather someone else. She was still spending as much time as possible with Vladimir whilst not on duty at the hospital.

On Friday Tatiana noted in her journal how she was spending time with the handsome *Volodia*. After her work, she sat with Olga's friend *Mitya* and played draughts with him in the hospital dining room. She then played ping-pong (little tennis) with *Volodia*. Afterwards she joined her friend in a card game with two of the other men, Opochkovitch and Gubarev.

Olga and Tatiana attended the liturgy on Sunday morning and were delighted to see Vladimir Kiknadze and also Dmitri Shakh-Bagov. As usual, the sisters returned home for lunch at the Alexander Palace.

Tatiana saw *Volodia* again on Monday at the infirmary. The two played checkers and afterwards sat together in the hospital corridor. As Olga felt unable to continue at the hospital she was replaced temporarily by her mother. It was an opportunity for Alexandra to see Tatiana in the company of Kiknadze for once. After dinner, Tatiana and her sister Olga chatted to their friends *Volodia* and *Mitya* over the telephone.

It was decided at this time that Olga was anaemic and in need of treatment. She returned to the infirmary only briefly each day in order to have a series of daily arsenic injections. It was a treatment for depression but one that was extremely dangerous. It is the same thing that over some years had almost certainly had killed the American author Louisa May Alcott in 1888. She too was one of four sisters.

A very good reason why Olga's nerves would have been shattered at this time was *Mitya*. In 1913, she had fallen in love with Paul Voronov and he had effectively been taken away from her and now, for the second time, she had fallen in love. She was naturally concerned that the same thing would happen again, that *Mitya* would suddenly marry someone else, but she would also have been extremely worried that he would die in the war as soldiers often did.

On his arrival at the port of Reval on Wednesday, Nicholas sent a hasty message to Alexandra. He had been impressed with the troops whom he had seen along the way.

That day, Alexandra had had visitors for lunch from the hospital in Petrograd including British aristocrat Lady Sibyl Grey, British Conservative politician Sir Ian Malcolm and Baroness Buxhoeveden. (Sir Ian's wife was Jeanne, the daughter of the famous actress Lili Langtry.) The Grand Duchesses Olga and Tatiana met this young British aristocrat on several occasions and were impressed by her dedication to nursing. The lady had gone to Petrograd in order to set up a hospital in Dmitri's palace.

Nicholas telegraphed Alexandra on Thursday from Venden after the rare treat of seeing British submarines. He later sent a note from Orsha after inspecting troops and hearing shooting in the distance. The Tsar sent a hurried note to Alexandra on Friday. The trip had been successful but the train had left rather late. Alexei had enjoyed accompanying his father on the visits. Alexandra was fascinated to know how her son reacted to the sound of gunfire. She was pleased that Nicholas was now free to travel about where and when he wanted – now he was in charge of the armies.

Meanwhile, that day, Tatiana continued her close friendship with Vladimir. She and Olga were enjoying life as ordinary young women for once without the usual restrictions of court life. Tatiana sat with *Volodia* and later her sister Olga arrived to join her. In the evening again the sisters chatted over the phone to their friends at the infirmary.

On his return to headquarters on Saturday, Nicholas found the time to compose a long letter to Alexandra. He spoke of his delight at seeing the British submarines at close quarters. Alexei had enjoyed climbing in them and the boy had asked many intelligent questions.

Olga was suffering from overwork at the hospital as the Tsarina confirms that day. The Grand Duchess had only risen that day for a drive out and spent most of the day on the sofa resting as Alexandra had done for years. The Tsarina explained to Nicholas that the arsenic injections that Olga was having every day would work better if she rested. (The injections were given at that time for depression or low spirits. They would not be used now for this. An X-ray would have showed the injection points up had anyone had the idea of checking for such marks on Olga's body as a form of identification after her death. Sadly, the body would have probably decomposed too much by the time it was found in 1979.)

That same day Marie sent word to her father whilst sitting in her bedroom. Her sisters were still sitting with their mother downstairs. She and Anastasia had visited their hospital that afternoon where they had been photographed with the men.

Nicholas sent a brief message home. Alexandra had asked him what was going on in Greece and Rumania. He had heard nothing about Rumania but had his concerns about Greece. He also explained that Alexei had hurt his arm but attempted to play it down, however, as it would have worried Alexandra.

Alexandra was delighted with her son's first letter home. Gilliard was also keeping her informed of her son's progress. The letters from her son were at times as comic as Anastasia's. Gibbes recalled Alexei at Stavka and how he had attempted to take home a valuable souvenir. However, Nicholas was not impressed. The boy intended to take home a big cut-glass ball that hung inside an electric chandelier. Nicholas shouted that it did not belong to him.

Anastasia had written to Nicholas that day about the concert she had attended at the Palace hospital. They had seen the Tolstoys and many other friends. Marie was currently playing records on her gramophone player whilst Olga was attempting to rest nearby. Marie joined Tatiana on a trip to the capital in place of her sister Olga that day, she added.

Nicholas found the time to compose a long, loving letter on Monday. He explained that Alexei had hurt his arm whilst playing the fool and pretending to fall from a chair and was suffering as a result. Nicholas sympathised with Alexandra who was once again complaining that her heart was enlarged.

That evening, Nicholas had a long chat with General Hanbury-Williams and spoke of his former English tutor Mr Heath who had taught him how to fly-fish some years previously.

Nicholas admitted in his journal that night how he had attempted to cover up Alexei's injury. The Imperial couple did not want everyone to know that the child was frequently ill.

Meanwhile, Alexandra congratulated Nicholas on the occasion of Olga's twentieth birthday. Olga's health was improving after she had rested indoors more often. The injections appeared to be working.

Olga thanked her father for a birthday gift. She had been given a piece of furniture for her room: a new couch. Most of her presents had been given to her in her bedroom. There had been a special *Te Deum* held at 12.30 in the Tsarina's Maple Room. Whilst Olga rested at home, Tatiana returned to the hospital once more.

Tatiana informed Nicholas that day how badly Marie had reacted to the formalities of committee meetings in town. She had been overwhelmed by the attention in public. When Marie was formally presented to the committee, she was so terrified she almost dived under the table.

Nicholas found time on Wednesday for a long letter. He was worried about the Tsarina. He too had arranged a *Te Deum* in honour of Olga the previous day.

Tatiana wondered how Nicholas had enjoyed his film show that Alexei had mentioned in a recent letter. She wanted to know where the film was actually shown. Was it in the hall or the dining room? That day, she had returned to the infirmary without her sisters. Luckily there were few dressings to be done. It had snowed heavily overnight but unfortunately it was too soft to be able to sledge as yet.

A rather bored Anastasia wrote to Nicholas. She could not understand why the Tsarina wanted the bedroom back to normal; she and Marie were happy with their beds in the middle of the room. She wrote whilst sitting on the toilet (water closet) listening to the gramophone in the distance.

Nicholas sent a brief telegram on Thursday before he left for the south. He would be seeing Khvostov before a letter from Alexandra arrived. Khvostov wanted the Tsarina to prepare Nicholas on several questions before the two met.

That day, Alexandra had an idea of selling her son's photograph as a postcard. Alexei had thought that a recent film of him was so bad that it made his dog look intelligent. In the film, he twirls around with his stick in the manner of Charlie Chaplin.

Marie complained to her father that day that she rarely saw her friend. She was only able to see him in church which was too public for the Grand Duchess. She had little chance for a private chat to him. The Grand Duchesses spent the evening upstairs in order to keep Olga company as she recovered her health. Marie was writing to Nicholas from the comfort of her shared bedroom. Lisa Ersberg, the sisters' former nurse, was lighting the lights next to the icons whilst she wrote and Olga was also writing in her room next door.

The sisters were intending to pay a call on Anya later that evening. Rasputin was also expected to be there. Marie suddenly overheard Olga in the next room. She was distressed when she managed to spill the ink out of her pot and got it all over her hands. It had annoyed her so much that she decided not to continue writing that evening. In the days before cheap all-in-one pens comprising of the ink already in the pen, letter writing could be a complex and often messy business.

An overjoyed Nicholas sent a message to Alexandra from Odessa on Saturday. He had clearly enjoyed the tour despite the cold weather.

That morning, the younger children had returned to their lessons whilst Olga rested as much as she could. She did briefly return to the infirmary but was convinced the daily arsenic injections were making her smell of garlic. That evening, Tatiana, Marie and Anastasia attended a funeral service of one of the young officers from the Catherine Palace hospital. They had dined early that evening because of the late start of the funeral.

The following day, Tatiana wrote to Nicholas and claimed she was keeping her mother company whilst he was away. She explained that the sisters normally dined with her in the playroom. That day, Emma Fredericks and Nini (Eugenia) Voyeikova had arrived for tea. (The family of Count Fredericks were well loved by the Tsarina and they proved to be loyal friends when such were needed in 1917. The Count and his wife had two daughters; one married Voyeikov, a member of the Tsar's household and bizarrely Alexei's mathematics teacher, and the other daughter was unmarried.) Tatiana also added, especially for Alexei, that she had seen Irina Tolstoy in church. Olga, she explained, had returned to the infirmary but was not actually working.

Nicholas sent another telegram to Alexandra on Monday after visiting Reni with his son. He was delighted to meet up again with his old friend Admiral Vesselkin.

Alexandra attended another funeral service that day, this time with Tatiana. General FV Dubrail Echappar was formerly an officer in the Tsarina's Own Uhlan Life Guards.

On Tuesday Nicholas informed Alix how he had met some old friends in Balta. He had an excellent memory and would have frequently seen people that he recognised.

Olga, meanwhile, tells Nicholas her news. It was Anastasia's turn to play the piano. They had just had tea in the company of old friends Anya and Lili. Tatiana was having a history lesson and Marie was reading a letter from Nicholas's brother-in-law Sandro.

Nicholas was greatly enjoying his tour of inspection and enthuses in a note to Alexandra on Wednesday. He would be leaving for headquarters the following evening.

Meanwhile, Alexandra had an awkward meeting that day, so used her daughters Olga and Anastasia as a protective shield. The Tsarina did not like Orlov and had no intention of discussing his recent dismissal. She later admitted to Nicholas that Olga was beginning to look better. Tatiana and Marie had gone to town that day. Olga was replaced by the eternally shy Marie once more.

On his return to headquarters on Thursday, Nicholas sent a hasty message home. He arrived to find a great pile of letters from his family. Later on, Nicholas found time to write to Alexandra at length. The Tsarevich had made quite an impression during the visit to the south. The locals had continually cheered him as he approached.

The same day, Alexandra admits her fears for the future of her unmarried daughter Olga. She hoped that her daughters would be as happy as she was. (Her daughters never married.)

Nicholas sent an affectionate message home on Friday, the eve of their twenty-first wedding anniversary.

That day, Alexandra wrote in remembrance of her mother-in-law's birthday. Nicholas and Alexandra had married on the birthday of the recently widowed Dowager Empress. They had chosen this day as court mourning was temporarily abandoned for the birthday of the Empress Marie. The day was also later chosen as the day of Olga's baptism in 1895.

Olga wrote unusually lovingly to her mother. She had been spending more time than usual in her mother's company due to her recent illness.

Marie sent a letter to Nicholas to congratulate Nicholas on his wedding anniversary and on his mother's birthday. She explained that she, Tatiana and Anastasia had had tea with the Dowager Empress the previous day and would return to her the following day, Saturday. Anastasia was sitting near to her reading as she wrote. Marie again complained that she had been unable to see her friend Nicholas Demenkov for some two weeks. (It felt like a whole lifetime to the sixteen year-old.)

On the following day, Nicholas thanked Alexandra for the anniversary gift of a small picture frame. She added that was not an easy matter to obtain and deliver gifts during wartime.

That day, Alexandra informs Nicholas how she had arranged with Anya for her children's friends to be present at a small gathering at Anya's. She obviously knew of Olga and Tatiana's close friendship with Shakh-Bagov and Kiknadze and Marie's friendship with Demenkov, but she did not seem overly concerned. She thought they would appreciate seeing their friends as they had not been to the hospital that day. She also invited Rita.

That morning, Tatiana, Marie and Anastasia had attended church in the company of their chaperone for the occasion, Madame Narishkin (*Madame Zizi* as she was known). The Tsarina, Olga and the remainder of the household had a *Te Deum* in the Maple Room once more.

Olga informed Nicholas that her younger sisters have gone to visit the Dowager Empress for a birthday visit. She was having a lie-in.

On Monday, Nicholas wrote a brief but affectionate message to Alix. He was looking forward to returning home and was counting the hours until they were reunited. Nicholas and his son returned shortly after.

That day, Tatiana wrote to her father of Anya's party. She had evidently enjoyed spending time with her friend Vladimir in the informal surroundings of Madame Vyrubova's small house a few days previously. She casually mentioned Dmitri Shakh-Bagov of the Erivansky Regiment and Vladimir Kiknadze of the Tsar's Strelak of the 3rd regiment. She added that Olga's friend *big* Rita was also amongst the guests. (The young lady was tall rather than fat.)

She was more forthcoming in her journal that evening. She had spent much of the day with *Volodia*. She sat with *Volodia* and *Mitya* before Olga arrived at the infirmary. She played the piano with Vladimir, and the two sat close together in the early afternoon. She spoke on the telephone later to *Mitya*.

Tatiana details an evening spent with Olga, Volodia and Mitya on Wednesday. The four seemed to be constantly together. Tatiana chatted on the telephone with her friend after she had arrived back at the palace.

The following evening, Tatiana again spent time with *Volodia* and Olga with *Mitya*. The sisters were spending a great deal of time with their friends. Thursday had begun like any other weekday for Tatiana with lessons. She had returned to the infirmary straight after where she had spent some time sitting with *Volodia* and *Mitya*. She returned to the palace for lunch and helped the recently returned Alexei prepare his lessons. She later spoke to her friend again over the telephone.

Before he left home once more, Nicholas wrote a letter to leave behind at the palace for Alexandra. He was concerned that she should not overtire herself. Earlier on Tuesday, Nicholas had attended a reception along with the French Ambassador.

On Wednesday, Nicholas telegraphed briefly on arrival at headquarters. He had once more taken his young son to the military headquarters with him. On this occasion, however, Alexei had left his dog Joy at home in the care of his mother and sisters.

Nicholas later found time for a letter on Thursday and he admitted that he and Alexei were missing Alexandra and the Grand Duchesses.

That day, Alexandra had explained in a letter to Nicholas that she had gone to church that day accompanied by Olga, but that her daughter left for the infirmary straight after whilst she returned home. She sent for Joy as he had been missing Alexei so much. He fell asleep at her feet.

In a letter that same day, Tatiana explains her annoyance at onlookers being moved away from her path by the secret service men. The previous day she had gone for a walk with Baroness Buxhoeveden towards Pavlovsk but had been angered when the people had been moved out of her way.

On the following day, Nicholas sent a brief message. Nicholas Sablin had left for a new post elsewhere. He had decided to join the army.

Unusually the day before, Alexandra had gone sledging with her daughter. It was extremely rare that the Tsarina joined in the wild games of her children. She explained in a letter to Nicholas on the Thursday that her room had felt so stifling that she had gone out in the fresh air.

That evening, Anya had dined with the family and all *worked* whilst singing religious hymns. Olga accompanied them on the piano. Olga returned to the infirmary on Friday morning and Alexandra returned to the palace to continue with her correspondence.

That day, Valentina Chebotarieva noted in her journal that Olga and Tatiana had arrived at the infirmary at nine that evening to clean the instruments. Kiknadze had sat near Tatiana on the stairs. The sisters were in a good mood, she noted, as Alexandra had given the order that Kiknadze be allowed to remain at the infirmary as an orderly.

Nicholas managed to find the time for another letter on Saturday. He asked Alexandra to send seventy more tiny icons for members of the Kouban Sotnia who were about to leave for the front. Voyeikov had just arrived with a plan of the proposed tour.

In a candid letter to Nicholas on that day, Marie admits how she and her younger sister played wild games in their classroom. The two youngest Grand Duchesses were often involved in wild games along with Olga, although the more sedate Tatiana did not take part in such games. Marie explains how she and Anastasia had been playing tennis in their classroom. They threw the ball against the wall and knocked a few things over; luckily nothing broke.

That day, the Tsar's young cousin Grand Duchess Marie Pavlovna arrived for tea at Tsarskoe Selo. The youngest Grand Duchess was rather fascinated by her short hair. As Tatiana's hair had been the same length the previous year, it should not have been such a shock to Anastasia. In a few years' time, it would become the fashion.

The next day, there was a party at Anya's, according to Alexandra on Sunday evening. Once more, the Grand Duchesses met up with friends at Madame Vyrubova's. Amongst the friends that night were Nicholas Demenkov, Boris Ravtopolo, Shurik, Alexander Shvedov and Victor Zborovsky. That day, Anastasia wrote of meeting Victor at Mass. As he was at the parties so often, it seems likely that he was a special friend of the youngest Grand Duchess. In letters to her father Anastasia had even admitted that she envied Nicholas when he was near Victor.

Later, Alexandra wrote that she and her four daughters had spent the evening with two officers. It was not normally done to take tea just with officers and without the Tsar being present. The men in question were Navruzov and Chavtchavadze. Later, she and the Grand Duchesses attended a Requiem Mass.

On Monday morning, Nicholas had more time to compose a long letter home to Alexandra. He spoke of conversations he had recently had with Khvostov and of the comings and goings at headquarters.

Alexandra wrote that day of her concerns for her friend Sonia who had been ill for many years. Sonia had been confined to a wheelchair with a spine-wasting disease and had her own rooms within the Alexander Palace. She had urged Dr Derevenko to see to her.

Later that same day Nicholas sent a telegram to Alix expressing his shock after hearing of Sonia's sudden death.

Marie and her sisters were predictably in a quiet mood that day. Alexandra was in a state of shock after the sudden death of her friend. Marie sat on the floor, as she often did, in her mother's room. Alexandra was lying on the sofa. Anya had made a successful bid for Nicholas's chair and the other sisters were sitting on chairs, attempting to *work*.

According to Baroness Buxhoeveden, Sonia had died in the arms of the Tsarina. She was with Sonia until the end as she had promised to do some years earlier.

The Baroness also felt that, had she lived, Sonia might have been a good influence on Alexandra and possibly even prevented some of the disasters in later years. She had been determined to carry on despite her illness and even attended parties in her wheelchair. Her honesty was something that Alexandra missed in later years and her common sense. She was actually the niece of a former Liberal Prime Minister and had great intellect.

The next day, Alexandra informed Nicholas of Sonia's final day. She was shocked at the speed of events. The aunt of Sonia had told Alexandra to rest for a while at 4.15 but at 5.10 she was called back as Sonia lay dying. The Dowager Empress was intending to go to the funeral service but, that evening, Olga and Tatiana went to town in order to collect donations and attend a committee meeting.

When Sonia died in the Tsarskoe Selo where Alix was tending wounded soldiers, Alexandra refused to change into black mourning clothes and went directly to the memorial service in her nurse's uniform. She, along with Olga and Tatiana, attended the service in their nurses' uniforms.

That day, officers of the Combined Regiment carried Sonia from her room in the Alexander Palace to the church. Alexandra drove behind the coffin accompanied by Olga and Anastasia whilst Tatiana and Marie walked on foot.

Nicholas wired that Alexei had a cold on Thursday but did not appear worried. He was taking the precaution of keeping him indoors. Alexei's condition worsened later in the day as Nicholas explained in a wire. His nose refused to stop bleeding and Nicholas decided to return to Stavka on the advice of Dr Feodorov.

That morning, Alexandra attended Holy Communion and prayed for Sonia. She wrote to Nicholas from Tsarskoe Selo that day of her visit. She had been accompanied to church by her eldest daughter Olga and Anya Vyrubova.

Nicholas became concerned for his son's health during the train journey but did not inform Alix of his concerns – as he confided in his journal that evening. Alexei had started a cold the previous day and that morning had a slight nose bleed and was sneezing.

That day, Anastasia sat with Marie in *Orchie's room*. The Tsarina's former nanny had died several years previously in England but her room was still known as *Orchie's*. The sisters had removed to her room after Anastasia had managed to fall on the floor when a chair broke. Luckily she was uninjured.

The following day (Friday), Nicholas was still concerned about Alexei although he was beginning to show signs of improvement. The bleeding had slowed down. They arrived at headquarters at 12.15. Later in the day, Nicholas finally admitted his concerns to Alexandra yet tried to reassure her. He had nevertheless decided that it would be best to return home. The boy's temperature had risen again. He was intending to leave at

3pm and would arrive home late in the morning on the following day.

On Saturday, he sent another wire later on with some reassurance for Alexandra that the boy was holding his own. The temperature was now more or less normal and he was eating well. That evening, Nicholas again wired Alexandra with more news. He stated that Alexei himself was surprised that they were returning home but thought it best that no one be allowed to see the boy on his return to the station.

That day, Sonia was buried.

Meanwhile, a friend of the Grand Duchesses, Valentina Chebotoarieva, detailed some remarkable events concerning the Grand Duchesses Olga and Tatiana. She was deeply concerned about the reputations of both Olga and Tatiana. She feared the situation would get out of hand. She observed that, as soon as Tatiana had finished her work for the day, she and Olga went straightaway to sit with Kiknadze. He sat at the piano at the infirmary and played the instrument with one finger, all the time talking in a low voice to Tatiana. Shakh-Bagov was running a temperature and Olga had sat for quite some considerable time at his bedside.

Valentina's colleague Varvara (*Bibi*) was horrified and greatly feared that Madame Narishkin (*Zizi*) would find out the truth of how much time Olga and Tatiana were spending in the company of their two friends. Olga was spending all day sitting on *Mitya's* bed. The previous day they had looked through photograph albums together.

She noted how Tatiana looked red-faced and excited when in the company of Kiknadze whilst he attempted to remain cool. She knew that others were becoming jealous of their constant attention towards the two patients. Valentina was worried that rumours were spreading in town. Luckily, she noted (Princess) Vera Ignatievna (Gedroitz) had an idea to send Kiknadze to the Crimea, out of the way. Vera had also heard that, when he was drunk once, *Mitya* had shown Olga's letters to fellow soldiers.

Meanwhile, on Thursday morning, Alexei's condition was more alarming as Nicholas detailed in his journal. The boy was taken up to his room immediately on arrival home and the doctors decided to cauterise the wound. Tsar spent the afternoon with his two younger daughters Marie and Anastasia but Olga and Tatiana returned to the hospital where they probably saw their friends!

Nicholas was able to spend his name's day at home. Alexei's condition slowly improved after a second cauterisation. That afternoon Nicholas went for a walk with Tatiana, Marie and Anastasia. That evening Olga and Tatiana were torn between returning to the infirmary and sitting with their seriously ill brother; it is more than likely they chose the latter.

Nicholas soon after returned to Mogilev on the 14th – without his son. The Tsar sent a telegram from Kiev after meeting up with his sisters Olga and Xenia that day. He was reassured that his son was improving.

Tatiana's dog was evidently missing the Grand Duchess whilst she was working and decided to spend the day with the Tsarina, as Alexandra notes in a letter to Nicholas that day. Ortipo had jumped up on her bed in the absence of Tatiana who had naturally returned to the hospital. Anastasia had gone to the dentist's.

Nicholas stopped briefly in Podvolochisk on Tuesday but could not get his son out of his thoughts. He recalled him in every place he went. The following day (Wednesday), he wrote enthusiastically from Bakhmach after the reviews of the previous day. He was comforted by the news that Alexei was continuing to improve.

That day, Alexandra spoke with pride about her son and went on to explain that she had been fitted with a false tooth. She made Alexei tell her sister Elisabeth the previous evening all about his recent trip. Alexei was writing a letter to Nicholas and Petrov was assisting. Joy was asleep happily by the side of his young master.

On Thursday, Nicholas wrote in great detail of his successful visit to the troops. Once more, he showed his great joy when inspecting the troops. He was at his happiest with them. He clearly took comfort in army life.

Alexandra wrote of her son that day. He had to be careful what he ate as the cold had gone to his stomach. He was hoping to be able to be up and dressed by the following day.

Olga joked about her Aunt Ella's visit in a letter to Nicholas. Elisabeth was falling asleep whilst attempting to crochet. She was sitting in Nicholas's chair and kept dropping off. Alexei was amusing himself by knitting a scarf for Dr Derevenko's wife, presumably for Christmas. Marie was on the floor (again) putting postcards into an album.

Marie complains of the cold (probably the cold floor) in her letter to Nicholas that same day. She explained that she and her sisters played cards upstairs with Alexei in his playroom but as yet they had not argued which indicates they often did.

Nicholas wired home on Friday from headquarters. It was already the 30th of December in the rest of Europe. Russia's calendar was still thirteen days behind as it had never been changed, unlike that of Britain.

He later wrote in more detail of his plans. He hoped to be home for the Russian Christmas holidays. Nicholas later telegraphed again with good news. To his delight, King George V had promoted him to the rank of Field-Marshall in the British army.

Alexei wrote briefly to Nicholas and wanted to know if Papa would be home for Christmas. (He was missing his father after spending so much time with him for the past few months.)

Nicholas wired home briefly on Sunday after attending another inspection.

Alexandra was delighted to hear that Nicholas would be home during the evening on Christmas Eve. She was rushed off her feet with all the Christmas decorations that needed to be done. Lili Dehn's son was coming later in the day as he was about to be baptised into the Russian Orthodox Church. He was her godson. There was good news concerning Alexei: he was finally able to play outside.

Olga's mind was elsewhere that day, as usual. She could think of nothing but her *Mitya*. She sat with him in the hospital that day.

Tatiana wrote to Nicholas of the film show she had seen but complained that there were not enough comic films shown. They had attended a cinema show at the Catherine Palace hospital the previous day but they had only showed one comic show. Most of the films shown to the wounded were films of recent events at the war.

On Monday, Nicholas wired in high spirits. Once more, his spirits had been lifted by seeing his troops.

That day, Alexandra admitted that she had sat with Anya so that her children could see their friends. (Small parties of guests were regularly invited by Madame Vyrubova, but the Tsarina never invited anyone to the palace. The Grand Duchesses saw their friends only at Anya's so would have naturally always been keen to visit her house.)

Tatiana was more concerned with her growing friendship with Vladimir that day. She had been delighted to meet his sister Elisabeth for the first time.

It was an important day for the Imperial couple: the name's day of the Grand Duchess Anastasia on Tuesday. Nicholas congratulated Alexandra in a telegram that day.

Meanwhile, Alexandra congratulated Nicholas! Alexei was now well enough to go into the garden with his dogs and even she was considering going out into the fresh air herself – a rare event. Her son had just gone out into the garden with his second dog Shot.

Nicholas sent another message to Alexandra after yet another inspection on Wednesday. He remarked that it was his final inspection on the Western Front of the Russian army.

Meanwhile, Olga notes in her journal of another meeting with her friend. She delighted in his company and thought of little else. She had spent much of the day in his company at the infirmary again.

Tatiana notes in hers that she did not see Vladimir in the evening and was disappointed, yet she had seen him earlier in the day. That evening, she had met up with Rita and *Mitya* however. It was possible that his absence was no coincidence as that evening Alexandra had accompanied her daughters to the infirmary.

On Thursday, Tatiana confides to her journal that she would have preferred to spend more time at the hospital that day. She had sat with Vladimir that morning but the approach of Christmas inevitably meant that she had to attend church and be with her family.

The Grand Duchesses gave presents to wounded officers at their hospitals at Christmas (in imitation of Nicholas himself). One of the wounded men Felix Dassel later recalled that the Grand Duchesses handed out cigarette cases and watches to honoured friends.

On Christmas Day, the family assembled at church and, to the delight of Olga and Tatiana, their friends *Mitya* and *Volodia* were there. The family lunched together and, in the afternoon, they handed out gifts to members of the Combined Regiment before going on to the infirmary. Tatiana made the most of the occasion and sat with *Volodia*, and Olga naturally sat with her friend.

The following day, Valentina Chebotatieva found out what had happened over Christmas. The two eldest Grand Duchesses had actually hatched a plan to secretly visit Vladimir Kiknadze on the twenty-fourth. It had been already planned on the eighteenth that he should be sent out of harm's way to Eupatoria in the Crimea. Madame Vyrubova had invited Shakh-Bagov and Kiknadze to her house for a party on the twenty-second. The Tsarina was also there and was persuaded to let Kiknadze stay on until the end of the holidays.

Chebotatieva was concerned about the plan to see Kiknadze. Chebotatieva thought that Tatiana in particular was inviting gossip.

On the Monday, Olga attended the *Church of the Sign* along with her sisters before going on to the infirmary where she contrived to sit with *Mitya* and Tatiana with *Volodia* again.

Olga returned to the infirmary for her shift on the Wednesday morning. One of her new light duties was to take the temperatures of the patients. Afterwards, she sat with *Mitya* again and returned home for lunch. The Dowager Empress had arrived. The family attended another Christmas tradition at one of the hospitals later but learnt that *Mitya's* regiment had to leave for the Caucasus at the end of the week. Olga retired to bed early that night. She was in shock.

It is probable that this was either a coincidence or that her parents had struck again in order to remove any potential danger.

Nicholas wrote in great detail on the final day of the Russian calendar after his valet had handed him a surprise letter from Alexandra. He relaxed by reading English novels in the evening. They were ones normally read by his teenage daughters so would have been, as he felt, soothing to the brain. It was a novel by A W Marchmont entitled *A Millionaire Girl*. It was one that had been a favourite of his daughters Tatiana and Marie.

Meanwhile, Alexandra sent a New Year's message to Nicholas. She noticed how the sun shone when he left just briefly as it often did. She intended passing the New Year in church, but her daughters had no intention of spending it so quietly. They were going to a party. She stated that the sun had shone for five minutes before he had left. She pointed out that even Shakh-Bagov had noticed that the sun shone for Nicholas.

Olga sent New Year's greetings to her beloved father from Tsarskoe Selo that day. She and her sisters were going to spend the evening at the infirmary. It was a cold night and she was suffering from a cold. The paper she had written on was a gift from her parents.

As the year ended, Olga must have wondered if she would ever see *Mitya* again.

Chapter Thirteen

New Year 1916

Nicholas spent New Year's Day at headquarters (Mogilev), sending a brief telegram home to the Tsarina explaining that he had ended the prohibition concerning the use of tramways by off-duty soldiers. Previously they had been banned from using this useful mode of transport. He agreed it had been a very unfair law and was happy to be able to change it.

Meanwhile, back at the Alexander Palace, the Tsarina had sent word to Nicholas explaining that their beloved son Alexei had received a telegram from all his friends at headquarters. The boy had made quite an impression in the short time he had been there with his father the previous year. He had been particularly close to the foreign military attachés. The message was, they said, in memory of all the happy times they had chatting before lunch during *zakuska* (hors d'oeuvres).

She explained that Alexei had been forced to remain at home due to a sore throat but his sisters had gone to Mass that morning. Alexandra then described how her children were in the next room at the time and making rather too much noise whilst eating.

That day Tatiana also took time out from her heavy schedule to write to Nicholas. She had returned to the infirmary early that cold morning before joining her sisters at church for Mass. The Grand Duchess revealed that her mother had spent much of the day resting but the ever thoughtful Anya had invited the children to her house for a party and they had been joined by Olga's friend Rita and her younger sister Lyuba (a friend of Anastasia) plus Alexei's beloved Irina Tolstoy. The five children enjoyed playing hide and seek in the dark in the cramped conditions of Anya's small villa after turning out the lamps.

Alexei had been given the gift of a journal by his mother and enthusiastically began to record the main events. On the first day, he noted how he had risen late and that his mother had rested all day as she felt ill. He was unwell himself and stayed in with a cold. His sisters lunched with him and in the afternoon (when his sisters returned to their respective hospitals) he went to Dr Derevenko's where he played with his little friend Kolya. He returned for dinner at six but the rest ate as usual at eight.

The young Tsarevich recorded the events of his day – the names of the people he met, studies, etc. When he became ill, one of his sisters (often Marie) wrote on his behalf in his yellow, silk-covered, gold-edged notebook.

The four sisters studied to various degrees: Olga very occasionally, Tatiana between her hospital shifts, and the two youngest Marie and Anastasia more or less enduring lessons each morning before visiting their hospital in the afternoons. As they did not actually work at the hospital, they duly returned later to their studies. The Tsarevich, on the other hand, had a more rigid programme. The children all had lessons on a Saturday.

A typical day for Alexei would begin with a lesson between the hours of nine and ten (possibly mathematics) and a drive in the park. He then had two hours of lessons beginning at eleven – maybe history, followed by English with Sydney Gibbes. He then rested after lunch and resumed his lessons for an hour at five and had an early dinner. The Tsarevich was then permitted to play or go for a drive but was expected to go to bed by 9pm. One of his older sisters, in the absence of Alexandra then listened as he recited his prayers. Nicholas frequently complained that the boy did this far too rapidly.

The young Tsarevich generally studied for an hour on Saturday morning then again before his dinner and during his free time, he would play with Dr Derevenko's son Kolya. He was outgrowing Andrei Derevenko's young sons; as he grew older, the age difference felt far larger than it had done in previous years. Alexei was growing up and had become fond of Irina Tolstoy a girl who was a few years older than he. (He had two special friends at headquarters too: Vasya Agayev and Zhenya Makarov.)

Meanwhile on Saturday, as Nicholas continued his life back at headquarters, he happened to mention (in his journal) that he had slept well as he usually did there. At home, Alexandra as a restless sleeper had undoubtedly woken him on occasions as she often took hours to get off to sleep.

Nicholas played the old-fashioned game of dominoes that evening with one of his men. It was a game that he had previously played with Alexei. Earlier he had written to Alexandra expressing his concern over the state of her health and urged her once again to take care.

The Tsar had attended a religious service on New Year's Eve but had gone to bed early accompanied by a headache. He realised that the Erivansky was the only regiment who had wired their congratulations which seemed a little odd. (It is interesting to note that amongst those Nicholas had chosen to take to headquarters was Colonel Silaiev of the Erivansky who just happened to be a senior member of the same regiment as Olga's favourite Dmitri Shakh-Bagov.) The reply that Alexei had composed to his friends at headquarters proved a great success, according to his proud father.

That same day, Alexandra explained to Nicholas how her son was now filling in his journal assisted by the ever obliging Marie. The Tsarina complained that she had begun the day badly as she had yet again barely slept and she blamed the headaches. She went on to explain that Marie and Anastasia had attended Mass earlier, accompanied by Anya. Olga and Tatiana were of course working at the infirmary.

After the Tsarina's letter was delayed for six hours on Sunday by heavy snow, Nicholas took the decision to send a telegram. He admitted his worries over Alix's health and wished her a speedy recovery.

As the late arrival of the train delayed Nicholas's usual paperwork, he was able to write more fully later. He was surprised that no one else had recalled that it was the first anniversary of the train accident that had almost killed Anya. He went on to explain that Prince (Valia) Dolgorukov was unwell and Nicholas had paid a call to his sickbed.

(Valia repaid his thoughtful gesture later by travelling with the family to Siberia.)

Alexandra had chosen to send Nicholas a whole pile of letters plus a postcard of Alexei taken at headquarters. She was greatly impressed by the picture of her handsome son. The Grand Duchesses were eating in the next room whilst she attempted to concentrate. They had been playing with toy guns in the dark. Alexandra had spent the day in bed but ventured as far as the couch.

Olga sent word to Nicholas explaining that Alexandra was actually reclining on the sofa whilst enjoying a game of patience. Tatiana and Marie were doing likewise. Olga then noted the arrival of Anya on her crutches.

However the Grand Duchess Olga confided in her journal that evening how she had sat with Mitya, who was shortly to leave for the city. His mother, who looked a great deal like her son, had arrived to see him.

Valentina Chebotarieva revealed in her own journal how she had noticed real suffering on Olga's face at the news of Mitya's imminent departure that day. She was aware how much the young man adored the Grand Duchess.

After the train was yet again delayed, Nicholas wired a brief message to Alexandra on the fourth. He explained that he had already sent word and hoped that she was feeling a little better.

Meanwhile Alexandra revealed to Nicholas that day how Olga and Tatiana had visited Colonel Silaiev's family once more the previous day. Anya was determined to set up a little hospital to the wounded and Alexandra was attempting to help. Alexei had quickly become bored with his new journal and was now writing in advance of the things he was expecting to do later in the day. Olga and Anastasia had both come down with a cold. Whilst Olga continued her routine Anastasia (in imitation of her mother) had taken to the sofa.

Marie had an amusing story concerning Olga to tell Nicholas. One of the officers on duty had failed to recognise Olga's voice on the telephone. Two days previously, their Aunt Olga had telephoned her namesake and asked that she visit one of her wounded men. Olga had rung the duty room and a man had asked who was speaking. She replied that it was *Olga Nicolaevna*. The man on duty (Kulyukin) had no idea who she was. He asked which *Olga Nicolaevna* and she had attempted to explain that she lived nearby but modestly failed to mention that she was a Grand Duchess. He was still confused.

He was then baffled and when she began laughing nervously he accused her of making a crank call. A disgruntled Olga had hung up and recounted the incident to Tatiana. Tatiana telephoned the man in question, who recognised her voice immediately. Afterwards, he admitted that he thought it was a joke and begged Olga's forgiveness.

Nicholas wired home on Tuesday morning after receiving a letter from Alexandra and attempted to reassure her that he was feeling well despite the cold.

The Tsar later found the time to send word and expressed his delight when two letters arrived as none had come the previous day. He explained that he was thinking of asking Boris Sturmer to become Prime Minister. He had already asked Khvostov his opinion but although, he had praised the man, Khvostov had been concerned about his age. (Unfortunately, leaving Alexandra in charge of the government proved a disaster.

She constantly changed the ministers and caused a great deal of upset. By the end of 1916, Russia had had four different Prime Ministers plus five ministers of the interior, four ministers of agriculture and a further three ministers of war within just sixteen months.)

Meanwhile that day Anastasia, Olga and Alexei were all unwell but the Tsarina had little sympathy for Valia. She explained that Anastasia's cold had been worsened by the return of *Madame Becker* and as a result she was unable to sleep. Olga and Alexei on the other hand had less heavy colds.

Anastasia managed to summon the energy to compose a letter to Nicholas. She explained that her mother was resting and how she and her siblings usually ate near their mother and even had tea in her bedroom. She confided that she, Olga, Marie and Alexei hid from each other and then shot at each other in the dark with their toy pistols. Alexei was sometimes scared. (Tatiana, true to her usual pattern, chose not to take part in these wild games.)

On Wednesday Nicholas replied to Alexandra's recent letter and admitted that he was delighted with her idea of sending Grand Duke George, along with Ilya Tatishchev, to Siberia in order to discover the conditions of the prisoners of war. (Tatishchev was amongst those who travelled to Siberia later with Nicholas and was held prisoner.)

Whilst he was writing, never an easy process for him, Nicholas received a wire explaining that Anastasia was suffering from bronchitis. He sent off a quick message stating that he hoped that she would quickly recover from such a tiresome illness.

The Tsar had gone to the traditional *Blessing of the Waters* ceremony but rather than the usual occasion on the River Neva in the capital Nicholas attended a local version. The troops who were stationed nearby attended, along with a vast crowd of locals. It was immensely cold, roughly twenty degrees below zero, and the ice had to be broken so that the ceremony could begin.

Unfortunately Anastasia's condition appeared to be deteriorating and it was decided as a precaution to move her from the room she shared with Marie. Grand Duchess Marie was accommodated with Olga and Tatiana next door. The doctors initially thought she had measles then influenza before finally agreeing on bronchitis.

Alexandra later confirmed to Nicholas that her youngest daughter was suffering from bronchitis and having difficulty swallowing. The young Grand Duchess had a headache and had coughed through the night. Anastasia naturally made light of the situation and explained to her mother that, although she was indeed pale, she also claimed that she looked quite foolish in her opinion.

The two invalids Anastasia and Alexei sent the day resting whilst Shura read to them. Olga had been given the honour of dictating her brother's journal that day. In her own journal that evening though, she admitted to being miserable when not in the presence of her beloved Mitya.

Olga and Tatiana had attended church that day before returning for their shifts at the infirmary. Tatiana arrived back to the palace quite late after spending the evening cleaning the surgical instruments.

On Thursday, despite the fact that Anastasia was still suffering from bronchitis, Alexandra chose only to speak to her by telephone from the floor below. This was something she often did in an effort to *save her legs*. (There was a lift between the two floors but she did not use it. The children, however, preferred to push each other down the stairs in the dark.)

Alexandra explained to Nicholas that day that Alexei had felt able to go downstairs that evening in his dressing gown. Anastasia was improving, her head ached less and her cough was now less troublesome.

Tatiana explained to Nicholas that lessons had restarted that day after the holidays. One of the patients had been teaching Olga how to play chess.

On Friday morning the Tsarina reported there had been a further improvement in the condition of her two youngest children after they had slept well. She was intending to go upstairs and see them that afternoon. The evening before, she and Marie had played patience. She had taken tea upstairs with the three youngest children and though Anastasia still looked a little green, she was improving. Olga and Marie had visited Anya several times the previous day.

Olga and Tatiana attended church on Saturday morning, accompanied by Marie, but Anastasia and Alexei remained at home, Alexandra explained to Nicholas. However, she assured him that both were continuing to show signs of improvement. Alexei had spent much of the previous day playing bezique with his English tutor Sydney Gibbes yet Anastasia had been forced to remain in bed a few more days. She still looked rather green. Alexandra had rested in the playroom with her two youngest children for a couple of hours the previous afternoon.

On Sunday Tatiana revealed to Nicholas that Anastasia and Alexei were sleeping around the Christmas tree just as they had done as small children. The Tsarina had joined them and was lying on the sofa nearby. The Grand Duchess explained that she and Olga had travelled to *Golsinforsk* the previous day and that an old friend Nicholas Rodionov had recently arrived. She had not seen him for almost a year.

After receiving a letter in celebration of her name's day, Tatiana composed a reply to Nicholas on Monday. Anastasia also wrote to her father to reassure him that she was improving. She was spending the mornings in bed whilst Shura (Tegleva) read to her and in the afternoons she usually joined Alexei in the playroom. The two of them played together before Alexandra arrived in time for tea. Alexei had been in a particularly amusing and giddy mood.

Nicholas reassured Alexandra on Tuesday that he had done as she had asked. He had been sent a small bottle of Madeira wine from Rasputin and she had insisted that he drank it.

Alexandra congratulated Nicholas on the occasion of Tatiana's name's day and went on to explain that Olga and Tatiana had already gone to the infirmary. She intended to hold a special Mass in her room later in Tatiana's honour. Anastasia and Alexei had improved enough to lunch with their siblings downstairs. Two old friends Nicholas Sablin and Nicholas Rodionov were expected to pay a call that evening, she added.

On Wednesday the Tsar sent word to Alexandra explaining that in two days' time he intended to visit the Trans-Baikal Division at Bobrouisk and would to leave for Orsha afterwards before returning to the palace where he would spend eight or nine days. He reported that Tatiana's name's day had been celebrated in the town with a concert and play. A copy of the Grand Duchess's portrait had been sold in aid of charity.

Whilst Anastasia recovered, Marie continued her studies alone. She had lessons on Wednesday morning in history and French. She then lunched with Alexei, Anastasia and Olga Butzova (one of the Tsarina's ladies) as Alexandra reclined on a couch nearby.

Olga and Tatiana spent the day at the infirmary but returned in due time for dinner. The four sisters ate together whilst Alexandra relaxed on a sofa close by.

On Thursday Nicholas composed his last letter before his intended return to the palace. There had been a meeting of the generals the previous day where they had discussed the never-ending problem of supplies. The president of the local council had been surprised to see him there rather than his predecessor Grand Duke Nicholas. (Nicholas later wired briefly before leaving for a tour of inspection.)

That same day Alexandra had sent word to Nicholas complaining that she had felt extremely ill in the night with stomach pains and felt quite faint. She had called for Madeleine Zannotti to fill up her hot-water bottle and asked her for some opium. She thought the pains may have been caused by the Adonis vernalis (herbal) heart medicine that she frequently took. The Tsarina went on to explain that Olga and Tatiana had been to town the previous day. They felt that the Dowager Empress appeared rather thin. The Grand Duchesses had then gone on to a committee before calling in on Xenia. Alexandra revealed that Nicholas's *friend* Nadezhda Plevitskaya had arrived. She had presented Olga with a donation from the fees she had earned from a series of concerts. (The two had met previously at Olga Alexandrovna's parties. The singer had been recently widowed).

Nicholas sent a wire on Friday explaining that he had just held an inspection and had been delighted with all that he had seen. He sent yet another message upon his return to headquarters later in the day.

The opium took its toll on Alexandra on Saturday as she admitted when she sent word to Nicholas and revealed that she was struggling to keep her eyes open. The children were well, she reported, but Olga had suddenly been sick in the night. (She failed to explain why this had occurred.)

Tatiana had gone to the infirmary that day where an operation had been performed to remove a kidney. The Grand Duchess had begun the day with a German lesson and had returned to the schoolroom after tea. The sisters later returned to the Grand Palace hospital where a concert was being held.

On Sunday, Nicholas arrived home and the family lunched *en famille*. During the course of the evening the Tsar read *A Millionaire Girl* a British novel by AW Marchmont whilst the others worked. The Grand Duchesses played hide and seek in the dark with their brother afterwards. They were happy enough to behave like children at times.

Meanwhile, returning to their more adult persona's, Olga and Tatiana represented their mother Alexandra at the opening of the Anglo-Russian Hospital in Petrograd on Tuesday chaperoned by Baroness Buxhoeveden and escorted by their grandmother the Dowager Empress. It had been arranged in one of the palaces belonging to Grand Duke Dmitri.

The elder Grand Duchesses had spent the morning at the infirmary after visiting the *Church of the Sign* and they returned in time for lunch. (Olga and Tatiana alternated between the adult world at the hospital and retaining their normal lifestyle as the Tsarina's children once they returned to the confines of the palace.) Once they returned from the capital, Olga and Tatiana paid a call on their cousin Tatiana and played with her young son and baby daughter. (It was generally Olga who chose to play with the children whilst Tatiana chatted to her namesake.)

Olga admitted in her journal on Sunday how she was still missing Mitya. (She was bored without him as she had been in previous years without Paul Voronov.)

The Grand Duchess Olga was delighted when Mitya arrived at the infirmary at noon on Monday. The two conspired to sit together in the corridor.

Nicholas travelled to the capital on Wednesday in the company of all four of his daughters. They visited a hospital before paying a call on the Dowager Empress in time for tea. Once again Alexandra was absent.

Nicholas left for military headquarters afterwards. On Thursday he confessed how much he missed his wife and family once he was back at headquarters – his nest. He hoped to return on the eighth. His only consolation now was seeing his troops.

That same day Alexandra had written to Nicholas after a most unwelcome proposal had been presented on behalf of his cousin Boris to Olga Nicolaevna. She was horrified yet Olga was even more so. She had only one man on her mind – Mitya. The Tsarina urged Nicholas never to divulge Olga's real secrets. It is evident she knew of them!

Meanwhile Nicholas sent a brief wire home on Friday expressing his delight after another troop inspection.

Alexandra explained to the Tsar that her children had asked permission to see their old friend Nicholas Rodionov the following evening. (He was a constant feature in their young lives and a good friend. He was a reminder of happier days before the war, playing tennis.)

Nicholas later sent an enthusiastic message home on Saturday after inspecting Tatiana's regiment of Uhlans amongst others at a large inspection.

He sent yet another telegram on Sunday after seeing more troops and thanked Alexandra for her recent letters.

Alexandra revealed to Nicholas that Tatiana had been delighted to hear that he had made a satisfactory inspection of her own regiment. The Tsarina went on to explain that Rodionov had dined with Anya the previous evening before calling at the palace to see them.

Olga sent word that day to her father disclosing that they were due to attend yet another charity concert that afternoon. They had only just risen and had not yet dressed. The three younger children had joined her and Tatiana in their room. Joy, her brother's spaniel, had not returned yet. (He was apt to wander and, in Tobolsk, he pounded the streets alone in the absence of his imprisoned family.)

At the beginning of the following month, Nicholas detailed his recent visit to the troops. He noted a few old faces but was concerned at the unhealthy appearance of General Pheve who was one of the most able generals of the war and had worked successfully in Poland before transferring to the Northern Front the previous autumn. He needed to find a replacement for him. (It was no easy task for the indecisive Nicholas. The Tsar preferred to defer to Alexandra at home and was rapidly becoming reliant on her to run the Empire. The results were catastrophic.)

Meanwhile, Alexandra was concerned that Nicholas would be lonely without the constant yet lively presence of his young son. In a letter that day, she explained that she knew how difficult it would be for him. On a lighter note, she explained that the previous evening their children had enjoyed themselves immensely at one of Anya's concerts. She prompted Nicholas to remember that it would be Anya's name's day was on the third. Tatiana, who had already written to her father, was currently bidding farewell to Rodionov on the telephone.

It was Tatiana's turn to write to Nicholas on Monday. She explained that she and her siblings had attended a small concert arranged by Anya the previous day. The five children and the wounded men had thoroughly enjoyed themselves. The entertainers included old favourite Delazari who sang and had told amusing stories. (Whilst Tatiana was composing her letter, her Russian teacher Peter Vassilievich Petrov appeared to be daydreaming. She ignored him on the occasions he attempted to speak as she was determined to finish the letter.)

On Tuesday it was Marie's turn to write to her father. He had an unending commentary of their everyday life as a result of the endless stream of letters, but he was in no position to reply to each one. That morning Marie had attended Mass at the lower church whilst Tatiana had gone on to the infirmary. Olga had a late start that morning and attended Mass later in the company of the Tsarina, Alexei and a partially recovered Anastasia. Her mother had spent much of the day resting on the sofa as she was suffering from pains in the jaw. Marie went on to complain that she had not seen her friend Nicholas Demenkov for some three weeks.

On Wednesday Nicholas wired with great news: Erzerum had been taken. He added that he had just seen Prince Alexander of Oldenburg (known as Alek he was the father-in-law of Olga Alexandrovna) who had demonstrated some gas masks.

That same day the Minister of the Interior Alexei Khvostov had been dismissed and the aged Goremykin had finally retired as President of the Council of Ministers. Boris Sturmer had the honour of replacing both men. There had been rumours that the first man had been in a plot to kill Rasputin. Alexandra was greatly shocked as she had seen him as a friend.

Meanwhile back at the Alexander Palace Alexandra was still feeling unwell and complaining of a severe headache. She disclosed in a letter to Nicholas that, the previous evening, Olga and Anya had taken turns to read her stories about children by *Avertchenko*. She had told Alexei that, as a special treat, there would be *blinis* (pancakes) for lunch. He had felt guilty eating whilst she was unwell but she had assured him that seeing him happy would make her feel better. Olga and Tatiana had gone to the capital during the course of the afternoon once more in order to collect charity donations.

On Thursday Nicholas went into more detail concerning a series of bizarre gas experiments. He had observed men wandered around a railway carriage filled with a poisonous gas but confessed he was completely bewildered as to why they were doing it. He went on to explain that he was intending to return on the eighth but would only make a brief stay as there was a military conference he needed to attend on the eleventh.

The Tsarina had met Miss Eady, the British former nurse of her nephews Don and Lu (George-Donatus and Louis – the sons of her brother Ernie) that same day. It had been decided that the lady would be safer out of Germany in the circumstances.

Olga's friend Mitya had meanwhile sent word to Anya. He was intending to remain in the city until the following day on regimental orders. He had written to Anya and also to Varvara in the knowledge that the two ladies would pass on his news to Olga.

The following day Nicholas wired merely to say that he had been for a drive and a walk and to thank Alexandra, Olga and Anya for their recent letters. Once again he referred to Anya as *Her*. (Alexandra often referred to Anya as *the Cow*.)

Alexandra sent word to Nicholas that day of news of their son after a recent health scare. He had had both arms bandaged but Rasputin had reassured her that he would be well in a couple of days. She explained that he had probably hurt himself whilst holding the cord on the sledges which had been tied together.

Tatiana had also written to Nicholas explaining that she had participated at an operation and had gone to the capital to attend a meeting with Olga. Tatiana confessed that she had become bored of the continual visits to Petrograd. On a more positive note she added that her mother's jaw pains were finally subsiding and that they were reading a book together that evening named *Olive*.

Nicholas put pen to paper to Alexandra on Saturday concerning Pleve's replacement. He would be succeeded by the controversial General AN Kuropatkin as Commander of the Northern Front. He knew the appointment would be criticised but he had too few good men to worry about such things.

On Sunday Alexandra had news for Nicholas concerning a friend of Olga's. Nicholas Karanagozov had written to Anya. He revealed that although the weather in Odessa had been delightful it was snowing in Kiev. His regiment had only been given leave in the south rather than at Tsarskoe Selo, so his mother and sister had arranged to meet him in Odessa.

The Tsar Nicholas and his younger brother Grand Duke Michael briefly visited the Russian Duma (government) on Tuesday the ninth/twenty-second in order to attend a *Te Deum* in celebration of the taking of Erzerum. Nicholas was warmly received and loyal speeches were made. It was a brief period of understanding between Nicholas and his government.

Meanwhile the Grand Duchesses had continued their usual routine but, whilst Alexandra reclined on the sofa, the four sisters lunched and dined with their father. However, Olga still had Mitya on her mind and that same evening noted in her journal that he had sent a postcard to her friend and colleague Varvara. (Despite the brief return of her beloved father Olga was still thinking of Mitya and she was constantly wondering when they would be reunited.)

Nicholas wired Alexandra with the latest news after his return to military headquarters. He had been met by all the military commanders upon his return.

He went on to explain that the military conference was due to begin at 6pm the following evening.

Just as Olga could not get Mitya out of her mind, Alexandra had been unable to think of anything but Nicholas since he left. The previous evening she and her daughters had either *worked* or played patience. Tatiana and Anastasia had even resorted to taken turns to read aloud but she could not concentrate.

Nicholas sent a detailed letter home on Friday concerning the conference which had dragged on until after midnight. He had been, on the whole, satisfied with the result but felt unable to discuss it in too much detail until he returned home.

Meanwhile, back at the Alexander Palace, Olga composed a quick letter to Nicholas before she hurried back to the infirmary. She complained that a photograph was being taken that day of everyone. (There were in fact many photographs taken of Olga, Tatiana and the patients and staff during the two years that they nursed at the hospital. The sisters appear inside the hospital and outside on the lawn with the various men they nursed. The sisters were still recognisable despite wearing a white scarf that completely covered their hair. Volodia Kiknadze appears on a couple of photographs, Mitya in several, and Marie's friend Kolya Demenkov was shown in a few shots and in a couple was quite clearly shown looking at Marie.)

Nicholas had more time to put pen to paper on Saturday when he complained that the conference had taken up far too much of his precious time and had lasted for some six hours. He had too much to do and far too many people to see. He had also needed to speak to some of the generals; his brother-in-law Sandro who had recently arrived; his cousin Boris after a review; Polivanov and Admiral Phillimore. He went on to explain that he had promoted Count AS Zamoisky to Wing-Adjutant (ADC). He had *inherited* the Count from Grand Duke Nicholas who had been commander-in-chief until the previous autumn.

Alexandra meanwhile returned to the vexed subject of Grand Duke Boris. She could not get over her disgust. She clearly understood that her young daughter would have been thrown into quite a different set on marriage to Nicholas's cousin. She disliked Boris's mother (Marie) and everyone who was associated with him. (Alexandra disapproved of society in general and was in many ways as Victorian as her late grandmother, Queen Victoria, if not more so.)

The young Grand Duchess Marie also sent word to Nicholas that day. She began by admitting how much she missed her father and went on to reveal that Lili Dehn and her husband had arrived the previous day. Tatiana's little dog Ortipo was hiding under the table and frustrated that she could not leap onto her knee. (Tatiana and Olga were of course at the infirmary, and the dog was attempting to cuddle up to Marie. The dog frequently launched herself onto an unsuspecting Alexandra.)

Nicholas composed a hurried note on Sunday. He naturally thanked everyone for their most recent letters and explained that he had been for a walk out of the town. (Although Nicholas did often have walks, the routes were of course checked out in advance by scouts.)

That day Nicholas had chatted to the British officer General John Hanbury-

Williams and confirmed that he had decided long ago to stick out the war until the bitter end. The two also spoke of Grand Duke George's recent visit to Japan and of Nicholas's younger brother Michael.

Whilst he was at headquarters Nicholas liked to read in the evenings and, during February, he got through *The Room of Secrets* by William le Queux and, the following month, he read *The man who was dead* by AW Marchmont. The Tsar had previously enjoyed tales of the past wars on an evening but in the current circumstances he had quite understandably chosen to read adventure stories and even novels of a romantic nature, such as those by Florence Barclay, in an effort to relax after a long day spent dealing with the various aspects of running the vast Russian Empire during wartime.

Meanwhile Olga, Tatiana, Marie and Anastasia had all attended concerts that day, as the Tsarina explained to Nicholas. The two eldest daughters had gone to a concert in the hospital whilst Marie, Anastasia and Alexei had gone to Anya's refuge. Anya's parents would also be attending in an effort to cheer them up. Recently, Anya's mother had received a malicious a letter about Anya which had obviously greatly upset her. The children had been joined by Nicholas Demenkov, Irina Tolstoy, Dr Vladimir Derevenko and Sydney Gibbes.

Nicholas announced on Monday to Alexandra that he would shortly be returning home and was intending to arrive late on Thursday morning. He had been given a thorough check-up by Dr Botkin, and proudly informed Alexandra that he was in better health than he had expected.

Meanwhile Alexandra explained to Nicholas that Anya was constantly urging her to go out but she felt sure that it would be unwise with her bad cough. It had kept her awake all night. Marie had a cold too, but she and her siblings were still determined to attend a concert at the Catherine Palace later.

Olga composed a long, detailed letter to Nicholas that day concerning the soldiers' concerts. She had enjoyed the balalaika piece but they had played too little for her taste. There was yet another concert today. Alexei had been teased by Dr Derevenko about the distorting mirror and she had to explain how it worked to him. They had seen two different scenes – *The Distorting Mirror* and *The Intimate Theatre*.

What Olga failed to mention that day to her father was a letter that arrived at the hospital from her beloved Mitya. As Valentina Chebotarieva observed, the letter had sent Olga into raptures. Olga had even asked Valentina if it were possible that she could have a heart attack at the age of twenty from the sheer excitement and joy.

In recent months Olga had been assigned to more menial duties at the infirmary but Tatiana had retained her previous position. Olga was now dealing with the administration side of the hospital along with taking temperatures and even making beds. Tatiana continued to take part in operations. The Grand Duchess Tatiana took her work at the hospital very seriously and one evening Tatiana had complained to Valentina that she should have been allowed to deal with the dangerous carbolic acid which was used for sterilizing the instruments and the floors at the hospital. She wanted to know why she was allowed to breathe in carbolic acid yet Tatiana was not. The Grand Duchess was then permitted to help.

Meanwhile Anastasia had also put pen to paper that day. She had been particularly taken by a ten year-old girl who had danced to the sound of an accordion at one of the charity concerts she had attended.

Nicholas was officially presented with a British Field-Marshal's baton by Sir Arthur Paget the next day. It was merely a political move on behalf of the British, Russia's allies, but one that appealed strongly to Nicholas who had a real love of all things military.

Alexandra explained in a detailed letter to Nicholas on Tuesday that their old friend Nicholas Sablin's brother had arrived for a brief visit. Olga had played the fool by sitting on a small table which she succeeded in breaking. Alexandra added that she was naturally delighted to hear that Nicholas would return in two days' time.

Nicholas duly arrived home as promised on Thursday morning as Tatiana noted in her journal that evening. The sisters had met him at the station and then gone for a service at the small *Church of the Sign*. That afternoon Nicholas and his children got down to the serious job of building a snow tower in the garden with the assistance of eight willing sailors. That evening, whilst his wife and daughters *worked*, Nicholas read aloud from an English book entitled *The Woman in the Car*. Tatiana found the story very interesting despite the uninspiring title. (Whilst Tatiana often seemed happy enough to join in with any amusements however boring they may have seemed to her sisters, Olga and Marie often admitted at this time to be bored without Mitya or Kolya.)

The family returned to church on Friday and Tatiana returned to the infirmary. Later, all the children, with the exception of Olga, attended a concert with their chaperone for the occasion, Countess Hendrikova, in the men's gymnasium.

On Saturday Tatiana noted in her journal how she had again returned to the infirmary to continue with the ever mounting number of patients who needed bandaging. The five siblings attended lunch with their beloved papa. Later two British visitors General Paget and Lord Pembroke paid a call on the Tsar. The younger children meanwhile continued working on the snow tower and Nicholas's ailing Uncle Paul arrived in time for tea.

The Tsar and his four daughters attended Mass together on Sunday. Nicholas and his children and the Tsar's aide-de-camp Anatole Mordvinov took a pleasant walk that afternoon and returned to the snow tower. The children were treated to a series of English movies later.

On Monday morning at the beginning of Great Lent, the Tsar and his five children attended church. The children including Alexei then went out in the garden and proceeded to energetically jump off the tower into the snow. The entire family attended church that evening.

After the usual lessons on Tuesday and yet another visit to the church for the Tsar's children, they spent the afternoon jumping off the snow tower once again.

The next day the youngest four children returned to their daily lessons before going to church with their father. In the afternoon Marie and Anastasia paid a call to their own infirmary. The five children later returned to their beloved snow tower and a series of photographs were taken showing them jumping off it into the snow with real enthusiasm. They were joined by the Tsar and Alexei's friend Kolya.

The following days were spent by the children continuing to jump off the mountain of snow when they had the time, between visits to church and the various hospitals.

Nicholas received the retiring American Ambassador of the USA, Mr George T Marye on Saturday. He received his important visitor in the Corner Sitting Room and the Ambassador officially handed Nicholas his letters of recall.

Valentina Chebotarieva noted on Tuesday that Olga and Tatiana had hatched a plan with Rita so that they could see Vladimir Kiknadze. They felt certain that he would arrive back at the infirmary by train. Valentina observed Olga and Tatiana at the station late that evening and was surprised and shocked to see them out so late. It transpired that they had permission to go to the cemetery. They had, they said, met him before going to the cemetery.

Early on Wednesday afternoon Nicholas left Tsarskoe Selo for military headquarters. Tatiana, Marie and Anastasia visited a local cemetery later that morning and were almost late for lunch when their car broke down in the snow. Marie was determined to find the grave of particular soldier and eventually did so but fell in the deep snow. Meanwhile, Tatiana and Anastasia had wandered off to see if they could find Sonia's grave nearby. Olga and Tatiana had arrived earlier than usual at the infirmary as Nicholas was due to leave at noon.

Nicholas wrote to Alexandra on Thursday expressing his concerns about leaving her when she was so unwell. He, on the other hand, was so exhausted that he managed to sleep some ten hours. He finished his letter on Friday morning and would go for another drive along the main road in a car later that day.

Meanwhile back at the Alexander Palace Alexandra was still suffering from pains in her jaw and Dr Derevenko was using an electrifying device in an effort to help. (The small boxes contained electrodes which were placed onto the 'patients' affected area and a small electric current was passed into them. The earlier ones produced an electric shock by means of a turning handle.) Olga and Anastasia, the Tsarina explained to Nicholas, had been visited by the dreaded *Madame Becker*. Anya was suffering from a worsening cough.

That day Marie explained in great detail to her father all about her exciting trip to the cemetery the previous day where she had managed fall in the snow. She had asked a guide to help her find the grave. Marie confided that she had initially put flowers on a grave that she thought was the correct soldier's name but subsequently discovered it was the wrong man so continued in her efforts to locate the correct one. Tatiana and Anastasia had wandered off to find Sonia's grave and had been waiting for her but the car broke down. They began to walk home, but luckily the vehicle had come back to life shortly after.

Marie then asked her father about the book that he was reading. (He often read ones that Tatiana and Marie had already read and he was currently reading *Olive* which had been given to Marie by her grandmother.)

Nicholas sent a brief telegram to Alexandra the next day and admitted that he had been greatly impressed by Marie's detailed letter. (The Grand Duchess was probably the most descriptive letter writer. She had a rare skill of saying something even when very little happened.)

Olga sent word to Nicholas that day concerning the progress of the unusually large snow tower that they had been building in the Alexander Park. She explained that, on the first day after he had left, they had gone for a sleigh ride with Baroness Buxhoeveden and then gone on to the tower. They had, in keeping with Lent, had no bells on the sleigh, she explained. Whilst one of the men was assisting, small lumps of snow had fallen from the tower onto his cap but he had not seemed to mind. Olga explained that she was sitting in her mother's room whilst Alexei rested, Tatiana studied and her younger sisters had gone to the Grand Palace hospital.

On Saturday Nicholas thanked Alexandra for taking the time to speak to Sablin. She had been concerned that a plot to murder Anya had recently been uncovered yet Nicholas had received a long letter from Khvostov explaining his devotion to the Tsar and an admission that he had failed to understand why he had been dismissed.

Anastasia admitted that same day that she had been amused how various officers had attempted to take charge of the construction of the snow tower. She and Olga had not been to see it recently, but Tatiana and Marie continued to do so. It was beginning to melt.

Alexandra explained to Nicholas on Sunday that Tatiana, Marie, Anastasia and Alexei were due to go to Anya's hospital within the hour for a concert featuring a conjurer.

Olga meanwhile informed Nicholas that day that the snow tower was still growing. Although she had not seen it recently, she would do so on Monday. Her siblings had gone to Anya's hospital to see the conjurer. She watched as Alexandra read. The book was so frightening that the Tsarina was literally holding her breath and wriggling around on the sofa whilst she attempted to concentrate.

On Monday Nicholas complained of being overworked. He had been receiving visitors until late into the evening. He went on to admit that he was dismayed at the accusation that Admiral Nilov was a bad influence on General Voyeikov. Alexandra had casually informed Nicholas that Voyeikov's wife had informed her that she felt that Nilov was influencing him against Anya Vyrubova.

That day had been fairly predictable for Alexandra and her children, but after dinner Lili and Charles Dehn, Anya Vyrubova, Baron Taube (who had recently been treated in Olga and Tatiana's infirmary) and an old tennis partner LM Kozhevnikov all arrived to spend the evening. (The Tsarina very rarely had guests after dinner with the exception of Madame Vyrubova or Madame Dehn.)

On Tuesday, Nicholas briefly mentions the Battle of Verdun in his daily letter to Alexandra. He urged her not to mention it but it seemed that the Russians had taken the initiative of attacking whilst the enemy was at Verdun. The previous day he had seen a silent film of Erzerum and afterwards there was a comic film starring Max Linder. (He was a great favourite with the children and was very similar to Charlie Chaplin.)

Tatiana, whose turn it was to write to Nicholas, explained that the snow tower was so extensive it had several floors to it. The sailors had helped with the construction work and, on the previous day, Lili's son Alexander had played with them. That evening they had bid farewell to Sablin who had gone to join the army.

On Wednesday Nicholas wrote at great length to Alexandra after she had sent some lily of the valley flowers. He was delighted with them and went on to explain that he intended to appoint General Ivanov as a military adviser at his headquarters. Nicholas continued his letter the following morning but had little to add.

Meanwhile Marie wrote to Nicholas to explain that Olga and Tatiana were leaving for Petrograd whilst she and Anastasia were about to leave for their infirmary. She was hoping to see Demenkov there.

Alexandra sent word on Thursday explaining that Tatiana had participated in an operation that morning on one of the wounded officers. Olga was by now working in a different capacity and wrote out prescriptions, handed out medicines, fed some of the more disabled men and even made beds and sewed torn pillowcases.

Two days later, Olga informed Nicholas by letter that, once Tatiana had finished her lessons and her younger sisters returned from their hospital, the four were intending to visit the snow tower. The sailors, meanwhile, had been working long hours on the construction, but the sisters enjoyed distracting them by throwing snowballs at them. She liked to hit Mr Botsman in particular as he pretended nothing had happened.

Tatiana had also written that day of the snow tower. She had joined in the fun which was fairly unusual for her. She remarked that Anastasia had taken several photographs of the tower. (The sisters would build another such tower in Siberia later to amuse themselves and, again, Tatiana would join in.)

Nicholas showed great concern in a telegram on Sunday after hearing that the pains in Alexandra's jaw had returned. He had little to impart. (She may have been suffering from neuralgia but was also prone to toothache.)

Meanwhile, Alexandra was rather more forthcoming – especially about his eldest and favourite daughter Olga. All the children had all gone to church and she felt very lonely despite them. They had quite different ideas to their mother, even the youngest (Alexei). Alexandra complained that they had little idea of how she saw even the smallest things. (Evidently they had minds of their own.) They found it difficult to understand when she talked about how things were when she was a child. (As a child brought up strictly under the dominance of her grandmother Queen Victoria, it was inevitable that there would be something of an age gap. Normally, children feel a different generation to their parents, which is understandable, but with Alexandra it was more like two generations.)

Alexandra admitted that, when she spoke quietly with her daughter Tatiana, she often understood her mother's point of view but Olga, on the other hand, initially resisted every idea. When she was angry with her, Olga sulked, she claimed. (Olga was missing Mitya and her beloved father and had not adapted to nursing in the same way as Tatiana had.)

It was clear that the war and the often intense physical pain she was in had got to Alexandra. She was effectively attempting to keep the government in order yet was managing to make new enemies every day. She also had the knowledge that her daughters were growing up, something she never came to terms with. Although Tatiana was nearly always obedient, her younger children and Olga were liable to do much as they pleased out of her sight. It was significant that, when her siblings played with toy guns, Tatiana had not joined in and it was she who made the most efficient nurse as the work was so close to her character. She had spent years pandering to the whims of her mother, helping her brother, and even her siblings had nicknamed her the *Governess*. When Olga had reached the age when she was able to go out into society, when she *came out*, it is significant that Tatiana went with her. She was the more confident sister, and Olga felt happier in her company when they were out *officially*. A young girl came out into society once she left the schoolroom and was effectively on the marriage market yet Alexandra had no intention of letting her precious daughters grow up let alone marry if she could help it.

Count Grabbe who knew the family well confirmed that it was Tatiana who was the family organiser and had a more serious nature than her siblings.

The children's English tutor Sydney Gibbes said much the same. She was, he felt, treated as the elder sister, rather than Olga. She was, of all the sisters, the one closest to her mother and was restrained and the most capable of dealing with everyday affairs. She had the character to sit contently with her needlework and had good powers of concentration (unlike Olga). It was actually Tatiana who later took control of the household when her parents left Tobolsk. She was put in charge.

That same day when Alexandra had complained about Olga's moods, the Grand Duchess had written to her beloved father. She explained that she and her siblings had worked on the snow tower the previous day and Anastasia had taken some photographs as a keepsake. She had even sympathised with her mother and informed Nicholas that Alexandra was still suffering from pains in her face but that it was helped by the electric treatment. She joked that the younger members of the choir appeared to have been ill as only the older members were really singing *To your cross*. (Olga was immensely fond of music and a talented pianist with a good *ear* so knew when the music was not quite correct.)

Nicholas finally had time to compose a letter home to Alexandra and the children on Monday. The Tsar rarely wrote to the siblings individually unless it was perhaps for a birthday. He explained that he had been unable to put pen to paper for three days due to pressure of work. He was struggling to deal with the constant comings and goings of the various ministers and was eternally searching for someone new. He also admitted that the Allies had suffered heavy losses in places.

Alexandra once again admitted to feeling bad that day. She had spent three hours alone desperately attempting to read as her daughters had gone to see Marie's ambulance train the previous evening. She made a point of remarking how Tatiana was working well at the hospital but merely added that Olga had just left on foot in the company of Shura. (Olga enjoyed time out in the fresh air and walked rather than went by carriage or car if she could, but she could never get rid of the chaperone.)

She went on to explain that Anastasia was having lessons but would go out for a walk with Trina later because her religious teacher was needed at the church. Marie was also writing to Nicholas and Alexei was out in the garden.

Meanwhile Marie in her letter that same day explained that her friend Nicholas

Demenkov had left on Saturday but at least she had been able to speak to him on the telephone. She asked Nicholas if he recalled that she had made her friend a shirt earlier. (She did actually make shirts for other men who were about to leave for the front of course.) She had asked Kolya how he liked the shirt and he had said that it fitted well. (He was tall and rather well built.)

She was writing in *Orchie's* room. (It had formerly used by Alexandra's English nanny who came to Russia in 1894. She had left Russia when Marie was a tiny child.) Her mother Alexandra was lying on the couch whilst Dr Derevenko gave her electrical treatment on her aching face.

Nicholas felt frustrated that he was unable to comfort Alexandra whilst she was suffering so much. In his letter on Tuesday, he explained that the expected thaw had resulted in the trenches where the soldiers were dug in becoming waterlogged. (It gave the men *trench-foot* as a result but, on the other hand, it drowned the rats.) The men were unable to sit or lie down to rest. The artillery and the transport were also stuck.

He sent a wire later in the day after the arrival of yet more letters. The level of the nearby river was rapidly rising and it was also very foggy.

That day Alexandra had sent word to Nicholas remarking that her cousin Missy (now Queen of Rumania) had sent Olga one of her pretty fairy-tale books. (Perhaps she was hoping that her son Carol would still marry Olga. It was, however, her mother-in-law who was a writer.)

She revealed that she was suffering with terrible pains in her head and eyes, and a nurse had been massaging her face, head, neck and shoulders in an attempt to ease the pain. (A physiotherapist would have been more appropriate as he or she may have been able to relieve the tension the Tsarina was undoubtedly suffering from worry and incessant pain.)

Nicholas was becoming alarmed at the rise in the river level after the ice had broken up and also that the fog had not lifted. (If the conditions were the same at the nearby battlefields, the results would have been horrific.)

Meanwhile, Alexandra explained that she had been spending time with Marie playing patience on an evening. Olga and Tatiana had gone to Petrograd for yet another committee meeting and would take tea with their grandmother in town. Alexandra was intending to have Lili's son Alexander's hair cut that afternoon. It had been left long and she felt it was time to make him look more like a little boy. He was seven years old.

On Thursday, the Archpriest of the Russian Army and Fleet George Shavelsky spoke to the Tsar regarding his concerns over Rasputin's influence. Nicholas, on this occasion, took no offence but usually, when anyone spoke out about Rasputin, they were dismissed from their post, whatever it was.

Nicholas wrote to Alexandra that day and entrusted the letter to General Shuvayev to deliver it to her. The Tsar admitted that sitting surrounded by fog for three days had had a depressive effect on everyone. He had gone for a drive the previous day and the route reminded him of a visit he had made previously with Alexei. He had been impressed by the sight of the river covered in ice and the occasional noise of the ice crashing together. It had revived his spirits.

That day, a French hospital ship the *Portugal* had been torpedoed in the Black Sea by a German submarine, with the loss of 115 lives.

Alexandra had written to Nicholas that day of the return the previous evening of a friend of Tatiana's. Dmitri Malama, who had presented her with her dog, arrived after a gap of eighteen months. He looked well and she admitted what a perfect son-in-law he would have made. She wondered why foreign princes were not as nice. He was shown Ortipo. Alexandra explained to Nicholas that Malama was the dog's father. (She meant of course that Malama had given the dog to Tatiana.)

Nicholas sent Alexandra a hurried message on Friday and admitted that he was glad that he would soon be able to return home.

Nicholas finally had the opportunity to attend church in the company of his immediate family on Sunday. They lunched *en famille* yet Alexandra remained on the sofa. The children went later to a concert at one of the hospitals in the company of Madame Vyrubova. It gave the Imperial couple some quality time alone for once. The children returned in time for dinner which was taken with their parents, Anya and Nicholas's aide Colonel Silaiev. (The children had often visited the officer's wife and children in previous months. It is significant that Anya had gone to the concert with the children as Alexandra had often complained that Anya was always there when she and Nicholas finally had free time together.)

That afternoon, Tatiana remarked in her journal that Alexandra had actually gone out into the garden and had a ride on a sledge. It was the very first such occasion that year, according to her daughter.

Olga and Tatiana returned to the infirmary for just over an hour in the early evening to assist Rita in cleaning the medical instruments. Afterwards, they sat and chatted with some of the patients. They returned back in time for dinner.

The Tsar's children resumed their usual routine on Monday, including lessons for the four youngest. Tatiana, however, went on to the infirmary immediately after her morning lessons where she assisted in an operation on a damaged thigh.

Olga returned to the infirmary along with Tatiana on Tuesday, but had begun the day with a massage before going on to *The Church of the Sign*. As Alexandra had been having a series of massages for her head, it was decided it may help release the inbuilt tension in Olga. Olga at this time was doing less heavy work at the hospital and dealing with the paperwork. She returned in time for one of her few remaining lessons. She usually practised music or French at this time of day. Alexei was complaining of a sore arm after playing the fool.

Nicholas went back to military headquarters soon after.

Alexandra sent word to Nicholas on Saturday and reported that their young son was endeavouring to continue with his journal but finding it irksome. The five siblings were due to go to a concert that afternoon at Anya's small hospital where there would be singers and conjurers, but she had declined to attend, despite Anya's prompting. She did not feel well enough to go out.

Olga wrote to Nicholas later detailing the concert and it appears that Alexandra had been persuaded to attend. She explains that there had been a couple of acrobats who, she thought, could have been father and son. Their antics were quite breath-taking. Later, once they had returned to the palace, Alexandra played a card game with an obliging Marie.

Olga and Tatiana returned to the infirmary on Monday and, to their surprise, Alexandra appeared later. Three new men had arrived for treatment. After lunch, the sisters returned to the hospital and afterwards sat out in the garden where the Tsarina joined them. The sisters later joined their younger siblings at the snow mountain. Alexandra once more joined them.

That day Tatiana had found time in her busy schedule to send word to her father. She explained that she and her siblings had been working in the ice that day, and Alexandra had sat nearby watching from her armchair. Whilst they were outside, members of the Convoy Escort passed by singing but stopped once they saw the family. Tatiana ordered them to continue. She had played at being Tsar, she explained. Whilst she was writing, her dog Ortipo sat by her feet chewing her football. She set the scene. Mother was reading and Olga and Marie were amusing themselves making up silly songs about the other nurses. Tatiana thanked Nicholas for leaving the sisters some cigarettes. She had just shared one earlier with Olga.

On Tuesday Nicholas wrote of his recent visits. He had enjoyed the review despite the wind, hail, and rain and he had the opportunity to visit a couple of hospitals.

In a letter to her father that day, Marie revealed that her sister Olga was having what she described as a reprimand. Tatiana was playing cards and the two youngest had already gone up to bed. (It is probable that her mother was rebuking her for something or other. As Anya had also arrived it may have been over a fight for the all-important chair belonging to Nicholas.) Earlier, Anastasia and Alexei had been playing the balalaika whilst Olga accompanied them on the piano.

On Wednesday Nicholas wired again after a review just before he left for another.

Alexandra had explained that day in her daily letter to the Tsar that three people had arrived from the film company *Pathe* and had generously brought the Tsarevich a gift of film apparatus and some large round tins containing films. She went on to remark that yesterday Tatiana had had a lesson on the balalaika and she hoped that she would be able to play with Alexei and the others.

Alexei had proudly managed to type a letter in French that day to his father. He explained that a French gentleman had brought him a gift of his own cinema and had showed him how it worked.

Meanwhile Olga and Tatiana had returned to their infirmary. Olga had once again received a massage early in the day. Alexandra, Olga and Tatiana later visited the Red Cross where they gave out crosses to those who had recently earned them. Nicholas's Aunt Olga, the Queen of Greece, had been expected for dinner that evening but she had a chill so decided to remain at home. The other visitors, the widowed Mavra (wife of the late Grand Duke Konstantin) and her daughter-in-law Elena, however arrived at the palace.

The Tsar found sufficient time to compose a letter to Alexandra on Thursday after a busy day. He had been reading an English book by Florence Barclay entitled

Through the Postern Gate, or *Little Boy Blue* as Nicholas referred to it. (He would use it as a nickname in the coming months. He enjoyed the gentle novels of Florence Barclay and her books were read avidly by Tatiana and Marie. Their mother would have approved of the author who was the daughter and wife of a vicar and had actually spent her honeymoon in the Holy Land. Olga, on the other hand, had rather more sophisticated tastes.) Nicholas had seen two old friends on his travels: Olga's old friend Alexander Shvedov and Anastasia's favourite Victor Zborovsky.

Olga had visited the Winter Palace again that day in order to accept donations whilst Alexandra escorted Tatiana on a visit to a small church at Bari. They later met up at Xenia's.

Chapter Fourteen

Spring 1916

At the beginning of April, Nicholas sent a wire after enduring a long and exhausting conference. He had little opportunity to go out in the beautiful spring-like weather. Normally, he went for a walk after lunch but, at headquarters, he had less opportunity to do so.

Olga and Tatiana had spent Friday morning as usual at the infirmary where there had been an operation. It meant that they returned for a late lunch before they joined their younger sisters at yet another charity concert. The entertainments included singing, music, dancing and comedians. The Grand Duchesses made their exit after a couple of hours and the younger ones, including Tatiana, returned to their lessons.

Anastasia described the evening she spent at home with her sister Marie. She played the balalaika as Marie attempted to play the piano. Anastasia admitted that it sounded better when Olga accompanied her but she had gone to bed early.

Nicholas wired home on Saturday after receiving a letter and the gift of a small icon. He was enjoying the weather now the conference had finished.

That day, Tatiana sent word to Nicholas and remarked that she had enjoyed the comedians Lersky and Dolsky the previous day. There had been singers too at the concert. The group was made up of amateurs who had volunteered their services for free. (Unfortunately, Tatiana's letters lacked the clarity of Marie or the comic talent of Anastasia. It was more a list of happenings rather than how they sounded or what they wore or how she felt.)

Marie, however, managed to accurately set the scene. She was downstairs and her mother and sister Tatiana were playing a card game. Anya Vyrubova was biting her nails and one of the servants, Volkov, was running around the room asking questions in a boring manner. She explained that tomorrow Queen Olga of Greece was expected and would bring her son Christopher. (The Prince had previously shown an interest in Olga but had been brushed off successfully by Nicholas.) Dmitri would arrive later in time for tea.

Meanwhile, Alexandra complained of Marie to Nicholas. She added that Marie was in a particularly grumpy mood and was bellowing at her. (The Tsarina also said that Marie and Olga had been visited by *Madame Becker* which may well have meant that she thought this was at least part of the reason. Marie was normally amiable but was at times rather difficult. Alexandra was convinced that Olga, however, had been less moody recently.)

Nicholas sent flowers for Alexandra on Palm Sunday along with a note. He admitted that, now he was no longer seeing the troops, letters were his only consolation. (They gave a vivid image of life at Alexander Palace. Each gave a different aspect of home life and kept Nicholas's spirits up.) He enclosed three flowers that he had found on his walk the previous day. He complained of being overwhelmed by visitors and hoped that he would be left alone in Holy Week. He appreciated Alexandra's gift of a book. He enjoyed reading in his free time – not that he had much.

That day Alexandra mentioned Marie's letter. She knew she could rely on Marie to give Nicholas a really detailed letter. Marie had written to him about what she termed the nonsense on the ice. Marie had been in the water.

Marie explained what she had been up to. It illustrated her immense strength. One of the men had lost some scrap iron in the middle of the pond and, when another man went to help him, they both almost fell in. She assisted by holding on to their uniforms. The men were on a piece of ice at the time and the other sisters held it with hooks. One of the other men was sitting on the bank giving orders. Alexandra sat in her armchair nearby and observed the action.

Olga had also written to Nicholas and was worried that the flowers would become frozen as the weather had cooled. Some had already begun to bloom.

On Monday Nicholas replied to a particularly loving letter he had just received from Alexandra. He had found great consolation in the religious service and was pleased that Father George Shavelsky had not gone on too long. He admitted that he had forgotten to take any Easter cards or eggs to send to the children. He asked Alexandra to assist him by getting some to him – so he could send them back.

That day Anastasia had told Nicholas by letter how her mischievous brother needed to be kept occupied. He was liable to injure himself when his time was not rigidly organised for him. Anastasia and her sisters had no lessons, but Alexei was forced to continue with his studies.

The five children had attended church that morning with the Tsarina and they had all returned later in the day for another service. Despite all the services, the sisters managed to return to their respective hospitals.

Nicholas wrote home on Tuesday with news of a great victory. He was especially pleased that it had come in time for Easter, which is far more important in the Russian Orthodox Church than Christmas. He complained that the weather was always good when he had to work but it rained when he had free time. (It is a common complaint today and a feeling shared by many.) The Russian troops had occupied Trapezound, he revealed.

He later wired after hearing of Alexandra's slight accident. She had fallen on the balcony whilst at Anya's little house.

The Tsarina struggled after her fall, as she admits that day in a letter to Nicholas. She was feeling shaky even just holding her knitting needles or needlework. She sent Nicholas eight Easter cards so he could return them for his four daughters, two sisters and Anya. She suggested that she send them on Friday.

Meanwhile, Tatiana had also written to Nicholas and admitted how boring she was finding it going to church without him. She had been working at the hospital as usual and asked his opinion on book *Through the Postern Gate* which he had been reading.

General Hanbury-Williams spoke with Nicholas on Wednesday concerning the problems experienced by the British Admiralty. He explained to the Tsar about the heavy workload of the British navy. They needed to assist the people of France, India, Australia and parts of Africa, according to the General.

Meanwhile Nicholas wrote at length to Alexandra and admitted that he had been rather baffled as to why Voyeikov had told Anya that he (Nicholas) was coming home soon. Alexandra sent presents to Nicholas so that he could return them to the children. She had already sent a collection of cards for him to sign and send on. She also enclosed some Easter eggs and a book. Her arm was better, she admitted, but had bruised badly in the accident. Alexei was suffering after hurting his left arm (whilst using a spade) and was struggling to sleep. His sisters had sat with him.

She went on to explain that Olga and Tatiana had gone to the infirmary and would return later to sit with Alexei and help paint the Easter eggs. That afternoon Marie and Anastasia had gone to their hospital to observe how the new X-ray machine worked.

Alexandra took the decision to write later in the day after her son's pains increased. She had spent the afternoon in the playroom with her son painting eggs whilst Sydney Gibbes read to the boy. He was suffering greatly, although he kept falling asleep briefly. He awoke soon after once the pains returned. He was quite unable to eat, and she found that he was best distracted whilst being read to. He had confession along with his two youngest sisters at home as he was unable to go to the church. Olga and Tatiana went to confess at church at ten.

Nicholas wrote again to Alexandra on Thursday, but only briefly due to pressures of work. Once again he complained that the weather seemed to get worse each time he went outside. Nicholas explained that his thoughts would be with Alix the next day, the eighth, as it was the anniversary of their engagement. He reminded her that he had fought for her then, like *Little Boy Blue* in the Florence Barclay story he had recently read entitled *Through the Postern Gate*. Nicholas identified with the character Guy Chelsea in the story. He enclosed a photograph album for his son that had been given to him by a British military photographer.

Luckily, Alexandra had good news for Nicholas that day: Alexei was better. He had begun to eat again which was a good sign. She had been with him whilst painting the eggs again and Mr Gibbes had read to him.

Olga struggled to concentrate as she wrote that day to Nicholas. Her sisters (probably not Tatiana) and brother were talking so loudly she could not hear herself think. She reported that some gifts had arrived from Grand Duchess Elisabeth and some beautiful eggs from the Mother Superior.

Marie also wrote to her father. She began by asking his forgiveness (as is traditional at that time of year, the day before Good Friday). She had spent much of the day with her brother but had visited the infirmary with Anastasia in the afternoon. The four sisters had visited the church that morning with them to receive Communion and had returned in the evening to hear the *12 Gospels* read.

Nicholas wrote on Friday, the twenty-second anniversary of his engagement to the formerly hesitant Princess Alix of Hesse in 1894, recalling happier times. He remembered a concert they had attended in Coburg, the Bavarian band that had played, and how his Uncle Alfred had kept falling asleep during the concert. He finished his letter the following day and thanked Alix for the gifts he had received, including some small eggs and a bookmark.

He explained that, at church, there had been lots of people there for Holy Communion. Many of the children stared at him and, as a result, forgot to look where they were going and tumbled into each other.

Nicholas later sent a wire that he hoped would arrive in time for Easter Day. He wished them all the best. It was so hard to be away from his family at this particular time.

On Friday, Alexandra expressed her appreciation to Nicholas for the beautiful blue flowers which had arrived. He had sent them in such profusion that she was able to gift some to her ladies-in-waiting to their great delight. (Nicholas may have sent blue flowers in memory of *Little Boy Blue*.) They were intending to visit church at two for the traditional carrying out of the Shroud from the church and would return at six for the (ritual not actual) burial, she explained. Alexei had recovered and had only woken up a few times during the previous night. He was eager to be able to attend the morning service. They had lunched near Alexei's bed as he was feeling rather dizzy after all the medicines he had taken. (It indicates that he may have been given something unusually strong.)

When Nicholas had dinner that evening at military headquarters, General Hanbury-Williams had spoken of Nicholas's visit to London in 1893. Nicholas had been mistaken for his first cousin George, now King George V. (Their mothers were sisters and were both originally Danish princesses, which is why Nicholas was able to speak a little Danish.)

Olga and Tatiana returned to the infirmary on Saturday. One of the patients Tatiana had bandaged that morning was an old friend – Baron Taube. Marie and Anastasia went back to their own hospital to see the patients where they generally played dominoes or cards with the men or read to them. They did not work as such, but made a contribution nevertheless.

Another old friend arrived for tea to Tatiana's delight – Nicholas Rodionov, an old tennis partner of hers. Alexei's little friend Kolya also arrived to spend time with the invalid. Nicholas's daughters took the opportunity to write to Nicholas to thank him for their cards and eggs. Tatiana admitted again how bored she was without him, and Anastasia said much the same.

On Easter Sunday Nicholas thanked Alexandra for the gifts which he claimed brightened up his bare rooms at headquarters. He distributed the eggs alone which was something he had never done before. He had previously done it with his parents or Alexandra. He had good news however: he hoped to be home by Wednesday.

He handed out the eggs to the members of his suite. Alexandra had sent a list of who the eggs were for but he may not have stuck to it to the letter. She had explained that the four big eggs were intended for Father George Shavelsky, General

Ivanov, General Alexeiev and Admiral Nilov (Count Fredericks had one already, she stated). The smaller eggs were intended for General Voyeikov, Count Grabbe, Prince Valia Dolgorukov, Dmitri Sheremietiev, Colonel Silaiev, Anatole Mordvinov, Kira Narishkin, Dr Feodorov, the recently promoted Count Zamoiy and Pustov.

That day, Alexandra explained how she and the children were spending Easter without Nicholas. Once more, she complains that Olga was in a grumpy mood. The Grand Duchesses had not wished to change into one of her nicer dresses and had preferred to remain in her uniform. They had attended the Easter service together and had then eaten with Andrei Derevenko and Klementy Nagorny. She had had to wake Alexei in time for morning Mass that morning. Tatiana had helped Alexandra with the handing out of the eggs in the absence of Nicholas. The sisters later returned to their respective infirmaries.

Tatiana put pen to paper to thank Nicholas for the gifts. She had enjoyed the service the previous morning and found that the air was so still outside that they had been able to take their candles out of the church without resorting to holding their hands over the flames. She explained that they were going to a concert the next day at the Catherine Palace. Anya had arrived in time for tea.

Nicholas wrote home on Monday in a cheerful mood. He had exchanged Easter greetings with some 900 soldiers during the course of that day. His cousin George had arrived to add to the feeling of festivity.

That day, the four Grand Duchesses attended the morning service in the company of their mother and many of the wounded soldiers. They returned for a celebration lunch but without Nicholas for the first time. Anya arrived in his absence however. The family then travelled the short distance to the Catherine Palace hospital to distribute yet more Easter eggs and later Alexei proudly held a film show with his new Pathe equipment and they enjoyed an American movie.

Olga, Marie, Anastasia and their chaperone Baroness Sophie Buxhoeveden visited Olga's ambulance train on Tuesday. Olga then returned to her duties at the infirmary. The children later attended a concert at Anya's small hospital.

On a hot day Olga walked to the infirmary on Wednesday in the company of Marie, Anastasia and their chaperone Catherine Schneider. Nicholas arrived in mid-afternoon with Colonel Silaiev. He soon got to work digging up what remained of the ice in the park under the bridge, accompanied by the sailors and his daughters. It was like the old days before the war. Despite Nicholas's return, Olga and Tatiana chose to go back to the infirmary on Thursday morning but they came back for lunch. That afternoon Nicholas escorted his eldest two daughters to the capital where they had tea with the Dowager Empress and later called in on his sister Xenia. The evening ended as it often did on holidays: the ladies worked whilst Nicholas read to them.

Olga and Tatiana resumed their duties at the infirmary on Friday. Later, they returned and, together with Nicholas and their younger sisters, walked towards Bablova. Anya accompanied the party, and Alexandra was pushed along in her wheelchair which she used from time to time. The party enjoyed tea at Pavlovsk in the company of Nicholas's Aunt Olga of Greece, her son Christopher and the late Grand

Duke Konstantin's family Ioann, Elena, Igor, Vera (10) and George. Upon their return, Olga Nicolaevna attended one of her infrequent lessons: singing and she later joined her sisters sitting in the dark on the balcony.

The following day, the sisters resumed their usual Saturday morning routine and returned to their respective hospitals. The family reassembled in time for lunch. Nicholas's cousin Grand Duke George had arrived as had the aged Count Fredericks and Dmitri Sheremetiev, and Nicholas was reunited with some of the staff who had been to headquarters with him in recent months.

After lunch, Nicholas escorted his four daughters on a walk. Whilst he had been away, they had to make their own arrangements. The family then went kayaking, with the obvious exception of Alexandra and probably Alexei too. They returned to the palace in time for tea and, afterwards, Nicholas resumed his usual holiday occupation of reading aloud.

The Tsar along with Alexandra and his daughters attended the regular Mass on Sunday morning before returning to the palace for lunch. Marie and Anastasia attended a wedding chaperoned by Countess Hendrikova but they returned in time for dinner. There were often weddings amongst the wounded men and they naturally invited the Grand Duchesses from the hospital concerned.

The children resumed their usual lessons on Monday morning after the Easter break. Olga and Tatiana returned to the infirmary and Marie and Anastasia to their hospital that day. Tatiana was still fitting the two in together somehow and managing to see her dog and have lunch and visit church during the early part of the day. Olga's start had been more leisurely with a relaxing massage.

That afternoon, there was a break from the usual pattern when Nicholas and his two youngest daughters Marie and Anastasia rode on their bicycles whilst Olga and Tatiana were driven in a small motor car for a visit. Meanwhile, the Tsarina's older sister Elisabeth had come for one of her brief visits and sat with Alexandra. She stayed for lunch and dinner. Alexandra was still feeling unwell and remained on the sofa that evening, even during dinner.

The children resumed their lessons and work as usual on Tuesday but, after lunch, the Grand Duchesses and their brother joined Nicholas, Alexandra and Elisabeth for a trip to a nearby cemetery for a memorial service in honour of all the soldiers who had died. The four sisters then went for a walk with their father and rode in one or two of the boats on the pond.

Nicholas had an important meeting on Friday with the newly appointed American Ambassador Mr David Roland Francis in the Corner Sitting Room of the Alexander Palace. Nicholas had recently met the retiring Ambassador. Mr Francis naturally presented his papers to the Tsar.

On his last full day at the Alexander Palace, Nicholas and his family returned to church for a special service for his safety whilst at headquarters. A service was normally held on his arrival and departure. Nicholas then enjoyed a ride on his bicycle and in the boats on the pond in the company of his four daughters. The family then had tea on the balcony, and afterwards the girls later returned to church with Nicholas.

The four Grand Duchesses returned to Mass with their parents on Sunday and all met up again with Alexei, in time for lunch. Nicholas left for military headquarters in the afternoon after a walk in the park with his daughters. The girls then went back to the hospitals and returned in time for tea, which was again taken on the balcony with Alexandra and her friend Anya.

That day whilst Nicholas travelled back to military headquarters he wired home from Malaia Vishera complaining that the carriage was too hot and he was missing his family already. (He hated leaving his wife and children. They visited him occasionally but the house where he lived was so small and crowded that they were forced to live aboard the train. The Grand Duchesses did not mind the cramped conditions though; they enjoyed the change of routine and the chance of seeing their father and new scenery. The eldest Grand Duchesses were working hard at the infirmary and it was important that they had the occasional break.)

Nicholas arrived back at headquarters on Monday and admitted to Alexandra that he had tears in his eyes after reading the ultra-romantic novel *The Rosary* by Florence Barclay. (It was a great favourite of Tatiana and Marie and a best-seller in that era. It is a more elegant version in some ways of *Jane Eyre* and concerns the plain heroine the Honourable Jane Champion who falls in love with the artistic and sensitive Garth Dalman. He falls for Jane once he hears her beautiful singing voice.)

He later wrote at some length of his journey and other matters. He had struggled to remain calm when he had parted from his family but reassured Alexandra that her letter had managed to help him and he had reread it several times. Nicholas had passed a hospital train on his travels and had met the wounded men along with their doctors and nursing sisters. He again praised the book that he had just completed. It was a shame that he had finished it but he had some other books to read. He finished his letter the following morning as he often did. He was intending to row on the nearby river.

Meanwhile, back at the Alexander Palace, life went on as normal for the remaining inmates. The children returned to their studies and work at the hospitals. Madame Vyrubova had arrived in time for lunch. On Nicholas's recent trip home, Alexandra had contrived to keep her away as much as she could.

The Tsarina had tea with her four daughters on the balcony. Alexei often dined alone as his mealtimes were different to those of his sisters and he was relegated to the nursery. He dined at six but the Grand Duchesses dined at eight with one or other or both their parents. He was eleven and a half so not treated as an adult of course, not that his sisters were.

That evening two old friends arrived in time for dinner – Nicholas Sablin, who had recently joined the army (he had previously been a senior officer on the Imperial yacht), and Tatiana's old tennis partner Nicholas Rodionov.

Nicholas showed his true romantic character in a wire to Alexandra on Tuesday. He described himself as *Boy Blue* after one of the men in Florence Barclay's book *Through the Postern Gate*. The character had so reminded him that he had chosen to adopt the name.

He found time to write again later in the day. He explained that he had really enjoyed the trip on the river with members of the suite. Not all his men were in the best of health, it seems.

Nicholas and his party had travelled in three dinghies down the river. He had been accompanied by Prince Igor, Dr Feodorov and Dmitri Sheremietiev but they had gone in a motor launch. The Prince, he declared, could not row and, after just a few strokes, coughed and spat up blood. He has only twenty-two years old. It became too hot so they all eventually moved into the launch. Dr Feodorov had an idea to test their fitness. (Prince) Valia's pulse was 82, Nicholas's 92, Voyeikov reached 114 and Kira Narishkin 128. The others then teased Narishkin about being a vegetarian. It did not appear to have done him any good. Ten minutes later, their pulses were taken again. Nicholas and Valia Dolgourkov had returned to normal, unlike the other two men. He had seen two little dogs chasing each other that morning out of his window. The guards were equally amused at the sight. (It reminded Nicholas of spring and, probably, his children's dogs Ortipo and Joy.)

That day Alexandra explained that Sablin and Rodionov had arrived for dinner the previous evening and had sat out with them on the balcony afterwards until 10.30 but had both left soon after to catch their train.

Olga cheerfully wrote to Nicholas of their recent visitors. They had greatly enjoyed their company. Earlier, she and Marie had sat on the window sill and watched as two men, a non-commissioned officer in the Cossacks and another soldier, played draughts. They were not the only ones watching; a large crowd had gathered. The sisters laughed as they observed the way the men were playing the game. (The girls had been surrounded by soldiers their entire lives and were familiar with them, and often their friends were amongst them. The three eldest undoubtedly fell in love with soldiers and, as for Anastasia, she appeared to mention the name of Victor Zborovsky too often in writing for it to be a mere coincidence.)

Olga had started the day with another massage before returning to the infirmary. On this occasion Alexandra accompanied them. There was an appendix operation which seemed to be quite a common complaint amongst the men. She later helped Alexei prepare his lessons.

Alexandra sent Nicholas the sequel to *The Rosary* named the *Mistress of Shenstone*. (I being one of the few people alive having read the works of Florence Barclay can confirm that, although rather sweet, they are a little on the dull side for the modern reader. They were ideal for the sensibilities of the age.)

On Wednesday Nicholas thanked Alexandra, Olga and Alexei for their recent letters, and discussed the possibility of taking out a loan for the costs of the war. He had also heard from his sister Olga who wanted a divorce. He finished his letter the following morning by which time he had had a further letter from Alexandra and one from Tatiana. He explained it had been very cold in the night and that he had had to close the window.

That day Tatiana revealed to Nicholas that it had been warm enough to sunbathe on the window sill. (The sisters enjoyed bathing in the sun at any opportunity.) She had wanted to restart her horse riding but was unable to as the horses were still at Gatchina.

On Thursday afternoon Alexandra had escorted her four daughters into the capital to the English hospital which had been set up at Grand Duke Dmitri's palace. They went on to tea at the Dowager Empress's palace and returned in time for dinner. Alexandra was naturally exhausted by then and, whilst her daughters sat at the table, she remained on the couch. She had not taken Alexei as his leg was still bent and he needed carrying.

After dinner, Olga and Alexandra read aloud in turns from an English novel which they had forgotten they had. The other sisters continued with their needlework.

Nicholas wrote at great length on Friday and outlined the itinerary for Alexandra's proposed visit. (The family would go to the Crimea for a well-earned break but would not return to Livadia on this or any subsequent occasion.)

The next day Nicholas complained once again to Alexandra of being overworked. He was constantly attending receptions and his free time was now taken up with reading newspapers (and replying to Alexandra's letters amongst others). He had no time to play dominoes in the evenings as he used to.

According to Alexandra, one of Olga's former suitors (Prince Christopher of Greece) had arrived for tea that day along with Tatiana Konstantinovna's young children. She found it difficult to concentrate as her children were all talking at once whilst they ate.

Olga had also written to Nicholas that day and enclosed some cards on behalf of Tatiana. She explained that yesterday her grandmother sent her and her sister Tatiana a Red Cross medal of the 1st degree. The Dowager Empress remained as head of the Red Cross. They had also seen Silaiev's wife and children the previous day.

At the beginning of May, a conversation on the subject of shooting almost got out of hand. Nicholas almost knocked over a bottle of wine in his excitement. He had been chatting about duck shooting with General Hanbury-Williams, and the Tsar had become so animated during the talk that he nearly sent the wine flying.

Nicholas found time to write later. He was greatly looking forward to having a holiday with his family in the Crimea in the coming weeks. They would only stay on Odessa for twenty-four hours, he explained.

In a letter to Nicholas that same day, Tatiana briefly discussed The Rosary. She explained that her mother had told her that he had just read the book and praised it highly. She thought it was wonderful. (Sunday was the one fairly quiet day for Tatiana when she had much time to write.)

Nicholas wired home after a trip on the river again on Monday. He had been greatly amused by the turbulence. He had been tossed around by the waves. It brought back memories of Alexei who had been at headquarters previously.

The two elder Grand Duchesses meanwhile carried on with their usual duties at the infirmary. On Tuesday, after the usual bandaging, Tatiana sat around in the company of Sedov, one of the patients, and later chatted to Varvara, known as Bibi. After lunch, Olga and Tatiana returned to Petrograd where they visited the refugees' registration desk before going on to their usual committee meetings. They later returned to the infirmary where Tatiana again chose to sit with Sedov.

Olga and Tatiana attended a service at the *Church of the Sign* on Wednesday. They were joined by the Tsarina and her son on this occasion. They met Varvara en route and she was given a lift by them to the infirmary. There was a festive atmosphere that afternoon as Olga played the piano, Anastasia accompanied her on the balalaika and everyone sang together. It was like a scene from *The Sound of Music*.

The Tsarina and her five children, along with a small entourage including Baroness Buxhoeveden and Resin, left soon after for Nicholas's military headquarters. They arrived after lunch on Thursday. The reunited family then went for a drive to the River Dnieper. They had tea on the train that evening.

On Friday, the Tsar and all his immediate family attended a service at a nearby garrison church. They were joined at lunch by Nicholas's cousin Grand Duke Kyrill and Prince Igor. The Tsar and his five children then went for a walk along the railway track returning to the train in time for tea. The family were then treated to a film show and sat out in a nearby village for tea. It was the Tsar's forty-eighth birthday.

That day General Hanbury-Williams met the Tsarina once more and they chatted about the British nurse Lady Sybil Grey (daughter of Albert, 4th Earl Grey) whom she had recently met. The Grand Duchesses had been particularly impressed by her bravery. The General found the Tsarina far easier to get on with than he had expected. Her reputation had preceded her, but the Englishman had something in common with Alexandra. She had spent much of her youth at Windsor, Balmoral and Osborne whilst staying with her late beloved grandmother Queen Victoria.

Alexandra admitted to the General her intense shyness on coming into a room filled with so many dignitaries. He later noted in his journal that Alexei had been recently promoted from private to colonel and was now exactly the same rank as his father. (Nicholas had been promoted to colonel by his late father and had always refused to alter the rank.)

Nicholas was asked by the men on Saturday if he would bring Alexei back to military headquarters on his return from his visit to the Crimea. The family again lunched in the nearby village, accompanied by Kyrill and Igor. The family left for the south soon after. The train travelled south towards the Crimea via Kiev, Vinnitsa, Bender and Odessa before arriving at Sevastopol.

The train arrived in Kiev on Sunday morning and Nicholas was briefly reunited with his mother and sister. The family arrived at the small town of Vinnitsa in the early afternoon. The Tsarina took the opportunity to visit a nearby ambulance train, train depot, warehouse and hospital.

They entered Bender(y) early on Monday morning where the Tsar reviewed the Czech-Slovak legions, formed from the former Austrian prisoners of war. The family arrived in Odessa late in the afternoon where they visited the cathedral and a warehouse. Tatiana noted with excitement in her journal her first sighting of the sea that year.

The family visited an iodine factory and a sanatorium on Tuesday. (Iodine was a valuable commodity as it was used for cleaning the wounds before operations as it is today.) They left Odessa at 9pm and went on to the next destination.

The train arrived in Sevastopol on Thursday morning and the Imperial family visited the Romananovksy Institute and lunched with the admirals. During the afternoon the Tsar's family inspected the new *Catherine the Great* ship. They walked on deck and below. It was a first for the excited Grand Duchesses. They then inspected the *Empress Maria*.

That day, the children's tutor Professor Petrov had sent word to Tatiana explaining that the palace was in a terrible mess. There were renovations going on in the children's rooms and Alexei's suite of rooms was being altered.

On Saturday morning the family (apart from Alexandra) returned to the Empress Maria where a Mass was performed. They then travelled to the Marine Corps base and the aviation school. The children were delighted at the sight of a gyroplane as it flew over the water.

The following day was spent quietly and the family simply sat on deck and went ashore to the St George Monastery and visited nearby forts.

The Imperial family finally arrived at Eupatoria on Monday where they visited the Karaim, an ancient Christian religious group. (They worshipped in synagogues and were part Christian, part Jewish. The head of the Karaim at that time was the Patriarch Gahan.) The family also visited the cathedral and hospitals in the area.

They met up with Olga's best friend Rita and the family then enjoyed the rare pleasure of spending time on a public beach. They saw Anya Vyrubova who had rented a dacha nearby. The children enjoyed sitting and looking for shells on the beach where they were joined by Rita and Anya, who was still on crutches. The family left for the north later in the day and Nicholas returned to headquarters.

Nicholas's spirits were low after the family split once more. He had enjoyed the brief holiday which had been their first since the outbreak of war. He wired from Gloushkovo on Tuesday as he travelled back to headquarters and admitted that he was feeling sad and empty without his wife and daughters.

Nicholas talked over a proposed visit by Lord Kitchener to Russia with General John Hanbury-Williams on Wednesday. Nicholas was keen that he be invited to Russia. It would, however, end in disaster. Meanwhile that day he composed a short letter to Alexandra. He was greatly missing his wife and his daughters, but luckily he had been joined by his son on this occasion.

Later, Nicholas wired to say that he and his son had played on the beach that day, like they had in the Crimea. They were keeping up the holiday mood.

Alexandra composed a long letter that day to Nicholas. The Grand Duchesses took the opportunity to sunbathe. Despite this, Olga, Marie and Anastasia were complaining about the weather, she remarked. They played ball or the piano in an effort to get warm. Tatiana meanwhile (as placid as ever) got on with her needlework.

Alexandra explained that the previous day, whilst Louise Tutelberg (known as Tudels) was arranging the Tsarina's compartment, the girls were laid out on the floor with the sun full on them in an effort to get brown. She wondered where they got such an idea. (A Victorian lady simply would not do such a thing. They had to be pale and interesting.)

After they arrived home, Olga complained in a letter to Nicholas of the endless quiet at home. She missed the bustle of the train and the towns they had visited. She was writing whilst sat in her mother's famous *Mauve Boudoir*. It was evening and the lamp nearby was lit but she felt odd and wished she were still in the Crimea.

Meanwhile, Alexei was missing his mother and decided to write. He was greatly amused when he realised that he was able to smell her familiar perfume on the pillow and curtains. He had been playing Nain Jaune (Pope Joan) with Dr Derevenko the previous day and had managed to win a lot of money.

Nicholas spoke to General Hanbury-Williams again on Thursday about Kitchener. He wanted to speak to the man personally as he valued his opinions. The General explained that he had no doubt that Lord Kitchener would be forthcoming with his views.

The Tsar later composed a short letter to Alexandra, after he had received a quite unexpected one from her. He reported that Alexei had settled back into the routine of headquarters easily enough.

That day Alexandra explained that they had unexpected guests for dinner. (They were not used to inviting anyone for dinner). Nicholas Karangozov, one of the wounded Olga had treated, had suddenly turned up, as had Anushevitch and Captain DS Yedigarov of the 17th Nijni Dragoons. The latter was about to leave the following day.

Olga and Tatiana had of course returned to their infirmary after their brief holiday. There was little to do, however. In the afternoon, Olga and Tatiana joined Alexandra in a visit to the Uhlan regimental hospital and all four of the Grand Duchesses later called at the Grand Palace hospital. To Olga's delight, she met Mitya Shakh-Bagov and his friend Boris Ravtopolo on her travels. It was, she remarked in her journal that evening, the first anniversary of Mitya's injury.

Tatiana complained of her boredom in a letter to Nicholas that day. She was missing the warmth of the Crimea and had little to do at the infirmary. She explained how they had visited church that morning and returned to the infirmary, but there were only two dressings for her to do that day. In the afternoon, they had all visited the Tsarina's Uhlan hospital and all the regimental ladies had been there. There had been a church service and they had been treated to tea and chocolates. It was odd to see so many ladies as, in recent times, Tatiana had only seen the men of the regiments (apart from the nurses of course).

The Tsarina could not get used to being without her son and, each time she passed the child's dining room at six, she was confused as to why the table was not set for his dinner. (The ladies dined at eight.) She could not get used to the lack of noise either, not that her two youngest daughters were quiet.

Nicholas wrote at unusual length to Alexandra on Friday. He wanted to reassure her that Alexei was all right and coping without her. After he had left with Alexei, the boy had remarked, on smelling her perfume in the carriage, how much he missed his mother. He had enjoyed a trip out to the beach where he had played happily. Dr Feodorov had even let him walk about barefoot, to his delight. He assured Alexandra that Alexei behaved well at the table and sat quietly next to him. He had missed his son very much when the boy had returned to the palace.

Alexandra was still praising her recent visitor in her next letter to Nicholas.

Captain DS Yedigarov told them a great many fascinating things. (Nicholas had a terrible habit of describing in his journal that he had seen a great many interesting things and never going into detail of the subject.) The Tsarina had been interested in hearing the news from the battlefront even though the horrific conditions must have been difficult for her to imagine. She adds that they had bid goodbye to Yedigarov that morning at the infirmary. She had photographed the men including Boris Ravtopolo and (Olga's friend) Mitya Shakh-Bagov.

According to Olga's journal, the four sisters were photographed that day. Boris Ravtopolo and Dmitri Shakh-Bagov had both appeared that day to her delight – shaven-headed after their recent exploits.

Meanwhile, Tatiana mentioned Olga's friend in a letter to Alexei that day. She explained that Ravtopolo and Shakh-Bagov had been to the infirmary that day and she had taken photographs of them all on the balcony.

Marie explained to Nicholas that evening that Olga was playing the piano whilst Tatiana read quietly. Anastasia had gone to bed and the Tsarina was looking through some petitions. Yedigarov had eaten with them the previous evening, she explained, and it was rather interesting. She also informed Nicholas that all were wearing shawls from Eupatoria as they felt so cold.

General Hanbury-Williams, who was living at the Hotel Bristol at the time, had personal reasons for remembering Saturday evening for the remainder of his life. He suddenly had a horrible premonition. The General had woken up at 3am and his weary eyes had rested upon some of the pictures he had pasted onto the wall including one of Lord Kitchener. The Englishman suddenly thought to himself had he done the right thing. He knew that the decision was the correct one but nevertheless, he had a feeling of trouble ahead. After a short interval, he looked once more at the collection of pictures, laughed and returned to his slumbers. Shortly after, Kitchener would die in tragic circumstances as would the General's eldest son.

Nicholas later wrote at some length to Alexandra. He was delighted that she had met Captain Yedigarov and explained that he had just received Trepov who had recently returned from the Caucasus. He had visited the front at Trapezound and met up with Grand Duke Nicholas who had been Commander-in-Chief before Nicholas had taken up the mantle. Trepov had explained that the local people had become more loyal since Nicholas's cousin had been in the region.

Meanwhile, Alexei had written to his mother. He had proved to be as mischievous as ever despite Nicholas's recent praise of his improved behaviour. The boy admitted that the previous morning, whilst Nicholas was still asleep, he had gone up to his father and tickled him with a pillow and tormented him.

(The Tsarevich enjoyed life at headquarters. He was in the type of environment many little boys would enjoy. He had spent all his brief life playing at soldiers and now he was at a real military headquarters in wartime with his beloved father. No other heir to the throne had ever been taken on such a journey in recent times. As a child, he had played with toy guns, soldiers and fortresses for hours on end with his sailor companion Derevenko as he rarely saw other children.)

Meanwhile, back at the Alexander Palace, the Grand Duchesses' lives continued as usual. That morning, Tatiana had been present during an operation. She and Olga then returned early for lunch before going back to the infirmary. That evening, it was not only Olga and Tatiana who assembled at the hospital but also Marie, Anastasia and even Alexandra. They all helped clean the instruments for the following day's work. The sisters were joined by Valentina, Mitya and Boris.

Nicholas wired home on Sunday and explained that the weather had improved enough to be able to eat outside again in the tent, and he and Alexei had been for a boat ride along the river.

The Tsar later wrote with important news from Britain where the Battle of Jutland had just taken place. (It would be the only naval battle in the Great War and there would be no outright winner. The Tsar's nephew Prince Albert, later King George VI, had a minor part in the battle.) Nicholas thanked Alix for a recent gift of two pansies. He had given one to his son.

Meanwhile, Alexandra wrote of her daughters' work at the hospital and she went on to add that the previous evening they had all spent the evening cosily at the infirmary. Olga and Tatiana had cleaned the instruments with the help of Dmitri Shakh-Bagov and Boris Ravtopolo. They had visited Colonel Silaiev's family the previous day too and had tea with them along with Shakh-Bagov and Ravtopolo. (The three men all belonged to the same regiment – the Erivansky. Alexandra failed to mention whether Olga was so delighted when she and Tatiana and their close friends had been joined by their mother and noisy younger sisters.)

By coincidence, Olga had written to Nicholas that day complaining that her two youngest sisters Marie and Anastasia were being noisy. She also explained that the soldiers had been given their own workshop to keep them occupied. They were making items for an exhibition. She had been comfortable on the balcony yet it was now too cold to remain. The armchairs which had formerly been covered in a red fabric had been recovered into something lighter. She was delighted to report that the large basket that had been there before was still there and full of earwigs. She finished her letter the following day after eating on the balcony. The Tsarina was receiving guests and, at three, they were all due to go out for a drive. Tatiana was intending to ride a horse.

That morning the Tsarina explained to Nicholas she had attended Mass with her four daughters. The ladies had been joined at lunch by Baroness Buxhoeveden and Countess Hendrikov. After lunch, Alexandra and her elder daughters travelled to Pavlovsk. In the evening, they had returned to the infirmary and, after cleaning the medical implements, Olga played the piano. The Tsarina and ever watchful Valentina were sitting nearby.

Nicholas finally had some very good news to impart on Monday. He wired that the Russians had had their very first victory in the south-west region.

He later wrote on the eve of Alexandra's birthday – her forty-fourth to be precise. He was upset that he had not been able to get her a gift or even see her on the day in question.

Alexandra explained to Nicholas in a letter that the previous day she had driven to

Pavlovsk in the company of her elder daughters Olga and Tatiana. She was intending to go out again today, she remarked, accompanied by Olga, Marie and Anastasia. Tatiana was intending to go horse riding.

That day Tatiana had gone for an early morning walk in the company of Anastasia and their chaperone Catherine Schneider. (They had probably taken the dog.) Tatiana made a brief visit to the *Church of the Sign* before joining Olga and Alexandra at the infirmary. There was yet another operation. The ladies later sat out on the hospital balcony with some of the patients. Whilst they relaxed, Boris Ravtopolo and Dmitri Shakh-Bagov appeared and they sat together. The four sisters reassembled back at the palace in time for lunch with their mother. Afterwards, the youngest children returned to their lessons. The two eldest sisters later returned to the infirmary to clean the instruments in the company of Boris and Mitya. The sisters left shortly before midnight.

Nicholas sent Alexandra a birthday telegram on Tuesday but unfortunately he had nothing to send. He later attempted to make up for the lack of a gift by composing a long letter. He also enclosed one he had received from his sister Olga as a bonus.

That day, the Grand Duchesses Olga and Tatiana had returned to the infirmary as usual. Tatiana and her mother, who had also arrived, took part in yet another appendix operation. Tatiana then returned to the usual bandaging and Olga's friend Mitya appeared yet again. The sisters returned to the palace in time for lunch which was taken on the balcony. Tatiana went out for a ride before dinner. Nicholas's ailing uncle, Grand Duke Paul, arrived in time for tea. The eldest sisters returned to the infirmary yet again afterwards where they continued with the instrument cleaning. They were joined in their tasks by Mitya and Boris. The sisters left after midnight again.

There was tragic news on Wednesday and, according to General Hanbury-Williams, the Tsar felt responsible. Horatio Herbert, Lord Kitchener, had died whilst travelling aboard the cruiser *Hampshire* to Russia. The ship had struck a mine off Orkney. He was sixty-six years old. Nicholas had gone up to the General after he had heard the news and said that he wished that he had not asked Kitchener to come, but admitted that such things were bound to happen during wartime.

Nicholas only briefly mentioned the news in a wire to Alexandra that day. He explained that the loss would be particularly hard on his cousin George.

In Britain, the country would always remember him as the face of the famous poster declaring *Your Country Needs You*. It was, of course, a recruitment poster.

Alexandra briefly mentioned Kitchener in her letter to Nicholas, but chose not to dwell on the death. Men were dying every day during the war, and she saw it on a more personal level than Nicholas.

That same day Olga had sent word to Nicholas explaining that her two youngest sisters had gathered flowers from the Children's Island for their mother. The lilac was beginning to show in the garden here and there. The lilac was, of course, Alexandra's favourite colour and her famous sitting room contained lilac and white furniture.

The four sisters later joined their mother on a visit to Anya's little house. The hostess had other visitors including Rasputin and a relative of hers Maria Golovin. The ladies returned to the palace for dinner before the four sisters returned to Olga and

Tatiana's infirmary. It was now becoming a place of social gathering not just for Olga and Tatiana but for their younger sisters Marie and Anastasia. In May 1916, Marie was almost seventeen and Anastasia nearly fifteen.

The next day Nicholas sent Alexandra a rather brief but baffling wire. He thanked her for her recent letters and then mentioned that there were now some 50,000 prisoners of war, starting from the beginning of the war. He mentioned the weather then said that he had received Anya's photos and wanted to know if he was to send them to Alexandra or not. He was wandering from one subject to another, something Alexandra had done for years in her letters.

He later wrote in more detail and sent Alix a piece of *lucky* lilac to add to her collection of flowers. It was in the way of a small token of his affection on the recent occasion of her forty-fourth birthday. He had found it in the garden.

Alexandra in her next letter to Nicholas that same day complained that she was somewhat irked that Anya Vyrubova was due to return shortly. (In recent years, she had felt that Anya was herself always complaining.) Anya would be returning in a week, but Alix had felt that it was she who had been on holiday – apart from Anya. She disliked the infirmary, according to Alexandra, and her children made faces at her imminent return. (In the coming years, the Tsarina would see Anya for her true worth and what a real friend she was.)

That day Olga and Tatiana had returned to the infirmary by ten and, to Olga's delight, Mitya and Boris arrived later. The sisters returned to the Catherine Palace hospital accompanied by the Tsarina after lunch. Olga decided to go to the island and pick flowers with her sisters later. As Olga and Tatiana returned to the infirmary that evening, they were joined again by Mitya and his close friend Boris.

The Tsarina's personal physician, Dr Eugene Botkin, meanwhile left to travel to the Crimea to collect his daughter Tatiana, so she could attend her brother's wedding.

Nicholas thanked Alexandra for the flowers on Friday. She had sent them to headquarters and to General Hanbury-Williams who had been quite delighted. Nicholas wondered if Alix had found a letter he had included in a large envelope.

He wrote again after the arrival of one of the Tsarina's letters and agreed that Anya always seemed to be in the way.

Alexandra meanwhile explained that her children had been gardening. Marie and Anastasia had decided the flowers would look a lot better without the surrounding weeds. (The park had been neglected recently which was understandable as the men who usually did the gardening were almost certainly away in the war. The old men would have been the only ones left and would have struggled to keep up appearances.)

She had, she explained, sat in the garden whilst the others played croquet. Olga and Tatiana were amongst those playing croquet along with Mitya and Boris, naturally. Olga had a committee later but returned to the infirmary at ten to help with the tidying up for a couple of hours, as she normally did.

That day, Tatiana had also written to Nicholas and she attempted to explain the changes that had recently been made. The children's rooms had been cleaned and, after the train, looked huge. She was never very descriptive, unlike Marie.

Anastasia had also written and complained about the weather. She was convinced that it rained every day. Despite this, they still continued to have their meals on the balcony. (The Tsarina's balcony was enclosed by heavy curtains by this time.)

General Hanbury-Williams observed on Saturday how happy everyone at military headquarters appeared to be. They were overjoyed after the recent successes against the Austrians. It had been reported that some 64,000 prisoners of war had been taken since the offensive had begun.

Nicholas explained in his next letter that he was intending to bring the icon of the *Borgia Mater* into the local garrison church which he regularly attended. He had little time for writing.

Olga sent word to Nicholas that day after assisting her youngest sisters in a spot of impromptu gardening. She took a great deal of interest in flowers and delighted in the signs of the coming spring. She explained that the lilac was now beginning to blossom at last and the trees were turning green. She had attended a committee meeting the previous day of the *executive department*. She was not overly impressed. (Olga would rather be in the infirmary.)

The Grand Duchess Olga had returned to the hospital as usual that morning after church and had written out prescriptions. Her friend Rita arrived from the Crimea. In the evening, Olga once more returned to the infirmary in the company of Tatiana. On this occasion, Valentina was close by as Olga spent more time with Mitya. She was often on duty as an unofficial chaperone to the elder Grand Duchesses.

That afternoon, Princess Paley, the second wife of Grand Duke Paul, met the Tsarina and explained that she had a late birthday present for her. She had ordered an expensive dress from Worth's in Paris. (The Tsarina was not overly impressed. She had taken the decision not to buy any new dresses during the war and use her allocation of dress expenses on charity. Alexandra was not really interested in dresses and often wore hers until they were threadbare and had little time for the recently created Princess.)

On Sunday Nicholas wrote to Alexandra on the occasion of Tatiana's nineteenth birthday. The Tsar on this special day spoke of Tatiana being a consolation in their old age. They seemed to assume that she would remain unmarried and stay with her aging parents as Nicholas's cousin Toria had (daughter of his aunt Queen Alexandra).

He hoped that she would remain as loving and patient as ever. Nicholas was so hot, he explained, that sweat was pouring down his pen. Yesterday, the troops paraded the icon along the streets. It reminded him of Borodino in 1912 (the 100th anniversary of the Battle of Borodino).

The Tsarina chose to remain out on the balcony in the heat, despite the palace rooms being much cooler. Her heart was complaining of the heat, she believed. (Her thoughts turned naturally to that day when Tatiana had been born at the little house nicknamed the *Farm* close to Peterhof. Her three younger siblings had been born in the recently renovated Lower Palace nearby. Olga, of course, being born in November had been born at the Alexander Palace, like her father.)

Tatiana thanked Nicholas for the gifts, letter and telegram she had received on her special day. She had received a telegram from a friend of Marie's, Nicholas Demenkov, which had been a nice surprise. Yesterday, she explained, Sablin had had tea with them. She also congratulated Alexei on his recent promotion to Lance-Corporal.

Meanwhile Marie chose to write to Nicholas about her recent gardening session. They had pulled out the weeds that had grown between the lilies of the valley. It was stifling their growth. They had done half the job and would return later to finish the work. She explained that now she joined their sisters at the infirmary each evening to help clean the instruments. Her sister Anastasia, on the other hand, joined in playing tiddlywinks or snooker with the injured men.

On Monday Nicholas complained of the excessive heat. He added that Alexei had particularly enjoyed getting a good soaking during a welcome shower of rain.

The Tsar sent word once again to Alexandra on Tuesday. He was delighted to report that the weather had improved vastly since the recent downpour. He had been to the woods for a walk with Valia Dolgorukov whilst his son played by the side of the road. They had then gone to the cinema and they were intending to go for another walk today. He was happy that the war was going better generally. Some of the Austrian troops and German divisions were making a desperate attempt to attack their flanks though at one point.

Meanwhile Alexandra explained that day that she too felt a lot cooler. She had been to church and to the hospital and was about to go for a drive along with Olga, Marie and Anastasia; once again Tatiana intended to ride.

Anastasia revealed to Nicholas how she had listened eagerly as his and Alexei's letters were read aloud. She apologised for changing the ink in the middle of the letter. After lessons that morning, she and Marie had played on the giant strides (stilts) as they had often done in the past.

Princess Paley arrived with a chiffon dress that she had ordered for Alexandra. Despite her initial annoyance, the Tsarina was impressed with the extravagant gift.

On Wednesday, at the beginning of June, Nicholas had good news to impart. Some 31,000 prisoners of war had been taken during the fighting at Lokachi and Kolki.

Meanwhile, Alexandra explained that she and Marie had attended a service at the cemetery in memory of the sixth-month anniversary of the death of her late friend Sonia. Olga and Tatiana had left for Petrograd and, after receiving the usual donations, they were going on to see Nicholas's late cousin Konstantin's widowed daughter and her young children. Marie and Anastasia were at their hospital, and the Tsarina intended to collect them shortly so they could go on a drive.

Later, the sisters joined their mother in time for dinner. Olga, Tatiana, Marie and Anastasia then returned to Olga and Tatiana's infirmary where the younger sisters played tiddlywinks with the men and the elder girls helped in the cleaning. Alexandra and Anya later joined the sisters. (It was becoming fairly obvious that the Tsarina was again keeping a close eye on Olga and Tatiana.)

Nicholas revealed on Thursday that his son kissed Alexandra's signature each evening after his father had read her letters. The boy listened whilst lying in bed before he said his prayers.

Meanwhile, Alexandra explained to Nicholas in her latest letter how she had been amazed by the reaction of her visit to the hospital. That morning, she had made a call at the infirmary with her daughters. The wounded had never seen Olga and Tatiana out of uniform and stared at their rings and bracelets. They wore dresses and hats and looked very different; normally their hair was hidden under the nurse's headdress. (For once, the men noticed Tatiana's beautiful auburn tresses and Olga's thick golden chestnut hair. It was not Alexandra that impressed the men but Olga and Tatiana.)

Marie and Anastasia had gone for a ride with Mlle Catherine Schneider that afternoon and had bought some flowers from a lady they met; some lily of the valley. They later returned to their hospital and amused themselves by swinging on the hammock outside.

The Tsarina and her daughters made only a very brief visit to the hospital before leaving for Petrograd. They attended Mass at the Fortress of St Peter and St Paul. Alexandra had heard that day of the death of the son of her old friend Toni Becker. (The nineteen year-old had been one of her uncannily unlucky godchildren.)

Nicholas admitted on Friday how the Tsarina's letters were a great joy to him. He ran out into the garden in order to relish each line in private.

He wired his thanks to Alexandra on Saturday for the photographs she had sent. They had been taken by Alexandra, Tatiana, Marie and Anya. He reported that, although the weather was terrible, the news was good. He went into no further detail.

Later, Nicholas thanked Alexandra again for the large number of photographs. He had been delighted with them and wished he had somewhere to put them. He had no photograph albums with him.

That day, Olga noted the arrival of two old friends at the infirmary: Victor Zborovsky who had been wounded in the chest and Alexander Shvedov who had contracted typhoid. She was thrilled when Boris Rovtopolo and his friend Dmitri Shakh-Bagov appeared before lunch. She returned to the palace along with Tatiana in time for lunch. That evening, the four sisters returned to the infirmary for a couple of hours and were joined by Boris and Mitya once more.

Nicholas sent his greetings to Alexandra on Sunday on the occasion of the birthday of their youngest daughter Anastasia who was fifteen. He had good news appropriately: Chernovitzi had been taken by the Allies.

Meanwhile, Alexandra congratulated Nicholas on their youngest daughter's birthday. She explained that they had been out for a drive but Olga had complained of the cold.

Anastasia spent the day in the company of her sister Marie. They visited their own hospital and later sat with Countess Hendrikova and looked at photo albums together. That day, she had been presented with a signed poem by the poet Nikolai Gumilev. It was signed by those officers who were currently recovering at the Grand Palace hospital. The poet had in fact grown up at Tsarskoe Selo. The birthday girl sent word to Nicholas to thank him for the gifts she had received. She also complained of the bad weather and reports that Victor Zborovsky, of whom she seemed particularly fond, had been shot in the chest right through.

Nicholas wrote in good spirits the next day. He explained that he had been for a drive with Alexei and they had been soaked by an unexpected downpour. Alexei had managed to sneak inside one of the cars and kept dry.

Meanwhile, Alexandra sent her congratulations to Nicholas for the recent victory. She had insisted Tatiana immediately telephone the hospitals with the news. She had joined her daughters at the infirmary there. Olga and Tatiana had been with Boris Ravtopolo and Dmitri Shakh-Bagov, and they had all been preparing material for the dressing station. The younger sisters had been playing games again with the men.

Olga wrote to Nicholas that day explaining that that the lilac and honeysuckle were still in bloom and the snow tower was still in situ but was rapidly shrinking. That day she had attended the baptism of a baby girl named Ludmilla at the cave church before visiting her ambulance train and handing out medals. In the evening, she and Tatiana had returned to the infirmary along with her mother, Marie and Anastasia. (It had been Mitya's final day in town before he returned to the front. Olga missed him a great deal and insisted that the date on the calendar at the infirmary remain on the day he left.)

Nicholas thanked Alexandra on Tuesday for the paste she had sent for the photographs. It reminded him, he explained, of how they used to spend quiet days on the yacht. The Tsar went on to write tellingly of General Alexeiev's views on Alexandra's interest in military affairs. He had listened silently and kept his opinions to himself yet managed to betray his innermost thoughts by his smile.

That day Valentina Chebotarieva noted how Olga had frantically searched for Mitya's knife. He had left it behind and she had been determined to find it and finally she did. In her own journal Olga had admitted how bored she was without Mitya.

Tatiana explained to Nicholas exactly which films would be shown that afternoon in the Manage for the soldiers – they would be films of the recent action at Erzerum and Trabezound.

Nicholas took the opportunity to send Alexandra a postcard on Wednesday. The Tsar recalled with his usual thoughtfulness and remarkable memory that it was the anniversary of the time they had spent at Walton-on-Thames in 1894 before their marriage. (Alix was at the time staying at a house close to the river that had been rented by her sister Victoria and her husband Louis of Battenberg.) He also sent a sprig of acacia via Count Benkendorf who was about to depart for Tsarskoe Selo.

Meanwhile, life went on much as usual at home. Alix reported that Olga was being teased by Count Alexander Vorontsov-Dashkov – one of Nicholas's many aides. (In previous years, both Tatiana and Anya had a crush on him and used to fight to sit next to him.) He was on three weeks' leave and was living at home with his wife and mother.

Marie explained to Nicholas that day how she and Anastasia had played with Anastasia's table-tennis set. It had been one of her birthday presents. Marie complained that she was tired of having to get down onto the floor to find the tiny ball again and again. (Marie was physically very strong but inclined to laziness as her weight indicates at this time.)

The Tsar again revealed military secrets on Thursday, unaware that Alexandra shared them with Rasputin. She asked the man for his advice and his blessings. Alexandra was not a spy but felt she could not trust the ministers. She trusted Rasputin for his apparent ability to cure her son. He obviously had little military knowledge but he did often show a lot of common sense. On one occasion, he had advised that the trains stopped the usual timetable so that supplies of food could get through.

Nicholas wired Alexandra later after the arrival of more letters and some very welcome additions to his growing collection of photographs. They would have been a delightful reminder of home and family.

Olga had written to Nicholas that day with an idea that she had had. She thought that it would be a nice idea if the wounded saw only comic films. They were usually given mainly news of the war and perhaps one comic film. She had asked the Tsarina if she could do something about it.

Meanwhile, Anastasia also wrote about her new table-tennis set to Nicholas. She revealed that her mother was going to town with Olga and Tatiana for a meeting of the Supreme Council (possibly for the refugee fund). She had played on the hammock with Marie that day. The two were apt to tip each other off it. She revealed that her young cousins Vera and George had been fighting, (as siblings often do).

The Tsar proudly boasted to Alexandra on Friday of their son's language skills. Alexei was not yet twelve years old but had conversed easily in French with a visiting prince. The Tsarevich had chatted amiably in French with the brother of the late Shah of Iran, Prince Zilli Sultan.

That day the Tsarina and her daughters had visited the local church on the occasion of the opening up of the relics of St John of Tobolsk. (The family were later imprisoned in that very town and later that year Alexandra's friends Lili Dehn and Anya Vyrubova visited Tobolsk along with her other friend Rasputin.)

Nicholas had only the time to send the shortest of wires on Saturday. Alexandra had asked him detailed questions regarding the ministers, but he had no time to answer. He urged her to speak to Boris Sturmer.

That day, Tatiana had explained to Nicholas that they had been to a memorial to one of their former patients, Zhukov. He had committed suicide. The Tsarina had taken all her daughters along to the service. Tatiana also revealed that Victor Zborovsky had been transferred to Marie and Anastasia's hospital. (It would have inevitably thrilled Anastasia.)

The next letter from Nicholas found him in a serious mood. He was greatly concerned about the lack of ammunition. The Russians never had enough weapons of any description.

Meanwhile, Alexandra was amused how Olga and Tatiana were teasing each other. They had kept calling each other thick skulls. She had noticed how Victor Zborovsky pretended to have no pain but his face gave him away.

Marie wrote to Nicholas and was delighted to report that she had a letter from Demenkov. He had not forgotten her.

Nicholas sent a telegram to Alexandra on Monday with a message for Marie. He congratulated her on her upcoming birthday (Tuesday). The family usually had their gifts the night before their actual birthday.

That day Olga Nicolaevna reported to Nicholas that she noticed that the gardeners were no longer cutting the grass. No weeding had been done either and there was just a small mark where the snow tower had been. She and Tatiana had returned to the infirmary as usual that morning. Tatiana had taken part in an operation and afterwards had sat outside in the sun. The sisters returned to the infirmary that evening to help with the tidying up. (Tatiana had employed her needlework skills in sewing the torn pillowcases).

The next day Nicholas briefly reminisced about happier times, but was quickly on to more serious matters. He congratulated Alexandra on the seventeenth birthday of Marie. He could not believe how time had flown. He went on to discuss the need for more officers as so many had been killed in the war already.

Meanwhile, Alexandra explained to the Tsar that Tatiana had found a box of cigarettes intended for general use. She was about to leave for Marie and Anastasia's new hospital, which had been built next to the old one, with her younger daughters. There would be a special *Te Deum*. Marie, she revealed, had been delighted with the letter from her father. (He rarely had time for individual letters to his children.)

That morning Alexandra and her four daughters had attended a special service *Te Deum* at the *Church of the Sign* for Marie's birthday. Tatiana began her day by sorting the laundry and later joined her mother and sisters at the new hospital. Olga and Tatiana later returned to the infirmary later in the evening. They left after midnight. Mitya had sent a telegram to Varvara, undoubtedly in the hope that she would pass on his news to his beloved Olga.

Marie had written again to Nicholas that day and enclosed more photographs. (She was a skilled photographer and even had the ability to develop them herself, as she proved in Siberia later.)

The Tsar wrote again to his family on Wednesday and explained that he had a great deal of paperwork to complete each day and endless meetings with ministers. He had managed, however, to find time to go for a row on the river and visit the local garrison church and cinema.

The Tsar's daughters were busy too, according to Alexandra, as she revealed in her daily letter to Nicholas that day. Olga and Tatiana had gone to town for a committee meeting. She was intending to go for a drive later with the younger children.

Tatiana had written to Nicholas that day and explained that she had found her younger sister's new hospital to be both comfortable and well arranged. She had seen Victor Zborovksy on her visit.

Nicholas was angered by a letter he had received from his aunt and explained his feelings in a letter to Alexandra on Thursday. She had asked why he had not done as she had asked.

That day, Alexandra informed Nicholas of how her daughters were spending their precious free time. Olga had remained on the balcony with her *work* whilst the other sisters had gone out horse riding.

Tatiana admitted to Nicholas that day that she now had even less time due to the increased workload with the new infirmary. On the first day they had, she explained, three new officers to treat and a further ten men of the lower rank. Four of the men had been critically ill and one just a mere boy of sixteen. The previous evening, they had been to a concert held at one of the hospitals. She hated to pass the old infirmary; it was not even empty as some men were waiting to leave.

Olga meanwhile had attended the *Church of the Sign* that morning in the company of Marie before returning to her shift at the infirmary. It was a warm day and, in the early evening, she went out picking flowers accompanied by Derevenko's young sons. She and Tatiana returned to the infirmary after dinner for the usual clean up that evening.

Nicholas wired Alexandra on Friday to explain how an old friend Count Keller had managed to get wounded again. He had wounded his other leg previously.

Nicholas later wrote candidly of future military plans and weaknesses. He explained that their second offensive was due to begin on Tuesday. He also explained that, had they had enough ammunition, it would be fairly easy.

That day, Alexandra had attended the funeral of another of their former patients. An old colonel they had operated on a few days previously had died.

In the afternoon, the Grand Duchesses attended a film show, intended for the wounded. Olga explained to Nicholas that there would be a French film called *Our Troops in Marseilles*. She thought there would be a comic film at the end as there usually was. Late the previous afternoon she had picked flowers with the Derevenko boys, she explained, and had then returned to the infirmary along with her sisters.

Meanwhile Marie sat on the balcony with her mother and Anya, listening to the approaching thunder in the distance whilst writing to her beloved father. She was due to go with Anastasia to their infirmary soon. The Grand Duchess revealed that she and Anastasia were now going with their older sisters to their infirmary each evening where they played *dobchinsky-bobchinksy*. She also explained that Rita and Baron Taube fought. (Marie failed to explain whether they fought in jest or seriously. It was either a remarkable coincidence or by design that the Tsarina was now going to the infirmary so frequently or sending her younger daughters along in her absence. Alexandra may have had worries that Olga and Tatiana were spending a little too much time not only away from her but in the company of Mitya and Volodia. Marie's favourite Nicholas Demenkov was an obvious cause for concern and Anastasia's frequent mentioning of Victor Zborovsky cannot have gone unnoticed.)

Nicholas admitted again on Saturday to Alexandra how he was struggling to find enough time to write. The Tsar blamed old General Ivanov for talking too much after lunch. He remarked that he and Alexandra had never been parted for so long previously.

He later praised the bravery of the Russian troops and exclaimed that the Odessa Rifles were particularly lion-like yet receiving heavy losses.

Tatiana too was having problems finding time to do all she wished to. They had been quite unable to go boating as they had in previous years. She commented to Nicholas on the French film that they had seen the previous afternoon and which she had found very interesting. She then pointed out that they only went for a drive or to visit some hospital or other, rather than walk as it reminded them too much of Nicholas's absence. The weather was warm and stuffy and it led to continual thunderstorms, but the Tsarina and her daughters and Anya remained on the balcony nevertheless. Whilst Alexandra and her three eldest daughters *worked*, Anastasia joined Anya in pasting photographs into an album.

It was Monday by the time Nicholas managed to find the time to write another letter complaining about the unpredictable weather. He also revealed more military secrets and his own future travel arrangements. (Alexandra kept a map on her desk in order to keep track of events in the war which could have been seen by anyone who went into her rooms.)

On Tuesday Nicholas discussed what he saw as the outrageous behaviour of his cousin Boris. The Grand Duke had unfortunately spoken of the inevitability of war with England in the future. The British Ambassador (Sir George Buchanan) and Foreign Secretary (Sir Edward Grey) were incensed. (The matter was later reported to the British Foreign Office and, as a result, Sir Alfred Knox and the British Intelligence Officer Thornhill visited Boris and insisted he withdrew his allegations.)

Nicholas later sent a brief message after hearing that one of the British aristocrats who was working in Russia as a nursing sister had been wounded. Lady Sybil Grey, whom the Grand Duchesses had so admired, had been injured in the face.

That day, Alexandra reported that Anya had had a slight heart attack the previous day. Anya naturally thought the end had come. (Anya would outlive her Imperial friend by as many years as Alix lived.) The Tsarina had spent the evening by her friend's bedside. She was intending that Anya lie out in the garden later and then the family would take tea with her as well as Victor Zborovsky and another old friend Yuzik. She had been greatly amused by her son's letters. (Alexei was still at military headquarters with his father and had sent his mother a begging letter asking for his pocket money after she had failed to send it.) She heard most days from Gilliard who had promised to keep her informed of her son's progress.

In his next letter home on Wednesday, Nicholas showed his real frustration at the lack of progress in the war. He was convinced that many of the commanding officers were idiots. He worried that the offensive at Baranovitchi was developing much too slowly.

Alexandra had been delighted with the photographs of her beloved son and asked Nicholas for more copies of the ones that Derevenko had taken. She needed them for an exhibition she was planning and had no really recent ones of him. She asked for ones of him with his toy gun, running, studying and with Nicholas in the boat. She added that she was about to go for a drive with Olga and Anya. Tatiana was out horse riding and the two youngest sisters were still at their hospital, she explained.

Tatiana recalled to Nicholas the enjoyable musical evening they had attended the previous evening. One of the wounded men (Kasyanov) played the violin and she had been impressed, especially as it was not her favourite instrument. Olga had played the piano later and three people had sung traditional Russian songs exceptionally well. They had both left after midnight. That afternoon, Olga picked flowers in the company of her mother and the partially recovered Anya Vyrubova.

Nicholas wrote again to Alexandra on Thursday. There had been recent heavy losses but he was still confident that things would get better. He had dined the previous evening with Rashpil and Skvortzov, two junior officers of the Imperial Cossack Convoy, and asked Alexandra to receive them on their return to Tsarskoe Selo on the twenty-fifth.

That day, in a letter to her father, Tatiana mentioned a couple of Russian dancers she had seen. They had been at a concert at Marie and Anastasia's hospital and two men of small stature had danced, one dressed as a woman. The twin brothers were aged twenty-five, she explained. She remarked that they were full of pity for the men. The sisters were sitting at the back as they usually did, with the wounded in front. They wanted to introduce the dancers to the Grand Duchesses but the men were unable to reach the back of the room easily past the vast crowd of soldiers, so some of the wounded lifted the men onto their shoulders and handed them to the back of the room. That day Olga and Tatiana had returned to their infirmary as usual and later hammocks had been hung outside for the men. Later, the violinist Kasyanov performed again at the hospital and some of the men sang. (The infirmary was becoming an impromptu music hall in the evenings.)

Nicholas described a thunderstorm in a letter on Friday. He was uncharacteristically descriptive. The electric wiring appeared to have been struck during a thunderstorm. The wires had begun to glow as if on fire. The storm had not died down until after dinner, but the heavy rain returned in the quiet of the night.

Alexandra chose to write to Nicholas that day of her friend Lili Dehn's recent visit to Japan. Madame Dehn had been at Anya's that evening where they had caught up with the news. Lili had spent two weeks in Japan and had brought some lucky ivory elephants back for the children. She had brought seven which was supposed to be luckier still so Alexandra had kept a couple for her son. The Tsarina explained that Lili had lodged in the same house in Kyoto where he had stayed in 1891 on his ill-fated Japanese leg of the Far East tour.

That day Olga and Tatiana had returned to their infirmary in the company of their mother. Olga had continued with her usual duties including sorting out the laundry. She had later sat on the balcony and in one of the new hammocks. She and Tatiana had then played croquet with some of the inmates.

Marie and Anastasia had been laid out on the grass in front of their balcony, according to a letter from Anastasia that day to Nicholas. She also explained that, the previous day, all four sisters had decided to make a bonfire and jumped over it as they often did at New Year.

Olga and Tatiana returned to the capital that evening and afterwards went back to the infirmary where Olga amused herself by playing the piano in the dark. (She hated being on show.) Other members of the group sang and Kasyanov played his violin. The sisters left well after midnight.

Nicholas discussed governmental matters in his daily letter to Alexandra on Saturday. He ridiculed the Duma President's (Michael Rodzianko) ideas for change but he had never really liked the man. (Nicholas, like his father before him, had always preferred to maintain the status quo – if in doubt, do nothing.)

Olga explained to Nicholas that day how she had very shyly played for the wounded men the previous evening. She had been so embarrassed that she had turned the light out so they could not see her. She explained that she was often invited to play in the evenings after the work had been finished. The others, she stated, sat close by and sang. As she played by ear, she had no need of light.

That day Olga and Tatiana had returned to the infirmary as usual and had returned to the palace in time for lunch. Accompanied by their mother and Countess Hendrikova, they visited the cathedral later for a special service on the occasion of the return of the 1st Hundred (regiment).

They later returned to the infirmary where they played croquet with their sister Marie and the patients, including Syroboyarsky. (In later years the Tsarina kept in close contact with Colonel Vladimir Syroboyarsky's wife. She also had a son named Alexander of the same rank.) That evening, Kasyanov had again played the violin whilst Dannikov chose to sing.

Nicholas admitted to Alexandra in his daily letter on Sunday that he was mystified why his daughters were expected to attend the opening of an exhibition of military trophies. He had little else to say due to lack of time.

That day the Tsarina had written to Nicholas explaining that she sympathised with Olga and Tatiana having to go so often to Petrograd. They had gone there again whilst she was about to take Marie and Anastasia out for a drive. Later the dentist arrived to treat her.

The Tsar's brother-in-law Sandro made a rare visit to his sister-in-law and nieces that day. He arrived for lunch which was taken on the balcony. Olga and Tatiana had then gone to town chaperoned by Baroness Buxhoeveden for the consecration of a hospital for 250 refugee children. Olga was bored yet nevertheless impressed by the accommodation. The sisters later returned to the infirmary where they played croquet.

In his next letter Nicholas agreed with Alexandra's request that Anya be permitted to visit military headquarters along with the Tsarina and her daughters. (He had always tolerated the Tsarina's friend but her frequent presence had in recent years become irksome to them both. They wanted to spend some time alone when they had the rare opportunity to do so.) He remarked that it would be more restful without her, though.

On Tuesday Nicholas wrote in haste. Once again, he had little time to himself. He had received Boris Sturmer. Later he had met with Admiral Grigorovitch and Admiral Roussin who had stayed on until late in the evening. The rest of the men had arrived during the course of day for the conference. He would be needed and had no time for writing. (He had however managed to write to Tatiana to request that she send him ten boxes of Serbian tobacco. He was a heavy smoker and the work did not make him smoke any the less.)

Wednesday was again hectic for Nicholas. He sent a brief telegram explaining his predicament. He had to receive three ministers that day and had no time for a letter.

Meanwhile, Olga returned to the subject of the untidy lawns. They were mowing the lawns at Pavlovsk but no one appeared to be doing anything about the grass at the Alexander Park. No one was doing any weeding and the gardens looked sadly neglected.

The sisters had gone as usual to their respective hospitals that morning and were reunited at dinner with Alexandra which they took on the balcony. The youngest sisters had eaten alone on the balcony with the Tsarina and Baroness Buxhoeveden at lunch as their eldest sisters visited town. The four sisters were reunited again in the evening at the infirmary where they played croquet.

A distracted Nicholas finally had a free moment to compose a letter on Thursday. He had finally seen the last of the government ministers but had no time to think. He added that Count Grabbe had requested that Victor Zborovsky be sent to the south for the good of his health and had asked if it were possible to place the man in the Escort's barracks at Livadia perhaps, along with his aged mother and sisters. The Tsar added that Alexei constantly wanted to know if she would arrive in time for his birthday on the 30th of July.

After he had made a decision about the exhibition, Nicholas wrote to confirm that it was not necessary for his daughters to attend. He then thanked Olga for her recent collection of photographs.

Meanwhile that day, Olga and Tatiana had returned to the infirmary where Baron Taube was again being treated. His leg was troubling him and he was due to have an operation on it. The Tsar's cousin Grand Duke George arrived for lunch at the palace. Later, the Grand Duchesses and the Tsarina returned to the hospital where the elder sisters helped clean the instruments and mend the torn pillowcases. They sat on the balcony to do the sewing.

Chapter Fifteen

Summer 1916

Nicholas was in good spirits on Friday as he wrote home to Alexandra. He sent a large bundle of photographs taken by Derevenko for Alexandra to pick out the ones she liked.

Meanwhile, back at Tsarskoe Selo, the Tsarina and her daughters had officially watched the departure of the 4th Squadron of Cossacks in front of the Catherine Palace and bid farewell to them as they went off to rejoin the war.

Marie explained to Nicholas that she had begun the day with her usual lessons then she had lunched on the Tsarina's balcony in the company of her mother, three sisters and Baroness Buxhoeveden. Pierre Gilliard, who had recently returned from military headquarters for a rest, dined with the Tsarina and her daughters that evening. They asked him numerous questions about their brother. They wanted to know how he was getting on and what he did during the day. He had been a constant presence in their lives and all were missing him.

Nicholas casually revealed more military secrets to the German-born Alexandra on Saturday. (It was as well that she was not a spy. He gave her all the information any foreign agent would have needed. Luckily, he always used a secure messenger service.) There was a temporary lull at the front, but that would end on the seventh, he revealed. The young Tsarevich had been amusing himself and everyone else with his antics. Nicholas wrote with wet sleeves and boots as the boy had managed to spray him with water from the fountain in the yard. He reassured Alexandra that he kept an eye on things so Alexei would not go too far (and injure himself).

Anastasia had explained to Nicholas that Gilliard had dined with them the previous evening and told them all about their father and Alexei. She also explained that there had been a prayer service held in front of the Catherine Palace before the troops had left the previous evening. She also revealed that the men actually sang as they left for the war. Anastasia went on to cheerfully admit that she and Marie had been playing on the hammock and they tipped each other out.

Nicholas had time to write on Sunday but little to say on this occasion. His Aunt Olga, the former Queen, had passed through by train but unfortunately he was too busy to see her. He and Alexei were eagerly looking forward to seeing Alexandra and the sisters soon.

That day Olga described to Nicholas some of the films that she had recently seen. The previous day they had seen some films of military training in Orianda and the

Crimea and films of Nicholas at reviews. There were comic items by Max Linder and something about the comedian Glupyskin (known as Cretinetti in the West).

Olga had returned to the infirmary after attending Mass at church on Sunday morning. She had written out prescriptions on that occasion. Later she and Tatiana left the infirmary and went to the Catherine Palace with their mother to the hospital there. In her free time, Olga had joined Tatiana and some of the recovering wounded in a game of croquet. They had, of course, returned to the infirmary that evening in the company of Alexandra to clean the instruments. They had resumed the croquet too.

Anastasia explained to Nicholas how much she was looking forward to seeing him. (They were about to leave for headquarters soon to join Nicholas and his son.) She also mentioned the film shows that she and her sisters and mother had attended. Anastasia confirmed that she and Marie were playing on the hammock and Marie often tipped her off. (Marie is often seen as rather saintly but the letters and journals reveal otherwise.)

Nicholas attempted to explain his busy schedule in his letter to Alexandra on Monday. He described Mogilev, where the military headquarters had been set up, as being similar to a large hotel with people constantly coming and going. He mentioned that his son had been swimming, but again made sure that Alexandra understood that the boy was constantly supervised in case of accidents. He went on to explain that his cousin Grand Duke Nicholas Mikhailovich (Sandro's brother) had arrived to discuss various questions regarding the Imperial Historical Society and confirmed that he would receive an officer that Alexandra had requested he see.

Meanwhile, Alexandra had asked if they could bring someone with them. (Although Nicholas had answered the letter, it is a matter of form that his letters are written out before hers. The children's letters, etc, are of course explained in age order unless they connect directly to one of the earlier family replies.)

The Tsarina had asked if Silaievich be allowed to come to headquarters with them. She explained that she and her daughters had invited (Anastasia's favourite) Victor Zborovsky and (Olga's old friend) Shurik for tea that day.

Nicholas's sister Olga Alexandrovna had asked the Tsar by letter if she could be permitted to mention her relationship with Nicholas Kulikovsky in her correspondence with his daughters. She hated hiding things from them. (If she and Olga Nicolaevna were as close as she had claimed, the sisters would have known. He had always appeared at her parties, after all. Olga and Anastasia would have been perfectly capable of picking this up in the past. Tatiana and Marie may have been less likely to notice.)

Tatiana had also put pen to paper and written to Nicholas that day to thank him for the beautiful photographs he had sent. The Tsarina, she revealed, had shown the pictures of her beloved son to the wounded. She (Tatiana) was due to participate in a hernia operation later.

Meanwhile, Marie mentioned the new hammock in her letter to Nicholas but she failed to mention the occasion when she tipped Anastasia out of it, but Anastasia had done the same to her undoubtedly. (They were sometimes filmed pushing each other down steps.) The hammock had been hung between two trees close to the balcony, she explained. Luckily, the trees were very strong, she revealed, but not saying why they needed to be. (She wasn't the lightest young lady, to say the least.) She and Anastasia had gone for a drive with their mother before dinner and later had gone for a walk with Tatiana, Anastasia and Catherine Schneider, their chaperone for the occasion. They had walked towards the railway station.

On Tuesday, Nicholas sent a wire to Alexandra thanking her for some pretty cornflowers and a pile of letters.

Meanwhile Alexandra explained to Nicholas that she was intending to bring Baroness Buxhoeveden with them on their trip to Mogilev as Countess Hendrikova had become ill.

On Wednesday morning the Tsarina and her eldest daughters had attended a service at the *Church of the Sign* before ten. The sisters had briefly called in at the infirmary but left at 10.30 as they were due to leave for headquarters. They collected the rest of the family and suite and drove to the railway station. They drove through the night towards Mogilev.

The Tsarina and her party arrived at Mogilev after noon on Thursday and they were met by Nicholas and Alexei in the pouring rain. The ladies were all wearing their coats (and hats of course) despite it being July. The reunited family lunched together and then, after a walk, went for a trip by car to the other side of the River Dnieper. They returned in time for tea which was taken on the balcony but the rain never ceased all day. The Tsarina and her daughters later returned to the train for the night. There was no room for them in the Governor's House where Nicholas lived with Alexei. Some of the Tsar's party lived at the Hotel Bristol.

On Saturday morning Nicholas continued his work whilst his son went for a walk and the ladies remained on the train. In the afternoon, the family went for another drive in the car. The driver in his carelessness managed to run over a dog which distressed the children greatly.

The Tsarina and her daughters spent much of the following morning confined on their train. Marie spent her time catching up on her correspondence before wandering off to a nearby field with her sisters to pick flowers. After lunch, the family reassembled and went for a motorboat ride on the River Dnieper. The Tsarina and her daughters later returned to the train for the night. Meanwhile, Marie and her sisters had a go at shooting with a revolver, as her journal reveals. It was the first time they had attempted to shoot with a real gun. Olga later acquired a gun of her own and, of course, she, Marie and Anastasia had played with toy pistols at home.

On Sunday General John Hanbury-Williams had the opportunity to thank the Tsarina in person for the flowers that she had sent recently to him as he sat next to her at dinner that night. Earlier in the day, the family had attended Mass together at the nearby garrison church. Tatiana, Marie and Anastasia had then gone for a walk with Count Grabbe in the city park. The family had another boat ride on the river later. After tea, which was taken in a tent, the family enjoyed a film show. There was a drama and a comedy piece.

The Imperial family visited the nearby monastery on Tuesday morning and, after lunch, went on another car journey. They then walked in the countryside. At tea, the family were joined by Anya Vyrubova, Baroness Sophie Buxhoeveden, Count Ressin, Golushkinym and two engineers. Alexandra, her daughters and other members of her party left in the late afternoon to return home to Tsarskoe Selo.

Nicholas sent Alexandra a wire on Tuesday the fifth/eighteenth of July to reassure her that all was well after her recent visit. He explained that Alexei was well but was already missing her, as he was.

On Wednesday Nicholas thanked Alix for her recent letters. He had greatly appreciated her visit and had been thrilled to see her again after so long apart.

That day, the four Grand Duchesses had spent the day quietly onboard the train. They lunched and dined in the company of Anya Vyrubova, Baroness Buxhoeveden, Ressin, Golushkinym and the two engineers. The weather warmed up as they returned. Olga read *Chekov* and the girls took the opportunity to walk when they stopped at some of the stations including Bologoye. The sisters returned to their respective hospitals upon their return and Marie and Anastasia went to sit with the recovering Victor Zborovsky and the others. The sisters returned home for tea which was taken on the balcony.

On Thursday Nicholas admitted to having nerves before decisive battles. He did, however, regain his usual inner calm as soon as the battle commenced. He added a note to request Tatiana sent him a *blue box* of notepaper.

Olga was delighted to see her friends at the hospital. Her friend Varvara (*Bibi*) had a welcome letter from Mitya. He was well. The sisters returned to the palace for lunch on the balcony and in the evening returned to the infirmary once again. The evening was enlivened by the playing of the violin and the piano.

Tatiana had written to her brother that day and had a message for Dr Derevenko. She thought that he would be interested to know that they had forty-eight patients at the infirmary currently. She admitted how much she missed her brother and father. She had really enjoyed the visit to headquarters. It was pleasantly warm sat out on the balcony. The Grand Duchess explained that she had just come back from the Catherine Palace hospital with Marie and Anastasia. She asked her brother to tell his father that Sister Movutsina was cross-eyed.

Nicholas mentioned his concerns about Greece in his letter on Friday to Alexandra. He had been chatting to his cousin Prince Nicholas of Greece and the Prince was intending to see his mother (Queen Olga) before calling in on the Tsarina, he explained. The Greek Prince had brought his cousin copies of official documents from Greece where his older brother Constantine (Tino) was now King. He was worried about the Greeks' position regarding Venizelos. Constantine was convinced that the current policy would endanger the dynasty.

General Hanbury-Williams discussed Serge Sazonov with the Tsar on Saturday. The British King had decided to award Sazonov with the GCB which was awkward as Nicholas had just dismissed the Foreign Minister.

Meanwhile Nicholas had news to impart to Alexandra. He explained that the Guards had attacked the previous day and had moved forward considerably. Many enemy troops had been captured together with fifty-five guns.

After Alexandra confirmed by letter that her daughters had fully accepted their aunt's relationship with her friend Nicholas, Olga Alexandrovna explained her delight in a letter to the Tsar. She was not certain whether the Tsarina had told them or not.

Marie had written to Alexei that morning on some bright red notepaper. She explained that she had been to the infirmary accompanied by Anastasia and their chaperones Anya Vyrubova and Catherine Schneider. The previous evening the Tsarina and her daughters had called in on baby Roman who would be baptised the following day. He was the grandson of Colonel Loman.

Nicholas had rather mixed news to tell Alexandra on Sunday the seventeenth/thirtieth. Despite heavy losses, the Russian troops appeared to be making progress against the enemy.

On Sunday morning, the Tsarina had attended Mass along with her daughters and had been present at a christening. (The baby Roman was the grandson of Colonel Loman of the Mixed Regiment of Guard at the Palace and he was also Starosta of the Feodorovsky Cathedral. Roman was the son of Nadia Sirotina. The Tsarina and the baby's other grandfather old Sirotin were the boy's godparents.)

Nicholas apologised to Alexandra on Monday for having little to say. He reported that Dr Feodorov had arrived, however, and would take over from Dr Vladimir Derevenko. He went on to candidly admit how deeply he loved Alexandra.

Meanwhile back at the infirmary close to the palace at Tsarskoe Selo there was not a great deal to do for Olga as she spent part of the morning working out a puzzle on the table. That evening, the Grand Duchesses returned to their infirmary and Olga took up her needle to sew torn pillowcases whilst Kasyanov played his violin once again.

On Tuesday Nicholas thanked Alix for a telegram she had sent from Sablin. He admitted that his constant fear was that the troops would go forward in a reckless manner.

He had received Count Vielepolsky and Count Olsoufiev; the latter, he explained, had lost his head over his cousin the Grand Duke Michael's two daughters Zia and Nadya. He had told Olga and Tatiana the same thing when he had seen them at Baroness Buxhoeveden's. (It seems bizarre that the Count should have noticed the beauty of the young Zia and Nadya but failed to mention the even more obvious appeal of Olga and Tatiana.)

That day, Tatiana confided to Nicholas her dreams of travelling abroad. Anya had recently received a letter from one of the Grand Duchesses' former tennis partners, LM Kozhevnikov from Hong Kong. (Lili Dehn had also recently returned from Japan. It would have sounded so exciting to the young Grand Duchesses who had never been anywhere really since the brief trip to Rumania two years previously. They had never been out of Europe on their holidays, unlike Nicholas who had travelled widely at their age.) They had received a letter from Kozhevnikov at the end of June and she was convinced that it would be good to go on such a journey. She would happily go. (It was very rare for Tatiana to express anything of this nature as usually she kept her thoughts and dreams very much to herself. Unlike Olga and Marie, she was not prone to wearing her heart on her sleeve.)

That morning, the Tsarina and her four daughters had attended a religious service at the Pestcherny Chapel (cave church) where there was a procession of the Cross on the anniversary of St Seraphim of Sarov. The sisters later returned to their hospitals. Olga gave out the prescriptions once more. That evening, the four sisters returned to Olga and Tatiana's infirmary where the youngest ones played *ruble*. Marie sat with Baron Taube for part of the evening and Kasyanov later obliged by playing his violin.

Nicholas reminisced about happier days on Wednesday. He recalled the day in 1914 when he had visited the Winter Palace at the outbreak of war. It was the second anniversary of that day. He reminded Alexandra of the huge crowds they had seen that day.

Meanwhile, Alexandra had news from Mogilev from a visitor. Dr Derevenko had recently returned back to Tsarskoe Selo and intended to work at the nearby hospitals.

That day Olga and Tatiana returned to their infirmary and, later, they sat on the balcony and played croquet with some of the inmates. In the afternoon, the two elder Grand Duchesses had returned to the capital to receive donations again. They returned to the infirmary that evening. The usual entertainment had been cancelled as Kasyanov was in bed with a sore throat and a temperature. Alexandra went off briefly with Anastasia to see her daughter's ambulance train. (Marie and Anastasia had gone to the Catherine Palace hospital that day.)

Nicholas revealed in his daily letter to Alexandra on Thursday that he had been discussing the end of the war with Voyeikov. Nicholas urged Alexandra to stop Count Fredericks from returning too soon from his health cure. The old Count only listened to the advice of the Tsarina, according to Nicholas. Voyeikov had just managed to rid himself of his Kouvaka business. It was a mineral water factory that he had owned. Nicholas explained that he had advised his friend to be self-confident in his dealings, especially in regard to the end of the war.

Meanwhile, Alexandra explained that the previous evening she and her youngest daughters had been looking over one of the ambulance trains. It had brought a great many wounded and they had travelled long distances from the battlefield.

Nicholas wired a message for Marie on the occasions of her name's day on Friday. The good wishes had come from him and her younger brother. He also thanked Alexandra and Anastasia for their recent letters. The weather was not in a pleasant mood; it was raining.

Later, Nicholas explained that it was not up to him to interfere in regimental appointments after Alexandra had asked for his help. He did not know what to suggest regarding Captain Yedigrov.

That day, the four Grand Duchesses had attended Mass with their mother at the Fedorovsky Cathedral and had later gone to a concert in Marie and Anastasia's hospital, returning in time for dinner. The sisters reassembled at Olga and Tatiana's hospital that evening.

The following day Nicholas showed great concern for his son. Alexei was suffering with his arm which only bent with great difficulty. He was not suffering any great pain luckily. He later blamed the damp weather for his son's malady as it had been raining very heavily. That morning, the child had calmly announced that he would spend the day in bed. He was unfortunately well versed in illness. Alexei was currently playing *Nain Jaune* with his tutors Voyeikov (Mathematics) and Petrov (Russian). (The appointment of Voyeikov as a tutor was merely on the grounds of economy as he was not actually a tutor.) He had some bad news: one of his pages had suddenly died that very morning. The former soldier had died whilst shaving himself before breakfast.

That day Tatiana had explained to Nicholas that they had called in on his Aunt Miechen the previous day, as her name's day had been the same as the Tsar's third daughter. They had also seen his cousin Kyrill and his wife Victoria-Melita (Ducky). They had then gone on to a concert at Marie and Anastasia's hospital where they had seen two very tiny men dance.

Nicholas had much better news of Alexei's health on Sunday. He had also been visited by his brother-in-law Sandro who had word of Nicholas's mother and sisters. Alexei had been allowed to get up but the doctor had forbidden him to go outside yet.

That day the sisters had gone to Mass with the Tsarina again and, in the evening, had bid farewell to one of the wounded men. Syroboyarsky was amongst those leaving soon. The Tsarina dined that evening with her daughters and Madame Vyrubova. (She often appeared in the absence of Nicholas.)

Nicholas only wrote a brief message the following day. He had spoken to Prince Alexander of Oldenburg, his sister Olga's father-in-law, about the impending divorce for Olga and his son Peter.

That day had been a fairly normal one at Tsarskoe Selo. In the evening, the four sisters returned to Olga and Tatiana's infirmary where they were entertained by Kasyanov on the violin whilst the youngest sisters played *ruble* again. Marie had been delighted to receive yet another letter from Nicholas Demenkov.

The Tsarina and her daughters left once again for Mogilev on Monday, arriving the next day. On this occasion, Alexandra was accompanied by the recently recovered Countess Hendrikova, Ressin, Grabbe and Dr Botkin. Once again, the Tsarina and her daughters lived aboard the train.

On Wednesday morning the Tsar and Alexei met the ladies at the railway station and everyone lunched on the train soon after. (The children no doubt had a multitude of news to catch up on. Anastasia and Alexei were particularly close and once they were reunited it meant Marie would have inevitably felt a little left out.)

The next day Alexei returned to his usual studies and had a mud bath. The Grand Duchesses had spent the morning lying in a nearby field and the family reunited in time for lunch which was taken on the train. They went for a motorboat ride along the River Dnieper during the course of the afternoon and once again the sisters enjoyed playing with the young local village children. (The Grand Duchesses were dressed very casually in great contrast to the way society ladies were expected to dress and the members of the so-called elite sometimes complained that the sisters dressed provincially which was a great shock to the people concerned. However the Grand Duchesses did not care how they were perceived, after all they had made friends with the most ordinary people throughout their short lives and all, including Anastasia, had fallen for a soldier or sailor and not a rich or handsome prince or duke.

Olga had had the prospect of marrying for position or wealth but had chosen a more normal path and she intended to wait for the right man.)

The next day, Alexei received many gifts for his upcoming birthday and, as usual, the birthday boy was given his presents the evening before the actual day. The family had gone for another boat trip that afternoon on the Dneiper. They were quite happy with simple pleasures.

On Saturday, the young Tsarevich reached the age of twelve years old. The day began with a celebration service at the nearby garrison church and a festive lunch. The boy received more gifts afterwards. He was presented with a pretzel by his little friends and, in return, he generously gave the boys boots and balalaikas.

The holiday mood continued on Sunday. The family went sailing on the river once again and enjoyed a trip to the local cinema. The sisters had spent the morning playing with the local children once again.

The festivities continued the next day, at the beginning of August. Alexei politely composed short messages of thanks to all those who had given him gifts. Lunch was taken in the tent and the family enjoyed a quiet walk along the river bank.

The Tsarina chatted to General Hanbury-Williams on Tuesday. He was about to leave for England as he had been recalled. Alexandra entrusted him with letters for her British relatives, including her sister Victoria. She also spoke about the education of her daughters and hoped that they would remain as simple and unaffected as they were.

Alexandra and her daughters left soon after.

Nicholas wrote to Alexandra on Wednesday and admitted that he hated to see her leave. He revealed that he had felt such calm when she was with him and thanked her for coming. Nicholas finished the letter the next day and hoped that she had slept well overnight. He felt so lonely without her and sent her passionate and tender kisses by post.

The Tsar composed a particularly loving letter to Alexandra on Thursday. He felt so miserable without her and felt the bright sunny days had gone with the departure of his Sunny. (Oddly, her nickname was indeed Sunny which must have seemed ironic to those who knew her as an adult. It was a name given to her by her late mother Princess Alice.) Meanwhile, the Grand Duchesses resumed their usual routine. Olga and Tatiana returned to the infirmary (after a brief visit to the *Church of the Sign*). Three new patients had arrived in their absence. Olga, Tatiana and Rita later played croquet with some of the inmates. The sisters all congregated at the infirmary that evening, along with the Tsarina. The ladies either sewed torn pillowcases or played *ruble*.

The next day Nicholas once again apologises for having little time for letters. He was too busy receiving an endless round of ministers. He was also intending to speak to General Prince Yuri (I) Trobetztoy, a former Commander of the Imperial Escort who had recently arrived. He wished Anya a happy journey. (She was about to travel to Tobolsk along with Lili Dehn and Grigory Rasputin.)

Meanwhile, Alexandra complained that her daughters were not interested in going to confession, yet Marie's subsequent letter proved that they had gone to vespers.

Marie revealed what had happened that day to Nicholas. She had gone for a drive along with Anastasia and their chaperone Baroness Buxhoeveden and all four sisters had tea on the balcony with their mother and had later dined with her. She had been with Anastasia to their hospital. The four sisters, she then confirmed, all went to vespers with their mother.

All four Grand Duchesses visited Olga and Tatiana's infirmary that evening where Marie had played *ruble*. She added that Anya's sister Alya and Rasputin had called in at the hospital to see Anya.

Nicholas again complained on Sunday of having little time for writing letters. His sister Olga's father-in-law had turned up unexpectedly. (He had probably arrived in order to discuss his son's upcoming divorce.)

Meanwhile Marie had written to Nicholas concerning a funeral service she had attended. She noted that they were constantly attending such services. The previous day they had visitors and Marie sat between her uncles (Grand Duke) George and (Grand Duke) Paul and their comforting presence had helped her. She had to go as she needed to change into a black outfit yet again.

The Tsar admitted on Monday that he had been thinking particularly of Alexandra the previous evening. He was imagining her at the small chapel she regularly attended and could visualise it well. Nicholas asked Alexandra to thank Rasputin for the flowers that he had thoughtfully sent. He added that Mr Gibbes had just arrived and Alexei was delighted to see him.

Nicholas agreed to the Tsarina's request that Sablin should be appointed as the Commander of the *Standart* but added that it seemed unfair to Zelenetsky. He explained that he needed to find the current commander a new position first. Nicholas ended by asking Tatiana to send him one of the silver cigar cases.

That day Olga and Tatiana returned to their infirmary as usual and left shortly before lunch. They rejoined the rest of the ladies to eat on the balcony. It was a very hot day but luckily it later rained that evening. The four sisters returned to the infirmary that evening. Olga was suffering a little as she had managed to hurt her leg again, as she had in 1913.

Marie and Anastasia had begun their day at their usual studies and in the afternoon they visited their own hospital. Later, Olga chose to read to Marie before the four were reunited at dinner with their mother and they returned to the infirmary together.

On Tuesday Nicholas confessed that he had little real news to impart to Alexandra. He remarked that the tutor Sydney Gibbes was settling in nicely at Mogilev. (That evening Anya Vyrubova and Lili Dehn left for Tobolsk.)

Nicholas had some news on Wednesday for Alexandra as his cousin Grand Duke Kyrill had arrived after a visit to the Guards. They had spoken about General Besobrazov who had been accused of being responsible for the recent losses. Nicholas had talked the matter over with General Alexeiev too. In a rare lapse of memory, Nicholas admitted that he had quite forgotten about Captain Zelenetsky. He needed to find a new position for him as they were thinking of replacing him with Sablin. (Nicholas was beginning to struggle to cope with the responsibilities of being Commander-in-Chief. Despite spending so much of his leisure time reading about wars and his brief career as an ordinary soldier, he had little practical experience.)

Later Nicholas sent a telegram to Alexandra, Olga and Tatiana to congratulate them on the second anniversary of their beginning work at the hospitals.

Tatiana had reminded her father of the second anniversary in a letter that day. She asked him not to forget to send the key she needed to his cupboards. (She had been put in charge of his stocks of cigarettes, paper, etc as a natural organizer.) The previous evening Lydia Krasnova the wife of a general had played the violin at the infirmary in one of their impromptu concerts. Tatiana confided that she was particularly concerned about one of her patients as he was worried that his young wife would leave him if he did not recover soon. He was very weak and was suffering from excessive bleeding.

The Tsar again showed signs of distress on Thursday when he spilt some ink on the letter he was writing to Alexandra. The normally immaculate Nicholas would have never have done this but he blamed the new pen. He went on to ask Alexandra if she would receive the Japanese Prince Kanin (a cousin of the Mikado) who was due to arrive in September.

Alexandra explained that day that her four daughters had had their photographs taken that afternoon. (The photographer Funk had been given the task but, unfortunately, as the results show, the pictures were far from successful. They were taken in the Tsarina's reception room as they had been in 1913 and 1914, but lack the clarity of the earlier ones.) Olga and Tatiana needed individual ones to hand out at their committees.

That evening Olga and Tatiana had returned to the infirmary as usual accompanied by the Tsarina. On this occasion they cleaned the instruments but later Tatiana and Varvara boiled silk for the dressings. It was well past midnight when they left.

Nicholas's spirits were lifted the next day after the arrival of his favourite: Nicholas Sablin. The two old friends sat up into the early hours chatting. Sablin had plenty of news since joining the army. The Tsar confided that his sister Olga did not want her divorce mentioned publicly for a few more days yet.

Nicholas later replied enigmatically to a wire from Alexandra. The time had not been settled but it had to be settled soon. He was referring to his sister's divorce.

That morning Olga and Tatiana had returned to their infirmary where there was an operation on Baron Stakelberg's arm. (Olga was not taking part in the theatre work by now of course as she was working in an administrative position.) After dinner, accompanied by the Tsarina, Olga and Tatiana returned to the hospital to clean the instruments and roll bandages.

Meanwhile, Anastasia had begun to write to Nicholas just before her first lesson of the day and was intending to finish it later. She and Marie later walked to their hospital with their chaperone and played table tennis, with some of the wounded. The other men looked on.

Nicholas had little to report on Saturday, but had at least decided on Besobrazov's replacement. (He was constantly replacing men, and finding someone to fill the vacant post was something of a nightmare to the reluctant and extremely hesitant Nicholas.)

Meanwhile, life continued much the same for Nicholas's daughters. There was another operation at the infirmary but Olga's duties that day included feeding one of the wounded men who was barely capable of doing it himself.

The Tsarina and her daughters lunched on the balcony that day despite the heavy rain. The heavy curtains ensure they remained dry. Afterwards, Olga and Tatiana made a rare visit to the Catherine Palace hospital in the company of their mother. They returned to their own infirmary that evening with Alexandra and assisted with the cleaning up. They were joined by Olga's close friend Rita and they all later rolled bandages.

Nicholas thanked Alexandra on Sunday for taking time out to explain to Count Benckendorf in person about Olga Alexandrovna's divorce. He felt that it would have been unfair to tell the old man about the situation by post. He was still having problems with government appointments, and the never-ending matter of supplies was troubling him.

Meanwhile Alexandra and her daughters had attended Sunday Mass at the cave church but they had visitors later. The Tsar's niece Irina and her husband Felix arrived in time for tea. The four Grand Duchesses later travelled the short distance to Olga and Tatiana's hospital for the inevitable cleaning and to roll some more bandages. The younger sisters preferred to play *ruble*.

On Monday Nicholas went into great detail to his wife about recent events in Rumania. Now that Rumania had finally declared war on Austria, he hoped it would be of assistance to the Russians. Part of the Russian Fleet had been sent to Constanza (where he had been as recently as 1914) to help protect them against German submarine attack.

The Grand Duchesses meanwhile attended Mass in the cave church with their mother and reassembled at lunchtime and dinner. The sisters visited their respective hospitals and in the evening the ladies returned to the infirmary to either roll bandages or play *ruble* again. The youngest sisters were regularly joining their elder sisters.

That day Marie had written to Nicholas and complained that it had been too cold for tennis recently and it continually rained.

Nicholas admitted in his letter to Alexandra on Tuesday how he was struggling in the choice of governmental and military appointments. (He never knew who to trust and was unfortunately never given impartial advice. Alexandra merely endorsed anyone who she thought was suitable and *not* hostile to Rasputin.)

That day Olga and Tatiana returned to their infirmary where an operation was performed on Petrov. Olga, meanwhile, sorted out the prescriptions for medicines for each of the patients. The four sisters returned to the infirmary that evening for the cleaning of the instruments. Olga was persuaded to play the piano and someone else, probably Kasyanov, played the violin. They returned at midnight.

Meanwhile Anastasia explained to the Tsar how sometimes she, Marie and Olga rode their bicycles indoors. They often rode their bikes at great speed and often fell off. Olga and Anastasia had chased each other. There had been no lessons that morning so she and Marie had a welcome lie-in.

The stress was clearly beginning to get to Nicholas and in his next letter to Alexandra he wandered from one topic to another in an almost random fashion. He explained that he was sending some photographs, mentioned the arrival of Grand Duke Dmitri, the return of Father Shaevlsky, accounts of his brother Michael, his chats with Gourko and of Besobrazov. He then turned to the subject of the weather and his son's friend who was about to leave.

That day Tatiana had mentioned in her letter to Nicholas the visit of Lady Muriel Padget – one of the nurses who worked at the English hospital in the capital. She had worked alongside the Guards, Tatiana explained. The Grand Duchess was delighted to spend time with the lady whom she so admired. She had travelled so far simply to nurse the wounded and had not remained in the hospital either. (It would have been both exciting yet frustrating to see the British aristocrat. Tatiana and her sisters never got very far and were continually chaperoned. She had complained recently of the security guards that surrounded their every move.) Tatiana then asked if Nicholas needed more cigarettes or tobacco.

Meanwhile, Olga continued in her administrative position at the hospital, handing out medicines and feeding the less able patients.

On Thursday Nicholas composed a short letter to Alexandra. She had not been able to understand which Gorko he had appointed. He explained that it was the man who had been in Moscow. He had a message for Tatiana. He had run out of tobacco and wanted her to bring eight boxes of Serbian tobacco on her next visit to headquarters.

That day Olga and Tatiana had resumed their duties at the infirmary before going on to the consecration of one of the many hospital ambulance wagons. They later returned to the infirmary and continued rolling an endless collection of bandages.

On Friday the Grand Duchesses returned to their respective hospitals. Tatiana attended a class before she went to the infirmary and visited the *Church of the Sign*. Later Olga and Tatiana visited the Red Cross with the Tsarina. The evening was spent quietly at home and Marie had elected to read aloud in the manner of her father. She read the best-selling American book by Elizabeth Vezerell entitled *Wide Wide World*. (It was written in 1851 and it concerns the exploits of the young heroine – Ellen Montgomery.) They later returned to the infirmary for the regular clean-up and to roll bandages with Bibi (Varvara).

The following day Nicholas composed a short letter to Alexandra and explained that his sister Olga's divorce had finally been sorted.

Alexandra wrote to him that day stating that she was about to bid farewell to Anya Vyrubova's sister Alya who (she claimed) saw her as a second mother. (Alya was the mother of three young daughters. The first two had been named in honour of her respective godmothers' Tatiana and Olga, and the third born in 1914 had been named Alexandra.) She went on to explain that she would be bringing Dr Botkin with her to headquarters as her other physician was going away shortly.

Anastasia also sent word to the Tsar that day but she had little to say other than the fact that Madame Zizi (Narishkin) and Shura (Tegleva) had joined them for lunch.

On Sunday morning the Tsarina attended Mass as usual with her four daughters and they called in briefly at their respective hospitals before they left for Smolensk.

The ladies arrived in Smolensk on Monday where they immediately went to visit some four local hospitals before boarding the train again and leaving for Mogilev where they were met by Nicholas on their arrival that afternoon.

The Imperial family visited the *Hotel Bristol* on Tuesday and later enjoyed a film show. The film on this occasion was entitled *The Secret of Nagorka*. The four sisters later dined with their parents and Prince Igor.

The next day the Grand Duchesses again played with local children and, after lunch, the family enjoyed a motorboat trip along the River Dnieper. The Cossacks obligingly danced later for Nicholas and his family. That day, they had lunched in a tent but tea was taken back onboard the train. The Tsar's children later played hide and seek. (Although Olga was now twenty years old, she was happy enough to join in and play the part of a child at times.)

The next days were spent at Mogilev and the outlying villages. The Tsar escorted his family on various boat trips whilst the ladies returned to the train each evening for the night. The four sisters once again adopted a casual way of dress which included a blouse, sturdy skirt, wool cardigan and boots. They often topped the outfit off with a casual knitted hat. They saved their prettiest dresses for official occasions.

On Sunday, the family attended Mass at the local garrison church and later went for yet another boat trip. They lunched in a nearby village. Anya had accompanied the party on this occasion and spent time with Nicholas and Alexandra, probably to the irritation of both.

The family continued their usual pattern on Tuesday of Mass followed by lunch in the nearby village. They did not go on the river however as they chose to go for a drive instead. In the evening, they watched the next part of the film *The Secret of Nogorka*. Dmitri arrived for dinner.

The following Sunday Nicholas and his five children attended the regimental holiday celebrations for the Cossack Escort at Mogilev. The event was filmed as most such occasions were and the four sisters wore hats and full-length fur-lined coats on what appeared to be a chilly day. Later that day, Alexandra and her daughters left for home.

Afterwards a grateful Nicholas wrote to Alexandra at some length after he unexpectedly came across a note in his pocketbook she had left for him. She had thanked him for letting her come to Mogilev, but he explained that he thought it was him who should thank her. He greatly missed their evening chats and was convinced that everyone else enjoyed her visits too. (He was sadly mistaken.) He explained that Dmitri had been sad to see his cousins go as it always put him in a good mood. Nicholas was also convinced that Igor missed the Grand Duchesses and admitted that he had no intention of asking the prince about it. (It appears that he was particularly fond of the sisters, although which one in particular is not explained, unfortunately.)

Nicholas later began a second letter shortly before he went to bed. He felt quite desperate to find some way of speaking to Alexandra but was at least glad to hear that she and the girls had arrived safely. She had remarked how cold it was and he admitted that it was the same where he was.

Alexandra wrote at great length on Tuesday and, for the first and probably only time, showed some jealousy. She had heard rumours that a certain lady was to be introduced to Nicholas. She had been convinced by someone that Count Grabbe intended to introduce her husband to a certain lady named Madame Soldatenko. She was worried that the lady, if she appeared, would make a play for Nicholas.

That day, an extremely bored Olga wrote to Nicholas. She explained that a telephone had been installed for the use of the Grand Duchesses but it was situated in their bathroom. The first person Olga spoke to was Baron Ungern-Sternbdusky (a Cossack). She remarked that it was dull without him, despite the sunny weather. She was sitting in her classroom as the heating stove made a loud howling noise, and the clock annoying her, by ticking too loudly.

Earlier on Tuesday morning, Olga and Tatiana had attended a service at the *Church of the Sign* before returning to their duties at the infirmary. There had been several visitors that morning including Boris Ravtopolo (Mitya's friend) and Volodia (Vladimir Kiknadze), Tatiana's close friend. The sisters were reunited at lunch where they were joined by the Tsarina and Baroness Buxhoeveden. The Tsar's uncle, Grand Duke Paul, arrived in time for tea. That evening, as usual, the four sisters returned to the infirmary to clean the instruments or simply play *ruble*.

Nicholas discussed some recent appointments on Wednesday in his daily letter home to Alexandra. He began by explaining that her last letter had failed to arrive due to a mix-up with the trains. Nicholas then went on to reveal that Admiral Grigorovich had arrived with Roussin. They had spoken of the Baltic Fleet, and none were satisfied with its current Command. Nicholas blamed the illness of Admiral Kanin for the deterioration. He felt that it was a convenient time to replace him. The person he had decided upon was Admiral Nepenin. He was a friend of Admiral Kolchak (later leader of the *White* army).

Alexandra praised her son's letter that day in a letter to Nicholas. It had been written in French without assistance. She enclosed the boy's pocket money and then went on to explain that Tatiana had taken over from her at a meeting whilst she sat and watched. She revealed that there had been guests at lunchtime: Colonel Silaiev and Boris Ravtopolo. (The men may have had news of their colleague Dmitri Shakh-Bagov.)

On Thursday Nicholas reassured Alexandra that he had no intention of seeing the lady in question. He could not understand how the rumour had started. He urged her to ignore Anya's stories. (The rumour had evidently come from her.)

Alexandra had attended Mass that morning along with her four daughters. The sisters had each returned to their respective lessons and/or infirmary but were reunited once again that evening at Olga and Tatiana's infirmary. The four then either assisted with the cleaning or played *ruble*. As usual the two younger sisters chose not to help with the chores.

On Friday Nicholas questioned Rasputin's opinion, something he very, very rarely did. He began by thanking Alexandra for her recent letter and for the message she sent from her friend. He then went on to say that he thought Rasputin's opinions of people often to be rather strange.

That day Alexei had written his first letter to his mother in English instead of his usual Russian. He had taken his pet cat out into the garden but she had run off towards the balcony. She was now sleeping on the sofa and his spaniel Joy was under the table.

Meanwhile Alexandra briefly mentioned her daughter Olga to Nicholas that same day. She stated that Olga was convinced that one simply must visit town as the weather had improved that morning. Alexandra on the other hand had other things she had to do.

However Alexandra was later forced to visit the city when she discovered that Countess Hendrikova, the mother of her lady-in-waiting, was dying. She left accompanied by Anya Vyrubova and Baroness Buxhoeveden and arrived back at one. That evening the four sisters were reunited at the infirmary as they washed and polished the instruments or simply played ruble. The eldest sisters *worked* whilst their younger siblings played.

Nicholas apologised again on Saturday for having little time to write. He had greatly appreciated the photographs that he had been sent by Marie's friend Nicholas Demenkov but was shortly expecting the Japanese prince. He sent his condolences after hearing of the death of the Countess. Nicholas added that he wished he was able to return home for a day or two – to see Alexandra and his daughters, and simply to have a long soak in his own bath.

That same day Alexandra had written briefly of her recent visit to Peterhof. She had been accompanied by Olga, Anya and Ressin. She and Olga (and Ressin) had left Anya at her parents' house, whilst the others had driven to a nearby hospital and on to a tiny Red Cross station.

Meanwhile the Tsarina and her daughters attended a service at the *Church of the Sign* that morning. Olga and Tatiana had then gone on to their infirmary where Boris Ravtopolo was once again visiting. Later, the sisters simply lay out on the balcony after their morning's duties were over. That afternoon, the Tsarina and Olga, on behalf of Tatiana, visited a new military medical ambulance that had been named after Tatiana. It had been presented to Russia by the Americans. (Tatiana was of course needed at the hospital, unlike Olga.) The sisters later attended a concert at the barracks of the Hussar regiment with their mother before leaving for a memorial service in town for the late Countess Hendrikova.

On Sunday Nicholas was visited at Mogilev by the Japanese prince. The Tsar wired Alexandra very briefly just before he went to meet the prince who had arrived by train.

Later the Tsar sent a second telegram after the conclusion of the visit and recalled an earlier visit in 1900 made by the same Prince (Kotohito) Kanin in that year. He was greatly impressed by his illustrious visitor and admitted how beautifully he conversed in French.

Meanwhile the four Grand Duchesses attended Mass at the cave church that morning. Olga and Tatiana returned to their hospital where Alexandra arrived later. She handed out medals. Yet again, Boris Ravtopolo was at the infirmary. The four sisters later visited the Catherine Palace hospital to see the patients and staff.

Tatiana had sent word to her father that day and explained that Gilliard had written to her about the serial film *The Mysterious Hand*. She added that they had been the previous day to see the young Countess (Anastasia) Hendrikova whose mother had just died. She informed Nicholas that Boris Ravtopolo was still there. (He had not left and was, it appears, quite happy where he was.)

The following day Nicholas went into more detail about the recent visit by the

Japanese prince. He had been given expensive gifts from the Emperor of Japan as had his young son. He intended to send them to the Alexander Palace so that Alexandra could admire them. The most beautiful item was a cloisonné picture that represented a peacock which was immensely heavy. His mother was receiving the prince in Kiev that day, he explained. He went on to request that Alexandra see their honoured guest on the fifteenth.

Meanwhile Alexandra had decided to go for a drive as the weather was so good. Tatiana and Anastasia had gone out horse riding.

Olga and Tatiana had been at the infirmary earlier, where Olga had done the prescriptions. She admitted in her journal how much she was missing Mitya and wanted to go and see him. The four sisters returned to the infirmary that evening as usual and Mitya's friend Boris Ravtopolo had also appeared. (He would have been a reminder of Mitya as the two young men were fairly close, and the two were from the Erivansky regiment.)

Nicholas bravely took the part of his widowed aunt against his wife in a letter to Alexandra on Tuesday. It was indeed a rare challenge. He insisted that he take Miechen's part. She had left a letter for him a few days previously and had asked for permission to stay at Livadia in one of the houses nearby under the court jurisdiction as it was not convenient to stay at a hotel in Yalta on this occasion. Nicholas had agreed and insisted that he had no alternative. He then swiftly changed the subject. He was sending Alix a letter from Konstantin's widow Mavra and a few illustrations that he found in a newspaper he thought would interest her. They had begun archaeological excavations nearby, and Alexei had taken a great interest, he explained, although mainly due to his soldier-like love of digging holes.

Meanwhile Alexandra, who had been unwell, decided to go out for a drive with Olga and Tatiana as the weather was so pleasant but she had been persuaded by her daughters not to attend the funeral of her lady-in-waiting's mother Countess Hendrikova. She had taken some pills which did not seem to have helped, although she was convinced they usually had in the past.

Meanwhile Olga and Tatiana had returned to the infirmary as usual. Anya arrived in time for lunch and afterwards the four sisters had returned to Olga and Tatiana's hospital where they had sat with Varvara either knitting or playing *ruble*.

On Wednesday Nicholas wrote to an ailing Alexandra. He was concerned that she was feeling so weak and urged her to take care of herself. He had forwarded a letter from Colonel Drenteln to Count Fredericks, he added.

Nicholas again showed concern for the military situation and remarked that he had no time to include the Guards in the reserves and they had hurried off to their new positions. The enemy had increased their troop numbers and heavy artillery which made the situation more worrying.

Luckily it was quiet at the hospitals so Alexandra had little to do, even if she had been able to. She wrote to Nicholas that day and explained that she let Tatiana do most of the work. The children had gone to Mass and she intended to join Olga and Tatiana at the infirmary later. That evening, the four sisters again returned to Olga and

Tatiana's infirmary where the youngest played *ruble* and Olga and Tatiana got on with the usual cleaning *work*.

Nicholas thanked Alix for her usual letter on Thursday before admitting that he had become involved, unintentionally, in the squabbles of others. He sent a letter from the former wife of Prince Kotchuby (Baroness Daria Grevenits) who had insisted on seeing him. She was, as the daughter of the Duke of Leuchtenberg, demanding the title as Duchess of Leuchtenberg. (The Tsar was outraged. He was convinced it was a plot to get money from lands associated with the title. As an absolute monarch, Nicholas normally had to deal with such issues but, during the war, he had less time than ever and he had been forced to ask Alexandra to take on some of his burden as regards the government. Unfortunately, it was a disaster. Everything had begun unravelling. The ministers were angered by her continual changes and the influence of Rasputin over decisions, and Nicholas was hardly proving to be Alexander I. Sadly, Alexandra did not have the skills of Queen Catherine, of Aragon, who ran the country so successfully when King Henry VIII was away in France.)

That day Alexandra held a reception for the visiting Japanese prince in Nicholas's absence. She was incredibly nervous as Nicholas usually took charge of the official entertaining. Alexandra was no natural hostess, to put it mildly. Nicholas could put anyone at their ease; Alexandra virtually no one. Luckily, the event turned out a great success but due to her daughters!

At least three of the Grand Duchesses were present at the reception and may have helped divert the attention away from Alexandra on that occasion. They could hardly be missed, all so beautiful and so charming, yet shy. They were enchanting. Tatiana seemed to have made a particularly good impression on the visitor, if the press were to be believed. (There were some bizarre rumours of her engagement to the visitor who was already married.)

Alexandra spoke unflatteringly about Olga in her daily letter to Nicholas. She had insisted that Olga sit near her at the table so that she would get more accustomed to meeting official guests and seeing how things were done. She described her eldest daughter as a clever child but not using her brains often enough.

However, in the same letter, Alexandra disclosed that she had presented the Japanese prince with a pair of china vases. She always thought vases were the most suitable gift for any occasion and these may have been valuable but their origin may have had potential to cause offence. She had presented the prince with a big pair of china vases – wood in winter and summer and two large crystal vases with eagles on. (Whether the vases were merely made of china or were Chinese is not clear. If they were Chinese this was a tactless move. The first two were possibly Chinese and the second possibly Russian with the eagles. It is interesting that Alexandra should have, in the same letter, complained that Olga rarely used her brains.)

Tatiana later wrote to Nicholas about the rumours of her impending marriage. There had been a rumour in town that she was about to marry the prince. It seemed odd as he was already married and not even a Christian, she explained. The hairdresser (Delacroix) had been curling Marie's hair with tongs and was about to do Tatiana's. She had sat next to Grand Duke Andrei and Grand Duke Nicholas Mikhailovich at the dinner.

That morning Marie had attended her usual lessons, including German and French but, by lunchtime, she had rejoined the adult world once more as she attended a special luncheon for the visiting prince. The Grand Duchess later returned to her more normal routine with a music lesson and that evening accompanied her sisters to the infirmary for the evening, no doubt with plenty to talk over after the reception. (Marie was now entering the twilight world somewhere between childhood and adulthood. Although Marie, like her older sisters, was more than happy to be seen as an adult, the Tsarina was reluctant to see her girls as grown-ups.)

Many commentators who knew the Grand Duchesses complained that they acted like little children at times, but this was probably due to the sisters having no specifically defined demarcation between childhood and adulthood. On odd occasions they were indeed expected to behave like adults, but more often than not they were treated like children. Alexandra even referred to them as the children, even when she meant Olga and Tatiana. Olga was now almost twenty-one and Tatiana nineteen.

Later Nicholas sent Alexandra a telegram congratulating her on the success of the visit after he heard that it had gone well.

Unfortunately the Tsar felt the need to sort out some potentially awkward issues with Alexandra on Friday regarding the yacht. The situation with Sablin's potential appointment had still not been sorted. There had been a misunderstanding as Nicholas had asked Admiral Grigorovitch to look for a post for Captain Rostislav Zelentsky in the future as he wanted Sablin to replace Zelentsky, but he had not ordered the change.

Meanwhile, according to Alexandra, her *children* went to see another military ambulance train and attended yet another funeral, that of the priest's son at the Feodorovsky Cathedral. (They were not spared the harsh realities of war, especially when it suited their mother to have them replace her when she was unwell.)

The four young Grand Duchesses visited Olga's ambulance train early that morning accompanied by their chaperone the Baroness Buxhoeveden. There were four new men bound for the infirmary, not including Tatiana's friend Vladimir Kiknadze who had been wounded again. He had been shot in the back. Anya Vyrubova arrived in time for lunch and afterwards the Grand Duchesses once more called in on Colonel Silaiev's wife and played with their children. It was a welcome relief after such a difficult morning. Olga chose to stay with her mother that evening as she was complaining once again of an enlarged heart.

On Saturday Nicholas attempted to make light of his son's injury in his daily letter to the boy's mother. It was raining incessantly and Alexei had hurt the instep of his foot. He was not able to put on his shoe(s). Luckily, he was not suffering any pain. He was dressed, but remained inside. On such days, Nicholas reminded Alexandra, usually when in the Crimea or on the *Standart*, they usually pasted photographs into albums.

Alexandra meanwhile mentioned in her letter to the Tsar the return of Tatiana's friend Kiknadze. He had spoken to Tatiana at great length about the sailors he had seen. She added that there were another four wounded apart from Kiknadze.

Meanwhile that morning Marie studied German, French and Mathematics. The four sisters were reunited at lunch. Olga and Tatiana had, of course, been to the hospital where Tatiana would naturally have been delighted to see Kiknadze again despite his recent injuries. (He may have been injured but at least he was alive. If he was in hospital then at least he was not in danger of being shot and killed on the field of battle.)

On Saturday afternoon, the four sisters visited the cemetery of Kazan with the sister of one of the men who had recently died. The four sisters returned to the palace for dinner before heading back to Olga and Tatiana's infirmary.

It was Anastasia's turn to write to Nicholas and she explained that she and Marie often played tennis with some of the wounded men but, as the men practised often, they had become very skilled, despite their injuries.

Nicholas was able to inform Alexandra on Sunday of their son's improvement. His foot was now much better, he was quite cheerful and they had played Nain Jaune together earlier. He went on to explain that he had been visited by Prince Alexander (Alek) of Oldenburg who had just returned from Reni and Rumania and had much to talk of.

Meanwhile Olga had written to Nicholas that day and she explained that she had spoken of Pierre Gilliard's letters with her mother. He had been asked to write every day about the progress of her son and he had often simply written about an American series they had seen at the cinema when the girls visited. (The film was entitled *The Mysterious Hand of New York* and it was a constant source of conversation amongst Gilliard and the children.)

That morning, the four Grand Duchesses had attended Mass together and had gone for a drive later. Later Olga had read to her two youngest sisters before all four returned to the infirmary for the evening. (It was snowing which was not unheard of in mid-September in Russia.)

Despite maintaining that his son was improving, Nicholas was now not only struggling to cope with the war but with his ailing son. One commentator noted that he was now paying more attention to the hour set for his meals than affairs of state. He was quite unable to rule the Empire and command the army. It was obvious that something had to give.

Nicholas appeared to be in a curious mood on Monday. He remarked that Alexandra's letters had been numbered wrongly and spoke about a strange friendship between Goutchkov and General Alexeiev. He had been told of their increasing closeness by Alexandra and wanted to know how she knew about it. He had been wondering about recent thefts at Tsarskoe Selo of military equipment. A colonel who was in charge of the heavy artillery had recently visited him. He had confided in Nicholas that every battery had one sentry on guard and that, on two nights, thefts had occurred. On one occasion, the sentry himself proved to be the thief. He explained how expensive British components for British guns were, constantly been taken en route from the port at Arkhangelsk to Tsarskoe Selo.

Meanwhile Tatiana questioned Nicholas in a letter that day about a book. She wanted to know if anyone had read *A Millionaire Girl* by AW Marchmont. (He had, in fact, read it the previous autumn.)

Nicholas II was finally beginning to see the inevitability of revolution in Russia. He revealed to Alexandra on Thursday that General Alexeiev had shown him a letter he had received from Prince Obolensky, the President of Supplies. They were still having real problems with every type of supply – from arms and ammunition to even some supplies of food and fuel. Obolensky had admitted that he was unable to alleviate the problem, the prices were continually rising higher and higher, and people were beginning to starve. Nicholas admitted that he understood where this would lead. The start of the long Russian winter would only make things worse and it had already started snowing at Tsarskoe Selo. Nicholas knew that Sturmer (the Prime Minister) could do nothing to help. He had only one possible way out and that was to put everything into the control of the military, but that could lead to more problems. Nicholas admitted it was an impossible situation and that he had never been a business man. (He was finally seeing the truth and it was too late to do anything.)

Meanwhile the Tsarina had written to Nicholas complaining that his niece Marie Pavlovna Junior seemed to have no maternal instinct. She had left her son in Sweden with his father and doting grandparents. (The couple had split up and, as things turned out, he was safer in Sweden. Alexandra, however, as a mother of five could not understand her actions, nor could her daughters who were all fond of children, especially Marie and Olga.)

(Grand Duchess Marie Pavlovna had grown up without a mother of her own and had been brought up by the Tsarina's sister Ella – hardly noted for her own maternal skills and who was childless. It had always been Ella's late husband Serge who had shown real affection for Marie and her brother Dmitri. Marie's father had lived mainly abroad when she was a child and had remarried and had another three other children whom Marie had rarely seen until recent years. It was hardly likely that Marie understood how she should deal with a child of her own.)

Marie Pavlovna had come for lunch that day, Alexandra added. She too was working as a nurse. Tatiana had been sent a sweet postcard of Lennart, Marie's son by Ingeborg (of Sweden, the sister-in-law of King Gustav and also a daughter of the Tsar's cousin King Frederick VIII of Denmark), and Alexandra saw a healthy and handsome boy and could not see why Marie had seemingly abandoned him. (Unfortunately, life is never that simple.)

The Grand Duchesses Olga and Tatiana had meanwhile spent much of the day at their infirmary. Olga had got down to her administrative work and, after lunch, had gone to see the ambulance train along with Tatiana and Marie; more wounded had arrived.

Wednesday found Nicholas in a more cheerful mood. The sense of depression of the previous day had worn off, as his letter to Alexandra indicated. The train had been delayed once more and Alexandra's most recent letter had failed to arrive. He thanked Tatiana for the photographs she had sent and asked her to send some notepaper from a *blue box*.

He had instructed General Alexeiev to order General Broussilov to halt the attacks which he felt were useless and to withdraw the Guards and other troops from the front lines. He wanted to give them time to rest and regain their strength. He intended that the men would later launch an attack near Galich and south of Dorna-Vastra to help their new allies, the Rumanians. They would need to cross the Carpathian Mountains before the real winter set in and it would be impossible. On a lighter note he added that it was the birthday of his Uncle Paul and also the name's day of his cousin Grand Duke Dmitri and Dmitri Sheremietiev, so everyone drank a glass of champagne in their honour.

Meanwhile Olga and Tatiana returned to their infirmary whilst Marie and Anastasia resumed their lessons. Marie and Anastasia dined with their mother but Olga and Tatiana accompanied by their chaperone left for the capital. Later, Rasputin and his wife made an appearance at Anya's. It was rare to see them both together. The sisters had gone there with Alexandra after dinner at home. The Grand Duchesses later left for the infirmary as usual. It had been a cold and frosty day and the ponds had frozen over again.

Nicholas had a change of heart on Thursday. He had become caught between the conflicting wishes of his wife Alexandra and General Broussilov. Broussilov had asked for permission to continue the attack as Gourko was intending to help him with the right flank. He had permitted it to continue.

He had also received an enormous pile of letters which had been passed to General Alexeiev in order to draw the Tsar's attention to the high prices of food. They had come from a wide variety of people, officers and ordinary soldiers alike, plus their families.

That day the four sisters attended a service at the *Church of the Sign* before going their separate ways. Olga and Tatiana went to their infirmary and the youngest sisters returned to their studies. The sisters reassembled at lunchtime when Anya appeared. The sisters later called in on Colonel Silaiev's wife and family before returning to the palace where Olga read to her sisters. She read *The Keeper of the Door* by Ethel May Dell. (It was a recent book as it had only been published the previous year and the name of one of the main characters Olga Ratcliffe would have appealed to the Grand Duchesses.)

Nicholas wrote again to Alexandra on Friday before she had time to react to his news. Astonishingly, he asked her to maintain peace and harmony amongst the ministers – most of whom hated her. He admitted how tired he was now of Mogilev.

Later, just as the Tsar had feared, Alexandra wrote explaining Rasputin's feelings. He had made his opinion quite clear. The attack must stop. She assured Nicholas that he would not tell a soul about it but she had to ask for Rasputin's blessing. (She of course referred to him as Our Friend and never spoke of him as Rasputin.)

The Tsarina was expecting Prince Nicholas of Greece to arrive in time for tea. She was pleased to note that her daughter Marie had gone out horse riding; normally only Tatiana rode anymore.

That day as the weather had improved Olga had walked to the *Church of the Sign*. She then went by automobile to the infirmary. She had fed one of the less able patients by hand and done some paperwork. Tatiana had remained at home as she was still having lessons.

Meanwhile, Tatiana, who was sitting waiting patiently for her teacher to appear, heard her youngest sisters making a real racket. They were playing their beloved gramophone player. They listened to a series of military tunes including *Raise the flag, The March of the Guard*, the Russian Imperial National anthem and then some of the marches that were often played on the yacht. (They were all usually played on the *Standart*, of course.) That evening, the four Grand Duchesses returned to Olga and Tatiana's infirmary where they elected to roll bandages, knit or play *ruble*.

Nicholas attempted to reason with Alexandra on Saturday. He urged her to inform Rasputin that he had taken sensible measures. They had more than enough troops to cope, he explained. He also diplomatically thanked Alexandra for her help with the ministers. (She had been able to speak to them and keep an eye on them, but she was never able to influence them unless it was against her.)

However, Rasputin was not happy to hear of Nicholas's decision. He explained that it would lead to many losses. Alexandra hoped Nicholas would understand.

Understandably on Sunday Nicholas decided on a change of topic. He sent her a recent photograph of himself taken in the Crimea that spring. He asked if she would come by the 3rd or 4th of October as he was looking forward to seeing her again.

Alexandra, however, refused to give in and again urged Nicholas to stop the advance. She urged him to stick to it this time.

Meanwhile Olga had written in a more light-hearted mood and she joked about the antics of her two youngest sisters. Marie and Anastasia had brought their bicycles into the house and were riding around the corridors on them. Luckily nothing had been broken – yet. Tatiana as usual was sitting quietly nearby – reading something in French. The two youngest sisters were being noisy and shouting. The four sisters all later went to the infirmary. (It had become their place for socialising, away from the restrictions of the Alexander Palace. Although Alexandra did join her daughters on occasions, she generally was too tired by the end of the day.)

That day Anastasia had written to Nicholas and asked him to thank Pierre Gilliard for the further updates on the story of *The Mysterious Hand of New York*. They had been to Mass that morning and to the infirmary where they had seen her friend Victor Zborovsky and Olga's friend Alexander Shvedov.

Nicholas attempted to reply to Alexandra's long list of questions on Monday. He was in a hurry though and was not happy about some of her ideas for governmental changes. (Nicholas was becoming sick of the merry-go-round she had created but had not the heart to complain as she was doing what she thought was her best. Unfortunately, it was a disaster and things were getting worse, not better. She had managed to annoy practically everyone by now.)

Sydney Gibbes, the children's English tutor, who had known Alexandra for many years, believed that she had failed to understand the Russian people. He felt that the Russians in a way acted out their lives and it was something she had never grasped. Her shyness was often misunderstood and seen as arrogance and she seemed to most to be haughty and distant, as Tatiana could do on occasions, but it was merely shyness. Alexandra was, of course, further embarrassed by a terrible Russian (and French) accent, speaking too quietly, becoming increasingly deaf in later years, and a face that went red easily.

That day, the Grand Duchesses Olga and Tatiana had returned to their infirmary. Olga was now doing administrative work but also helping with the beds, sorting out the medicines and feeding some of the weakest of the men. The four sisters later went to the Grand Palace hospital but they returned to the infirmary that evening as usual, where Baron Taube had again returned – injured once more.

Nicholas finally gave in the following day to Alexandra's wishes and the advance ceased. The confused Brussilov asked whether he should send back those incoming troops or allow them to continue. (The Tsar knew that once Alexandra had an idea in her head she was not liable to change her mind so the best way was to give in. It was something he knew from experience. It was difficult enough to cope fighting the war without having the Tsarina hectoring him.)

Nicholas thanked Alexandra on Wednesday for the instructions SHE had given him regarding what to say to the new minister. He thanked her for the precise details of what he should say to A D Protopopov. (She had always taken the lead in household decisions and now for the sake of having some peace he was letting the Tsarina tell him what to say to his own ministers.)

Meanwhile Olga and Tatiana had visited their infirmary as usual and saw that there had been some new men arrivals overnight including the Tsar's former aide-de-camp Prince George Eristov, a Colonel in the Life Guards. Later, the sisters called in on Madame Silaiev and enjoyed tea and sweets recently sent from the Caucasus with her. They returned to the infirmary that evening where Olga sat with one of the patients and played *ruble*. There was some news from Mitya who had sent a telegram to Varvara (Bibi).

That day Marie wrote to Nicholas about the book she was reading: *The Rosary* by Florence Barclay, the English author whose books were of a distinct religious nature. Nicholas had already read it.

Nicholas acknowledged Alexandra's latest letter on Thursday and bought her up to date with the news. He had spent two hours chatting to Protopopov the previous evening and sincerely hoped that he would prove a successful new minister, with his excellent knowledge of internal affairs. He added that he was excited at the prospect of seeing Alexandra and his daughters again soon and hoped that she would arrive by teatime on Monday.

That day Olga and Tatiana once more returned to their infirmary and Sonia Dehn arrived for tea. Afterwards, the sisters all gathered at Marie and Anastasia's hospital where a concert was taking place.

Anastasia's letter to Nicholas that day reveals that she and Marie had been joined on their bicycles by Olga, and she and Olga had been chasing each other. Sometimes they had fallen off in their excitement.

Nicholas informed Alexandra on Friday that he was about to receive a delegation of Serbian officers who had brought military medals for all the family. He was rather surprised and had no idea what the medals would even look like as he had never seen any before.

Meanwhile Olga went into more detail when she wrote to Nicholas about the concert they had attended the previous evening. There had been a symphony orchestra from the Life Guards' Vosnysky Regiment and they had played very well. It reminded Olga of happier times on the yacht in 1913. She had thoroughly enjoyed the concert.

The day had been spent fairly quietly by the Tsarina. Whilst her daughters lunched and dined alongside her, she remained on the sofa. The girls later went for a walk and passed one of the hospitals. Anya arrived for tea and persuaded Alexandra to visit her. The Tsarina then spent the evening at Anya's where Rasputin had also appeared, whilst her daughters returned to the infirmary. Tatiana's friend Volodia was amongst the crowd that evening. (Olga's friend Mitya was still away but at least Olga had the comfort of recently hearing from him via another friend.)

Chapter Sixteen

Winter 1916

On the first Saturday in October the Tsar detailed his appointments in his next letter home to Alexandra. He went on to discuss the Erivansky Regiment. Nicholas was busy looking for someone to replace Colonel Silaiev. He had been advised by General Kondzerovsky that the best candidates were either Colonel Michabelli, Prince Shervashidze or Colonel Gelovani. The previous day, a General Yurihich and two ambassadors arrived from the Crown (Alexander) Prince of Serbia with medals for Nicholas and his son. Nicholas had been presented with the Serbian Military Cross and he had been mightily impressed by the Serbians' dignified behaviour. He had also been presented with handsome crosses, the crosses of mercy, for Alexandra and her daughters. (The Crown Prince was the brother of Elena, wife of Prince Ioann of Russia, an old friend of Grand Duchess Olga.)

Alexei had received his medal with the inscription that it was for bravery. The boy wrote to his mother explaining that he had assumed it was for fighting with his tutors.

Meanwhile, back at Tsarskoe Selo, Olga and Tatiana returned to their infirmary before rejoining their youngest sisters and Madame Zizi (Princess Elisabeth Narishkin) for lunch. During the course of the afternoon, the sisters went to yet another concert at the Catherine Palace hospital. Tatiana, in her letter to Nicholas that day, admits her boredom of the endless charity concerts. The sisters returned to the infirmary that evening with the Tsarina to help clean the surgical instruments, sew the torn pillowcases and join in with a game of ruble. The game proved so popular that evening that it spread over two tables. Olga, Tatiana and their sisters played with Vladimir Kiknadze, Nicholas Karangozov and Bogdanova amongst others.

The Grand Duchesses Olga and Tatiana returned to the infirmary on Sunday after first attending Mass at the small cave church nearby. They joined their younger sisters, Countess Anastasia Hendrikova and Mlle Catherine Schneider in time for lunch at the palace. Afterwards the sisters joined their mother for a service at the *Church of the Sign* before they all left for Mogilev by train.

Meanwhile Nicholas sent a brief wire to Alexandra on Monday explaining that their son had an upset stomach so would not be at the station with Nicholas to meet them later.

The Tsarina and her daughters arrived at headquarters soon after and, on Tuesday morning, Nicholas and his children attended a parade of the escort. After lunch, the

The Grand Duchesses Olga and Marie on the balcony of the Alexander Palace,
Tsarskoe Selo, 1913

The Grand Duchesses Olga, the Tsar Nicholas II of Russia,
Nicholas Rodionov and Paul Voronov

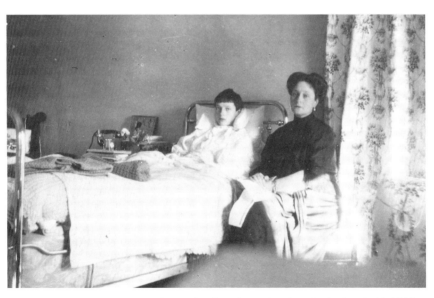

The Grand Duchess Tatiana with the Tsarina Alexandra after she had typhoid, 1913

The Grand Duchess Tatiana on the Imperial yacht, *Standart*

The Tsar and Tsarina at tea with Anya Vyrubova (foreground), Tatiana and Olga (far left), Marie (centre), Anastasia (standing), Nicholas Sablin (centre), 1914

The Grand Duchesses Marie, Tatiana, Anastasia and Olga with their cameras, 1914

The Grand Duchesses Tatiana and Olga, 1914

The Tsar and Tsarina with Anastasia, Olga and at right Tatiana,
Marie and Anya Vyrubova at tea, 1914

The Tsar and Tsarina at tea with Anastasia, Olga, Tatiana, Sablin (foreground) and Anya Vyrubova, 1914

The Grand Duchess Olga with her godchild, niece of Anya Vyrubova

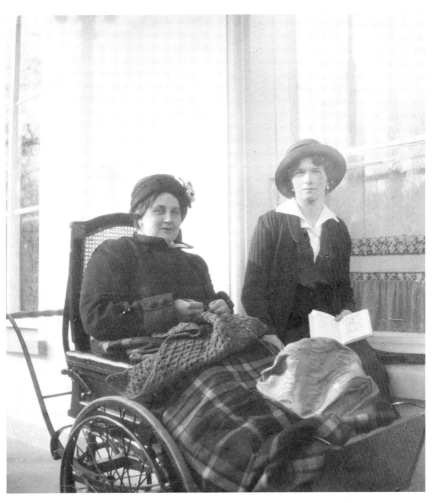

Anya Vyrubova and Grand Duchess Olga, 1915

The Grand Duchesses Anastasia, Tatiana, Marie and Olga (left to right) with the Tsarina Alexandra, 1916

The Grand Duchesses Olga, Tatiana and Marie
on the Imperial yacht, *Standart*

The Tsar and Tsarina with (left to right) Marie (hidden), Olga, Anastasia (front) and Tatiana

The Grand Duchess Olga (back 2nd to right) and Tatiana (seated)

The Tsarina and Grand Duchess Olga and Anya Vyrubova, Grand Duchess Tatiana
in front as nurses at their infirmary

The Tsarina (seated) with Olga and Tatiana (near door) and Anya Vyrubova
(to right of Tsarina) with patients and staff at their infirmary

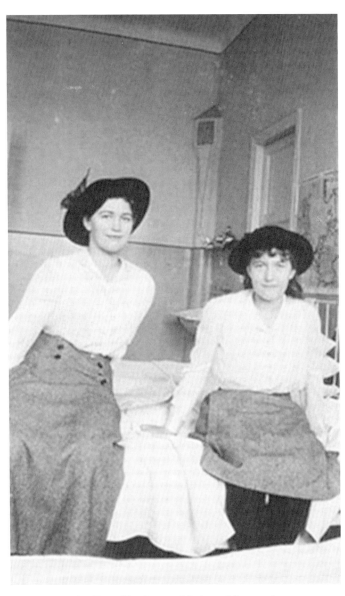

The Grand Duchesses Marie and Anastasia
at their infirmary

The Tsar at Tobolsk with Olga (left), Anastasia and Tatiana
on the roof of the greenhouse at the Governor's house at Tobolsk

Marie (left) with Tatiana (back) and Olga (seated), June 1915

Livadia Palace, 1942
(Photo from the author's own collection)

Massandra, near Livadia Palace, 1942
(Photo from the author's own collection)

2,000 year-old statue of a nymph from Livadia, which has since vanished
(Photo from the author's own collection)

Ai-Petri in the Crimea where the Tsar often walked
(Photo from the author's own collection)

View of Yalta from Livadia Palace, 1942
(Photo from the author's own collection)

Livadia Palace, 1942
(Photo from the author's own collection)

Livadia Park, 1942
(Photo from the author's own collection)

Oreanda near Livadia, 1942
(Photo from the author's own collection)

Feodosia in the Crimea, 1942
(Photo from the author's own collection)

Cossacks obligingly sang and danced for the delighted guests. The family then visited a nearby ambulance train. After dinner, Nicholas read to his children one of the many comic stories by *Teffi* (Nadezhda Alexandrovna Buvhinskaya).

The next day General Hanbury-Williams arrived back at military headquarters on his return from England. He had arrived on the Tsarevich's name's day. The Tsar received the General at lunch and insisted that they talk over his recent trip to Britain. (Nicholas had not been to Britain since 1909.)

The General was again received by the Tsar on Thursday which happened to be the General's birthday and also General Janin's from the French military mission. The British Ambassador Sir George Buchanan arrived with a gift – a GCB for the Tsar.

It was Buchanan's one and only trip to Mogilev. The Tsarina did not attend luncheon which was followed by an audience. Buchanan was seated on this occasion next to Olga and one of her other sisters, so Buchanan had no chance to speak to the Tsar. After lunch, a *cercle* was held but General Hanbury-Williams assured the Ambassador that the Tsar would be sure to ask him to talk to him later in his study. The Tsar later thanked the Ambassador for coming, but nothing more.

The Ambassador was forced to interrupt Nicholas and said that he had some things to talk about. On receiving the Tsar's permission to talk to him, Buchanan explained that Nicholas would soon be receiving the retiring Japanese Minister for Foreign Affairs, Viscount Motono. He suggested the Tsar try to enlist the Minister's help in arming Russia. Nicholas was not disposed to make any concessions towards his former enemies, however.

The Tsarina had a long chat with General Hanbury-Williams on Friday concerning his recent trip to England. She wanted to know all about his family, including his two sons, both of whom had been recently wounded – one seriously. (The General had married in 1888 and had four children. His son John married Princess Zenaide Cantacuzene in 1928.)

The Tsar and his family attended Mass on Sunday morning at the nearby garrison church and they later went for a walk along the highway, naturally without Alexandra. Later an Italian guest, Lieutenant Marsengo, played the guitar and sang for the assembled guests. The four sisters then dined with their mother and played hide and seek (probably on the train).

On Tuesday the Tsarina sent General Hanbury-Williams some more flowers and asked to see photographs of his children. Later, the General was presented with a picture of Alexandra with her own son.

That day Olga took the opportunity to write to her Aunt Xenia. She explained that, despite the continual rain, she had enjoyed their time at Mogilev. They had been at military headquarters for some nine days already and were due to return on Wednesday. Her mother, she revealed, had begun to go on the outings with her family, which was a rare event. The trips often involved a walk in the nearby forest and ended with a big bonfire where they baked potatoes with Derevenko and the designated drivers. (Alexei's favourite end to any day trip was to bake potatoes.)

Nicholas wrote to Alexandra on Wednesday shortly before she left. He thanked her for returning to Mogilev and noted that she was going back to her work and never-ending cares. He hoped that they would meet again in another two and a half weeks' time. He would miss her, especially in the evenings when they had time to spend alone at headquarters.

On Thursday Nicholas had important news. He was fairly certain that he would be able to leave for home on the 18th and spend two or three days at the palace. Meanwhile, the Tsarina and her daughters finally returned home that day.

Nicholas explained to Alix on Friday that their son was suffering from a stomach upset again. He had, he admitted, originally just thought the boy was missing his mother. Alexei had played in the wood the previous afternoon but his temperature had risen and he was sick. Alexei had to get up twice in the night to make a quick dash to the bathroom. He had improved by morning but had been confined to bed as a precaution. It must have been something he had eaten, Nicholas assumed.

Nicholas introduced General Hanbury-Williams to the new Russian Finance Minister Peter Bark at dinner on Saturday. The General was suitably impressed with the minister.

That day, Nicholas assured Alexandra that Alexei's health had improved. Mitya Dehn and Dimitri Sheremetev had just arrived to replace Naryshkin (Kira as he was affectionately known) and Prince Igor. It was beginning to get colder and there had been a slight frost. (The long Russian winter was about to begin.)

That day, the Grand Duchesses returned to their usual routine and, whilst the eldest sisters went back to their infirmary, Marie and Anastasia resumed their lessons. They reassembled in time for lunch with Alexandra, Catherine Schneider and the visiting Prince Gavril. In the afternoon, the four sisters returned to the Catherine Palace hospital and Anya arrived in time for tea.

The sisters returned to Olga and Tatiana's infirmary that evening where they sat with Rita and some of the patients, including Vladimir Kiknadze and Syroboyarsky. The sisters joined in games of *ruble* with their friends. Olga simply stood and chatted to Mitya who had recently returned, to her obvious delight.

Nicholas chatted with General Hanbury-Williams at dinner on Sunday about Constantinople. It had been Russia's aim for many hundreds of years to gain Constantinople as part of the Empire. It was never achieved.

That same day, Nicholas day wrote to Alexandra explaining that Alexei had been put on a strict diet after his recent stomach upset and was not amused. The boy continually complained that he was hungry as a result. He went on to reveal that, the previous day, all the army quartermasters had arrived for a conference. He had discovered that the army required 2,676 wagon loads each day just to feed the men and horses which took up 400 trains each day. (When this total was added to by the food and fuel needed by the ordinary population and the gradual slowdown of the service due to the heavy snow of winter, it is fairly obvious that trouble would occur. The supplies of food would inevitably dry up for everyone.)

Meanwhile Marie complained of being bored in a letter to Nicholas. She had enjoyed her time at Mogilev and found the usual routine of lessons, their hospital, the

Catherine Palace hospital, a walk in the afternoon followed by a visit to her older sisters' infirmary each evening thoroughly predictable. Whilst she was writing, she set the scene as she often did. Olga and Tatiana were reading close by, Anastasia had returned upstairs and her mother was also writing to him.

Nicholas candidly admitted one of his faults to General Hanbury-Williams on Monday. They had spoken about *tempers* and the Tsar stated that, although he very rarely lost his own temper, when he did it was very, very bad indeed.

The Tsar admitted to Alexandra that day that he had mistakenly thought that he had written his last letter to her, before his return. (Nicholas, usually the most organised of men, was beginning to get a little ruffled.) The previous evening he had been very busy and had spent almost two hours speaking with Protopopov. He added that his aide Mordvinov had not sneezed when Anastasia sent him a letter that had allegedly contained some type of sneezing powder. Mordvinov had laughed at the trick but complained that in the past couple of years he had not had the opportunity of getting his own back on the practical joker.

Anastasia meanwhile explained that the previous day she had seen Victor Zborovsky. (Although she was never known to have a *boyfriend* (platonic) like her elder sisters, he appears to have been the most likely candidate.)

Nicholas wired the Tsarina on Tuesday to explain that he would prefer to attend Mass in the fortress later.

That day Olga and Tatiana had returned to their infirmary and discovered that there had been two new arrivals. Olga, accompanied by Countess Hendrikova, had gone into town that afternoon as the Grand Duchess had one of her committee meetings to attend. She returned in time for tea and was concerned to see that Mitya was unwell. In the evening, she, along with her sisters, returned to the infirmary where she kept him company.

That evening, according to Olga's journal, she had sat on one bed with Mitya whilst Tatiana had sat on another with Volodia. The sisters left at eleven. (Once again, the eldest Grand Duchesses were probably causing some consternation amongst certain members of the nursing establishment and even the other patients who may have been jealous of the attention two of the men were receiving. The matter would, however, soon resolve itself in quite an unexpected way. There are a couple of photographs of Tatiana with Volodia and in one of them another of the patients is quite clearly seen staring hard at Volodia as if annoyed.)

The Tsar returned home on Wednesday afternoon along with his young son. Later, he walked in the garden with his daughters Olga, Marie and Anastasia. That evening, Olga was presented with a kitten by her brother. Nicholas read aloud to his family that evening. Olga had worked at the infirmary earlier in the day and had, as usual, seen Mitya but she did not return to the infirmary in the evening.

The Imperial family visited the capital on Thursday where they attended a special Funeral Mass in memory of the Tsar's late father, Alexander III. It was the twenty-second anniversary of his death. The family later lunched together and the four sisters went for a walk with Nicholas. Prince Igor arrived later for dinner with Nicholas and his daughters. (Previously, Nicholas had hinted at Igor's fondness for the sisters.)

Olga and Tatiana returned to their infirmary on Saturday. They were photographed. Some pictures they had taken recently had not worked so they were photographed again. After their shifts, the sisters sat and relaxed in the company of their friends, including Kiknadze. They played tiddlywinks.

Olga and Tatiana attended Mass at the lower church on Sunday morning. Olga spotted Mitya as they passed the infirmary. The family were treated to a film show in Alexei's small cinema upstairs that evening and, afterwards, Nicholas read some of the comic stories by Teffi.

The two eldest Grand Duchesses returned to their infirmary on Monday morning – naturally Tatiana did the dressings whilst Olga attended to the administrative work. They sat with the patients later before returning for lunch. That evening, Nicholas again read some comic stories by the Russian lady known as Teffi and Tatiana later rang the infirmary to make sure that all was well.

There was a wedding at one of the hospitals on Tuesday. The Tsarina acted as the groom's mother and Dr Botkin as the bridegroom's father. Alexandra and her daughters then went out for a refreshing drive. Later Nicholas and his son left and returned to Mogilev by train via Smolensk.

On Wednesday the twenty-sixth, Nicholas thanked Alexandra for a letter he had found on his table. He explained that he and Alexei had watched as the car had taken her and her daughters back home. Alexei had gone to his cabin to play and, later, Nicholas played a quiet game of dominoes with Dmitri before retiring early to bed. He had been reading an English book for most of the day. The book was entitled *The Man who Dined with the Kaiser*. He intended to send it to Alexandra later to read. He added that Alexei had had a nosebleed but it had been quickly stopped by the intervention of the doctor. He went on to reveal how much he had thought of Alexandra and his daughters since his departure. Nicholas found it quiet without the wild shrieks of his youngest daughter or Marie who constantly tormented his aide Mordvinov. Alexei's cat had run away at one point and had stubbornly refused to come out of its hiding place.

Nicholas simply composed a brief wire home on Thursday. He had just finished lunch and was about to go back to the train. They were leaving early that evening for Kiev.

Meanwhile Alexandra wrote to Nicholas from the Alexander Palace complaining that it was so dark in her room that she could barely see to write. The children had gone to the Catherine Palace hospital. (She was still referring to them as *children* and yet Olga would be twenty-one years old in a matter of weeks.)

Nicholas and his son Alexei arrived in Kiev on Friday where they met up with the Dowager Empress, Grand Duke Paul (the Tsar's uncle) and his brother-in-law Grand Duke Alexander Mikhailovich (Sandro). As Nicholas was driven through the streets lined with troops and schoolchildren, he suddenly remembered his former Prime Minister Peter Stolypin who had been murdered at Kiev in 1911. He then lunched with his mother and young son. (It was rare for Alexei to dine alone with his father and grandmother; probably the first such occasion as it was certainly the last.)

On Saturday, Nicholas met his sister Olga who had lived in Kiev for some time and was working at one of the local hospitals as a nurse and was due to marry within a few days. He did not stay for the wedding. Nicholas visited Olga's hospital where there had been a young deserter who had been condemned to death. The Tsar spoke quietly with the young man and afterwards decided that he should be freed. He had been frightened after running out of ammunition. The Tsar knew only too well that there were shortages of weapons of all types. It had been a constant worry to him.

Sir George Buchanan, the British Ambassador, later revealed that, on this occasion, the Dowager Empress had spoken seriously with Nicholas about the political situation.

Meanwhile, the elder Grand Duchesses returned to their infirmary in the morning where Olga dispensed the drugs and dealt with the beds. Later, the Tsarina and her four daughters left for the city. Olga and Tatiana went to one of their committee meetings whilst Alexandra accompanied by her two youngest daughters visited the hospital at the Winter Palace. They had tea on the train and afterwards the four sisters returned to Olga and Tatiana's infirmary. Olga played the piano and, to her delight, Mitya appeared later.

Nicholas found the time to write to Alexandra on Sunday after he returned by train from Kiev to Mogilev. He began writing before he left the train so that he would be able to hand the letter to his courier as soon as possible. He revealed that he had enjoyed spending time with his mother and they had some long conversations in the evenings. He had also twice had the opportunity to see his youngest sister Olga. Olga was hoping to be married on the 5th. The Dowager Empress was intending to remain in Kiev as she had really enjoyed her stay there.

The Tsar wrote again on his arrival after finding a letter waiting for him from Alexandra. He explained that he had seen his sister Olga and spent about an hour with her and had also met two of the doctors and some of the other nurses at the hospital. The wounded arrived to see him and, more particularly, his son.

Marie was busy that day finishing off some shirts for a couple of the wounded officers who were about to leave her hospital. She explained to Nicholas that day that they were about to go to the Catherine Palace hospital for yet another concert. It was two years since the hospital there had been established. Nicholas's old friend Lersky would be there. She enjoyed seeing him as she found him easy to talk to and very amusing. On this special occasion, the famous singer Maria Kuznetzova was also appearing in the line-up.

Nicholas wired Alexandra on Monday but had little news. He urged her not to overtire herself.

Alexandra admitted to Nicholas that day how much she had enjoyed the concert. She was impressed by Maria Kuznetzova's singing and even her Spanish dancing. It was the first time she had seen Lersky, and he reminded her of Nicholas who had so often spoken of this man in the highest terms. (Nicholas is rarely seen as a man of humour, but he did collect the comic sayings of his late brother George and often reread them in his study.)

Olga heard that morning the bad news that Mitya was soon to depart for the Caucasus with his mother. She and Tatiana worked at their infirmary as usual but that afternoon went for a ride to Pavlovsk.

That day, Anastasia explained about the concert as her mother had done. She also remarked that the kitten (Vaska) her brother had recently brought Olga was now quite grown-up and was rather handsome. (Alexei also had a cat and Marie may also have had one, possibly a Siamese.) That evening, the four sisters returned as usual to the infirmary. They returned home later in an open car despite the fact that it was lightly snowing.

On Tuesday, at the beginning of November, Nicholas sent a brief message back to Alexandra after meeting up with an old friend – Rear-Admiral Veselkin.

Meanwhile, in Kiev, the Tsar's youngest sister, the Grand Duchess Olga Alexandrovna, who had recently divorced, married Nicholas Alexandrovich Kulikovsky, a captain in the Cuirassier Regiment. It was a quiet and extremely low-key ceremony despite the presence of the Dowager Empress and her son-in-law Sandro (Grand Duke Alexander Mikhailovich). The bride went back to work on the ward that same evening.

That day, Anastasia sent word to Nicholas. It was their last lesson with Petrov for a while, she explained, as he was about to leave for Mogilev to teach Alexei. She admitted that she was struggling with such a scratchy pen. They had written to Anastasia's former nurse Tatiana Gromova. (The nurse had, in previous years, worked on Anastasia's back which was said to have been weak, not that you would have known. She was an energetic and lively child.) Yet again, she managed to include Victor Zborovsky in the letter. She had seen him.

On Wednesday, Nicholas sent his congratulations to Alexandra on the eve of their eldest daughter's twenty-first birthday. He could hardly believe it was twenty-one years since her birth. He added that it had snowed heavily in the night and the cars were finding it difficult to get through the streets.

That day, Alexandra admitted that she had only slept for a couple of hours the previous night and explained that, for the first time, Tatiana had been permitted to give the chloroform during an operation. (It was used to put the patient to sleep temporarily so that they could be operated on.)

The Grand Duchesses meanwhile stuck to their usual schedule. The sisters returned to their respective hospitals and they joined their mother at the palace for lunch and dinner. In the evening, the four sisters returned to Olga and Tatiana's infirmary. The Tsarina visited Anya Vyrubova, and Rasputin also called in on his friend.

On Thursday Nicholas wrote to Alexandra and explained that Alexei had injured his right leg. Dr Feodorov had ordered the boy to remain in bed for the day. He was nevertheless enjoying himself in the company of his three tutors and Nicholas could hear the noise from the next room from the foursome.

Alexandra explained that day to Nicholas her delight in being able to speak to her son over the telephone. Unfortunately she had some difficulty in hearing him; although she would not admit it, she was rather deaf. There had a special *Te Deum* that morning to celebrate the twenty-first birthday of Olga Nicolaevna in the hospital and then at the palace.

Marie had also written to Nicholas of her joy at speaking to her brother. Her hearing was clearly better than her mother's. She had not only heard her brother but had overheard the engineer switch himself off just before her brother's voice came through.

Alexei had written to his mother that day and asked about Olga's cat. He explained that it had been difficult to hear him because the line was made of steel instead of copper.

Meanwhile, the birthday girl Olga had begun the day at the *Church of the Sign* before returning to her infirmary but there were few cases that day. She received a great many telegrams on her special day. The sisters returned to the infirmary that evening where one of the inmates played the piano to amuse the guests. Olga's day was made when she heard that Varvara had received a telegram from Mitya that day from Mozdok.

On Friday the Tsar explained in his usual letter home to Alix how their son had bravely attempted to keep quiet so as not to disturb his father, despite being in great pain. Dr Feodorov had said that the swelling was going down though but had insisted that his patient stay in bed for a week.

Nicholas later realised his mistake in sending letters unread to Alexandra. A letter had been given to him, although reluctantly, by Grand Duke Nicholas. The Grand Duke had been less than complimentary about the Tsarina, unknown to the Tsar.

The Tsarina was deeply offended by the letters. She could not believe that he could say such things about her.

Nicholas apologised again to Alexandra on Saturday and admitted that he should have looked at the letters before forwarding them. He had no idea of their content. He was always in such a hurry, he explained. The Grand Duke had not so much as even spoken about her recently, he stated. Luckily, there was good news – Alexei's leg was improving.

On Sunday the Tsar thanked Alexandra for her latest letter and he confirmed that their son was still improving. It had been a busy day. It was the holiday of the Guards' Equipage and he had several other visitors to receive.

Meanwhile, Alexandra, Olga and Tatiana attended Mass before returning to the infirmary. There were just a few men to treat. The weather was becoming more like winter as the trees were covered in snow. Later, the ladies returned to the hospital where Alexandra handed out some medals. The sisters went back to the infirmary after dinner but they mainly sat around chatting as there was little to do.

On Monday Grand Duke Nicholas and his brother the Grand Duke Peter arrived from the Caucasus. According to General Hanbury-Williams, who was also invited to lunch that day, Nicholas seemed genuinely pleased to see the Grand Duke. In his daily letter home that day, Nicholas pointed out that the Grand Duke had left behind two particular members of his suite. The brothers had left Orlov and Yanushk in the south.

The Tsar had seen Dr Sirotinin who explained that General Alexeiev needed a rest in the Crimea for the next six to eight weeks. He was exhausted by overwork. As Nicholas himself had noted some time previously, he was a particularly hard worker.

Meanwhile, Alexandra had sent her son's pocket money. Once more, she had forgotten to send it and she apologised to the boy.

Meanwhile, the infirmary where the eldest Grand Duchesses worked was fairly quiet. Boris Ravtopolo had returned as unfortunately he needed to attend his mother's funeral. That afternoon, Olga joined her two youngest sisters at the Catherine Palace hospital where they sat out on the balcony for much of their visit. That evening the Tsarina and her four daughters paid a call to Anya's little house for an impromptu party. She had also invited Olga's friend Rita, Yuzik, Gromatin and Anastasia's friend Victor Zborovsky.

On Tuesday Nicholas wrote to Alexandra. She had suggested that Boris Sturmer should take a holiday rather than leave his post. He thought it was a good idea that the old man disappear for a while as the Duma and the entire country seemed to dislike him. Nicholas was convinced the man was hated simply because they supported him. He hoped that Alexandra would be able to visit him on the 14th.

Meanwhile, an old friend had returned to the infirmary. Olga and Tatiana's friend, the talented violinist Kasyanov, had come back with a bullet wound in his side. That evening, the Tsarina and her daughters returned to the infirmary where Olga played the piano and everyone sat around cosily playing *ruble* and chatting.

On Wednesday Nicholas resumed his conversation with Alexandra about Sturmer in his letter to Alexandra. He admitted that no one had any confidence in the man and he would have to go. (The man had two posts: President of the Council of Ministers and the Foreign Minister. Nicholas had often doubled up some of the various ministers with two positions as he was so unsure who to trust.) Nicholas candidly admitted to Alexandra that Sir George Buchanan, the British Ambassador, had told him that the British consuls had predicted serious disturbances if the man stayed. There was much he wanted to say but he had no time to write much more.

The Tsar later wired after speaking to Boris Sturmer. He explained simply that he had spoken to the old man and would inform her of his decision soon.

That day Anastasia had taken her turn to write to Nicholas and she explained that Olga's little cat had been given a collar so she could be heard coming. The bell was fitted to a blue ribbon.

Nicholas wired Alexandra on Thursday after dismissing Sturmer. He simply stated enigmatically that he had done it.

He later sent another brief message concerning Alexandra's travel arrangements. He was sending Voyeikov back so that he could accompany the ladies to Mogilev. Nicholas wrote yet again to Alexandra at great length concerning the recent governmental changes. He also begged her not to drag Rasputin into this.

On Friday Nicholas spoke of the famous *Angel of Mons* story to General Hanbury-Williams. British troops had reported seeing angels over the battlefield at Mons in August 1915. The story may have been told to Nicholas by his daughter Tatiana. He stated that one of his daughters spoke at about the same time to a wounded Russian soldier who had claimed that some Russian troops had seen a vision of the Virgin Mary.

On Saturday Nicholas wired Alexandra and wished her a pleasant journey. (She and her daughters were due to visit Mogilev.) Alexandra and her four daughters duly arrived at military headquarters shortly after.

Nicholas and Alexandra dined together on Monday evening and celebrated the birthday of the Tsar's mother. The Dowager Empress had been born in Denmark in

1847. It was also, of course, the twenty-second wedding anniversary of Nicholas and Alexandra.

On Tuesday General Hanbury-Williams had another opportunity to chat to the Tsarina. He sat next to her at luncheon and, once again, she asked about his children, particularly his wounded son.

As the Tsarina and her daughters settled down to life at Mogilev once again and they were again forced to sleep on the train, the young Tsarevich was delighted to be reunited with his mother and sisters. He had recovered from his recent accident and on Wednesday he enjoyed a game of football with General Hanbury-Williams and other members of the party.

On Friday, according to General Hanbury-Williams, Nicholas and Alexandra celebrated the birthday of Queen Alexandra. (The widow of the late King Edward VII was a sister of Nicholas's mother and also a sister-in-law of Alexandra's late mother.)

The Tsar's daughters made the most of their free time on Saturday and played with some local children. They later walked towards the monastery. It was a welcome break for all the sisters, whether from work at the hospital or as a change from constant lessons for Marie and Anastasia.

On Sunday General Hanbury-Williams spoke with the Tsar of the vexed question of supplies. That day the family had attended Mass at the nearby garrison church and went for a drive that afternoon. After dinner, the family sat around in the company of the members of the suite and household.

On Tuesday the Tsar and Tsarina and all their children attended tea with an excited Princess Paley at Mogilev. She and her son Vladimir set about finding as many unusual sweets and fruits as they could. Her chef made up a number of sandwiches, cakes and petit fours. The family had tea with their hosts. Nicholas, according to his hostess, appeared pale and tired yet Alexandra (unusually) seemed in a happy mood. Alexei looked rather pale but was as charming as he usually was with ladies. The sisters shyly placed themselves next to Dmitri at one end of the table. Olga (Princess Paley) seated herself at the other end of the table as hostess. She sat close to the samovar (Russian tea urn) and cups. The Tsarina was seated on her right and Nicholas on her left. Grand Duke Paul sat on the other side of Alexandra.

The party went well until Alexandra asked the Princess her thoughts on Livadia. Nicholas interrupted and stated that it was hardly a fair question as the Princess had a most beautiful palace of her own and Livadia was more of a family home.

The younger members of the party retired to the drawing room and played happily together. Princess Paley's son Vladimir had played host to the younger members and the children enjoyed their time together. Vladimir was a talented poet like Olga Nicolaevna, and the two would have had this in common but would have had little chance to talk of poetry in such a lively environment and in the company of the excited Alexei, Anastasia and Marie. The Tsar had great difficulty getting Alexei away at seven. That evening, Nicholas and Alexandra attended a film performance and had dinner back at the Governor's House.

Nicholas returned home to Tsarskoe Selo the following day with his family. He remained there until shortly before Christmas. They arrived home on Friday. Anastasia had been amusing Ortipo on the long journey home and played ball with her. The family arrived home in time for tea.

On Saturday Nicholas attended a gathering of the Order of St George at the People's Palace in Petrograd, along with the Tsarina and their young son. It was a bitterly cold day for an open-air service. Nicholas was awarded with the Order of St George and Alexei with a St George medal as a result of their having come under enemy fire. Nicholas had been reluctantly pressed into accepting the decoration by an old friend Prince Anatole Bariatinsky. (Nicholas only removed the medal a few days before his death.)

On Sunday the family returned to church for Mass as usual and the sisters returned to visit their respective hospitals. Life carried on as usual for the children. Marie and Anastasia continued with their studies.

On Tuesday, Marie had her usual German, French and history lessons. Although it was later denied that the Grand Duchesses knew German, they did. Marie later attended music and Russian lessons before the four sisters were reunited at dinner with their parents. During the day, Marie and Anastasia had found time to visit their infirmary, and their older sisters, of course, spent much of the day at their own hospital.

On Wednesday Olga took the opportunity to write to her Aunt Xenia and she explained that there was not much work currently but whilst they had been at Mogilev another three new patients had arrived. One of the men was shell-shocked. He was suffering from concussion and was unable to speak.

The youngest Grand Duchesses continued their usual lessons that day. Marie had English, history and Russian lessons that morning. She later joined her sister Anastasia for a visit to their own hospital. Olga and Tatiana as usual had worked at their infirmary. That evening, as Olga read to her youngest sisters, they knitted. The Tsarina's sister the Grand Duchess Elisabeth made a rare but brief visit that day.

As December began, there was little evidence of the horrific incident soon to occur. Despite his return, Nicholas was kept busy and, on Friday morning, he received General Voyeikov; then before lunch he gave audiences to Trepov, Peter Bark, Polovstov and Shakhovksy. The rest of the day was spent in a quieter vein. He accompanied Alexandra on a walk, although she rode in her small carriage. The four daughters also walked with them. He later spent time reading, a rare luxury recently and, finally, the family visited Anya. She had another visitor – Grigory Rasputin.

That day, the Grand Duchesses had returned to their usual duties – Olga and Tatiana to their infirmary, and Marie and Anastasia to their lessons. The Tsarevich once more at the palace resumed his usual routine. It would have been difficult to readjust to the more feminine household consisting of his mother, four sisters, the ladies-in-waiting, maids, nurses, servants, etc. He had been used to an entirely grown-up male environment at Mogilev. It was only ever altered when his sisters and mother visited occasionally. The sisters attended another concert at the Catherine Palace hospital that afternoon but returned for dinner.

On Saturday Nicholas and Alexandra were joined for tea by Grand Duke Paul.

He somewhat boldly asked his nephew to grant a constitution but Nicholas refused to do so. He explained that he had sworn on his coronation day to hand over his full autocratic powers to his son on his death. The Tsarina sat silently. Paul spoke openly about the influence of Rasputin. It was now Nicholas's turn to remain silent whilst Alexandra defended her friend. The Tsarina even stated that every prophet is damned in his own lifetime. (To be fair, he was damned in death too.)

Meanwhile, the eldest Grand Duchesses returned to their infirmary and, on this occasion, Alexandra joined her daughters along with her son. The Tsarevich stoically stood by and watched from the doorway during an operation. There could be no doubting his bravery and patience. Later, Olga stood in the corridor and chatted with the patients, including Kasyanov. That evening, as Nicholas sorted out his photographs, Tatiana took a turn at reading aloud. She read some short stories written by NA Leykina in 1893.

On Sunday the family attended Mass together and afterwards Nicholas left for Mogilev with his son. The children went to yet another concert at the Catherine Palace hospital. The sisters then joined their mother for dinner before returning to the infirmary once more.

Meanwhile, Nicholas composed a long and loving letter to Alexandra in the train. The journey back to Mogilev took some twenty-five and a half hours. He apologised for being in a temper at one point during his recent visit.

The Grand Duchess Tatiana wrote to Nicholas on Monday offering her congratulations. The following day would be Nicholas's saint's day – St Nicholas Day. She was sorry that he would not be able to spend it with his family. She added that the snow had not stopped since his departure. The sisters had gone out sledging earlier and their mother had joined them for the first time in quite a while.

Nicholas duly arrived back at military headquarters on Monday evening. He attended a special service at the nearby church in honour of his name's day on Tuesday. Nicholas received messages from King George V, amongst others. The Tsar sent a telegram of thanks to Alix that day. Their son had presented Nicholas with a pile of gifts from the family the previous evening as usual.

Later, Nicholas wrote and thanked Alexandra again for the presents. He was in a light-hearted, celebratory mood. He had got out at each station along with Alexei and had a brief walk and they had stretched their legs. They had arrived to find deep snow. Nicholas had been reading yet another of Florence Barclay's novels *The Wall of Partition* and had felt soothed by it.

Alexandra wrote that day with worrying insight into Rasputin's knowledge of her daughters. He had told Alexandra that he had been contented with the Grand Duchesses as they had such heavy courses (periods) for their age and their souls were much developed.

That same day, Olga had written to Nicholas in a happy mood. She had sat in her father's place at lunch. They had several guests including Count and Countess Benckendorf, Madame Zizi (Narishkin), Ressin, Apraksin, Anya Vyrubova, Countess Hendrikova and Baroness Buxhoeveden. She sat between the two old women (Madame Benckendorf and Madame Zizi) and tried to amuse them, but it was not easy. She blushed so easily. They had been celebrating St Nicholas's Day in the absence of her father.

Despite her jolly letter, Olga's journal revealed that she was actually bored. She was cheered later with the news that she had been given another regiment. The four sisters returned to Olga and Tatiana's infirmary that evening, and Olga obligingly played the piano for the assembled group.

There was a crushing blow for General Hanbury-Williams on Wednesday: he heard that one of his sons had just died. The news was not unexpected, but still came as a terrific blow. The Tsar sent his young son Alexei to comfort the General. The boy explained that his father thought that he might feel lonely.

Nicholas had been overwhelmed by the number of telegrams he had received the previous day. That day he wrote of the film he and his son had been watching together for some time. He explained to Alexandra that the villain had finally been revealed in the film *The Mysterious Hand of New York*. The baddy turned out to be the cousin and fiancé of the main female character. The news came as a great surprise to everyone in the cinema.

Meanwhile Olga had been delighted with her birthday gifts, according to Alexandra that day. She had been appointed to a second regiment (Plastini). She was already the Colonel-in-Chief of one of the Hussar regiments. She had been so excited at the news that she had been unable even to read the words of the telegram aloud. She sent off a wire to her new regiment at once. Once again, they had spoken to Alexei over the telephone but his voice carried less well than Gilliard's far deeper sounds.

On Thursday Nicholas wired Alexandra with news of the General's loss. The two men had become fairly close over recent months.

Later the Tsar reassured Alexandra that he knew exactly what to say to Trepov (the Minister of Communications) when they met on the 12th. Trepov was hated by the Tsarina. Nicholas urged her not to worry herself about the matter. Trepov was coming to talk to Gourko about the problems with the railways. Nicholas revealed that each evening he read a chapter of Florence Barclay's *The Wall of Partition*. Alexandra had sent him another short volume by Count Leo Tolstoy. It was a posthumous work entitled *Hadji Murat*.

That day Alexandra wrote to Nicholas. She had decided to visit Novgorod and was making the arrangements. She ended her letter by urging Nicholas to be firm and to be the master.

Tatiana had written to Nicholas that day and admitted that she was pushed for time and was actually writing at the infirmary. She also confessed that she had been unable to hear her brother on the telephone. (It is not impossible that Tatiana, like her mother was a little deaf. She may have lost some hearing when she had typhoid in 1913 and she certainly had hearing problems after she had measles in 1917.)

On Friday Nicholas wrote to the Tsarina after hearing of her intended trip to Novgorod. She had wanted to go there for some two years. Nicholas informed her that the Governor of Novgorod, named Islavin, was an excellent man and one he greatly admired. He had decided to see Trepov on Saturday instead, he added.

That evening, the four Grand Duchesses had returned to Olga and Tatiana's infirmary as usual, whilst the Tsarina visited Anya. Madame Vyrubova had two other guests – Lili Dehn and Grigory Rasputin.

On Saturday, Nicholas wired on his son's behalf. They had read Alexandra's latest letter with interest and the Tsarevich, he explained, quite understood that she was unable to write. He later wrote more fully and revealed that he (Nicholas) had visited Novgorod in the summer of 1904. The previous day he had prayed before the icon of the Mother of God, which was something Alexandra had wished him to do.

That day, Olga had noted in her journal that the Tsarina had seen Protopopov at Anya's. They had attended the vigil service at seven and, later, they had called in on Anya. Rasputin and his wife were at Madame Vyrubova's and had dined there. The Tsarina and her daughters had then gone on to the infirmary, but there was little to do. The Tsarina and her four daughters left at eleven by train for Novgorod.

Marie also reported that she had gone with her mother and sisters to Novgorod that evening. The four sisters, she confirmed, had then gone on to the infirmary with the Tsarina before leaving for Novgorod and travelling through the night.

Nicholas had no time to write on Sunday so sent a brief wire to Alexandra. He was about to go to church then would go on to the reports and a big lunch. He intended writing more fully on Monday, he explained.

Meanwhile, the Tsarina and her daughters arrived by train at Novgorod and they went straight to the Sophia Cathedral where there was a Hierarchical Liturgy. The party then visited the various religious relics and on to the Archbishop's residence. There was a hospital in the lower part of his house. Alexandra and her daughters dined with Anya Vyrubova, Countess Hendrikova, Ressin and Apraksin, amongst others. That afternoon they visited the Zemstvo hospital and a shelter for refugee children. They then visited the monastery and hospital. The party had tea with the noblemen and returned to the train. They spent a total of two nights on the train.

Nicholas finally had time to write to Alexandra on Monday but only briefly. He had been chatting to a civil engineer named Weinberg who had just returned from Germany and told Nicholas many things. (Yet again, the Tsar failed to explain what he had spoken of.) Nicholas had issued a manifesto to his troops explaining that the Germans had made a peace offer, but the time for peace had not yet come.

That day, Alexandra wrote of her recent visit which had been, she believed, a success. She had asked Olga and Anastasia to write more detailed accounts. She had been impressed with the cathedral which she thought rather beautiful. She regretted that it had got too dark to see much of the town. They had spent over two hours at the cathedral and they had knelt before each of the saints. They went to a hospital and museum straight after and they had returned to the train for lunch. She had eaten on her bed. The Grand Duchesses had lunched in the company of the Governor and Prince Ioann. They were then received by the Governor's family with the traditional bread and salt of welcome and went to the small Zemstvo hospital.

The party had then travelled to the *Dessiatinni monastery* which contained the relics of St Barbara. They saw an old woman named Maria Mikhailovna who was alleged to be over 100. She had spoken to Alexandra enigmatically that the war would soon be over and that her daughters would marry. (It is sometimes said that she actually said that they would marry Christ or even death. As Alexandra was fairly deaf and the old woman a little indistinct, the words could have been muddled easily.) The Tsarina complained that she had little time to chat and had wished to but it had been too fidgety around. (That was often used by Alexandra as a way of indicating her irritation with people.)

They had later visited a home for boys from Tatiana's committee and some of the girls came too from their home. Alexandra and her daughters later arrived home and afterwards dined at Anya's. They were joined by Rasputin. The sisters later went to the infirmary where they played *ruble* and chatted to the patients and staff alike. They made no distinction.

Nicholas finally had more time to write on Tuesday. He had enjoyed Alexandra's detailed letter about her visit. She had managed to see more than he did on his visit in 1904, he admitted. He thought it would be nice if they could both go together the following spring. (They did not, of course.)

Meanwhile, Alexandra was still attempting to get Nicholas to be more forceful towards his ministers. She had seen Rasputin and he too urged Nicholas to be firm. She had spent much of the day writing Christmas cards. (She and Nicholas had a large family and it would have taken quite some time writing to them alone. The cards to England and Germany had to be sent at an earlier date, as Russian Christmas was of course thirteen days later than in the West. They would have been sent by courier rather than by the ordinary post. The cards of the era were one-sided, rather than the two-page versions of the twenty-first century. The sisters usually signed jointly as *OTMA* on each card they sent.)

That day Olga and Tatiana had returned as usual to their infirmary after a brief visit to the *Church of the Sign*. Alexandra, however, remained at home as she was exhausted after the recent trip. There was a new patient at the hospital: an eighteen year-old. Olga played tiddlywinks with Tatiana and Kasyanov in a spare moment. They later visited town to attend a committee meeting and, on her return, Olga heard that Mitya was due some leave.

On Wednesday Nicholas rather jokingly thanked Alexandra for the severe scolding she had given him in her last letter. He claimed to have read it with a smile as she had spoken to him as if he were a child.

Meanwhile, there was some trouble at Marie and Anastasia's hospital. One of the officers, Alexandra explained to Nicholas that day, had been thrown out for mocking her journey to Novgorod. The doctors decided he had to go. She changed subject swiftly. The girls had been out for a drive and had come back complaining of the cold and wanting their tea, she explained. (The nearest she would have got to making it was pouring out the tea and handing around the biscuits.)

The eldest Grand Duchesses had been busy that day and had attended the *Church of the Sign* together before going to the infirmary. They later visited the Grand Palace hospital and, in the evening, returned to their own hospital once more. The Tsarina remained at home.

In his letter to Alexandra on Thursday, Nicholas admitted (after her recent scolding) that he was a mere weak-willed hubby. She had asked him so many questions he barely knew where to begin. He was overwhelmed by work and worries.

Meanwhile, Alexei had spent the afternoon playing in the nearby woods in the snow with his tutors and others. He later played hide and seek in the dark. (He enjoyed the game as much as his sisters, although probably for different reasons.) Olga had a committee meeting that afternoon in town.

On Friday Nicholas attempted to calm Alexandra after her recent letters. He explained that he was not angry at her and understood her wish to help him in his hour of need. He hoped to have some chance of leaving on Sunday - after the conference. Again, he signed himself as her weak-willed husband.

That day Alexandra complained that the treatment she was receiving was making her ill. Dr Botkin had advised her to rest after giving her something stronger than usual. She was intending to rest for most of the day. It was cold outside and everywhere was covered in a thick blanket of snow. She explained that, yesterday, Olga had gone to town for a committee meeting. Olga had observed that Prince Vladimir Volkonsky, who usually smiled at her, never once did so. She was proud to see how her daughters were learning how to watch people's faces.

That same day, in his own journal, the French Ambassador Maurice Paleologue confirmed the Tsarina's worst fears: everyone hated her. He had spoken to a famous Moscow dressmaker who confirmed the truth. She admitted that Nicholas would be booed if he appeared in Red Square but that the Tsarina would be simply torn to shreds. Even the saintly Grand Duchess Elisabeth was scared to leave her convent.

Anya Vyrubova was sent on an errand that afternoon to Rasputin's lodgings to take an icon to him from the Tsarina. He was expected to attend a late supper at Princess Irina's, the wife of Prince Felix Yussopov. When Anya later informed the Tsarina of the plan she was convinced that it was a mistake; she knew that Irina was in the Crimea and not in the capital.

Rasputin had been invited to the Moika Palace by Prince Felix (according to the Prince's later admission) on the pretext of seeing Princess Irina. Although Felix had often recently visited Rasputin in town, it was unusual for the Prince to invite the man to the palace and the late hour made it stranger still.

The Prince and his friends (Grand Duke Dmitri Pavlovich, the politician Vladimir Purishkevich and Dr Stanislaus Lazovert) had prepared a cellar room at the palace especially for Rasputin's visit. A samovar stood on the table along with some cakes and the sideboard was filled with glasses and bottles. According to the Prince, his friend Dr Lazovert had put a quantity of crushed cyanide of potassium crystals into the middle of each of the small cakes. Each cake was sufficient to kill a man, if not several.

The intended victim duly arrived at the palace dressed in his best embroidered silk blouse, black velvet trousers and shiny new boots. He smelt as if he had washed but with the cheapest of soaps. The Prince escorted his guest into the cellar and explained that Irina was upstairs at a party and would join them shortly. He had attempted to make the impression of a party in the room above by playing the gramophone and

Rasputin could hear the sounds of Yankie Doodle playing from the room above.

The Prince offered his guest a cake. After initially refusing, Rasputin took two and swiftly ate them with relish. Felix was baffled as to why his intended victim remained alive. Rasputin then asked for some Madeira wine which the Prince duly proffered knowing that it too was poisoned. Rasputin drank two glasses yet still remained upright although his head was beginning to trouble him a little. He took some tea in order to clear his head.

Rasputin suggested that the Prince sing for him and Felix obliged by singing one song after another. The intended victim meanwhile sat nodding and grinning. The other conspirators, meanwhile, huddled together at top of the stairs not daring even to breathe. Purishkevich, Grand Duke Dmitri and the others listened whilst Felix endeavoured to continue with the impromptu concert. After waiting more than two hours, the terrified Prince rushed upstairs not knowing what to do next. Lazovert had no idea what they should do and had already fainted once. The Grand Duke suggested that they give up the plan and go home but Purishkevich disagreed. They could not leave the man half-dead. The prince then volunteered to finish the task. He took the Grand Duke's Browning revolver and returned to the cellar with it concealed behind his back.

Rasputin was seated and breathing heavily but asked for more wine. He then suggested they go visit the gypsies but the Prince led him to the mirrored cabinet and showed the man the ornate crucifix. Rasputin stated that he preferred the cabinet. The Prince then insisted that he look at the crucifix and say a prayer. Rasputin simply glared at him and turned to look at the cross. The Prince then fired and hit Rasputin in the back. He fell down upon the white bearskin rug. The other men rushed downstairs and the doctor took the victim's pulse and swiftly declared him dead. A moment later as the Prince stood alone with the corpse, he noticed that Rasputin's face was twitching. He began to wake. Rasputin opened first his left eye and then his right. He then stared with hatred at the Prince.

Rasputin appeared to be foaming at the mouth and grabbed hold of the Prince by the throat. The terrified Felix struggled free and fled upstairs only to be followed by Rasputin on all fours. Purishkevich then heard an inhuman cry – it was the petrified Felix who yelled at him to fire at once. The Prince then rushed towards his parents' apartments in desperation.

Purishkevich dashed outside into the courtyard, where Rasputin was heading for the iron gate and would soon escape into the street. Rasputin was shouting that he would tell the Tsarina what Felix had done. Purishkevich shot at Rasputin and missed – he shot again and once more managed to miss. He then attempted to steady his aim and fired again; this time he hit the target in the shoulders. Rasputin stopped and Purishkevich aimed once again, this time he hit the victim in the head. He then ran up and kicked Rasputin hard with his boot. The victim could not rise but ground his teeth in anger. The prince suddenly appeared and proceeded to hit Rasputin with a rubber club.

The body was then rolled into a blue curtain and tied with rope and taken to the River Neva where Purishkevich and Lazovert pushed it through a hole in the ice. When the body was found three days later it was clear that he not died from drowning;

his lungs were filled with water and he had even managed to get one arm out and raise it as if in blessing.

Meanwhile on Saturday, quite unaware what was happening in the capital, Nicholas sat down to compose a letter to Alexandra. He had finished work earlier than expected and explained that, when he returned, they would consider some of the things she had asked about concerning the government appointments. Meanwhile Alexei had been out to buy Christmas presents and visited the Hotel France. He was naturally quite unaware of any problems.

Baroness Buxhoeveden recalled some years later that stories had begun to circulate about Rasputin's disappearance. The Tsarina remained visually calm despite the talk. Alexandra was holding a reception of ladies when she heard the rumours. She spoke quietly with Madame Vyrubova and then continued her meetings. Madame Vera (Witte) Narishkine was seen by Alexandra straight afterwards, but the Tsarina remained composed as she chatted about a workshop for disabled servicemen.

Alexandra voiced her concerns for Rasputin's safety when she wrote to Nicholas that day. She appears to have added to the piece during the day as she did not mention her friend until well into the letter. She suddenly remarked that they were all sitting together worried that something terrible must have happened to Rasputin. Anya had told her that he had been due to visit Irina's house the previous evening and knew that it was odd at the time as Irina was away. Now her fears seemed to be confirmed. He had vanished and there had been reports of an incident at the house. The police were investigating it but she refused to believe that he was dead. She had decided to keep Anya nearby as she feared for her safety too.

Meanwhile Olga Nicolaevna attempted to carry on as normal. She and Tatiana had been to the *Church of the Sign* before returning to the infirmary. Olga had assisted in making up the beds and noted that one of the patients, Sokolov, had deteriorated during the night. She played tiddlywinks with Tatiana and Kasyanov before the two sisters returned to the palace for lunch.

Marie and Anastasia had also continued with their usual schedule of lessons that morning. Anya arrived in time for tea and then the Tsarina, her friend and the four Grand Duchesses had huddled close together, worrying about Rasputin's fate. He had disappeared during the night. They all waited up for a telephone call. The sisters all slept together. (Anatole Mordvinov observed the sisters that evening huddled up together on a sofa in their reception room. They were visibly upset.)

Still unaware that anything was amiss, Nicholas wired later. He was planning to leave Mogilev with Alexei soon. He did not see Alexandra's letter until later. After reading Alexandra's frantic letter on Sunday morning, Nicholas sent a telegram to his wife from Orsha. He admitted how horrified he was at the news. He was quite shaken and confirmed that he would arrive the following afternoon.

Meanwhile the Tsarina and Anya had received Communion that morning and the girls had attended the liturgy together. Olga confirmed in her daily journal that Anya would be staying with them. Late that morning Olga and Tatiana had gone to the infirmary but there was little to distract them. Anya and Lili Dehn spent much of the day consoling the Tsarina. Nicholas Sablin also made a brief appearance. At one point, Olga, accompanied by Countess Hendrikova, decided to take Marie, Anastasia, Madame Dehn and her young son out for some fresh air probably in an effort to get the little ones away for a while. Marie and Anastasia also visited their hospital.

That evening Olga and Tatiana chose to remain with their mother. Tatiana slept on the sofa and Olga took Nicholas's place besides Alexandra. (Marie's journal indicated that they already suspected that Dmitri and Felix were connected with Rasputin's disappearance and Olga had noticed that morning that there appeared to be a strange bright light in the sky but she could not explain it.)

On Monday morning, Olga and Tatiana returned to the infirmary as usual. They had begun the day at the *Church of the Sign* but again they had little to do at the hospital. Olga went with Kasyanov into the drawing room. The doors were closed and no one else was around. The two amused themselves with some music. She played the piano whilst he sang. She noted that he was very sweet. She had grown quite fond of him. He shared her love of music and was an excellent violin player. Olga then went to hand out the prescribed medicines before returning to play some more music. She was in dire need of some respite after such a difficult few days.

Olga then went back to work and attended to the dressings before she and Tatiana joined Kasyanov for a game of tiddlywinks again. The sisters returned for lunch and finally the Tsarina was officially informed that Rasputin had indeed been murdered. (Alexandra had asked Alexander Protopopov, the Vice-President of the Duma, to find out what had happened and keep her informed.)

They had tea with Anya and Lili and, according to Olga, they all felt Rasputin's presence around them. They went out to see if Nicholas had arrived at five but, realising that he had not, returned at six. They were happy to be reunited, especially in the circumstances. Later, Protopopov arrived and also the Tsar's Uncle Grand Duke Paul (the father of the young Grand Duke Dmitri who had been involved in Rasputin's disappearance and was present when he had been killed).

The youngest sisters had begun the day as usual with lessons. Marie studied arithmetic and history, but real history was been made outside the palace walls.

Anya Vyrubova later revealed that Alexei had asked his father if Rasputin's killers would be punished like Stolypin's had.

Paul had made an appeal on behalf of his son (who appears to have been involved in the disappearance of Rasputin but *not* in his actual murder). On Tuesday, Nicholas replied and explained that he was unable to lift Dmitri's house arrest until the end of the initial investigation.

Meanwhile, Olga and Tatiana resumed their usual work after a visit to the *Church of the Sign*. Olga wrote out the usual prescriptions, assisted by Kasyanov. The two stood together for some time near the lockers. She did very little that day. Later, Olga and Tatiana played tiddlywinks again with two of the patients, Kasyanov and Meyer. Olga's feelings for Kasyanov appear to have begun to confuse her. She confessed that she felt uncomfortable and could not play without him. She was missing Mitya but was beginning to have feelings for someone else. The family later lunched together.

Meanwhile Marie had endured lessons in German and history. She was never the happiest student, unlike Olga. The four sisters walked with Nicholas in the early afternoon, as in former days, and the four sisters later dined with their parents and Anya.

On Wednesday the Tsar and his wife and four daughters attended the funeral of Rasputin who was buried in a half-finished church nearby. Father Vassiliev performed the service but there were few other mourners apart from Madame Vyrubova and Lili Dehn. It was a glorious morning, the sun shone and the snow glistened. The mourners had to walk across planks of wood to get to the service. Madame Dehn arrived first, swiftly followed by Anya. The rest arrived soon after. The Tsar and Tsarina threw earth onto the plain coffin and Alexandra distributed flowers amongst the mourners to throw onto it.

Olga and Tatiana later returned to their infirmary where once more Olga wrote out the prescriptions whilst Kasyanov dictated. (It was reminiscent of 1913 with Olga and Voronov. Despite her evident feelings for Mitya, she was growing closer to Kasyanov.)

Marie's journal confirmed that all the sisters were at the funeral. The family later visited Anya where Rasputin's daughters had gathered.

On Thursday Olga noted her concerns for her parents in her journal and she asked God to help them. That morning, she and Tatiana returned to the infirmary as usual but Olga's friend Kasyanov had gone to the city. At noon, to Olga's great relief, Mitya appeared. She noticed that he looked healthy and sunburned.

Marie and Anastasia had visited their own hospital that day and Anya and Lili came for lunch, but that evening the four sisters ate alone with their parents.

Tatiana was greatly affected by the death of Rasputin and collected his sayings in a notebook, but subsequent events show Olga was less upset. She was more concerned with the manner of his death. (It may be significant that Mitya greatly disliked Rasputin, as Valentina's notes indicate.)

On Friday, Olga and Tatiana made their devotions at the *Church of the Sign* before leaving for the infirmary. Olga was delighted to see that Kasyanov had returned. She spent much of the morning sorting out the laundry with Varvara. Later she joined the others in a game of tiddlywinks.

That evening, Grand Duke Dmitri left for Persia (Iran) and exile. Felix had been confined to one of his personal estates. Nicholas felt hurt that Dmitri had gone against him. He had effectively brought him up and the pain of this was worse than anything. Dmitri must have known how the Tsarina relied on Rasputin.

A petition was later signed on behalf of Dmitri. They begged the Tsar not to exile the Grand Duke. In truth, he was safer there than in Russia, although no one realised that at the time. The petition had been signed by the Dowager Queen of Greece (Olga, the Tsar's beloved godmother); Grand Duke Kyrill and his brothers Boris and Andrei; Grand Duke Paul; the Tsarina's own sister the Grand Duchess Elisabeth; Prince Ioann and his wife Elena; Princes Gavril, Konstantin and Igor, amongst others.

The names included those of whom the Tsar thought highly, including his godmother Olga and, to a lesser extent, his Uncle Paul and Konstantin's sons, but it had no positive effect.

On Christmas Eve the Grand Duchesses Olga and Tatiana returned to the infirmary but, as a result, managed to turn up only for the end of Mass later. Nicholas and his younger daughters were already there when they arrived. A familiar old face Nicholas Sablin turned up in time for lunch and, afterwards, the Tsar and his children went for a walk before they distributed gifts from the Christmas tree in the hallway. Olga received an early present: a green ring. The family returned to church in the early evening.

Although Christmas 1916 occurred on a Sunday, a cloud of sorrow and fear still hung around the day. The Imperial couple felt betrayed and alone. Even their closest relatives had recently spoken out against them in the petition, including Alexandra's own sister. They were beginning to feel like the sole survivors on a sinking ship, or a desert island. The number of people they could count on was rapidly diminishing.

That day the French Ambassador had spoken to Nicholas and found him completely overwhelmed by recent events. The only topic they spoke of with any enthusiasm on the part of Nicholas was Napoleon Bonaparte, who was a great hero of the Tsar.

That morning the immediate family attended Mass and they later carried out their usual traditions, including a visit to the Convoy Christmas tree in the arena. The Tsarina obligingly distributed some of the gifts.

On Tuesday the family returned to the tiny *Church of the Sign*. Olga was delighted to see Mitya there and contrived to stand with him and Varvara during the service. The family later saw an episode of *The Mysterious Hand of New York*.

Olga and Tatiana returned to their infirmary on Wednesday morning where once again Olga wrote whilst Kasyanov dictated. Marie and Anastasia later attended a concert where the famous singer Nadezdha Plevitskaya made an appearance.

On Thursday morning Olga and Tatiana returned to their infirmary and some of the men were transferred that day, including Olga's new friend Kasyanov.

Nicholas was unwell and had been suffering from influenza. It had been many years since he had been so sick and it was as though his body had simply had enough.

That day the Tsar had received the British Ambassador Sir George Buchanan. Nicholas appeared very pessimistic on their last meeting. Nicholas attributed the severe food crisis to the breakdown of the railways. The meeting was a very difficult one and, after the Ambassador had spoken at length about the government, Nicholas had insisted that it was up to him to pick the ministers and no one else. They spoke of the situation in the city, but Nicholas was still doggedly convinced it had all been exaggerated. The Ambassador warned Nicholas of the abyss that awaited him. (Nicholas was always someone who believed in fate and, like many Russians, he felt he could not go against what was his fate. He had never been proactive and probably, in his heart of hearts, knew that things could only get worse. Like his great hero Napoleon Bonaparte, who he had spoken of to the French Ambassador, he knew that exile awaited him, if not worse.)

On the last day of the year, Nicholas attended church and prayed that God would show mercy on Russia. Would He?

Chapter Seventeen

New Year 1917

It was less than evident that anything different was about to happen on the first day of the New Year. The Tsar's brother, the Grand Duke Michael, arrived at Tsarskoe Selo on Sunday afternoon and the two brothers headed off for a reception at the Catherine Palace. It was the usual diplomatic reception that happened every year.

Nicholas received the congratulations of the Diplomatic Corps. It was intensely cold and, as the ministers approached the Catherine Palace by covered carriage from the station to the palace, the thick frost obscured the view for the entire journey. The guests were greeted by the Director of Ceremonies and, soon after, Nicholas arrived, accompanied by his aides. The Tsar greeted all his guests in his usual formal yet impersonal manner. There was no hint of any possible problems indicated by his behaviour. He rarely if ever showed his feelings in public.

The Tsar behaved as he usually did towards the British Ambassador Sir George Buchanan. In a recent interview between the two men, they had met and disagreed.

That evening, life went on as normal at the Alexander Palace, despite the metaphorical gathering of storm clouds all around the Imperial family. Nicholas read one of the short stories by Chekov to his children. It may have been *The Princess*. He read on special occasions and holidays aloud to his family but usually he read alone in the peaceful study he spent most of the day in.

Meanwhile Tatiana had written a note to Alexandra in a positive mood. She hoped for the end of the war. (It would end soon, but not before the revolution had begun.) The children often sent their parents little notes. Although they lived in the same wing of the palace, Alexandra often remained downstairs for most of the day whilst her children lived on the upper floor.

On Monday Nicholas received the new President of the Council of Ministers: Prince Nicholas Golitzin. The aristocrat warned the Tsar of the dire state of Russia but with little success. The Tsar, once again, took no notice of the prophecies of doom. He was an autocrat and not used to listening to the advice of anyone; even if he solicited someone's assistance, he rarely did anything other than what he wished. He preferred, on balance, to maintain the status quo or, more simply, to do nothing.

That evening, the Tsar continued his holiday readings to his family. Once again, he chose a couple of short stories by Anton Chekov. The stories were *The Trouble* and *How Awfully Tired I Am*. They could not have been more aptly titled.

The next day the Assistant Minister of Finance NN Povrovsky urged Nicholas to rid himself of AD Protopopov. Yet again, the Tsar was implacable. Nicholas had insisted that things were not as bad as he had been told. He was convinced that any troubles were simply an exaggeration.

Meanwhile he continued his nightly readings to the family. He read another of Chekov's stories; this one entitled *The Teacher*. (He would soon become his own son's temporary teacher.)

Earlier that evening, Anya Vyrubova decided to copy down the letters of the late Grigory Rasputin. Olga Nicolaevna obligingly copied them for her. Tatiana also collected his words in a notebook. The Grand Duchesses had also been greatly shaken by his death, but Tatiana had taken it more personally than Olga. Olga was able to see the bigger picture and not just see it from a personal point of view.

Despite the warnings, life went on exactly as normal at the Alexander Palace. A Rumanian orchestra came to the palace each Thursday evening. The Tsarina's friend Lili Dehn later recalled how Alexandra derived a great deal of pleasure from the concerts. Madame Dehn generally attended the weekly concerts along with other members of the household including Prince (Valia) Dolgouruky, Madame Voyeikov, Colonel Grotten, the Tsar's ADC Linevich, Colonel and Mrs Rebinder, and some officers from the Imperial yacht. It was a regular get-together. (Alexandra and particularly her daughter Olga loved music and both were talented pianists.)

By coincidence, on Saturday, the Crown Prince of Rumania arrived in Petrograd along with the President of the Council, Mr Bratiano. Crown Prince Carol and Mr Bratiano were both invited to lunch with the Tsar the following day. It was the return of one of Olga's former suitors yet on his previous visit he had been more interested in her younger sister Marie.

The Rumanians arrived at the Alexander Palace on Sunday as expected. The visitors lunched with the Tsar and his family, and later there was a large reception held in the Corner Room for the important guests. The Rumanians were still Russia's allies – whether or not they were likely marriage connections in the near future. It was not to be.

On Monday Olga confided in her journal that the preparations for the visit had made her quite furious. She was not particularly fond of the Crown Prince and was rapidly becoming irritated by the formality of such occasions, as her namesake Aunt Olga Alexandra had done in previous years and indeed her late grandfather Alexander III. Olga preferred spending every waking moment at the infirmary. It was somewhere where she felt at ease.

Meanwhile, Nicholas remained at home for a full two months after Rasputin's murder. He was hoping that a quick and successful spring offensive would end the war and put a halt to the constant food and fuel shortages. He kept maps in his large study and spent hours staring at them, trying to think of ways to bring the war to a peaceful conclusion. It was a quiet time in the Russian battlefields as the heavy snow stopped an advance on either side. Unfortunately, the snowstorms also put a stop to the railways and food was beginning to get scarce in the capital and Moscow alike.

On Tuesday the Tsarina and her daughter Olga visited Rasputin's grave. It was his name's day and his grave was within the newly built church, in the grounds of the palace.

Despite the obvious cold, the Tsarina determinedly sat out on the balcony on the following day. She often sat outside in all weathers – wrapped up in coats and furs. There was a lot to think about after Rasputin's death. He had predicted shortly before his death that he would be killed. Rasputin had also stated that, if he was murdered by members of the Tsar's own family, the consequences for the Imperial family would be horrific. It would mean the end to the life of the Tsarevich within a couple of years. Sadly, he would prove accurate. Alexandra had always believed wholeheartedly in him and now feared for her family, especially her son. When the boy had been ill in the past, she had always felt that Rasputin could be relied upon to help him. Now she felt quite alone without his support.

The situation was not just deteriorating in the capital, but closer to home as well. At this time, the commander of the mounted guard regiment, stationed inside the Alexander Palace, Major-General Ressin, informed the Tsarina's lady-in-waiting Baroness Buxhoeveden that the morale of the men was low and that revolutionary propaganda was rife amongst them. He was seriously concerned about the loyalty of the men to the Tsar.

On Monday, the Allied delegates arrived in the capital and held a preliminary meeting for the conference. The meeting included the British Ambassador Sir George Buchanan, the French Ambassador Maurice Paleologue, the Italian Ambassador the Marchese Carloti and others.

Nicholas received the members of the various embassies at the Alexander Palace late on Tuesday morning.

One day the Tsar's children had come into close contact with a young cadet and he had come down with measles. They had been playing out in the snow and on Thursday the vulnerable young Tsarevich was the first to show signs of a slightly raised temperature.

There had been a special film show for the Imperial children held in the playroom earlier that evening. As Alexei's temperature began to rise, his sisters Olga and Anastasia visited him in his room.

Nicholas received the heads of the delegates to the conference on Saturday in a private audience and afterwards invited all the delegates to a gala dinner at the palace. The British Ambassador Sir George Buchanan found himself seated to the Tsar's right and took the opportunity to speak about the food crisis. The Ambassador was convinced it had been as a result of a lack of organisation between the Ministries of Agriculture and Transport. There was no system installed to distribute foodstuffs. The Tsar agreed that the Agriculture Minister needed to get the *zemstvos* (unions) to help or it would inevitably result in further food shortages and strikes.

The next evening the Imperial children watched films in the Tsarevich's large playroom. (He had his own projector and stock of films that had been given to him generously by the *Pathe Film Company*.) The Grand Duchesses later went to sit with Madame Vyrubova who had been moved into the palace in recent weeks for her own safety after the death of Rasputin. There had been threats to her life too.

Earlier on Sunday, Olga had been visited by a British nurse, the young aristocrat

Dorothy Seymour who worked at the Red Cross hospital based in Grand Duke Dmitri's palace in the capital. (He had been given the palace on his twenty-first birthday by his widowed aunt, the Grand Duchess Elisabeth. She had no need for material possessions once she decided to start her own religious establishment.)

The visit to the hospital showed the Tsarina in a rare positive light. She had found her true vocation in nursing and was happy to talk about something she was so fond of. For the first time, she felt she was doing something useful and, like Olga, felt thoroughly at home in the nursing uniform including the headdress which covered the hair entirely. Sadly, it was too late for the general public to appreciate the move. The Tsarina had always been disliked ever since she had married Nicholas in 1894. Alexandra had the unfortunate knack of putting just about everyone she ever met on edge as she spoke to them. She spoke too quietly and often mumbled. Alexandra was by now increasingly deaf and she had the unhappy gift of making enemies wherever she went. Her mother-in-law the Dowager Empress was an outgoing party lover who shone in company, which made the situation even worse. The two women were obviously quite different. Apart from Nicholas, the only thing the two had in common was a strong dislike of the other woman.

One of the nurses at the Red Cross hospital, a Miss Seymour, was impressed by the Tsarina. She was moved by her beauty and even, remarkably, Alexandra's sense of humour. This was an aspect of Alexandra very rarely seen in public. Olga was wearing her nursing uniform and was relaxed and informal. Dorothy spoke to Olga for a couple of hours and came away with the idea that Olga was a pacifist and showed a real horror of war and suffering.

The time that Olga had spent in the hospital had given her a real dislike of war. She had seen only too clearly the results of warfare and had been moved at the sight of the horrific injuries. It had affected her so much that she preferred to work out of the operating theatre. Tatiana remained unmoved by the suffering and continued her work as normal. She had always been a practical girl whereas Olga had always been a thinker and quite impractical.

On Tuesday, there was yet another film show held in Alexei's playroom. The hairdresser appeared and Olga and Tatiana had their hair washed and curled with tongs. As the two soon came down with the measles, washing their hair may not have been a wise move. The four Grand Duchesses only had their hair curled on special occasions.

Meanwhile, Nicholas's journal gave little away of his mood. He had taken a walk on Sunday afternoon and had worked outside in the snow. He had a meeting with his emissary Klopov later. Maybe he had news.

Alexei must have been in great pain on Monday as, late that afternoon, Olga's journal records that he was injected with a half a syringe full of morphine and that he had slept from six.

On Tuesday, Nicholas again met members of the conference.

At the beginning of February, Olga confided in Valentina about Rasputin's murder. She had admitted to her friend that perhaps it was necessary to get rid of him but the manner of his death was particularly brutal. She had too many dead, dying and mangled men in recent years and saw the reality of it first-hand at the infirmary. It was the very reason why she had transferred from the operating theatre to more routine duties at the hospital.

Whilst Tatiana and Marie, like their mother, remained devoted to the memory of Rasputin, Nicholas, Olga, Anastasia and Alexei seem to have been less clear in their convictions. It may be no coincidence that the more intelligent of the children appeared to be able to see more than the others. Nicholas did not so much care less about the death as was fatalist about everything that happened in his life.

Dr Derevenko once told Pierre Gilliard that he had heard Alexei make amusing remarks about Rasputin, not complimentary, and did not feel that he was influenced by the man.

As a young boy, Nicholas had been present when a fireball had gone through the church close to Peterhof, and he had seen how the Emperor stood unflinchingly throughout. When Alexander II was murdered shortly after, Nicholas could not but recall the incident. Some years later, his younger sister Olga Alexandra had seen Nicholas act in exactly the same way when a fireball came through the same church when Olga was a girl. Nicholas had not moved when, in 1905, it appeared he was being shot at from the St Peter and Paul Cathedral. He had asked Olga on that occasion, when she had asked about the incident, what else he could do. He had long ago decided that his fate was predetermined. He had been like a ship without a pilot for many years heading towards the inevitable iceberg.

One evening the Tsarina's friend Lili Dehn had noticed how she had been somewhat preoccupied. Madame Dehn was sat listening to the Rumanian orchestra one Thursday evening when she noticed that Alexandra was looking more than usually sad. (Alexandra, despite her nickname of Sunny, was never exactly known for being overly cheerful.)

Madame Dehn asked the Tsarina why she was feeling so sad that particular evening. Alexandra could not quite understand how to answer. It may have been the sad music, but she thought that her heart was broken. (The Tsarina was not just coming to terms with the death of her friend Rasputin but with the inevitable outcome. It was his gloomy predictions that were weighing on her mind.)

That same evening Anya Vyrubova showed a monumental lack of tact. She suggested that, as everyone was so out of sorts, they should each indulge in a glass of champagne. The Tsarina was greatly angered by the suggestion and declared that her husband hated wine and could not bear to see women drink it. Yet, she declared, what did it matter as the people believed that he was already a drunkard. In recent months, there had been constant unpleasant rumours about Nicholas and Alexandra – none of them complimentary. (Many had alleged that Alexandra was Rasputin's lover or that Anya was the lover of Rasputin *and* Nicholas. Alexandra was alleged to be a German spy. There had been no end of rumours.)

That same day, as Alexei recovered from his recent attack of the measles, his eldest sisters continued their work at the infirmary. They were quite unaware that they too would soon fall victim to the virus. Olga dealt with the arrangement of the beds and distributed the medicines as normal. She could not help noting in her journal that evening, however, that it had been the twenty-fourth birthday of Mitya. (Olga missed him desperately when he was away. Once he returned to the front, he was in constant danger of being killed.)

She later returned to the palace to sit with her brother. The Tsarina had returned to her bed, complaining of her heart, and even Nicholas had a cold. Olga herself began to feel seriously unwell.

On Friday Grand Duchess Olga remained in her room and she was diagnosed with a middle ear infection. She got up later for lunch where there was a visitor.

That day, the Tsar's brother-in-law Sandro arrived at the palace and he had dined along with Nicholas, the four Grand Duchesses and the aide Linevich. Olga and Tatiana spoke to him of their nursing and seemed more mature to their uncle who had not seen them for two years. The sisters were in a jovial mood, despite Olga's infection. They had no idea how seriously ill they would soon become.

Sandro later spoke to Alexandra who was lying in bed. Nicholas had come into the room with Alexander and the Grand Duke had noticed at once his sister-in-law's wary expression. It was as if she knew he had come to cause trouble. He had wanted to speak to Alexandra alone, but Nicholas had chosen to remain close by. The Grand Duke spoke of the political situation and the propaganda. Alexandra interrupted him and declared that the nation was still loyal to Nicholas. She then turned to the Tsar and stated that it was only the treacherous men of the Duma and the society of the capital who were their enemies. Sandro admitted that she was indeed partly right.

The conversation went further downhill at this point. Sandro spoke of Rasputin and her interference (as it was seen) in politics. He urged Alexandra to keep out of politics and concentrate on her children. She looked at Nicholas who remained smoking but said nothing. (It was typical of his character that he never took on an argument. He was passive to a fault.)

Sandro continued to speak about the dire situation in the country. She eventually simply declared that Nicholas was an autocrat and he could not possibly share his divine right with a parliament. Sandro then dramatically announced that Nicholas had ceased to be an autocrat in 1905. As the conversation continued, Alexandra declared that he was exaggerating the danger. She refused to continue the talk and the Grand Duke left. As he left, he saw Linevich chatting to Olga and Tatiana in the Tsarina's sitting room. He was surprised to see the aide in the next room. That evening Nicholas barely mentioned his brother-in-law's visit in his journal. He merely explained that he had arrived for a long chat with the Tsarina in his presence.

The Grand Duchess Olga was by now beginning to suffer badly as the infection had taken a hold on her. That afternoon, Nicholas had taken a walk in the company of only Marie. He noted in his journal that Olga's ear was aching and that he met Rodzianko (Duma President) before tea.

Olga was suffering with complications following measles. She had little time or energy to be able to complete her journal on Saturday evening and she spent the day lying in the Red Room, which was the ante-room to the children's bedrooms.

At about this time, General Sir Henry Williams met the Tsarina for the last time. He recalled how he was taken to the famous *Mauve Boudoir*. The two chatted about the old days, of tennis parties thirty-six years previously at Darmstadt. She remembered many of the names he had forgotten and was delighted with the memories. She spoke of the difficulties of having close relatives during the war living in Germany, England and Russia. He noticed that her hair was by now sprinkled liberally with grey. (It was hardly surprising in view of recent events.)

On Tuesday the Tsarevich attempted to get up again but, as his left arm and left leg proved to be extremely painful, he decided to return to bed after breakfast. He spent most of the day in bed and later lunched with the other invalid Olga. Sydney Gibbes attempted to keep the boy amused. His colleague Gilliard was also unwell.

The next day, it became clear that the virus was spreading. Anastasia was beginning to feel unwell and Pierre Gilliard had taken to his bed with what was believed to be influenza. Olga and Tatiana were already ill (they shared a room). When one of the children became ill, it was inevitable that the rest would do so soon after and, as with the typhoid outbreak in 1913, the rest of the household were also vulnerable.

Anastasia was confined to her bed by Thursday and Olga joined Marie and Anastasia late that afternoon for confession in her younger sisters' bedroom. Marie was still showing no signs of the virus but the others were all sickening, Alexei was improving but had an attack of his old enemy – haemophilia – unfortunately.

Tatiana, who was also suffering from the effects of the measles, wrote to her mother. She apologised for not coming when called. She had felt that she would have shown herself up in front of Anya by crying. Tatiana admitted that she had been in a terrible mood that morning and something, she explained, had made her rather snappy. She was seriously ill and was not sure what to do with herself. One of the earliest signs of the measles virus is sometimes a feeling of irritation. It was unusual for Tatiana to behave in such a manner as she was prone to think of her mother first in every situation.

(Tatiana had probably never forgiven herself for being the one who had accidentally spoken out against Rasputin's visits to the nursery in the spring of 1910. It was no coincidence that, later that same year, the family went to Germany and stayed there a very long time. She had never quite got over being the one who was inadvertently responsible for the scandal that blew up in 1910. He had visited the bedroom of Olga and Tatiana, and she had let on to one of the nannies about this. The nanny was furious but, when Alexandra had found out, it was the nanny whom she was angry with, not Tatiana. The notes between Alexandra and her daughters at this period indicate that Marie was baffled as to what was going on, but the ever vigilant Anastasia had a good idea what had happened. Tatiana was mortified.)

Meanwhile, that same day, Sydney Gibbes noted that his youngest pupil Alexei was showing signs of improvement. Alexei played with his tutor during the morning and the priest arrived at noon to give the boy Holy Communion. The child was well enough in the evening to have his hair trimmed and have a bath. The Tsarina read to her son that night from one of the Tsarevich's favourite books: *Helen's Babies*. The book was rather an old one and had odd stories about babies and their behaviour.

On Sunday the Tsarevich remained confined to his playroom but later was permitted to lunch downstairs with his parents and elder sister Tatiana. Olga and Anastasia were unwell and Marie may have chosen to remain with her sisters upstairs. (She was normally inseparable from Anastasia. Marie had felt quite left out by her older sisters when she was a small child and had at times been bullied by them, so Anastasia was her friend. Sadly, at times, she had to share Anastasia with her brother.)

That day, Baroness Buxhoeveden had briefly visited the capital and everywhere she heard people speaking openly against the monarchy. She even spotted the words *Down with the Tsar* written on a wall not far from the Winter Palace. She was spat at through the window of her carriage the next day. The carriage may well have had the Imperial insignia on it.

Meanwhile, the young Tsarevich was still confined to bed on Tuesday. He had developed a cough which was especially worrying for him as a bad coughing fit could bring on bleeding. Sydney Gibbes attempted to keep the boy calm by reading to him. The Tsarina had given him a new book of Russian fairy tales. (It was, deliberately or not, a memory of Rasputin who told the boy traditional Russian fairy stories on his previous visits. Even Nicholas had been enchanted by Rasputin's stories.)

On Wednesday, Nicholas finally decided to leave the peace of the Alexander Palace to return to Mogilev. He saw his children before he left. Nicholas visited Olga before lunch whilst she lay in bed. She later went to sit with her brother. She already had the virus but it was not yet clear whether Marie had.

Nicholas did not seem overly concerned about the state of his children's health. Alexei was improving and, although most of them were ill, it had not been confirmed as measles. They were frequently ill at the beginning of the year. He did not see much to worry him.

The Tsar's brother the Grand Duke Michael made a rare visit and stayed for lunch. Nicholas and Alexandra made their traditional visit to the *Church of the Sign* before his departure to pray for his safe return.

Earlier that day, however, Nicholas had almost changed his mind. Had he stuck to his original decision, things might well have ended quite differently. Protopopov, the deputy Duma President and Minister of the Interior had arrived at the Alexander Palace. He spoke first to the Tsarina who had informed him that Nicholas was intending to leave for Mogilev for a month. She had been (unusually) unable to make him change his mind. Nicholas then entered the room and told the Minister that he intended returning home in three weeks.

Protopopov begged him to remain at the palace. Nicholas was obviously moved by his concern and promised to return, if possible, within a week. At one point later that evening, Nicholas summoned several of the ministers, including the Prime Minister Prince Golitsyn and announced his intention of going to the Duma the following day to personally announce the appointment of a responsible government. Later, the Prince was summoned once more, only to be informed by Nicholas that he had changed his mind. The chance for saving the monarchy had been lost.

Shortly before he left, Alexandra composed a letter for Nicholas to read later. She urged him to be strong and wished that she could help him with his heavy burden. She explained that gentleness would not be understood; he had to be firm. She was probably right, but again it was too late.

Nicholas later sent a wire to Alexandra en route for Mogilev. He was thinking of her and felt lonely and sad without her but was grateful for the letter she had left for him.

Meanwhile, Alexei's cough was becoming more tiresome and his temperature was beginning to rise. Alexandra returned to sit with her children. Later, Rasputin's widow appeared with a two week-old baby girl. (The child was shown to Olga, which seemed a bizarre thing to do when the children were so ill. The child named Aninov Korovnitsv's life was put in great danger but, at the time, no one knew that Olga had the measles.)

On Thursday, Nicholas telegraphed home on his arrival. He had only just begun to throw off a cold and attempted to explain that he was coughing less. He thanked Alexandra and Alexei for their messages.

Later, the Tsarina wired confirmation that Olga and Alexei were both suffering from the measles and Olga's face was covered in a red rash. The Tsarevich had a sore mouth, a bad cough and his eyes were very sore. The children, she explained, were lying in the dark. She and her daughters were all wearing summer skirts and white dressing gowns. She hoped the others would catch the virus quickly if they were going to do so. She felt that it would be over quicker if they were all ill together, and it would be better for them.

That evening, Nicholas replied as if with frustration rather than worry. He thought it was a nuisance that they were ill. (He had no concept that the illness could prove dangerous. Alexandra had had the same illness in 1898 and had been extremely ill.)

There was only one of the children still up – Marie. That day she had written to Nicholas explaining how things were progressing. She was in her bedroom and Olga and Tatiana were resting in their room next door. The Tsarevich was in his bed in the playroom. Sydney Gibbes was sitting with him but wearing a doctor's smock to avoid spreading germs. She thought it looked rather amusing. The Tsarina, Marie and Anastasia were also wearing overalls.

Whilst the young Tsarevich was confined to his room, Sydney Gibbes read to the boy. One of the books he read was Sir Samuel Baker's *Cast Up By the Sea*. According to the tutor, the book had a great impact on Alexei. He had been so caught up in the character of Ned that, when he had finished the book, Alexei insisted on a repeat performance. On occasions, the Tsarina sat nearby and listened to the story.

There was soon yet another casualty of the measles epidemic – Anya Vyrubova. She had begun to get terrible headaches and took to her bed. Even when Tatiana explained that Olga and Alexei had measles, Anya did not suspect that she had it. Later in the day, Tatiana had become seriously ill. She had been generally unwell for a while, like Anastasia had at first, but suddenly became worse. The Tsarina now had four invalids – Olga, Tatiana, Alexei and Anya. Anastasia did not appear to be too ill so far but, later on, she too became worse.

Lili Dehn later explained that she believed that the Tsarina had inherited some of her late grandmother's tenacious spirit. Madame Dehn felt that Alexandra was in many ways a typical Victorian lady. According to Lili, the Tsarina was especially expert at making a bed and changing a patient's nightclothes swiftly and easily without disturbing the patient. Alexandra, like her daughters Olga and Tatiana, had worked as a nurse recently and that was probably part of the reason for the Tsarina's evident nursing ability.

Alexandra had inherited some of her late mother's nursing skills. Alice had worked in two wars in Germany before Alexandra was even born. The Princess was also pregnant on both occasions. Alice had met Florence Nightingale in Balmoral in the 1850s and had been inspired to nurse. She was only twelve at the time.

Meanwhile on Thursday, people broke into the bakeries in the capital in order to take food as they were beginning to starve. A peaceful protest was held in the capital mainly by women who demanded food. It was like a rerun of the French Revolution. At that time, Queen Marie-Antoinette had countered with, *Let them eat cake*. She had no idea of the seriousness of the situation and, in Russia, Alexandra had the Queen's portrait on her wall and must have felt a sensation of history repeating itself.

It was, of course, mainly the women who were demanding bread as the men were away fighting in the war. It was only the old and wounded men who remained at home or in hospitals.

Meanwhile, within the walls of the Alexander Palace, Tatiana admitted in a letter to her father that everyone had cried when he had left. Although Tatiana was herself ill, it was Olga and Alexei who were the most seriously unwell at this point. She explained that all the remaining family sat with the invalids. Olga was in her bed and Alexei in the playroom. The sisters (Tatiana, Marie and Anastasia) took turns to sit with their siblings.

That evening, Nicholas wrote to Alexandra after finding a free moment. He had found a letter she had left for him in his train compartment. He hated the idea of leaving after spending two long months at home. He admitted that he had not expected that Olga and Alexei had the measles. He urged Alexandra to keep visitors away.

It appears that Olga and Alexei were not the only ones with the measles. Nicholas reported that the number of boys from the 1st and 2nd Cadet Corps with the measles was increasing.

Nicholas greatly missed Alexandra and the quiet time they had spent each evening together with the children playing with one of the puzzles. He explained that he intended to start playing dominoes again when he had the chance. He had previously played with Alexei when he had accompanied him to Mogilev.

That day, Alexei was in good spirits, according to his tutor Sydney Gibbes, despite the measles being more developed. He helped the boy cut out paper houses and stick them together to make his own village.

Nicholas sent word once more to Alexandra on Friday after hearing that Tatiana and Anya had also been diagnosed with the measles. He was surprised how rapidly it was spreading and actually encouraged Alexandra to make sure that Anastasia and Marie got the virus. (They did, but Marie became very seriously ill as her illness developed into pneumonia too.) Nicholas thought it would be a good idea to go to Peterhof later so the rooms could be disinfected.

The Tsar continued the following day. He was pleased to hear that there appeared to be no complications at least. He explained (probably after chatting to Dr Feodorov) that the temperature was high in the first days but would gradually decrease towards the end. He was somewhat amused to think that Anya was naturally suffering more than the children. As an adult who had recently suffered a serious train accident and a minor heart attack, apart from being rather overweight, she would naturally have suffered more. She certainly complained more.

In her letter to Nicholas on the Friday, Alexandra informed him of the rioting in the capital. She had more idea of what was actually going on than the Tsar had as he was much further away and had other things on his mind.

However, the multi-tasking Alexandra had spent the day nursing her sick children and Anya, taking their temperatures, and had even managed to see some of the ministers. She added to her letter throughout the day, between nursing.

She explained that there had been riots the previous day in the Nevsky Prospekt. Some people had broken into a bakery and the Cossacks were called in to assist. She had heard the news unofficially, probably from members of the household.

Alexandra had taken turns with Peter Petrov to read to Alexei *Helen's Babies*. Olga and Alexei were both running a slight temperature, as was Anya. Olga was looking fairly well, yet tired. Alexandra had insisted that Marie and Anastasia return to their own room. She had not taken Nicholas's advice to expose them to the illness. She was struggling to cope with four invalids and did not need more. She wandered between one sick room (Olga and Tatiana), or Alexei or to Anya. Mr Gibbes, she explained, was reading to Alexei and she sat with her elder daughters writing quietly whilst they rested.

She had meetings with various ministers and had been to church, but had left her youngest daughters with Shura Tegleva (the children's former nurse) as all three were suffering from a sore throat. Anya constantly coughed. Olga had spots on her face, but the Tsarevich's spots were mainly on his legs.

According to Baroness Buxhoeveden, the Tsarina held receptions on Friday and Saturday whilst her children were ill but told each of the men concerned that they risked infection. They spoke to her at their own risk.

Late on Saturday evening, Nicholas finally heard of the rioting that had been going on for some three days already.

Earlier that day, Nicholas had wired Alexandra and had sent messages of sympathy for the invalids. He also thanked Marie for her recent letter. (Marie would continue to be her mother's help for as long as she felt able, to the detriment of her own health. She attempted to take over the role of the eldest sisters when Olga and Tatiana had become ill. She became what Alix later described as her legs. She took over Tatiana's role of her mother's main help. As a result, Marie saw far more of her mother during these crucial days. It showed Alexandra a side of Marie she had never previously seen, although it was there. The Tsarina began to rely on Marie just as she used to do with Tatiana only. Lili Dehn later recognised that Marie appeared to have suddenly grown up at this point.)

That same Saturday, Alexandra wrote to Nicholas admitting that she was greatly concerned about events in the capital yet firmly believed that it would soon pass, assuming that the Duma did not inflame the situation by allowing the most hostile speeches to be printed and distributed. She was still concerned about her family. Anya remained the most seriously ill and had a terrible cough and very high temperature. Olga and Tatiana's temperatures were normalising. She had been convinced that Anastasia would become ill that day as she looked unwell the previous day, but her temperature was stable. Later, Olga and Alexei showed a worrying increase in their temperatures, yet Tatiana did not seem a great deal worse.

The situation in the capital was worsening. Most of the people were on strike. There were no trains, trolley cars or taxi cabs. People appeared in the streets with banners declaring *Down with the German Woman! Down with Protopopov! Down with the war!* The cabinet was gravely concerned and met all day. They begged Nicholas to return. The entire cabinet, except Protopopov, offered to resign and asked Nicholas to appoint a new ministry acceptable to the Duma but he refused.

Later that same evening, Alexandra continued her letter to Nicholas. She was determined, she explained, to carry on her duties. The Tsarina had the rather sensible idea that the people should each be issued with a ration card for bread which was now in short supply. She explained her source of news: it was Lili Dehn who had spoken to the taxicab men. She had just been to the nearby *Church of the Sign* accompanied by her daughter Marie. They had placed candles and been to see Rasputin's grave.

Meanwhile only Marie and Anastasia were now up and they sat for most of the day in the semi-darkness of their oldest sisters' room next door. The two youngest daughters ate with their mother. That day the Tsarevich lay quietly in his playroom again. He was read more Russian fairy tales by Sydney Gibbes. According to the tutor, the boy seemed in good spirits. After dinner, he was carried across the hall to see his oldest two sisters.

Alexandra was aware of the situation in the capital, more so than Nicholas, but she kept herself busy with the day-to-day worries over her children's health and that of Anya.

On Sunday, Nicholas received a telegram from the Minister of War informing him that soldiers were now refusing to open fire on the rioters and were even joining the rebels. Despite the rather worrying news, Nicholas showed little emotion in his journal that evening. He mentions attending Mass, dealing with the reports, writing to his wife, walking down the road to the chapel and playing dominoes. He seemed quite unconcerned.

However, in a letter that day to Alexandra, the Tsar admitted that, earlier in the day, he had suffering an excruciating pain in his chest for some fifteen minutes in church. His face was covered with perspiration but he could not understand what it was as he had no heart palpitations. It suddenly vanished as he knelt before the icon of the Holy Virgin. He urged Alexandra to see more of Lili as he thought she was a sensible friend.

That day, Alexandra had written to Nicholas unaware of his recent heart scare. She had been overjoyed at receiving his letter and admitted covering it with kisses. She felt lonely. Anya was very ill but had plenty of visitors, including Rasputin's widow. She explained that Marie and Anastasia were calling themselves *assistant nurses*. They constantly chatted and kept her spirits up. Gilliard was still very weak after his recent illness, but Gibbes was constantly in attendance on Alexei. The two tutors had no children of their own to risk infection, but Petrov did.

An old friend Nicholas Rodionov had sent Olga, Tatiana and Anya each a pot of flowers – lily of the valley. The youngest sisters were constantly with the other patients so likely to become ill themselves, she explained. It was too late now anyway. Tatiana had a terrible cough and Olga and Alexei had a high temperature, only surpassed (naturally) by Anya's. Alexei was covered in spots like a leopard, Olga's red spots were large flat ones and Anya was covered too. All complained of sore throats and eyes.

Alexandra spent her days between the sick beds of her children and Anya, whose room was situated at the far end of the palace. That day, according to Baroness Buxhoeveden, the Tsarina had kept working and had met Professor Madsen of the Copenhagen Serum Institute. He had come to talk about the tetanus serum.

The Tsarina had attempted to contact the Tsar that day by telegram, but without success. She had sent the Baroness a note that day detailing the temperatures of the invalids: Olga was 39.9 (or 103F); Tatiana 39.3; Alexei 40 (104F); and Anya 40.3 (104F). They were all seriously ill.

That same day, Countess Anastasia Hendrikova, left Petrograd on a visit to her sick sister in the Caucasus. As soon as she arrived, she heard of the situation in the capital and chose to return to the side of the Tsarina. (She would remain loyal for the rest of her life – which was roughly as long as her loyal mistress. She was later murdered by the Bolsheviks alongside Catherine Schnieder.)

On Monday, Nicholas wrote what he assumed would be his last letter home. He was intending to return home in the next couple of days, but it was not to be. He saw frightened faces all around him on his return to Mogilev, but still failed to see any sign of danger ahead – or he chose to ignore it and resigned himself to fate. He wanted to know why the Grand Duke Paul had not taken a hand in the situation. (The man was seriously ill so it was a very unfair complaint against him. He later died of cancer and it does not exactly make you feel well as one has found out.)

There was an improvement in the health of the Tsarevich that day. As soon as he woke up, he was taken to see his elder sisters and spent the day with them. (He was generally a cheerful child; as someone who spent so much time seriously ill, he appreciated the times when his health improved. It takes serious illness to make many people appreciate good health, and Alexei knew only too well what it was like to be very sick.)

That day, Baroness Buxhoeveden had informed the Tsarina of the desperate situation in the capital. Alexandra was far better informed than Nicholas, but was less able to do anything about it. She was now unable to contact Nicholas, and he seemed to have resigned himself to fate.

The Tsarina had asked the Baroness to invite Madame Sazonov to lunch that day, but the lady was forced to decline the offer as she was not even able to reach the railway station. There was fighting in the streets and the members of the Preobrajensky Regiment (who had their barracks opposite) had mutinied and were firing with machine guns. The Baroness then spoke to Madame Sazonov's brother Senator Neidhardt who gave her the latest news. Three different regiments had mutinied the previous night, he explained. He asked the Baroness to inform the Tsarina.

The Tsarina asked the Baroness to send for Colonel Groton, the Acting-Commander of the Palace in the absence of General Voyeikov. He reported that, despite the mutinies, the troops who guarded the palace had remained loyal. He had heard that the Tsar had ordered General Ivanov with some trustworthy troops to put down the riots.

Meanwhile, the Tsarina had problems closer to home. Tatiana had developed abscesses in her ears and Olga had developed pericardiatis. Anastasia joined her sisters in the sickroom but Marie had stoically remained at her mother's side, fending off the signs of illness. She knew she was ill but refused to rest.

Later that evening, the President of the Duma, Rodzianko, telephoned Count Benckendorf for news of the health of the Tsarevich and begged him to ask the Tsarina to move the children to a place of safety. It was impossible to move them when they were so ill, however, and the Tsarina felt it would look like she was fleeing. (She would never leave without Nicholas and he would never leave.)

That night, Marie and Anastasia arranged a bed for Lili Dehn. She was accommodated on a sofa. Anastasia lent Lili a nightgown and Marie gave her a lamp and icon. The two sisters thoughtfully framed a photo of her son Alexander to make her feel at home.

The night was not yet over. Later, the Tsarina sent an urgent wire to Nicholas stating that concessions were inevitable as street fighting continued. Many regiments had gone over to the other side, she explained. Rodzianko had also sent Nicholas an urgent telegram that evening but his Chief of Staff Alexeiev fatefully decided not to wake the Tsar. The telegram had urged the Tsar to act at once or all would be lost. As he received no reply, Rodzianko sent another frantic message. The final hour had come, he explained, when the fate of the monarchy would be decided.

Meanwhile, in the capital, General Khabalov had attempted to put up notices declaring a state of siege, but neither paste nor brushes could be found. The offices of the secret police were already on fire and the angry mob refused to let anyone put out the flames.

Monday proved to be the turning point. The Volinsky Regiment who had returned to their barracks the previous evening stayed up all night arguing. At 6am, a sergeant killed a captain who had struck him the previous day. The other officers quickly fled and the rest left to join the rebellion. It quickly spread to the other regiments including the Semonovsky, the Ismailovsky, the Litovsky and the Or-Preobrajensky Guard. Soldiers assisted civilians erect barricades. The Law Courts were set alight and also the Ministry of the Interior and several police stations. By noon the Fortress of St Peter and Paul had fallen. By nightfall, some 66,000 soldiers had joined the revolution.

At 9am, word reached the Alexander Palace that several regiments had mutinied. Baroness Buxhoeveden took the message and relayed the news to the Tsarina. Alexandra listened with self-possession and remarked that it was all up (for the monarchy) now.

On what appeared to be the longest night in history, Nicholas finally made a note of the, by now, critical situation in his journal. He noted that riots had begun in the capital several days before and, to his great regret, troops had also taken part. He was frustrated at being so far away and receiving only fragmentary news. He had decided to return home and got onto the train. He sent a wire to Alexandra explaining that he would be starting for home the following day.

Meanwhile Pierre Gilliard telephoned his colleague Sydney Gibbes on Monday evening and explained that the Tsarina had said that she need not come on Tuesday. Alexei would spend the day with his older sisters. His temperature was too high to do much else, he explained.

Finally, Tuesday dawned. It was to be another difficult day. Nicholas left Mogilev at 5am and sent Alexandra a wire explaining his movements. He sent a second telegram at 9.27 which was received half an hour later at the palace. Nicholas explained that he was hoping to be back the following morning. It was at least a twenty-five-hour journey – on a good day without delays. The Tsar's train was stopped at Vishera and he was diverted to Pskov. He would be unable to reach home as he intended.

Meanwhile, that day in the Russian parliament, Alexander Kerensky had declared that the ministers were mere fleeting shadows and that, in order to prevent a catastrophe, the Tsar had to be removed, by force if necessary. These words were of course treasonable and Protopopov began proceedings to deprive Kerensky of his parliamentary immunity and enabling him to be prosecuted. It was already too late. There were serious shortages of food and fuel. The army was short of food and, of course, ammunition. The railways had no fuel and could not hope to supply six million soldiers at the front or even move them around. The price of food had soared and the general chaos was added to by the extreme weather. Heavy snow blocked the railway lines and the engines burst. No supplies were getting through.

According to Count Grabbe, who later recalled events in 1917, the Tsar and his entourage only heard of the events in the capital when they had boarded the train at Mogilev at around 6am that morning. They were so far away from the capital and communications appear to have broken down.

Although the Tsarina had refused to move due to her children's health, she instructed Baroness Buxhoeveden to secretly begin packing. As Alexandra packed things herself, she put Lili Dehn temporarily in charge of the children. She did not want the rest of the household to know what was happening. As always in these situations, what does one pack? She probably packed some clothes, books, medicines, icons and pictures. Her jewels would have been an afterthought.

The Grand Duchesses heard gunfire in the distance but said nothing to the Tsarina. Once she had left the room, Olga asked Lili Dehn what the gunfire was about. Lili attempted to reassure her that it was nothing to worry about and the hard frost made the noise sound worse than it was. Olga did not believe her and persisted. She wanted to know if Madame Dehn was sure that was all as her mother seemed to be very nervous and she was worrying about the Tsarina's health. Olga asked Lili to urge the Tsarina to rest. The girls were always concerned about their mother's health.

Later in the day, when the sisters heard that the Guarde Equipage were to remain in the Palace, they were delighted. It was just like being on the yacht again, they explained.

On Tuesday evening, Anastasia shared a room with Lili Dehn whilst Marie stayed with her mother. (They often stayed with their mother when Nicholas was away.) Olga, Tatiana and Alexei were still very ill and unable to move around.

Anastasia and Madame Dehn were unable to sleep. The Grand Duchess repeatedly asked Lili if she was asleep. The two looked out of the window at one point in night and saw a huge gun in the courtyard. Anastasia was greatly shocked and thought aloud how shocked Papa would be at this move.

Meanwhile, Nicholas later wrote of the main events of the day in his journal. He had spoken to General (Nikolai L) Ivanov and instructed him to restore order in the capital. They had travelled through Vyazma, Rzhev and Likholshavl.

Anya Vyrubova was later convinced a move the Tsarina had made earlier that evening to speak to the soldiers guarding the palace had been a life-saving move. At about eleven, she had gone outside to speak to the Naval Guard and the Convoy Cossacks who were the only men remaining on duty that night. She took Marie with her. It was a freezing cold night and Marie was already showing signs of the measles but the Grand Duchess had insisted on remaining with her mother.

The two then spoke words of encouragement to the men and voiced their confidence in them. It may have been this action alone that kept the men at their post overnight. The next day, they disappeared. Unfortunately, even if some had wanted to stay, in the time of revolution it would have been dangerous for them to remain against the wishes of the majority.

Although she later became seriously ill as a result, it was more likely Marie's actions that made the difference. The Tsarina was never popular but her daughters were. Marie had probably been a familiar fixture in their lives for many years and her pretty face may have at this point made a difference. Once she was no longer there, however, instinct took over. They joined the revolution.

The Tsarina sent for Grand Duke Paul. He was one person on whom she could rely to tell the truth. Later, Baroness Buxhoeveden was told by Marie that their interview had been a stormy one. Alexandra had been angered at the realisation that all the troops in the Petrograd military district were actually reserves from the local factories. Apart from one disagreement, Marie explained, the Grand Duke was kindness itself towards his niece (by marriage).

Anya Vyrubova later explained that it was Paul who had informed Alexandra what was actually happening and it was he who later informed her of the abdication. No one else had dared speak to her officially. All the news she had previously was via Baroness Buxhoeveden, Lili Dehn or others she trusted within the household. Lili's news had come via the taxicab drivers.

That day, the last day of the month, the Tsarina had written the main events of the day in her journal. It shows what really mattered. It began with a list of the temperatures of her children: Olga (39.1), Tatiana (39.5 ½), Alexei (37.7) and Anastasia (37.7).

Alexandra knew what was going on in the capital, but what could she do about it? All she could do was nurse her invalids and hope for the best.

The Tsarina went on to explain that she had sat with Anya Vyrubova, Count Benckendorf, Groten and Boriov. Later, she sat with Linevitch upstairs. She later listed the temperatures of Alexei (37.3), Olga (39.8 ½) and Tatiana (39.8) at 1pm.

She had tested the children again at six and Olga had worsened. She had been measured at 40.3 whilst Alexei had improved, and Tatiana was beginning to stabilise.

Alexandra spent most of the day in the company of Marie and her most worrying patient Olga. At nine, she again checked the thermometer and Olga showed a little sign of improvement but Tatiana appeared to have worsened a little. Anya's situation remained critical. The Tsarina ended by explaining that she had passed the troops in the garden that day.

Chapter Eighteen

Spring 1917

At 5am on Wednesday morning, Anastasia and Lili Dehn slipped quietly into the Tsarina's room where she too was awake but Marie still sound asleep. The events of the previous night had finally worn out the young Grand Duchess. Alexandra explained that the Tsar's train appeared to be late and she now expected him to arrive at ten.

Madame Dehn was profoundly shocked and insisted on knowing why the train had been delayed. The Tsarina merely smiled and said nothing. Anastasia however declared that the train was never late. The Grand Duchess was concerned that, if Nicholas failed to come, soon she would be too sick to see him upon his return. She was already ill but not as yet as seriously as her eldest sisters. She had felt so useful to her mother for once. Olga and Tatiana had been treated as adults in some ways recently, but it was only now that Alexandra had begun to see her two youngest daughters as useful.

Luckily, the day found the Tsarevich in better health and his temperature had finally stabilised. He spent the day in the playroom with Sydney Gibbes who noticed an improvement in the boy's condition. He also remarked in his journal that evening that the Tsarina was extremely worried as she had not heard from the Tsar. They had been quite unable to communicate.

It was deadly quiet outside as the soldiers who had mutinied elected to join their comrades in Petrograd. The only communication the occupants of the Alexander Palace were able to maintain with the outside world was via a direct telephone line to the Winter Palace. Those who managed to arrive at the Alexander Palace from the capital described particularly gruesome murders of army officers and policemen. There was no longer a train service. The palace guards wore white armbands to prevent themselves being forcibly removed from the palace. It was a signal of truce.

That day Alexandra wired an absent Nicholas ensuring him that all her thoughts and prayers were with him. She firmly believed that God would help and added that the children's temperatures were still high and they were all coughing. Nicholas was having problems of his own as he was unable to return home.

On Thursday the second/fifteenth of March he wired Alexandra explaining briefly that he had arrived at Pskov at dinner time, hoped that everyone was better and able to meet soon.

That morning, the commander of the north-western and northern fronts, General Nikolai Ruzsky arrived to speak urgently with Nicholas and talk over the long telephone conversation he had had with Michael Rodzianko. He explained the situation in the capital and admitted that a government of Duma members would be powerless to do anything. Nicholas's abdication was now needed. Nicholas agreed after he received replies from each of the Commanders-in-Chief. All had urged him to abdicate before it was too late. At around 9pm Alexander Guchkov and Vasily Shulgin arrived from the capital on behalf of the Duma and the Council of Workmen's and Soldiers' Deputies. They intended to insist that he abdicate but Nicholas had already decided to do so. He would abdicate not only for himself but for his son. He had spoken at length to Dr Sergei Feodorov and he had convinced Nicholas that the boy would be better off with his parents. If the Alexei had remained as Tsar, he would have been a puppet in the hands of others. Nicholas abdicated in favour of his younger brother Michael.

Nicholas then returned to Mogilev to bid farewell to his beloved troops and see his mother. He knew that both meetings would prove difficult.

Meanwhile, on the second, Alexandra sent two detailed letters to Nicholas via two of the Cossacks, Soloviev and Gramotin. The men had her words sewn into the stripes of their trousers in an attempt to make sure that Nicholas received at least one of the letters.

Alexandra admitted a feeling of helplessness knowing that she could do nothing in his hour of need. It was obvious that they were keeping them apart and she urged him to sign nothing, not knowing that she was already too late. She had attempted to explain the situation to their son and went on to reveal that Olga was beginning to show some signs of improvement but Tatiana had problems with her hearing and her ears in general. The children slept peacefully whilst she wrote. Alexandra urged Nicholas to wear Rasputin's cross, even if it were uncomfortable, and reassured him that nothing could divide them.

Sydney Gibbes's journal that day for the first time betrayed a feeling of panic. Although Alexei's condition had improved, the situation in the capital was a real concern – for the adults. The cable in the Tsarina's personal lift had broken which made it difficult for the Tsarina to walk upstairs to her children and she became breathless just walking a short distance.

The Archpriest Afansy Beliaev had been one of the few visitors permitted to see the Tsarina, or rather the ex-Tsarina, that fateful day. The church warden at the Feodorovsky Cathedral, Dmitri Loman, had called on Beliaev to explain to him that he had been invited to take the miracle working icon of the Heavenly Mother of God from the *Church of the Sign* to the palace where the Imperial children lay seriously ill.

Beliaev later entered the palace with ease, although it was guarded by the combined regiment. He was escorted upstairs to see the Imperial children who each lay in their individual camp bed. The priest placed the blessed icon on a table but the rooms were so dark he was barely able to see the Tsarina, dressed in her nurse's uniform, standing next to her son's bed, surrounded by the nurses and nannies. A few thin candles were placed and lit in front of the icon before he began a thanksgiving service. News came soon after that the Tsar had been detained and arrested. He may even have abdicated!

Alexandra prayed with fervour before the icon and begged her heavenly counterpart for guidance. She insisted that the icon be taken to her daughters and then to Madame Vyrubova. He later left with the icon and all those who chose to remain were arrested.

According to his daily journal Nicholas had slept well on the night on the second/third of March despite the events of the previous day. The difference between an absolute monarch and an ordinary man was a vast one and the sense of relief palpable. He spent the day talking over the events of the past day with others but chose to read for much of the day. The subject was coincidentally *Julius Caesar* and the date in the West was the fifteenth of March or *The Ides of March,* a fateful day for the Roman Emperor and indeed for Nicholas.

Nicholas arrived at Mogilev shortly after 8am and was met by a mixed group of soldiers, and chatted with General Alexeiev. The General had the latest news from Rodzianko and Nicholas learned to his astonishment that his brother Michael had also abdicated. Nicholas was quite convinced his brother had been coerced into signing the manifesto.

Meanwhile at 4am that morning, the new revolutionary commander of Tsarskoe Selo knocked on the door of Grand Duke Paul's home and announced that Nicholas II had abdicated in favour of his brother, not knowing that he too had also renounced the throne. Paul felt it his duty to inform Alexandra as he knew no one else would be likely to do so.

Paul Alexandrovich arrived to inform Alexandra of her husband's abdication and was taken to the Crimson Drawing Room where the two spoke. In the adjoining study, Marie and Lili overheard the loud voice of the Grand Duke and the agitated replies of the former Tsarina.

A greatly apprehensive Marie wished to know why the Grand Duke was shouting at her mother. She was convinced that they should go and see what was happening yet Lili urged her to remain quiet. Marie declared that Lili could remain, but she intended to return to her room as she could not bear to imagine that her poor mother was under such stress.

The Grand Duke was at that moment informing Alexandra of the abdication and the exclusion of her son. She refused to believe him, initially declaring that it was impossible, just another newspaper lie. She reaffirmed her belief in God and the army and refused to believe that either would desert her.

The Grand Duke replied that the army was now on the side of the revolution. She answered bitterly that now it was *Misha* after all. Alexandra then burst into tears and wandered out into the Green Drawing Room. Madame Dehn saw her totter into the room. Lili rushed to her aid whilst Alexandra struggled to stand up against the writing table. She took Madame Dehn's hands in her own and, in a broken voice, uttered the single word – *abdication.*

The Tsarina was inconsolable. Madame Dehn, fearing for her sanity, succeeded in calming Alexandra after reassuring her that the most important thing was that Nicholas remained alive. Alexandra insisted on knowing what Lili intended to do, and Madame Dehn proudly affirmed her loyalty. She urged Alexandra to send word to Nicholas as he would be desperate for news of her, and she agreed.

Madame Dehn then went to find Dr Botkin who gave her a composing draft for the former Tsarina. Alexandra initially refused to take it but Lili insisted.

Lili suddenly saw Marie weeping bitterly in a corner. She had quite clearly heard everything. She was the first of the Tsar's children to hear of his abdication.

Just at that moment, as if to break the tension, Alexei Volkov appeared and announced that dinner was ready. Meanwhile Alexandra demanded to know where Marie was. Lili remained to comfort the young girl and knelt down as the Grand Duchess rested her head upon her shoulder. Lili kissed Marie's tearstained face as she attempted to soothe her and urged the girl to remain strong for the sake of her mother. The Grand Duchess agreed and gradually regained her composure. She later explained to Anya that her mother was grieving and she too cried, but they all had attempted to smile afterwards at the meal table.

After her talk with Lili Dehn, Alexandra sat down to put pen to paper to pledge her support to Nicholas. She confessed that her heart bled for him and how it was maddening not knowing what was happening. She had heard nothing but the vilest rumours and hoped that he had received her latest letters. These were being sent via an officer's wife. Alexandra enquired after Voyeikov and explained that now only Marie remained up. In the evenings she and Marie continued to make their rounds amongst the men. She assured Nicholas that Grand Duke Paul had informed her of everything and that she quite understood why he had abdicated in favour of his son.

Marie had witnessed first-hand the humiliation of her mother's discovery of Nicholas's abdication and henceforth took it upon herself to write to him, fully aware that she was the only one of his daughters able to do so at this point. Even though she was feeling unwell she promised her father that she would spend as much time as she was able with her mother. Marie spoke positively of her brother's recovery and of Lili Dehn. She mentioned the soldiers who surrounded them, including one particular old friend Victor Zborovsky.

She assured her father that her thoughts and prayers were with him. Her sisters were still being kept in semi-darkness but Alexei, who was feeling better, had become bored of the gloomy atmosphere and moved into his playroom where he had opened the curtains.

Earlier she had assisted her brother and Gilliard cast lead bullets out of a tin. It had greatly amused Alexei. She added that her mother was cheerful apart from some slight heart problems. Marie revealed that she was sleeping with her mother, so as to be on hand at all times. Lili was staying in the Crimson Room, the ante-room to the Grand Duchesses' rooms, where Olga had slept when she was ill at the end of 1915.

Marie revealed that they were able to see the soldiers from their windows and on the previous day she and her mother had paid a call on them in the basement. It was completely dark as there was no electricity. She also went on to explain about the icon from the church being brought to the palace.

Marie attempted to set the scene. She was seated in the middle of her bedroom, her sisters and brother scattered around her. They had been all moved into one bedroom. Olga was speechless due to her incessant cough, and Tatiana's head was swathed in bandages and she was unable to hear. Only the two youngest were sufficiently well enough to be able to chat.

Alexei had attempted to jump in his bed but had been forbidden to do so. Lili was sitting on the floor and speaking in a low voice to her mother, who was reclining on a sofa. Marie had divided her time between sitting with the invalids and simply gazing out of the window. Anastasia was in bed drinking tea and each of them had their dog for company.

The previous day, when Anastasia had still been up, she and Marie had watched the soldiers and Cossacks from the window. The men pretended to fight one another in an effort to keep warm. She had spotted the Cossack Victor Zborovsky amongst the group and had spoken with him. He chatted amiably with the other soldiers and attempted to keep up morale by recounting various amusing stories. He smoked and offered his cigarettes around the men in a spirit of friendship.

The previous afternoon, the two had observed the Cossacks from Shura's window. The men were singing or simply standing around whilst their horses ate the hay that had been brought for them. The Cossacks ate at one of the mobile kitchens hurriedly set up in the courtyard. (Marie had as usual explained the situation in great detail and, in her description of the troops, she hoped to reassure Nicholas. He knew at least that his family were safe, for now at least.)

Meanwhile Pierre Gilliard had noted in his personal journal how he felt that no one could possibly understand how greatly the former Tsarina suffered from lack of news from the Tsar and concern for her children's health. He had observed Alexandra in her son's room that evening and noticed how she was determined to remain strong and calm for the sake of her children.

That evening, Dr Botkin had gleefully informed his children Tatiana and Gleb that the ever-complaining Anya Vyrubva naturally had seen herself as the greatest victim that day. She was making the most noise and Dr Botkin joked that, to hear Anya, one would have thought the revolution had occurred simply to spite her.

Baroness Buxhoeveden saw the former Tsarina after dinner accompanied by Count Benckendorf and Count Apraxin. Alexandra had received them in her daughter's schoolroom. She appeared deathly pale and barely able to stand. The three spoke of their devotion and Alexandra kissed the Baroness whilst Sophie, quite overcome, murmured some words of affection. Benckendorf held tightly onto her hand as the tears streamed down his face. Even before the three left, they could hear Alexandra sobbing bitterly.

Tatiana at this time was suffering from abscesses in her ears and was deaf. Anastasia's health suddenly deteriorated and Marie, who had caught cold whilst the rash was developing had contracted double pneumonia. Marie later became seriously ill and feverish. At one point, Dr Botkin confessed to the Baroness that he feared for Marie's life, but she decided against mentioning the fact to Alexandra. If the Tsarina had not realised already, it would worry her even more.

The Dowager Empress had in the meantime travelled up from Kiev for a reunion with Nicholas on Saturday, the fourth of March. A great deal had happened since they had last met and the two sat and chatted for quite some time. Two telegrams arrived later from Alexandra much to Nicholas's delight. General Alexeiev and Count Fredericks were received by Nicholas after tea and afterwards he drove to dine with his mother returning at nightfall.

Nicholas wired Alix explaining his delight at the prospect of meeting his mother. There was another snowstorm, he added.

Grand Duke Alexander, who had accompanied his mother-in-law from Kiev, observed that his she sobbed yet Nicholas simply stood looking down at his feet whilst smoking a cigarette. Nicholas and his brother-in-law embraced, but Sandro was lost for words.

After hearing his voice on the telephone the former Tsarina wrote joyfully to Nicholas. The already hard of hearing Alexandra admitted that it had been quite difficult to understand the words he spoke, as someone was clearly listening in. All the girls were now lying in the room in the dark but Marie was still determined to write. She explained that she had finally read her husband's manifesto that morning and another from Michael who had since abdicated.

The couple had spoken on the telephone very briefly about the situation. Each had begun by asking how much the other knew then both had gone on to speak of the children. When Alexandra had heard the announcement that Nicholas was on the telephone, she had jumped up with the enthusiasm of a schoolgirl, according to the Baroness.

Sydney Gibbes observed that the young Tsarevich knew little of what was happening, but knew that something was wrong. He spent the day casting more lead bullets with his English tutor as his contribution to the war effort. He also built paper model houses. The Tsarina called in on her son from time to time to check on his progress.

Alexandra received a wire from Nicholas later. In an attempt to stay positive he remarked that his despair appeared to be passing. He had received Alix's telegram that evening.

Nicholas attended Mass at the usual garrison church on Sunday, but as Count Grabbe observed at the time, everything had changed. Nicholas stood in exactly the same place during the service yet the words had been altered to avoid mentioning him by name. Many of the congregation were so overcome that they were reduced to tears.

Nicholas sent a brief telegram to Alexandra that day and in a rare show of affection his mother added a message to her. He hoped the invalids were improving. He sent a second telegram later concerning the wife and daughters of Count Fredericks.

After receiving General NI Ivanov, Nicholas took his leave of Count Fredericks and General Voyeikov who were leaving for the country. Nicholas dined with his widowed mother that evening onboard the train.

Meanwhile, back at the palace, things took a distinct turn for the worse. Gibbes noted that Alexei was not quite as well as he had been formerly. They had removed to the boy's classroom, as it was impossible to keep the large playroom warm. There was no running water and it now had to be fetched from the ponds.

Alexander Gutchkov arrived at the Alexander Palace to see Alexandra that evening accompanied by a surly entourage of men who abused the servants and suite alike for working for the former monarchs. A terrified Alexandra hurriedly telephoned Grand Duke Paul for assistance and he duly arrived shortly before midnight. Alix was asked by Guchkov and Kornilov, the new commander of the Petrograd military district, if she had everything she needed. She replied that she had but asked that they make sure that the local hospitals had enough supplies. Shortly before the telephone was cut off, a few loyal friends sent messages of support to Alexandra and asked after the children. She felt quite touched at the gesture. The loyalty of those who had previously served the monarchs was mixed. One of the doctors informed the Tsarina by letter that he no longer wished to attend at the palace, yet the Tsar's dentist Dr Serge Kostrisky came despite the danger to himself. The former Grand Duchesses gratefully replied to any letters of support they received but further communication ceased as the recipients were inevitably too scared to show any connection with the former monarch's family. It would have put them in danger, and yet some bravely persisted.

On Monday evening, a greatly relieved Nicholas noted in his journal with satisfaction that he had received two letters from Alexandra plus a further two from Marie. They had arrived via the wife of Captain Golovkin.

The day had been far from ordinary, according to Count Grabbe. Nicholas spent the morning arranging his paperwork and after lunch went to a staff hall where all the military personnel serving at military headquarters had assembled. Nicholas had chosen to wear his Cossack uniform, which was especially appropriate as they had proved to be one of the most loyal of all the various regiments.

According to Sir Peter Bark, Nicholas graciously thanked all his staff for their hard work and expressed his belief that Russia and her allies would win the war. He confessed that he was submitting to God's will and willingly laying down his post as Supreme Commander. Everyone was moved to tears.

On Wednesday the 8th, Nicholas met his mother for the last time. He signed a farewell order to the armies and then personally took leave of all the officers of the Headquarters' staff and administration in the duty house before he bid farewell to the officers and Cossacks of the Convoy and the Combined Regiment. He found it particularly painful. Nicholas had wished to ask Konstantin Nilov, his adjutant general of the Imperial Suite, to accompany him back to Tsarskoe Selo but was denied this seemingly simple request. Nicholas finally left Mogilev at 4.45pm accompanied by four members of the Duma.

Later Count Grabbe explained that, in his opinion, it was the loyalty of the Cossacks that had saved the life of the Tsar that evening. They would have willingly fought to the death to protect him. Sadly there was quite a different attitude from the men of most of the other regiments. Count Grabbe had been informed that a large number of mutinous troops were intent on marching towards Mogilev and to the Governor's House the following morning.

The Count duly ordered two Convoy Cossack's squadrons to be alerted, and they stationed themselves along the road which led from the station to block the approach of the men. The Cossacks had determined not to let anyone near Nicholas and, on hearing that the Cossacks had arrived, the others fled. It was a close escape and Nicholas's choice of dress that day may have encouraged their continued loyalty.

There were a few more positive signs. Once the trains began running again, the Tsar's aide-de-camp and old friend Captain DV Dehn arrived from the capital to place himself at the former Tsarina's disposal. He offered to come with his wife, a distant relation of Nicholas, and remain in the palace. The former Tsarina gratefully accepted his offer but unfortunately Dehn was arrested and not permitted to return. Alexandra was almost exclusively surrounded by women, sick children and aged men.

Others also came to offer their services, including the Tsarina's former lady-in-waiting Princess Elisabeth Obolensky yet she too was denied permission to remain. Madame Eugenie Voyeikov and Countess Sophie Fersen came simply to express their support.

When the palace guard and the Cossacks were forced to leave despite or because of their loyalty, each went to personally take their leave of the Tsarina, and some of the men openly wept.

Others who showed their open support included the Tsar's sisters and Grand Duke Paul and his second wife, who had been ungraciously treated in the past by Alexandra. The Tsar's aged godmother Queen Olga of Greece and her niece Princess Elena continued to call at the palace and often sent letters and flowers to Alexandra. Alexandra's sister Elisabeth however was not even permitted to communicate with the former Tsarina.

Meanwhile Alexei was showing signs of improvement yet, according to Gibbes, had sore eyes and ears. Alexei had spent the morning peacefully then had lunched with his older sisters. He then slept peacefully before dinner and afterwards once again constructed model houses with Gibbes and the two enjoyed playing dominoes together.

Olga's journal confirmed that although Marie finally became ill that day, she determinedly refused to go to bed. She wished to be able to greet her father when he finally returned. Lili Dehn assured her that she would remain by the side of the Tsarina but Alexandra did not wish Lili with her in case something terrible happened. Olga and Tatiana nevertheless urged Lili to remain.

General Lavr Kornilov arrived at the palace that morning along with the new Commandant of the Tsarskoe Selo guard, Colonel Eugene Koblinsky and Captain Paul Koztebue the new Palace Commandant and placed the former Tsarina under arrest yet politely apologised for having to do so. Kornilov explained to Alexandra that it was merely a precaution to safeguard her and the children from the mob. Nicholas had also been arrested at Mogilev and once he returned and the children were sufficiently recovered the Provisional Government intended to send them to Murmansk where it was hoped a British cruiser would take them to England and into exile.

Alexandra explained to Pierre Gilliard immediately afterwards that both she and Nicholas were now under arrest and that everyone who did not want to be kept in close confinement at the palace would need to leave before 4pm. Gilliard, like Lili Dehn, decided to remain with the family. She then asked Pierre Gilliard to explain the situation to his pupil Alexei. Nicholas would be returning tomorrow and the boy needed to be informed beforehand. She was intending to inform her daughters. Unfortunately Alexei failed to take it all in initially so Gilliard decided to change tack. The tutor explained that Nicholas no longer wished to be Commander-in-Chief. The boy was greatly moved and shortly after Gilliard gently added that Alexei's father also no longer wished to be Tsar. Alexei wanted to understand why this had happened. Gilliard simply explained that his father was very tired and had had a lot of trouble recently.

Later Alexei put a question to his mother. Would he be ever permitted to return to Mogilev with his father? She explained that it was no longer possible. He then asked if he would be permitted to see *his* regiments and his soldiers. When Alexandra replied in the negative the boy was close to tears. He was more concerned about not seeing his friends and the soldiers again than anything else. The boy had no thoughts for his own *position*.

The former heir then asked about the Imperial yacht. Would he be able to see the *Standart* again? Unfortunately the answer once more was no because the yacht no longer belonged to his father.

The Tsarina had the difficult task of explaining things to her daughters. Marie already knew something of what had happened. Tatiana proved to be the most awkward to get through to as she was deaf and her sisters were forced to write the details down for her.

Anastasia questioned Lili Dehn afterwards as to how she had managed to keep it all a secret from them and remain so calm? Lili admitted that the former Tsarina had been her inspiration. Anastasia defiantly stated that she did not care, so long as her father was returning.

Alexandra spoke at some length later to Victor Zborovsky about the incident and he confirmed that she appeared to have confidence in General Kornilov despite his actions that day. The members of the Convoy were instructed that they had to leave or be arrested. The members of the household who chose to remain included Baroness Sophie Buxhoeveden, Lili Dehn, Anya Vyrubova, the Count and Countess Benckendorf, Madame Narishkin, Mlle Catherine Schneider, (Countess Anastasia Hendrikova who arrived later), Pierre Gilliard and others. Count Apraxin remained initially but then decided he would be of more use if he represented Alexandra in the capital.

As the members of the Convoy Cossack regiment left, the Tsarina presented each of them with small icons and gifts from the family. As each man received his presents, he dropped onto one knee. Alexandra then led Victor Zborovsky into her daughter's room in order to take their leave. Anastasia's friend had proved his worth. She had chosen well.

The palace entrances were securely locked and sealed and the keys were now in the charge of the newly appointed *Commander of the Palace,* Colonel Paul Kotzebue. He was in a very awkward position as he was constantly spied upon by the men who became increasingly unruly. He was unfailingly courteous to the former Imperial family, but the soldiers were ultimately the masters and he had to be guided by their moods and whims.

Nicholas finally returned home on Thursday accompanied by his loyal friend *Valia*, Prince Dolgourukov and Sergeant-Major Pilipenko of the Convoy. When he arrived, the former Tsarina was in Alexei's playroom with her son. Anya Vyrubova was still confined to bed at the time but that morning, whilst Dr Botkin was seeing his patient, Lili Dehn burst into the room exclaiming that Nicholas had arrived.

However Nicholas was no longer arriving home as Tsar of Russia but as a simple prisoner. Alexandra ran downstairs to meet him. The couple spent much of the day in the company of their children and finally at four Alix went to see Anya. Alexandra admitted that Nicholas had sobbed like a child on his wife's breast. Nicholas had gone out into the garden and they saw him through the window with his faithful *Valia*. They were surrounded, however, by six soldiers who, armed with rifles, pushed Nicholas this way and that. They refused to let him walk this way or that and insisted on addressing him as *Mr Colonel*. Nicholas remained unmoved and with great dignity walked back to the palace, but Anya passed out due to the shock and weakness.

Later Nicholas, Alexandra and Lili called in on Madame Vyrubova. Whilst Nicholas chatted amiably with the patient, the other two ladies sat at the table with their needlework. Anya spoke candidly with Nicholas for some time and eventually he admitted that, even if the whole country begged him on their bended knees, he would not return as Tsar. He spoke with tears in his eyes as he recalled the men whom he thought were his friends.

He also revealed that, after he had abdicated, he had met two Cossacks and told them to take his initials from their uniforms. They had asked to be permitted to kill Guchkov and Shulgin but he had said that it was too late now. Anya asked if he thought the riots and strikes could be put down but he replied that he could not see it happening for at least two years. He just wanted to remain in his own country maybe as a simple farmer and to be permitted to earn his own living. He did not want to go abroad.

As he confided in his journal that evening, Nicholas found his *welcome* rather different than usual. He had arrived shortly before noon and straightaway was aware of the change in attitude of the men on duty. He had noticed guards on the streets and some sort of ensign on the entrance to the palace. (To someone who thrived on order this was, to say the least, disturbing.)

He had been reunited with Alix and the children upstairs where she attempted to appear cheerful. The children were lying in a darkened room but Alexei had revolted and made his playroom his domain. Marie was the most worrying case at the moment and lay seriously ill. The couple lunched and dined in their son's playroom. Nicholas was delighted to see another friendly face – old Count Benckendorf. He confessed in the journal to going for a walk with *Valia* and not being able to get far. That evening they had visited the members of the household in the other wing, including Anya. He was remarkably restrained in the circumstances.

Earlier Marie had briefly regained consciousness and questioned Lili Dehn about her father. She could hardly believe that he was finally home. As she drifted back in delirium, she had visions of crowds of people. She was convinced that they had come with the intention of killing Alexandra and she wanted to know why.

Once again, the Archpriest Afansy Beliaev had been asked to call in at the Alexander Palace to conduct a service. He was met by the new Commandant of the palace along with the duty guard. He was also met by Nicholas's valet who explained that the Tsar, he refused to call him anything else, wished to speak to him about the forthcoming service. The young ensign who had accompanied the visitor explained that it would not be permitted to do so.

The valet was outraged and demanded that the meeting take place, or he would be forced to speak to the Tsar about the matter. The guard, unmoved by this, refused to alter his initial response. The priest was then led to the church and was met shortly afterwards by Count Benckendorf. He explained that the Tsar had asked that Beliaev conduct services at the palace on Sundays and holidays. At the end of the vigil, the Archpriest asked the Commandant how he was expected to behave during the services. He was informed that the Commandant had no such instructions but added that any conversation with the Tsar had to be non-political and in the presence of the duty guard. He explained that it was best not to address Nicholas directly, but admitted that he had called Nicholas *Your Majesty*. The Commandant went on to explain that there could be no personal meetings in the Tsar's room, and tactfully attempted to remind the priest that it was best not to offend the guard in any way.

Nicholas and Alexandra stood behind a screen during each of the religious services and left by a separate entrance. On the first occasion that the priest had to refer to the Russian State and the provisional government, rather than the devout autocrat during the service, he struggled and was close to tears. He stumbled over the exact wording which was both unfamiliar and distressing.

The new regime was something the Grand Duchesses found difficult to adjust to yet they saw the funny side. On one occasion, Anastasia had broken a vase in the drawing room but had light-heartedly assured Lili Dehn that it did not matter. It no longer belonged to them and was the property of the government.

Nicholas appeared to be in a better frame of mind on Wednesday. He had slept well and had decided to sort out his papers as he had done at military headquarters. He took the decision to burn some of them. Alexandra had already destroyed some of her own.

Nicholas was relieved to finally be at home with his beloved family. He sat with his children until after two and then went for a walk once more with *Valia*. Luckily, the two ensigns who had accompanied him the previous day behaved in a more gentlemanly fashion. Now he was free of work for the first time since 1894, he took the opportunity to play in the snow. He spent the evening in the company of his family again. Usually, he worked well into the evening, and it was something of a relief to have time to spend with his wife and children without having to worry about the build-up of papers.

Although the guards had behaved well that day, it would not always be the case and, on one occasion, Nicholas lost his temper when one of the guards intentionally stood on his heel. He made sure it would not happen again. Nicholas swung his cane backwards, without moving with much force, as if by accident, so that the man involved never tried the trick again, nor did anyone else. Dr Botkin explained the story to his daughter Tatiana later. He was one of the few permitted to come and go at will. He had children, but his wife had left him years before so his case was a special one. Since his appointment years before, he had daily informed his young children about the antics of the Tsar's children, and the two families had become friends. Nicholas once said that *The Doctor* was his best friend. In the coming months, the doctor's loyalty became apparent.

Nicholas was delighted to learn on Saturday from Count Benckendorf that it had been decided that he and his family should remain at the palace for the foreseeable future. The former Tsar spent much of the day burning his papers. His children remained in the sickroom. Anastasia's ears were now aching. The same thing had happened previously with Olga, Tatiana and Alexei. Anastasia's measles had begun much later than that of her other siblings and Marie remained seriously ill. The second most ill, after Marie, had been Olga. It would be some time before Marie and Olga were able to go outside. When Marie finally was able to go outside into the park with her siblings, she was confined to a wheelchair.

Nicholas decided that he wished to go out into the garden and the remaining members of the suite assisted as Nicholas, Tatiana and Anastasia began to dig a vegetable garden. He had always wanted to be a farmer; now he had the chance and it gave him the opportunity to do something useful and remain out-of-doors for long periods in the fresh air. He had always craved physical exercise and this was an excellent way of providing food for the family. He later spent time cutting down dead trees in the park which would be used for firewood later in the year. That evening Alexei felt able to have his first bath since his illness. (When one is physically weak it takes a great deal of energy to do simple things that most take for granted.)

Nicholas relaxed and enjoyed the simple pleasure of reading on Tuesday. He had rarely had time to read books in the past. He had only ever been able to read after work, late at night or on his holidays. He now had as much time as he wished to read as he no longer had to spend endless hours at his papers and reports, and no longer had to receive ministers and attend receptions. Although he had been crushed by the turn of events, in practical terms he was happier now and he felt free for the first time. Sadly, in the coming months, he would come under an increasingly harsh regime. Had it stayed the same, it would have been tolerable for Nicholas. He had all the time in the world now to read, spend precious time with his family, or out into the garden for walks or do work of some description.

Nicholas began to act as if he had simply *retired* and life at the Alexander Palace went on fairly peacefully on the whole. Nicholas, Tatiana and Anastasia went about their task of planting out a vegetable garden along with the other volunteers. One of the guards later remarked that Nicholas was so methodical in the planting and supervising of the rows of carrots and cabbages that, had he not been Tsar, he would have owned the country anyway.

Nicholas had always enjoyed spending time outdoors and it was a familiar way of life for him. Olga, Marie and Anastasia had long had a great love of flowers and only recently they had spent their free time weeding the garden. They had often spent hours simply picking flowers, usually lily of the valley for their appreciative mother. She adored flowers and filled her rooms with them to excess.

Nicholas was tireless in his weeding and tilling the ground. It kept him busy, and it was an extremely useful occupation, especially when there had been a food shortage. He was literally taking responsibility for feeding his family. On some occasions, work had to stop as crowds gathered next to the palace gate. They were fascinated to see the former Tsar working like a simple peasant. Some chose to mock him and his party whilst others simply felt sorry for them. No one had ever shown any real animosity against the former Grand Duchesses, and most hated the former Tsarina rather than the Tsar. She was the target of most of the hatred, not her children due to her German origin and lack of public appearances. The young Grand Duchesses with their simple ways, beauty and great personal charm made friends easily when they had the opportunity. Marie and Anastasia were especially keen to chat to anyone they met.

The former Tsar and his family lived quite well. The dinner menu on Friday evening for Nicholas, Alexandra and the children included *consommé* (clear soup) with beetroot, *kasha* (buckwheat) and *pirozhki* (meat pasties). It also included boiled perch (fish) with hollandaise sauce, roast turkey, salad and semolina pudding. That day, members of the suite who may have dined with them signed the menu card including Countess Hendrikova, Count Benkendorf and his wife, Madame (Zizi) Narishkin, Prince (Valia) Dolgorukov and Baroness Buxhoeveden. Only the Countess Hendrikova stubbornly chose to sign with her former title as a sign of defiance.

On Tuesday afternoon, there was a surprise visit from the leader of the new provisional government Alexander Kerensky. Nicholas silently fumed in his journal. He was angered by the two arrests made that day whilst he had been out in the garden at the time and felt quite helpless.

Anya Vyrubova was still bedridden, recovering from the after-effects of the measles, yet Kerensky had been quite determined that she be removed at once to prison. She had been as much of a hate figure in the eyes of the public as the Tsarina herself. Lili Dehn had been in the room at the time but had cunningly evaded Kerensky by rushing out just before he went in. Madame Dehn went to seek the Tsarina who urged her to hide from him.

Lili went into Marie's darkened room where she was sleeping as she was still confined to bed. Lili hid in the semi-darkness behind one of the convenient screens that divided Marie's and Anastasia's shared room. As she hid, Kerensky entered the room, ignoring the bedridden Marie. The Tsarina and her two elder daughters followed him to the room but he had already gone in the short time it took for them to get there. He was wandering around the palace as if he owned it.

Anya Vyrubova pleaded with Dr Eugene Botkin to prevent them taking her away. She knew that she was still too ill to move and was naturally terrified of being hauled off to prison. Unfortunately both the Doctor's Botkin and Derevenko had declared her fit. They probably realised that had they caused a fuss it would cause trouble for the Imperial family.

Kerensky insisted that Lili Dehn be removed at the same time. Alexandra, having little free time of her own, asked Madeleine Zannoti to pack a suitcase for Madame Dehn. Tatiana was reduced to tears but Olga and the Tsarina were determined to remain calm, at least on the outside. Lili had time to bid farewell to Anastasia, but not to Alexei or the sleeping Marie. Alexandra asked Zannoti to find a small sacred icon which she duly presented to Lili. Tatiana gifted a small leather case containing the portraits of Nicholas and Alexandra to Lili. It would be a reminder of her parents, she explained.

The former Tsarina and her two eldest daughters escorted Lili down to the waiting car. She was joined by Anya Vyrubova, and the two reluctantly climbed into the vehicle. Madame Vyrubova struggled to do so as she was not able to walk without her trusty sticks. Tatiana continued to cry as the ladies were forcibly separated.

Alexandra had spoken briefly to both of her friends before they left and assured them that they would meet again in heaven. Tatiana had begged Anya for a token of remembrance. Madame Vyrubova had little to give but presented the Grand Duchess with her redundant wedding ring.

That evening Nicholas noted in his journal that the weather had been as revolting as their mood. Despite everything, Marie and Anastasia had managed to sleep for most of the day.

Nicholas had a brief walk on Thursday morning. He sorted out his books and slowly began to put things aside as he was fully expecting to go in exile to England. He went for a walk with his eldest daughters after dinner and spent the rest of the evening quietly as usual. He was continuing his new regime.

In order to simply go out into the garden was no easy matter. Any members of the former Imperial family who wished to go out for some fresh air had to wait in the semi-circular entry hall for the officer on duty to appear with the appropriate key. This farce was re-enacted each time they wanted to go out.

After spending the twenty-fifth of March which was Palm Sunday (the last Sunday before Easter when Jesus riding a donkey had entered Jerusalem) under house arrest, Nicholas admitted in his journal how he felt frustrated that he was unable to contact his mother or siblings. Late that morning, he attended the liturgy at the palace's own chapel accompanied by Olga and Tatiana. The Archpriest Afansy Beliaev again conducted the service in the absence of Father Vassiliev. He gave each member of the congregation a small twig of the consecrated willow branch as usual at this time of year. The conditions however were far removed from normal.

The former Tsar's mood did not improve on Tuesday, the twenty-seventh. Kerensky appeared after Mass and explained that, for the foreseeable future, Nicholas and Alexandra would only be permitted to meet at mealtimes. He claimed that it was on the orders of the Soviet of Workers' and Soldiers' Deputies as he needed to interview them both separately. Initially it had been decided that Nicholas would remain with the children but after it became clear that Alexandra was needed to supervise the invalids it was altered so that Alexandra remained with the children instead. Nicholas was however able to see Tatiana as she had suffiently recovered although Anastasia chose to stay with Marie and the rest of the invalids. Nicholas felt compelled to submit as he was greatly concerned lest the guards resorted to violence. He took a walk with Tatiana later. Olga had a slight relapse during the course of the day. She took to her bed with a sore throat. Luckily Marie and Alexei were showing signs of improvement. Nicholas spent the evening in the company of Tatiana and, after she retired to bed for the evening, he read alone.

Another religious service was held for the former Imperial family on Wednesday the twenty-eighth and again the Archpriest officiated. He performed the liturgy to a congregation of three. He then read prayers for those who wished to confess and gave a short sermon on how to approach repentance. The servants' confession began at 2pm and this lasted for some three hours. In all, fifty-four people arrived in order to confess. The Archpriest had lunched at one. The meal was a frugal one consisting of shredded cabbage with pickles and potatoes, and *kissel (*fruit soup*)*. During Lent, meat and dairy is not taken. The former Imperial family probably ate the same fare.

He began Matins at six with the singing of *When the Glorious Disciples* by four soloists from the court choir. The service lasted a couple of hours. The Archpriest had been visited by the Commandant that day and was impressed with the man's humane and noble bearing. The priest ate at eight – he was presented with a meal of mushroom soup, dry biscuits in a sweet syrup accompanied by a slice of pineapple. Again it was probably the same meal the Tsar and his family ate on this day as it had neither meat nor dairy.

A special funeral service for the anti-royalist victims of the revolution was held in the grounds of the palace on Thursday. Beliaev attempted to carry on as normal despite the difficult circumstances. The liturgy was performed and the former Imperial family took part and prayed most fervently and then took Communion. It ended at noon. Meanwhile thousands of soldiers and workmen came to attend the ceremonies which lasted for much of the day but the Easter service continued. The *Shroud* of Christ was brought from the nearby cathedral along with a special table on which to place it. A large book containing the Gospels was also brought and the festal Easter vestments. The altar and the table of oblation were duly covered with the black vestments and black chasubles.

The group then separated and went to lunch. The priest later revealed that his meal consisted of rice cutlets with mushrooms, fried smelt followed by fruit compote. The family probably ate a similar meal.

At six, the vigil and reading of the Gospels began but, on opening the window a couple of hours before, the priest could clearly hear singing. The men outside were playing military music including the *Marseillaise* and funeral marches as they buried the dead. Inside the service was attended by a congregation of a hundred in the presence of the duty guard. The service, despite the noise outside, was both reverential and moving and the choir sang especially well that day. The performance by the four soloists during *The Wise Thief* was outstanding. Although the service had to be shortened the *Twelve Gospels* were read and, after each, a hymn was sung. The service lasted an hour and forty minutes whilst the rival service continued outside. Ultimately it was the weather that helped disperse the men. A fierce snowstorm soon emptied the park leaving only a few of the more determined. Dinner was served at eight including cabbage soup with mushrooms, roast meat and raspberry jelly. Again the family probably ate the same.

On Good Friday everyone, with the exception of Olga, attended confession separately. Baroness Buxhoeveden was the first to confess at noon and she could not help but notice a soldier positioned next to her. She realised that he fully intended to hear the former monarch's confession too. She asked the guard if he would leave as she was about to confess but, just as she suspected, he refused to move. The two then had a lively debate and, remarkably, the Baroness came out ahead. She had argued that even condemned prisoners were allowed privacy during confession and urged him to speak to his superior Kerensky. The man decided not to bother the provisional leader with the matter and agreed. The priest was allowed to continue with the confessions in private. The doctors Botkin and Derevenko were amongst those he saw.

That day the procession of the *Shroud* or *Holy Winding Sheet* took place in the palace church. The servants headed the procession dressed in funeral black; then came Nicholas and Alexandra and their daughters Tatiana and Anastasia, the household and the priest. (The former Tsarina had been allowed the concession of attending church with her husband.) They each carried lighted tapers which threw huge shadows on the dimly lit walls. Luckily, the men on duty that day were less militant than some and the ceremonies went on in peace. The service began at 2pm and the *shroud* was taken to the middle of the church. It was respectfully placed on rugs, surrounded by entire bushes of lilacs, roses and other fresh flowers. The priest spoke of the sad act which was performed in all such Russian Orthodox Churches: the bearing out of the *shroud*. It symbolised the sacred image of Christ who died for the good of all.

Later the priest was escorted to the Grand Duchesses' apartments where four of the children were gathered in one room. He met Olga who remained in bed, Alexei who was sitting in a chair in his light blue dressing gown, Marie reclining in her wheelchair, and her inseparable sister Anastasia. He spoke firstly to Olga as the other three left the bedroom. Anastasia pushed Marie's wheelchair. Afterwards the priest held confession for the three youngest children together in an ajoining room. Beliaev went away impressed by the mildness, restraint, moral purity and obedience of the children to their parents. It took an hour and twenty minutes to finish confession with the four. Matins was held at 7pm and afterwards the priest heard the confessions of four of the other ladies of the household. The priest heard the confessions of Tatiana, the former Tsarina and Nicholas that evening. Each spoke to the priest alone. Beliaev had the brief chance to talk to the former Tsar afterwards and Nicholas spoke of the abdication. He admitted that he had been told of the anarchy in the capital and rebellion and had decided to go not to Petrograd but to return home. He was unable to travel back to Tsarskoe Selo as the railroad had been cut off so thought he would return to the front but that line had also been cut. He then confessed that alone without a close adviser he had been deprived of his freedom like a criminal and had signed the act of abdication for the good of the country. Afterwards the Tsar and his wife spoke on general topics including the health of Father Vasiliev but later the conversation turned to family and Nicholas suddenly said that he was misunderstood; he had only wanted to do good.

On Easter Sunday morning, Olga Nicolaevna, who had been confined to bed due to a secondary infection, sent a cheerful note to her father. She wished him a happy Easter, kissed him by proxy and then signed with her second military rank: a Plastuni.

Meanwhile, Nicholas had returned to bed after the late-night subdued celebrations. The previous evening he and Alexandra had been given special permission to eat together but the celebrations had been made difficult by the presence of the guard and, although the couple had been joined by Tatiana and the normally talkative Anastasia, the party had been unusually quiet and everyone had found it difficult to know what to say, especially Alexandra who had barely spoken to her neighbours at the table Count Benckendorf and the priest. Nicholas took a walk in the park after breakfast on Sunday morning. Alexandra then presented the servants with the remnants of the china eggs from stock. Later Nicholas worked on the ice near to the bridge with Tatiana and they began to break it up as he had done in former times. They were briefly joined by Anastasia and Alexei.

Unfortunately, a crowd had gathered to observe the former Tsar at work again and they had to move back towards the garden itself. A service was taken in Alexei's playroom at seven so that the children would participate. As Nicholas was still not allowed to sit with Alexandra, he returned to his study and read aloud to Tatiana. He had been sleeping on the large ottoman sofa in his study. Olga and Marie were still largely confined to their beds and Anastasia had chosen to remain with her mother and siblings unless they went outside with their father. The family was still divided and Nicholas spent most of the day in the company of Tatiana which was unusual as Tatiana was normally inseparable from her mother. As Olga was too ill to move it was Tatiana who sat with her father rather than Olga as would have happened formerly. The Queen of Greece had bravely turned up at the palace that day to leave a gift for the former Tsarina. She asked the officer on duty to pass on an Easter egg to Alexandra.

Nicholas continued working outside in the park on the ice on Monday. He had begun the day with a walk, accompanied by his friend *Valia*. He then attended the liturgy along with Tatiana and Anastasia. The three were then joined by Alexei and they broke up the ice together just like old times but once again a crowd appeared again and refused to move. The group carried on despite the gaping crowd. That evening, Nicholas attended Mass and, during the evening, he sorted through some old postcards. He later read aloud to Tatiana in his room for a while.

The new routine established itself. The former Tsar, accompanied by some of his children, went out into the garden twice a day but, on each occasion, they had to wait for the officer on duty to appear with his keys for the gate. They went out for an hour from eleven and then again at two thirty for a further two and a half hours. Alexandra remained inside with Olga and Marie who were barely able to move.

Nicholas recalled in his nightly journal on Saturday the twenty-third anniversary of his engagement in 1894. It was a whole world away from the present situation. In the morning, he spent time walking with his son and Nicholas revealed in his journal why the guard had been so surly the previous day. They had been drawn from the ranks of the soldiers' deputies. (Later, they had been changed and the new group were friendly. The latter party were from the reserve battalion of the 4th Infantry Regiment. In the weeks to come, Nicholas noticed a great difference in the guards – some were very friendly and others were more aggressive.) He later worked on the ice near the pier and enjoyed the warmth of the sun despite the crowd of onlookers. Later, he attended the vigil with Tatiana, Anastasia and Alexei.

Kerensky returned on Wednesday, the twelfth. On this occasion, Nicholas (who was sitting with Tatiana) was extremely concerned lest Alix be arrested and taken away. Alexander Kerensky had come to examine the former Tsar's papers. Nicholas had silently handed over the key to his desk to him. On seeing the sheer amount of material involved, Kerensky handed the task over to his friend Colonel Korovichenko who was a military lawyer. Nicholas and the Colonel continued the work alone.

Meanwhile Kerensky cross-examined Alexandra about the political role she had played. The former Tsarina answered him in a straightforward manner and he was impressed by her candour and precision. Nicholas felt under great pressure whilst she was being interviewed, and Tatiana later revealed to the Baroness how he had been ready to rush to her aid at any moment. The interview had seemed endless to Nicholas and Tatiana. Afterwards Kerensky informed Nicholas that Alexandra had been honest. Nicholas replied that he had known it all along. The couple had been separated a month. Whilst Nicholas had slept in his small study, Alexandra had spent all day in her daughters' rooms resting, exhausted. Luckily that evening the couple were permitted to return to normal and they spent the evening together and finally were able to sleep in the same room again.

The guards dressed casually and their slovenly appearance did not impress the eternally ordered Nicholas, even though he wore his clothes until they were threadbare, as his late father had done. He was a stickler for order and found it difficult to adjust to the undisciplined behaviour of the guards. One day Baroness Buxhoveden and Tatiana noticed that one of the duty guards at the front of the Alexander Palace had selected an armchair to sit in. He was sitting back enjoying the view with his rifle resting casually across his knee. The Baroness sarcastically noted that all he needed was a pillow. He suddenly disappeared and came back with some sofa cushions and a footstool. The guard then sat reading a newspaper with his rifle on the ground beside him. Others took potshots at the unfortunate swans or tame deer in the park. The men came and went to and from the palace as they chose, doing what they termed their *rounds*. On another occasion, one helped himself to the gold and silver items belonging to the Baroness one evening when he was convinced that she was asleep. Prince Dolgurkov was forced to prevent a member of the guard from entering Alexandra's room whilst she was dressing. A guard was later permanently placed outside her room so she was compelled to dress behind a screen. Luckily she and her daughters possessed them in their rooms as they were now very necessary.

There were endless indignities and these came one by one, day by day. Each parcel was opened and examined carefully; even the laundry was searched. Luckily the family were allowed to retain their cook, and he was provided daily with the ingredients for the simple meals that they were given. They were forbidden fruit at first as a luxury, and even the plants in the rooms were confiscated. As a result, Alexandra was moved to tears when someone presented her with a single flower or branch of lilac. She had been used to rooms filled with flowers. The family had no problems eating simple meals as none had a taste for luxury; the only privation was the lack of sweets for the younger three children and the initial lack of fruit which had been a staple part of their diet.

On another occasion, the Baroness and Tatiana were quietly sitting on a window sill and a voice came insisting that they move at once. They were instructed to close the window immediately. He announced that he would fire if they failed to move. They objected as it had previously been allowed and it was hot. The guard merely shouted that they would obey orders or be shot. They quickly closed the open window, despite the heat.

Church services had been permitted, but they were often made an occasion for much talk amongst the guard often leading to physical abuse. The guardroom was situated directly under the former Tsarina's bedroom so she was able to hear them. The guard later insisted that each detachment should hand over their prisoners personally. Luckily, the diplomatic skills of the aging Count Benckendorf came in handy. He suggested that both the current and future officers walked into the family's rooms and were presented to the Tsar and his family together. On one such occasion however, one of the officers refused to take the hand of Nicholas. He retorted that he was a man of the people and refused to lower himself by shaking hands with the tyrant.

Meanwhile Pierre Gilliard had a conversation with the former monarchs on the sixteenth on the subject of Alexei's lessons. There was a distinct lack of tutors for the boy so alternative arrangements needed to be made. Nicholas elected to teach his son history and geography and Alexandra would be in charge of her son's religious education. Baroness Buxhoeveden (in the temporary absence of Mr Gibbes) would teach Alexei English; Mlle Schneider would instruct him in arithmetics; and Dr Botkin would teach the boy Russian.

Nicholas was angered when the guards decided to celebrate May Day. Although it was still the eighteenth of April in Russia, it was the beginning of May in the West. It was the first occasion on which the day was celebrated in the country. Nicholas felt it ridiculous that they should have parades through the streets, singing, music and the new red flag everywhere. The men also came into the park to lay wreaths of flowers on the recently dug graves. He went out into the garden for a walk that afternoon, once the noise had ceased. He was delighted to see that the sun came out too. It had snowed heavily during the celebrations as if the weather had conspired to interrupt the proceedings once again. Nicholas worked in the garden afterwards with Tatiana, and that evening he read aloud to the children from one of the books he had read whilst at Mogilev – *The Millionaire Girl* by AW Marchmont a great favourite of the younger sisters.

On Saturday morning Nicholas took his son out into the park for a walk. The boy played on the Children's Island whilst the guards stood on the other side of the garden watching. The weather had improved sufficiently for Nicholas to continue his work in the garden. The family attended the vigil that evening and, before dinner, Alexandra received some rather modest gifts from what Marie had termed the *arrested*. It was the eve of her name's day and, as usual, the gifts were presented the night before. Nicholas read aloud later.

Olga presented her mother with a poem on Sunday the twenty-third she had spent time over. She and her siblings had written out verses from famous poems when they were small. Olga was a talented poet. The observant Olga noted how her mother failed to hide her sadness. The piece revealed that her mother would weep for herself if only she realised how grief-stricken she really was. Alexandra had taken the abdication far worse than Nicholas. The former Tsar was more upset by the lack of manners and change of routine than anything else. Nicholas was delighted that Alexandra had some fine weather for her name's day. It was the one thing that the provisional government had no influence over, and yet it often seemed as if the Almighty had.

The members of the household all came to congratulate Alexandra on her special day. The family returned to the garden that afternoon and broke up the ice again. They went back inside before tea. Nicholas read in his study before dinner and again read aloud to the family.

Chapter Nineteen

Summer 1917

At the beginning of May, Nicholas threw himself into his new work. To him it was finally the beginning of May yet to the rest of Europe and indeed to the Russian government it was already the fourteenth. The former Tsar gave his son another geography lesson. He had begun what was another warm day with a pleasant walk. Nicholas then worked on the vegetable garden despite the increasing heat of the day. He then read alone until dinner and aloud to the rest of the family in the evening. He read Sir Arthur Conan Doyle's masterpiece *The Hound of the Baskervilles* set in Devon. Alexei was a particular fan of the Sherlock Holmes' stories and would have relished it.

Nicholas noted in his daily journal that, the previous day, General Kornilov had given up his post as Commander-in-Chief of the Petrograd Military District and that Alexander Gutchkov had just resigned that evening. Both men had complained of the interference of the Soviet of Workers' Deputies and other even more radical elements. Nicholas wondered what yet was in store for Russia. He was no longer Tsar yet was still deeply concerned for her future.

Tatiana finally got round to writing to her former Russian tutor Peter Petrov on the fifth. He had been unwell and she was concerned on hearing the news. Although he did not travel with the family, probably due to ill health, his devotion to them never waned. Tatiana felt rather ashamed that she had not taken the time to write before but assured him that she had not forgotten him. It was possible, she reminded him, to be friends and not actually correspond. She had been very upset to hear that he had been unwell. She asked if he had any news from his nephew, presumably a soldier. She wanted to know how he was – was he confined to bed? Tatiana expected that he would have heard, possibly from one of her siblings, that they were planting a kitchen garden. She admitted how sad she was that they had not seen each other for quite some time.

Tatiana's letters are far more stilted than those of her sisters or even her brother. She seemed to have inherited her father's problem with putting her thoughts down on paper. She did not write with the same ease and ability as Olga and Marie.

Meanwhile Nicholas's thoughts turned to his mother on his forty-ninth birthday. He knew that she would inevitably be thinking of him too. On the positive side, he was now able to spend more time with his wife and children. He found it painful not being able to correspond with his mother. The only things he knew of her movements came from newspaper articles which were less than flattering. Although it was a Saturday, it felt more like a Sunday to Nicholas. He had attended the liturgy and spent part of the morning playing with a wooden puzzle. He had worked in the garden on the new vegetable patch where they had begun to build individual beds and later spent the evening reading and simply enjoying precious time with his beloved family.

Tatiana sent word to Olga's close friend Rita on Sunday asking her why she and the other former nurses at the infirmary did not correspond with the former Tsarina. Rita had only corresponded with Olga and Tatiana and not with Alexandra, who nevertheless continued to correspond with her. (It was an awkward situation for Rita who felt unable to say that she and the others felt much of the blame for the revolution lay at Alexandra's feet.)

Nicholas was clearly enjoying the novelty of growing his own food. On Tuesday, he revealed in his journal that they had spent the afternoon working hard in the garden and had even begun to plant some of the vegetables. Tatiana and Anastasia joined in enthusiastically but Marie and, to a lesser extent, Olga were still a little too weak.

According to Klaudia Bitner, a former nurse who was later brought in to teach the children, the family normally rose at eight and had prayers before breakfast. They went out in the garden twice a day. When there were no lessons, Alexandra and her daughters once they had sufficiently recovered stayed inside attending to their sewing, knitting, crochet or embroidery. They never sat idle. On other days the Tsar and his children were more than happy to clear the paths of snow or leaves, or fell trees for firewood. In the evening, Nicholas read aloud from the Russian classics or a British novel.

Olga, who had finished her own education, taught her younger sisters English (along with the Baroness); the Countess taught history to Anastasia; Dr Botkin explained the finer points of Russian literature to Alexei; and Dr Derevenko taught the boy science. Gilliard, of course, continued with French, the now redundant court language. The Tsarina taught religion to the youngest four children. Countess Hendrikova also held art lessons with Tatiana. Later, Olga and Alexandra taught German to Tatiana and Marie. Catherine Schneider, the court reader who had formerly helped Alexandra to learn Russian, had Russian grammar lessons with the four youngest children.

On Saturday, Nicholas went for a stroll with his son in the morning before continuing with the vegetable garden. Later Tatiana and Alexei went boating on the pond. That evening, Nicholas read aloud in French. The book in question was *Le Parfum de la Dame Noir* (The perfume of the lady in black) by Gaston Leroux.

The former Tsar reminisced about his coronation on Sunday the fourteenth. He could scarcely believe how times had changed since the day in 1896 when he had taken his coronation oath. Luckily, the weather was some consolation. He went for an early morning walk with his son before liturgy and spent the afternoon on the pond in canoes and boats in a suitably festive mood. The family later worked on the vegetable plot. They dug some more beds on the Children's Island. Nicholas read in the evening again.

On Monday afternoon, the family returned to the garden to carry on with the vegetable plot. According to Nicholas's journal, the former Tsarina planted vegetables along with her daughters.

The temperature rose to over 90°F in direct sunlight (68 in the shade) on

Wednesday; nevertheless the family chose to spend the day outdoors. Nicholas began the day with a long walk with his son before they returned inside. Nicholas gave Alexei a history lesson. The afternoon was spent gardening, walking and rowing, or simply soaking up the sun next to the pond. Nicholas chose to ride his bicycle later accompanied by his four daughters. It was more like the old days. After dinner, it rained heavily and the new farmer appreciated the live-giving properties of the water on his plants.

Nicholas returned to the garden on the morning of Whit Monday. He went for an early morning walk with his children Olga, Anastasia and Alexei. They dined at noon but again spent much of the afternoon outside. It rained later, and Nicholas enjoyed the beautiful fragrance that came from the garden through the windows and into the palace. He was once again appreciating the simple things in life. It was the anniversary of the start of the Russian offensive by the armies of the south-western front, Nicholas recalled. The former Tsar still had a remarkable memory but it only reminded him of happier times. It was coming to something that such an anniversary should be seen as better than the situation he now found himself in. Nicholas appreciated the time he now had to do as he pleased, but still, at the back of his mind, he worried about what the future would hold. Would he be permitted to remain in the background or would he be put on trial? The constant reminder of the image of Queen Marie-Antoinette on his wife's wall must have weighed heavily on his mind. Would the Tsar end up like the French King had done? In an effort to keep himself away from such thoughts, at least during the day, Nicholas kept as busy as possible and filled every moment with some activity.

At the end of May which was a Wednesday – as if one day was any different to another – Nicholas's thoughts turned to his late father. He had decided to look through Alexander III's papers and that evening Count Benckendorf took off the seal to the cabinet where the paperwork was kept and Nicholas leafed through the pages.

The days turned to weeks and the weeks into months but little changed. On Saturday the third of June, Alexander Kerensky returned to the Alexander Palace without warning. He spoke to Nicholas briefly and asked him to send on papers to the Investigation Committee concerning internal politics. That afternoon Nicholas, assisted by the former lawyer Paul Korovichenko, sorted out his papers and later Colonel Koblinsky assisted the Commandant with the paperwork.

Nicholas returned to the garden and sawed some wood later but there was an unfortunate incident concerning the former Tsarevich. The boy was playing on the Children's Island with his toy gun and the soldiers noticed it and insisted that the officer remove it. It was taken with due solemnity to the guard house despite the fact that it merely a wooden toy. The officers then had to send it to the common hall. The officers were as much the pawns of men from the lower ranks as Nicholas was.

On Monday, Alexandra wrote to her old friend Lili Dehn and confessed that she was happy to hear that a new Commander-in-Chief of the Baltic Fleet, Admiral Rostosov, had been appointed. She hoped that it would be the beginning of better times and hoped that he would restore order. The former Tsarina readily confessed that she could not reconcile herself to the new way of life. She found it hard to understand the new soldiers who were so unlike the brave heroes she had tended in the infirmary.

Nicholas now read the newspapers with tears in his eyes, she added. She admitted that the new guards were an improvement but the men were changed frequently and nothing remained the same for long. The letter would have to go via a trusted friend or it would never arrive at all. There was to be a prayer service that day at noon to celebrate Anastasia's birthday – her sixteenth. She could barely realise where time had gone.

She had resigned herself to fate; what else could she do. Alexandra admitted that she saw it as a trial by God – an examination. She still believed that God was merciful. Now she thanked God for each day that passed without incident. It had been three months since the revolution and yet nothing had altered for the better.

According to Baroness Buxhoeveden, the former Tsarina still thought of her friends despite all that had recently happened. Sophie's mother was seriously ill and Alexandra took it upon herself to ask that, should a telegram arrive concerning the lady, she should be told first so that she could tell the Baroness in person. The expected wire duly arrived on the evening of the former Tsarina's birthday. Alexandra broke the news of the death to the Baroness the following morning.

The former Tsar's thoughts turned to his abdication on Friday. It was now three months since he had arrived at the palace from Mogilev for the final time but he was more concerned about the lack of news from his family than anything else. Nicholas felt they were being treated like convicts but he had not been convicted of any crime. Although it was 97°F in the sun outside and 77°F in the shade he noticed the unmistakable smell of fire in the air outside. (Then, as now, bonfires always seemed to be lit on the hottest days when one desperately needed fresh air and the windows open.)

Nicholas decided to teach his son in the cooler conditions of his study that day. (The small study he spent most of his time in was dark and had little light, but his new study that he very rarely used was a large and airy room effectively on two floors. Alexandra remained inside most of the day as she had a real dislike of heat.) The family went out into the garden that evening. It had cooled down considerably by then. Nicholas walked alone without Alexandra but in the company of his four of his children. Despite his abdication, Nicholas was still fascinated by the progress of the war. He noted in his journal that evening that he had news of the launching of a new offensive on the south-west front. They had broken through enemy lines and had taken many prisoners. The news cheered the former monarch. He was still proudly Russian.

Late on Saturday evening, there was some excitement after a hot and stuffy day when a shot was suddenly heard by the family. Anastasia who was sitting next to an open window had continually covered and uncovered lamps whilst sewing and the reflections had been mistakenly taken as signalling to the outside world. It was quickly realised that it was a mistake. The Tsar had been reading aloud to his wife and daughters whilst they *worked*. The lamps concerned, according to Pierre Gilliard, had green and red shades.

Baroness Buxhoeveden later revealed that there was a suspicion of spies everywhere at the time. She believed that some of the underservants spied on the senior members of the household. The Baroness explained that they had once found a footman kneeling against a door and listening to the conversations inside the room.

That day, the former Tsar's valet Teteryatnikov was replaced by Terenty Chemodurov. In normal circumstances, each of the senior members of the household stayed for a designated period of service and was replaced by another man or woman of the same rank. It is still the same today in Britain for Queen Elizabeth II.

Pierre Gilliard noted in his journal on Thursday that they had by now finished the vegetable garden. They had planted five hundred cabbage plants plus carrots, lettuce, beans, turnips and squash. Each of the servants had been allocated their own plot and had been permitted to grow whatever they wished. All the family assisted in digging the plots of their servants. There was no distinction of rank involved. The Tsar had now begun to fell the dead trees for firewood, which provided the household with fuel for the coming winter and exercise for Nicholas and his children, and the members of the household who chose to join in.

Olga wrote to her former tutor Peter Petrov on Tuesday, the nineteenth. She was delighted to hear of an improvement in his health. He had returned to Tsarskoe Selo after spending some time in the capital. Olga assumed that he had already heard from Gilliard recently. She explained how they now went for a walk in the garden from two until five in the afternoons. The former Tsarina also came outside, as long as there was sufficient air. Alexandra sat out on a sofa under a tree near the pond whilst Nicholas and others went deep into the park in search of trees to fell. Alexei enjoyed playing on the Children's Island and ran around barefoot and, on occasions, went swimming. Mlle Schneider amused herself by continually weeding and watering the flower beds, including the roses, and the former Grand Duchesses often assisted her.

Olga explained that she was now assisting Marie with her English studies and heard Marie read aloud. Sometimes Olga did a dictation, if the weather was not too hot. Twice a week, she and Marie studied Russian history together. They were currently studying folklore heroes. Olga also studied medieval history twice a week with Anastasia from the Alexander Nechvolodov's work entitled *Tales of the Russian Land*. She admitted that her memory was not as it was but she was nevertheless determined to continue her studies. Olga was reading things that she admitted she found boring – the history of art, French history and Russian literature according to Galakhov's illustrated history of Russia.

Meanwhile, Nicholas was in a good mood that day as he had heard news concerning the new military offensive. The Russians had broken through enemy positions and had taken many thousands of prisoners.

There had been a celebration *Te Deum* on Tuesday in the field church for the recent military successes. Gilliard noticed how the former Tsar had proudly given his son a copy of the evening newspaper with the news.

Olga sent word to her aunt Grand Duchess Olga and godmother on Wednesday. She had been touched by her aunt's recent letter and admitted how she regretted not having time for a chat during their last meeting in Kiev. She also revealed that her mother was extremely bored and quite unable to get used to the new regime. Olga hoped that they would all be reunited in the Crimea where the rest of the family were. Olga Nicolaevna regretted greatly that she had not seen Olga's baby son, who was now living the life of an exile with his parents. (He was luckier than his elder cousins as he had a commoner father; the little family were granted a little more freedom.)

Meanwhile Tatiana had written that day to *her* godmother, her father's other sister, the Grand Duchess Xenia. Had Xenia had received the postcard that she had sent? She was delighted to hear that everyone was in good health and that Xenia had been reunited with her six sons. Her father had just received a letter from Xenia before he went out for his walk. She went on to explain that, sadly, some of the Grand Duchesses' usual tutors had been unable to come so both of her parents, the former Tsar and Tsarina of Russia, were their teachers. In the mornings and afternoons, she accompanied her father out into the garden but she also sat with her mother at two for the remainder of the afternoon – some three hours.

Whilst they went out into the park, they often walked in the woods where their father had begun to cut down some of the dead trees for firewood. He was joined by some of their friends and his children in this occupation. They were all thoroughly enjoying working in the kitchen garden and they were now eating the food they had grown themselves. On an evening her father read aloud whilst the rest *worked* or did something else. She added that all four of the sisters had had their heads shaved after they had the measles as their hair had begun to fall out. Hopefully it would thicken up as it regrew.

Pierre Gilliard noted in his journal on Thursday how the four Grand Duchesses had insisted on removing their scarves when having their photograph taken by him. They had all lost a lot of hair since their illness, their heads had been shaved and they were now quite bald. The sisters all removed their scarves simultaneously at Olga's word. They thought it would be amusing to see the look of horror on their parents' faces when the pictures were developed.

Tatiana wrote to her old friend Zinaide Tolstoy on Friday after the sisters each received the most welcome and unexpected gift of an embroidered bag. Tatiana had chosen the blue one decorated with multi-coloured flowers and Olga had picked the blue bag with yellow roses. Marie had decided upon the all yellow bag and Anastasia the one in pink. The bags were proving to be very useful and were a constant reminder of their generous friend. The bag that Zinaide had sent for her mother was used for transporting her book into the garden when she went to sit out. She wondered if her friend's husband read aloud in the evenings, as her father did. They were almost finished with the sixth volume of *The Count of Monte Cristo* by Alexandre Dumas. Did she know the book?

On Sunday morning, Nicholas escorted his son for a walk before the family gathered for the liturgy. Despite the continuous rain showers during the afternoon, Nicholas took his usual walk with his children. The group later felled a fir tree and chopped it up for firewood. Nicholas then watched as members of his much reduced staff cut the grass. The family ambled back to the palace after sitting next to their precious vegetable patch. Nicholas read again that evening.

He was spending more time with his son than he had before the outbreak of the war. They had naturally grown closer in the times they had spent alone at military headquarters.

The peace and tranquillity was ruined on Monday for Nicholas after he learnt from Kobylinsky that, in future, he should not hold his hand out to greet the officers or the sentry. There had been occasions when the man in question had refused to take his hand. The Commandant thought it best to avoid any direct confrontation. It was a sad reflection of the deterioration of civilities. Nicholas, however, had nothing but praise for Colonel Kobylinsky. He was a former veteran of Petrograd Life Guards who had been wounded twice at the front and he remained loyal to the former Tsar.

Nicholas meanwhile resumed his teaching and he gave another geography lesson to his son. Nicholas was someone who had been very well travelled in his younger days. He had not only travelled to Germany, Britain, Finland and Rumania but, in previous years, had travelled to Italy, Denmark, France, Sweden, Japan (where his life almost ended), China, Hong Kong, Java, Thailand (Siam), Vietnam and Singapore.

That day, the woodcutters tackled a huge pine tree near to the orangery fence. The sentries even showed an interest in helping. Nicholas finished reading *The Count of Monte Cristo* that evening. (The book by Alexandre Dumas published in the 1840s was set in France, Italy, islands of the Mediterranean and the Levant in Western Asia. It was set in the years 1815-38. Despite being directly descended from the Emperor Alexander I of Tolstoy's *War and Peace*, set at this time, Nicholas was quite fascinated by the history of his ancestor's greatest rival: Napoleon Bonaparte. Nicholas's daughter Olga was suitably interested in Bonaparte's only son.)

Nicholas suddenly remembered on Tuesday that he had forgotten to write in his journal the previous day of the recent victory. It was a major breakthrough for Russians. Nicholas was still proud of his country even if it was no longer his empire. He was still a Russian through and through.

That afternoon, the four Grand Duchesses collected up the recently mown grass. They were certainly not above doing the most menial of tasks. Nicholas and his helpers cut down two pine trees. The former Tsar and his daughters then spent some time in the orchard before returning for dinner. That evening Nicholas began reading a different story aloud to his family. The book was by a rival of Sir Arthur Conan Doyle, a French writer named Maurice Leblanc concerning the rather brilliant fictional character of *Arsene Lupin*.

Nicholas had more good news on Wednesday. He heard that the Russian army had captured Galich the previous day, with a number of prisoners. He continued his usual routine of a walk and lessons with Alexei. He later cut down a total of three fir trees with his assistants. His daughters were not above *assisting*. Marie had been ill recently but was immensely strong as she had inherited the physical skills of her late grandfather. During the course of the evening Nicholas once more read aloud.

Baroness Buxhoeveden recalled how happy Nicholas had been at the news of the recent great victory. He had always hoped that his personal sacrifice would lead to a victory in the war. She went on to disclose that the former Tsarina and the children were equally delighted.

Nicholas and, later, Alexandra had begun to appreciate Kerensky's patriotism. The former Tsar even admitted that the politician was a man he felt could have been of great use to him as a minister. The former Tsar would never utter a single word of resentment against the members of the provisional government nor did he complain when Kerensky used his private possessions, including Nicholas's car. The former Tsarina even worried about the health of Kerensky and sincerely hoped it would not break down before things were put right in Russia.

The former Tsar began to worry at the beginning of July about the chaos taking place in the capital. He had spent Wednesday as usual in the park but his journal revealed his fears for Petrograd. Nicholas had heard reports of disorder and shootings and was concerned that many soldiers and sailors had arrived in Kronstadt with the express purpose of overthrowing the current regime.

Nicholas was in a calmer mood on Thursday. He was greatly relieved to learn that most of the troops had chosen to remain loyal to the provisional government in the capital. Order had been restored. The weather was delightful and Nicholas took a pleasant walk in the company of Tatiana and his friend *Valia*. During the course of the day Nicholas and his merry band of helpers managed to cut down four trees. That evening he began a new book entitled *Tartarin de Tarascon* by the French author Alphonse Daudet.

Nicholas went for a walk on Friday accompanied by a recently recovered Marie and *Valia*, and the entire escort of the guards of the 3rd Rifle Regiment. (It is fairly obvious that it was his daughter who was the attraction.) That evening he glued photographs taken since the revolution into an album. It inevitably included ones of his daughters with no hair. All the pictures were taken in the garden and showed the former Imperial family working the land.

On Saturday morning Nicholas walked in the garden accompanied by his daughters Tatiana and Marie. He was delighted to note in his journal that evening that the men of the 4th and 5th Rifle Regiments had chosen not to follow the family during their walk. He noted some governmental changes. Prince Lvov was no longer Prime Minister. He had been replaced by Kerensky. The new leader had also retained his posts as Minister of War and Navy. He was also in charge of the Ministry of Commerce and Industry. Nicholas was convinced that he was the right man for the job – all of them. The more power he had, the better.

On fine days Alexandra came out into the garden and sat herself on a rug close to the pond under the shade of one of the trees. Once she was sitting enjoying the sun with Baroness Buxhoeveden. When the lady suddenly rose briefly in order to go elsewhere, a soldier of the guard decided to sit next to the former Tsarina. Alexandra instinctively moved away a little but the man chose to question her. He began by asking her why she failed to travel around the country and was so seldom seen in public. She calmly explained about her ill health and gradually the man warmed to her to his surprise. He then asked her about her German origins but she replied that although she had been German in her youth she had married a Russian and was proudly patriotic of her adopted homeland. The two then began to discuss religion calmly when the Baroness arrived back with an officer, thoroughly expecting trouble. The soldier politely took his leave of the former Tsarina and admitted that he had been quite mistaken in his thoughts of her character.

On Tuesday, the Grand Duchesses' former tutor Petrov replied to a recent letter from Olga. He sent word in remembrance of her name's day on the eleventh of July. He had posted it the day before so it may well have been delayed in the post, which was less than reliable.

He explained that if the good fairies from the storybooks really did exist, he would ask them to wish her all the best wishes. Petrov confessed that he was not a fairy but, nevertheless, wished her all the best he could. (The reference to the fairies indicates that the Grand Duchesses were obviously fascinated in the fairies or why else would a grown man mention them. The two oldest sisters would indeed take books about elves and goblins to Siberia which is remarkable considering they were both in their early twenties. On the wall behind Olga's bed at the palace later photographs show a picture of a winged figure with a child, a fairy or an angel. The Grand Duchesses had after all spoken with Nicholas some years previously about the famous *Angel of Mons* story where a large group of soldiers all claimed to have seen the figures of three angels above the battlefield.)

Nicholas heard on Tuesday of a possible move south, hopefully to the Crimea. He noted in his journal that evening that Kerensky had again appeared and during the course of their conversation it had become clear that he thought the family should be moved for their own safety. That morning Nicholas had gone for his usual walk, on this occasion accompanied by his young son. There had also been a religious service in honour of Olga's name's day. Nicholas returned to the park later to cut down more trees and noted that they had cut down some seventy trees so far.

The former Tsar had just finished reading the third part of *Dmitri Merezhkovsky's Trilogy of Peter* (the Great). Although he readily admitted that it was well written he found it painful reading.

In his journal on Thursday night, Nicholas noted regretfully that many of the Russian troops were now deserting and refusing to fight the Germans and Austrians. Many of the units had been affected by the propaganda, and the enemy had naturally taken advantage of the situation. As a former soldier himself, Nicholas found this particularly upsetting and humiliating. He also heard that the death penalty had been reinstated. As Nicholas was expecting to be moved soon he had begun collecting up his precious books and other items to take into exile.

Nicholas remembered the start of the war on Wednesday the nineteenth – exactly three years previously. It felt like a whole lifetime to the former Tsar. He hoped that God would help save his precious Russia. It had been a very hot day and once again on his regular walk that morning Nicholas was accompanied by his daughters Tatiana, Marie and Anastasia and, again, a whole convoy of men made up from the 3rd Rifle Regiment decided to join them. Despite the heat, Nicholas felled more trees and finished off the ones they had begun earlier. He decided to read another of Merezhkovsky's works a novel on the Emperor Alexander I.

Nicholas went out into the garden with his children for an hour on Friday morning and, after tea, he finished the first volume of his ancestor Alexander I. He had hoped that Kerensky may have turned up as Nicholas wanted to know once and for all where and when they would leave the Alexander Palace. Marie received some gifts after supper in honour of her name's day. The former Tsarina presented her with a gold bracelet with a green heart-shaped stone. The bracelet was one of Alexandra's own. She had no new gems to give her daughter.

Nicholas noted in his daily journal on Tuesday that a new government had been formed. It differed little from the previous provisional government as Kerensky remained as leader. Nicholas had spent the day cutting down four fir trees and had then gone indoors to read. He finished the book he had begun earlier on Alexander I.

The former Tsar heard via Count Benckendorf on Friday that the new government was not intending to send the family to the Crimea as had been hoped but somewhere remote in the east. He had no idea where but he still counted on a stay in the Crimea. Nicholas's mother and sisters were there after all, so it seemed possible. Nicholas spent much of the day cutting down a large fir tree and later read another of Sir Arthur Conan Doyle's well known Sherlock Holmes stories *A Study in Scarlet* aloud to his family.

Saturday proved to be a beautiful yet humid day and that morning Nicholas walked towards the greenhouses and spotted a guard sleeping on the grass. The non-commissioned officer who escorted Nicholas went up to the man and removed his rifle. That day, Nicholas and his assistants managed to fell nine trees and cut up a fir tree.

Alexei received presents that evening on the eve of his thirteenth birthday. Nicholas had by now finished his packing including many books and the rooms had begun to look rather empty. Only the pictures remained on the walls.

It was the birthday of the former heir on the thirtieth. The icon was brought that morning from the *Church of the Sign* and the family prayed in front of her image. Later, Nicholas and his party went out into the garden where they continued cutting up trees.

Alexandra had chosen to send word to her friend Lili Dehn that day to thank her for the letter she had sent recently and apologised for not replying sooner. The Commandant had to read through all letters that were sent out and he was very busy, she revealed. Alexandra confessed, suprisingly, that she had been pleased to have made his acquaintance. She understood that Dr Botkin had recently managed to see Lili. She was delighted that he had been able to do so. She was unable to explain where she was going but cleverly hinted at the trip Lili (and Anya) had made the previous year to Tobolsk.

Alexandra complained of her heart and head and admitted that she was struggling to sleep. On the positive side the icon had been brought from the *Church of the Sign* in honour of her son's birthday. After Alix had sent her best wishes and kisses to Lili and her son, Nicholas added his kindest regards. Olga added her thanks for the little icons Madame Dehn had sent and asked if Rita could write to an old friend, Colonel Syroboyarski, as Alexandra had done. She also added that she remembered *Faith, Hope and Love*. Alexei also thanked Lili for her congratulations on his birthday, and Olga repeated her thanks for the postcard and icon she had received.

(An icon of *Faith, hope and love* had been placed on the wall of the young Tsarevich's bedroom at the Alexander Palace when he was a baby. Faith, Hope and Love aged twelve, ten and nine or in Russian *Vyara, Nadazhda and Lyubov* were the daughters of St Sophia the Martyr, a very important saint in the Eastern Orthodox Church from the time of Hadrian. The sisters named after the virtues and mentioned by St Paul in the *Corinthians* were murdered one after the other, and their mother died three days later. The irony of the three murdered sisters was remarkable when one considers later events in Russia.)

The former Tsarina also chose to write to her friend Anya but it was more difficult to get letters to Madame Vyrubova who was in and out of prison, and it was smuggled out later.

Alexandra admitted that her heart was too full to write and she was struggling to know what to say. She again hinted that they were due to be sent to Tobolsk and revealed that she had prayed for Anya when the icon had been brought from the *Church of the Sign*. She knew how much Anya had suffered and that she was imprisoned in far worse conditions than she was at the time. Alexandra also enclosed a box containing Madame Vyrubova's jewels which she had been looking after.

Nicholas's brother Michael suddenly appeared the next evening accompanied by Kerensky. It was an awkward meeting and the two hardly knew what to say to each other. Later, the guards began moving the family's luggage into the hall. The family and the servants sat around waiting to move as the departure was continually delayed. Alexei was so tired that he had gone back to bed on occasions but was unable to sleep.

The family and their party left at dawn on the first of August and they left under heavy guard in two cars to the railway station. The group included General Ilya Leonidovich Tatischev (the Tsar's aide-de-camp), Vasily Alexandrovich Dolgorukov (the Marshal of the Court), Pierre Gilliard (Alexei's French tutor), Sydney Gibbes (the children's English tutor), Dr Eugene Sergeyevich Botkin (the Court physician), Countess Anastasia Hendrikova (the Tsarina's personal lady-in-waiting), Catherine Schneider (the Court reader), Baroness Sophie Buxhoeveden (the Tsarina's lady-in-waiting), Anna Stepanova Demidova (a parlour maid), Elisabeth Ersberg (a former nanny of the children), Ivan Sednev (the children's servant), Klementy Nagorny (Alexei's companion), Ivan Kharitonov (the cook) and Alexei Volkov (a valet). There were also servers, scribes, hairdressers, lackeys, a wardrobe attendant and a wine servant.

Count Benckendorf had been told by Kerensky that there were going to be elections in November 1917 to the Constituent Assembly and it was quite possible that a future government might free Nicholas. It did not happen unfortunately.

Chapter Twenty

Tobolsk Summer 1917

Soon after the Tsar and his family left the Alexander Palace, Lukomsky ordered that all the drawers and cupboards in the palace be sealed along with some forty doors. The contents of each of the rooms were photographed for posterity and even the calendars were kept to the date of the Tsar's departure for Siberia.

Alexandra and her daughters were rumoured to have taken with them millions of roubles worth of jewels. The family took the things they felt they could not do without, including lamps, carpets, photograph albums, a gramophone player, the children's own nickel-plated camp beds (the children had slept on these all their lives and they were moved from palace to palace), various books, clocks, religious icons, silverware including various teapots, sugar basins, jugs, spoons etc, even a small basket for visiting cards and, obviously, clothes and food. The children brought their pet dogs but the cats unfortunately had to remain behind.

Amongst the clothes the former Imperial family chose to take with them were Alexandra's black coat, Nicholas's khaki shirts and forage cap, boots, his silver cross of St George, an ordinary soldier's shirt belt with a brass buckle and the wide trousers he usually wore with a crimson stripe. Alexei took his soldier's greatcoat with epaulettes, lance-corporal stripes and his forage cap. The sisters took navy travelling suits, plus various skirts, blouses and their woollen cardigans and hats. They all took clothes suitable for hot or cold weather. If they were going to Siberia, it was not always cold as many believed as the summers could actually be stiflingly hot. Nicholas had briefly visited the area after his trip to the Far East.

The family were transferred to a sleeping car on the train. Alexandra was physically helped aboard the train by Colonel Artabolevsky. Although it was very hot, stuffy and even dusty, Nicholas managed to get to sleep for a few hours. Later in the day, Nicholas and his children disembarked and had a walk with their guards, the riflemen, and they picked flowers and berries. The meals were taken in the train's own restaurant.

Anastasia wrote of the journey in a composition some months later for her English tutor Sydney Gibbes who arrived to rejoin the family in October. She wrote in English in the form of a letter with copious spelling mistakes. She began by explaining that they had begun the journey early in the morning and, once they got onto the train, the former Grand Duchess and the others all fell asleep. They were all exhausted having not slept at all the previous night.

It was very hot and dusty onboard the train and they were forced to keep their curtains or blinds closed as they passed through the stations. Once, late in the day, she was looking out of the window and they stopped close to a small house. As there was no station there, they had been permitted to look out. A little boy had come close to Anastasia and asked her if she had a newspaper. The child called her *uncle* which confused her. She explained that she was an *auntie* and had no newspaper. She was initially baffled as to why the boy had thought she was male but then suddenly recalled that she had very short hair. The soldiers thought it was very amusing. (The sisters normally wore scarves over their shorn hair but probably had taken them off due to the heat in the carriage.)

A routine was quickly established on the train; morning coffee was served at ten and lunch was taken at one. Nicholas and his daughters ate in the restaurant but Alexandra chose to remain her compartment with her son. Tea was served at five. The family had a walk each evening after the train made a brief stop along with the family dogs. Dinner was served at eight as it had been at home and, once more, the family split into the same two groups; Alexandra always ate with her son. As the train crossed the Ural Mountains into Siberia, the air became much cooler. The forests became deeper, the rivers wider and the fields seemingly endless.

According to Baroness Buxhoeveden, the former Tsarina was greatly disappointed that she had not been able to go to Livadia as she had hoped. Alexandra attempted to remain positive and tried to see as a good sign the fact they were travelling towards Tobolsk where Lili and Anya had gone a year previously. Nicholas had to keep away from the engine lest the driver recognised him. It had been decked out as a Japanese Red Cross train in an effort to avoid confrontation with the locals.

The young Grand Duchesses, after their initial disappointment at leaving their home, began to take a great interest in their new surroundings. The men had been chosen by Colonel Kobylinsky as being the most reasonable and they chatted amiably with the children and, on one occasion when the group picked cornflowers, they were presented to Alexandra.

However Nicholas complained bitterly in his journal on Wednesday about the Commandant's request that they keep their curtains drawn at each of the stations. That afternoon, Nicholas and his children had their half-hour walk with the dogs at *Svecha*.

Meanwhile Sydney Gibbes, who had been refused permission to join the former Imperial family, visited Alexandra's close friend Anya Vyrubova. He took a close-up photograph of the lady so he could take it to Alexandra later. He was still hoping that he would be given permission to go to Tobolsk. He was able to join the family later.

The train passed through Rasputin's home village of Pokrovskoe on Thursday and all the family gazed upon his house. The two-storey house was easy to spot amongst the simple huts in the village. As they passed the village, Alexei Volkov overheard Alexandra talking tearfully about Rasputin who had predicted that she would see it eventually. Nicholas and his children had their by now traditional early evening walk at Perm.

Nicholas noted on Friday that it was getting cooler. Early in the morning, they passed Ekaterinburg (the place where the family would ultimately go after Tobolsk). They eventually arrived at Tyumen late that evening. It had been deliberately timed so that no one was around and the party then transferred to one of three steamboats as there was no railtrack to Tobolsk. Nicholas and his family were housed aboard the *Rus*. It took most of the night to load the luggage from the train to the boat. Nicholas was concerned that his son had another late night as he normally went to bed a great deal earlier. The other members of the party followed behind along with much of the luggage on the *Kormilets* and the *Tyumen*. The convoy left at three in the afternoon after Nicholas and his children had stretched their legs at the Kosmakova landing.

The journey to Tobolsk continued by boat on Saturday and the group ate aboard and took their daily walk in the morning at Trakhtair. The convoy of steamboats duly arrived at Tobolsk wharf at four thirty. The house that had been assigned to the family was not ready unfortunately which meant they were forced to live on the boats for longer than expected.

As they landed, the Commissar, the Commandant and *Valia* went off to inspect the house intended for use. Nicholas was informed later by *Valia* that the Governor's house was unfurnished and dirty. It had been used as a military barracks in recent times rather than a home. It had to be repainted and cleaned. The luggage had already been taken off and had to be returned to the steamboats temporarily. Nicholas noted in his journal that evening that he had joked how it had not been possible just to arrange him lodgings. It did not seem a great imposition.

The family lived aboard the *Rus* until the Governor's House was ready for them. Meanwhile they went for extended walks along the river bank and on short boat trips. It reminded Nicholas and his family of the journey they had made in 1913 along the River Volga. They gained the illusion of freedom for once.

The town of Tobolsk looked impressive at first sight and most the town had been built on the high points of the river where the River Tobol joins the Irtysh. The pretty domed churches were a comforting image to the family. The Archbishop Hermogen had offered his own residence for the former Imperial family, a generous thought considering how he had been treated after admitting his opposition to Rasputin. The house had its own garden and even a private chapel, but sadly the rooms were not suitable so it was declined with thanks.

Monday and Tuesday were spent again aboard the steamboat, and Nicholas and his children walked along the river bank in the afternoons. They had a boat trip along the River Tobol during the mornings.

Nicholas and his children, in particular, were enjoying the boat trips and it reminded them of time spent on their own yacht. On Tuesday evening Nicholas noted that they travelled up the River Irtysh for about six miles (or ten versts) and, after landing on the right bank, the family went for another walk. They climbed a high bank and enjoyed the beauty of the scenery. Alexandra, never one to even go so far as her own garden at the Alexander Palace, remained on the steamboat.

The *cruise* continued on Wednesday and there was a boat trip along the same route during the early afternoon followed by a half-hour walk for Nicholas and his children.

Unfortunately bad weather on Thursday prevented any further trips.

That same day Anastasia had written to a friend Vera G Kapralova and explained how they were now living aboard a steamboat as the house intended for their use was not quite ready. It was the first wet day on the trip. Marie was having a lie down as she had caught a cold but she was improving, however. (Marie had only fairly recently recovered from the measles and double pneumonia so her immune system would have been weakened by the prolonged illness.)

Anastasia urged her friend not to forget them. It was a constant fear for all the family that their former friends, especially those they had made recently at the infirmaries, would forget them – as if they ever could. It was more of a case that the *friends* concerned were too terrified to write to the former Grand Duchesses. On the other hand, no one actually wanted to stay in contact with the former Tsarina.

It is sometimes said that the Grand Duchesses *chose* to accompany their parents into exile but, after all, where else could they go? Even had they been able to, they would probably not have wanted to stay with their grandmother as they were never particularly close. The only possible exception may have been their father's youngest sister Olga Alexandrovna whom they knew very well. However, they were never given the choice.

The family enjoyed the same boat trip excursion to the River Tobol on Friday. Nicholas and three of his daughters enjoyed a walk but Marie and Alexei remained onboard with their mother.

The former Tsar's sister Xenia noted in her journal on Saturday remarks she had recently heard from her relatives about Nicholas and his immediate family. Xenia had heard her brother spoken of as a real saint who took everything with such patience. Olga, she revealed, was now very nervous and Nicholas much the same. Marie was quite unable to get over the events she had seen that spring. The Dowager Empress,, it appears, had received letters from her sons Nicholas and Michael and another from Tatiana. (A great many of the letters they sent had disappeared. Alexandra and her daughters often complained that they failed to receive letters and parcels they had expected. The contents of the boxes they had been sent were often missing, especially if they were items of food.)

The house was finally ready for the family and they left the *Rus* early on Sunday morning. Alexandra was taken by carriage to the Governor's House, accompanied by Tatiana. Nicholas along with Olga, Marie, Anastasia and Alexei walked to the house which was sited on the newly named Liberty Street in the centre of town.

That evening, however, Nicholas's spirits were low and, in his journal, he revealed his disappointment. They had been allocated rooms on the first floor. The family visited the rooms downstairs where the dining room was situated and the household were to be lodged and the house opposite where other members of the staff were housed. It would be their only visit to Kornilov House. They were also given a tour of the kitchen and guard house. The former Tsar was not impressed with the small orchard and rather ugly kitchen garden. Nicholas placed his few treasured possessions in the study and the dressing room he now shared with his son. There was also a half-cellar where the family's other possessions were housed in cases. The house had been furnished by local people but Nicholas and his family personalised it with their own pictures, lamps, etc. One trunk that was stored in the cellar contained Nicholas's old photograph albums.

He had also brought an old suitcase containing his old journals and letters.

Although compared to the opulence of the Winter Palace and even the Catherine Palace, the Alexander Palace had been fairly small, still the Governor's House felt cramped to Nicholas. He was used to a large park where he could walk but now he was restricted to a tiny garden. The house was a white-painted building containing two storeys with balconies on the ends of the second floor. These would be used by Alexandra who was used to sitting out on her balcony at home but these balconies were not enclosed like the one she usually sat on and yet had the benefit of being off the ground.

The house had a large compound and it contained several outbuildings, a greenhouse, a woodshed and a barn. A balcony of sorts was later built on the roof of the greenhouse, and Nicholas and his daughters spent many hours sitting up there. The town had some 20,000 residents and it contained dusty, unpaved streets, log houses, some stone buildings, a few ornate villas and, of course, a church. A wooden fence was erected around the house and a small section of the side street was included for extra space.

According to Sydney Gibbes, who arrived later, Nicholas quickly became bored in the confined space of the small garden. During his leisure time, Nicholas walked up and down the small yard forty or even fifty times in an hour and felt like a caged animal in a zoo. He began to saw logs again when given the opportunity. The garden became extremely muddy after rain and contained neither trees nor bushes. The only greenery was in the form of cabbages.

There had been talk at first of the four Grand Duchesses being given some liberty but, in the end, it came to nothing. They were not under arrest and had joined their parents willingly, as had members of the household. According to Baroness Buxhoeveden, Eugene Kobylinsky had even hoped at one time that Nicholas might be able to go shooting once things were settled. Again, it never happened. The former Imperial family would only be permitted to leave the compound under armed guard. The only place they were permitted to go (and that stopped later) was the local Russian Orthodox Church on Sundays and holidays.

Marie, on the other hand, quickly made herself at home and learned the names of all the soldiers and their wives and children. Nicholas and his wife shared a bedroom, Alexei had a room to himself as the only boy, and the four sisters shared a corner room. Klementy Nagorny was given a room close to Alexei's. Gilliard slept in the large drawing room downstairs whilst the rest lived in the house opposite named Kornilov House. Nicholas was allocated a study and Alexandra a drawing room. The large hall in the Governor's residence was later turned into a small chapel with icons and lamps.

Monsieur Gilliard was amongst those who lived at the Governor's House along with Countess Hendrikova and Catherine Schneider. They all ate with the family and were able to wander back and forth to the house opposite – for now.

Nicholas retrieved his old photographs of the cruise he had taken in his youth on Monday. The recent steamboat trips had brought back memories of the cruise on the *Memory of Azov* with his brother George and cousin Prince George of Greece in 1890-1891. He spent all day sorting out the old pictures and reminiscing. The past is a safe place.

Within three days of their arrival, Alexei's spaniel Joy was bitten by a local snake but luckily he quickly recovered. He along with Tatiana's French bulldog Ortipo relished visiting the rubbish heap in the yard and eating as much as they could. Anastasia's little dog Jemmy, who had been given to her by Anya not long before, was more refined and stayed indoors sedately with her mistress.

Nicholas spent much of Wednesday on the balcony, sunbathing with his entire family. It was yet again a reminder of the old days and they took breakfast there. It also had a good view of the surrounding area – something Alexandra's closed balcony at the palace did not have. Many years later, a local resident at the time recalled seeing the family on the balcony. He noticed the girls all had short hair and assumed it was the new fashion – it was, but not until the 1920s.

Dr Vladimir Derevenko and his family arrived on Thursday to Nicholas's delight. The doctor was an old and trusted friend and his young son Kolya was Alexei's close friend. Olga's friend Rita also appeared. She had come from the capital, and spent some time with Countess Hendrikova. She had foolishly brought a collection of letters hidden in a cushion. These were found and the Countess's room searched later.

The former Imperial family spent an hour in the garden on Friday, and they returned in the afternoon for a further couple of hours. Nicholas set up a trapeze or exercise bar for himself, similar to one he had at the palace. Meanwhile, the Countess was still having problems and was punished for Rita's actions by being restricted to the Governor's House for several days. Rita had been ordered back and went by evening steamboat.

Rita was taken back to the capital and interrogated about a Cossack organisation. No evidence of anything was found and she did not betray Anya Vyrubova whom it appears had sent her. Anya was deported to Finland and then rearrested. Her mother bravely spoke to Leon Trotsky and, as a result, Anya was again released. Meanwhile, the former Tsar amused himself by sawing wood with Prince Dolgorukov or General Tatishchev or anyone else who cared to join in.

Nicholas felt frustrated on Tuesday that he was unable to go further afield on his daily walk on such a beautiful day. He had been accustomed to a great deal of space in the park at the Alexander Palace. It would have been pleasant to have been able to walk alongside the river as they had done previously. They simply read on one of the balconies instead.

Nicholas noted in his journal on Wednesday that it was now a full two years since he had arrived for the first time at Mogilev as Commander-in-Chief of the armed forces. Now he had no power at all.

Nicholas's frustration was evident on Friday evening when he admitted how tedious he was finding his walks in the tiny garden of the Governor's House. The small garden made it all the more prison-like. It felt quite different than the Alexander Palace to Nicholas, as obviously it was far smaller and, as a result, made the conditions feel even more irritating.

At the beginning of September, a new Commissar Vassily Pankratov arrived at the Governor's House with his surly assistant Alexander Nikolsky. The latter made a poor impression on the former Tsar who thought he looked very untidy and unkempt.

He was to be the censor of the family's letters to their relatives and friends.

Unfortunately there were problems with the plumbing at the Governor's House and the downstairs water closet overflowed with waste from the ones on the floor above. As a result the family had to stop using them and the baths for a while. Nicholas asked Dr Botkin to draw the attention of the Commissar to the impossible situation and he was duly shocked. As the house had initially been altered to include bathrooms, it was obvious that the septic pits were too small. No one was in a rush to clean them.

Meanwhile Nicholas continued to take an interest in the politics of Russia. On Tuesday, he remarked in his journal that wires arrived twice a day at the Governor's House but they were rather ambiguous. The government appeared to Nicholas to be in something of a muddle. General Kornilov, it appeared, was under arrest.

Meanwhile, Alexandra was worried about her friend Anya Vyrubova. Despite the fact that she had in recent years continually complained about Madame Vyrubova, Alexandra now appreciated her true loyalty. She was one of the few who remained friends with Alexandra and had suffered greatly for her friendship. She had been treated very harshly.

On Thursday, she noted in her journal that she had heard that Anya was now on her way to Sweden. She had been seized at Helsingfors and was now imprisoned on the former Imperial yacht the *Polar Star*. It was quite ironic as in previous years Anya had been a guest on that yacht as she had on the other yacht the *Standart*.

The family were permitted to attend the local Russian Orthodox Church on Friday, the eighth. It was their first visit to the Church of the Annunciation but the experience was spoiled by the presence of crowds of fascinated onlookers close to the entrance.

The weather continued to be extremely warm. Nicholas was amazed how pleasant it was for the time of year. On the afternoon of Monday the eighteenth, Nicholas played *gorodki* (a type of skittles) with *Valia*. He had not played it in years. Olga had been unwell recently, possibly due to the inadequate plumbing, but she was now improving and sat on the balcony in the sun with Alexandra that day.

Nicholas was delighted when a former palace official, Baron Bode, arrived on Friday with a parcel of household items from the palace and some of their personal items. It was like Christmas all over again. That morning it had even snowed quite heavily but it had melted away by the end of the day.

The simple arrival of some crates of wine belonging to the former Tsar caused uproar over the next few days according to Nicholas's journal on Saturday night. When the soldiers heard, they were incensed. They insisted on the destruction of all the bottles stored at Kornilov House. It was eventually decided to pour it away in the river. Nicholas and his family watched as that evening the wine was taken away in a cart. The Commissar positioned himself next to the wine, armed with an axe. He was followed by a whole convoy of armed riflemen. (It was rather out of proportion and like a scene from a farce.)

Pankratov continued his petty, one-sided squabble against Nicholas. On the twenty-ninth, the former Tsar learned via Dr Botkin that Kerensky had allowed them to go on trips outside the town. Unfortunately Pankratov decided that they could not go for security reasons. Nicholas did not believe a word of it. The family were indignant but helpless to do anything. That day, Nicholas finished reading *Ramuntcho*, a love and adventure story by Pierre Loti. It concerned contraband runners in the Basque province of France which presumably had been read to the family whilst the *illegal* contraband wine was being taken away.

Nikolsky insisted that the former Imperial family be photographed – like criminals. It was now their turn, he explained, as he had been forced to have his photograph taken in former years, and everyone now had to have their own identity card containing a photograph. The restrictions on Nicholas and his family worsened under the new regime. Dr Botkin's two youngest children, Tatiana and Gleb, arrived in the town, and the former Tsarina hoped the two would be company for her own children as the *Doctor* was already living with the former Imperial couple and their five children. The two children were, however, refused permission to enter the house.

Many years later, Gleb recalled that, on their arrival, Alexandra had asked Pankratov to allow him and Tatiana to study with the Grand Duchesses but Pankratov had refused to even consider the suggestion. Gleb was a year older than Anastasia, and Tatiana Botkin nearer the age of the elder Grand Duchesses. The only way the former Grand Duchesses and their brother could communicate with Gleb and Tatiana was via the windows. They could wave to each other and send little messages via the *Doctor*. In the years that the two families had known each other, the usual form of communication had always been via their father; he was one of the few still able to come and go.

Gleb drew his cartoon animal pictures for Marie, Anastasia and Alexei. The drawings were elaborate ones showing various animals dressed up as real people. They wore regimental uniforms and the depictions were so accurate that even Nicholas was impressed. The animals had now passed through the revolution and Gleb did a series of the illustrations which actually mocked the new authorities. The monarchist figures that he depicted were more active than reality and he depicted the new government as monkeys. Gleb had the storyteller's ability to end the stories as he pleased, and the monkeys invariably came to a sticky end. Nicholas was impressed by the uniforms and informed Gleb, via the *Doctor*, of his approval of the new designs.

Gleb also found that he had something in common with Olga. They both shared a great love of poetry. Olga became very interested in his verses and he sent the work to her. She helped the boy by giving him advice and exchanging opinions about the rhymes and rhythms of the pieces. Previously, Gleb had little connection with the eldest Grand Duchess but now they shared a common passion. Gleb Botkin had not seen his friends for several months and noticed instantly that Anastasia had recently put on weight. She had replaced Marie as the overweight member of the family. Since her illness, Marie had become much thinner. Despite everything that had happened in the past six months or so, Gleb still recognised Anastasia as the same boisterous and lively girl she had always been. She had the gift of brightening any situation.

Chapter Twenty-one

Tobolsk Winter 1917

The former Tsar's daughters and wife frequently sent word to their friends and relations but Nicholas chose not to. He rarely wrote to anyone except his own closest relatives and usually merely added a few words to a letter by Alexandra. He had never been a natural writer and, now he no longer had the need to spend all day at his desk, he preferred to enjoy every waking moment outside, if at all possible. The letters that the ladies wrote appear to have often gone astray, and the ones posted to them also vanished. It was often months before they received letters. As October began, the weather changed. Despite the intense heat, the leaves on the trees began to fall.

On Monday, Tatiana sent word to an old friend Zinaide Tolstoy. She had received a letter from the lady some time before but had only just got around to the reply. Tatiana was not the greatest communicator but now even her letters began to improve. There was little to do, so she described what had happened. Madame Tolstoy had written at the end of August but a combination of the tardy post and Tatiana's reluctance to reply meant the answer came rather later than expected. Tatiana admitted that she often thought of her friend and sincerely hoped she was in good health. Tatiana explained that the Governor's House was not large yet it was comfortable enough. They had a balcony to sit out on and a small garden situated behind the kitchen. It had a vegetable plot in the middle and was so small that it took but three minutes to walk around. They spent their leisure time walking to and fro in the tiny plot.

There was a wooden fence surrounding the yard and, despite having several large holes in it, it performed its purpose. (It kept them in.) The windows of the family's rooms gave them ample opportunity to see the people go by in the streets. It was their one real distraction. The former Imperial family were confined to one place and they watched the free people go about their everyday business. The only real consolation to the family was to visit the nearby church. They were permitted to attend on certain occasions but services were often held in the large hall at the Governor's House. They had a splendid view over the mountains from the windows and could see the cathedral and the city. Unfortunately, they were unable to see the river.

The family had little to do. The children passed their time by *working,* reading or playing the piano. They went out for walks in the small garden and attended lessons. Tatiana wondered how her friend was passing her time. She wondered if Zinaide's husband would be able to write. She explained that letters to her had to go via the

Commissioner Pankratov. (All letters were read before they were given to the family.)

Tatiana also took the opportunity to write to Princess Nadezhda that same day but wrote a remarkably similar letter. She confirmed that everyone was all right and, although the house was small, it was quite cosy. The garden was so small that one was able to walk through it in a matter of minutes. They were having religious services in the house, she explained, but it was not the same as actually going to church.

That same evening, Nicholas explained in his journal that now their staff were permitted only to take walks in the neighbourhood when accompanied by one of the riflemen guards.

Sydney Gibbes finally arrived as the Indian summer ended and came equipped with a huge pile of books, much to the delight of Nicholas. The former Tsar noted in his journal on Saturday evening that, on his arrival, Gibbes had told them many interesting things about life in the capital. Once again, Nicholas's lack of description is frustrating.

Gibbes had been unable to arrive any sooner due to a series of railway strikes. He told Nicholas of vigilantes, drunken soldiers and violent strikers. It was obvious that the new government was struggling to maintain order. Gibbes was allotted a room at Kornilov House.

Gilliard had refused to share with his English colleague as the two men did not get on. Gibbes had refused to live anywhere without the services of his maid Anfisa. The two were later allotted their own lean-to apartment close to the kitchens. The Grand Duchesses were much amused by his insistence on having his personal maid. It was almost certainly for her hygiene skills and domestic abilities as Gibbes was known to be especially keen on cleanliness. He was probably one of the few men who was known to travel everywhere with his own personal porcelain sink.

The Englishman later recalled that Nicholas had been delighted to see him and hear news of the outside world yet failed to understand why the British press were so hostile to him. At first, he seemed to blame Gibbes personally. He quite understood the hostility of the revolutionaries in his own country but was devastated by the reaction of Britain. They had, after all, been Russia's allies in the war and his own cousin George V was king.

The three youngest children now resumed regular lessons which helped to maintain a sense of normality. They had been taught previously by Nicholas and members of the suite including Countess Hendrikova, Baroness Buxhoeveden and Dr Botkin. Now that Gibbes had returned, the usual routine was re-established. A former teacher and nurse Klaudia Bitner also arrived to assist with the teaching of Russian and mathematics to the sisters. The children's lessons began punctually at nine in the morning and stopped for an hour at eleven. They then escorted Nicholas in his daily walk in the tiny garden as they had done in the past – but now the space was restricted. The lessons were taken in the large hall as there was obviously no schoolroom at the Governor's House. Alexei was taught either in his own bedroom or Gilliard's room.

The family and members of the household who lived on the ground floor including Gilliard assembled in the downstairs dining room at one. Alexandra, however, ate in her own room with her son. Nicholas, his children and members of the household went out into the garden again at two o'clock for a couple of hours. Lessons were resumed for the younger children for a further two hours. The household were invited to spend the evening with Nicholas and his family in the large hall. They played various games including bezique to while away the hours. When it became very cold, the group reassembled in Alexandra's drawing room. Nicholas read aloud whilst the ladies *worked*. Alexandra often played bezique with General Tatichchev before she returned to her needlework, or simply sat quietly in her armchair. Alexandra's comfortable drawing room was in a way the equivalent of the *Mauve Boudoir* but naturally in vastly reduced circumstances. She kept her treasures around her and her precious pictures on the walls.

Baroness Buxhoeveden, who had previously taught English to Alexei before the arrival of Gibbes in October, had been impressed by the boy's manner. He was immensely polite and greatly appreciated the time she took over his lessons. She later recalled that the former Tsarevich thanked her after each lesson. In a clever imitation of his father, he extended his hand and smiled and told the lady that it was very nice of her to teach him. The Baroness knew that he felt some sort of obligation towards her as she was not one of his regular teachers. He even worked especially hard, she revealed, as he knew that she had made an effort to provide him with lessons. He felt he owed her that at least.

Klaudia Bitner was shocked how little the younger children knew of Russian literature. They had read very little of the classical writers such as Pushkin and Lermontov. They had not even heard of Nekrasov or any of the others. Alexei, she revealed, had little understanding of geography and little mathematical knowledge. Klaudia read the children Nikolai Nekrasov's narrative poems *Russian Women* and *Red-Nosed Frost*. Marie and Anastasia were enchanted and wondered why no one had ever told them about the poet. It was not only the young sisters who enjoyed the poems; the former monarchs came to hear her speak as well. Olga, of course, was well versed in poetry and read widely but her sisters were not so well read. Luckily, Sydney Gibbes was about to increase their knowledge of the classics – although he naturally gave them British classics to read.

He had brought with him a collection of English books including *Ivanhoe* by Sir Walter Scott which Tatiana and Anastasia read. He also had a number of books that included stories that had been retold for children apart from *Ivanhoe* – *Dombey and Son* and *David Copperfield* by Charles Dickens and *The Tower of London* by Ainsworth about Lady Jane Grey. *Ivanhoe* was of course set partly in Gibbes' native Yorkshire at Conisbrough Castle and was the boy's favourite story. Alexei enjoyed Gibbes reading these books to him in this particular order.

Sydney Gibbes also brought another great favourite of Alexei's: Rider Haggard's *King Solomon's Mines*. He had to reread it immediately afterwards at the request of the boy. Mr Gibbes had also brought Sir Arthur Conan Doyle's *Memoirs of Sherlock Holmes* which ends dramatically with Holmes tussling with his arch-enemy Professor Moriarty and tumbling over a cliff at the Reichenbach Falls. The girls also read William M Thackeray's *Vanity Fair*. The book's anti-hero Becky Sharpe was surely a great favourite with the rebellious Anastasia. The book's other main character Amelia would have been more to the taste of Tatiana. It was first published in 1847-8 and was a satire on society of early eighteenth-century Britain, set at the time of the Battle of Waterloo. Its title of course comes from John Bunyan's *Pilgrim's Progress*.

It is unlikely that the girls read Thackeray's excellent comic sequel to Scott's *Ivanhoe* entitled *Rebecca and Rowena*. The writer, like most readers of the famous novel, wished that Ivanhoe had married Rebecca instead of Rowena and set about giving the story a different ending.

Gibbes also brought other British books including *Quentin Durward* by Sir Walter Scott set in fifteenth-century France in the reign of King Louis XI; *As You Like It* one of William Shakespeare's comedies; *The Maid at Arms* by Yorkshire-born writer Raymond Wilson Chambers; *Mr Wycherley's Wards* by L Allen Harker; *Under the Red Robe* by Stanley Weyman; *White Dove* and also *Idols* by WJ Locke; *The White Prophet* by Sir Thomas Henry Hall Caine; some animal stories including *The Biography of the Silver Fox* and *Monarch: The Big Bear of Tallac* by Ernest Thompson Seton; and, oddly, Talbot Baines Reed's *The Fifth Form at St Dominic's (school)*.

Nicholas's reading tastes included the Russian classics or anything with a military aspect. Tatiana and Marie preferred the novels of the British writers Florence Barclay or Arthur William Marchmont. Olga read widely and liked history and poetry, and Alexandra chose religious works almost exclusively and encouraged Tatiana to do likewise. Whilst it is always assumed that Tatiana actually preferred these books the reality was quite different. As many stated it was impossible to know her thoughts, she did on rare occasions speak of longing for foreign travel and amongst the books she took to Tobolsk were ones by Paul du Chaillu which were adventure stories. One of the books she chose to take to Siberia was Chaillu's *The Country of the Dwarfs* which begins with a list of things he decided to take on his travels to equatorial Africa. He mentioned simple, obvious things like pocket handkerchiefs and specially made boots, and goes on to say that his clothes were for wear and not for show. These were exactly the sentiments the Grand Duchesses had when packing for Siberia. They did not take expensive silk dresses but simple sturdy skirts, blouses and cardigans. The sisters also took the volumes likely to be read over and over again, and this book was one that was eminently useful as it included the drugs to carry in one's medicine cabinet which included quinine, castor oil, Espsom salts and laudanum as well as needles, thread and cotton. These details would not have been found in the average fashionable novel. Tatiana's sense of practical, common sense is shown by her choice of reading material. When one fails to appreciate the books a person reads, one cannot possibly hope to understand the character.

Whilst Olga suffered from boredom in exile, as her tutor Gibbes admitted, her thoughts would have inevitably wandered to *Mitya*. Would she ever see him again? Tatiana never mentioned *Volodia* in public and resumed her normal existence as her mother's helpmate but, as her later letters show, a tinge of bitterness appeared. Her letters had a tone of sarcasm which Olga's did not.

Reading books was one of the few pleasures left to the former Imperial family. It was fortunate indeed that the Tsarina had encouraged her daughters to *work*. It gave them something to keep them busy and provided a method of mending or altering clothes, occasionally even making them. They were capable of knitting woollen socks or cardigans or sewing shirts or blouses. They were unable to buy new clothes so were forced to mend their old ones. Occasionally, they used some scrap material to make something else. A scarf later became a diary cover. It also enabled them later to sew their jewels into the cushions and undergarments. Luckily, the house, like most in that era, had the use of a piano, which was a great comfort to Olga in particular. Luckily Olga would not have needed to take sheets of music as she had an excellent memory for tunes and was able to play by ear. She could play a piece after hearing it without resorting to the music. Sadly it was less pleasant in the garden by autumn as the small kitchen garden had turned into a muddy bog after recent heavy rain, so one needed other forms of occupation.

Olga remembered to write to Petrov on Tuesday and confessed that she had forgotten entirely to answer his letter. Although Tatiana had written, Olga, who was usually more efficient in replying to letters than her sister, had failed to write. She was pleased to hear, from his recent letter, of an improvement in his health. She added that everyone was well. Her younger siblings had begun their lessons again, she explained. Nicholas was sitting close by as she wrote and he and the others sent their best wishes to him. They often spoke with Monsieur Gilliard about the time when they had tormented Petrov during lessons. (Anastasia was not above doing the same to Gilliard.)

Alexandra decided to write to Anya on Saturday and explained that Gibbes had recently arrived at Tobolsk. Alix was greatly worried about her friend and knew that she had suffered immensely simply for the crime of being the Tsarina's confidante. Alexandra asked about Anya's legs and her heart. (Alexandra had been the centre of Anya's world for several years and it would have been a shock simply to be apart, never mind the constant fear of being in and out of prison.) She reassured Anya that everyone was well.

Olga wrote to her friend Rita on Tuesday whom she had not seen since her unfortunate visit to Tobolsk. She sent her best wishes to Rita on her special day. She had sent a postcard to Rita previously via Varvara (Bibi) but had no idea whether it ever arrived. Olga asked about some of their mutual friends. Olga and Tatiana had attempted to keep in contact with the friends they had made at the infirmary in recent years – nurses and patients alike. She had written to some of her friends from the hospital but rarely received any answer. They had been sent a letter but the parcel said to be accompanying it had got lost. She was not quite sure whether letters should be addressed directly to her or via the Commissar. (Tatiana in her earlier letter stated that they should go through him.)

The weather was good and it felt more like early autumn. It was not very cold and there was little snow as yet. She felt unable to complain as the sun continued to rise each day and she felt its warmth. They did not go out for walks so much now and they had little to do. There was not yet enough snow to play in but it was too cold to play other games outside. She went on to ask about Rita's younger sister Lyuba, who was a particular friend of Anastasia, and about Tatiana's friend Dmitri Malama, and of Marie's favourite Nicholas Demenkov. She asked Rita to let her know if there was any news. She also asked of Ippolit Mocholov who had been on the yacht in former days as an engineer. Olga added that her younger siblings had restarted their lessons and, in the evenings, they sat together playing various party games. On occasions, one of them read aloud something from *Chekov*. They liked to read his comic short stories. She asked again about other friends including Olga Butzova and Zinaide Tolstoy. (It is more than likely that her sisters had asked Olga to ask about their various friends in the letter.)

As the anniversary of his father's death came round once more, it only reminded Nicholas of how things had changed since that day in 1894 when he had reluctantly taken up the mantle of Emperorship. He felt sorry for Russia in the circumstances but was helpless to do anything. The previous evening, a requiem had been held.

Alexandra decided to write once more to Anya on Saturday after receiving a letter from her friend. She was delighted to hear from Madame Vyrubova and kissed her in her imagination. Alexandra tried to explain that, despite their being apart, there was no such barrier against friendship. She finally understood the friendship that Anya had so freely given for so many years. She wrote to the address she had previously been given and hoped the letter would arrive. Alexandra admitted that she had been thrilled to have a recent image of Anya, brought by Gibbes. She admitted to shedding many tears on first seeing it. Alix asked if Anya had news of Rasputin's children. (She never used his name as such and merely called him *Our Friend* as she had always done.)

They thought of Anya often and she prayed for her safety. Everything was in the hands of God. Tomorrow she was dearly hoping to go to Holy Communion. They were having services at home now and they had a service for the dead the previous evening (for her late father-in-law); tonight they were having confession. She longed to be able to talk to Anya but it was impossible. Alexandra had not heard from Lili Dehn for some considerable time. Alix had been suffering from neuralgia for some time but, luckily, her dentist Dr Serge Kostritzky had recently arrived to treat her.

Alexandra had heard that things were difficult in the Crimea but at least her sister-in-law Olga was happy with her baby son Tikhon. She had been forced to nurse the child herself as she had no servants at all. Olga and her husband were forced to do everything for themselves. (It was something that Olga would not have minded. After so many years of having no children she was more than happy to nurse the baby herself and had never liked the fact that she had so many servants. As she had married a commoner, she had more freedom than her mother or sister.)

Alexandra revealed that the weather had deteriorated in the past few days and she had not been able to go outside. Her heart was not so good but she was finding much consolation from reading the Bible. She often read it to the children and assumed that Anya also read it often. She had been overwhelmed by the gifts Anya had sent – a jacket, a blue dressing gown, red slippers, a silver tray and spoon, and a stick (possibly a walking stick). She often wore the icon that Anya had sent earlier. She asked about the people Anya was now staying with; it may have been a priest from Peterhof but Alix could not remember. Anya moved around frequently.

The same evening, Nicholas had written in his journal that they had seen the funeral from their window of a member of the 4th Rifle Regiment. The school band that marched in front of the procession had performed rather badly though. They had attended Mass at home late that morning and they had attended confession at 9pm. Nicholas had sat for much of the afternoon chatting with the dentist. He had so few chances to talk to anyone new these days. It made a welcome change to speak to someone who had seen the outside world. Gibbes' arrival had been the last such chance.

Nicholas was comforted after Communion on Sunday. The entire immediate family had attended the liturgy early that morning and each had received Communion. It was a fairly mild day and, despite the continual snow, Nicholas and his children spent much of the day out in the small garden.

In the early hours of Thursday, the 26th of October (or 8th of November in the West) the provisional government surrendered to the *Bolsheviks*. The current government were originally called the *Mensheviks* (majority) and the *Bolsheviks* (minority). The two had made a dramatic split many years previously. The *Bolsheviks* had believed in assassination as a means to an end but the majority preferred to use other methods. Initially, the *Mensheviks* had gained power but they had now lost to the *Bolsheviks*. It was bad news for Nicholas. Alexander Kerensky had been a man who Nicholas could speak to but the leader of the *Bolsheviks* Vladimir Lenin, whose own brother had been hanged after a disastrous assassination plot many years previously, was quite another matter.

Kerensky went into hiding and eventually escaped via Murmansk. He ultimately fled to the United States of America. He was said to have hidden at one point in the underground caverns under Gatchina Palace where Nicholas had grown up. Had Nicholas told him about the escape route? It is unlikely but not impossible.

As a result of the overthrow of the provisional government, food became scarce, as Volkov later recalled. When the Imperial family had been imprisoned at Tobolsk, the locals initially came with food supplies. They received quite a lot of provisions from the nearby Ivanovsky Convent. Until the October Revolution, food at the Governor's House was plentiful, but the family ate with moderation. The main meal of the day was served at 8pm and simply consisted of two main dishes. On special occasions, a sweet/dessert appeared but normally there was nothing more. Morning tea was taken at eight and lunch was served at one. Afternoon tea was taken at five and included tea and buns.

Olga Nicolaevna turned twenty-two on the third of November. The situation was quite different to all her previous birthdays. It must have seemed to her that, each birthday since 1913 onwards, the day was bleaker each time with the war and revolution coming soon afterwards. The day would have been celebrated with a special service but held within the house itself. Any gifts would be home-made or taken from her mother's stock of jewels or her father's precious stock of books. They had little to give. The cook would have saved as much of his diminishing stock as possible to serve the best meal he could.

The shrewd cook Kharitonov had taken quite a stock of food from the kitchens at the Alexander Palace and had proved to be very astute at collecting things that would prove not just useful but long-lasting. Alexandra ate very little but preferred pasta. The cook had a good stock of pasta, rice, flour, tinned foods, etc. He had been presented with meat, fish, eggs and milk on occasions, but these were in short supply in later months. It was difficult to obtain fresh food of any kind. The yard had some chickens which would have helped with supplies. The kitchen garden did contain cabbages but the family had little chance of planting their own vegetables as they had done at the Alexander Palace. There was little space and the ground was often too muddy.

There would have been quite a few things that were around in 1917 in tin, jar or packet form such as custard (to make up), jam, jelly (jello), tea, powdered chocolate for drinking, mustard (to make up), syrup in tins, tinned fruit or meat or soups. The resourceful cook would have taken biscuits and crackers, cheese, etc which were fairly long-lasting and, of course, wheat flour. They would have been able to get local mushrooms and radishes as these grew fairly easily, but other foods would have been in short supply. Luckily, there was a river close by and game from the forests but, after the October Revolution, it was increasingly unlikely that fresh food would be brought.

Meanwhile, after Nicholas had received a most welcome letter from his sister Xenia with encouraging news about his beloved mother, Nicholas wrote to his sister on Sunday. He rarely wrote. It was a remarkable letter as it was the only one to recount the abdication.

Xenia had sent word on the fifteenth of October, although it is not exactly clear how long it took for it to arrive at Tobolsk from the Crimea. Nicholas had been concerned about his mother's health as she had gone through a great deal. She had lost her husband in 1894 and her son George in 1899 and her sons Nicholas and Michael had both renounced the throne. She was now living in the Crimea along with her daughters and grandchildren, but they too were restricted in their movements.

He had written just after they had returned from the liturgy and it was still dark. They had been permitted to attend the local Russian Orthodox Church but had to pass through the town garden in order to do so and cross the street. Although the journey was merely 500 paces, the riflemen guard surrounded them at all times. The men stood in a loose chain as the family left church and some of them then followed them home. It felt like being rounded up like sheep and they all found it particularly funny.

It had been snowing for the past two days yet it did not seem like winter. The snow kept melting each time but the air was fresh and pure. Nicholas felt that they were living their life at sea. Every day was much the same as the last one. He attempted to explain what had happened to him recently. When he had arrived back from Mogilev, the children had been very ill, especially Marie and Anastasia. He had spent all day sitting with them, wearing a white smock. At first, an officer of the guard had accompanied the doctor on his rounds twice a day. Some of the guards had even entered the room whilst the patients were being examined.

He had taken walks outside with *Valia* Dolgorukov and one of the officers of the guard. No one had cleared the paths of snow since the end of February so it gave Nicholas something to do. The guards always accompanied him and the family were only permitted to walk where the guards were situated. They were in a narrow chain of guards and could go no further. Colonel Korovichenko had promised that they would be allowed to go out further into the park when it became warmer. Nothing happened so, one day, Nicholas had taken it upon himself to go further into the park, accompanied by four armed riflemen. Afterwards, he was permitted to go further out. He had gained a small victory. He spent much of his time chopping down dead trees and sawing them up for firewood. They were not permitted to use the balcony at the palace as someone had decided to lock the door. They had to go into the garden with members of the suite. Each time they went out, they were watched by the other riflemen in a mocking manner.

In the summer, they had been permitted to stay outside until eight. He spent the days watering the vegetables in the patch they had made or riding his bicycle accompanied by his daughters. In the evenings, they sat by the windows and watched as the riflemen sat on the grass, smoked, read, sang and generally horsed around.

The riflemen who came to Tobolsk were quite different types as most had served at the front, and many had been wounded and received the St George Cross. They had made friends with them. (When they left the palace, Kobylinsky had deliberately sent a more agreeable sort of man with the family, who were more sympathetic towards the former Tsar.)

Nicholas suddenly remembered that, in the spring, there had been processions in the streets and musicians playing the *Marseillaise* (the French republican tune that had been banned in Russia for many years) and Chopin's *Funeral March* over and over again. They were burying what they termed the *victims of the revolution* in the park. Due to the ceremonies, the family had been forced to go out later. The haunting funeral march had accompanied them for long afterwards and they had spontaneously kept whistling it until it had sent them quite mad.

Nicholas hoped that one day he could tell Xenia all that had happened to him in person. So much had occurred. He was convinced that he had bored her by the end of the letter. His hand had grown numb. Nicholas ended by admitting that his thoughts were constantly with her and his mother. He signed off 'from the *Beputons*' which was a family in-joke.

Olga chose to write to her Aunt Xenia on Saturday. Nicholas's sister was living in the Crimea with her mother and sister. She had last written to her aunt a month ago and wondered if she had received that letter. Olga Nicolaevna began by asking how everyone was – Xenia, Olga and their mother the Dowager Empress. She reassured the Grand Duchess that all was well with them at Tobolsk and they were all in good health. It was now the beginning of winter, she explained, and getting much colder. She had little news as so little happened. They were able to take walks around the garden. The locals, she explained, dressed from head to foot in furs. The hats that they wore had all the same hanging flaps and they often wore bright red boots. She found the tiny sleds that they used very interesting. The horses appeared to run faster and seemed more like racehorses.

Olga felt warm inside when the sun shone. It was comfortable next to the window and there were some plants, including three pots containing cyclamen. She had received them as gifts on her birthday. (There was little else to give and they may have been from her three sisters.) There was a small tree in the hall but she had no idea what it was called. She had dug it up from the greenhouse where the chickens lived. The birds had belonged to a previous owner of the house; either the governor or the soldiers who had used it as a barracks fairly recently. She was not sure that the tree would survive as it was so dusty. She had washed it and kept on watering it occasionally. She only remembered to water the tree when the leaves started to wilt, she admitted. Olga confessed that she could not get used to the time change. The government had altered the clocks. It seemed that they had put the clocks forwards, backwards and then back again. The sun continued to rise at the same time, no matter what time it was said to be. She asked if Olga had seen her granddaughter. Irina's daughter of the same name had been a baby when Olga had last seen her. Tatiana added her best wishes at the top of the page.

Gleb Botkin was convinced that Olga Nicolaevna appeared to understand the general situation better than anyone else, including her own parents. He felt that she had little illusion of what was in store for them: death. As a result of this, she appeared to often be nervous and worried. He was convinced that Olga had a certain sweetness about her that prevented the others being affected by her depressive tendencies. He saw her as a woman of great intelligence. She was an avid reader and a talented poet. She felt close to *the Doctor* and felt at ease in asking him questions on any subject. She admired his intelligence and in her letters to him she addressed him as *Dear Well*. To Olga, the doctor was a deep well of profound ideas.

Nicholas spent Friday sawing wood outside in the yard. The weather was a little warmer. Later, he finished reading the first volume of *1793* and that evening he read an old favourite aloud to the family: *Memoirs of a Hunter* by Turgenev.

Gleb Botkin later remarked on this old favourite. Nicholas and his ancestors had read this book avidly and learned all that they knew about the peasants from it. Unfortunately, it was taken far too literally.

Nicholas admitted in his journal on Saturday that he was becoming concerned over the lack of news from the outside world. They had received neither newspapers nor telegrams from the capital for quite some time. The four sisters meanwhile amused themselves by jumping off the swings into the snow. It was not something their brother could join in, sadly. It was too dangerous. There was a religious service held in the hall that evening.

One evening at around this time, Nicholas had a long chat with Dr Botkin about his late father the Emperor Alexander III. The doctor later recalled the conversation to his son Gleb. The doctor explained that Nicholas had always venerated his father and had retained the rank of a colonel that had been given to him by his father. He had refused to take a higher rank because it would have meant removing his father's initials from his shoulder straps.

Nicholas had told *the Doctor* that he now believed that his father had a peaceful reign simply because it had been a short one. Nicholas stated that he had maintained peace by sheer terror. He also felt that his father had messed up the affairs of administration so much that things were in total chaos when he died. The former Tsar Nicholas II was starting to think that the revolution was actually the fault of his father. Nicholas felt that Alexander had antagonised every foreign power and, had he lived longer, things would have gone wrong sooner. Nicholas claimed that, during the twenty-two years of his reign, he had attempted to unravel the tangle he had inherited from his father. He insisted that Russia's situation before the war had been a great deal better than it had been at the time of his father's death in 1894. Nicholas had to go through the

Japanese war and the revolution of 1905–1906. He felt the latter had been a result of his late father's time in office. Nicholas blamed his father for the current disaster. He had opened his father's desk up after his abdication and read Alexander III's reports. This extraordinary view is not one that history recalls.

According to Gleb, the former Tsarina had firm views on the monarchy. She also had a surprise in store for Dr Botkin. There had been a conversation between Alexandra and *the Doctor*. He had asked Alexandra why, instead of abdicating, the Tsar had not granted a parliamentary form of government. Originally the liberals had merely demanded this. Many felt that, had Nicholas yielded to this demand, the revolution would not have taken place. If he had agreed, he would have won the support of all but the extremists. According to Gleb, when he mentioned parliamentary reform, Alexandra would have none of it. She was indignant and wanted to know why people could not understand that he could never have granted a parliamentary form of government. It would have been even worse, she explained, than the abdication itself. The Tsar had pledged a solemn oath when he had been heir to the throne to preserve the autocratic power impaired and bestow it on his successor (Alexei) exactly the same as he had been given.

It appears that Nicholas had given his oath that, as long as he reigned, he would remain an autocrat. If he had granted a parliamentary form of government, it would have meant he had broken the oath he had sworn. The abdication was therefore a way of not breaking his oath. The doctor was thunderstruck. He wanted to know the way out as Russia could not remain an autocracy forever. She agreed. Nicholas had thought of that too, she admitted. He had already had it in his mind that he would not demand of his own son the kind of oath he had sworn to his father. Alexei would then be at liberty to grant any form of government he chose.

On Thursday the fourteenth/twenty-seventh of November, it was the birthday of the Dowager Empress and Nicholas and Alexandra's twenty-third wedding anniversary. The menu at the Governor's House on that festive occasion included for luncheon sturgeon soup with *Rastegai* (an open pastry); cheese pancakes with sour cream; goose with cabbage and meat balls; and pancakes with syrup. It looked fairly impressive but the day was a special one and the ingredients had been kept for this occasion. The syrup would have been from a tin and the cabbage from the garden.

Baroness Buxhoeveden later admitted that the menu was usually rather restricted. The only vegetables that they were able to procure in such a severe climate were cabbage and carrots. Any potatoes had to be brought specially from Tyumen but luckily fish and game were plentiful.

There had been a special religious service at noon but the choir, according to Nicholas's journal that evening, managed to muddle things up and sang out of tune. It was probably because they had not rehearsed. That afternoon Nicholas amused himself by rereading some of his old journals which had been stored in the shed. It gave him the chance to relive happier times – his marriage, the births of their children, holidays, and possibly the time he had been stuck in the bathroom in Windsor Castle in 1984 and Alix had to get him out.

Nicholas finally found out via old newspapers what had been happening in past weeks in Petrograd and Moscow on Friday, and he became frustrated. It was worse than he had expected. The weather was not very promising either; it was very windy.

He was even more shocked on Saturday after seeing what had been happening in more detail. He was especially crushed when he heard of a likely armistice.

Nicholas noticed a change of behaviour in the guards who surrounded him on Monday. They had not been paid and were later given money only after a loan had been taken out. Nicholas kept himself busy by dealing with the firewood.

After closely observing Nicholas at this time, Dr Botkin spoke candidly to his son Gleb. He spoke highly of the former Tsar. Nicholas was highly educated and very intelligent yet lacked confidence in his own judgement. The doctor was convinced that, had he acted on his own opinion, things would have never have got so bad. He had so often seen Nicholas yield to the persuasion of others when his own judgement was perfectly sound. He further elaborated. Nicholas, he explained, did not lack willpower or courage but it was his own modesty and his genuine respect for the opinion of others that was a terrible failing. If he were not Tsar, Nicholas would have been seen as a pleasant and intelligent man, but, as Tsar, he was an autocrat and needed to be decisive and firm. It was, of course, something that Alexandra had frequently told him.

The expected religious service was cancelled on Tuesday as Pankratov refused to permit the family to attend. As it was a pleasant, warm day, Nicholas and his children worked in the yard.

Olga replied to a recent letter from her former Russian tutor Peter Petrov on Thursday. It had taken a month to arrive. She noted from the postmark that it had actually arrived on the last day of October but arrived with her twenty-four days later. She was perplexed as to where it had been all this time. The former Grand Duchess joked that she was writing in red ink. It was, after all, a fashionable colour. (She was referring to the *Bolshevik* party that had recently taken power and who were known as the *Reds*.) She admitted that almost everyone had read his recent letter as they were desperately short of news. Olga had little to impart; Gibbes had already written to him. She had little to say as their life was very predictable.

Olga went on to explain the daily routine. On Sundays they attended vigil at eight thirty but in the hall of the house itself rather than the nearby church. They had an amateur choir sing during the service. Olga was not impressed with their particular style of singing. She disliked the concert style although she confessed many liked it.

She explained that they had been warned that the climate in Siberia would be extreme but so far it had been quite mild. (The Tsar's children had spent every winter playing out in the snow so they were quite used to the cold.) One day, it was frosty with a slight wind but, other days, it was rather warm. The nearby river, the Irtysh, had come to a halt some time ago as it was frozen over and no traffic could pass on it. They were about to begin building a snow mountain. So far however there was not enough snow in the small compound. Her father spent much of his days sawing wood, making firewood and stacking it up in a pile. Alexandra came out if it was not too cold as she complained that the extreme cold made it difficult for her to breathe. The dogs Joy,

Ortipo and Anastasia's tiny Jimmy were all well, she explained. Joy and Ortipo had to be constantly stopped from eating filth from the rubbish tip.

Olga signed it as usual as his pupil number one. Alexandra had done something similar when writing to her former teacher Miss Jackson. She had called herself PQ3 which meant, bizarrely, Poppet Queen Number 3. The governess had taken Elisabeth, Irene and Alix but presumably not Victoria, the oldest sister as she was by then a little old and extremely intelligent. Her son Lord Mountbatten regarded her as something of a walking encyclopaedia.

Alexandra sent word once more to Madame Vyrubova on Friday after she had received a letter the previous day. Again, it appears the post had been deliberately slowed down as Anya had written on the sixth, yet the letter had arrived only on the twenty-third.

Alexandra was nevertheless delighted to hear from Anya yet concerned that Anya was now living in unpleasant conditions. She was forced to climb stairs which was not easy for someone who could not walk without the aid of crutches. She had nowhere to take a walk even if she could do so. Alexandra explained that each day she read from a book that Anya had given her some seven years previously. The book was entitled *Day by Day*. She enjoyed reading it as it was so nicely written. The weather was constantly changing. On occasions it was frosty and sometimes it was sunny. It was often dark and the snow thawed all the time. It was dull for those who thrived on long walks yet were deprived of them. Lessons were continuing. She and the four Grand Duchesses were already busy making simple home-made Christmas gifts. Alexandra could hardly believe how quickly time flew. It was almost eight months since they had met but she reassured her friend that God would not forsake her.

Mostly everyone was well apart from the colds and chills they often had in the winter weather. Alexei's arm and one of his knees often swelled up, but he was not in any pain. Her heart was playing up again. She spent much of her days reading and simply thinking of the past but believed in a brighter future. She had not heard from Lili Dehn in three months. She would be thinking of Anya much in the run-up to Christmas. Alexandra asked Anya to kiss Rasputin's widow and children for her. Liza Ersberg had not arrived, she explained, nor the other young maids.

Alexei also wrote that day to Anya as it was intended to be included with his mother's letter. He explained to Anya that he often thought of her and her little home which made him sad. They had often cut wood and it was used to heat their baths. The days seemed to pass quickly.

In one of his entries in his journal at this time, the former Tsarevich had disclosed his real feelings. He was beginning to understand at Tobolsk the word *truth*. He now believed that everyone had lied at Tsarskoe Selo. If he ever had the opportunity to become Tsar, no one would ever dare lie to him. He intended to sort things out, if he was given the chance. (He was referring to the fact that the servants and soldiers had seemed loyal, but in reality were only paying lip service.)

On Sunday, the twenty-sixth, Nicholas noted in his journal with bitterness that the men who had been awarded the St George Cross were not even permitted to attend the traditional celebrations that day. It was a holiday in honour of those who had been awarded the St George Cross. A dinner was given yet those at the Governor's House were not permitted to attend it.

Pierre Gilliard had sent word to his former colleague Petrov that same day to bring him up to date on his former pupil Alexei's progress. He had only just received a card that had been sent on the fifteenth. Alexei had been shown the postcard and felt guilty that he had not written recently to Petrov. Gilliard explained that the boy's only possible excuse was his lessons. He was having twenty-eight hours of tuition each week. Alexei had promised Gilliard that he would compose a letter the following day during his French lesson. (It was a clever ploy by the boy who would, as a result, miss a French dictation.)

He was glad to hear that Petrov was now feeling better. He added that, if Petrov was having problems sleeping, he was not alone. It appeared that most of the inhabitants of the Governor's House and even those across the road were suffering from insomnia. Gibbes, despite his British imperturbability, was also unable to sleep. (Alexandra had always been a bad sleeper, as had Olga in recent years.)

The Swiss citizen Pierre Gilliard admitted that, in the past twelve years, he had begun to love Russia, with its sad, dreamy, idealistic and even childish ways, but he was confused as to the sudden change in attitude. He went on to remark how delighted he was to hear that all was well with their colleague Monsieur Konrad and his family. He had received a letter from Madame Konrad after she and her children had arrived in Switzerland. (The couple had taught the Grand Duchesses in former years – music and mathematics. The lady had taught the latter and it is likely that the children missed Monsieur Konrad's lessons more than Madame's.) They had hoped that M Konrad would be able to travel to Tobolsk but it did not seem possible.

Unlike Gibbes and Gilliard, he had a wife and children to consider. It is no coincidence that, with the exception of *The Doctor,* all those who travelled with the former Imperial family to Tobolsk were unmarried. In later years, Gilliard married Shura Tegleva. Anna Demidova, the Tsarina's maid who later travelled with the family to Ipatiev House, had unfortunately fallen in love with Sydney Gibbes. He did not show any interest in women in general.

Meanwhile Nicholas recalled one of his former regiments on Monday. It was the regimental celebration day for the Nizhegorosky regiment and he wondered what had become of them. Were they even still alive?

Alexandra wrote to her friend Lili Dehn on Wednesday as she was concerned that she had heard nothing from her friend in recent months. Letters often did not get through at all. She asked if Lili had received the postcard that she had sent on the twenty-eighth of October. The former Tsarina reassured Madame Dehn that everyone was well but her heart was not good. She stayed inside most days as the cold air made it difficult for her to breathe.

Alexandra asked after Lili's son Alexander, her godson. She had heard that one of Rasputin's daughters had married and that his son was living in the capital. She recalled that it would very shortly be the first anniversary of Rasputin's death. Alexandra admitted that she now had to wear spectacles in order to read, draw or embroider. She often thought of Lili and promised that she would pray for her. She added she was reminded of Lili by the scent of Verveine (a type of perfumed *toilette water*).

As December began, Nicholas struggled to complete his daily journal. Nothing ever changed, and if it did it was not for the better, so it all seemed so pointless. He merged Friday and Saturday together, something he had never done previously. He explained that, after their daily walk, the family gathered together for rehearsals. The tutors had decided it would be a good idea to get the children to rehearse and take part in a series of plays.

Despite Nicholas's protestations, the days were now more interesting for the children at least. They spent most of the week rehearsing and performed a play on Sunday evenings.

On the first Sunday of the month, it was so cold that Alexandra and Alexei were unable to attend Mass. After their return from church, the four Grand Duchesses and their brother got down to the serious business of rehearsing for the weekly play. A stage was set up in the drawing room, and the furniture and various screens were moved around to make it look like a theatre. It was all put back to normal afterwards. Nicholas and his children walked in the yard until dusk. As the long winter evening continued, Nicholas read aloud from Turgenev's *On the Eve* whilst the others played bezique.

According to Sydney Gibbes, during this period Alexei often played cards in the afternoons including his favourite game: the oddly titled *The slower you ride, the farther you go*. He would partner either Gilliard or Gibbes against Valia Dolgorukov and Mlle Schnieder. Trina took the game most seriously and frequently swore that each game would be her last. Alexei was equally determined to win but, when he did not, he simply went quiet and carried on as determined as ever to win.

Three of Alexandra's personal maids attempted to gain access to the Governor's House at Tobolsk on Tuesday. They were refused entry as there were already enough domestics. The three included Madeleine Zannoti and Anna Utkina.

That same day Olga Nicolaevna wrote to her friend Zinaide Tolstoy, after the lady had generously sent the gift of some perfume shortly before. Olga thanked Zinaide for the expensive gift and her recent letters and postcard. She greatly appreciated the letters that she sent so frequently. A letter had arrived the previous day which had been sent on the eighteenth of November. They had finally heard from Lili Dehn who had not written for some considerable time. Alexei's little friend Kolya Derevenko had been spending some time with them and had made a welcome addition to the household. The weather was finally beginning to become cold. The long Russian winter they had been warned of had finally arrived yet nothing much ever seemed to happen. Now that the local river had frozen, Tobolsk was effectively cut off from the rest of the world. Olga believed that, although this delayed the post, it did eventually arrive now. She ended by sending her very best wishes and signed the letter simply as Olga. Tatiana added her signature but signed as Tatiana R(omanov). They had no pretension of rank.

The family's clothes were beginning to fall apart by the end of 1917. Nicholas's trousers had torn and needed darning and the girls' underclothes were rags. Alexei asked his mother to knit him some socks as all his contained holes. They would have found it difficult to wash their clothes as they would either have been sent to the state laundry which was very rough on their clothes, some of which may have been delicate including the underlinen, or the ladies of the household had to assist with the laundry. They would have not had access to the washing machines that the Tsarina had previously, so everything would have had to be washed, probably with cheap soap.

Luckily Alexandra and her daughters Tatiana and Marie were especially adept at needlework and would have nimbly mended torn clothes and remade items from scraps of material. Finally, the skills Alexandra and her daughters had learnt were proving very useful. They may have been short of wool, but anyone with Alexandra's consummate gifts would have unravelled any old socks or even cardigans and used the same wool for new items.

A special service was held in honour of Nicholas's name's day on Wednesday at noon at home. The gifts that he had received that day included three pies and he thoughtfully sent one of them to the guards. When he had gone out into the garden, the men of the 4th Rifles congratulated him on his special day and he was quite touched. That evening Nicholas performed in one of the plays along with Marie, Alexei and Gilliard entitled *Le Fluide de John*. He felt it went well and there was a great deal of laughter.

Nicholas and his son often slipped into the guardhouse to play cards with the men of the 4th Regiment, such was the rapport between the men and the former monarch and his family. Unfortunately these men were not always on duty which meant that the situation was not always so friendly.

Alexandra sent word once again to her old friend Anya on Friday and confessed that she was constantly in her thoughts and prayers. Anya had recently had a misunderstanding with one of her own close friends. Alexandra warned her that it was a time when she needed the few close friends she had. She admitted that the times caused a strain on all relationships. Alexandra felt far removed from the rest of society but it had its compensations. When she read of what was happening in the capital, she realised that it was safer to be somewhere isolated. She was angered by the constant fear and suspicion and still hoping that Madeleine Zannoti and the other maids would be given access to the Governor's House.

She went on to complain of the coldness of the rooms. There was a strong draught that came through the ill-fitting windows. The pretty jacket that Anya had sent was now very useful. Everyone was suffering from chilblains on their fingers, just as Anya had done in her tiny house without foundations at Tsarskoe Selo. Alexandra explained that she was writing whilst having a brief rest before dinner. Anastasia was playing the piano and little Jemmy had decided to sit next to Alexandra. (The dogs would have given the family some warmth by sitting close to them and the dogs would enjoy the closeness.)

Alexandra then went on to briefly mention the plays. The children were committing to memory a new French piece. She thought it was an excellent idea. The evenings were usually spent with Nicholas reading aloud whilst she embroidered. She was making some Christmas gifts. They painted ribbons for bookmarks and decorated their own cards. She was now taking the children for their religious lessons as a priest was no longer permitted to come for the purpose but she was enjoying the lessons as they brought so many happy memories. She had begun reading for pleasure the works of the *Archbishop Wissky* and about St Tikhon of Zadonsk. She was relieved that she had been able to bring her favourite books with her.

Alexandra wondered if Anya had read from the Bible that she had given her. She explained that there was now a more complete edition. She had given one to the children and had managed to obtain a large copy for herself. There were some very beautiful passages in the Proverbs of Solomon.

She thanked Anya for so many happy recollections. Alexandra admitted that she now lived very much in the past. No one could take away her memories. She had heard via one of her correspondents that one of the former wounded soldiers they had treated was again wounded. Prince George Eristov was back in hospital. She did not know what had happened but asked Anya to pass on her greetings to the Prince. Alexandra wondered where Anya's brother Serge and his wife Nina were. She was delighted to hear that Anya had now resumed her maiden name – Tanyev. She asked Anya to pass on her greetings to Emma Fredericks and Anya's parents. They had the service for Nicholas at home as they had been told there had been some sort of disturbance. She had not been outside for four weeks because of the cold which affected her heart.

She had shown Anya's photograph to *Valia* and Gilliard but not to the ladies. Alexandra complained that the Countess was too distant. She admitted that the young lady was very sweet but did not seem near to her and all her real friends were far away. She was sitting surrounded by Anya's precious gifts: the jacket, dressing gown, slippers, silver dish and spoon, and the icons. She wanted to send Anya something yet knew it would not arrive. Nicholas, she revealed, had been touched by the congratulations she had sent for his name's day. She confessed that she could only think of Anya now with tears in her eyes.

Alexandra decided to write to Anya again the following day Saturday and reminded her friend that it was the feast day of the Virgin of Unexpected Joy. She recalled that it was the anniversary of their journey together to Saratov. The holy woman that they had met had since passed on but she had kept the icon she had presented her with. It was now nine months since they had been taken prisoner and they had been at Tobolsk for a further four months. She was surprised to hear that Nini Voyeikov and her family had failed to receive the little icons she had sent them before leaving home. Alexandra apologised that she was unable to give anything for the Christmas tree of Anya's servants. It may well have got lost along the way had she sent anything.

She was writing whilst still in bed and Anastasia's little dog was sitting practically under her nose and interfering with her writing. Ortipo was sitting on her feet which kept both of them warm. Alexandra had been touched when Commissar Makarov had sent on some of her most treasured possessions to her a couple of months previously via the Baron. They had included Nesterov's *Annunication* from her bedroom, four small prints from her Mauve study, five beautiful pastels by Kaulbach of her children, some photographs of Livadia, and even a small carpet from her bedroom. She had also received her wicker chair which was now in her bedroom. It had a cushion containing rose petals that she had been given by some Tartar women. She had slept with it on the train, the boat and ever since. The former nurse Klaudia Bitner had arrived and was giving lessons to the children. She asked Anya if she would write to Gilliard. She hoped to be able to send Anya some macaroni and coffee soon if she wanted it. Alexandra was finding it awkward to take the meat out of the soup without eating any of it, as she preferred not eat the flesh. She found it easy to fast and to stay indoors yet was unable to sleep. Her heart had improved, however, as she rarely did a thing. She was grey and thin now and her dresses hung like sacks.

Alexandra explained that everyone was in good spirits. They had all suffered but their souls were at peace. She went on to ask about old friends who had worked at the various hospitals. Madame Orlov had written to inform her that her grandson had died but she rarely received letters of her own. Alexandra warned Anya, as she often did, to burn her letters lest they be taken as evidence against her. Madame Vyrubova had been in and out of prison constantly since the spring.

Tatiana also took time to write to Madame Vyrubova that day. She reassured Anya that they often thought of and prayed for her. It was hard to be apart. The sisters often wore the dresses that she had kindly sent them. They lived very quietly and the days seemed to pass quickly. They had lessons in the morning then they walked in the small garden which had been enclosed by a high fence. The family lunched together downstairs in the dining room but usually her mother and brother ate in her father's study upstairs. The children accompanied their father into the garden in the afternoon, assuming it was not too cold. They went upstairs again for tea and then they either read or wrote letters. Their father frequently read aloud to them in the evenings. All the days were much the same. On Saturday evenings at nine a service was held in the big hall upstairs. The priest was unable to come before that time. Sometimes they were permitted to go to church on Sunday mornings at eight. They walked there, escorted by the guards and had their own separate Mass.

On the sixth, they had been forced to have the service on her father's name's day at home. It was sad not to be able to attend church but one could not have everything. At least Anya was able to attend church. Tatiana then went on to ask about Anya. How were Anya's legs? She wondered if Serge and Nina had a child yet.

All the letters they received, she explained, had to go via the Commissar. She was glad to hear that Anya was getting on well with Prince Eristov's parents. She knew him but had never met his parents, she admitted. Tatiana then asked if Anya had seen Baroness Buxhoeveden. She had not arrived at Tobolsk. On this occasion, Tatiana simply signed herself as T.

Tatiana had also written to her former colleague and close friend Valentina Chebotarieva that day. She wondered if Valentina had received the letter she had written on the twenty-ninth of November and asked her to let her husband also see her correspondence. She expected that Valentina was missing her friend Lydia Feodorovna, the wife of General Krassnov. The main thing though was that the couple were happy together. She worried about Filatov who was still at the infirmary as he had been there for quite some time now. Was it possibly the same wound that was causing the problem or perhaps something else? She also asked about another old friend Baron Taube.

It was so cold recently that the wind seemed to cut through one's face but happily today the wind had dropped and the sun was shining. The weather was quite different at Tsarskoe Selo at this time of year. She wished her friend well and sent her love to Valentina's daughter of the same name and her other friend Olga Grekova.

Meanwhile Sydney Gibbes who had returned in the past couple of months had snapped one day when Anastasia had been unusually talkative during class. He told her to *Shut up*. She had not heard this phrase before and was amused by it and it was adopted as her nickname and she noted it down on the front of her English notebook. Anastasia's notebooks were found some time later and each of the ones that they found contained her Russian and German lessons. Her Russian book was filled with spelling mistakes. Gibbes kept the one that Anastasia had written *Shut up* on the front. The two youngest sister's handwriting was in a remarkably similar style in scratchy pens and spluttering pen nibs. They both had a heavy left to right slope and a large script.

Marie's lessons with Sydney Gibbes at this time included translations of poems into prose. In one of the stories, she wrote of the Chieftain of Ulva's Isle who promised to give a boat man a lot of money if he would row him ashore. In the poem by Whittier called *Maud Miller*, she used poetic licence and decided to marry the heroine to a peasant rather than the judge as in the original version. She had lots of children with which she occupied herself. Marie also wrote of Robert Browning's *Herve Riel* and of the *Old Armchair* of Eliza Cook. She renamed it the *Cane Bottomed Chair*.

Anastasia's handwriting was even more difficult to understand than Marie's and she wrote of the young knight *Lochinvar* and *King Richard of Sicily* and the tragic tale of the young *Evelyn Hope* who had just died.

Olga was photographed at this time pulling around, Alexei in his sledge. She was often bored but spent a great deal of time reading, something she was luckily extremely fond of. On occasions she composed poems and on an evening mended clothing items along with the others. She had the luxury of a piano and as someone who particularly adored music this would have been a great comfort.

Nicholas composed a short note of thanks for Anya on Sunday. He now rarely wrote at all but a parcel was due to be sent to Madame Vyrubova along with several letters written over a couple of days so he made a small contribution. Nicholas thanked Anya for the kind wishes she had sent on the occasion of his name's day on the sixth. He reminded her that she was always in their thoughts and prayers. Alexandra read aloud all of her letters and he had been horrified at her recent sufferings. They were all well, he reassured her. It was a shame that she was not with them. He passed on kisses and blessings and signed off as her loving friend. Nicholas urged her to give his love to her parents. (He had known Anya's father for many years as he was a senior court official.)

Alexandra decided to write once more to Anya that day to thank her for the most generous gifts including the blue silk jacket and the pastilles. She had little to send in return and found herself writing in English again. It was a real risk sending the parcel, she admitted, and urged Anya once more to burn the correspondence. She repeated her thanks for her letters which were a real joy to her. She urged Anya to forget all the terrible things that had recently happened to her – throw them away, she suggested, like your married name. The perfume that she had sent had been greatly appreciated and reminded them all so much of Anya. Alas, she had no *White Roses* perfume to send her. Nicholas and the children appreciated the things she had sent them and she dearly hoped that the food that she had posted recently had arrived safely. They sent five painted cards which she and her daughters had made.

Alexandra reaffirmed her faith in God and appreciated his small mercies. She apologised for writing so badly and blamed the bad pen and the cold weather. Her fingers were quite stiff. At least they had the rare pleasure of attending church that morning. The maids still had not arrived and it was said that they had not the correct papers yet. The Commandant and the guards felt they already had enough staff. She thanked Anya for standing up for her. Very few had done so.

Alexandra went on to explain that she was kept busy teaching religion to Tatiana, Marie, Anastasia and Alexei. The lessons began promptly at nine and she taught German to Tatiana three times a week and once with Marie. She also read with Tatiana or simply sewed, embroidered or painted whilst wearing her spectacles. Sometimes she read the Bible. She regretted that the family were able only to exercise behind a high fence in the tiny garden. Nicholas was meek and, uncomplaining and she regarded Alexei as an angel. She dined with her son and often lunched too. The daughters were also uncomplaining. They had no news from her family in England or from Germany. They had heard that the Dowager Empress who was imprisoned in the Crimea had grown old, sad and tearful.

The priest was not allowed to give lessons and, even when they had the opportunity to see him at services, they had the guards and Commandant standing listening to every word. When they went to church, Volkov wheeled her in her chair. At least, now she did so little, her heart was better. She recalled the visit to Novgorod the previous December and her friend's (Rasputin's) murder. Now their letters and parcels were examined each time they arrived. Nicholas and Alexei were so sorry that they had nothing to send her. She worried for her friend trapped on the sixth storey and barely able to walk. It would be their first Christmas apart for many years. She explained that they had better write to each other less as she feared the letters would all be stopped.

Olga too composed a letter and expressed her appreciation for the letter and the small gifts. She was happy to see the familiar handwriting of an old friend. The perfume she enclosed so reminded them of Anya who they often thought of. She went on to explain how the four sisters now shared a blue corner room, which had been arranged very cosily. Nicholas's dressing room which he shared with his son was opposite. Alexei's bedroom came next. Nicholas and Alexandra shared a brown bedroom. When it was very cold, the draughts came through the gaps in the windows. Finally Olga wished Anya a peaceful and sunny Christmas. When so much had happened in the past nine months, it was as well to wish for peace.

Olga appears to have written a second note to Anya in which she thanked her again for the gifts and added that she hoped Madame Vyrubova had received the postcard she had sent.

Tatiana put pen to paper in order to send another note to Anya after the parcel came. She admitted that Anya was often the topic of conversation. They spoke constantly of Madame Vyrubova with Gilliard, *Valia* and Gibbes. She could not get over how odd it was that they were now imprisoned in the same house that Anya and Lili had previously stayed in. Tatiana always wore the bracelet that Anya had given to her on her name's day and wondered if Anya could still remember the cosy evenings they used to spend by the fireside. The Governor's House was very draughty and the heating was not adequate. She went on to ask if Anya still saw anything of Grotten and Linevitch.

Anastasia's letter to Anya after the arrival of gifts was again an attempt to explain the way they were now living. They had arranged their joint bedroom comfortably and they often sat on the window sills watching the locals go by as a form of distraction. They also walked in the garden behind the high fence and had begun to act in some little plays.

Anastasia's remark that the sisters often sat and watched the passers-by indicates how bored they were and would have made them feel like birds in a cage looking out at the ordinary people who were free, unlike them. She had by far the greatest acting ability and one of her tutors later indicated that she would have made a career as a comedian had the circumstances been different. As the conditions gradually declined Anastasia's comic antics cheered the rest of the family.

Alexei also composed a note for the package and added that he hoped that she had received the postcard that he had recently sent. He too thanked her for the little mushroom. The perfumes reminded him strongly of her. He prayed each day that they would all be reunited and be together.

The former Tsarevich had not shared his mother's faith in Rasputin, it appears. One day, Klaudia Bitner had rushed to retrieve a small icon that had fallen on the floor. He had laughingly remarked that it was not an icon and she need not pick it up. It was a picture of Rasputin. Had he had the same faith in the man as his mother he could not have let the picture remain on the floor. He along with Olga or Anastasia had all seen him as a human, not a saint.

That same day, Baroness Buxhoeveden finally arrived at Tobolsk and she stayed at Kornilov House for some weeks before she was able to find lodgings nearby. She was denied access to the Governor's House as the others had been. She had been delayed due to a recent appendix operation.

On Sunday morning Alexandra composed a note for the Baroness which was duly passed to her across the road to Kornilov House. She hoped that Isa had slept well. (Sleep was a rare and valued commodity at the Governor's House, as Alexandra, Gilliard and Gibbes had all admitted.)

She enclosed an icon and explained that Saint John of Tobolsk's remains lay in the cathedral on the hill. Sadly she had never had the opportunity to see them. She urged the Baroness to wear the icon so St John would be her guard and guide. They would be having a service at noon and she hoped that the Baroness would be permitted to join them.

The brutal reality of life at Tobolsk was brought home on Tuesday. Nicholas was incensed when he found out that one of the soldiers from the Second Rifle Regiment had carved some offensive scribble on the plank of wood that the children had used as a swing, and he naturally removed the offending article. The young Alexei had just been about to investigate. The men of the Second Regiment continued to behave in a boorish and obstructive manner towards Nicholas and his family, but the men of the First and Fourth Regiments continued to act in a more gentlemanly manner towards them.

Alexandra sent word once again to Anya on Friday and again complained that her maids had still not been allowed to join them despite being in the town for some eleven days. She explained that the Baroness was ill again. She had been assured that she would be allowed in but she doubted it. She understood that Anya had been upset that the Baroness had failed to visit her, but perhaps she did not know where she lived.

She sincerely hoped that Anya would receive the gifts she had prepared for her at Christmas. Anna Demidova and Alexei Volkov had helped her pack the parcel up. She urged Anya to let her know when the parcels arrived. They had been sent by two different messengers. She made a note in her journal each time she wrote. Had she received the postcards she had sent? She had drawn them herself. Alexandra then promised she would send Anya some flour soon.

Alexandra observed that the bright sun made everything glitter and sparkle in the frost. Her poor family could only walk up and down in the yard. She dearly longed to take Communion again, they had last taken it on the twenty-second of October but they had to ask permission now before they did anything. She was currently reading about *Solomon* and *St Seraphim*. It was fortunate that she still had the photograph albums of Anya's safely with her own in the trunk. She longed to see them but knew it would only bring back memories of happier times and make her feel sad.

She then went on to paraphrase some words she had written in Nicholas's diary in 1894 when he had explained about his previous *encounters*. She explained that everything for them was now in the past; she had no idea what the future would hold; only God knew and they had given everything to his safe keeping. She asked Anya to pray for them and for Russia. She had asked Chemodurov to take a slip of paper on Sunday with everyone's names on so that the priest could pray for them. Alexandra asked where Anya's old grandmother was and hoped that Anya's brother would be able to wish her a *Happy Christmas* at least by telephone. She went on to ask about other old friends including Alexander Linevitch who had recently married, Colonel Grotten, Countess Marie Rebinder, and the Bishops Isidor and Melchisedek. She wondered if it were true that Protopopov was seriously ill. Her life was so strange she confessed that she could write volumes.

She confided that her old friend Zinaide Tolstoy and her husband were living at Odessa and Rita was lodging with them and were expecting Lili Dehn to join them shortly there. She asked if Anya knew anything of Tatiana's old friend Dmitri Malama. Had Prince Eristov given her the letter Tatiana had written? She also confirmed that Mr Konrad was still at Tsarskoe Selo but luckily his family had managed to escape to Switzerland. She went on to add that the children wore the brooches that Madame Soukhomlinov had sent them.

On that same day, Sydney Gibbes composed a very detailed letter on behalf of the former Tsarina to Miss Jackson. Alexandra had been a former pupil of the lady who was living at a home for retired governesses in Regent's Park, London. It was hoped that she would take it to the British royal family and perhaps help in an escape attempt. It went via Gibbes, an Englishman, so as to arouse less suspicion. It was a clever plan but there was one key flaw: Miss Margaret Jackson was seriously ill and died on the twenty-eighth of January 1918 near London. She would have been in no position to do anything. The letter was said to have originally included a detailed map of the house, which was taken out before it was sent.

Gibbes went on to say that he assumed that she had read in the newspapers what had been happening. They had been taken to Tobolsk in Siberia which was some 300 versts from the nearest railway station and lived in the former Governor's House. The town was grouped around the foot of a steep hill leading to a plateau where the Bishop's Palace and the Assizes Courts were housed. The churches were, as was the custom in the area, whitewashed with a green painted roof.

They were situated in two houses, one either side of the street. He described in detail the Governor's House. He explained that, on mounting the main staircase, one entered the saloon on one side which was being used as a study by Nicholas and on the other side a drawing room (Alexandra's sitting room). The next rooms included the main bedroom then a room shared by the four daughters. The latter contained the girls' camp beds and treasured possessions. The youngest child had a room to himself on the other side of the corridor. He used it as both bedroom and classroom. The dining room, he explained, was downstairs which was more convenient for the kitchen.

Each day was much the same apart from Sundays and holidays and their eves when the old local priest came to read prayers. They were sometimes permitted on Sundays to visit the local church. They were also permitted to have a small choir visit the house. (This may have been a possible way of entering the house.)

The youngest (four) members of the family had their lessons each morning then they all took exercise in the small fenced-in plot. They had little to do except saw wood. They were all generally in good health and spirits despite the difficult times through which they were living. They knew nothing of the outside world, except what they read in the newspapers which did not come regularly (and were not known for their accuracy).

He stated that it was ages since she had written, or was it simply that they had failed to arrive? (She was unlikely to write being a month short of her own demise.) Gibbes urged her to write and send news of everybody, including David (the then Prince of Wales, later Edward VIII). He had heard that he was now in France. The weather had now turned very cold. The ground was covered with snow and winter had set in late that year as it had been warm until fairly recently. It was very dark in the mornings until a week ago and it had been dark when they visited church. They had made their way there through the deserted town garden, but now the clock had been changed and it was already light when they set out. The sentries were positioned every few yards in the dark. The same priest officiated at the services, but was assisted by a deacon and the choir. It lasted little more than an hour and the procession then reformed and returned by the same route.

The letter remained unanswered and, in May 1919, Gibbes wrote to the British High Commission in Vladivostock explaining that he had written the letter at Alexandra's request but did know Miss Jackson personally. He later heard that the letter had got as far as Petrograd. The former Tsarina had hoped that she would pass it to the British royal family. He urged them to find out what had happened to the letter.

Meanwhile, on Tuesday the nineteenth, Alexei decided to send word to his former Russian tutor Peter Petrov. He sent him his best wishes for the coming New Year and hoped that he had received the previous letter from him. He asked after the tutor's health, which had not been good recently. Alexei then went on to complain that there had not been enough snow yet to build a snow mountain again. His spaniel Joy was growing fat as he was eating rubbish from the refuse tip. He was continually being chased away from the heap by people using sticks, but to no avail. The dog often ran away and appeared to have many friends in town. (He was the only member of the family to freely wander around Tobolsk.)

The boy wrote to Petrov during his French lesson as he complained of having little free time. He promised to write more often during the Christmas holidays and duly signed the letter as Petrov's fifth pupil. (It had probably been Gilliard who urged him to write.)

Whilst he was at Tobolsk, Alexei began to collect old nails as he was convinced that they would be useful one day. In a world where everything was slowly vanishing, he may have had a point.

In the build-up to Christmas, Alexandra and her daughters spent many an hour working on the gifts they would later distribute. Unfortunately, the children of Dr Botkin were not permitted to join the family for the festive season. The former Tsarina attempted to make sure that no one was left out. She sent the Baroness a drawing she had done of some holly to remind her of an English Christmas. According to the Baroness, Olga informed her that she and her siblings put a brave face on for the sake of their parents. The younger children, she was convinced, did not understand the danger they were in. One day, Marie had told Sydney Gibbes that she was quite happy to remain forever at Tobolsk.

On Christmas Eve, Alexandra spent the day arranging the carefully made gifts and decorating the Christmas tree. It was a balsamic fir which smelt strongly of oranges. The tree was also decorated with thin silver-coloured strings known as silver rain. There was a religious service in the hall at noon and afterwards the family lunched together in the downstairs dining room. The former Tsarina also presented some of the guards with a small Christmas tree and some food, and gave each a copy of the Gospels with a handmade bookmark.

The family dined in the downstairs dining room accompanied by Alexei's friend Kolya. The Baroness was forbidden to join them. There was a distribution of gifts later from the Christmas tree for the members of the suite. A large choir sang at evening service and even the guards appeared. The members of the suite and the tutors were treated as part of the family, much to the delight of the children, according to Pierre Gilliard.

Alexandra and her daughters presented members of the suite, the servants and tutors alike with handmade gifts they had made including knitted waistcoats. Tatiana gave her mother a lilac-covered notebook to use as a journal which she had made out of scraps of material from Alexandra's old scarf. She had also embroidered a swastika on the front which was an ancient symbol of faith.

Although *The Doctor* lived at the Governor's House with the former Tsar and his family, his children resided at Kornilov House across the road and the children were not permitted to see their father even at Christmas. Alexandra learned that Gleb was thinking of training for the priesthood and she sent him a book on theology as a gift. Gleb also received a gift from Anastasia: an embroidered letter case. According to Dr Botkin, the former Tsarina was the only person who really seemed buoyed up with hopes for the future that day. Alexandra sent a letter to the Baroness expressing her good wishes and hopes for the future. She added her greetings to Miss Mather who shared lodgings with Isa.

On Christmas Day, the former Imperial family rose early and went to church at 7.30 am. Upon their return Alexandra spent the remainder of the morning resting and painting whilst wearing her spectacles. The family lunched together in the downstairs dining room at noon and saw the Baroness through the window from across the street. After lunch, Alexandra sat for a while on one of the balconies and watched as Nicholas cleared away the snow outside. Alexei's little friend Kolya arrived in time for tea. The children then rehearsed for their play whilst Alexandra looked on. The family dined downstairs at eight as usual and once again Kolya joined them. Nicholas read aloud to the family in the evening as he often did.

That day at church, the deacon had prayed for the health of the Tsar and his family and then uttered the words *A long life* afterwards. These particular words had not been spoken since the abdication, and afterwards Pankratov called for the deacon. He claimed that he had acted under the orders of his superior, Father Alexei. There was an inquiry held the next day and, as a result, the Tobolsk Soviet instructed Pankratov be held responsible and told to keep a much stricter regime in future.

That day Olga had written to her friend Rita shortly after receiving a most welcome letter which had been written on the seventh despite already having written to Rita two days previously. Olga explained that the Christmas tree had been placed in the corner of the hall and was a balsamic fir tree which smelt delightfully of oranges. It was not like the ones they had before at Tsarskoe Selo and the resin continually flowed down its trunk. They had no decorations apart from some silver rain and the wax candles. They had distributed the gifts after dinner on Christmas Eve. Most of the presents were things they had embroidered in recent weeks.

A vigil service had been held at ten in the evening and the tree was then lit. It was beautiful. The choir came and sang but in the concert style. Olga complained that they had not heard from Lili since August. Had she forgotten about them? She was writing to her friend on the large hall table, close to Alexei's toy lead soldiers. Nearby, Nicholas sat drinking coffee with her four siblings but her mother had remained in bed.

The sun was shining onto the writing paper near to her right arm. It had snowed recently and they had been able to add to the snow mountain. She revealed that the

Baroness had arrived but had not been permitted to see them yet. They had only seen her from the window. Olga ended the letter by sending her greetings. Alexandra added hers. Anastasia added a brief note to Rita and revealed that she had on occasions received letters from Rita's younger sister Lyuba.

Tatiana thanked Petrov on Wednesday for the postcard that he had sent her. She asked if he had been able to have a Christmas tree that year. Tatiana explained that they had a strongly scented balsamic fir tree and, delightful fragrance had enchanted all. She hoped that things were going well under the rule of what she termed an illiterate janitor. She could not understand how it was a benefit to Mother Russia at all. Tatiana went on to ask Petrov to pass on her regards to those she knew, including Monsieur Konrad who remained at Tsarskoe whilst his family had fled abroad. Their lessons had ceased for now, due to the Christmas holidays. Some evenings, the family were forced to play hymns on the piano to drown out the revolutionary songs played by the men below. (Olga was the most likely to play, and they often played the famous Cherabim Hymn.)

Tatiana had also written to her friend Olga Voronov that day and had casually informed her that a photograph of Olga and her family hung on the wall beside her bed. (Whether her husband Paul was in the photo or not, she does not explain. He was, of course, Paul Voronov and his photograph may have been on the wall of the room Tatiana shared with her three sisters including Olga. It was Paul's birthday on the twenty-ninth. Was this why she wrote that day? Was he still on Olga's mind? Was the letter a subtle way of Olga reminding Voronov he was not forgotten?)

Nicholas confessed in his journal on Thursday that he had spent much of the day outside in the sunshine but he had been angered after hearing that Father Alexei was now being examined by the authorities and under house arrest after the recent service on Christmas Day. He blamed the men of the Second Rifles and Pankratov for this move.

On Sunday Nicholas and his family spent the evening apart after tea but reunited shortly before midnight on New Year's Eve. They hoped the next year would be happier and bring better tidings. It did not.

Chapter Twenty-two

Tobolsk New Year 1918

There was hardly an auspicious start to the New Year of 1918 for the former Imperial family as both of the eldest Grand Duchesses went down with rubella or German measles as it is sometimes known. Nicholas noted in his journal how they had attended church that morning without Olga and Tatiana. The family attended the service at the nearby Church of the Annunciation where the liturgy was celebrated by Father Vladimir Khlynov in the absence of Father Alexei Vasiliev. The latter was in deep trouble after his deacon had the audacity to use the names and official titles of the Tsar and his family during the service on Christmas Day. The deacon had claimed that he had been acting under instructions from his superior.

In an echo of the events the previous year, Olga and Tatiana had both fallen ill at the same time but happily it proved to be nothing too serious this time. The former Tsar's children were frequently ill at the beginning of a year. Dr Botkin and his associate Dr Derevenko were convinced that it was the rubella virus and both the girls had presented with a slight fever. Alexandra spent most of Monday attending to her daughters and constantly took their temperatures. Tatiana's peaked at 38.5 and Olga's rose to 37.7. Alexandra noted in her journal that Tatiana had a strong rash, a headache and bloodshot eyes.

Alexandra lunched and dined with her two eldest daughters before competing against Nicholas in a game or two of *bezique*. He later read aloud whilst his wife knitted. Despite the events of the previous year the evenings ended much the same as ever but with a smaller cast. The household was vastly reduced and some now lived in the house opposite. One notable absentee was, of course, Madame Vyrubova. In previous years Nicholas and Alexandra had spent many evenings in the company of Anya Vyrubova but they would never see her again. She had been a constant feature in the life of Alexandra, in particular, and the children had scarcely ever been apart from her.

On Tuesday Nicholas noted in his journal that, although it had been confirmed that Olga and Tatiana did indeed have the virus, they appeared better. (It is a fairly mild illness compared to measles and often, apart from the rash, it remains undetected.)

When Nicholas had gone outside, he found little to do and was consequently bored as he desperately needed to keep busy and active. The annoying presence of the guards and the restrictions of the tiny yard were a constant reminder of the current situation. The only trips the former Imperial family had were to the church – under armed guard. Alexandra, however, remained busy nursing her sick children and keeping up with her somewhat limited correspondence, on this day with Lili Dehn and Madame Maria Syroiarskaia. Olga's rash was now more developed and Tatiana spent the greater part of the day coughing and sneezing. Once more, Alix chose to eat with the invalids. Although she had frequently complained of heart pains or headaches in the past, whenever she had an invalid to nurse she appeared to forget her own ailments.

Nicholas finished reading *The Nest of the Gentry* by his favourite author Ivan Turgenev that evening to his family. Alexandra and her daughters preferred English novels on the whole and usually Nicholas obligingly read one to their taste.

There was something of a crisis of confidence for Eugene Kobylinsky on Wednesday and he confessed to Nicholas that he was convinced that power was slipping through his fingers. He felt that he could no longer be of any use to Nicholas and begged the former Tsar's permission to leave. His nerves were completely shot and he felt unable to carry on. With tears in his eyes Nicholas begged him to remain on behalf of his wife and children. He insisted that if they had to endure all of this so did *he*. Nicholas then embraced Kobylinsky and he duly changed his mind. Despite his position, he had grown fond of the family, which was something of a disadvantage as he disliked upsetting them. He was intelligent enough to see how things could end. Nicholas did not want to lose someone he trusted and dreaded who would replace him. As they say *better the devil you know…*

Meanwhile Nicholas admitted in his journal that evening that he had been quite devastated over the matter of the epaulettes. They would have to be removed. He had been given his by his late father so they meant more than his mere rank or a connection to the monarchy. Happily, Olga and Tatiana were showing signs of improvement but Alexei was now unwell Luckily the illness proved fairly mild.

Alexandra again spent the day nursing her children and later lunched with Olga, Tatiana and Alexei. Unlike Nicholas, Alexandra had little time to be bored, and yet the former Tsarina was still furious that Vassily Pankratov was still refusing to allow the Baroness, Madeleine Zannoti, Anna Demidova and Annushka Ukina access to the overcrowded house. He thought that they had quite enough staff. After tea Alexandra played bezique with the as yet still healthy Anastasia. That evening she dined with the three invalids. Tatiana had by now managed to rise for at least for part of the day. She had recovered a great deal quicker than she had done the previous year when the children had all gone down with the measles.

Unfortunately Marie had joined her sisters on the sick list by Thursday and was absolutely covered in spots which meant that Alexandra was now nursing four children. It was inevitable that all the sisters would eventually come down with the virus; not only were they inseparable, but they shared a single bedroom and the remainder of the household was now confined in a much smaller space than in the palace which would increase the risk of further infection.

Alexei happily noted in his journal how he had more spots than ever. He spent the morning playing checkers with Klementy Nagorny and admiring his growing collection of red blotches. The former Tsarevich proudly noted that he and his father had failed to remove their epaulettes despite the guards being ordered to remove theirs. (It was a small victory – for now.)

That day Alexandra lunched and dined with her four invalids but the former nurse Klaudia Bitner relieved her for a while so she had the opportunity of resting before dinner. The long nights were proving difficult for Alexandra. That evening Nicholas read whilst Alix *worked*.

Nicholas chatted with the friendly riflemen of the 1st and 4th Regiments concerning the decision to remove all the military epaulettes on Friday. They too complained of the outrageous behaviour of the men of the 2nd Regiment. The difference in the behaviour between the two camps was quite astonishing. Nicholas and the children had felt so confident in the company of the men of the 1st and 4th that they played cards together. General Tatishchev and Prince Dolgourkov, with the assistance of Alexandra, finally succeeded in convincing Nicholas to remove his epaulettes later that same day. If he had not done so, it would have risked a hostile demonstration by the men of the 2nd Regiment.

Alexandra's mood was far more positive than Nicholas's on Friday and she ignored the matter of the epaulettes in her journal as she once again spent the day nursing, but significantly she chose to go out into the garden during the afternoon to chat with the men of the 4th Regiment. The general mood was lightened at three when Father Khlynov arrived for the traditional *Blessing of the waters* ceremony. It is the equivalent of Epiphany and marks the date when Jesus Christ was baptised by his cousin John the Baptist in the River Jordan. Normally, Nicholas attended this important religious occasion in the capital on the River Neva.

Alexandra, meanwhile, had lunched upstairs with the two remaining invalids Olga and Marie, the same two who had proved the weakest in the previous outbreak. Tatiana and Alexei had been able to join the rest of the family and suite downstairs. The same arrangement was repeated at dinner. That evening Nicholas read aloud to his wife and recovering children.

Alexandra was at her happiest when she had something to do and she greatly enjoyed nursing. She always had great empathy with the sick and children as well as old people and members of the clergy. Unfortunately, she usually struggled to deal with anyone who did not fit into either category.

The family were permitted to attend the Epiphany service at church on Saturday, but only under armed guard. Nicholas was accompanied by Alexandra and his children Tatiana, Anastasia and Alexei. The other children remained indoors, probably tended to by the obliging Dr Botkin. Olga and Marie were able to dress but remained indoors due to the excessive cold. Alexandra lunched in Nicholas's study with them later and the same small party dined together at eight in Alexandra's drawing room. Later, Nicholas read aloud once more. It was a pleasant end to a largely predictable day and a novel would give the family a chance to imagine themselves elsewhere – anywhere else.

That day a partially recovered Tatiana sent word to Zinaide Tolstoy and she thanked her friend for the postcards. However she explained that the letters that Zinaide had sent had as yet failed to arrive. The wire she had sent arrived on the first of the month. (It appears that telegrams were more difficult to lose than letters.)

She asked Zinaide how she had spent the New Year and then went on to reveal that they had been ill with rubella. It had been transmitted to them via Alexei's friend Kolya. She had been in bed for three days, but that morning she had been able to attend church with Anastasia. She had not as yet caught the virus. It had been a very cold day but the sun was rather hot and they had sat out in the garden.

The Baroness had finally arrived in the town but was living in a house on the opposite side of the street. She had not been permitted to see them. (The Baroness was living with Miss Mather, a friend of her late mother.)

Tatiana confessed that she had no idea how long they would remain in Tobolsk as they were never actually told anything. She was pleased to hear that Rita was staying with Zinaide and she sent her best wishes to them both. She added that she would like her greetings sent to all those who remembered her. (It was unlikely that anyone would have forgotten her, but many would have been too afraid to admit that they had known her.)

Nicholas put pen to paper in order to reply to his sister Xenia on Sunday after receiving a most welcome letter. He found it extremely hard to live without news as the papers only told of new horrors. He was convinced that Russia's former allies must despise them by now. Nicholas revealed that the best part of the day was the night, when he could forget everything for a while. He had been angered by the decision a few days previously to remove the epaulettes which had only been decided by a small majority. He went on to explain why it had happened. In Tsarskoe Selo, they had already been removed, and they were concerned that local soldiers and hooligans would forcibly rip them off in the street. It was the same everywhere: one or two bad cavalry soldiers influenced the others. All the children, with the exception of Anastasia, had become ill with rubella over the New Year holidays but they had now recovered. The weather was at least pleasant as it was nearly always sunny, despite a slight frost on the ground. He confessed that his sister and mother were always on his mind.

Alexandra had read the service and prayers that morning before lunching with Marie in Nicholas's small study. Later he read Leskov to the family. Alexandra dined with Marie at eight in the former Tsarina's pleasant drawing room. It was said to be the only comfortable room in the entire house. The others dined downstairs with Nicholas and the members of the suite. That evening he finished reading *Bretteur* and began reading one of Ivan Turgenev's short stories entitled *Three Portraits*. He tried to vary the books he read.

As Alexandra resumed her lessons with two of her daughters on Monday there was a Siberian snowstorm. She gave Tatiana a brief German grammar lesson and then Marie read from the Bible *Psalms 94-104*. She enjoyed the religious studies, but may have found the German lessons a little more difficult as they would have inevitably brought back memories of her childhood. She then spent the hour before lunch giving her son a similar lesson. They read together from the *Gospel of St Mark chapters 6-7* from the Bible and *Meditations on the Divine Liturgy* by Nikolai Gogol. The children slowly read from the same book of the Old Testament Bible on each occasion.

At one the family were finally reunited at lunch in the dining room with the suite. That evening, however, Alexandra again chose to dine in her room with Alexei. Nicholas read later that evening. In the past, he had only read aloud in the holidays, but now it was a regular feature of the evenings. He was an excellent reader, according to Madame Vyrubova, and spoke several languages well. Now he was getting plenty of practice. Catherine Schnieder had been the official court reader, but Nicholas had now taken over the post.

That day Olga had written at length to her friend Rita. She explained that she had received a total of four letters that day from Rita plus another two postcards from Odessa. Her reply was sent via Pankratov as it was assumed that it would inevitably stand a better chance of arriving at its destination. She advised Rita to use the same route.

It had become very cold recently even inside the house. The wind blew hard against the ice-covered windows and the warmest places in the house were the corridors where they tended to congregate. It was warm in the kitchen but unfortunately it was full of cockroaches. She went on to explain that the balsamic fir Christmas tree was still standing in the hall and showed no signs of decay. When they rubbed the branches it smelt of oranges.

Nicholas kept his morale up on Tuesday by cleaning up the yard and filling the shed with useful firewood. He was assisted by Orlov of the 1st Regiment who, like Nicholas, was formerly a member of the Preobrazhensky Regiment. Nicholas's daughters joined them as they were perfectly happy to help with any type of work. In the past, before the revolution, they had frequently assisted Nicholas break up the ice.

(The sisters had all previously enjoyed bicycle riding and canoeing and were very much out-of-doors types like their father. Marie was inclined to be a little lazy but nevertheless also enjoyed being outside, once she got there.)

Over the past two evenings, Nicholas had begun to read a book by *Golodnikov* on the locale of Tobolsk. He read aloud to the family after dinner as usual later. He had probably never read so much in his life and it was far more pleasant than spending a long day at his desk and papers and having little time out in the fresh air.

Meanwhile Alexandra chose to thank Anya for her recent letters and gifts. The perfume that she had sent in October had finally arrived suitably on Christmas Eve. She wondered if Anya had ever received the parcels she had sent. Alexandra had sent sausage, flour, coffee, tea and noodles. Alix admitted that she frequently wore the mauve and light blue jackets that Anya had sent due to the excessive cold in the rooms.

The children had recently been infected with rubella, she explained. All of them had been sick apart from Anastasia. Olga and Tatiana had been forced to spend the New Year in bed. Marie had been very ill and her temperature had risen as high as 39.5 (103°F).

The good news was that the girls' hair was now growing well and lessons had resumed. She had given three lessons the previous morning but she had none today so was catching up with her correspondence in her free time. She had little time presently for reading but they had some very good books. Alexandra spent her days knitting, doing embroidery, drawing or giving lessons. She was having problems with her eyes still so used her spectacles.

On Wednesday a bored Alexei complained in his journal that the day was just like the previous one. He had played in the garden that afternoon with Kolya Derevenko and they had run, jumped in the snow and he had watered the snow mountain so that it did not shrink. He had fought and wrestled with his friend.

Alexei found, like his sisters, that playing outside in the snow and reverting to childhood was a great distraction but, unlike them, he had to be careful not to injure himself, much to his frustration.

Alexandra wrote to Colonel Syroboiarsky on the eleventh informing him of the wild antics of her daughters. They sledged on the snow mountain and constantly fell over. It was remarkable that they had not hurt themselves but they were covered in bruises.

Alexandra had a busy morning – she instructed Anastasia on the *Fall of the Roman Empire*, gave religious instruction to her son and then assisted Tatiana with a German reading. Tatiana read *Freie Bahn* by Werner. The former Tsarina then sorted through her finances with Olga. (Olga had begun working in the administrative department at the infirmary but was not as naturally organized as her sister Tatiana.)

Alexandra then saw the oculist about her eyesight and he ordered her some new spectacles. After tea, she played bezique with Olga. As the eldest Grand Duchess now did little studying, she suffered from boredom more than her sisters. She did have some lessons where she acted as more of a teaching assistant than anything, but she still continued to learn.

Tatiana wrote to Victor Zborovsky's sister Ekaterina that same day and mentioned her dog Ortipo who was well-known to snore. The dog was turning really lazy, according to Tatiana, and spent the entire day either lying close to the stoves or on the divans.

That same day Tatiana complained of the increased restrictions in a letter to Rita. She had been delighted to receive a letter and postcard from Olga's friend and revealed that Rita's sister Lyuda often wrote to Anastasia. Another friend and former nurse Olga Kolzakova often wrote but her letters appeared to have got lost along the way. They had only received the fifth one that she had sent. Tatiana was quite disgusted. The post was rather unpredictable.

Tatiana admitted that they had all been surprised to hear of Olga Grekova's recent marriage to Baron Dmitry Taube. Whilst she was glad for Olga she admitted it spoilt things for her.

(Tatiana had disliked the idea of marriage since childhood despite her romance with *Volodia*. Her former nanny Miss Eagar's tales of *Villikins and Dinah* as a small child had done little to help. The tale of suicide was hardly suitable for such a sensitive child. Dinah had killed herself rather than marry a rich man against her wishes. Each time one of her relatives or servants had married when she was small, Tatiana failed to understand why they wished to leave their mother. Tatiana would never leave hers.)

The former Grand Duchess Tatiana was angered that so many men had lost their lives for Russia and now it had come to this. All those who had fought now had no rank. They had fought for nothing, it seemed. She was very sad at what was happening to Russia and hoped that one day God would teach them a lesson.

Tatiana went on to explain that the sisters were now working in the courtyard and bringing firewood in to the shed. They had built a tower of snow but it was clear that the soldiers were not at all happy about it. When the children stood on the hill, they could see over the high fence into the distance.

(Tatiana's obvious irritation was evident in the letter to Rita. In many ways, her words echoed those of her mother. Alexandra always remained fairly bitter about her fate as did Tatiana and Alexei, the two who were probably the closest to their mother and consequently often spoke in a similar manner. Tatiana had not maintained the inner peace her mother had previously stated that all had achieved. She had obviously been affected by Nicholas's upset over the matter of the epaulettes. Tatiana had grown closer to her father since the days after the revolution when she had spent the long evenings with him, when her parents had been forcibly separated, and she was the only daughter fit enough to spend time outside the sick room.)

Pierre Gilliard's journal indicates a rare spirit of togetherness between the former Tsar and his guards on Friday. It had been Tatiana's name's day and a special service of thanksgiving, a *Moleben,* was held in the hall which doubled up as a makeshift chapel. Afterwards Nicholas, his children and Gilliard had been amongst those working on the snow mountain that day, and some of the soldiers of the guard actually came to assist them.

Despite the service and the building of the snow mountain, Alexei still felt bored, as he admitted in his journal. He declared that whole day had been just the same as the previous one. He had spent a great deal of time in recent years with his father at military headquarters where he had enjoyed being able to see so much more than he ever had before, but now he could do nothing and go nowhere. It was frustrating. At headquarters, he had felt quite *grown-up*, but now he was clearly seen as a child.

Olga and Tatiana had had a similar experience as they had worked as nurses between 1914 and 1916 and had gradually begun to carve out a life of their own away from the restrictions of court life and etiquette. They had made friends, fallen in love, and enjoyed spending time with ordinary people of their own age for the first time. They had stayed out late at the infirmary and had jobs. Now they had nothing. As Olga played bezique with her mother after tea that evening it must have surely frustrated the former Grand Duchess who had recently held a responsible position at the infirmary. She was now reduced to amusing her mother with a game of cards. She did not resent her mother, merely the lack of opportunity.

However Nicholas was in a happy mood on Saturday as he contentedly sat out on the platform that had been built on top of the greenhouse. There were several photographs taken of the family enjoying this vantage point. They included Nicholas and his four daughters. Obviously, Alexandra never scaled the heights of the greenhouse roof. It was a place where they could see far into the distance and soak up the sun on a warm day. Marie was often absent in the pictures as she was the main photographer.

Tatiana had another religious lesson with her mother that morning on the explanation of the parables. Later Marie had a German reading with her mother from the book *Vineta* by E Werner. After lunch Tatiana returned to the subject of the parables with Alexandra. The former Tsarina's knowledge of the Russian Orthodox Church and Christianity in general was vast and she was totally dedicated to her faith.

After tea the family held a dress rehearsal for a French play that was due to be held on Sunday evening. Nicholas for once would be amongst the cast. A new priest arrived to conduct the all-night vigil service that evening. (It is a special service that combines vespers and matins on the eve of a holiday.)

There was an Obednitsa *(Te Deum)* held on Sunday morning at the Governor's House. It was held as usual in the hall. After lunch Alexandra sat knitting as Tatiana read to her. The two had always been close and Tatiana was thought to be her favourite daughter. She was certainly the one most likely to do whatever her mother requested. Her compliant nature had ensured that she later became a good nurse. Tatiana's devotion to duty and order had equipped her well for the post. Olga was more of a free spirit and did not deal well with the blood she saw spilled in the operating theatre. It had disturbed her deeply and caused her to become ill. In a way, she had a form of shell shock such as the soldiers had on the battlefield.

That evening a French play entitled *Les Deux Timides* (Two shy people) was performed. It was a vaudeville comedy in just one act and lasted only thirty minutes. The performers included Nicholas as *Thibaudier,* Anastasia as *Cecile,* Tatiana as *Annette,* with Pierre Gilliard as *Jules Trimoussin,* Prince Dolgorukov as *Anatole Garadoux* and General Tatishchev as *Souffleur.* It had a small audience – Alexandra, Olga, Marie, Alexei, Dr Botkin, Dr Derevenko with his son Kolya, Sydney Gibbes and the maids.

On Monday, Anastasia took to her bed. Her acting the previous evening may have exhausted her and she finally came down with the rubella virus. Meanwhile Alexandra continued with her lessons. Anastasia's illness meant that she spent the whole day in bed and her brother was bored. Not only was she not available to keep him company, but his friend Kolya had remained at home with a cough. The former Tsarina was also occupied elsewhere. That morning Alexandra gave Marie religious instruction. The former Grand Duchess spent fifty minutes with her mother reading from the Bible *Psalms 104-109.* Alexandra then spent the hour before lunch teaching her son and he read from *St Mark 7-8.*

In the afternoon Olga joined her mother for a game of bezique. The two had become closer in recent years as Olga had always been extremely religious, this was one of the things that brought the two together in their times of trial. Alexandra later dined with her two youngest children. Anastasia was still suffering from the effects of the virus and Alexei had been increasingly bored without her company. Nicholas read aloud to the rest of the family that evening as usual.

On Tuesday Alexandra found time to write again to Anya Vyrubova despite spending most of the day nursing Anastasia. She named Anya *Sister Seraphine* and herself *the sinful sister Feodora.* When she had converted to Russian Orthodoxy, she had taken the name Alexandra Feodorovna, so presumably this was a reference to that.

She wished Anya or Anna well on her name's day and reassured her friend that God would one day hear their prayers and end the gloomy days they were currently enduring. She urged her not to despair. The children were well now, apart from Anastasia. She spent her days outside in the sunshine or, on colder days, knitted socks in her *cell.*

The Baroness, she complained, had arrived long ago but had still not been allowed to see them. The others had all gone to dinner but she had remained behind with Anastasia. In the evenings, she added, they embroidered items for the church. Tatiana and Marie worked with great skill and zeal. Nicholas read aloud to them as they worked in unison.

That evening Alexandra dined with her two youngest children upstairs whilst the rest ate downstairs to the dining room as usual.

Alexandra resumed her lessons with her children on Wednesday whilst the wind whipped up a gale outside. She gave Tatiana a scripture lesson for an hour, but she spent much of the day with Anastasia. The two also lunched together. Later, Alexandra once again instructed her son and he read from her Bible again: *St Mark 8-9*. Alexandra dined with her two youngest children at eight whilst the rest ate in the downstairs dining room. The evening ended much as it usually did with Nicholas reading aloud as the ladies *worked*. Although it was 1918 it could have been any household from the late Victorian era, except they were all held captive in Siberia.

Whilst Anastasia rested on Thursday, her siblings continued their lessons. Tatiana had a German reading with her mother that morning and, shortly after Marie, arrived for her regular scripture lesson. The children had not been taught by their mother previously, but during their childhood she had sometimes sat in on their lessons, much to the consternation of the tutor.

Alexandra later dined and spent most of the afternoon in the company of her youngest daughter. She later dined upstairs with Anastasia and Alexei. Nicholas read aloud later. The days were quite predictable but also fairly cosy as everyone attempted to make the best of the situation. Nicholas probably suffered the most with having so little work to do and being restricted to a small yard for his exercise. The revolution had given him far more time with his family and more time to read, but the inevitable feelings of powerlessness were frustrating. Although he had no desire to be Tsar again, naturally he would have appreciated having some control over his own destiny and especially that of his wife and children.

As Anastasia was finally able to get up on Friday, her mother was able to spend a more relaxing day painting and knitting. There was always something that needed making. She was able to lunch downstairs with the rest of the family and household as she no longer needed to sit with any of the invalids.

Later that day Alexei spent half an hour working on the *Old Testament* with his mother learning about *David and Jonathan*. Although Anastasia was quite recovered she later chose to dine with her mother and brother upstairs. Once again Nicholas read aloud after dinner. It was a reminder of happier times when his own father had done the same with his children. In the days before the television or the mass production of the wireless radio, it was one of the few pleasures available to a family in the evenings. Olga and her sisters occasionally played the piano.

The obliging Pierre Gilliard and Prince Dolgoukov watered the ever growing snow mountain in the yard on Saturday. They carried a staggering total of thirty buckets of water between them but the water was so cold that it was frozen by the time it travelled the brief distance between the tap and the snow mountain. It simply *steamed* when it arrived. The delighted children would be able to begin tobogganing the following day but in reality they preferred just jumping off it.

Meanwhile Alexandra spent most of her day simply knitting, apart from a brief religious lesson with Tatiana. An all-night vigil was held at 9pm in the house.

An *Obednitsa* was held late on Sunday morning before the family gathered together to lunch downstairs. Alexandra again spent most of the day knitting. She continually had some project in hand as there was always someone who needed new socks or a scarf. It was extremely cold and knitting was rather relaxing in tense circumstances but sadly on many occasions her hands struggled to hold the needles due to the excessive cold.

The French play entitled *At the Door (A la Porte)* by Eugene Vercousin was performed by the former Tsar's children that evening and it was repeated later. On this occasion Tatiana acted alongside her brother and Pierre Gilliard. Tatiana's part was simply that of *une dame*. Gilliard played Rolande Delavney and Alexei had two parts: *Balthazar* and *un cocher*. Anastasia had not been well enough in the past week to rehearse but may have played Tatiana's part well had she had the chance. She was not only a talented actress, but she also had an excellent French accent as her tutors later admitted. Gilliard naturally preferred to put on French plays whilst his colleague Gibbes chose British ones.

That day Alexandra sent word to Olga's closest friend Rita in Odessa. She thanked Rita for her recent letter and the perfume and requested that she thank Madame Kadbish for the icons and the rosary beads they had sent. It was comforting to know that they were not forgotten.

She urged Rita not to lose heart and keep her courage. Alexandra was convinced that eventually God would spare Russia but it meant that all would need to remain patient in the meantime. God had storms as well as sunny weather, she explained. They were grateful when the sun shone on them and warmed them up. She suggested Rita take a look at nature as it was a great comfort; although horrors occurred all around them she placed her trust in God as he knew best. Life is difficult and all tread a thorny path yet she was certain that they would gain peace and calm in heaven. She felt sure that God would hear the prayers of those who had already reached heaven and prayed for those in danger on this earth. God gave her strength and peace of mind and once life was over He would show His endless love and mercy.

Alexandra then changed the subject and went on to explain that no one was permitted to wear epaulettes. She thought it was horrid and understood that now everyone was forced to wear civilian clothes. On a more cheerful note, she added that her friend and former wounded soldier Alexander Vladimirovich Syroboyarski had moved in with an English family and was now studying the language. He had been very weak after surgery yet God had chosen to save him.

They were delighted to hear that the nurse Olga Porfina Grekova had married one of her former patients Baron Taube. The children had now all recovered from their recent bout of rubella. Her heart was now in better condition as she rarely went out. She sent her regards and those of Nicholas and her son. She thanked Rita for the prayers and the photograph of Nicholas Demenkov. She confessed that she had struggled to hold her pen due to the extreme cold.

The former Grand Duchess Marie had constantly asked about Nicholas Demenkov in any correspondence that had been sent to Rita or Zinaide as he was also in Odessa. A photograph of him had been sent for Marie and would almost certainly have been given pride of place in her small collection of photographs and icons on her wall next to the bed in her shared room.

It was again very cold on Monday morning and Alexandra who was suffering from chilblains struggled to hold on to her pen whilst she wrote to Anya. She had unexpectedly received a letter from Anya dated the first of January and a postcard of the tenth although it was now the twenty-second. Alexandra explained that she was again sending food but had no idea whether it would arrive. (Any parcels containing food were likely to be intercepted. Much of the vast country was still short of food, so it was understandable.)

They thought of her often, she had last written on the sixteenth and sent the letter via the hospital and a card the day after by Sydney Gibbes plus others on the ninth. The letter writing stopped abruptly after Alexandra dropped and broke her favourite pen. She admitted that it was extremely cold as the wind blew straight into the house. It was especially cold in the bathroom. Everyone else was outside despite the cold. She hoped that Anya wore the grey shawl she had sent which smelt of the *verveine* Zinaide had sent from Odessa.

She went on to explain that they had hung the cross sent by Anya over the children's beds whilst they were ill recently, although it lay on the table during a religious service. She added that they had just heard from an old friend Olga Porfirievna Grekova, a nurse at one of the palace hospitals. She had also written to another former nurse Olga Kolzakova.

Of the few people that Alexandra and her daughters now corresponded with, most were former nurses and patients from the palace hospitals and they had little if any contact with members of society. It was the ordinary nurses who proved to be the most loyal friends to the Grand Duchesses.

Olga also took the opportunity to write to Anya and she admitted that she too was finding it hard to cope with the extremes of the climate. It was blowing a gale outside. They had just returned from their walk. She had recently noticed that the name *Anna* had been written on their window. Who had done it? It was odd that they were now living in the same house Anya had stayed in back in 1916.

As the letters would no doubt have been sent via the same messenger, Marie also sent word to Anya and confessed that it had been some time since she had written. She felt so sad that they no longer met but hoped that one day God would arrange that they could see each other. Like Olga she found it remarkable that they were now living in the same place that Anya and Lili had done so recently. Did Anya remember the layout of the rooms? They managed to be quite comfortable with some simple adjustments. They walked in the small garden twice a day and some of the soldiers were kind. She thought of Anya each day and had seen the photo that Gibbes had taken of her, and the perfumes she had sent reminded them strongly of her.

Alexei's contribution also had cold as the theme of his piece and he described how they coped with the cold. His father had taken to wearing his thick Circassian Infantry coat indoors. The whole family spent much of the day seated close to the heated stoves and they had stuffed paper and old rags into the gaps in the window frames. He was pleased to hear that Anya had received their gifts. Today there was some twenty-nine degrees of frost. There was a strong wind yet it was sunny and they had been out in the yard and he had gone on skis.

The previous evening he had acted in a French play along with Tatiana and Gilliard. They were currently preparing another piece. He also revealed that he sometimes played games with some of the soldiers in their rooms and on occasions he was visited by Kolya Devenko. He shared his room with Nagorny. They had four (male) servants – Volkov, Sednov, Trupp and Chemodurov. It was lunchtime so he came to an abrupt halt after asking that God would bless his friend. He then kissed and embraced her.

Baroness Buxhoeveden later revealed why the house felt so cold in the winter. It had previously been fitted with an expensive system of heating and now there was little fuel and, as a result, the family suffered. The former Grand Duchesses who had frequently complained of the cold, with the obvious exception of Tatiana who rarely spoke out, wore as much warm clothing as they could find – at the same time.

Alexandra was concerned that Anya would also be cold so had knitted her some over-sized, man-sized socks. She had been touched that Anya had chosen to send some money but urged her not to send any more. They had enough – for now. (Nicholas never carried any cash and later it became clear that the only one with any cash with them was Anastasia.)

She complained that she had not heard from Lili Dehn or her sisters Victoria and Irene for a year and had only received a single letter the previous summer from Elisabeth. Happily her sister-in-law Olga who was nursing her baby son corresponded often. Olga had informed her that the Dowager Empress was now becomming very old and sad.

Anastasia's little dog was sat on her lap, warming her knees. It was very cold yet she knew that, in the capital, they no doubt had worse – hunger, cold and lack of light. She dearly hoped that God would help Anya bear all her trials with patience. She believed that the worse one endured in life the better it would be for them in the next world.

She would shortly run out of wool as she spent much of her days embroidering and knitting. The children had received a letter from their old nurse Miss Eagar in England, the first they had had from England. She could not believe the rubbish they had printed in the newspapers about Tatiana. (They once stated in the British press that she had escaped and was living in England – Tatiana read the article.)

It was so very cold, Alexei had just put on a sweater and the girls wear *valenki* (felt shoes) in their rooms. Sednyov had just brought her a cup of cocoa to warm her up. Did Anya pray with the rosary beads? Alexandra longed to be able to go to church but they were only permitted on special days. They hoped to go on the second of February and, on the third, she would be able to say prayers for Anya's name's day. Alexandra confessed that she often thought of Livadia and wondered where the *Standart* was now. She could hardly believe it when she heard that Anya had been imprisoned on the *Polar Star.*

Nicholas and his family dearly hoped that they would one day be permitted to travel to the Crimea to their estate Livadia. It was close to where the Tsar's relatives were kept under house arrest and, being on the coast, a likely place to escape from. Nicholas and Alexandra, however, never wished to leave Russia. They would have been content to live the life of exiles in the temperate climate of the Crimea which was ideally suited for the health of Alexandra and her son in particular. The palace with its private grounds, church, terraces and statues was somewhere that would be both quiet and remote. It had been built in the Italianate style with gardens studded with ancient Greek marbles from local Crimean ruins and even had its own 2,000 year old *Nymph* statue from ancient Pompeii in the grounds. The naked female figure with its urn was matched by the Pompeian vestibule built into the palace. Yet their idyll would soon be covered in ivy, the grass unmown and the flowers choked by weeds.

The thoughts of the former Imperial family surely wandered to Livadia in their thoughts at night. Nicholas himself admitted that night-time was the best time of all when they could imagine a world where they were free to go where they chose. Olga's thoughts of the Crimea were no doubt mingled with the walks she had with Paul Voronov in years gone by in the years before the outbreak of war. The Grand Duchesses no doubt dreamed of the time when they attended balls and parties at the palace and their home at the Alexander Palace. The sisters would surely have recalled the time spent at the infirmary and their friends they had left behind. Marie thought constantly of Demenkov and mentioned him in her letters and ones sent to Olga and Tatiana's friends in Odessa who were still in contact with him.

Meanwhile Tatiana had written to her old friend Zinaide Tolstoy that day after receiving postcards from her. She had been delighted with the cards sent for her name's day on the twelfth. She thanked Zinaide for the perfume and revealed that although it had arrived quite safely, other packages (perhaps containing food items) which she knew had been sent had failed to appear.

The Grand Duchess also inquired about Marie's friend Nicholas Demenkov. What had happened to him? Tatiana revealed that the arrival, each letter was a great delight to all concerned. They took turns to read each one. She had luckily received a great deal of post on her name's day and ended by wishing her friend much happiness.

It was so cold on Tuesday that the family chose to have tea in the small dressing room that Nicholas shared with his son as it was too cold everywhere else. The room being so small would have retained the little heat the house had. It had been very windy day for most of the day. That evening Alexei dined upstairs accompanied by his mother and, afterwards, Nicholas read to his family.

On the morning of the twenty-fourth Nicholas recalled his sister Xenia but was unable to communicate with her. Tatiana read the *Spiritual Reading* to Alexandra that morning – a complete yearly cycle of brief homilies for each day of the year –with anecdotes for each of the seasons, something like Flora Thompson had done in England in the book *Lark Rise to Candleford*.

Alexei had a religious lesson with his mother after lunch yet he spent much of the afternoon in the yard with his father. He twirled a stick around in his hand in the snow as he had done in a film that had been made of him whilst he was at Mogilev two years previously. He closely watched Nicholas clear the snow off the roof and brought wood into the house but Alexei was bored out of his mind.

Anastasia attended her weekly religious instruction on Thursday morning with her mother and read from the *Book of the Prophet Isaiah 1-3*. As soon as she had finished, Tatiana arrived for a German grammar and dictation lesson with Alexandra. Alexandra kept busy that morning, and after an hour's break, Marie appeared to read the *Psalms 109-118*.

They were once again able to lunch downstairs. It had been too cold to do so the previous day. Alexandra spent the afternoon knitting again and later dined in the company of her son. Nicholas read to his family once again afterwards.

The soldiers' committee made the decision on Friday the twenty-sixth to replace Pankratov with a military commissar from Moscow. Pankratov and his deputy Alexander Nikolsky left soon after. Shortly before the two men left, Gleb Botkin was amused to see Pankratov using a cat as a handkerchief. The man sat crying whilst wiping his tears off on the bemused cat. Nikolsky was less overcome. That evening the two men bid farewell to everyone after they had been dismissed. Nikolasky shook hands with the teenager and admitted that he had never expected to leave whilst they were alive. Gleb agreed that he had thought much the same. When asked where he was now going, Nikolsky replied that he intended to find a refuge for his outraged feelings. Gleb hoped that he would find somewhere suitable.

Meanwhile Alexandra spent Friday morning catching up with her correspondence and later looked through the financial accounts with the assistance of Olga and Pierre Gilliard. It was the more economical Alexandra who dealt with household accounts rather than Nicholas.

Alexei who was prone to injuries was unable to go outside as he had hurt his knee but he was later able to spend an enjoyable sixty minutes learning about *David and Saul* with his mother once she had finished the family accounts. The two, mother and son, later dined *a deux*.

After spending the day outside in the yard sawing wood and sorting out the firewood for the house Nicholas then finished off the twelve volumes of the works of *Leskov* and began to read the Russian translation of *The Garden of Allah*. He was an avid reader like Olga.

That same day Tatiana had replied to two recent letters from her former Russian tutor Petrov and confirmed that everyone was in good health. She omitted to mention that her brother had injured his left knee the previous day. She explained that each morning they had lessons between the hours of nine and eleven and afterwards they all went out for a walk in the garden. They studied for a further hour before lunch and, in the afternoon, went back out into the yard. (The routine closely resembled that which they had adhered to in the years before the revolution.)

They remained outside until about four but, on days when the weather was particularly pleasant, they stayed out longer. The sisters *worked* until it was time for tea. Afterwards, they rehearsed for a play. They had already put on three and it was proving to be a great distraction and was good for their diction – English, French or Russian depending on the play.

Tatiana revealed that they had built another snow mountain in the yard and, as they had become quite bored walking up and down in the small area, they had taken to sliding down the snow mountain. There had already been a few accidents. On one occasion, Pierre Gilliard had ended up sitting on her head. She had begged him to move but he was unable to as he had sprained his ankle. She managed to crawl out. It was very amusing but, unfortunately, it meant that he had to lie down for a few days. On another occasion, she had slid down the snow mountain backwards and hit her head on the ice which felt very hard. She was convinced that she had smashed the mountain but, luckily, the mountain and her head remained intact. She must have a tough old block, she thought. It was very cold, there was an icy wind which seemed to cut your face, and it had even been cold inside in the rooms.

On Saturday Alexandra kept to her new schedule as her son took to his bed again after his recent injury. He would have been even more bored than usual as he was now unable to walk, but he had already spent the greater portion of his short life in bed.

The former Tsarina listened whilst Tatiana read the *Spiritual Readings* and then a couple of verses from *Jesus son of Sirach 35-37*. Marie then arrived for a German lesson and read to her mother. Alexandra then carried on knitting and managed to complete yet more letters before lunch.

Alexandra lunched with her son and she sat with him as he recovered, accompanied by her embroidery. She hated to sit idle and had made sure her daughters never sat without some sort of *work*. Olga preferred it to be a book but Tatiana and Marie had always been more obliging.

That evening another play was performed at the Governor's House entitled *La Bete Noir (The Black Beast)* by MM Mendale et Cordier. Marie happily played a male part as *Frederic Dortez*. Tatiana acted the part of *Madame Bellamara* and Olga *Maman Miette*. Other actors included General Tatishchev and Countess Hendrikova which inevitably meant that the cast was almost as large as the audience.

Alexandra resumed her lessons with the children on Monday morning. Tatiana read the *Spiritual Readings* before beginning her German literature studies and, after a brief interval, Marie arrived to read the *Spiritual Readings* before reading *Psalms*. The sisters almost certainly both read exactly the same piece. Alexei arrived for a lesson before lunch and read from *Mark 10-11* and Gogol's *Meditations on the Divine Liturgy*.

That afternoon a partially recovered Alexei played energetically outside with his friend Kolya. They slid down the snow mountain and, predictably, Alexei managed to injure himself, this time the ankle of his other leg. He spent the evening limping and later held a cold compress on his foot. He hated the restrictions placed on him as a haemophiliac yet the boredom led to him becoming even more reckless than usual. He had always known how easy it was to become injured but, like many before in his position, he chose to risk the consequences.

Alexandra rested and wrote letters before dining with her son at eight. They had often dined *a deux* even before the revolution. Once again during the evening, Nicholas read *Leskov* to his family. Nicholas often read a fashionable English novel to amuse the ladies. He was, after all, living in a household with more females than males – as he had four daughters but only one son.

On Tuesday as the wind howled outside, Alexandra cancelled her usual lessons to comfort her injured son. He had barely slept the previous night due to the excessive pain. She sat and sewed or played cards with him. She later rested and Tatiana came to read the daily *Spiritual Readings*. Nicholas read aloud later. In such reduced circumstances, books were a real solace and a chance to forget their current surroundings, if only briefly.

Alexandra held a brief lesson with Tatiana at the end of the month beginning with the *Spiritual Readings* and followed by *Jesus son of Sirach 37-40*. The Bible lessons that Alexandra gave to her children were almost exclusively from the Old Testament.

Afterwards Alexandra returned to sit with her son and the two lunched together. She then managed to go out for a rare half an hour mid-afternoon. She then returned to sit with her son whilst knitting. The two then played cards and the two once again had tea and dined together. Nicholas read aloud before Alexandra returned to sit with Alexei. She hated to leave him when he was unwell.

Whilst Alexandra went outside that afternoon it is probable that Tatiana or Olga replaced her and sat with Alexei. In past years, it was normally Tatiana who took it upon herself to sit with her brother on the occasions when he was unwell. Her nursing instinct had come in useful when she worked as a nurse at the infirmary but once she had finally found her true vocation the revolution robbed her of the chance of continuing.

As February began, Nicholas learned that it had been decided that Russia was to be brought into line with the rest of the world. The date was changed so, instead of being the first day of the month, it was actually the fourteenth. (In the eighteenth century, the rest of Europe had adopted a new calendar, but Russia had not. As a result, each century they had become yet another day further behind than in the West. As a result, Olga's birthday was on the 3rd of November or the 15th, but Anastasia's was the 5th and 18th as she had been born in the next century to her older sisters. It was quite baffling.)

Nicholas was convinced that the change would lead to no end of mix-ups. Alexandra's diary was double-dated as she had until 1894 lived in a different time zone in Germany.

That morning, the family bade farewell to many of the riflemen. It was, on the whole, the older men who left. It was no coincidence that they had been the ones who were more pleasant towards Nicholas and his family as there was a deliberate policy of getting rid of anyone who was too friendly towards the former Tsar and his immediate family.

Alexei had been unable to sleep until 4am so took the chance to catch up later and remained in bed for most of the day. It snowed heavily but happily it gave Nicholas an opportunity to clear the yard. Nicholas was bored easily and, despite being an ex-Tsar, he was not too proud to do manual labour. It was something he actually enjoyed. He had been brought up fairly simply by Alexander III of whom his contemporary Queen Victoria had once declared was no gentleman.

Meanwhile, as her son slept peacefully in his room, Alexandra resumed her lessons. Anastasia arrived for her weekly religious instruction. The lesson was reduced to half an hour in which she read from the Bible *Isaiah 3-5.21*. Tatiana arrived later to read the daily *Spiritual Reading* before reading in German. Marie joined her mother at noon and read from the *Psalms 120-139.*

Whether Anastasia's lessons were shorter due to her age or her well-known difficult nature is not clear. She had always been the one who gave the tutors the most trouble yet was unlikely to behave in the same way with her mother. Her English tutor Sydney Gibbes had found the lively child particularly difficult to teach, but she had calmed down a great deal since the revolution. She was still liable to cause hilarity however when she felt the occasion needed it. She was still bravely ridiculing her jailer only days before her death. She had realized that her gift for comedy was a way of breaking up the tension in difficult circumstances.

Later Alexandra lunched with her son. She spent much of the afternoon keeping him amused; they played a game of cards together or Alexandra simply sat and *worked* whilst he rested. She dined with him later and that evening there was another all-night vigil.

The guards had decided that the family would not be permitted to attend church on Friday, despite it being one of the Great Feasts, and the Nicholas and his family were greatly disappointed. The church was a great solace to Nicholas and Alexandra and they craved the inner peace it gave them more and more in the coming year. Although Alexandra had converted to the Russian Orthodox religion from the Lutheran church, initially reluctantly, she had accepted the religion with all her passionate nature.

On Friday morning, an *Obednitsa* was held shortly before noon on the occasion of the feast day dedicated to the *Meeting of the Lord* or, in the West, the feast of the purification. It is the celebration of the day the Virgin Mary presented herself and her new baby son to the church, forty days after his birth for the traditional *churching* of the mother after the birth of a child.

Afterwards Alexandra once again dined with her son. The weather was particularly fine and sunny so the former Tsarina again took the opportunity to go outside for three quarters of an hour. One of her daughters, probably Tatiana, would have remained with Alexei. She was the most likely of all the sisters to deputise for her mother and look after her brother.

Kolya arrived later and stayed for dinner. The two boys dined upstairs with Alexandra whilst the rest went downstairs to the dining room as usual. It was extremely fortunate that Alexei had a young friend as he had no one else of his own age to play with now. He was not permitted to make return visits to his friend. It was lucky that Nicholas's daughters were such good friends as they saw no other young ladies. They had had very little social life in the past, but now they had none. The only contact they had with the outside world was watching people go by and occasionally waving to someone they knew from the window or members of the suite who lived opposite. Nicholas read aloud to his family later as usual.

The following day was the name's day of Alexandra's friend Anya and she could not help but remember the date and noted it on the top of the page in her daily journal. Tatiana arrived to read the *Spiritual Reading* shortly after nine and then she read aloud from the Bible – again it was *Jesus, Son of Sirach 40-43.* She began from where she had left off on the previous occasion. The readings were relatively short.

Marie arrived for her German reading once Tatiana had finished. Alexei was now up and had dressed and he was able to lunch later with his mother in the comfort of Nicholas's small study. Afterwards, Alexandra went out into the garden before returning to her embroidery. She had always embroidered items for the church but now they were used for the makeshift chapel they had set up in the house.

Meanwhile Olga had felt the urge to write once again to her close friend Rita. The two had worked at the infirmary together and had seen each other more or less every day until the revolution, and Rita had even come to the palace when Olga was ill in the spring of 1917. Olga began by asking if Rita had received her letter of the twenty-first. She reassured Rita that everyone was in good health. The weather had been frosty yet sunny and it was possible to see a great many stars at night. They spent the days outside and playing in the snow. They had been kept busy learning various French and English plays.

Olga went on to complain that yet again three parcels sent by Zinaide from the Crimea had not arrived. Dr Botkin had heard that the people were starving in Moscow. They heard of suffering everywhere but believed that God would intervene and somehow help. Olga then asked Rita if she had any news of the recently married Baron Taube and finally asked Rita pass on her greetings to Nicholas Demenkov.

The former Grand Duchess Olga also chose to correspond with Zinaide Tolstoy that day which made sense as she lived in the same house as Rita. She thanked her friend for the carefully chosen and quite beautiful postcards. They were all healthy and walked a great deal in the restricted area of the small yard. The weather was clear and cold but bright. They had still not received the three parcels they had been sent.

Marie also put pen to paper to send word to Zinaide. She felt that time had simply flown by. The four sisters now slept together in one room and in the mornings, she, Anastasia and Tatiana kept themselves busy with their studies. Twice a day they walked in the small yard and garden or amused themselves by sliding down the snow mountain.

They rehearsed all week and then performed plays on Sunday evenings, she explained. They had been rehearsing that day and frequently took a male part. Her short hair helped her get into character. Unfortunately they were no longer allowed to go to church apart from on special occasions so usually held the service in the hall upstairs. It was comfortable enough but not the same as being in a real church. She could not help but think of the Feodovosky Cathedral where they used to worship. It would soon be Lent, but they were not sure how they would fast. She could hear her mother and sisters singing as they intended to join the choir. She had not sung herself though as yet.

Later Alexandra dined in her room with Alexei before the family attended another all-night vigil at nine. Nicholas read aloud afterwards whilst the ladies knitted.

Alexandra had also written a letter to Valentina Cheboratieva a former senior nurse at the infirmary despite the fact that the lady replied only to Olga and Tatiana.

Alix explained that her children played on the snow mountain and mentioned the religious service at home the previous day. She added that they spent time making embroideries for the church and knitting socks.

Shortly before noon on Sunday an *Obednitsa* held in the hall at the Governor's

House. The hall was kitted out with an altar and icons, and a bedspread of Alexandra's was used as an altar cloth. She used her skills to arrange a small chapel. In the past, she had often had the priest visit her and the children when they were sick or otherwise unable to attend church.

After the family attended lunch downstairs in the dining room Alexei went out into the garden, accompanied by his friend Kolya, and Alexandra sat out on the bench in the sun. The family reassembled for tea in Nicholas's study. It was taken there due to its sunny aspect on that particular day. Nicholas, his family and their guest Kolya dined a little earlier than usual as there was about to be a Sunday evening performance in the makeshift theatre.

After a repeat performance of *A la Porte* with Tatiana, Alexei and Pierre Gilliard resuming their previous roles, there was the premiere of *Packing Up* by B Gattan. The undoubted star of the farce was Anastasia who had a great gift for comedy and, on this occasion, caused quite a stir.

Dr Botkin later admitted to his son Gleb that he had never seen Alexandra laugh so heartily in all the time that he had known her. He was convinced that she would fall off her chair. Anastasia had by accident or design exposed her large backside during the piece. She wore a dressing gown and her father's underwear – the gown flew upwards at one point which caused great hilarity. In recent months, Anastasia's weight had increased, probably due to lack of exercise, and the underwear of her father's showed off her worst feature – her large backside.

Anastasia had played the part of *Mr Chugwater*, Marie for once had the female lead as *Mrs Chugwater*, and Alexei played a bit part of the *luggage man*. It was stage-managed by Sydney Gibbes. The evening ended quietly with Nicholas reading to the family. It was a peaceful end to an exciting evening; one they would never forget. It was now a rare occasion to enjoy themselves so much in the current circumstances.

It was back to reality on Monday morning as the children returned to their lessons. Tatiana continued with her German reading after beginning with the daily *Spiritual Readings*. After a short break, Marie arrived for her religious instruction with her mother. She also began with the same *Spiritual Readings*. It is interesting to speculate who read the piece the best; logically it was Marie as she had a greater ability with words in general.

After a brief rest, Alexandra's next pupil arrived – her son – and he continued reading *Mark 11-12* and Gogol's *Meditations of the Divine Liturgy*.

Alexandra felt compelled to send word to her old friend Anya Vyrubova later after hearing of the death of her friend's father Alexander, a senior Court official. Alix greatly sympathized with Anya as she too had lost her father. It was a greater tragedy as Alexandra was unable to comfort her friend in person.

The letter was, as usual, smuggled out by one of the maids as it was far safer to go via a trusted friend than by the usual post as most letters were intercepted. Any post between Alexandra and Anya would have been treated with more contempt than most.

They had heard of the death of Anya's father's death by telegram so Alexandra did not know when exactly he had died and what had happened. She gloomily recalled that it had been told that her father would die soon after her brother Serge had married.

Alexei, saddened by the news of the death, attempted to comfort Anya with a short letter. He began by mentioning the weather which was once again cold and windy yet sunny. He had been outside and had walked on skis and the previous day he had acted in a French play along with Tatiana. They were currently working on a new piece. He also revealed that, on occasions, he went to play games with some of the more congenial guards in their rooms. The letter ended abruptly when the boy joined his family in the dining room for lunch at one.

Alexei's journal that day however was less positive and he complained that everything was the same as ever. He had lessons and was thoroughly bored.

Olga had also composed a letter of sympathy to Anya. She reassured Madame Vyrubova that she was thinking of her and hoped that God would comfort her in her time of great need. Olga went on to explain that the mauve bottle that Anya had recently sent her mother was always placed with honour on her table as a constant reminder of their friend. The big corner room the girls shared was very cold, she explained, as was all the rest of the house. They were all well though and were able to walk in the yard. They constantly heard the sound of church bells in the distance. Olga confessed that she was sad that Anya's sister and brother were not with her as she grieved.

Alexandra spent much of Tuesday morning writing letters, including one to Anya's widowed mother. Despite having a bad cold she nevertheless decided to go out into the sunshine in the garden for half an hour before she came back indoors and resumed her knitting. The family lunched together but Alexandra again dined with her son. Nicholas read aloud later to his family.

That day Olga wrote at great length in the evening to her Aunt Xenia who had recently written from the Crimea. Olga had appreciated her aunt's particularly long letter and was pleased to hear that the evenings continued to be pleasant at Ai-Todor. She acknowledged that they were not suffering from the Siberian winter as yet. It had actually been rather warm in the mountains and fields but it was considerably cooler at Tobolsk and the wind could be very unpleasant.

Although it was now dark, the moon was bright and she could see many stars and the sunsets were spectacular. It had recently snowed and their snow mountain was progressing. It was in places the same height as the fence so they were able to see out which was a great advantage. On occasions people stood and stared at them but the guard quickly moved them on. At times the sisters had deliberately moved away so that a crowd would not form and they were not forced inside. That was their greatest fear.

They had worked hard in the snow but recently Marie had hurt her eye. It was still swollen and purple yet she did not complain. Marie often seemed to find some way of injuring herself. A local boy named Misha sometimes appeared; he was being educated by one of the guards from the 1st Regiment. She explained that she was writing whilst sitting on a chest in the corridor where it was warmer. Anastasia, who was sitting nearby knitting some socks, sent her aunt a kiss. Alexei had already gone to bed and Monsieur Gilliard was reading to him. Once he was settled, her parents would retire for the evening.

She revealed that the veteran soldiers were being sent away from the Governor's

House, and the people that were friendly towards the former Tsar's family were gradually being replaced. Olga went on to explain that Tobolsk was close to the railroad and approximately 300 versts from Tiumen. They continually heard rumours about what was going on elsewhere and, at times, if it were not for the suffering of people, it would have been quite amusing.

She continued her commentary. Her mother had gone to see her brother who was in bed, and Anastasia was now teasing Gilliard. She had some interesting news. Pankratov had been sent away and had been *thrown off*, as the snipers said. They occasionally heard from Princess Elena Petrovna and her mother-in-law Mavra had informed them that her son Ioann had become an archdeacon and was intending to carry on with his religious career. He was happy but his wife Elena did not approve of the move. She could sympathize with Elena, as to be a priest's wife was rather dull.

The former Grand Duchess suddenly came to a halt as she explained that she was needed to play bridge with Trina Schnieder, *Valia* and Dr Botkin. The rest were either playing bezique or simply *working* whilst her father was reading aloud from a book by Leskov.

She continued her letter later the following day but confessed that nothing much had actually happened in the interval. She had plenty of amusing stories she could tell Xenia if she had the chance. They had been saddened by the recent changes in the dates. It was rather confusing. During the week, they rehearsed and, on Sunday evenings, they performed various plays, she explained. It was often great fun. She then apologized for the disorganized letter as her thoughts wandered from one subject to another.

They had been learning how to develop their own photographs and Marie was proving to be the most gifted. Liza Ersberg had just come into the room and asked to respectfully kiss the hand of Xenia in her absence. The letter ended as she had to go off to rehearse the play.

Nicholas confessed on Wednesday the seventh/twentieth of February that he was utterly baffled as to what was going on. He was beginning to think that the war with Germany had resumed since reading in the telegraph bulletins that this had occurred after the truce period had expired. The army had already been demobilized and the heavy weapons had been abandoned. (It proved to be a false alarm luckily.)

The family stuck to their usual routine. Tatiana read the *Spiritual Readings* aloud to Alexandra before finishing off the readings from the Bible she had begun some time ago on *Jesus, Son of Sirach*. They ate in the dining room downstairs and then all trooped out into the garden. After tea, Alexandra enjoyed a game of *bezique* with her daughter Olga.

It was a date that Olga would have been unable to forget as exactly four years previously her beloved Paul Voronov had married Olga Kleinmichel. It must have seemed a thousand years ago, never mind four. She may have wondered where she would now be if she had married him.

Alexei resumed his religious studies for an hour before dinner with his mother. Once again he learnt about *David and Saul* in the *Old Testament*. He later dined with his mother and the day ended as normal with Nicholas reading aloud to his wife and children.

As Thursday came around once more, Anastasia had her weekly reading of *Isaiah* with her mother early that morning. As she finished, Tatiana appeared to read the daily *Spiritual Readings* and continue her German literature studies with her mother. Marie duly appeared later to read from the *Psalms*.

Alexandra lunched with her son later and spent the afternoon reading and *working* whilst keeping him company in Nicholas's study. He may have played with his lead soldiers or simply rested. The two then dined together whilst the rest walked downstairs to the dining room before Nicholas returned to his nightly readings.

The former Tsarina spent a sunny Friday morning catching up with her correspondence and painting. She later lunched with her son in Nicholas's study and afterwards she went out into the garden again. Alexei returned to his religious studies in the afternoon and read to his mother from the book of *Mark 12-13* and the *Meditations on the Divine Liturgy*. Alexandra dined with her son before indulging in a peaceful evening with her knitting. The family assembled later for Nicholas's evening reading session.

Tatiana and Marie again had lessons with their mother on Saturday morning. They had studied on Saturday morning as children, so it was nothing new to them. Tatiana read from the *Prophet Jeremiah 1-6* and Marie had a German reading lesson.

The family reassembled at lunch downstairs at one before they wandered out into the garden together. That afternoon Nicholas and Alexandra heard that more of the soldiers of the guard would leave the following day. It was obvious by now that it was no coincidence that the men who had been pleasant towards them were all gradually disappearing.

Alexandra spent part of the late afternoon looking through the accounts for the family and household. She later dined with Alexei and then did some more knitting before the family reassembled for an all-night vigil. There was no time for Nicholas to read.

Alexei noted the main events of the day in his journal that evening. He had spoken to some of the soldiers that afternoon and the family had wished all of them a pleasant journey. At six, his sisters had brought in an adjutant to see their parents and his mother had presented him with a small icon.

It was extremely difficult for the boy to part with yet more of his few friends. They would have reminded him of happier times at Mogilev.

Olga was certain to have remembered that that day was the birthday of her beloved *Mitya*. She had not seen him since December 1916 but she would have not forgotten him. He was twenty-five years old. They would never meet again but, with so little to do, he would have constantly crept into her thoughts whether she wished or not.

There was an *Obednitsa* late on Sunday morning and after lunch, all the family went out into the garden and watched the departure of the men of the 4th Regiment. They had stood on top of the snow mountain in order to see more. The men departed on sledges.

After dining, Alexandra played *Chicane* with Catherine Schneider and afterwards there was another performance by the children and their tutors. They repeated *Le Fluide de John* which had had its premiere on the Nicholas's name's day in December but the second piece was a new one entitled *In and out of a punt* by Henry Vernon Esmond.

In the first play, Marie went back to taking a male part, that of *Lucien*, Alexei was *John* and Monsieur Gilliard played the lead part of *Duplagne*. The second play was performed in English and Tatiana played *Margaret* whilst Sydney Gibbes, an experienced actor in his youth, played *Hugh*. Alexandra was suitably impressed and admitted that the performances were very well acted and most amusing.

Nicholas was devastated on Monday the twelfth when he finally heard of the humiliating peace terms that had ended the war. However the German-born ex-Tsarina failed to mention the terms in her journal that day but she had a German lesson with Tatiana that morning. She later heard Marie read from the daily *Spiritual Readings* and Alexei the book of *Mark 13-14* and the *Meditations on the Divine Liturgy*.

Alexandra spent a remarkable three hours that afternoon going over the household accounts with Monsieur Gilliard and later revealed her dilemma in a candid letter to Madame Syroboiarskaia. They would have to part with some members of staff, which greatly concerned her as they would then have no wages or pension. She felt extremely guilty but knew it was not her fault.

She rested afterwards as it had given her a headache. She later dined with her son and Nicholas resumed his reading after dinner as usual.

Alexandra continued to try to resolve the financial situation on Tuesday. She looked through the accounts with Pierre Gilliard during that morning and talked it over later with *Valia*. They would have to manage on 4,000 roubles a month from now on including 600 for each member of the former Imperial family so ten members of the staff and suite had to go.

That evening the household heard what proved to be false reports of the death of General I Ivanov and of the murder of the Metropolitan Vladimir of Kiev and Galicia. The news, when it did arrive, was not always accurate and often simply rumours.

Alexandra had written to her friend Syroboiarsky that day of her humiliation at the peace terms. She was convinced that the revolution would be exported to Germany. (It was but did not last for long – the *Spartacus revolt* was quickly put down.)

Meanwhile Nicholas noted his concern in his personal journal on Wednesday the fifteenth over the household cuts and the attempts to make ends meet. They would have to have substantial cuts in their domestic staff and in food too.

After having an hour's religious instruction with Tatiana that morning, Alexandra had spent a further couple of hours after lunch discussing the state of their finances with Pierre Gilliard. She spent a couple of hours with Alexei later reading of the exploits of *David and Bathsheba* before dining in the company of her son. She later returned to the vexed subject of the finances with *Valia* and afterwards Nicholas soothed the company with some reading.

The government had paid for the upkeep of the former Tsar's establishment up until now, but when the *Bolsheviks* had taken charge funds no longer arrived from Petrograd. Colonel Koblinsky had problems paying his own men and, in an effort to obtain food, Prince Dolgorukov and General Tatishchev had signed bills in their own names. They had a little money left from the amount that had originally been provided by Count Benckendorf for their journey but they needed to make economies to make sure it lasted. The servants were given a small pension upon their dismissal and the rest offered to stay on without pay. Alexandra would not hear of it, but their salaries were cut.

The family meals were, by now, fairly basic. At one, they were presented with soup and a dish of meat or fish, followed by stewed fruit. The evening meal comprised of pasta, rice or pancakes then vegetables. They were occasionally presented with welcome gifts of fish or game from local people. There were generally no second helpings and each person was rationed to three sugar lumps per day, and coffee was given only to the former Tsarina as she was prone to headaches and used it as a pain killer. The cook rarely had any butter as it was one of the few things he could not obtain. He had a good stock of basic ingredients but only those that had been able to last the journey from Tsarskoe Selo.

According to Baroness Sophie Buxhoeveden, the delicate underwear of Alexandra had given way under the merciless washing of the local laundry. They had never had to wash such delicate items before. The Grand Duchesses' items went the same way. They eventually took to washing some items themselves, including handkerchiefs and dusters. It is not inconceivable that those working at the laundry deliberately mangled Alexandra's clothes.

Anastasia had her weekly reading with her mother on Thursday morning. Once again, she read from the book of *Isaiah 10-13*. Tatiana appeared as soon as Anastasia had finished, in time for her German reading lesson. After a break of an hour, Marie arrived for her religious instruction and read from the *Book of the Wisdom of Solomon 1-5*.

The family reassembled for lunch downstairs in the dining room. Later Alexandra assisted by Gilliard sorted out the payments for the servants who were about to leave. They continued their task after tea accompanied by Tatiana. Alexandra then dined quietly upstairs in the company of her son; then she spoke about the money crisis with *Valia*. Yet again, Nicholas soothed the frayed nerves of Alexandra with some reading. He had not become involved as he hated to deal with anything that caused problems. That evening he read Nikolai Leskov's book entitled *Cathedral Folk*. The book had first been published the same year Alexandra had been born: 1872.

On the morning of Friday the 17th, Alexandra quietly read and wrote to an old friend of Tatiana – Dmitri Malama. She returned to sorting out the finances before lunch with Gilliard and this time Marie assisted as best she could. After lunch Alexandra carried on her task assisted by Gilliard and Tatiana. She then sat peacefully attempting to return to her embroidery. Alexei arrived at four for an hour's religious studies and he again read from the book of *Mark 14-15* and Gogol's *Meditations on the Divine Liturgy*.

Alexandra later dined in the company of her son before sitting with her daughters quietly *working* as Nicholas read aloud Count Tolstoy's tragic epic *Anna Karenina*.

Later the family heard that Prince Vladimir Orlov, a former major-general in Nicholas's suite, had suffered a stroke. There was still worse news – Sergeev, formerly of the Crimean Cavalry, had been killed and the former chief of staff General Yanushkevich had died in a train accident.

Nicholas noted the new changes to the household in his journal that evening.

General Tatishchev, *Valia* and Gilliard had now taken up the important duty of running the household. Nicholas's valet Volkov was to assist them. (He failed to mention that, on that day, it had been decided that butter and coffee should be excluded from the table as luxuries as from Saturday.)

On Saturday despite the increased hardship Alexandra continued her usual schedule of lessons with Tatiana who read from the book of *Jeremiah 10-16*. Marie appeared for her German reading lesson straight afterwards.

Alexandra chose to go outside after lunch with the rest of the family despite the fact that it was snowing but she only remained there for a half an hour. She later dined in the company of her son upstairs. An all-night vigil began at 9pm.

An *Obednitsa* was held before lunch on Sunday which was then taken downstairs. The family then went outside in the small garden but Alexandra remained outside for an hour. Nicholas had been out sawing wood earlier.

As the choir was no longer permitted to sing at the Governor's House, Alexandra, her daughters and Nagorny practised their singing. The family then rehearsed for the evening's entertainment and later dined downstairs accompanied by Kolya who had arrived for the evening.

Two plays were performed on Sunday evening. The first was *The Crystal Gazer*, a comic piece by Leopold Montague with just two performers – Marie as *Miss Bessie Blank* and Sydney Gibbes as the *Crystal Gazer*. It was followed by a more serious piece – Anton Chekov's *The Bear*. Olga played *Popova* whilst her father played *Smirnov*. Marie had the smaller part of *Luka*.

It had been a long evening for Marie as she had acted in two different pieces and Nicholas had some awkward lines to say to his daughter Olga. He admitted that he (as Smirnov) loved her like he had never loved before; he had left twelve women and a further nine had left him. He had never loved them as he now loved her.

In the first play, a bogus clairvoyant mixes up his clients and it leads to cross purposes about lost loves and even a lost dog. The clairvoyant remarked that the client had arrived without an appointment; it was not his fault she got the wrong message.

After the performances, Alexandra went behind the stage to admire the make-up and told Gibbes that the long white theatrical beard (which he later had in reality as a Russian Orthodox priest) made him look like a former Bishop of Wakefield she had known many years previously.

Meanwhile on this day the *Bolsheviks* signed away some four thousand square miles of lands in Finland, Estonia, Livonia, Lithuania, Courland and Russian Poland.

Lessons resumed on Monday morning. Tatiana had a German reading with her mother. Marie did a reading from the *Wisdom of Solomon 5-7*. Alexei arrived shortly before lunch and read from the book of *Mark* and the *Meditations on the Divine Liturgy*.

Nicholas and Alexandra received the news that Michael Rodzianko's son George, a captain in the Life Guards Preobrazensky Regiment, had been shot the previous month and news also came of the death of Felix Yussopov's cousin. Alexandra had initially thought they meant Felix.

Alexei had spent the afternoon with his friend Kolya, and the former Tsarevich made a wooden dagger with his knife. Kolya did the same and the two boys attacked each other with the weapons which seems rather dangerous in view of Alexei's illness.

Olga sent word to Rita that day and quickly apologized for the torn paper. She explained that she was having problems writing due to the conditions. Olga had been thrilled to hear from her friend *Ritka*. A letter from Rita had only arrived today after almost a month. Olga disclosed that she had written on the 11th and 21st of January and again on the 3rd of February. Whether or not the letters had arrived at their destination, she had no inkling. She had heard that fat Orlov had not died as they had initially heard but had had a stroke. His son was in good health; she had received a letter from the family that same day. Olga confessed that she found what was happening throughout the country quite horrible. They had to hold on to the hope that things would improve. She understood that it must have been extremely frightening living in Odessa. At least now things had calmed down. It seemed an age since she had any correspondence from Katya, but at least Rita had heard from her. She had recently heard from Olga Grekova with her great news and added that Alexander Syroboiarsky frequently wrote and now intended to travel to Japan. She also disclosed although Pankratov had gone Colonel Koblinsky was still at Tobolsk. She hoped that he would remain.

The weather was so far not too cold although it had snowed recently. There seemed to be so little to write about as nothing seemed to happen and they were no longer permitted to attend church. She had begun to chop up wood in the garden, but confessed that she had little talent for it. She went on to explain that Alexei and his friend Kolya were digging ditches and tunnels in the snow. The boys were particularly proud of their achievements and wanted the sisters to crawl in them on their stomachs.

She also revealed that her hair was growing well but all the sisters' hair was now rather scruffy, with the exception of Marie's which was nicely curling. Unfortunately, they now had no one to curl their hair for them. Olga seemed to recall that she had already mentioned the plays to Rita in a previous letter. They were going well and were often very funny.

Baroness Sophie Buxhoeveden had still not been given permission to move into the house with them but she lived nearby with an old Scottish woman, Miss Mather. The two ladies often gave lessons and were happy to have something to do. Unfortunately they had not heard recently from Lili Obolenskaia and had no idea where she was.

Olga wondered if she composed a letter for Katya, would Rita would forward it to her? The Post Office in Tobolsk was not accepting any letters for Petrograd, Moscow or Kiev. But it was evidently not a problem in the south of the country. Had she heard from Olga Butsova? Her Aunt Olga wished to send her regards to Madame Butsova if she was still in the area. She had been expecting to leave.

They had heard often from her Aunt Olga who appeared to be blissfully happy with her baby son. He appeared to be very cute from the photos she had sent of him and was quite big already. She went on to confess that she had heard about the capture of Kiev. How hard everything was now. Unfortunately they had failed to receive the packages Rita had recently sent but they had just received the first one she had posted. Did Rita know where Lili and Charles Dehn were now?

It had snowed all day and she had puttered around on the snow mountain. She had heard that the guards intended to destroy it and put it out to *pasture*. It was typical of the stupidity of the current situation. They had not heard from Victor Zborovsky recently, she revealed. She asked Rita to give her regards to her landlords, Zinaide and her husband and signed simply as Olga.

That evening, just as Olga had predicted, the soldiers chose to destroy the snow mountain. They had been irritated when the family had watched the departure of the 4th Regiment from the top of it. The children were greatly upset at this move as it had been their chief amusement.

Nicholas only discovered that the soldiers had destroyed the snow mountain when he went outside on Tuesday morning. He was greatly angered at this move which he found ridiculous. He had chosen to go out into the yard despite the snow and strong winds. Alexandra spent the day quietly reading and the family reassembled for lunch at one. The meal was somewhat predictable but nevertheless adequate. Alexandra returned to her sewing later and, after tea, she and her daughters practised their singing. That evening Alexandra dined with Alexei and afterwards, as Nicholas read, the ladies *worked*.

Anastasia had written to a friend that day and she recalled with sadness the time she had spent at the hospital. She knew that frequently friends wrote but frustratingly the letters failed to arrive. She had heard that Nicholas Nicolaevich Vasiliev had died. There were so many deaths in these times and she wondered if anyone ever went to tend the graves of their former friends now. She asked if her friend remembered the wounded soldier Lukyanov who was always playing with her bracelets like he was a baby. He had left his visiting card in her album but it had been left behind at the palace. Luckily she had some photographs of her former hospital on the writing desk. The sisters often spoke about their times at the various hospitals and how they had chatted on an evening over the telephone.

The former Grand Duchesses had lost so much. Everything they thought they had owned, they no longer did. All they had were the things they had managed to bring with them and even that could vanish – jewellery could be stolen unless they hid it, clothes were now in rags, food was becoming scarce, and those who guarded them were slowly becoming more unpleasant towards them. The men of the 1st and 4th Regiments who had been friendly towards them had been replaced by men who thought little of them. There would always be some exceptions but those who wished to be pleasant were intimidated by the majority. It is always the way.

Alexandra resumed her lessons with Tatiana at ten on Wednesday morning as she read from the book of *Jeremiah 16-24*. Alexandra simply sat and wrote afterwards before lunch.

Alexandra and her daughters practised their singing during the afternoon and after tea Alexei returned to the subject of *David* in his readings with his mother. The two dined together before they went downstairs to listen to Nicholas read to the assembled family.

On Thursday morning, Anastasia returned for her weekly lesson with her mother and read from the *Psalms 13-20* for some forty-five minutes. Straight after, Tatiana appeared for her hour of German reading and later Marie arrived in time for her religious studies at noon. She was still learning of the *Wisdom of Solomon 7-12*.

The family lunched downstairs later and after tea there was a brief snowstorm. Alexandra and her four daughters practised their singing once more but the regent, who normally led the singing, failed to appear. Alexandra later dined with her son upstairs whilst the rest of the family ate downstairs. Nicholas read later.

That day Alexandra had news that her former gentleman-in-waiting Vladimir Kondratiev had died, probably of old age.

Marie sent word to her grandmother on that Thursday and explained how she and her sisters spent the evening. They either played cards or simply *worked* as their father read aloud but she admitted she was not fond of card games.

When the four sisters were together they sometimes sang and it often ended up with them loudly pretending to be *zurna* (a musical instrument and a type of horn) and some of them even banged against the door or anything else in order to make a tune. They made such a noise that they were heard all through the house. (In his youth, Alexandra's brother had often pretended to be a musical instrument and he may well have done this to amuse his sister's children when they were younger.)

Tatiana returned for another of her Bible readings with her mother early on Saturday morning and again read from the book of *Jeremiah*. After a short break, Marie appeared for her lesson in German reading but the lesson was unusually long and lasted almost three hours.

The family ate together downstairs in the dining room at one and afterwards Alexandra sat out for a while on one of the balconies. Alexandra dined with her son later and that evening, at the all-night vigil, the choir appeared. The four women, a tenor and the regent all came without payment.

There was some bad news, however, as the family heard of the death of one of their former infirmary patients. Captain Gubarayov of the Crimean Cavalry Regiment had died heroically at the beginning of January at Simferopol.

An *Obednitsa* was held late on Sunday morning at the Governor's House. Alexandra was suffering from her usual heart complaint and decided to eat alone in her room. She rested for the remainder of the day and dined alone. She eventually went downstairs to watch a second performance of *Packing up*. Marie, Anastasia and Alexei repeated the play but unfortunately Anastasia failed to cause the sensation she had on the previous occasion when she accidentally showed off her underwear. It was nevertheless received well and was again thoroughly enjoyed by all concerned. It proved to be their final performance. Later Nicholas calmed the mood with some reading aloud upstairs.

According to Sydney Gibbes, Alexei had been learning his part for the play *Rats* by WA Mackersy but they had been unable to do the play due to the onset of Lent. The boy was exasperated as he had worked hard on the piece and was looking forward to acting again.

That day Tatiana had written once more to Zinaide Tolstoy after another letter arrived from her. The letter had been dated the twentieth of January so it had taken well over a month to arrive as it was now the twenty-fifth of February. She was delighted to hear that everything appeared to be going well with her friends. Other letters she had written had unfortunately failed to arrive and sarcastically Tatiana hoped that someone would enjoy reading them!

Tatiana asked if she had received the letter she had sent on the sixteenth of February. Little had happened and she assumed that Pierre Gilliard would have written recently. They had spent much of their free time rehearsing and performing plays recently. She praised the directional skill of Gilliard and Gibbes.

The Grand Duchesses wondered how Zinaide was and how she spent her time. Tatiana and her sisters had been assisting their father with the firewood outside. Luckily, the weather was more like spring than winter. She wished Zinaide all the best and sent her greetings to the lady's husband Serge Petrovich Tolstoy and her daughter Nathalie and promised to write again.

Monday brought back memories of Nicholas's late father Alexander III as it was his birthday. It was also the beginning of the *Week of Cheesefare (Maslenitsa)*. It is sometimes known as butter or pancake week as it is the last week before the Great Lent and therefore the last opportunity to eat dairy food which is not traditionally eaten during Lent. Meat, fish and eggs were also not strictly allowed.

Tatiana began the day by reading the usual *Spiritual Readings* to her mother. Marie arrived later for her religious instruction with Alexandra. On this occasion the lesson lasted for the more usual sixty minutes. After an hour's break, Alexei appeared and he read a portion of the Bible – on this occasion, it was from the book of *Luke 2-4*. He then went on to read from the *Meditations on the Divine Liturgy* once more.

Alexandra lunched in the company of her son upstairs and then, as it snowed, outside spent the afternoon with him after he hurt his toe. He had to keep the foot up or to lie on the floor and was unable to put his boot on. He spent the afternoon looking at newspapers. She dined with Alexei that evening and later listened as Nicholas read.

Alexei spent the day indoors again on Tuesday in the company of his mother and the two dined together. He was delighted when pancakes, one of his great favourites, appeared at lunch and he managed to force down nine of them. When he was ill, he rarely ate, so seeing him eat was a great pleasure to Alexandra.

That day Tatiana replied to a letter that had just arrived from Rita which had been posted on the 8th of January and had taken several weeks to arrive from Odessa. Tatiana numbered the letter (3) as she had written twice before that year to Rita. She wondered if the other letters had arrived. She had heard that another friend, Olya, had recently married someone called Malinovsky but she had only heard the news second-hand. She was delighted to announce that the sisters' hair had now grown to the length her hair had done so by the summer of 1914. Did Rita recall the photographs they had taken where she was wearing the blue ribbon? She was convinced that their hair had grown quicker this time as they had been shaved twice and had worn scarves rather than wigs. The wigs were uncomfortable (and the constant pulling them on and off pulled out any hairs that were beginning to grow). The first time Tatiana had lost her hair in 1913, she felt quite ashamed about it, but this time all the sisters had suffered the same as they had all lost their hair the previous spring.

(However valiantly Tatiana and her sisters had attempted to cope without any hair, it would have nevertheless been an upsetting and humiliating experience. They attempted to deal with it as if it were funny and perhaps they even convinced themselves it was.)

Tatiana admitted how she longed to see the ocean again. Until a few days ago, the weather had been quite spring-like but it had become very cold once again. She asked Rita to give their best regards to Nicholas Demenkov. She hoped that his health had improved. Tatiana begged Rita to write again. They had had no letters from Lili Dehn recently. She recalled that a year ago they had listened to the Rumanian orchestra in front of the fire. She wondered if Rita remembered.

(Once again Tatiana admitted that she longed to travel. Although she rarely complained and seemed quite compliant, in reality Tatiana longed for adventure and during her imprisonment probably read the stories of travelling equatorial Africa she had brought with her. She longed to return to the warmth of Livadia and to warmer climes in general. The sisters preferred the warmth rather than the cold and Tatiana had leafed through her father's photographs of his tour of the Far East in the 1890s and imagined the warmth of the palace where the heating system was adequate and the nights were cosy and they had no need to wear layers of clothes inside the house. It seemed a million miles away but the stories her father read each night gave them all a chance of escape and something pleasant to think of in difficult circumstances.)

That evening, the injured Alexei dined in the company of his mother upstairs as he was unable to get downstairs as his foot was causing some trouble.

On Wednesday, Alexandra recalled the death of her own father. The Grand Duke of Hesse had died in 1892 and ,only a few days previously, it had been her father-in-law's birthday. The couple had both lost their fathers in the space of two and a half years.

That morning, Tatiana appeared to read the *Spiritual Readings* to her mother and then read from the book of *Jeremiah*. She read it to the end. Alexandra then rejoined her son and the two lunched together. That afternoon, Alexandra listened as her son read about *Solomon and Sheba*. He was still working through the Old Testament. Meanwhile Nicholas had spent much of the day outside in the yard sawing wood. He was assisted by Tatiana after her lesson. He finished reading *Anna Karenina* by Tolstoy and began reading *Lermontov* that evening.

(The suicide of Anna Karenina in front of a train at the end of the Tolstoy epic cannot have been a happy ending and may have even reminded Olga, Tatiana and Marie that they were all parted from their true love and had little hope of a reunion reducing them to tears. To Alexandra however, Anna like Sheba was an unfaithful wife and she would have seen the moral in the story.)

Nicholas was delighted to report in his journal that evening the arrival of most welcome gifts of butter, coffee, biscuits and jam for tea. Some people who had heard of their recent economies had come to their rescue. He was greatly appreciative of the presents. The Grand Duchesses had always adored fruit jam so it was a great treat for them. They had often bought pots of jam on their walks.

Chapter Twenty-three

Tobolsk Spring 1918

A memorial service or *Panikhida* was held on Thursday in honour of Nicholas's late grandfather, Emperor Alexander II of Russia who had been murdered exactly thirty-seven years previously.

Earlier Anastasia had returned for her weekly forty-five minute religious instruction with her mother where she had read aloud from the book of *Isaiah 20-26*. Marie arrived at noon for her weekly session where she spent a peaceful hour completing the *Wisdom of Solomon*.

Alexandra and her son again lunched and dined together privately upstairs and later Nicholas read aloud to the family after dinner.

Tatiana took it upon herself to reply to a late arriving letter from Zinaide Tolstoy that day. It had been jointly addressed to herself and Olga. As it had been clearly dated January 1918, Tatiana admitted to being rather baffled as to why it had suddenly appeared after over a month. Had Zinaide yet received the letter she had written on the twenty-fifth of the previous month or the one she had done a couple of days later to Rita? She went on to reveal that they had finally heard from Lili Dehn. Tatiana then urged Madame Tolstoy to continue with her correspondence despite the obvious delays and asked if she had heard about yet another of their old friends, Nicholas Rodionov. She had heard the sad news of the death of Captain Gubaryov who had been killed at Simferopol in the Crimea.

On the first anniversary of his abdication, Nicholas recalled the final days of his reign and voiced his fears for Russia's future in his daily journal. His thoughts returned to the final days he had spent aboard the train at Pskov and he confessed that he did not even know what to wish for any more yet willingly placed his trust in God.

Meanwhile, Alexandra spent most of Friday morning composing letters to old friends including Count Fredericks' daughters Emma Fredericks and Eugenia (Nini) Voyeikova, Lili Dehn, Anya Vyrubova and Nicholas's Aunt Olga, the Dowager Queen of Greece. They were amongst the few who continued to correspond with her personally and those who remained the most loyal in the dark days of exile. In her journal she recalled the anniversary of the death of the young soldier David Grabovoi, an officer of the 14th Georgian Regiment in 1915. His death had been especially painful for her at time as he had died in the palace hospital in her care.

She lunched and dined in the company of her son and at lunch there had been pancakes much to the delight of her young son who particularly appreciated them.

The young former Tsarevich had drawn whilst his English tutor Mr Gibbes read aloud to him. He was finally able to fit his boot on to his injured foot by the end of the day after having endured a compress on his toe all afternoon in an effort to improve it. The evening ended as usual upstairs with Nicholas reading aloud to his family.

On a cold and windy Saturday, the former Tsarina looked through the accounts once again with Pierre Gilliard. He was amongst those who had been recently appointed to take care of the household. She again lunched and dined with her son. The delighted Alexei confirmed in his journal later that he had a remarkable sixteen pancakes at lunchtime as they were serving them for the last time before the onset of Lent. He later had the luxury of a warm bath as his foot had sufficiently improved to immerse in water.

Alexandra had written another three letters including one to Zinaide Tolstoy. She was one of the most frequent correspondents of the family. There was an all-night vigil at nine, a service that combines vespers and matins and is held on the eve of an important holiday.

The former Imperial family attended an *Obednitsa* late on Carnival Sunday morning. It was *Forgiveness Sunday* when Russian Orthodox believers ask one another's forgiveness for past sins. The children trapped inside the house were only able to observe the local people enjoying the festivities from afar. They could hear the sound of bells, singing and mouth organs, and hear the sledges pass by. Unfortunately they could see nothing due to the high fences that surrounded them.

Alexandra lunched with her son before she again dealt with the household accounts assisted by Pierre Gilliard. After tea, Alexandra and her daughters practised their choir singing and afterwards Alexandra dined with her son upstairs whilst Nicholas and his daughters Olga, Tatiana, Marie and Anastasia dined downstairs in the dining room with the rest of the household. The diners included General Tatishchev, Prince Dolgourkov, Pierre Gilliard, Countess Hendrikova and Catherine Schneider.

The season of the Great Lent began on Monday morning with a service at the Governor's House. As the choir had been unable to come, Alexandra and her daughters had practised their singing skills and the five ladies sang under the direction of the new deacon, but not very successfully, according to Alexandra. They had had no proper rehearsal, despite their recent attempts at using their vocal chords. They sang again in the evening service at seven with the deacon who had remained at the house during the day.

Alexandra had lunched separately again with her son whilst the others ate downstairs. She later sat out on the balcony accompanied by the Countess. After the evening service, Alexandra dined with her son once more. The evening was spent without the suite and Nicholas read about the life of St Nicholas.

In a letter to Anya, Alexandra explained that she had been sitting on the balcony writing out the music for the prayers. Despite her admissions in her journal about the singing earlier, she chose to tell Anya that the singing had gone well. They had attempted to sing some new prayers with the new deacon and she dearly hoped the second service would be better. They were permitted to attend the eight o'clock services at the church on Wednesday, Friday and Saturday mornings which was a real comfort.

On the morning of Tuesday the 6th of March, a service was held, followed by half an hour's singing rehearsal. Tatiana later read the daily *Spiritual Readings* to Alexandra. The former Tsarina lunched with her son upstairs once again and she caught up with her correspondence, read and painted. The Romanov ladies' choir practised again before tea.

The evening service was held at seven and luckily the singing improved due to the constant rehearsals. Alexandra dined in the company of her son later but she chose to retire to bed early that evening. It had been an unusually busy day for her.

According to Pierre Gilliard, Nicholas had spoken to him about the Treaty of Brest-Litovsk that afternoon which had ended the war with Germany. Nicholas had been very depressed and announced that he found it a disgrace. He would have never agreed to it and could not believe that the Germans would have dealt with those he termed as traitors. He was convinced that it would ruin the country. Later, when Prince Dolgorukov mentioned the clause in which the Germans had demanded that the Imperial family be handed over to them unharmed, Nicholas was convinced it was a way of discrediting him, or some insult. Alexandra added that, after what had happened to Nicholas, she would rather die in Russia than be saved by the Germans.

On Wednesday, Alexandra noted in her journal that it was Orchie's birthday. Her former nurse, Mary Ann Orchard, had died in England in 1906. It was also the anniversary of the death of her late paternal grandfather, Prince Carl of Hesse and, on a more positive note, the twenty-ninth birthday of her nephew Prince Waldemar of Prussia, the son of her sister Irene. He was known as *Toddie* and had been a great favourite of hers when he was a small child and, like Alexei, was a haemophiliac.

That morning, the former Imperial family had finally been permitted to attend church once more, as they had been promised, and they duly attended the *Pre-Sanctified Mass* a pre-Lent celebration at eight in the sunshine. Alexandra lunched with her son upstairs and afterwards Tatiana read the daily *Spiritual Readings* to her mother. The day was spent fairly quietly and another service was held at home at seven. The singing went well. The service was held in the hall close to the piano where plays had previously been held. Afterwards Alexandra dined in the company of son and once more she retired early to bed.

On the morning of Thursday, the eighth, in the absence of her usual lessons, Anastasia had sufficient time to compose a letter to her Aunt Xenia. She politely thanked her for the postcard which had only just arrived and went on to ask about the Dowager Empress. She was worried about her grandmother's health. She added that they frequently spoke of Xenia and the family. Although the weather was pleasant and it was nearly always sunny, they were no longer able to slide down the snow mountain. The guards had not only wrecked it but erected a drainage ditch through it. It was still standing but they were unable to slide down it now. It had been bugging the guards for a while, so they had deliberately done this. She found the whole thing quite pathetic. Anastasia explained that their new hobby was chopping and splitting firewood which was both useful and enjoyable. They were already good at it. The sisters also helped to clear the paths of snow. She had not yet turned into an elephant but she expected she soon would as she had put on a great deal of weight. She thought it may have been through lack of movement. Anastasia begged Xenia to forgive her terrible handwriting as her hand was moving all over the page. They were all fasting that week, she revealed. They sang at home in the choir but they had finally been given permission to attend church. She wished to know how Xenia was getting on. There had been little happening with them that needed writing about. Anastasia came to a sudden halt as they were about to go out into the yard again to work. They all sent their best wishes and hugged them all. The sisters asked to pass on their best regards to her.

Alexandra had lunched and dined in the company of her son. During the course of the evening Nicholas read to the family of the life of his namesake St Nicholas.

Friday brought back painful memories for the former Tsar. He recalled that it was exactly a year since he had arrived back at Tsarskoe Selo after his abdication. He feared for the future and felt his only hope was to put everything in the hands of God.

However Alexandra was more concerned with being able to attend church that day and made no mention of the anniversary in her daily journal. They participated in *Pre-Sanctified Mass* at the nearby church. The state of the path made it impossible to use Alexandra's wheelchair so she was obliged to walk like everyone else. The chair had been bought for her recently by her daughter Olga. Alexandra relaxed on her return before lunch which was again taken upstairs with her son. In the afternoon, the former Tsarina and her daughters practised their singing again as they would be needed in the service at home that evening.

After dining in the company of her son, Alexandra joined the rest of the family at confession in the private chapel erected in the hall. Nicholas and Alexandra confessed, along with Olga, Tatiana, Marie, Anastasia and Alexei plus Prince Dolgorukov, Countess Hendrikova, General Tatishchev, Liza Ersberg and eleven of the men. The children had spoken first and their parents last.

Alexandra walked to the church and back, without the aid of her wheelchair, with the rest of her family on Saturday morning, almost certainly leaning on the arm of Nicholas. They attended Mass and took Holy Communion. They returned to the Governor's House where once more Alexandra lunched privately with her son whilst the rest ate downstairs. That evening there was a service at home where Alexandra and her daughters sang under the direction of the deacon. Olga and Tatiana were sometimes alleged to have good singing voices, but the art of blending the voices of different people of varying ages with degrees of ability was not proving easy.

On Sunday morning, as the weather improved, Alexandra sat out in the sunshine. An *Obednitsa* was held at home shortly before lunch. Once again, Alexandra lunched and dined upstairs with her son. Later she painted and sat out on the balcony despite the cold. The young former Tsarevich watched his father in the yard that afternoon, and Nicholas sawed wood, whilst his sisters chopped the logs and carried them into the shed. Alexei stopped work at one point and decided to throw snowballs at his sisters. Although Nicholas was tireless in his work he was joined on and off by various male members of the household including Gilliard or one of his daughters or, on occasions, as photographs of the time prove, his son. When Nicholas chose to play skittles he again proved to be far fitter than the rest of the household.

That evening, as he passed on the street, Serge Markov, formerly a cornet in Alexandra's Crimean Cavalry Regiment, caught sight of the former Imperial family as they gathered in the upper storey windows. As he slowly lit a cigarette, he noticed Alexandra nod to him cautiously. Somehow, she later managed to pass on to him a cigarette holder and note. On occasions very small items were smuggled in and out of the house at this stage, possibly in coat or hat linings or in the tops of bottles.

Alexandra dined in the company of her son that evening and later the family gathered together to hear Nicholas read aloud.

On the morning of Monday the twelfth, as the second week of Lent began, Tatiana read from the daily *Spiritual Readings* to her mother and Marie arrived later to read from *The Ray of Spirit*. Alexandra then relaxed for an hour and painted before her next pupil arrived. Alexei read from the book of *Luke 4* and the *Meditations of the Divine Liturgy* by Gogol once again.

The family separated at lunch. Alexandra ate upstairs in the company of her son and the rest walked downstairs to eat with the household.

Later, as Alexandra sat out on her balcony, she saw Markov once again. She also saw Vladimir N Shtein, the former Vice-Governor of Mogilev whilst Nicholas had lived there, who passed on a most welcome gift of some 250,000 roubles from the monarchist organizations. It had come at an opportune time for Nicholas and his family. It was possible that Anya Vyrubova had arranged for the men to visit and perhaps even organize an escape attempt. They also brought gifts of books and tea and, according to Alexandra, the family had recently received jams, biscuits, coffee and *pirozhki* which is a type of bun.

The money may have been smuggled in one of the books or the food parcel. It is possible that messages were smuggled into the family whilst they were at Tobolsk via Dr Derevenko or Dr Botkin who came and went frequently at this time.

Tuesday was spent quietly at the Governor's House. As there were no lessons Alexandra took the opportunity to send word to her old friend Anya Vyrubova. She lunched with her son and afterwards sat quietly in the sunshine on the balcony. The evening went according to its usual plan: Alexandra ate privately with her son whilst the rest of the family dined downstairs with the suite. Nicholas read Turgenev's *Spring Torrents*. The story may have been a personal interest to Nicholas as it concerns a young Russian landowner named Dimitry Sanin who fell in love with a young girl from Frankfurt, the town close to where his wife grew up in Darmstadt.

Nicholas was rather amused when the new *Red Guards* appeared on Wednesday. A detachment had been sent from Omsk and the current Commandant had been rather disturbed at the prospect of their arrival. He had strengthened the guard and put a machine gun in position. He thought it quite pathetic how the revolutionaries failed to trust each other.

The day was the feast of the *Feodorovskaia Mother of God*, the patronal icon of the Romanov dynasty. Alexandra had spent the earliest part of the morning quietly reading and writing. She then listened to Tatiana read for an hour of *Jeremiah's lament*, and from the book of *Baruch* sometimes known as the deuterocanonical book of the Bible. She then returned to her writing before lunching at one in the company of her son.

That evening Alexei returned to his religious studies and read about *Solomon and Jeroboam* on this occasion. Tatiana appeared later to read the *Akatharist* (hymn of praise) to the Feodorovkaia Mother of God appropriately to her mother. Alexandra later dined in the company of her only son and afterwards Nicholas read aloud to the assembled family.

On Thursday morning Anastasia returned for her religious instruction and for once she was allotted the full hour. She read from the book of *Isaiah 26-29*. Tatiana arrived at ten for her German lesson. The Grand Duchess studied from various texts and ended with a German reading.

Marie returned for her hour of religious studies at noon and read from the *Wisdom of Jesus, Son of Sirach 1-6*. Alexandra then lunched privately upstairs with her son. He had not been able to go out as he had developed a bad cough and a snowstorm raged outside. She read to him later from the journalist Nikolai Leikin's *Where the Oranges Ripen*, a lampoon on Russia's nouveaux rich on a tour of the European continent in 1892.

The evening ended predictably as Alexandra dined in the company of her son and the rest ate downstairs with the members of the household. Nicholas read again afterwards.

Friday was spent fairly quietly at the Governor's House as a snowstorm raged outside. That morning, Alexei had an hour's religious instruction with his mother. He read from the book of *Luke* despite his bad cough. He later lunched with his mother and then sat with her whilst she read to him. The two spent most of the day in each other's company and they dined together later. Nicholas read aloud to his family afterwards.

Tatiana and Marie returned to their lessons with their mother on the morning of Saturday the seventeenth. Tatiana spent an hour reading from the book of *Ezekial 1-14* and Marie followed with a German reading lesson straight afterwards. Later, Nicholas read to his wife whilst she quietly *worked*. It was unusual for him to be indoors for much time during the day as he preferred to spend as much time as possible outside. Alexandra had as usual lunched and dined accompanied by her young son, and an all-night vigil was held in the house from 9pm.

It began snowing again on Sunday morning and an *Obednitsa* was held shortly before midday indoors. The hall had been converted into a small chapel with the help of a table, icons and an arrangement of cloths and candles. Alexei's friend Kolya arrived to break up the monotony of the day. He then dined in the company of the former Tsarina and her son. Nicholas read to the assembled family later.

The third week of Lent began on Monday and, as usual, Tatiana read from the *Spiritual Readings* to her mother that morning. Marie came an hour later to read of the *Wisdom of Jesus, Son of Sirach*. Alexandra's third pupil of the day duly arrived at noon and Alexei spent an hour reading from the book of *Luke*.

Alexandra and her son lunched at one whilst the rest ate downstairs as normal. She was spending less and less time downstairs. At the Alexander Palace, she lived on the ground floor whilst her children had their suite of rooms on the floor above. Alexandra spent an hour on the balcony later and Alexei went out into the garden to join his father and sisters.

After tea Alexandra and her four daughters practised their singing once more. As she had little else to do and was a talented singer, Olga may have been given a more prominent role in the choir.

Alexandra later sent word to Zinaide Tolstoy, who was probably one of the most frequent correspondents, before dining in the company of her son Alexei. The evening was ended predictably with Nicholas reading aloud to his family. He was an excellent reader in several languages and many admitted that he had a good speaking voice. The one thing that Nicholas's late father had insisted upon with his children regarding their education was the ability to speak as many languages as possible. It was a sensible decision as the various royal families had intermarried and spoke varied languages at the dinner table. They often changed rapidly from one language to another in the course of a conversation.

The only other thing that Alexander III had insisted on was giving his children a love of nature. He succeeded with Nicholas as he did not like being inside unless absolutely necessary. After a long morning at his desk at the Alexander Palace, he had always gone out for a long walk, no matter what the weather. Now, he could only go out into a very small area and he naturally found it frustrating. He paced up and down the yard like the caged animal he was in effect.

As the weather finally improved on Tuesday, Alexandra spent the whole afternoon sitting out on the balcony. It was so much warmer that she was able to do so in a thin blouse, silk jacket and the inevitable skirt, of course. The jacket was one of the ones she had been sent by Anya. Of the clothes Alexandra wore in Siberia, the most luxurious were the ones she had been given only recently by Anya. She was said to have never bought a new dress since the beginning of the war.

Later, Alexandra looked through the household accounts assisted by Pierre Gilliard. She dined in privacy with her son that evening and, afterwards, Nicholas read to his assembled family whilst the ladies *worked* or played cards quietly.

That day the former Tsarina had written various letters and had informed Madame Vyrubova that, although the *Bolsheviks* had arrived, nothing had changed. Boris Solovyov, the son-in-law of the late Grigory Rasputin, had been arrested. It was said that he was organizing an escape attempt. Alexandra still had the belief that God would work a miracle.

Alexandra resumed her usual schedule of lessons on the morning of Wednesday the 21st. Tatiana arrived at ten to read from the book of *Ezekiel 14* and *Daniel 1-5*. Once Tatiana had finished, Alexandra ventured out to sit on the balcony for a while. After lunching quietly with her son at one, she went back to the balcony where she wrote to an old friend, Colonel Syroboiarsky. Alexei returned for his usual Old Testament readings late in the afternoon and read about Elijah ending with the death of Ahab, and Jezebel being eaten by the dogs. Alexandra and Alexei later dined together. Afterwards, the family bade farewell to three of the men who had completed their duties but had not yet returned to their homes.

That evening, as Nicholas read to his assembled family, Alexandra recalled that it was now exactly a year since Anya Vyrubova and Lili Dehn had been arrested and taken away. Luckily, Lili was released soon after but Madame Vyrubova had been through terrible times since.

On Thursday morning, as the snow began to thaw outside, the former Imperial family heard a band of rogue-*Bolsheviks* from Tyumen leave Tobolsk in fifteen troikas. They could clearly hear the sound of the sleigh bells, and the whistling and whooping of the men. The Omsk detachment had apparently run them out of town.

Anastasia returned for her weekly religious instruction early that morning and read from the book of *Isaiah 29-32*. After she had departed, Tatiana came for her German reading lesson. Whilst she read, Alexandra embroidered. She was not one to waste time, even though she now had all the time in the world. Unfortunately, *time* was the one thing that would soon be running out. Marie arrived for her religious instruction at noon and she again read of the *Wisdom of Jesus, Son of Sirach 11-18*.

Whilst her sisters continued their studies, Olga occasionally spent time in the greenhouse, tended to the few indoor plants, cut wood with her father, read from her stock of books, wrote letters or simply sat and stared out of the windows. It was a far cry from the past years when she had been working at the infirmary. Now, she had nothing of real importance to do. She was not even the nurse when one was occasionally needed. Tatiana took that position. Inevitably her thoughts may have returned from time to time to *Mitya* or to Paul Voronov.

That day Alexei had noted in his daily journal the reduced rations. The previous day he and his four sisters had been given a supply of half a pound of sugar which was to last for a whole month. He played outside in the yard that afternoon with his friend Kolya. He had made himself a bow and arrow and enjoyed shooting with it.

On Friday the 23rd, Alexandra recalled her that it was the birthday of her sister Princess Victoria whom she had not seen since the summer of 1914, and also of her brother-in-law Grand Duke Alexander or Sandro as he was known, the husband of Nicholas's sister Xenia. Sandro was in the Crimea under arrest with his family but Victoria was living safely in England. She lunched quietly with Alexei at one whilst Nicholas and his four daughters dined downstairs as usual. The weather was sufficiently improved for Alexandra to sit out on the balcony again. Later she looked through the financial accounts with Gilliard.

For much of the day, the bored guards sang and played their balalaikas. They had nothing to do, but Nicholas and his children had spent the day outdoors or on the balcony in the fresh air. Nicholas was less than impressed by their lack of ability to find something useful to do. After all, he had done so. He spent most days sawing wood or even sweeping the paths.

Alexei had his Bible studies shortly before dinner. He read from the book of *Luke*. He then dined in the company of his mother. Later, the family assembled so that Nicholas could read to them.

On Saturday morning, Tatiana returned for her religious instruction with Alexandra and read *Daniel 5-8* for an hour. The former Tsarina later caught up with her correspondence. She wrote to her old friend Madame Syroboiarskaia. Alexandra later lunched at one with her son as usual.

Alexandra spent most of the afternoon sitting on her balcony simply enjoying the view and the fresh air. Later, she dined with her son before attending a religious service which was again held in the hall upstairs at the Governor's House. The all-night vigil was held late that evening without the assistance of three singers and the regent. Unfortunately, they would not be able to come until late the following morning which meant that the Romanov choir was required again. The service was held on the eve of the Annunciation and also for the most holy Theotokos.

Alexandra and her daughters sang at the religious service held at the Governor's House at 8am on Sunday morning. The choir had been unable to arrive early enough for the service. It was a special day in the Russian Orthodox Church as it was the Annunciation, the celebration of the day when the Angel Gabriel appeared to the Virgin Mary and she was told that she would give birth to the Son of God. Jesus was born nine months later.

Nicholas noted that evening in his journal that his wife and daughters had sung that morning without any rehearsal yet failed to state whether or not he enjoyed it. Although Alexandra was said to have a fine singing voice, Madame Vyrubova once explained that he did not actually like it. She normally never sang whilst he was around as it was said to irritate him.

Later Alexandra dined in the company of her only son as she usually did and she later sat out on the balcony. The air was fresher as it had snowed a little that morning. Kolya Derevenko arrived for tea and stayed for dinner. He ate with Alexandra and his friend Alexei. That evening the former Tsar read to the assembled family members.

Anastasia wrote that day, whilst sitting close to the window, of the sisters' new routine which comprised of lessons, watching people pass by on the street, sweeping the yard and singing. They had few amusements so had to make their own. They had fasted in the first week of Lent. Lessons for the four younger children took place in the mornings and evenings, she explained. She went on to add that in fine weather they sat on the balcony and, when they went into the yard, they cleared the paths like janitors. Sometimes, they chopped wood or even sawed it.

That day a local businessman sent gifts to Alexei. He was given a sledge and a boat. Alexei and his friend Kolya began sliding down the internal staircase in the boat. It was a dangerous game.

On Monday the twenty-sixth at the beginning of the fourth week of Lent, the former Tsarina resumed her lessons with her children. Tatiana arrived first to read the *Spiritual Readings* and Marie appeared later to read from the same work, probably even the same piece. She continued however with *St John Chrystostom*. As Alexandra relaxed before her final pupil of the day arrived, it began to snow. Alexei arrived later and read from the book of *Luke* and continued with his reading of Gogol's *Meditations on the Divine Liturgy*.

Alexandra lunched with her last pupil at one, and afterwards she relaxed with a little painting and composed a couple of letters. Alexandra dined upstairs at eight with her son and afterwards Nicholas read aloud to his family from Nilus's *Protocols of the Elders of Zion*. Although Nicholas was not aware, the book had actually been fabricated by the secret police. The author claimed that they were the protocols of a Zionist organization bent on destroying civilization and creating a worldwide Jewish state. Nicholas found the work fascinating.

Pierre Gilliard noticed a worrying change in the atmosphere inside the Governor's House on Tuesday. The new Bolshevik Commissar who had arrived with the detachment from Omsk had insisted on being able to inspect the house. The soldiers who were on guard had refused to comply. Colonel Kobylinsky was extremely concerned that it would lead to conflict between the two groups. He had taken the precaution of doubling the sentries. The family spent a disturbed night.

Meanwhile Nicholas mentioned the book he had begun the night before in his journal and made a remark about the increased cold, but added that the previous evening there had been some unrest amongst their detachment due to rumours of the arrival of more Red Guards from Ekaterinburg. There was even talk of moving them to the priest's house nearby.

Alexandra was becoming alarmed and, that morning, with the assistance of Marie Tutelberg and the four Grand Duchesses, began sewing her jewels into items of clothing. They hid them in buttons, belts and even corsets. She then dined in the company of her son Alexei at one and then continued with the sewing project that afternoon.

The former Tsarina sat outside briefly but, after only fifteen minutes, was told to go back inside by the guards. There may have been an alarm; possibly something was happening in the street that looked a little suspicious. The guards were on edge and worried that something might start with the other troops. Alexandra returned indoors and continued with her embroidery before tea. She later gave Alexei a brief lesson in Bible studies for half an hour before dinner. They dined *a deux* once again and later that evening Nicholas continued with his reading, probably the same book by Nilus.

On the morning of Thursday the twenty-ninth, Nicholas noticed that someone new had appeared. During his morning walk, he spotted a gentleman known as the *Extraordinary Commissar Demianov*. He had made an inspection tour of the guards' accommodation and the garden accompanied by the Commandant and the riflemen. He actually commanded the Red Guard detachment at Omsk and had arrived in Tobolsk two days earlier.

Although there was a great deal of agitation, things could have been a whole lot worse, according to Gleb Botkin. Luckily, Demianov proved to be a native of Tobolsk and an extremely pleasant man. He was even a monarchist, it appeared. When Dr Botkin heard that another detachment were marching on the town from Tyumen, allegedly committing frightful atrocities along their path, he was convinced he would never see his children again but nevertheless chose to return to the Governor's House. Had he remained with his children, it is likely that he would have ultimately survived. One of the officers of the guard nearby informed Gleb that the *Bolsheviks* from Tyumen were intending to take the former Imperial family away. The men were arming themselves for a shoot-out. Luckily, nothing happened as the men finally arrived in the small hours and were attracted to the lights of a local club, and proceeded to loot it and got drunk. It was a narrow escape for Nicholas and his family.

That morning had been a quiet one for the family. Anastasia failed to appear for her usual weekly religious instruction. She was undoubtedly unwell so she was replaced by Alexei and he carried on where she had left off with the book of *Isaiah 32-34*. Tatiana arrived shortly after her brother had finished his studies for the morning. She read the daily *Spiritual Readings* before having a German reading lesson. Alexandra lunched and dined with her son again and that evening again Nicholas read aloud to his assembled family.

That day, Alexei made what would prove to be his last entry in his journal. He had never liked writing in it. He began by complaining that everything was just the same as ever. In the evening, he had shot at a target. He was almost certainly joined by his sisters. At Mogilev in the summer of 1916, Marie had indicated that they had done so then. Olga acquired a gun at one point, and it appears that Nicholas and his family had been sufficiently worried about their personal security to give the children lessons in shooting, including the twelve year-old Alexei.

The observant Alexei noticed that, during their morning walk, the extraordinary commissar had arrived to look at their garden and yard. (He may have been looking to see if there was any way the family could escape or, more likely, any possible opportunities for the men from Ekaterinburg to gain entry.)

On Friday morning, Alexei remained in bed in his room as unfortunately he had coughed so violently that he had caused a slight haemorrhage in his stomach. His mother sat with him and he managed to read from the Bible and read from the book of *Luke* and *Meditations on the Divine Liturgy* by Gogol. She lunched with Alexei as he recovered. Colonel Kobylinsky gave the orders that Catherine Schnieder, Sydney Gibbes, Countess Hendrikova, General Tatishchev, Prince Dolgourkov and their maids had to move out of Kornilov House and into the Governor's House. It caused a great deal of trouble as they now had to be found space in an already crowded house.

Alexandra spent the day with her son as he was in great pain at times. Nagorny, who had looked after the boy during the night, was now worn out by the constant worry and sleepless nights. During the day, Alexei's tutors Gilliard and Gibbes took turns in reading to him in an effort to distract him. The Doctors Botkin and Derevenko were still – for now – at liberty to come and go as both had young families living in the town. During the night, Alexei was unable to sleep and was sick on four occasions. He may have been given morphine for the pain as it is liable to make one extremely sick afterwards. Alexandra spent all of Sunday at her son's bedside. There was little possibility of the child sleeping that day either as furniture was dragged across the road for the new inhabitants. The boy appeared to improve during the day but then got worse again towards the evening. There was an all-night vigil held in the house late in the day.

As Alexei lay ill all day in bed with intervals of intense pain, the members of the household who had just arrived from across the road were informed that they could no longer go out into the street. Another seven people made the house even more crowded than it had been. The guards, according to Nicholas's journal, wanted to make sure everyone was living in a strict regime for when the new detachment arrived. They wanted as little trouble as possible.

Alexandra dined alone in Nicholas's small dressing room that he shared with his son. In the evening, she went to sit with the rest of the family.

On Monday, the 2nd of April, searches were made at the Governor's House and, as a result, Nicholas's dagger and, more bizarrely, *Valia's* and Gilliard's draughts set were confiscated. Alexei had not slept the previous night and Gilliard had sat up with him. Kobylinsky later explained to Nicholas that searches had been made to pacify the sentries.

Alexei finally fell asleep at seven, probably due to exhaustion. He well knew that long periods of continual, severe pain can be very tiring. He woke up at eleven then quickly fell back to sleep. Later Alexandra sat with the rest of the family as Alexei slept. Alexei's condition improved after a good night's sleep.

On Tuesday, Alexei continued to sleep for part of the day. Alexandra sat with him all day as Gilliard and Gibbes once again took turns to read to him. She again rejoined the rest of the family in the evening.

That day Tatiana had written briefly to Zinaide Tolstoy in anticipation of Easter. She was not aware at that point that it would prove to be an Easter where her family was torn apart. She sent the usual message of greeting given at this time of year: *Christ is Risen* and hoped that her old friend was in good health and everything was going well.

Wednesday was spent quietly by Alexandra sitting by the bedside of her son once more. He was still in pain but not as badly as the previous day and he began to eat a little. He ate some fish and a little *Kissel* or fruit soup. She rested later whilst Gilliard patiently read to the boy. Later that night, Nicholas read aloud to his wife and daughters from *The Great in the Small* by Serge Nilus.

Meanwhile, Olga took the opportunity to send word to her friend Rita after receiving the letter Rita had sent on the seventeenth of December with some verses. It had taken until April to arrive but, nevertheless, Olga was delighted to receive it. She wondered if Rita had got the letter she had sent on the 6th of January. She went on to explain that everyone was safe but the times were worrying. They had heard what was happening via the newspapers, but little else. The Red Guards had recently arrived but so far they had behaved well. The family had been to church on three occasions recently but now they had to attend both vespers or the evening service and the liturgy at home. The house was now becoming very crowded. The Countess, Catherine Schneider, Prince Dolgorukov and General Tatishchev were now also residing with them.

Life was much as usual. They spent their days sitting on the balcony, sawing and chopping wood, etc. Now that the snow was beginning to melt, the garden was becoming very muddy again. They were only able to see Baroness Buxhoeveden through the windows.

Once again, Alexei suffered a disturbed night. Alexandra spent most of the day keeping her son company but Anastasia appeared on Thursday morning for her usual weekly religious instruction. She read aloud from the book of *Isaiah 34-38*. Her brother had taken her place the previous week and read from the same piece.

Alexei was sufficiently improved to be hungry that day and ate more than he had on the previous day. Alexandra had tea again in Nicholas's small study and rested briefly afterwards. Towards evening, Alexei's pains returned and he became more restless.

He finally fell asleep shortly before eleven, and Nicholas read aloud to his wife and daughters as his son slept peacefully.

There was mixed news concerning Alexei on Friday the 6th. The pains increased intensely during the day. He was unable to eat and suffered greatly. Alexandra spent the day with her son; as he suffered, she did too. Dr Derevenko saw the boy in the late afternoon and was happy that the child was improving. Although he was in intense pain, the blood was beginning to be reabsorbed into the body.

Alexandra wrote to her friend Madame Vyrubova that day and explained how her son was suffering from backache as he was tired of lying constantly on it. She had, on occasions, attempted to help him by holding his leg. He was very thin as he had been unable to eat and had only just begun to do so the previous day. She thought that the recent coughing fit may have brought on the attack. It was bad enough to remind Alexandra of Spala in 1912 when the boy had almost died.

She went on to explain that the exhausted child eventually fell asleep. The pain had worn him out. Alexandra spent most of the day with her son but was relieved on occasions by either Monsieur Gilliard or Tatiana. The tutor read constantly to his pupil and warmed the child's injured leg with the *Fohn apparatus*. It was snowing outside but it quickly vanished and the garden became more and more muddy.

Alexandra explained that, recently, a new Commissar had arrived from Moscow. He was called Yakovlev and they were expecting to make his acquaintance later in the day. It got very hot and dusty in the summer, and Alexandra admitted that she was hoping that they would be transferred to a nearby convent. (The thick walls and lack of direct sunlight makes such places, like churches, eternally cool even in summer.) Unfortunately, she revealed, they often hinted that they would be taken into the middle of Siberia. They hoped that it would not happen.

As she wrote, Alexandra spotted eleven men passing by on horseback. All appeared quite friendly enough. They often saw men with the most frightening faces. They were not likely to feature in the painting she was doing of a garden. She imagined them outside the gates where the sunshine would clean the dirt from them. She had been delighted with the small mauve Easter egg that Anya had sent. It was unfortunate that she had sent money; she wished she could return it. She knew Anya needed it for herself. Alexandra then asked Anya to kiss her widowed mother from her. She had just seen the new Commissar and, to her, he seemed to have a kind face.

Sadly the former Tsarina once again proved to be a terrible judge of character.

Alexandra spent most of Sunday the 8th sitting by her son's bedside. Although he had slept much better the previous night, his pains began to increase again by early evening. The family attended the all-night vigil at nine whilst Alexei slept. Whilst sitting with her son, Alexandra had managed to write several letters during the course of the day.

There was some cause for celebration on Sunday the th as it was the anniversary of the engagement of Nicholas and Alexandra. She had finally agreed to marry him in the spring of 1894, just after her brother's marriage. There was a celebration *Obednitsa* late that morning which was again held in the hall. Alexandra again spent the majority of the day at the bedside of her son. He had slept on and off the previous evening.

After the service, Colonel Kobylinsky showed Nicholas a telegram which had come directly from Moscow. It confirmed his worst fears. Nicholas was forced to remove his epaulettes. He had hoped that the decision by the local committee would have been overruled.

Nicholas took the decision not to wear them when outside the house but he chose to wear them in private. He swore that he would never forgive the authorities for this move.

Meanwhile, Alexei suffered with pains at intervals throughout the day and had a slightly raised temperature. Nicholas spent much of the day working in the garden and, that evening, he attempted to calm himself down with a book. He read Vsevolod Solovyov's appropriately named *The Soothsayers*.

On Monday morning, as the sixth week of Lent began, there was worrying news when the Commissary from Moscow arrived with a small detachment of men. He later took tea with Nicholas and Alexandra. Pierre Gilliard regarded his arrival with great concern, and Marie and Anastasia were so disturbed by his arrival that they each burnt their diaries. They were convinced that he was about to make a detailed search of their belongings. The girls decided to sacrifice their journals rather than entertain the possibility of strangers, hostile ones at that, reading their innermost thoughts. It is not inconceivable that they had made disparaging remarks about some of those guarding them.

Meanwhile, whilst the snow fell and the wind blew outside, Alexei continued to show signs of improvement yet still suffered greatly at intervals. He did, however, manage to sleep fitfully. Whilst Alexandra had again spent much of the day with her son, she too decided to burn some of her letters and arrange her papers.

Alexei had sufficiently improved by the afternoon to be able to play cards with his mother. That evening Nicholas again read to his wife and children but overnight Alexei was quite unable to sleep as the pains returned.

According to Baroness Buxhoeveden, who never actually saw the family on her arrival in Tobolsk, the arrival of Jacob Yakovlev was a surprise to everyone, including Colonel Kobylinsky. She believed that Yakovlev had been given full powers and had arrived accompanied by a party of mounted men including the former sailor Paul Khokhariakov and an officer with the unfortunate name of Rodionov, who in no way resembled the Grand Duchesses' old friend. He assembled the guard and had allegedly praised them and informed them that they would be paid highly by the Government for their loyalty. The men all seemed impressed by him and he seemed to be someone who was well versed in handling the masses. He had also informed the men that he was now in charge and he had to be obeyed as he had the authority to shoot anyone who disobeyed his orders. Colonel Kobylinksy quickly formed the opinion that the man intended to take the family away somewhere.

On Tuesday morning, Yakovlev arrived earlier than expected and dashed about, going from one room to another. They had expected his arrival at eleven. He met the former Tsar and his daughters in the hall. Nicholas was convinced it was a deliberate plot to try and catch everyone out. It was as if he was attempting to ascertain whether Alexei was really seriously ill or not. He asked Nicholas if he was satisfied with the accommodation and the guard which was rather an odd question to pose to a prisoner.

Alexandra was not quite dressed. Yakovlev spoke to Nicholas then ran in to see Alexei, peered in the other rooms, and apologizing for the inconvenience, went back downstairs. He later returned upstairs where he met Alexandra, rushed back to see Alexei, as if trying to catch him jumping around the room, and then went back downstairs.

It was obvious that Alexei was seriously ill and would be unable to be moved. According to the Baroness, who may have got it second-hand from another member of the household, Yakovlev communicated with Moscow. He then informed Kobylinsky that he would be relieved of his duties on the fourteenth. He and Rodionov now gave all the orders. General Tatishchev, who appears to have been her informant, told the Baroness that he considered it the most dangerous crisis the former Imperial family had ever gone through.

Alexandra was very impressed with the new man whom she thought looked like an intelligent yet very nervous-looking workman, who could have perhaps been an engineer. She had again spent the day with her son. Alexei had felt able to play cards cheerfully with his mother for some of the day and slept for part of the afternoon. Nicholas read to the family that evening as usual.

Yet again, Alexei had a restless night. The changes recently to the household and the new men that had appeared would have left him feeling unsettled. As a sensitive and intelligent child, he would have sensed the tension around him. Sleep was something of luxury anyway at Tobolsk as Alexandra and Gilliard both admitted. The former Grand Duchesses' sleep would have been disturbed due to the constant snoring of Tatiana's dog Ortipo. The dog was a persistent snorer as Anastasia disclosed to her father in a letter as far back as 1914 when she slept in the adjoining room at the palace. She and Marie were able to hear the dog from the next room so as the dogs presumably shared the girls' room at Tobolsk, the snoring would have been more obvious than ever. Unfortunately dogs with a pug or snub nose are inclined to snore yet those with a pointed nose are less liable.

On Wednesday morning, Alexandra remained in bed and did some painting whilst Tatiana read to her from the daily *Spiritual Readings*. She then spent the remainder of the day with Alexei, either playing cards with him or *working* alongside him as he rested. Alexandra lunched and dined with Olga and Alexei that day.

It had been a pleasant and sunny day. Nicholas sat outside on the greenhouse porch basking in the sunshine. It was a favourite place for him and his daughters. They were often photographed there. Marie rarely appeared in the pictures at Tobolsk. The reason is obvious: she was the main photographer and even developed the ability to develop her own photographs. Nicholas later worked by the hill, clearing out a deep ditch. He was at his happiest when he had something to do outside.

Thursday proved to be a turning point. The day had begun on a positive note as Alexei had slept well. Early that morning, Alexandra returned to her normal schedule. Anastasia arrived for her weekly scripture lesson to read from the book of *Isaiah 38-42* and afterwards Alexandra sat with her son and the two played cards. Shortly before lunch, Marie appeared for her Bible studies and read from *Jesus, Son of Sirach*, verses 18-26 aloud. Tatiana had previously worked on this piece.

After lunch, however, Yakovlov appeared along with Koblinsky. Alexandra had intended to ask them about the arrangements for visiting church during Passion Week but she had no opportunity. Yakovlev announced that the Government had decided that they had to be moved but failed to say where. As he had observed that Alexei was ill, it had been decided that Nicholas should go alone, by force if necessary.

Alexandra had a horrific decision to make – should she accompany her husband or remain with her sick son? She eventually chose to go with Nicholas and Marie would join them. During the revolution, Alexandra had eventually begun to appreciate Marie's helpful nature. Alexandra was concerned that Nicholas would need her as he may have to go on trial.

Olga was to attend to her brother, Tatiana would deal with the household, and Anastasia was needed to cheer everyone up. She was especially needed by her brother who could not part with her as the two had always been together as children. Olga and Tatiana were both trained nurses and were well used to nursing their brother. Tatiana was an experienced nurse, perfectly capable of dealing with any crisis, level-headed and had assisted at complex operations in the infirmary, so was able to deal with practical concerns. As Olga had been the one who felt more disturbed than the other children during the recent events, it was a sensible idea to give her the responsibility of looking after her brother.

The ever-loyal Dr Botkin elected to accompany Nicholas and Alexandra, as did Prince Dolgourkov and the maid Niuta. Chemodurov and Sednyov would also go with them.

Alexandra, about to be separated from four of her beloved children, one of whom was seriously ill, spent the remainder of her time with Alexei. She sat with him during tea and dinner. The heartbroken family spent their last precious evening together and it was not until the early hours of the following morning that they left.

Pierre Gilliard later recalled that Tatiana had taken a key position in the decision for her mother. He had met two servants that afternoon sobbing in the corridor. They had been told that Nicholas needed to leave. Gilliard did not know what to do. He had not been *officially* told so took the decision to go back to his own room.

Tatiana knocked on his door soon after in tears. She informed Gilliard that her mother was asking for him, and Alexandra told him of their decision. She explained that anyone who wished to would be permitted to accompany Nicholas. She did not want her husband to go without her. Alexandra was convinced that the authorities wanted to separate the family. She was certain they would use the worry over his family as a lever to make him do as they wished.

She was certain that together they would be stronger and more able to resist. She was sure Nicholas needed her but was afraid for her son. She admitted that, for the first time in her life, she did not know what to do. At this point, Tatiana cut in and declared that her father had to go, so they must make a decision. Gilliard decided to offer a way out. Alexei was already better and they would all take care of him. After pacing the room for a while, Alexandra realized that it was the only possible outcome.

Alexandra agreed that it was for the best. She would entrust her son to Gilliard.

Nicholas arrived soon after, and Alexandra announced that everything was settled. She would accompany him with Marie. He could only reply that it was all well, if that was what she wished.

Tatiana had forced her mother to decide. Marie would accompany her mother. She was, according to Tatiana, an angel and the best amongst them. She was convinced that Marie would prove useful to her mother. Olga's spirits, she explained to Gilliard, were too low and she would be needed to look after her brother. She felt that Anastasia was too young even to be taken into account.

The children who were being left behind put notes into their father's pockets. Olga promised to look after her brother. She explained that God knew the reason for it all and would bring them out of it.

Alexei too wrote a note to his father promising to get better soon and that he would try to eat as much as he was able. He was happy that the sharpshooters were accompanying Nicholas.

Anastasia asked God and the angels to protect Nicholas but admitted she had no idea how they would cope without him.

Tatiana who had been so instrumental in the decision was unable to write anything at all. She was less able to put her words on paper than the others and felt too overcome to even attempt to.

The girls returned to their room in tears.

Chapter Twenty-four

Ekaterinburg Spring 1918

At about 4am on Friday morning on the 13th/26th of April 1918, the former Tsar and Tsarina left Tobolsk in wooden carts, four-wheeled springless carriages or *tarantass*, along with their daughter Marie. Unfortunately they were forced to leave the remaining children as Alexei was unable to travel. Alexandra and Marie were wrapped up warmly in Dr Botkin's fur coat and the *Doctor* in Prince Dolgorokov's rabbit fur coat. They were accompanied by Anna Demidova, the valet Terenty Chemodurov and the Grand Duchesses' manservant Ivan Sednyev, eight riflemen and a mounted escort comprising ten other men.

Nicholas had hoped to be able to travel with his wife and daughter but had been forced to travel with Commissar Yakovlev instead. It was a cold morning and the roads proved to be extremely bumpy, quite unmade. The party crossed the Irtysh River through a deep section and managed to halt four times en route during the course of the day. They covered some eighty-six miles or 130 versts and finally stopped for the night at the village of *Ievlevo* and were accommodated in what had formerly been the village shop.

They had changed horses at eight and again at noon on that Friday when they had stopped briefly for lunch. The meal was *ad hoc* made up of the cold provisions they had taken with them for the journey. As the horses were changed for a fourth time, the linchpin which connected the horse to the vehicle came out and the ladies were forced to climb out into a different basket. They changed horses for a fifth time, and Alexandra and Marie were obliged to move to yet another basket. The rest of the group constantly changed carriages at each stop.

That night, Nicholas and Alexandra shared a room with their daughter – they on their beds and the unfortunate but weary Marie on a mattress on the floor. They had finally got into their beds at ten by which time they were exhausted, and Alexandra complained of aching all over. She was not used to such difficult travelling conditions. Luckily, Nicholas was naturally more fit, and Marie had the elasticity of youth, apart from physically being very strong. Alexandra sent a note back via the first coachmen to her children.

At 4am on Saturday morning, the family had tea and packed again. They were due to leave at five but Yakovlev had understandably overslept. They crossed the river on foot via some wooden planks then onto a ferry. They were on the vessel only briefly.

The weather luckily was better that day but Yakovlev managed to irritate Alexandra by running around and getting what she termed *fidgety*. (It was a term she used when *she* was particularly irritated.) He was telegraphing his progress.

The road gradually became easier, but nevertheless they were constantly jolted around. The road was probably full of small holes. Nicholas worried about Alexandra who had never enjoyed the best of health. They changed horses about six times and at around noon arrived at Pokrovskoe. As they changed horses, the family had an excellent view of Rasputin's house. It was the only two-storey building in the village. His family appeared at the window as they arrived.

They later took tea using their own provisions of food at a local peasant's house in Borki. Just as they left the village, they spotted an old friend, Nikolai Sedov, formerly of Alexandra's Crimean Cavalry Regiment. They later stopped at a village school for tea but this was taken with the guards. Dr Botkin who had been shaken by the journey and was suffering from pains in the kidneys went for a brief lie-down at this point.

The group arrived at Tiumen at dusk and were quickly surrounded by a whole squadron who escorted them into the town. At midnight, they finally got onto a train. It was filthy but nonetheless comfortable after such a difficult journey. Nicholas noted in his journal that night that they all looked very dirty after the long journey. They got into their beds at ten, too exhausted to undress. Nicholas shared a compartment with Alexandra. He took the top bunk. Marie shared another compartment with Anna Demidova. Valia and the doctor shared another.

According to Jacob Yakovlev, the former Tsarina spent the entire journey in her compartment apart from when she went to the bathroom. He also claimed that she deliberately went to the bathroom at four or five in the morning in an attempt to avoid contact with the guards. When she did spot a sentry in the corridor upon exiting the bathroom she immediately changed her mind and locked herself back in until the sentry had gone.

Meanwhile, Olga attempted to calm her parents by sending an encouraging letter from Tobolsk. Alexei was gaining strength although still confined to bed. They would join them as soon as he was better. The weather was improving, she assured them. She ended by saying that she hoped that God would be with them.

Marie's message to her sisters and brother was not so positive. She complained of the journey being quite dreadful. They had been badly jolted on the roads.

As the train journey progressed, it slowly dawned upon Nicholas where they going. He knew that they were travelling towards Omsk. Luckily, they had all slept well, probably due to exhaustion, although Alexandra claimed that she had barely slept. As they rose, they began to wonder where they would end up. They all guessed the ultimate destination: was it Moscow or Vladivostok? Naturally, Nicholas was told nothing. Marie spent much of the day chatting with the riflemen who had their compartment at the end of the car.

It was Palm Sunday but Nicholas and his family had no opportunity of attending church or even a service. As they passed through Vagai station, the party were brought food. Nicholas found it delicious. They were given soup and a main course. They subsidised their meagre fare with provisions they had brought from Tobolsk, including tea. Alexandra did not eat meat and lived mainly on pasta. Later, Ivan Sednyov cooked cutlets for the party, with the obvious exception of Alexandra. After they had passed through Nazyvaevskaia station, Marie and Anna Demidova took the chance for a short walk on a couple of occasions during brief stops. Once again, they were forced to cover the windows as they went through the various stations. The holidays had meant an influx of people.

As they continued the journey on Monday, it soon became clear that they were changing direction as they passed through Nazyvaevskaia once more. Nicholas was baffled. Yakovlev had initially attempted to go via Omsk to avoid Ekaterinburg where it was known the locals were particularly hostile to the ex-Tsar. Unfortunately, he was ordered to reverse direction and go through Ekaterinburg. If the local Soviet insisted, he would have to transfer the prisoners to them.

Nicholas was delighted to be given the opportunity of having a stroll twice en route. As a result, everyone was in a cheerful mood despite the evident confusion. The party were brought food shortly before noon, but Alexandra merely required a drink of coffee.

At Masiankaia station with Nicholas and Marie, with members of the reduced household, were once again permitted to step out of the train for a brief walk. Alexandra remained on board. The train then sped off again yet, soon afterwards, the train suddenly came to a halt. The family were told that an axle on one of the carriages had caught fire and needed to be hooked off but this was not the truth.

That evening Sednyov prepared an enjoyable dinner for the family. Nicholas read the Gospels for the day to Alexandra and Marie. Alexandra began to suffer from her familiar problem: what she termed an enlarged heart. She sent word to the children as she had done each evening but most of the letters failed to arrive.

The train and its passengers – prisoners and guards alike – arrived at their final destination on Tuesday morning. Nicholas and his party waited whilst Yakovlev and his deputy Guzakov spoke with members of the local Soviet. They had arrived at their destination: Ekaterinburg at Station One. Yakovlev had given orders that the doors and windows be firmly locked and the curtains drawn before they arrived, as an extra safety measure.

The train remained for some three hours and was then moved into another station freight yard. The party were finally able to get off at a station, Number Two, nearby after yet another delay. Yakovlev had been forced, just as he feared all along, to hand over Nicholas and the others to the local Ural Soviet. Yakovlev had arrived at the first station at Ekaterinburg but, on seeing the angry crowds, had instructed a freight train to be driven between them and the crowds so that they could carry on to the second station and get off the train in privacy. He had no option but to hand the prisoners over to the local Soviet; there was no way out. Yakovlev officially handed over Nicholas and his party to the Chairman of the Soviet and members of the Presidium. He was given a written receipt as Nicholas was formally handed over like a parcel.

Nicholas, Alexandra and Marie were taken by car with a suitably large escort to

Ipatiev House or the House of Special Purpose as it was officially and rather sinisterly named. It was naturally surrounded by a high fence. One by one, the other members of the household arrived, including Dr Botkin, Terenty Chemodurov, Ivan Sedynev and Anna Demidova. However, *Valia* was not permitted to join the rest of the party. He was taken away and later shot. He had been accused falsely of aiding an escape attempt and harbouring weapons. The family were escorted by a new collection of guards; not the ones they had travelled with.

The former Tsar and his party were assigned just four rooms, including a corner bedroom, a lavatory, a dining room containing windows with a view of the small garden and parts of the town, and a large hall. They were not permitted to unpack for some time as the trunks were examined as if they had suddenly gone through Customs at the port. The new guards examined everything in great detail, down to Alexandra's medicine phials. Nicholas was outraged and complained to the Commissar.

Nicholas and Alexandra shared a bedroom (initially with Marie) which had yellow wallpaper. It housed two beds, a couch, two tables, a lamp, a bookcase and a single armoire. (This was a wardrobe where items had to remain flat and with no space for hanging suits, for example, as in a modern wardrobe.)

The valet Terenty Chemodurov later revealed that one of the men who conducted the search wrenched a handbag from Alexandra, and it was this that induced Nicholas to complain of the treatment. He remarked that, up until then, they had been dealt with by decent and honest people. One of the men, Boris Didkovsky, replied that the ex-Tsar must not forget that he was now under investigation and arrest. The bag had only contained a handkerchief, smelling salts and Alexandra's heart drops. There was no knife, gun or hand grenade as they seemed to have assumed.

The party finally had their lunch at half past four including *borshch* and a main course. The group, including the ex-Tsar and the maid, ate together in the dining room. That evening Nicholas, Alexandra and Marie were forced to sleep together in one room, without the luxury of a door. Anna Demidova slept in the dining room and the others were accommodated in the other room. The guards slept in a room close to the dining room. Unfortunately, when the family wished to visit the bathroom, they had to pass the sentry at the doors of the guards' room. There was a high fence erected around the house and a chain of sentries stood not far from the windows. They were also in the garden. The family were brought tea at 9.30pm after which the beds arrived and a basin for washing. They went to bed at eleven and Nicholas read aloud from the Bible.

Alexandra chose to remain in bed on Wednesday morning, complaining of an enlarged heart and a headache. Nicholas was grateful for small mercies. The previous year, he had been greatly angered by the May Day celebrations but, on this occasion, he merely appreciated the music in the distance. The family were not permitted outside in the garden. Nicholas would have much appreciated a long soak in the bath, but the pipes were not working. He was used to having a bath each day but, in the circumstances, even this was now impossible. Luckily the weather was particularly pleasant so Nicholas simply enjoyed breathing the fresh air through the open window.

Nicholas, Marie and the rest of the diminished household were given soup and eggs which had arrived from the local soup kitchen. Alexandra, who was a picky eater, preferred to just eat some bread, which she found rather enjoyable. Afterwards, Marie read the *Spiritual Readings* aloud to her mother. It was the one familiar thing they could do to remind them of the approach of Easter, as they were unable to visit church or have any sort of service, however brief.

Alexandra ate a frugal meal of tea, bread and malt extract. Later Marie read to her mother whilst Nicholas sat at his writing table in their shared bedroom. Alexandra sent word to the other children later that evening and Marie wrote to her sister Olga in anticipation of *Pascha* or Easter with notes added by each of her parents.

Marie told Olga, predictably, that the three of them thought constantly of the others. They spoke often of them and wondered what they were doing. Marie explained that the beginning of their journey had been very unpleasant and even depressing. It improved, however, when they were able to join the train. They had no idea what the future would bring, Alexandra added. Nicholas hoped that the Lord would protect his children. He embraced them all in the Easter greeting, kissing them each thrice, well, at least in thought. Imagination was the one thing the *Bolsheviks* could not take away.

Marie added that they kissed the nannies and ladies too. The nannies included Shura and Liza who had remained with the family despite the revolution. The Grand Duchesses had chosen voluntarily to go with their parents, and Shura and Liza who had known the girls for most of their lives chose to remain loyal to their former charges even though the youngest of the girls was almost seventeen.

Later Alexandra realized that the Commandant Avdeev's assistant Konstantin Ukraintsev had worked as a beater when the Tsar's younger brother Michael had gone shooting near Borzhom. It was even more surprising to learn that, fifteen years previously, Olga had played with him when he was a little boy at Gagri. (Sadly, the assistant was later dismissed as he appeared to be too friendly towards the family.)

On Great and Holy Thursday, in the run-up to Easter, Nicholas read from the Gospels. Unfortunately, the Romanovs now needed every little bit of spiritual guidance as conditions were rapidly worsening. That morning, Alexandra noted in her journal that the soldiers drank up all of the water out of the samovar or tea urn. Later, more water was brought so the family could have tea.

Official titles were now dispensed with. Nicholas was no longer even an ex-Tsar but merely Nicholas Alexandrovich. Alexandra, in particular, found this new form of address offensive.

Despite the petty annoyances, Alexandra admitted that her heart was feeling less enlarged. She was finally re-establishing some sort of routine. She dressed in a tea gown but remained sitting on her bed. She wrote some Easter postcards for the family and household, and Marie arranged her long hair. Lunch arrived at two from a local cafeteria. Later, the others walked in the small garden whilst Alexandra, again, remained indoors. She had rarely gone out even when she resided at the Alexander Palace.

After tea, Nicholas read from the book of *Job*. Nicholas had always identified with the eternally unlucky Job. Then Alexandra arranged the various religious images on a table. After dinner the seven members of the household sat together whilst Nicholas and *the Doctor* took turns to read from the *Twelve Gospels* as traditionally read at this time of year. The circumstances were substantially altered, however. The children Olga, Tatiana, Anastasia and Alexei were many miles away and no one knew when they would be reunited. That evening, Alexandra again wrote to her missing children. It was in many ways a reminder of the early days of the revolution when Alexandra was assisted by Marie whilst the others remained ill.

In an attempt to make light of the grim situation, Marie again sent word that day for her sisters and brother. It was no easy task. She assured them that her mother was feeling better and was lying down. The rest had spent a pleasant hour in the tiny garden. They had finally brought a barrel of water so that her father could have his bath before dinner that evening. He was allocated some nine litres.

She had been on the American swing with Anna Demidova in the garden and had walked up and down in the small yard with her father. Her mother was resting and was lying on her bed. She was slightly improved yet still suffering with her heart and head.

Marie added that the sisters would need to make a list of all those whom they wished to accompany them to Ipatiev House. The sisters had to give a reason for the presence of each of those they wished to bring. Oh, how very complicated things now were, she exclaimed. She longed for the peaceful life they had lived for eight months in Tobolsk. She felt so sorry for those who had yet to suffer the indignities of Ekaterinburg. She hoped that she would shortly have tidings of them. Marie prayed that the Lord would keep them. She signed with her nickname of Masha rather than Marie. (Marie would variously call herself Marie, Maria, Masha or Mashka, depending on her mood.)

It was Marie who had once exclaimed that she thought she could have been happy at the Governor's House in Tobolsk. The situation had changed dramatically and the restrictions were obvious. At Tobolsk, the guards had not been housed on the same floor as them.

It snowed overnight and through the morning. The following day was Great and Holy Friday, or simply Good Friday to those in the West. Nicholas continued his Bible readings that morning. He again chose Job and read from the Gospels. Alexandra got dressed before lunch but sat on her bed in a tea gown. She preferred this type of dress as it was far more comfortable and she had no need to wear a corset. Lunch did not appear until well after three. Tea arrived at six, as if to make up for the lateness of lunch. Nicholas and Marie had spent the previous half-hour outside.

In the evening Nicholas read aloud from Nilus's *The Great in the Small* and then continued reading from the Gospels. Dinner became supper as it arrived after ten. Whilst Nicholas and Marie ate what they were given, Alexandra ate *vermicelli* which had been prepared by Sednyov. Again, she wrote to the remaining children at Tobolsk. The letter was later lost but, according to Gilliard, it instructed them, in code, to hide their jewels. Alexandra's jewels were sewn inside two pairs of double brassieres, each weighing four and a half pounds. Tatiana and Anastasia wore these. The work of sewing the jewels into the clothes had begun earlier and was carried out by Alexandra initially but, after she left, it was continued by Shura Tegleva, Liza Ersberg, Olga, Tatiana and Anastasia, as Shura later recalled. The Grand Duchesses' jewels were sewn into a double brassiere in the same way. It was worn by Olga. Shura also recalled that they had sewn valuables into their hats, hidden between the lining and the velvet. They included a large pearl necklace and a large sapphire with brilliants. They also carried many pearls under their blouses.

The Grand Duchesses had outer garments of blue cheviot. The sashes held two buttons and the ladies replaced them with jewels, probably brilliants. They were wrapped firstly with wadding and then black silk. The girls' grey outfits of English tricot with black stripes had the buttons taken off and jewels sewn in them in black silk and wadding.

It was unlikely that the jewels hidden in the brassieres and buttons would be discovered but the pearls under their clothes may well have been. This was a clever double bluff in effect, as the finding of these jewels may have made the guards assume they had found everything. The jewels were later discovered, but only after their deaths.

Nicholas reported some good news in his journal that evening. The guards were now stationed downstairs which made the trip to the bathroom much less embarrassing. It also meant that the dining room no longer smelt of tobacco. He had heard rumours that Valia was no longer free. Despite the best efforts of *The Doctor*, they had not been able to communicate with him. As Nicholas was never one to put himself forward and the guards treated him with disdain, Botkin was now Nicholas's representative and asked for anything they needed.

On the eve of Easter, Nicholas read aloud from the Gospels. He then added a few lines to a letter from Alexandra and Marie. He drew a plan of the house. The drawing was intercepted by Alexander Avdeev later. Previously, Gibbes had sent out a plan of the Governor's House in Tobolsk to Alexandra's former governess Miss Jackson in England. She had not replied on account of being on her deathbed. Letters often took months to travel within Russia so one to England would have taken some time and Miss Jackson's letter had been only written a month before she died.

Nicholas and the rest of the household were brought their luncheon and afterwards Nicholas went for a welcome bath. Alexandra's meal was cooked separately by Sednyov and she ate a little later. He had prepared her some vermicelli again. Alexandra and the maid Demidova also had a bath. In previous years, it was something that would never have made Alexandra's journal: the fact that she had a bath. It had always been an everyday event, but now it was something of a luxury. It was an indication of how bad things had become.

Later, Alexandra rested and sent word to her children once more. The others had gone out briefly into the garden. After tea, Nicholas read to Alexandra and Marie as Alix arranged the images on the table. The priest Father Anatoly Grigorovich Meledin and deacon Vasily Afanievich Buimirov arrived after eight. Whilst they served matins, they were joined by the soldiers of the guard and the Commandant's assistant Ukraintsev. It was a great comfort to the family to be able to have a service. The soldiers came just to keep an eye on things. The family dined at nine, an hour later than they would have done in the past. Later Alexandra went to bed, and Marie, who was sharing her parents' room for the first time since she was a tiny baby, read to her mother.

Easter Sunday was spent by the ex-Tsar and his family in much reduced circumstances and far more simply than in former years. Marie read the *Spiritual Readings* to her mother and Nicholas read from the Gospels and a French book. The day's luncheon was not impressive. Sedynov reheated the leftover food from the previous day. Alexandra joined the rest of her somewhat diminished family and then went for a lie-down. She wrote once again to the missing children whilst the others went out into the small garden. Alexandra enjoyed a cup of cocoa and then Nicholas read again, this time from *The Great in the Small*. Alexandra mixed the words up in her journal and managed to rename the work *Small in the Great*.

As the family gathered for tea, the sun came out which was an encouraging sign. There were few positive signs recently. Later Nicholas read from the Gospels once again and Alexandra joined the rest for dinner. The family later sat with Botkin for an hour in his room. Nicholas and Alexandra had always been fond of *The Doctor* but, in recent months, they had come to rely upon him more and more and realised his true worth. The former monarchs chatted with Ukraintsev, who was of course someone they had met before and one of the very few who was friendly towards them now. That day, Nicholas drew another plan of the house, but it too remained unsent.

Meanwhile, back at Tobolsk, Olga, in the absence of her parents, distributed the Easter gifts to her sisters, brother and the remaining members of the household. Since the departure of the former Tsar life at the Governor's House had rapidly deteriorated. The new Commandant, Paul Khokhriakov appeared to be under the control of his assistant Rodionov, who introduced new and restrictive rules on a daily basis. The former Grand Duchesses were closely watched and submitted to the indignity of a daily roll-call. They were also ordered to leave their bedroom door wide open at night. Baroness Buxhoeveden was one of the few members of the household who had not been moved into the Governor's House and she continued to live close by with her mother's old Scottish friend, the redoubtable Miss Annie Mather. The Baroness was only able to see the former Grand Duchesses when they waved to her from a window.

The surly Rodionov had assembled the three sisters in a room one day and demanded to know which girl was which. He addressed them simply as *Olga Nicolaevna, Tatiana Nicolaevna* and *Anastasia Nicolaevna*. The man had not realised that the former Grand Duchesses were normally addressed thus within the Imperial household so the lack of title meant nothing to them. He also claimed that he could not tell them apart as there were so many of them.

(It was meant as an insult but to this day many continue to mix up the sisters, and Olga and Marie in particular are constantly confused, yet there are those, myself amongst the number, who are able to tell the sisters from the backs of their heads alone.)

Meanwhile back at Ekaterinburg Marie sent word to her sister to Olga. She explained that they drew comfort from the cross, which was all they could see of the church across the road. It was as well that they could not see the huge gun trained on the yard.

Marie began the letter with the usual greeting *Christ is Risen*. Marie was unable to see her siblings but, in her mind's eye, she kissed Olga three times. She sent her congratulations and hopes that everyone would spend the day quietly. (It was significant that quiet days were now precious, as anything else meant that they were submitted to something unpleasant. At Tobolsk, the children often complained that nothing ever happened, but now they hoped that nothing *would* happen.)

Marie then asked Olga to pass on her greetings to the rest. She was writing whilst sitting on her father's bed. Their mother was unwell, she explained, and having a lie-down. The three of them had slept well, in the cosy room with four large windows. The sun was shining, as it often did in the hall. The window had been opened and they were able to hear the birds singing outside. (The birds were not caged, unlike the Romanovs.) They could also hear the distant sound of the electric tram.

They had heard music on the 1st of May. Whilst they lived on the ground floor, they were still only able to see the very top of the local churches with the crosses on the cupolas.

Anna Demidova was now sleeping in the dining room and the others, Dr Botkin, Ivan Sedynev and Terenty Chemodurov, lived in the large drawing room (or hall). *Valia* had not been permitted to join them, and they did not know where he was. The men were now sleeping on beds that the guards had brought yesterday for them and the guards. The house, she remarked, was owned by the Ipatievs. The significance could not have gone unnoticed to the observant Olga. (*As it was in the beginning, so shall it be in the end* – the Romanov rule had begun at the Ipatiev monastery and was likely and did end at Ipatiev House.)

Monday the 23rd was spent peacefully by the residents of Ipatiev House. It was Alexandra's name's day but, naturally, it was not spent, as in former days, with great celebration. Nicholas simply continued reading the Gospels and *The Great in the Small.*

Alexandra sent word to her children once more and then lunched with the rest. Ivan Sednyov, who had previously been the Grand Duchesses' manservant, again took on the role of cook. Whilst Alexandra had a lie-down, the rest went outside. It was sunny again and had been snowing lightly overnight. That afternoon, Nicholas read aloud to his wife and daughter whilst Marie painted. After tea, Marie read the *Spiritual Readings* for the day.

The routine was re-established. Lunch had now returned to one and dinner at eight as in former days. The meals had been rather late initially. That evening, the family gathered in Botkin's room which was the large hall that he shared with the other male retainers.

On Tuesday the Commandant, Avdeev, informed Nicholas that the plan of the house that he had included in the letter three days previously could not be sent. The Commandant later revealed that, when he had told Nicholas that it was not permitted, the former Tsar had acted like a naughty schoolboy and protested his ignorance. He claimed that he had no idea that it was in any way wrong. The Commandant knew that it could be used as part of an escape plot. Marie's recent letter had described the family bedroom only too clearly.

Once again, Alexandra wrote to the missing children and Nicholas read from the Gospels and *The Great in the Small.* Sednyov prepared Alexandra's meal of vermicelli but the rest ate at two once their meal finally arrived from a local cafeteria. Alexandra had refused to eat it as it had too much meat in it for her taste. Afterwards, Nicholas read aloud once more. In the absence of any religious services, the reading of the Gospels was as close as they could get to a service.

Later, Alexandra remained indoors as the others went outside for a breath of fresh air. When Nicholas returned, he read aloud again. This time he read Maurice Maeterlinck's *La Sagesse et la Destinee* or Wisdom and Destiny. (He regularly alternated between Bible readings, Turgenev's *Spring Torrents,* the novels of Vsevolod Solovyov and John Richard Green's *Short History of the English People* and the above mentioned work.)

That evening, whilst Nicholas read, the others played *Chicane.* The household dined together at their usual hour of eight and, afterwards, Nicholas, Alexandra, Marie and *the Doctor* played bezique and cards together.

As so many letters sent from the former Tsarina had failed to arrive, Olga had the inspired idea to send a telegram – to their maid Anna Demidova. The plan worked as it was later mentioned in Alexandra's journal. Olga simply noted her thanks for the letters and all were well. The little one (Alexei) had already been out in the garden. She also assured them that they *were* writing.

Meanwhile, Anastasia had written to her sister Marie in the hope that the letter would be forwarded to her. She began by explaining that they had all been very happy to finally receive some news and to be able to share impressions of recent events. She apologized for the state of her handwriting and admitted that she was in a stupid mood. Anastasia wondered how everyone was getting on. They constantly heard rumours but hardly knew what to believe. Many of the stories were so disgusting. They only told them half of what was going on, and the sisters were convinced they were being lied to.

Klaudia Bitner was spending much of her time with Alexei and he was trying desperately hard to eat. She asked if Marie remembered how it was when she was there and when he was sat on the bench. They took turns to sit with him to encourage him to eat but now he ate happily without any coaxing. Anastasia assured Marie that they were all thinking constantly of them all. They felt quite sad and empty without their parents and Marie. They had attempted to make Easter as festive as possible in the circumstances. They had arranged the icons with spruce and flowers which was the local custom.

They had taken some photographs which she hoped would come out. She was doing some drawings and had been told that they were good. They had been on the swing and she had fallen off. She thought it was very amusing and spoke so often of it that her sisters were sick of hearing about it.

Her little spaniel Jemmy had caught a cold and was no longer going outside. The dog sent her regards. (It is often described as a male dog but the autopsy later proved otherwise.)

The weather had been very good and she had managed to tan rather more than her sisters. She thought she was far more boring than pretty though these days. Unfortunately, it had been much colder this morning and the sisters all felt frozen. They did not go outside.

She had forgotten to extend her best wishes for the Easter and wished to kiss her, not just three times but many. They had demonstrations nearby but it did not bother them. As the sisters sat together, they missed Marie. Anastasia then asked her sister to thank their father for the delicious figs he had sent them. They were savouring them; a rare treat. (He had little else to send but, luckily, they were one of the most long-lasting foods and could have easily come from the palace.)

She apologised for such a jumbled letter as her thoughts were all over the place; she simply said what came into her head. They would be going for a walk shortly. It was not summer yet and no flowers were in bloom but they were starting to come up. Although the sun had now come out, it was still very cold and she was barely capable of holding the pen. In the evenings, they sat together and told fortunes by using a book. Marie knew the book she meant. Sometimes they *worked*, and she explained that they always did everything they were asked.

She sent kisses to Marie and the other dear ones but could not say much. She knew that Marie would understand why. (The letters were read by the Commandant and others.) She thought sometimes that, although she thought Russia was a sweet place, she was angered that she seemed to be unable to quite understand the truth. She admitted that once she had been very rude (possibly to the guards). She must have written enough by now, she thought; all of it quite silly. She intended to read through it and maybe add some more later on when she had some free time.

She wished Marie all the best for the future and assured her that she prayed for her constantly. She and her parents were ever in her thoughts. She signed off simply as A.

It had been said that Olga had a small pistol that had been given to her by her father which she may have hidden in her boot. She was encouraged to hand it over to Kobylinsky before she left Tobolsk. This may have been what Anastasia meant when she said they had to do as they were told. Although it is often said it was unlikely that she had a gun, Marie's journals show that the girls DID have training in how to shoot at Mogilev and, later, Alexei mentioned shooting practice too.

Anastasia was desperately missing her sister Marie. The two had never been apart previously and Marie unlike her other sisters was always more tolerant of Anastasia's more eccentric behaviour.

The general conditions at the Governor's House were difficult to say the least and they were now constantly under suspicion. One day when Nagorny attempted to smuggle out a simple note from Alexei to his friend Kolya, General Tatishchev had to beg Rodionov not to have Nagorny court-martialled for the *offence*.

On Wednesday morning, Nicholas continued his daily readings of the Gospels and *The Great in the Small*. He later went out in the garden and was greatly amused and not a little bewildered by the strange array of hats and jackets worn by the newly arrived guards. It was as if they could not decide which uniform to wear. Several of the men were former officers, but the majority were Letts. When Nicholas and his party went out into the garden, all the off-duty men chose to go out into the garden to watch them. The men chatted and wrestled one another.

Once again, Alexandra ate separately from the others. Ivan Sednyov catered for the former Tsarina with some more vermicelli which she greatly enjoyed with some bread and butter. She ate little protein. The rest of the party ate later when lunch was brought from outside. As Alexandra lay quietly on her bed accompanied only by one of her headaches, the rest went out into the garden whilst the sun shone.

Meanwhile, Nicholas chatted with one of the former officers, a native of the Baikal region. He also spoke with the captain of the guard who stood close by. Nicholas was, of course, with Marie who was generally very happy to speak with the guards and was always popular with them. She was someone who appeared quite ordinary and, unlike Tatiana who was sometimes wrongly seen as haughty, she was quite at home in the humblest of surroundings.

When they returned inside, Marie read to her mother. Shortly after dinner, Ukraintzev delivered the telegram that had been sent by Olga to Anna Demidova. It was most welcome news as, unlike the letters, it came through fairly quickly. Most of the letters sent to and from Ipatiev House managed to get lost along the way – by accident or design.

The evening was a fairly jolly one as the family had had good news and were consequently in a more contented mood and played bezique. They could hear the sound of piano playing in the distance as the piano had been recently been moved into the guards' duty room. The meal had been an excellent one according to Nicholas's journal and not only plentiful but actually served on time. The one fly in the proverbial ointment was the worry over *Valia*. They could not find out what had happened to him.

Despite the good news, Alexandra was still struggling to sleep due to continuing headaches. That morning, there had been great agitation in the guard room as the telephone was constantly ringing. Nicholas noted that Ukraintsev was missing, despite the fact that he should have been on duty. He wondered what was happening but, as usual, the former Tsar was told nothing. Ukraintsev had been replaced by the Commandant whom Nicholas referred to simply as *Goggle-eye*. As no one chose to speak to the Commandant he accompanied the family on their walk in total silence.

That morning, Nicholas read to Alexandra and his daughter Marie from the Gospels and the lesson for the day. Alexandra was incensed that they now had to get out of bed for the guards, the head of the guards and the Commandant as they called in to check on the family. The men appeared to assume that they would vanish off in a time machine between shifts. Alexandra felt humiliated at the *roll call* but Nicholas, as an ex-soldier, took it more in his stride.

Avdeev later recalled that the family generally rose at nine, apart from Alexandra on occasions and had tea at ten. There was a *roll-call* then. It consisted of the Commandant's inspection of the rooms, in order to verify everyone was present.

Alexandra ate on time that day as Ivan Sednyov arrived with her usual order of vermicelli, but the rest did not eat for another hour. Their food arrived late again.

Marie assisted Anna Demidova in washing Alexandra's long hair. It was quite grey in parts now but still difficult to dry after washing as it was so long. The girls now all had fairly short hair and it dried far more easily. The rest of the household went outside and after tea, Marie read the daily *Spiritual Readings* to her mother and, then, Nicholas took a turn at reading aloud.

Luckily, after the fiasco at lunchtime, the meal arrived promptly at eight that evening. Alexandra ate with the others for once. Nicholas, Alexandra and Marie then sat in the hall, Dr Botkin's room, and played bezique. Whilst they were playing, the Commandant appeared with another man. They looked around the rooms and left.

Friday proved to be a particularly humiliating day. The Commandant told the family to get up shortly after eight as he wished to see them before the shift changed in fifteen minutes. They needed to check the rooms. The guard had been changed three times the previous day.

After Alexandra had written for the fifteenth time to her missing children, Marie read the daily *Spiritual Readings* to her mother. Nicholas took over the reading soon after. Yet again, lunch arrived late. Whilst Alexandra remained inside, the rest went outside for some fresh air. She later joined them for tea.

That evening, the Commandant arrived and asked Nicholas and the others in turn how much money they had. He then asked everyone to write down the exact amount and took the cash away for *safe keeping*. Nicholas never had any cash nor had his wife. Marie had some that had been given to her by Anastasia for the journey.

Marie wrote to her sisters that day and admitted how she was missing the peace and calm of Tobolsk. Each day now brought a nasty surprise, she explained. Just now, they had been asked to hand over their money. They had to sign for it. Her parents had nothing but she had the *16 roubles and 17 kopecks* that Anastasia had given her for the trip. Luckily they had left each with just a little cash. They had also warned them that there were no guarantees that they would not be searched later. It was hard to believe that after fourteen months it would come to this. She could only hope that it was better for her sisters and brother – back at Tobolsk.

Later Nicholas read Leikin to his reduced family. The family dined together shortly after eight and afterwards played cards in Dr Botkin's room and chatted with the Chief of the Guards.

The following morning, Marie continued her letter. She had no opportunity of posting it or even handing it to someone to take, so endeavoured to carry on. They had just risen and had lit a fire. The rooms were so cold, she explained. The crackling of the wood in the grate reminded her strongly of her time in Tobolsk. That morning they had given their dirty laundry to the laundress. Anna Demidova was doing a little of the work herself. She had washed Alexandra's dusters and the handkerchief. (The outer clothes containing the jewels would not have been sent to the laundry.)

She wondered if they had packed her things. She had taken very little. She expected that they would be leaving very soon. They had heard nothing from them. No letters had arrived. She was continuing to paint from the book by Elizabeth Bem. She hoped that they would be able to buy some white paint for her before they left. They had little left now. The previous autumn, Monsieur Gilliard had managed to find some which was in flat, round tubes of paint. She hoped that this letter would reach them before they left. She asked God to bless them on their journey and keep them from evil. They wanted to know who would escort them.

Marie finished the letter and admitted that they had no idea what had happened to *Valia*. She wondered if they played on the swing or was the plank broken again.

She signed as Maria. She varied her signature; some days she felt like a Marie and, on others, a Maria.

It was a remarkable coincidence that, soon after, the guards found a good use for some white paint; sadly not what they had in mind at all. (It was used to whitewash the windows.)

Happily Alexandra slept better overnight.

On Saturday morning, Nicholas returned to the reading of the Gospels and the lesson of the day for Alexandra and Marie and, afterwards, Alix wrote to her children once again. Whilst the rest walked outside before noon, another telegram arrived from Olga. The family sat together for a while as Nicholas read before lunch. Again, Alexandra chose to eat with her husband and daughter for once. The family reassembled for tea, after Nicholas and his daughter had been outside yet again. He read before and after tea. The dinner was brought late again and, by now, Alexandra was referring to it as supper. The group played cards again later.

Olga's wire simply thanked everyone for the Easter postcards. Alexei was slowly improving, she explained. She called him the little one. It was how they referred to him and it was less obvious in a telegram than Alexei. He was feeling well, she assured them, and kissed all warmly. She signed simply as Olga.

Nicholas's thoughts turned to the past on Sunday, the twenty–ninth. It was the anniversary of the attempt on his life in Otsu in Japan back in 1891. A local policeman had decided for some unknown reason to strike him with a sword or sabre. Nicholas was badly wounded on his forehead but recovered.

That morning Alexandra wrote another postcard to send to the children. They had their tea a little late. She had slept poorly the previous night due to yet another headache.

During the morning Nicholas read to his reduced family and they ate together later. Alexandra chose for once to go out into the garden with the others afterwards, possibly in an effort to clear her head. When they returned, Nicholas read again and they all had tea. Marie read the *Spiritual Readings* to her parents later and Nicholas finally finished reading *The Great in the Small* to his wife and daughter. The family then had dinner or supper and spent the evening playing cards before Alexandra had a welcome bath.

Meanwhile, back in Tobolsk, Olga decided to write to Dr Botkin's daughter Tatiana. It is clear that the Marie's letters to Tobolsk had a far better rate of arriving than Alexandra's had from Ipatiev House.

She thanked Tatiana for the recent letter she had sent. It had taken several days to arrive but that was not unusual. (At least it *did* arrive.) Olga explained that her sister Marie sent word of *the Doctor*. Dr Botkin usually wrote at night and on one occasion he fell asleep during his bath. She reassured her that everyone was well and thanked God. She asked to give her regards to Tatiana's younger brother and fellow poet Gleb. She signed as Olga R(omanov). She was simply Olga to her family.

The note about the doctor falling asleep in the bath was one of the few comic events that happened in such terrible circumstances.

Nicholas too was in a light-hearted mood that day after hearing that the Chief of the Guards had gone out – dancing. In his journal, he explained that the man had been absent for some three hours as he had been dancing at a ball. He had gone around looking quite sleepy all day as a result. Nicholas understandably had not seen guards and dancing as being things that were likely to go together.

That afternoon Alexandra had sat out on a bench whilst the rest went for their walk. Nicholas confirmed that the meals had arrived on time.

On Monday, Nicholas observed that no one was permitted to go anywhere near the house. An old woman and then a boy had attempted to get near to the fence just to look through the gap in the fence, but had been driven away and even made fun of. Avdeev had come into the garden but had kept his distance.

That morning, Alexandra had written yet again to her missing children. The others had gone out into the garden, but she had remained indoors. When they returned, Nicholas read aloud to her and Marie whilst the ladies played cards.

Once again, there was a problem with the catering. Whilst Alexandra ate at one, the rest had to wait over two hours before their food arrived. She chose to sit out again in the afternoon. After tea, Nicholas again read whilst the others played cards. The family played card games again after dinner.

On the morning of Tuesday the 1st of May, Nicholas, Alexandra and Marie were overwhelmed when several letters finally arrived all at once from Tobolsk. They spent the morning reading and re-reading them in their excitement. Alexandra immediately wrote back.

It was a pleasant warm day and, for once, things seemed a little brighter. Alexandra remained inside whilst the others went out for some air. They returned in time for lunch, which arrived on time. Dr Botkin was informed that they would from now on only be permitted to go out for an hour a day. It was, according to the Commandant, to make it seem more like a prison regime.

However, there was some good news as Nicholas noted in his journal that evening: they had been brought their own samovar so they no longer had to depend on the charity of the guards. They also had their own source of tea as they had brought it with them along with other provisions, but much of the food had been left at Tobolsk, of course. Nicholas read aloud to Alexandra and Marie before and after tea. The family played bezique after dinner. Nicholas noted in his journal that he had managed to gain four beziques during the card game.

When they could have the meals prepared in their own kitchen, the quality of the meals improved. Nuns from the *Novotikhuinsky monastery* brought gifts of eggs, milk, butter, cheese, eggs and pastries but, unfortunately, Avdeev and his men took much of the food for themselves.

That day Tatiana chose to write to her old friend and colleague Valentina Chebotariev. It had been quite some time since the two had met; a great deal of water had flowed under the bridge since, most of it poisoned.

She asked how Valentina had spent Easter. It had been a sad time for her as her parents had been taken away from them. She explained that Marie had gone with them and the others had remained behind to look after Alexei who was sick. They had not been told why they had been removed. It was not until a week later that they learned where they had been taken. They were now in Ekaterinburg. Her mother had been unwell, she reported, after the journey which proved harrowing.

Wednesday brought even more misery, as Nicholas noted in his journal that evening. An elderly house painter appeared and the man painted over each of the various windows with a whitewash. It gave the rooms a feeling as if they were living in a perpetual fog. It felt quite dismal. He had even painted over the thermometer. They could however see a little bit of the sky at the tops of the windows.

Nicholas and his reduced family lunched slightly late. Unfortunately, Ivan Sednyov who had been acting as temporary cook was feeling unwell with influenza and had lain down. Afterwards, Nicholas again read before all the family went out into the garden. They remained outside for an hour, which was the new rule. According to Nicholas's journal, they were outside for fifty-five minutes before they were herded home like cattle. None of the off-duty soldiers were in the garden when they went out. It was unusual as normally some were outside at this time of day. The Chief of Guards did not speak with them as they were being watched all the time by one of the Commissars. He not only observed Nicholas and his party but also the Chief of the Guards and the sentry.

The family returned to the house afterwards and found the contrast between the sunshine outside and the whitewashed windows inside quite depressing. The only room that appeared to benefit from recent changes was the dining room as they had taken down the rug that had previously covered the windows. Nicholas read aloud that afternoon, and Alexandra and Marie played patience. The family also enjoyed a game of cards after dinner. There was now little to do in the evenings and there was no longer a piano.

On Thursday morning, Alexandra was unable to work out what the temperature was as the painter had managed to smear the thermometer with white paint. That morning, as they were no longer permitted outside in the mornings, Nicholas read to his wife and daughter. Alexandra was still suffering from a headache. Ivan Sednyov was also still in bed but, luckily, his fever had abated.

After luncheon, the family were finally allowed out into the fresh air of the garden. After tea, Alexandra once more sent word to the children. That afternoon they received a very welcome gift from Alexandra's Elisabeth sister who was in Perm. She had sent coffee, chocolate and some Easter eggs. Nicholas taught his daughter how to play backgammon.

That evening, due to an electrical fault, the household ate by candlelight. It took several days for the lights to be fixed.

On Friday, after her sister Elisabeth had sent a welcome parcel of food, Alexandra was able to have a cup of coffee. It was a real treat for her. It was damp inside the rooms so the family lit a fire.

It was now three weeks since the family had been split up. Alexandra wrote again to her children, and she and Marie wrote to Ella in order to thank her for the generous gifts.

After lunch, which was late again, the family went out into the garden despite the light rain. They had only one chance per day of spending time outside so they took it, rain or shine. Even Alexandra went outside as inside, with the whitewashed windows, it was like living in a fog. They only remained out for half an hour due to the rain, though. Later, they heard that the children had set off from Tobolsk. (They had not.)

That afternoon, Alexander Avdeev opened up another room which was intended for Alexei. Nicholas was delighted to see that it was both larger and lighter than he had suspected. It had two windows and was able to be heated adequately with one of the stoves. Nicholas read to his family later that day. The family once again dined and played cards by candlelight that evening. The Commandant, his assistant and the electricians had been going through all the rooms fixing the wiring, but it was not yet completed.

Marie had sent word to Zinaide Tolstoy that day. Marie began with the traditional Easter greeting of *Christ is Risen*. She apologised for taking so long to answer. They had unexpectedly been moved recently and, hopefully, Alexei would soon arrive with her sisters. It was now just three weeks since they had left Tobolsk. It was very sad that the family had been split up. Luckily, the house was clean, although quite small. Unfortunately, as it was in the city, the garden too was tiny. She had no idea how they would manage when the others arrived as it was very crowded already. She was sharing a room with her parents for now. They spent most of the day in that same room, although they had just been out into the garden, despite the rain.

The journey from Tobolsk had been difficult with bumpy roads, but at least the weather had been favourable. They had lost some writing paper along the way and even some of the tobacco had fallen out of cigarettes but, oddly, the glass objects had remained intact. The drugs that they needed had arrived safely. They had travelled for two days and spent a night in a small village. The group had crossed the River Irtysh on horseback but had to go through the River Tura on foot. They had travelled a short way on a moveable bridge. Luckily, her mother had coped quite well but was extremely tired on arrival and now constantly suffered from headaches. They had travelled with Dr Botkin who suffered greatly during the journey with colic in the kidneys. Luckily, he recovered later.

She wanted to know if her friend had news of Lili Dehn's son or her close friend Nicholas Demenkov. She sent her best wishes to Rita, Zinaide's tenant and the children. It was unfortunate that they had never had the opportunity to see the relics of St John of Tobolsk. She signed simply as Marie.

Meanwhile back at the Governor's House in Tobolsk Alexei had one day begged his sister Tatiana to let him sit up in an armchair for the first time since his recent illness. After he had managed to remain seated for a few hours, the Commissar decided that he must be well enough to travel. Dr Derevenko, however, concerned that the boy was not ready for the journey, managed to postpone the date of departure by a few days.

Saturday the 5th was grey and cold but Alexandra took the opportunity to get outside of the hideous whitewashed world that had been created for them. Earlier, Marie had read the daily *Spiritual Readings* and Nicholas had taken his turn at reading afterwards. There was very little to do. Once more, lunch had arrived an hour late but

Alexandra had already eaten by then. She benefitted from having her meals prepared separately inside the house rather than having the indignity of waiting for it to arrive.

Once again in the evening, the former Tsarina ate on time whilst the others were forced to wait patiently for a further hour until they were fed. It may have just been an awful coincidence that the meals often arrived late, or more likely something of a power thing. Nicholas, who had now been stripped of all his earthly powers, was now forced to sit and wait for his dinner. Later, the family played cards and Alix enjoyed a bath afterwards.

It was Nicholas's fiftieth birthday on Sunday and the day on which the Russian Orthodox Church celebrated the life of the long-suffering Job. The older he got, the more Nicholas identified with Job. It was a day that was spent without four of his children and under arrest and incarcerated. At least the weather was pleasant as it was a day of bright sunshine. It was the one gift no one could deny him.

The priest and deacon arrived before noon to officiate at the Easter service of intercession. Nicholas and Marie were permitted to go out in the morning, but Alexandra chose to remain indoors. After lunch, they were given the luxury of sitting out in the garden in the sunshine. On this occasion, Alexandra joined her husband and daughter outside. They went back inside in time for tea after which Nicholas read once again. He read *The Blue and the Gold* by Arkady Averchenko. The family dined together that evening, half an hour late.

Nicholas and Alexandra were both perturbed that they had had no news of their children. Had they set off?

Meanwhile at Tobolsk the Baroness Buxhoeveden had attended a morning church service and on her way back had hoped to see the former Grand Duchesses through the window of the house. She failed to see them at first but finally she saw three heads appear above the sill at the very last window. They hastily nodded then vanished from view. The three had knelt before the window for some time and waited for her to appear, as they expected her to. Olga, Tatiana and Anastasia had been told not to appear at the windows but had been anxious not to disappoint the Baroness.

Pierre Gilliard's journal for the day revealed that they had not left Tobolsk. They would leave the following day. The Commissar had refused to let the priest come and, worse still, he had insisted that the Grand Duchesses keep their door unlocked at night. (The girls may have considered moving some heavy furniture in front of the door but, in the circumstances, they almost certainly decided against such a move.)

Later, Gilliard explained how Olga, Tatiana and Anastasia had spent that last day at Tobolsk. They must have known that life would get even harder when they reached Ekaterinburg. Luckily, they managed to have a little fun at the expense of their jailers.

That evening, they called for the two remaining bottles of wine. It was not possible to take them on the journey so it was decided to drink them. Whilst they did so, the Commandant attempted to find out what was going on. The group managed to hide the bottles and the glasses under the table when he came into the room. They were concealed by the long tablecloth.

He stood at the door of the room and the prisoners all suddenly had a fit of the giggles. The Commandant was even more confused. Luckily, he decided that such behaviour was not generally a sign of plotting and left.

Gleb Botkin saw Anastasia for the very last time that day. He had approached the house hoping to catch a glimpse of her. She was standing at a window and began to wave to him. He politely took off his cap but was spotted by Rodionov. He was warned that no one was permitted to look at the windows. He warned that they would shoot anyone who so much as looked in the direction of the house. They were to shoot to kill. As the sentries grabbed their weapons and those passing by in the street ran for cover, Gleb bowed again to her and turned into a side street. The two had been friends for several years, although their early friendship had been carried on via Dr Botkin who informed his children of Anastasia's latest antics and the children passed each other little notes.

On Monday, Alexandra was so surprised that lunch arrived exactly on time that she had to write the fact in her journal. She also noticed another alteration: the guard and the Chief of the Guards had also been changed for the first time in a week.

The former Tsar, his wife and daughter sat outside that afternoon for an hour. After tea, Nicholas again read to his family from the same work as the previous day. He then went off for a long soak in the bath. Marie read the daily *Spiritual Readings*, and the rest of the household, with the exception of Alexandra, dined an hour late. Alix either did not eat or had done so earlier. Once again they played cards by candlelight. The Commandant had scraped the paint off the thermometer so Alexandra was again able to read the temperature.

Nicholas, Alexandra and Marie were becoming concerned that they had still not had any news of the other children. Had they left?

On Tuesday morning, Marie read the usual *Spiritual Readings* to her parents. Nicholas followed her with a Gospel reading and the lesson for the day.

It was already three weeks since they had arrived. After lunching late again, they were informed that the children would probably arrive on Wednesday or Thursday. They were to be given a couple of rooms next to the dining room for their son and members of the suite were to be housed downstairs.

Nicholas and Marie went out that afternoon, without Alix who remained indoors. They reassembled in time for tea. As the ingredients for tea came from the stock of provisions they had brought with them, it was the one meal that was regularly on time. Before dinner, Nicholas began reading the fourth part of *War and Peace* by Leo Tolstoy. He had never known of the existence of that part previously. Marie was able to have a bath later. Nicholas and the rest of the household, apart from Alexandra, were reduced to dining almost an hour late again. Alexandra either ate earlier or did not eat. The family played cards afterwards.

According to Gilliard's journal, the rest of the family finally left Tobolsk that very day. They left the house and boarded the *Rus*, the same boat that had brought the entire family to Tobolsk the previous year. Baroness Buxhoeveden had been granted permission to join the party. The steamer had only just arrived with a cargo of German prisoners of war.

Olga, Tatiana, Anastasia and Alexei were joined for the journey by the Baroness,

Countess Hendrikova, Mademoiselle Catherine Schneider, Pierre Gilliard, Sydney Gibbes, General Tatishchev, Dr Derevenko, Alexandra (Shura) Tegleva and thirteen servants. They were escorted by Rodionov, Paul Khokhriakov and their men.

The Baroness confirmed that, after their departure, the Governor's and Kornilov houses were both looted. Everything was taken away including the horse and carriage that had been lent by the Archbishop to take the children to the landing stage. Olga complained to the Baroness that the Archbishop would need his carriage but the Baroness assured her that it was no use saying anything.

Once the steamer left the landing stage, for some reason the men decided to fire machine-gun volleys. However, Paul Khokhraikov, who was rather more considerate than Rodionov, took the precaution of reassuring Alexei not to be frightened of the noise.

When the former Grand Duchesses, their brother and the others sat on a bench on deck, a guard seated himself at the end of the same bench and everyone had to converse loudly in Russian so that the guard could hear every word. Alexei was able to sit out during the day in his wheelchair as the weather was fairly good. The guards amused themselves during the voyage by firing their rifles at passing seagulls.

That night, Rodionov insisted that Alexei be locked up in his cabin with Nagorny. Despite objections from the rest of the household that the boy may need a doctor at any time, their pleas were ignored. Nagorny, it appears, continually argued with Rodionov. The three Grand Duchesses, on the other hand, had to keep their door open at night.

There was a slight delay when the party arrived at Tyumen as the local Soviet wished to arrest everybody. The group were eventually able to board the train. The news of the former Tsar's children's arrival had spread like wildfire in the local town, and a crowd gathered. Some of the women threw flowers to the children, but they were rudely pushed aside by the guards.

Alexei had been separated from Monsieur Gilliard, to his great distress, as the party climbed aboard the train later. The group had been split into two separate parties. The boy was kept amused by playing games of cards with his sister Tatiana and the Baroness.

The four children had been placed in a carriage together with General Ilya Tatishchev, Countess Anastasia Hendrikova, Baroness Buxhoeveden, Mlle Catherine Schneider, Dr Derevenko, Klementy Nagorny and a maid. Each was put in separately by an armed guard. The two tutors Gilliard and Gibbes had been placed in a fourth-class carriage with the servants, and there was no way of communicating between the two carriages. Sydney Gibbes, however, the ever-resourceful Yorkshire man, made friends amongst the ladies in his carriage as he had the foresight to bring along a porcelain bowl for washing.

Luckily, at the last moment, Volkov had the presence of mind to run up and give the children's party a bottle of milk and some cold veal and bread. It was lucky as they would have had no food for two days. The General cut the meat and bread with his trusty penknife. The carriage was quite filthy and not ideally suitable for an invalid to travel in.

Paul Khokhriakov managed to hurt his foot when he stepped off a ladder. Olga, who had been a nurse only recently, offered her assistance. She would look at his foot and bandage it, but he rudely refused her thoughtful offer. According to the Baroness, the Grand Duchess continued to worry about the poor fellow.

As the train finally arrived in Ekaterinberg, Gilliard could only watch helplessly as he saw Nagorny carry Alexei from the train and his sisters struggle to carry their various personal belongings. Gilliard attempted to get out and help them, but was rudely pushed back into his carriage. He saw Olga and Anastasia attempt to carry their belongings and then Tatiana who was carrying her dog Ortipo and a heavy brown valise. Her feet continually stuck in the mud as she endeavoured to carry on. Nagorny came to her aid, but he was rudely pushed back by one of the Commissars.

Meanwhile, on Wednesday the 9th, whilst the children were still in transit, Nicholas and his daughter were absorbed in reading *War and Peace*. Alexandra spent a restful morning and only dressed at eleven. Once again, lunch arrived late, but Alexandra had already eaten. In the afternoon, the family sat out in the fine weather. Nicholas read aloud to his wife and daughter after tea, and later they played cards once again.

Finally, late on Thursday morning, Nicholas and Alexandra (and Marie) were reunited with the other children. The only people who had been permitted to join them were the cook Kharitnov and Sednyov's nephew. General Tatishchev, Countess Hendrikova and Mlle Schneider were taken away and never seen again. (They were all shot.)

Pierre Gilliard, a Swiss citizen, and the British-born Sydney Gibbes were free to go. The Baroness was also set free along with the servants. The group remained on board the fourth-class carriage for a further eleven days when they were told to leave.

Nicholas was naturally ecstatic when the children arrived. He had been greatly concerned for their personal safety after he had reluctantly left three young women and his seriously ill son, apart from a few members of the household and servants who were powerless, at the mercy of armed guards.

That evening, Nicholas detailed their arrival in his journal. It appears that they had been warned that the children were coming, that they had arrived at the station, etc. The children arrived at eleven, some nine hours after their train had pulled into the station. The children arrived only with as much hand luggage as they had been able to carry. It had been quite a struggle, especially for Tatiana and Anastasia who both had small dogs with them. The reunited family went out into the garden briefly after lunch. The beds failed to arrive so Alexei was given Marie's bed and the sisters slept on an arrangement of cushions and clothing on the floor in the room next door. Alexei managed to hurt his knee and kept his parents awake all night. He had slipped and hurt it when getting into bed.

The family had access to a kitchen and a bathroom now and the sisters were given their own bedroom, but the water was very rarely warm enough for a bath and the house proved to be very damp.

On Friday Alexandra recalled the birthday of her brother-in-law Prince Louis of Battenberg and the anniversary of the birth of her late sister Marie, known generally as May. Alexandra had lost both her mother and younger sister to diphtheria in December 1878. It could be said that she named her third daughter after her late sister; although Marie was the name of the Tsar's mother, she had previously been known as Dagmar. Alix and Marie had been inseparable as small children and now, forty years later, she was still remembering her sister's birthday, despite the fact that she had not been able to see her sister for so long. However she failed to record that it was also the birthday of the late Queen Victoria – Alexandra's beloved grandmother.

Alexei already quite weak from the journey, not to mention the weeks of illness he had gone through and the physiological trauma of being parted from his parents, suffered from an injured knee on Thursday night and had struggled to sleep overnight. Throughout Friday, he and his mother ate in the bedroom that they shared with Nicholas.

Dr Derevenko arrived during the afternoon to check on his patient and change his tight bandages which were usually used for treating haemophiliacs. The doctor was not permitted to chat with the family as Avdeev remained in the room. Alexandra had attempted to ask him about the ladies. As he was still at liberty in the town, she hoped that he would have some news of them. He was not permitted to speak so merely made a deprecating movement with his hands. Alexandra misunderstood and assumed that they had all been condemned to death. She burst into tears.

Nicholas took the decision to send his valet Terenty Chemodurov for a rest. He was replaced by Trupp. As the valet left, he was searched thoroughly and his clothes removed temporarily. That evening Alexei Trupp arrived with Nagorny and Alexei's dog Joy. They too were interrogated on their arrival. (The dog, however, was not searched which, considering the paranoia, was surprising.)

Nicholas sat with his wife and son throughout the day and continually read. He had begun reading *Unfinished Story* by Apukhtin.

Dr Botkin wrote to Avdeev asking for permission for Pierre Gilliard to be admitted to the house as he was needed for Alexei. A similar note to Beloborodov asking for Gibbes was sent. Both were refused entry, but in the event it saved their lives.

The girls slept on the floor as their camp beds had not yet arrived. They had not been able to bring them as they had only been allowed hand luggage. Alexei again had a disturbed night. He slept with Nagorny.

On Saturday the 12th, Alexandra recalled in her journal that it was the birthday of her aunt, Princess Helena of Schleswig-Holstein. She and her daughters Thora and Louie, as they were known, had been close to Alix as a child and teenager but, since her marriage, they had had little contact. Thora had, however, travelled to Russia after Alix returned to her homeland of Germany in 1897. The two spent a great deal of time together, and Thora was beginning to bring Alix out of herself. Unfortunately, Alix caught the measles and Thora later returned home. Had she stayed, she may have had a positive effect on Alix. When Thora was around, Alix blossomed and became far more sociable. It was Helena's lady-in-waiting who had once described Thora and Alix as behaving like the Bennet sisters from Jane Austen's *Pride and Prejudice*. She had remarked that whilst Thoras behaviour was similar to that of *Lydia,* the slightly more hesitant Alix nevertheless reminded her of *Lydia's* boon companion *Kitty.*

Meanwhile, Alexei spent the day in bed, surrounded by the attentions of his mother. The swelling had gone down a little but the intermittent pains were very severe. He was unable to eat and simply drank some tea and milk during the day as he rarely ate when in great pain.

Yet again, Dr Derevenko arrived to see his patient and once more Avdeev accompanied him. The trunks belonging to the Grand Duchesses finally arrived but this led to a lengthy inspection. Marie's baggage would have been searched on her arrival, but most of her possessions came with her sisters.

Nicholas again used Botkin as a mediator to ask for Gilliard. The doctor asked the Chairman of the Regional Soviet for permission. Once again, dinner arrived late. Alexei began to eat a little and finally fell asleep. Afterwards, a more contented Alexandra played bezique with Nicholas and then went to bed early. That night, according to Nicholas, everyone slept better, with the exception of Alexei and, presumably, Nagorny who was in the same room.

Alexei gradually improved on Sunday morning; although he was still in pain at times, the intervals between the bouts of pain increased. Once again, Dr Derevenko came to check on his patient. He was accompanied by the Commandant Alexander Avdeev and another man. Nicholas and Alexandra both mistook him for a doctor. Jacob Yurovsky had at one time trained as an army medical assistant but he was no doctor. The Commissar, the Commandant and the Chief of the Guards had again decided to examine the children's luggage.

Meanwhile, Nicholas began reading the books of the famous Russian satirical writer, Mikhail Saltykov which he had found amongst the books in the house. They had belonged to the previous owner Nicholas Ipatiev. They played bezique again after dinner.

On Monday the fourteenth Alexandra noted in her daily journal that it was the anniversary of the coronation. Nicholas had been crowned as Tsar in 1896 shortly before a horrific accident when many hundreds or even thousands of people had been killed at a field when some had rushed towards the stands where beer and other gifts were due to be handed out in honour of the coronation. A rumour had gone around that there would not be enough for all. The events of that day had haunted Nicholas's reign and his ill luck continued.

Although Alexei had another bad night, he improved during the course of the day. Dr Botkin had spent part of the night with the boy in order to give the exhausted Nagorny some rest. Yet again, lunch was brought late. Alexei spent the day in bed but, for some reason, Dr Derevenko did not come. Nicholas read a great deal and went out in the garden for an hour.

The four Grand Duchesses and Anna Demidova spent much of the day darning the linen. The local wash-houses had gradually ruined most of the things they were sent. After tea, Ivan Sednyov and Klementy Nagorny were called for interrogation by the Regional Soviet. Both were formerly sailors from the Imperial yacht *Standart*. They would not be permitted to return.

That evening the examination of the Grand Duchesses' luggage continued in their presence, which was naturally rather humiliating. The cases would have contained clothes including undergarments and their precious objects such as books and icons. Marie's precious camera was confiscated and not returned. Anastasia had used it a few times when they were in Tobolsk in the past weeks.

After 10pm the sentry who was standing under one of the windows suddenly shot at the house as he claimed that he thought that he had seen someone moving at the window. Nicholas was convinced that he was just fooling around with his rifle as he had seen the others do the same.

Klementy or Klim Nagorny was said to have been arrested after he attempted to stop a guard at Ipatiev House from stealing a gold chain that belonged to Alexei. He was spotted in the street after his arrest by Sydney Gibbes, Pierre Gilliard and Dr Derevenko on Vesnesensky Prospect and they witnessed him climb into a carriage along with armed Red Guards. Gibbes later claimed that he saw them but failed to betray his friends. He was driven off and shared a prison cell with the Prince Lvov for four days. Then Klementy Nagorny was taken out and shot.

Despite an improvement in Alexei's health on Tuesday, he still remained weak. He had been able to sleep better but had constantly woken during the night.

The family lunch arrived late yet again. Alexandra once more ate alone. The former Tsar and his daughters went outside for an hour after lunch. Dr Derevenko finally arrived but, yet again, Alexandra was unable to speak to him as Avdeev remained in the room. She asked about Nagorny but Alexander Avdeev explained that he had no idea when he would be permitted to return. Alexandra was concerned that he and Sednyov would not come back.

Alexei's pains increased towards the end of the day but, after he was given medicine, he appeared to improve. After tea, Alexandra cut her husband's hair. They had no hairdressers amongst the reduced household so she decided to take matters into her own hands as his hair needed a trim. Afterwards, cuttings were found indicating that the girls' hair was also trimmed at some time. Alexei was carried to bed after dinner as he was suffering again. Luckily, he had a better night and slowly improved.

On Wednesday, Tatiana sewed the remainder of her mother's jewels into some items of clothing. They were increasingly concerned about the searches. Alexandra and her son lunched in his room before he went back to his parents' room for a nap. Later, Dr Derevenko arrived and put Alexei's leg in a plaster of Paris splint.

Nicholas and his daughters, with the possible exception of Tatiana in the morning, walked in the garden twice, morning and afternoon. Later, Alexei was carried back to his own room, and Alexandra retired to her bed slightly earlier than usual with a headache.

Marie, who had been at Ipatiev House for far longer than her three sisters, appears to have had a more confident attitude with the guards, as an incident concerning Tatiana shows. One of the guards had told a tasteless joke in front of Tatiana, which upset her deeply. Marie spoke to the guard and complained of the man's behaviour. She asked why he was not ashamed of himself. Did he imagine that a well-born woman would be wooed in such a way? Did he expect her to think well of him? She advised him to act in a much more respectful and refined manner; then they would all get along.

Alexei spent Thursday in his parents' room. He continued to show signs of improvement. When Dr Derevenko arrived that afternoon, it was discovered that the swelling had gone down slightly. Unfortunately, this led to a higher temperature as the blood began to reabsorb. He was later taken back to his room as the pains increased once more.

Meanwhile, Nicholas and his daughters had again gone out in the garden during the afternoon and that evening Alexandra briefly enjoyed a game of bezique with Nicholas before she retired to bed for the evening.

Alexandra's health broke down once again on Friday and she spent the day in bed feeling giddy and complaining of sore eyes. Her ill health cannot have been helped by the noise outside. They were making the fences higher still outside Alexei's window. Dr Derevenko had been refused entry as Avdeev was not present. The hammering noise from outside made her feel worse. Whilst the others went outside, she remained in bed with her eyes closed. She was irritated when she realised that the family dinner arrived at six, but they were only given it at eight when it had been reheated. After dinner, Alexei was carried to his room again as his pains had increased once more.

Alexandra spent the day in bed again on Saturday after complaining of feeling weak and having a headache. Alexei was taken into her rooms and he slept a little whilst the others went outside. The children washed their handkerchiefs again, according to Alexandra, although by now they may have also taken to washing their own underwear by hand as everything got so badly damaged when it went out to the laundry. It would have been less embarrassing too. Dr Derevenko and the ever present Avdeev arrived after dinner to see Alexei. The patient was then carried back to his own room. He had a slight headache but quickly fell asleep. As Nagorny had not returned, it is likely that Dr Botkin stayed with him at night on occasions.

On Sunday morning, an *Obednitsa* was held at Ipatiev House. As Alexei had slept well, he was taken in his camp bed to the hall where the service was held. A new priest officiated – Protopriest Father Ioann Storozhev.

Nicholas and his daughters took the opportunity to get out into the warm air that afternoon. Nicholas found it unbearable to be forced to sit inside that evening in the fine weather. He hated being inside on any day and longed to spend time in the garden as he wished. The family were only permitted outside when their jailers allowed.

Later, Dr Derevenko and his shadow, Avdeev, arrived to check on Alexei's condition. The boy was later carried back to his own bedroom by Nicholas, assisted by Trupp and Kharitonov. He quickly fell asleep. Alexandra enjoyed a brief game of bezique with Nicholas that evening before turning in for the night. She was still complaining of feeling weak and unwell generally.

Father Storozhev later recalled seeing the family that day. Alexandra, who was wearing a loose-fitting dark blue dress, appeared tired, but he thought Nicholas seemed quite calm. He thought the sisters seemed almost happy. (They had recently been reunited so were quite content with that at least.) Alexei lay on the bed next to his mother. The priest was shocked by the appearance of the boy. He appeared very gaunt yet tall. He looked very sick yet his eyes seemed quite alive and bright. The boy was fascinated with the new face. (It was not just a new face but a rare welcome face.) The child was wearing a white shirt, possibly his nightshirt and was covered with a blanket. The priest would return some six weeks later.

It was a special day in the Russian Orthodox and Eastern Church on Monday. It was the day that had been chosen to celebrate the birth of the founder of the Orthodox form of Christianity: Emperor and later Saint Constantine and his mother St Helen. It was also the birthday of King George V of Great Britain, who was, curiously, a first cousin of both Nicholas and Alexandra, each via the maternal line.

Alexei had again slept well and he was carried the short distance between his own room and that of his parents late that morning. Once again luncheon arrived an hour late. The guards and Commissar controlled everything now – even the hour the food arrived. Nicholas had been someone who paid more attention to the time of his meals than to the state of the country, according to one commentator at the time of the revolution. Now, Nicholas was subject to the whims of his jailers. He may not have been in an actual prison but the outcome was much the same. He was allowed out briefly each day in the prison yard.

The day proved to be unusual as Nicholas and his daughters were permitted to go out for longer than normal. Alexei, meanwhile, spent the day in his parents' room with his attentive mother. Later, Nicholas finished reading the second volume of Saltykov. The family played cards and laid patiences. After dinner, Alexei was carried back to his own room and, again, he fell asleep quickly. It was as well that he was improving as, yet again, Dr Derevenko had not been allowed access simply because Avdeev was not there.

As Alexei slept peacefully, Alexandra played bezique with Nicholas before she turned in for the night at ten. It had been a warm day and the rain came down heavily during the night.

It had not been a totally peaceful day, however, as Nicholas noted in his daily journal. Downstairs, they had heard a gunshot. The Commandant had gone to see if the bullet had gone through the floor. Nicholas was not informed why the shot had been fired.

On Tuesday, Nicholas unusually complained of having slept badly. He was normally a good sleeper, unlike Alexandra, but had been suffering from pains in his legs and lower back. He also complained that the rooms were hot and stuffy.

Alexei spent the day in his parents' room once more. He was feeling better but his appetite had not fully returned. Nicholas and his daughters went out into the garden during the afternoon. Alexei had been told by Dr Derevenko (who arrived at seven with his usual minder, Avdeev) that he could be carried out into the garden the following day. The committee later gave Alexei permission to stay out in the garden as long as he liked, but the rest of the family would be restricted to an hour. It was unfortunately typical of the committee's unreasonable attitude. Alexei may have been permitted to go out with other members of the household, ie Dr Botkin, but this is unlikely.

Later, Alexandra had the rare luxury of a bath. That day, Vladimir Lenin, the Bolshevik leader, had given the order that clocks all over Russia were to be set two hours ahead for the summer season.

On Wednesday morning, the new clocks made everything seem confusing. Alexandra got up at half past six, but it was two hours later in the new time zone. It was not enough that the new regime had changed the date; now they were attempting to change *time* itself.

Alexei had a bad night due to the splint, which had kept the injured knee firmly in place, being removed the previous day. As it was such a lovely day, Alexandra asked

Dr Botkin to carry her son out into the garden. He sat out in his mother's wheelchair and enjoyed the fresh air for once. Tatiana joined her mother and brother outside and sat close to the newly altered fence. The rest of the family paced round their small yard like caged lions. Nicholas was still in some pain himself and not in a happy mood. Alexei was taken back indoors later as his leg was aching. Yet again, lunch was late – two hours late on this occasion.

After the family had gone back in, workmen arrived to erect even higher fences around the house. It would now be impossible to see the tops of the trees. There was a positive benefit, however, as they would be able to have the windows open. It was oppressive in the heat and the whitewashed windows made it seem even more so.

Nicholas and his daughters went out again in the garden after lunch, but Alexandra remained indoors as her son rested. Later, Dr Derevenko arrived with his minder, the Commandant Avdeev, and the doctor made up a new splint for the boy as his knee was so swollen.

An entry in the house logbook used by the guards reported that Alexandra spoke German to her daughters in the presence of the Commandant. She was given a second warning for using a foreign language in the presence of the doctor. (It had been forbidden to speak in anything other than Russian, mainly because the guards wished to listen in to all conversations and they could only, on the whole, speak Russian. In reality, Alexandra spoke English to her daughters, not German, but the guards spoke neither language so could not tell German from English.)

The family dined punctually at eight for once. The new time was causing problems as Alexei had to go to bed later as it was too light at his normal time. Nicholas and Alexandra played bezique later before they too went to bed. Nicholas struggled to sleep as it was still light outside.

On Alexandra's forty-sixth birthday, she spent part of the day outside in the garden in the sunshine. It was her actual birthday but, due to the change in the time zones between Russia and Germany and the additional one day each century, Alexandra's birthday was actually held on the following day now in Russia, yet still celebrated on this day in Germany and Britain. (One had to be a time travelling genius to understand the various dates and time zones at this time.)

As Alexei had had a better night, he was taken out with them that afternoon. Nicholas however remained indoors. After a predictably late lunch, Marie carried her brother out in the garden and he sat out on Alexandra's wicker chair for half an hour. Marie had inherited her late grandfather's legendary strength but was the only one of Nicholas's children to do so. Alexander III had been immensely strong. Nicholas had found it quite intimidating as a young man and it was probably one of the reasons why he had something of a mania for fitness himself.

Olga and Alexandra sat with Alexei later while the others, Nicholas, Tatiana, Marie and Anastasia, went back out again. It was hot and stuffy inside again. The house seemed to be cold and damp in winter, yet hot and stuffy in summer. It was not ideal in any sense. Once again, the doctor failed to arrive. Alexei was carried back to his bedroom after dinner. The former monarchs played bezique together that evening.

Nicholas, meanwhile, had spent most of the day in bed suffering badly from haemorrhoids and in great pain. In previous years, he had often complained of constipation and naturally the one had led to the other.

On Friday, in a complete turnabout from the usual established routine, Nicholas remained in bed for the day whilst Alexandra went out into the garden with her children. He had been suffering from pains in his legs and what he termed *other places*. He was, of course, suffering from haemorrhoids or piles and also rheumatism. He had not been able to sleep for the past two nights so decided to stay in bed. He had assured Alexandra that he felt better when he remained quiet.

At noon, Alexandra and her daughters accompanied Alexei into the garden. Alexandra sat out for a while and then went back indoors, Tatiana having been put in charge of her brother's care. She was usually second in command, after her mother when it came to Alexei's medical care. They had to go inside at one yet lunch failed to arrive for well over an hour. It was late yet again.

Nicholas and Alexei ate each of their meals in their rooms. Nicholas ate in an armchair and both slept briefly. Dr Derevenko failed to appear that evening, probably as his *minder* Alexander Avdeev was busy elsewhere. As the day progressed, Nicholas began to feel better. The rest had done him good. He began taking a small amount of iodine, in an effort to recover. (It is now only used for sterilizing skin before operations.)

That evening, in the absence of the tutors and even temporarily Nicholas, Tatiana began reading aloud to her brother. She read a historical novel by Henryk Sienkiewicz. The book entitled *The Crusades* would have appealed to Alexei whose favourite books included Sir Walter Scott's *Ivanhoe* which was, of course, set at this time. Nicholas and Alexei both slept well overnight, much to the satisfaction of Alexandra. Both her invalids were much improved.

Alexei was taken into his parents' room at one on Saturday but yet again lunch was delayed, on this occasion for an hour and a half. Nicholas had managed to sit up but, by two, he decided to go for another lie-down. (He may have become irritated whilst waiting for the lunch to arrive.)

As it continued to rain all afternoon, the family were told that Dr Derevenko would not be able to come until at least Thursday. They were informed there was an outbreak of scarlet fever in his house. (Overnight, the guards at Ipatiev House had become increasingly alarmed after hearing reports that there had been an anti-Soviet mutiny the previous day. Forces from the Czechoslovak legion had rebelled after attempts had been made by the Communist authorities to take away their weapons during their evacuation to Europe on the Trans-Siberian railway. There had been many arrests in Ekaterinburg as a result. This had panicked the guards.)

That afternoon, Alexandra amused her son with a few games of cards whilst his obliging sister Tatiana read to him. Nicholas and Alexei dined together in the bedroom before the former Tsarevich was carried back to his own room. Later, Nicholas played bezique with Alexandra. Alexandra continued to fuss over her husband and take his temperature, which had returned to normal by now. The guards made a great deal of noise in the evening. Nicholas was concerned that they had no recent newspapers and wondered what was going on.

Nicholas was finally able to get up and dress on Sunday morning. Alexei too had slept well and, at noon, Marie carried her brother out into the heavily enclosed garden. Alexandra followed them out and they sat with Olga and the maid Demidova in the sunshine. Tatiana and Anastasia remained inside with their father.

The family finally ate at well after two. Whilst Alexandra remained indoors that afternoon, Nicholas, Tatiana and Anastasia went out for an hour. They returned in time for tea. Once again, Tatiana read aloud to Alexei and her mother. After they had dined after a mere half-hour delay, Alexandra played cards with her son before he was taken back to his room. She later rejoined Nicholas and the two played bezique once more. Nicholas had spent much of the day reading. He was now working through Saltykov's twelfth volume *Poshelhonskaia starina* (old day in Poshekhon's). After a pleasant day, Nicholas was beginning to feel better.

Nicholas's happiness proved to be only short-lived, however. On Monday, he became irritated when the family's trunks that had been stored in the shed were constantly opened up, and objects and provisions taken out. It was completely unexpected. He realised that it meant that things could easily be stolen. He had also noticed recently that the guards were increasingly avoiding speaking to the family and household. He found it puzzling. The men seemed to be apprehensive about something.

Once again, the family split into two groups and took turns going outside. Alexandra went out for an hour at noon with her son, Tatiana and Marie. The remainder ventured out for an hour at five. They had been forced to remain inside until Avdeev arrived. Once again, lunch had been late. It was almost three before it was served.

In their free time (and there was plenty of it), Olga, Tatiana, Marie and Anastasia were now assisting Anna Demidova in darning their stockings and the linen, possibly including their underlinen which was continually torn by the local Soviet laundry. The girls were well used to *working*. They also spent time doing knitting or embroidery if they found anything to use, threads being occasionally brought by the local nuns. Items of clothes were continually remade and mended.

Whilst Tatiana read aloud to her brother and mother, Alexandra and Alexei played cards together. That evening, dinner arrived over an hour late, as if to make up for the late arrival of lunch. Later, Alexei was carried back to his room and Nicholas and Alix played bezique once more. It was very windy overnight but luckily it cooled down the overheated house.

It was the former Grand Duchess Tatiana's twenty-first birthday on Tuesday. It would normally have been celebrated with a special service at church and a lavish meal, but in the circumstances no such service was permitted. That morning Alexandra sat out in the garden, despite the wind, with her daughters Olga and Tatiana and her son. Later, Tatiana read the daily *Spiritual Readings* to her mother. Although, once again, lunch was over an hour late, it proved to be a special one. Kharitonov had done his best with a small stock of ingredients but had created a dish containing potatoes, beetroot, which was always plentiful in Russia, and a sort of compote. The girls continued with their new hobby – washing their handkerchiefs – whilst Nicholas had spent most of the day reading.

After the celebration lunch, Tatiana read to her mother and brother. Nicholas, Olga, Marie and Anastasia went out in the garden but Tatiana chose to remain indoors with her mother and Alexei. After dinner, Alexandra again played bezique with Nicholas.

It rained on Wednesday morning and once more lunch arrived late. Tatiana spent much of the day reading aloud to her mother and brother. She had replaced Gilliard and Gibbes as her brother's main reading companion. When they had read to him, it had calmed him and kept his mind on other things whilst he was suffering from pain or simply bored. Tatiana took their place.

After tea, Dr Vladimir Derevenko finally arrived. As his quarantine was not officially over until the following day, he was careful not to touch Alexei. The family dined at their usual hour and, afterwards, Alexandra played cards with her son. Alexei was taken back to his room soon after and his parents resumed their nightly game of bezique.

On Thursday, a priest was expected at Ipatiev House as it was a special day in the Russian Orthodox Church: the day of the *Ascension of the Lord,* the day when Jesus finally returned to heaven after he had appeared after his death. In preparation for the arrival of the priest, Alexandra took her son into the hall which was decked out as far as possible to resemble a chapel. She placed the icons on the table but soon after they were informed that all the local priests were busy at their own celebrations. Tatiana read to the assembled family before lunch, which naturally arrived nearly two hours late. To add to the misery, the family were not permitted to go out into the garden for their usual walk.

Avdeev had a long conversation with Dr Botkin. It appeared that Nicholas and the family might have to leave, possibly for Moscow. The Regional Soviet had become concerned over the actions of the anarchists. The household was told to prepare to leave. Avdeev had explained to the doctor that any packing should be done in private so as not to alarm the guards. He claimed that the actions of anarchists might require the family to depart quickly.

The Commandant came back later that evening to explain that they were now not expected to leave for several days. He also promised that Sednyov and Nagorny would be returned to the house and that they would be able to have the services of Dr Derevenko for the intended journey. He added that *Valia* and the rest of the missing members of the household had left three days previously for Tobolsk. This was not true. Prince Dolgorukov and General Ilya Tatichshev, Klementy Nagorny and Ivan Sednyov were dead.

Chapter Twenty-five

Ekaterinburg Summer 1918

On Friday morning, Alexandra sat out in the sunshine for an hour from noon along with her children Olga, Anastasia and Alexei. The former Tsarevich had not slept well the previous night. When they came inside, Tatiana read aloud to her mother and brother. Once again, lunch arrived over an hour late.

Nicholas and his daughters went outside into the garden that afternoon, but yet again Tatiana chose to remain indoors and read to Alexandra and Alexei. After tea, Dr Derevenko arrived along with his minder Alexander Avdeev. The doctor checked on the progress of his patient Alexei. After dinner, which arrived on time for once, Alexei was carried back to his own room. During the evening, Alexandra again played bezique with Nicholas.

It had been decided to keep the family at Ipatiev House and the family had been told that the anarchists had been caught. (A couple of nights before, at the Palais-Royal Hotel in the town, the Commissar Paul Khokhriatov had arrested two of the anarchists, one of whom had put up armed resistance.)

At noon on Saturday the 2nd of June, Alexandra went into the small enclosed garden along with her son, Tatiana and Marie. They came in after an hour. Tatiana read as they waited for lunch to arrive. It came after two. Nicholas and the other children had intended to venture outside that afternoon but, as it was raining, they decided to remain inside. Tatiana read once more to the assembled family whilst Alexandra played cards with her son. Tatiana continued reading after dinner. Alexei was carried back to his bedroom afterwards, and Alexandra joined Nicholas for their nightly game of bezique.

There was again no religious service at Ipatiev House on Sunday, although the family had hoped that a priest would be allowed to come. Nicholas spent much of the day reading Schilder's history of the *Emperor Paul I* as he had done all week. He was thoroughly enjoying reading about his illustrious ancestor. They had been told that Nagorny and Sedynov would arrive on Sunday, but both were in truth dead.

Alexandra sat out in the enclosed garden with her son, Olga and Tatiana. It was a fine morning and they were able to sit out for an hour. Tatiana read to her mother and siblings when they returned from the garden. Lunch arrived an hour late.

Whilst Nicholas, Olga, Marie and Anastasia ventured out again that afternoon, Alexandra remained inside accompanied by her son and Tatiana. The Grand Duchess continued with the story she had begun earlier and finished it. Later Alexandra and *the*

Doctor amused Alexei in a game of cards. Botkin was now spending a great deal more time than he had ever done before with the family. Nicholas had always seen the doctor as a good friend, and his constant presence, especially as he was a physician, was a great comfort to Nicholas and the family.

Meanwhile Nicholas along with Olga, Marie and Anastasia, walked in the narrow confines of the small garden. It was now truly a prison with its high fences and the constant presence of the guards. After dinner, Alexei was taken back to his own room and washed. Later, Nicholas and Alexandra resumed their nightly game of bezique.

On Monday morning, Tatiana read verses 8-10 from the book of *Daniel* from the Old Testament to her mother. It had been quite some time since Alexandra had given Bible study lessons to any of her children. At noon Alexandra went outside to sit in the sunshine, accompanied by her son Alexei and daughters Tatiana and Anastasia. They returned indoors after an hour. As lunch was now made by the former Tsar's cook Kharitonov, it was just about on time. It was only slightly late. He had literally been slaving over a hot stove in an overheated kitchen all morning. The smell of food now went all through the house. Previously, food had been brought from outside and reheated, apart from the few meals that had made in the house from provisions that had been brought from Tobolsk.

Alexei was now able to wander around the rooms in his mother's wheelchair. He had recovered much of his strength but not enough to walk far. He still had to be carried into the garden and back to his own bedroom. During the course of the afternoon, Avdeev arrived with a workman to discuss what to do with the windows. Later, Avdeev escorted Dr Derevenko on his rounds to the recovering Alexei.

After dinner, Alexandra and her daughters watched as Kharitonov prepared to make some bread. Alexei was carried back to his room later and his parents resumed their nightly game of bezique. Now that the family had their cook make all the meals, the food arrived on time and this was a great relief to all. The guards no longer had the power to make Nicholas wait for his meals. He needed to have a proper routine and he made a regular point of playing Alexandra at bezique each evening.

The Grand Duchesses Olga, Tatiana, Marie and Anastasia later returned to the kitchen where they kneaded the dough. It was a whole new experience for them to be able to become involved with the cooking. Previously, they had assisted with growing vegetables but were not normally involved in any other part of the food chain.

The days were duller than ever for the four young Grand Duchesses. They spent their time reading or doing needlework of some sort. Alexei spent his time playing cards with his mother or with his model boat. The piano had been taken out of their apartments before Olga had arrived thus depriving her of the ability to play music. They had the ability to sing however, and on occasions, the sisters may have made impromptu music as they had previouly at Tobolsk when they pretended to be a musical instrument.

It has always been stated that the Grand Duchesses were at all times *carefully chaperoned*, but it would have been almost impossible when there was now no lady-in-waiting at Ipatiev House to chaperone them. The only other female in the house, apart from Alexandra who spent her time with Alexei, was the maid Anna Demidova. She was now literally the maid-of-all-purpose. She had no one to help her.

The family had a cook, a kitchen boy and a valet, but it was Demidova who had to do much of the work herself. It now seemed sensible to let the girls assist her and help in the kitchen. Whilst Tatiana had always been happy to help her mother in anything, Marie was inclined to be lazy and was happier chatting with the soldiers when she had the opportunity. The Grand Duchesses had always been surrounded by soldiers, but these were not the same kind of men they had known before. They were not guarding them from danger, but simply guarding them as prisoners.

The girls by now were assisting Anna Demidova with some of the laundry and the ironing. They mended the linen and their own stockings and even washed the dishes. They were now beginning to learn how to make bread.

The Grand Duchesses who had been trained to be just that – Grand Duchesses – were now living in vastly reduced circumstances with clothes that were either torn or mended. The jewels that they had were all hidden away and the clothes that they had brought with them were not exactly the *gold dresses* that the rather naïve locals expected them to wear when they arrived in town. It was lucky in many respects that Alexandra had never spoilt her daughters, and they were quite used to staying inside, reading and sewing. They had little else to do.

Alexander Avdeev later spoke of Tatiana at this time. He confirmed that she could be pleasant towards the guards if they spoke to her in a way she found acceptable. Tatiana, he admitted, would even go up to one of the interior guards and speak to him about his life, etc.

Jacob Yurovsky confirmed Avdeev's opinion of Tatiana. He even went so far as to claim she actually flirted with the sentry outside her room. He was convinced she had done this to make sure the guards were in a good humour with the family.

Unfortunately, the four sisters had little knowledge of the real world and, to them, they were merely chatting *nicely* with the men, just as they had done all their lives with the soldiers they knew from their hospitals or those who had simply guarded the palace for many years. The sisters did not see it in the same way the Ipatiev House guards did. They were not flirting in their own eyes; just attempting to get by in a difficult situation.

Tatiana did appear to be influenced by the outgoing nature of Marie who had been at Ekaterinburg a great deal longer than her sisters. Jacob Yurovsky claimed that Marie spent much of her time flirting with the guards, but all she was actually doing was talking. Sadly, this was interpreted as flirting by those who had no previous knowledge of the Grand Duchesses. They had few friends and had always spoken in a friendly manner to anyone they met – male or female, rich or poor. They saw no distinction between anyone, unlike the *Bolsheviks* which is an irony in itself.

According to Yurovsky, Anastasia was also influenced by Marie's behaviour. He stated that he often saw Anastasia, at the side of Marie, making eyes at the soldiers and laughing at their replies. Unfortunately, he jumped to a conclusion about the sisters. He did not know them and only reported what he saw. He had no idea of their usual behaviour. Royalty are instructed from childhood to shake hands and chat to everyone without distinction. The girls were only doing what they had always done. As they now had no chaperone to stop them talking to what would have been previously seen as *unsuitable* types, they simply carried on as usual.

The sisters were not all the same though, according to another. Speranski later remarked that he saw *modesty* in Olga, something Sydney Gibbes had also said of her. He felt that the three younger sisters were less so and behaved in a coquettish way. He believed these three gave the guards reason to believe that more than a friendly feeling existed.

Olga was older than her sisters and had suffered the disappointment of losing Paul Voronov and again with Dmitri Shakh-Bagov. She had few illusions. It was often said that she knew that the family were doomed and she suffered from depression from 1915. It was not unknown within her family to suffer from this. Alexandra certainly had it, Alice of Hesse's letters indicate she had it, and Queen Victoria certainly showed signs of it.

After the revolution, Olga had grown closer to her mother, and the two shared an intense religious belief. Although it was sometimes said that Tatiana was also very religious, it was pointed out astutely by Gibbes, later an Orthodox priest himself, that Tatiana merely played it out. She had always been at her mother's beck and call and said exactly what her mother wanted her to.

Meanwhile, on her seventeenth birthday, the former Tsar's youngest daughter Anastasia spent the morning learning to bake bread along with her older sisters. There were few material gifts for the former Grand Duchess, but at least she had beautiful weather. The girls rolled out the bread and put it in the oven. As it cooked, Alexei was brought into his parents' room and Tatiana read the daily *Spiritual Readings* to her mother. The bread was served at lunchtime and everyone was suitably impressed.

In the afternoon, Alexei was wheeled out into the garden in the wheelchair Olga had bought for Alexandra. They enjoyed the warmth of the day and the scent of the lilac and honeysuckle. Alexandra noticed that the flowers were unkempt, however. After the family had returned, Alexandra had to rest up as she was finding it difficult to breathe. She often suffered in the hot weather. Alexandra resumed her nightly bezique game with Nicholas after dinner. The meals were now on time, much to the family's satisfaction. She had played cards with Alexei earlier before he was taken back to his own room. Despite a brief thunderstorm, the rooms remained stuffy.

Alexandra remarked in her daily journal that local nuns were now sending milk and eggs for her son and cream for the rest. Alexander Avdeev *generously* allowed the family to receive the milk, eggs and cream that day, as he recalled himself. The local convent had petitioned to be allowed to contribute food for the former Imperial family and, after discussion with the regional executive committee, it was decided to allow them to do so. It was clearly a matter of *control* as why else in times of food shortages would one have to ask about free food for your prisoners?

Kharitonov was being brought food every couple of days and was making meals out of the leftovers for much of the time.

It was clear how much control Avdeev now had over Nicholas and his family. He could even control the food they ate. It is no wonder they delighted in eating bread made by the sisters. Now that Ivan Kharitonov cooked the meals, Nicholas was no longer at the mercy of the bad timekeeping of those who had brought the food. It was a small victory for Nicholas. Meanwhile, Nicholas had spent much of the day reading again. He continued to read Saltykov's third volume and was riveted.

On Wednesday morning, Tatiana read the daily *Spiritual Readings* to her mother, but she and her sisters Olga, Marie and Anastasia were now working regularly in the kitchen. It was a hot day and the heat of the kitchen would have been intense, but they enjoyed their new vocation. The family ate lunch together at one. Now the meals were regularly on time and there was less stress involved over when the meal would appear. The food was made by the cook, his young assistant and the sisters. They had no fear of being poisoned as they may have had before. As the laundry had come back damaged by accident or design on so many occasions, it was not unlikely that someone along the food chain had sullied the food at some point.

The former Tsar and his family went into the garden that afternoon. It was hot outside and inside by now and the girls would have been hotter still in the heat of the kitchen. That evening, Alexandra resumed her game of bezique with Nicholas. The days seemed more peaceful now. But would it last?

On the morning of Thursday the 7th, Alexandra recalled the birthday of Grand Duke George's daughter Nina. She was the same age as Anastasia – but her fate was somewhat different. As a child, Anastasia had played with Nina and her sister Xenia, but now they would never see them again. The girls claimed that Anastasia was a particularly rough child. Alexei was carried through to his parents' rooms late that morning and luncheon again appeared on time. Unfortunately no one had thought to bring any new supplies of meat so the cook had used his initiative and made a macaroni tart for the family. It made no difference to Alexandra as she did not eat meat.

Later, Alexandra cut her husband's hair again. There was no barber amongst the much-reduced staff. The family then went out into the enclosed garden and sat out together for an hour. Dr Derevenko arrived before tea to see his patient, Alexei. Tatiana read the daily *Spiritual Readings* to her mother afterwards. Alexandra wanted a bath but was only able to have a sitting bath or hip bath as they were only able to bring the hot water from the family kitchen.

It was now four weeks since Olga, Tatiana, Anastasia and Alexei had arrived from Tobolsk and the family had been reunited. They had never been apart before for so long or in such difficult circumstances. After dinner, Alexei was taken back to his own room, and Alexandra and Nicholas played bezique. Alexandra decided on an early night as she felt extremely tired. It was at about this time that the first of four letters arrived, written in French, about a potential escape plan. Later, it was found that it was part of an elaborate plot to discredit Nicholas and use it against him.

That day, Olga had composed a suitable reply in French in which she explained the layout of the house and stated that, from the balcony, there were five windows on the street side and a further two onto the square. The windows were all glued shut and painted white, she explained. Alexei however was sick and unable to walk. She urged that no risks be taken unless they were certain of success. The family were always under close observation, she revealed.

On Friday morning, Alexandra rose and dressed earlier than usual as a party of six young women had arrived in order to clean the floors. After they had finished, Alexei was again taken into his parents' room. After lunch, Tatiana read the daily *Spiritual Readings* to her mother. Alexandra showed Tatiana how she did tatting. Meanwhile, Nicholas read to his son from a book he had found in the house – *Sea Stories* by AY Belomor.

It was extremely hot that afternoon and, when they went outside, Alexandra sought the shade of some bushes. They had been given an extra half-hour. Later Dr Derevenko arrived with his *minder* to see to Alexei's leg. He used some electrical apparatus. Once again, the visitor was not allowed to chat. The boy's left arm was also swollen. Alexandra played cards with Alexei and Dr Botkin before dinner, after which Alexei was returned to his room and his parents played bezique. Despite a series of thunderstorms, the house remained airless and intensely hot.

It was still very hot inside the rooms on Saturday morning and the family stuck to their usual schedule. Alexei was carried through to his parents' room late that morning, and the family lunched punctually at one. Whilst Nicholas and his children went out into the garden for the full hour and a half that afternoon, Alexandra chose to remain inside in the overheated rooms where she was joined by Olga. One of the girls generally chose to sit with their mother. One was normally *on duty*.

Someone arrived to look into the problem of the windows. The Commissar had insisted that the windows were secure, yet the heat inside was unbearable. A compromise had to be arranged. Alexandra played bezique with her son and Dr Botkin before dinner and with Nicholas afterwards. The doctor was by now part of the family. They appreciated the sacrifices he had made. He had chosen to remain with them despite having two dependent children – Tatiana and Gleb. The decision must have torn him apart, and his health was beginning to suffer.

The intense heat had still not abated by Sunday. Alexandra and Tatiana went to see what they could do for Dr Botkin that morning as he was suffering from pains in his kidneys. Tatiana, an experienced nurse, prepared an injection of morphine for him. He had been in agonising pain since early that morning and remained in bed. Mid-morning, two soldiers arrived and took out one of the panes of glass in the room shared by Nicholas and Alexandra. It came as a great relief to the occupants of the room as it gave them some much needed fresh air, and it also had the added bonus that one of the panes was no longer whitewashed.

The priest, Anatoly Meledin arrived shortly before noon to conduct a service. It was the *Day of the Holy Trinity*. It was the first time in some three months that the family had had the consolation of a religious service. Although it was naturally conducted in the hall and in the most difficult circumstances, they made the best of it. There was a table containing all the images belonging to the household, ie icons of the various saints, most in duplicate, and an arrangement of birch tree branches. The priest celebrated with a real *Obednitsa* and *vespers*. Despite the sparse conditions, it was nevertheless a cause for celebration. The priest had been permitted to come and they had some welcome news with the windows that morning. They were thankful for small mercies.

The rooms had been very stuffy, especially at night, and it had fallen to Dr Botkin, who was now ill, to apply for assistance. They had recently been granted the luxury of an extra half-hour's walk. They were granted a full two hours by Sunday. After lunch,

Alexandra and Tatiana sat with Dr Botkin who was still feeling very ill. He had spent many hours attending to the sick Romanovs, so they were finally able to look after him. He had attended to Tatiana in 1913 when she had typhoid, and he had become ill himself as a result. His dedication was rewarded, but not in the way one would hope.

Nicholas and his other children enjoyed the luxury of being outside for two hours that afternoon. Later, Dr Derevenko arrived. Botkin was moved back into the hall afterwards as it proved to be less hot and stuffy than most of the rooms due to its size.

For the first time, Alexandra and Alexei finally made it to the dining room for dinner that evening. Alexei had been ill since he had arrived at the house. He was later wheeled through the house by his sisters. Tatiana had chosen to sleep in her brother's room to keep him company. Her camp bed was moved into his room temporarily. The former Tsarina later played bezique with Nicholas and the bed-bound Botkin, and later she played bridge with her daughters. That evening, Nicholas and Alexandra had the delight of sharing a room filled with fresh air for the first occasion in quite some time.

The window was kept open overnight which gave the bedroom a much fresher feel but proved noisy. It has been said that the window may have been left open for an escape attempt. A series of letters were passed between the family, written by Olga in French and an unknown *officer* claiming that they would help them escape.

It was the *Day of the Holy Spirit* on Monday. The two patients Alexei and Botkin both appeared better after a good night's sleep. Alexei spent the morning being wheeled around in his mother's wheelchair by his sisters. He went outside with his father and sisters whilst Alexandra remained indoors complaining of her heart. Botkin was in bed.

Alexandra lunched in her own room accompanied by her son who sat on her wicker sofa. She remained inside again that afternoon with Marie whilst the others ventured out. As Alexandra lay close to the open window reading, Marie played cards, possibly patience, nearby.

Dr Derevenko arrived at six to briefly see his patients Alexei and Botkin. The family again dined together that evening. It was only the second time they had done so for some time. Later, Alexei's leg was massaged and he had a compress put back on. Many years previously, Alexandra's brother Frittie, who had died at the age of three, screamed when his tight bandages were put on to prevent bleeding. He had lived a brief life but had been constantly angered by the treatment he had to suffer. Whilst Frittie complained, his nephew Alexei was far more resigned to his treatment.

Once again, Tatiana chose to sleep in her brother's room to keep an eye on him. Her camp bed had been put close to his. When Alexandra went to bed at ten, she noted that it was actually slightly hotter inside the house than out. The house, unfortunately, retained the heat and the lack of open windows made the situation worse. The family had expected Siberia to be cold in the winter but, with the exception of Nicholas, probably had little idea of the intense heat in the long summer months. It was stiflingly hot on Tuesday morning. Alexei spent much of the morning being wheeled around the rooms by his sisters. Botkin was showing signs of improvement. After luncheon, most of the family went out into the garden but Tatiana remained inside the stifling house with her mother. She read the daily *Spiritual Readings* and then went on to read from the book of *Daniel 16-end* and *Hosea 1-5*. The family reassembled in time for dinner.

That day Olga replied to the letter from an *officer* concerning the escape attempt. She wrote in French once again. She was accomplished at writing in French but, as Gilliard later revealed, she and her sisters did not have the vocal ability, unlike their brother.

It was again stiflingly hot on Wednesday the 13th. Alexandra spent part of the morning *arranging things*. She may have expected an escape attempt after the recent letters. Alexandra lunched in her room, accompanied by Alexei in his wheelchair and Botkin in an armchair. The rest dined as usual in the dining room.

Nicholas and his children spent a couple of hours outside in the afternoon, but Alexandra again chose to remain inside and was accompanied by Olga. The two had never been particularly close but, in the days since the revolution, Olga had drawn near to her mother. They were joined by Dr Botkin or, as Olga termed him, *dear well*. She greatly admired his intelligence. He was a gifted linguist and spoke German too. Olga liked to chat with him as he was one of the few really intelligent and nice people she knew. She had little in common with Anna Demidova, the only other female in the house outside her own family. Dr Derevenko returned to visit his patients after tea. Both were much improved. Once again, Alexandra dined with her son and Botkin. She was keeping a close eye on both of them. She decided to let her son sleep in her room that evening as it was better aired than his room. Tatiana therefore moved back in with her sisters. Alexandra went to bed early but was unable to sleep for the noise. The open window had given them fresh air but exposed them to the noises of the street and the guards on duty.

They had received another letter that day from an *officer*. He had told them that, when the signal came, they were to barricade their part of the house from the rest. They would have to climb out of the window with the aid of a rope. The men would be waiting at the base, they explained.

This seemed a simple enough plan, but it was merely an attempt to implicate Nicholas in an escape attempt. The plot failed as the family flatly refused to climb down the rope. They were not all young and fit. Alexei was recovering from a serious illness, as was Dr Botkin. Alexandra had complained of ill health for most of her married life, so she too was not capable of climbing down a rope. However, Nicholas, who had remained fit since his soldiering days, and his daughters, who used to climb onto roofs as children, would have been quite capable.

It was the nineteenth birthday of the former Grand Duchess Marie Nicolaevna on Thursday but, unlike Tatiana's birthday a few weeks earlier, no special meal was prepared in her honour. It proved to be yet another excessively hot day. Alexandra spent much of the morning arranging her things. They had barely slept the previous night as they had sat up fully dressed expecting a possible escape attempt. They had received a couple of letters recently which had indicated that loyal friends were about to make a rescue attempt. Nicholas and the rest of the family remained on edge for the next couple of days as they expected something to happen.

Happily, Botkin was now able to sit up, and he spent the morning in the company of Alexandra whilst Alexei was wheeled around the rooms. After lunch, Nicholas and some of his children went out into the small garden. It was tedious but at least it got them out of the overheated house and into the air, even though it also proved to be excessively hot. Olga remained inside to keep her mother company. Dr Derevenko failed to arrive but the Military Commissar and the Chairman of the Committee came to look around the rooms. They refused to open another window, so it was decided that Kharitonov and Leonid Sednoy would sleep that night in Alexei's bedroom as it was less hot than their room which was close to the kitchen. The family dined at eight as usual.

That day Marie was allegedly smuggled in a birthday cake by one of the guards, Ivan Skorokhodov. It is also stated that the two slipped away for a quiet moment alone and were discovered by his superiors during a surprise inspection of the house. Some of the guards also reported that Alexandra and Olga were angered by Marie's behaviour and avoided her company. The young man was said to have been removed from the house.

Yet again, this is a story that is likely to have been totally fabricated as Alexandra's journal makes no mention of any such incident, and she did not avoid Marie nor did Olga. It is, however, symptomatic of the tension that had by this point built up between the guards. If anything had happened, it was merely Marie again chatting *nicely* with someone who had brought her a most welcome gift. It was nothing more than that. The sexual tension between the four young girls, all of whom were exceedingly pretty, and the young soldiers would have been incredible. The soldiers chatted with the girls and, occasionally, the words or actions of the girls, all of whom came from a very, very sheltered existence, were taken out of context. That is all. The sudden inspection was more likely due to the possible escape attempt, which was probably yet another rumour to discredit the family. To many a girl, being pretty seems to mean she is of doubtful morals; it is *not* the case. The tension was intense that day, and Anastasia stuck her head out of the window at one point and was shot at. A bullet became lodged in the window frame.

Friday morning sadly proved to be excessively hot too. Alexandra sat and *tatted*, just as she had shown Tatiana recently. She decided against going outside again after lunch. Olga kept her mother company. She was *on duty* again. The others went outside and, after tea, Dr Derevenko arrived. Alexandra dined with her son. Everyone decided to go to bed early as the heat had exhausted them. The family found that a sentry had been posted beneath their windows. No one was permitted to sit on the window sills. The sentry, they were informed, was watching for any signs of movement. It was almost impossible to sleep in the intense heat and in the knowledge that a sentry was standing under their windows listening to every sound they made.

Saturday the 16th proved to be yet another intensely hot day. Alexandra continued arranging her things and *tatting*. She was very tired as she, like the rest of the family, had barely slept for days. When Nicholas ventured outdoors after lunch, Marie chose to remain with her mother. (If she was avoiding Marie, Alexandra was not doing it very well.)

Later, Alexandra sorted through the various medical preparations with Dr Botkin. They almost certainly had morphine, iodine and arsenic. It is remarkable that it had not been confiscated previously. That evening, the Military Commissar arrived suddenly to make sure that everyone was still in the house. The heat and the pressure had taken its toll on Alexandra who, again, began to complain of suffering with her heart. She had never fared well in very hot weather.

Overnight, Alexandra had struggled to sleep due to the sentry outside who had been particularly noisy. The heat made sleep impossible anyway. She was disappointed that no service would be permitted on Sunday. She was feeling unwell again and spent the day arranging her things and tatting again. Anastasia remained inside whilst the rest went outside. It was rare for Anastasia to be the one who kept her mother company. It was more often one of her older sisters and again it meant that Olga was with Marie, who she was clearly *not* avoiding.

Dr Derevenko arrived again to see his patients and, after dinner, Alexandra and Nicholas played a brief game of bezique but she went to bed early once more. It rained heavily in the night which, to everyone's delight, cooled the house down. Alexandra felt far more positive after the heat finally subsided and there was a pleasant breeze in the bedroom which she shared with Nicholas and, occasionally, Alexei.

On Monday, it was the commencement of the two-week long Saints Peter and Paul Fast. Despite the fresher feeling, Alexandra chose to remain indoors after lunch accompanied by Marie, who she was again clearly not avoiding. The others went out for a walk in the restricted space of the small garden where the increasingly tall fences had truly given the place a prison feel. After dinner, Alexandra resumed her evening of bezique with Nicholas, but she did not stay up long.

Tuesday morning was pleasant but luckily not too hot. That day, the daily walk for the family and household was split into two. Nicholas and his children (with the exception of Tatiana who remained with her mother indoors) had been permitted a half-hour walk in the morning and a further hour and a half was spent outside after lunch. Although the girls were said to have taken turns sitting with Alexandra, Tatiana's turn appeared to come around a little too quickly and Anastasia's scarcely ever.

As Alexandra remained indoors, Avdeev demanded to know why she constantly stayed inside. She explained that it was due to ill health but he chose not to believe her. Annoyingly for those in charge, Alexandra could not be manipulated so easily. They never knew whether she would go outside or not. They wanted to retain an element of surprise – not to let her have it!

As if to break up the monotony of the day, Dr Derevenko arrived before lunch. He had usually been permitted to come in the early evening. It was undoubtedly an attempt to confuse the family in the unlikely possibility of an escape attempt. If they broke up the routine, it would be more difficult for them to tell any *friends* where they would be and what they were doing at any given time. The splitting of the hours outside was also done for a similar reason, in all probability. The guards had actually been told to vary the timings of the walks. To paraphrase the former Imperial Romanov national anthem, the prison guards wished to *confuse their (Romanov) enemies*.

Once again, Alexandra continued to arrange her things. They had been expecting a possible escape attempt but, in the increased security, it now seemed more unlikely than ever. A sentry had been placed under the bedroom windows of the former monarchs and he made sure that they remembered his presence. He was not exactly quiet but, when they had initially been locked up in the Alexander Palace, some of the guards had removed their heavy boots so as to avoid waking the sick Tsarevich.

444

The guards had gradually been replaced by men who were less and less well-disposed towards the family. Avdeev was now visiting the captives morning and evening in an effort to make sure they were just where he wanted them. That evening, once again, Alexandra and Nicholas resumed their nightly game of bezique.

On Wednesday, despite an increase in the temperature inside, Alexandra chose to remain indoors as the others ventured out in the morning. She was joined by Tatiana that morning and, in the afternoon, Olga took a turn of duty. Alexandra played bezique with Olga. The rooms were again very hot and airless. In an attempt to make her feel more comfortable, Marie and Anna Demidova washed Alexandra's long hair. It would have taken a long time to dry normally but, in the heat, it would have dried rapidly. After dinner, Alexandra had a bath. Happily, at the end of the long hot day, there was a thunderstorm with heavy rain. It cooled down the carpeted oven that was Ipatiev House. It was so badly ventilated that it managed to be hot in summer and cold in winter.

The heat had increased even more on the morning of Thursday the 21st. There was some excitement during lunch when the Chairman of the Regional Committee arrived with some of his men. Avdeev was dismissed – allegedly for the theft of the former Imperial family's items from the shed by his subordinates. He was replaced by Jacob Yurovsky and his aide Grigory Nikulin.

Alexandra found the younger man to be a decent sort but was not impressed with the rest of the men. Yurovsky immediately tightened security and brought in new men to guard the former Tsar and his family. The new guards proved to be largely foreign but, nevertheless, hardened Communists.

Yurovsky and his assistant insisted on seeing the jewels the family had retained, including rings and bracelets. The ones that they had hidden remained so – for now. The jewels were then taken away and receipts given. Alexandra was unable to take off two small bracelets that had been a gift from her uncle, Prince Leopold, Duke of Albany. As she had only been twelve when he died, the items were predictably tight. The children too each had a gold bracelet that had been given to them as babies that could not be removed. Nicholas was unable to remove his engagement ring either. Alexei was left with his watch, after Nicholas's intervention. Nicholas had long believed that items were being stolen from the trunks in the shed. The new Commandant later claimed that the jewels had been removed so as not to tempt the new guard from attempting to steal them.

After all the excitement, Nicholas and his children were finally able to spend some time outside. They had an hour outside from six but, once more, Alexandra chose to remain indoors. She was joined by Olga who appeared to be *on duty*.

On Friday, the new Commander arrived with the jewels and he then sealed them in a packet which was left on their table. He intended to come each day and check that the packet remained sealed.

That day the family also received the last of a series of letters from an *officer* regarding a potential escape attempt. It is likely that the letters were part of a plot to implicate the Tsar and his family by the Commandant in an escape plan, which would ultimately lead to their execution or to kill the family as they attempted to escape which is why the letters arrived with such apparent ease.

On Saturday, Alexandra recalled in her journal that it was the fiftieth birthday of their cousin Princess Victoria of Wales, known as *Toria*. She was the unmarried daughter of the late King Edward VII and therefore a first cousin of both Alexandra who was a daughter of King Edward's sister Alice and Nicholas, who was the son of Edward's wife's sister. Nicholas had once professed, in his youth, to be in love with Toria. It is fascinating to speculate how different his current life would have been had he married her.

The day proved to be a sunny one but punctuated by rain showers. Two young women came to clean the floors. The former Grand Duchesses assisted them when they went into their room. They were not permitted to talk, of course.

Whilst Nicholas and his children went out for a walk in the afternoon, Alexandra remained indoors, on this occasion with Anastasia. They were permitted to go for an hour and a half that day. During the walks, Yurovsky made sure that the guards had no contact with the prisoners, and anyone who disobeyed his order was dismissed.

After tea, Alexandra played cards with the two patients – Alexei and Botkin.

The Commander brought Nicholas's watch in its leather case which he found in one of the other rooms. It had been stolen from the trunk.

Nicholas also discovered that day that much of the food that had previously been stolen was now finally reaching the kitchen. The former Tsar spent much of the day reading as he usually did when he had nothing else to do. He had recently begun reading Saltykov's seventh volume. In the evening, Alexandra and Nicholas played bezique before Alexandra sank herself into a refreshing bath.

On Sunday, it was the *first Sunday after All Saints* and also the Eastern Slavic Holiday of *Ivan Kupala* which coincided with the *Nativity of John the Baptist,* Jesus Christ's cousin who baptised him. There was no religious service though. That afternoon, Alexandra went out in the garden with her family for the first time in quite a while. It was pleasant and not overly hot that afternoon. That morning, Dr Botkin had finally ventured outside. There was a thunderstorm that evening again and it rained heavily.

It was consequently cooler on Monday morning after the rain. Alexandra returned to her usual habit of remaining indoors early in the day whilst the rest went out for half an hour. She again stayed inside that afternoon, accompanied by Marie, whilst the rest of the household ventured outside for one and a half hours.

That day, lunch was slightly late due to men fixing the electricity in the rooms. It had been faulty for some time and they had resorted to candles at one point. Whilst the men were working, Tatiana arranged her mother's long hair. Alexei's health continued to improve, but Alexandra was disappointed that he had not been given Nagorny back. They had no idea that he had been arrested and/or was dead. Dr Derevenko had not come either that day. Luckily Botkin was able to see to the boy as he was now better. Alexandra and Nicholas played bezique that evening after dinner. It rained heavily during the night.

Nicholas was angry that the door to the shed had only just been sealed. He wrote in his journal that evening how he thought that it should have been done a month previously. He had heard rumours that some of Avdeev's men were under arrest for a series of thefts. Nicholas had also observed that some of the new guards were Latvians. They were not all soldiers; some were simply workers who had joined the army.

Tuesday the 26th was spent quietly by Alexandra. Although Nicholas and the children chose to venture outside on two occasions, she remained inside with Olga. She spent her time *tatting*, playing patience and playing cards with Alexei and Botkin and bezique with Nicholas. Her eyes were aching so she felt unequal to reading.

On Wednesday afternoon, despite being in great pain, Alexandra chose to go outside with the others. She was suffering from pain in her back and legs and thought it was somehow connected with the kidneys. Alexandra complained in her journal that no meat had been brought for the past two days. Kharitonov had to make do with the ever-diminishing provisions he had brought from Tobolsk. Alexandra did not eat meat so it did not make much difference to her but she did not wish her family to suffer. She later took a bath before playing bezique once again with Nicholas.

Despite the lack of food, it became clear on Thursday morning that Yurovsky was not going short. He had insisted that the family be up by ten for an inspection but he kept them waiting. He was having his breakfast and feasting on cheese which may have been sent for the family from the local convent. Alexandra was indignant that the family had not been permitted to have any more cream. She remembered that morning, and noted in her journal, that it was her sister Irene's fifty-second birthday. Alexandra must have wondered whether she would ever see her again.

In a humiliating scene, workmen arrived and began putting iron railings around the only open window, in Nicholas and Alexandra's bedroom. They had been worried that they would climb out of it. Alexandra must have wished she had been physically capable of doing so. She was in terrible pain still.

Later, the family were finally brought some meat. It was to last six days but there was scarcely enough to put in the soup. The Commandant was very rude to the cook; probably after he had asked about the diminishing food supplies. Alexandra remained in bed all day and did not feel like eating dinner that evening However Nicholas went outside in the pleasant weather accompanied by his children but Anastasia remained behind and read aloud to her mother.

Tatiana and Marie asked for the return of their camera but were refused. Marie had the ability to develop her own prints, but was denied the chance to further her skills. It would not have been something the Commandant wished to have – photographs of what was going on.

Later, Jacob Yurovsky recalled why the heavy iron grate had been installed over the open window in the corner bedroom. The former Tsarina had frequently stood in front of the window, and she could be seen looking out at the square where she would wave at people, hoping to be seen. The guards saw her do this often and Yurovsky had told her personally not to do this. She had refused and he had solved the problem by placing an iron grate over the window. It now meant that she would not be able to lean out at all.

Friday was the day dedicated by the Russian Orthodox Church to the *Holy Apostles Peter and Paul*. Alexandra, however, spent the day either in or sitting on her bed as she was still not feeling well. Nicholas and the children went out into the garden twice, but Marie remained with her mother. Each day, one of the sisters read the daily *Spiritual Readings* to their mother.

The family constantly heard the sound of distant troop movements. They identified the distinct sounds of the artillery, infantry and cavalry passing by during the course of the week. They could also hear the sound of the troops marching to music. The town was, in fact, in a stage of siege. More and more men were being sent to fight the Czechs and White Guards (anti-*Bolshevik* troops). The Executive Committee were sufficiently disturbed by the advancing troops that, that very day, they met and resolved to execute the former Tsar and his family without trial.

Alexandra recalled the birthday of her niece, Princess Louise of Battenberg on Saturday, the thirtieth. The Princess was twenty-nine years old that day. Alexandra had known the child well before her marriage but had not seen anything of her since they had last met in Russia in 1914. Olga and Tatiana had formed a close friendship with their much older cousin on that visit and had frequently corresponded for several years since they had met in Germany in 1910 and spent several weeks there. Now, it was barely possible to get a letter to someone within Russia, let alone in Germany or England.

It was a most beautiful morning but, as Alexandra was still feeling unwell, she again chose to spend the day lying on her bed. Her back caused pain when she moved. At least she had some fresh air from the window, even though she was now barely able to look out of it. When the children went outside with Nicholas, Alexandra remained indoors. She was joined by Anastasia in the afternoon. The family were informed by the Commandant that Nagorny and Sednyov had been taken back out of the immediate area. The two men were actually dead. Nicholas and Alexandra were continually told lies concerning the fate of the former retainers.

Alexei managed to get a bath early that evening. It was the first time that he had been able to do so since he left Tobolsk. The boy was able to climb in and out of the bath and his bed unaided, but was still unable to stand firmly on one of his feet.

Yurovsky later complained that the family were constantly bathing themselves several times a day which was rather unfair as they bathed infrequently. He disapproved of the former Tsar and his family doing anything that they may actually enjoy. Overnight, it rained again and the former monarchs heard the sound of three gunshots. Nicholas had complained in his journal that evening that he had had no recent news from the outside world. They had no idea what was going on.

On Sunday, at the beginning of July, a priest was finally permitted to return to Ipatiev House. It had been a difficult night for Alexandra as she had been unable to get to sleep due to the incessant pains in her back and legs but she gained much solace from the *Obednitsa*. The same team who had come recently returned – Father Storozhev and his deacon Buimirov.

Nicholas and his children walked in the garden before lunch for half an hour but, as usual, Alexandra stayed inside. She was joined by Olga on this occasion. They almost certainly spoke of the service. The two shared a great passion for their religion, and it had been a great consolation for them both.

Whilst Alexandra remained on her bed, the others went out again that afternoon but Tatiana chose to sit with her mother. She read from the *Spiritual Readings,* from the book of the *Prophet Hosea, chapter 4-14* and the *Prophet Joel 1-end*. Alexandra had spent much of the day, although sitting on her bed, *tatting* and playing patience. In the evening, her wicker sofa was taken into the hall and she sat there and played bezique with Nicholas. She later took another bath and then retired for the day. Despite Yurovsky's claims that the family bathed twice a day, Alexandra did not appear to have had a bath for ten days.

Father Ioann Storozhev later recalled his last visit to the house. He saw Nicholas walk into the room along with two of his daughters. Yurovsky asked Nicholas if everyone had arrived and the former Tsar confirmed firmly that they were all present.

The priest spotted Alexandra as he went beyond the archway. She was with her son and two of her daughters. Alexei was seated in his wheelchair and appeared to be wearing a jacket with a sailor's collar. (He was probably covered by a blanket to his waist.) The child appeared pale but better than he had on the priest's previous visit. Alexandra looked better but was clearly wearing the same dress as she had on his previous visit. Nicholas too wore the same clothes.

The priest noticed that Olga, Tatiana, Marie and Anastasia were all wearing white blouses and black skirts. Their hair appeared to have grown quite significantly. It was now shoulder length. Storozhev was convinced that Nicholas and his daughters appeared to be, if not actually depressed, certainly exhausted. (He did not indicate whether he meant physically or mentally, but it is likely he meant both.) They stood in exactly the same positions as on his previous visit in early June. On this occasion however, Alexandra's chair stood next to that of her son. She was a little further away from the arch, slightly behind Alexei and Tatiana. It was Tatiana who pushed the wheelchair of her brother when they rose to kiss the cross after the service.

He seemed to recall that Olga and Marie stood close by and that Anastasia was standing next to her father. He stood where he had done before: by the wall to the right of the archway. Dr Botkin stood behind the archway with the other servants – a girl (Demidova was hardly a girl), a young boy (Leonid) and two other men. Jacob Yurovsky was standing in the living room close to the same far corner window. There did not appear to be anyone else in the rooms.

During the service the priest read the usual *Who Resteth with the Saints* but noted that at this point the deacon did not read this prayer but began to sing it instead. He joined in, uncertain of what else to do. They had barely begun when he heard the family behind him fall onto their knees. After the service, they all kissed the Holy Cross. (Tatiana, of course, wheeled her brother to the spot.)

The deacon gave the *host* to Nicholas and Alexandra. (Yurovsky had agreed this beforehand.) As he was about to leave, the priest passed the sisters and heard the faint sound of the words *Thank you*. As he walked in silence away from the house, the deacon suddenly said that he was convinced that something had happened to the family there. The priest agreed; they appeared to be quite different. No one had even sung.

The words *something had happened* may have been significant as the behaviour of the family appeared quite different than it had previously when the priest and deacon had come. It is not entirely impossible that a member of the former Tsar's family or household accidentally overheard what was about to happen. Nicholas's children

Olga, Anastasia and Alexei were all extremely perceptive and may have seen or heard something suspicious. The most obvious change in recent months was the attitude of the guards: they had avoided speaking to them. Yurovsky did not want the guards to get close to the family, particularly as it would prove difficult to shoot someone whom you know well, especially the children.

On Monday, Alexandra lunched on the sofa in her bedroom as the women had returned to clean the floors. After they had gone, she lay back on her bed. She read *Jesus, Son of Sirach 26-31* with Marie. The family had gone out twice during the day into the garden, but Alexandra declined to go out. Tatiana read the daily *Spiritual Readings* to her mother that morning. Alexei was able to have another bath before dinner. Afterwards, Alexandra and Nicholas played bezique again and Alexandra returned to bed fairly soon after. Again, the family heard the sound of a single artillery shot in the night and several other revolver shots.

Earlier that day four women had been despatched from the union of professional housemaids to wash the floors at Ipatiev House. Eudokia Semyonovna later recalled the visit in great detail. She revealed that all of the girls were excited at the prospect of seeing the house where Nicholas and his family had been imprisoned. They had been escorted to the house by Commandant Medvedev. They were confronted by Nicholas, Alexandra and all the children sitting at the dining room table as if they were having some kind of meeting, although Alexandra claimed she was sitting in her own room at this time.

The girls bowed their heads in greeting and the family responded by smiling at them. The four former Grand Duchesses each got up and went with the girls to their bedroom. The sisters lifted up their camp beds for the cleaners. Eudokia explained that none of the former Grand Duchesses appeared to be either scared or in the least worried. They appeared in high spirits, their short hair was disarrayed, and their cheeks were rosy like red apples. They dressed quite unlike she expected Grand Duchesses to dress. They wore short dresses or skirts of black with white blouses. She could even see a bit of décolletage (maybe as they bent down).

The Commandant Yurovsky was watching nearby. He stood listening at the open door and glared at the four girls as they exchanged both jokes and pleasantries with the four Grand Duchesses. After this silent warning, the girls spoke in hushed tones.

At one point, he moved his head away from the door, and Anastasia turned towards the doorway and made a rude face at him. The girls laughed and she put her tongue out and thumbed her nose at his back. She herself burst into laughter but quickly checked herself.

The Grand Duchesses, Eudokia revealed, were perfectly welcoming and friendly. (They had seen no other young girls for a considerable time.) They had moved the furniture to assist the cleaners and had even got down on their knees to help them wash the floors.

Eudokia was able to hear Yurosky in the dining room whilst she was cleaning, talking about Alexei's health. As the Grand Duchesses moved the camp beds back into place, they could not resist joking. They teased each other and one demanded that the little peasant urchin move the bed to the left a little. (Marie was particularly strong physically, and Sydney Gibbes once admitted that she was quite capable of lifting him off the ground.)

The Grand Duchesses appeared joyful, and the cleaner revealed later that she had always seen Nicholas as a figure of divinity but she saw that he was no giant. He was smaller than his wife and quite drab. He did not appear to be evil, but rather common-looking if anything. She noticed he had a small nose, a low forehead, thin hair and had a bald patch on his skull. He had narrow shoulders and his legs appeared to be short for his body. Alexandra, however, appeared sick and tired; she still appeared proud and one could see the sadness in her eyes. The cleaner could see a slight resemblance to each of the girls in their mother's features, but still lacked their smiles and laughter. She lacked their colour too. She looked quite pale. (She never went out much, unlike them.)

Alexei remained in his wheelchair the whole time, about half an hour. He was moved around from room to room by his father. His face was the colour of wax. (It was often thus after a bad attack.) His face was quite transparent and his eyes appeared sad with big dark circles around them. He smiled at the girl and giggled when she bowed to him.

Although she conceded that the Grand Duchesses were full of spirit and breathed a love of life, he looked as if he were no longer of this world. The girls had highly polished nails, she revealed, but all had chipped nails after assisting the cleaners. She saw the family not as gods but as mere mortals.

Tuesday morning (the 3rd/16th of July) began much as usual but it proved to be the last full day for the former Tsar and his family.

It began as a grey morning but later it would be another beautiful day. The young Alexei had caught a slight cold. According to the former Tsarina's journal, she and Olga spent much of the morning arranging their collection of medicines. They had quite a collection of iodine, morphine and arsenic. Yet it may have meant that it was now possible that they had resewed some of the heavier items of jewels as more thread had arrived. *Arrange medicines* had previously been used as a code to sew the jewels into the clothes to hide them.

That day, eggs, milk and thread had been delivered from the nearby convent. Nicholas and his children ventured outside that afternoon, but Tatiana remained indoors with her mother. Tatiana had earlier read the daily *Spiritual Readings* then she read from the book of the *Prophet Amos* and the *Prophet Obadiah*. Whilst her daughter read, Alexandra *tatted*.

After dinner, Leonid Sednyov was suddenly sent out of the house, allegedly to see his uncle. (He was by now, unfortunately, dead.) Alexei had grown quite fond of the fourteen year-old boy and the family wondered if they would see him again. That evening, Alexandra played bezique as usual with Nicholas before she turned in for the night at 10.30.

According to Yurovsky, he had sent the boy away that morning under the pretext that he would join his uncle. He revealed that Botkin, the usual intermediary, had asked about Leonid's fate and then Tatiana had wanted to know where he had gone and why. She explained that her brother was missing him. Tatiana calmed down after receiving some sort of explanation.

Yurovsky later went into more detail about what he termed Tatiana's outburst.

He claimed that she had been quite hysterical. She stated that Alexei was missing the boy and she demanded that he be returned. He had to calm her down but could only say the same as he had to Botkin. Yurovsky lied in order to get rid of her and said that the boy would return soon. She was then finally happy and went back to her family.

It had been decided that the former Tsar and his family should be shot. Later, Yurovsky recalled the events of that fateful night when the Romanovs had their date with destiny. He prepared some twelve revolvers and designated who was to kill whom. He had been informed by Philip Goloshchyochin that a truck would arrive at midnight, the men would then give a specified password and they would then hand over the corpses for secret burial.

Yurovsky assembled his men, the executioners, at 11pm. He handed over the weapons and announced that they would shortly shoot the prisoners. He made sure that Paul Medvedev checked the guard outside and inside in a thorough manner. Medvedev and the guard commander were to keep a constant watch over the area surrounding the house and inside where the external guard had been stationed. He instructed them to keep in constant communication – they had no radios of course. Yurovsky informed Medvedev that he would let them know at the very last moment that he was ready. He must then inform the guards not to be alarmed at the sound of firing inside the house.

The truck failed to arrive until 1 am. Yurovsky then went to wake the prisoners. Dr Botkin slept in the room closest to the entrance and came out to see what was going on. He was told to wake the household. Yurovsky explained that there was unrest in the town and it was therefore unsafe to remain on the top floor of the house. He would move them, he revealed.

It took about forty minutes to assemble the prisoners who had naturally spent time dressing. He led them into the room that he had earlier designated, down some steps into the basement. Yurovsky later admitted that he had not realised that the windows, small though they were, would let out the noise of the gunfire. He had not bargained for two or three of the victims to be standing against a solid wall which meant that, if they missed it, would be extremely noisy.

Each man was given a target. Some would have been harder than others to kill as shooting the former Grand Duchesses would have taken a great deal of determination.

Unfortunately for the murderers and the gathered victims, they had collected various objects such as pillows with jewels sewn inside and bags, even one or two dogs. This made the killing so much more difficult. The extra items made the shooting even more hazardous.

Yurovsky had ordered them to stand along the wall but Alexandra had wanted chairs to be provided as she intended to sit. Nicholas carried his son into the small room. Yurovsky ordered that two chairs be brought.

Alexandra duly sat down and the four Grand Duchesses and Demidova stood next to her. Next to them, Alexei was sat in a chair; behind him was *the Doctor*, Kharitonov and the others. Nicholas, he explained, stood opposite his son. (In some reports he was said to have sat with his son on his knees.)

Yurovsky ordered the men to go to their places and wait for the command to be given. Nicholas had managed to stand in such a way that he appeared to be shielding his beloved son. Yurovsky attempted to explain to Nicholas that his relatives had wanted to save him but the Soviet of Workers' Deputies had resolved to shoot them.

Nicholas was thunderstruck and said simply, *What?* He turned towards his son in a manner of protection. At that moment, Yurovsky shot Nicholas and killed him outright.

Then the men began firing in a totally disorganised manner. They had all been instructed to aim for the heart but most failed to do so. The room was tiny, a mere sixteen by eighteen feet, and many of the bullets began to ricochet, despite the men standing in the doorway to shoot. One of the bullets managed to injure one of the men shooting.

When the firing died down, Yurovsky realised that many of the victims were still alive. Alexandra, Alexei, some of the sisters and Demidova were not yet dead. Some had perhaps merely fainted. He shot the petrified Alexei. The men proceeded to shoot the girls but they failed to shoot them in the head and they survived the volleys.

They continued firing. Eventually, everyone died. It was later claimed that Demidova ran around the room screaming, protecting herself with a cushion, and that she and Anastasia, who had merely fainted, were killed with bayonets afterwards. Anastasia's dog Jemmy was also killed. Joy was spared, but it was never explained satisfactorily what happened to Ortipo but she almost certainly died. The jewels hidden in the bodices of the girls initially saved their lives, but ultimately prolonged the agony.

Yurovsky knew that it would be difficult to dispose of the bodies but someone came up with the idea of stretchers. They took the shafts from sledges and placed sheets onto them. The men then checked for signs of life in each of the bodies and placed them on the stretchers. There was blood everywhere. He ordered that some woollen military cloth be put onto the stretchers and used to line the truck.

He instructed Michael Medvedev and Peter Zakharovich Yermakov to remove the bodies. Once they had moved the first of the bodies, one man said that another had taken some of the valuables. Yurovsky stopped the removal and demanded the return of the valuables and, eventually, two men owned up.

Yurovsky then threatened to shoot anyone who looted the corpses. He moved the two men who had taken things and instructed Nikulin to escort the bodies and make sure everything was in order. He collected everything that he could and sent it to the office.

He gave orders that everything should be cleaned and washed thoroughly, and the party left at 3am with the bodies. They were driven towards the Verkh-Isetsky works yet, before they arrived, the group was met by a whole group of people on horseback and carriages. The visitors wanted to know if the family had come dead or alive. The truck got stuck soon after between two trees. They spotted several more men taking valuables. Yurovsky ordered the men he had posted to keep everyone away from the truck.

Yurovsky asked if it was far. Yermakov, who had decided on a particular site, replied that it was not far to the works, beyond the railroad beds. There was a marsh behind the trees. They could not move the truck. They attempted to lighten its load, but to no avail.

They arrived at a gully close to a mine, but peasants were sitting around the fire after spending the night at the local hayfield.

It was already daybreak. It was impossible to unload the truck without being seen.

Yurovsky did not know what to do. He had to get rid of the peasants. He realised that they were now in the village of Koptyaki or close to it. Yurovsky ordered his men to cordon off the area, explaining that Czechs were nearby. He ordered his men to keep everyone back, and some of his men were sent into the town as they were not even needed.

He then ordered the remaining men to take the clothes off the bodies in the truck. The bodies were thrown into a mine. He wanted the clothing burnt and ordered bonfires to be lit. The men then discovered that the Grand Duchesses and even the former Tsarina had jewels sewn into their clothes. The girls' bodices contained diamonds mainly. These had acted as a type of body armour. They found more valuables in the ashes of the fires. They had still not buried the bodies, though.

Yurovsky later realised that the bodies needed to be taken out of the mine and moved elsewhere. It was obvious that people knew what had gone on. He set up a guard post, removed the valuables and left. He spoke to the Regional Executive Committee and explained his dilemma. It was later decided to move the corpses. Men were sent to exhume the bodies. It proved difficult to get them out of the mine. The men worked through the night and were exhausted by the effort.

Yurovsky then went to the Town Executive Committee to ask their advice. Did they know where they could hide the bodies effectively? They proposed using a deep abandoned mine nearby. It was on the Moscow High Road. He obtained a car and went with some help to look for the mine but the car broke down. It was getting more and more difficult to finish the task, and it was ending up more and more like a sick version of the Keystone Kops. Everything that could go wrong did. It was as if the former Tsar really did have a divine power.

Yurovsky left the driver behind to fix the car and carried on by foot. The others then looked over the mine and deemed it suitable. They went back to the car but it had to be towed. They waited for a passing car. Later, some people arrived on horseback. They seemed to recognise him. They were rushing towards the nearby plant and, reluctantly, they gave up the horses.

Whilst they waited, Yurovsky's men attempted to burn the bodies but no one knew how to do it. They decided to get some carts so that, if the worst came to the worst, they could bury the bodies in more than one place. It seemed eminently sensible as it was rapidly descending into a farce.

The road leading to the Koptyaki was clay near to the gully. If they buried them there, it would be impossible to find them again. If they buried them and drove by with a string of carts, it would be suitably confusing. The cart tracks would lead in a circle.

He could find no more cars so went to the head of the military transportation to see if he could find one. There was one, but it was with the chief. He got it and drove to Voikov who was head of supplies in the Urals and requested some petrol or kerosene, sulphuric acid too to disfigure the faces, and some spades for digging. He then commandeered ten carts from the prison, but without the drivers.

They loaded everything up and went back. The farce continued. The truck was sent and Yurovsky awaited the arrival of Polushin, but he failed to arrive. He waited in vain until 11pm. Polushin was the main specialist in burning.

Polushin had ridden off on horseback and had managed to fall off. He had hurt his foot and was unable to ride. Yurovsky decided to go on horseback as he did not want to risk getting stuck in the car. He finally arrived at the place where the bodies had been moved to. He also had bad luck with the horse. It hesitated and dropped to its knees and managed to fall on its side. It came down on Yurovsky's foot. He lay there in pain for some time before he was able to remount the animal.

When he finally arrived, the work on extracting the corpses was already going on. They decided to bury them in a pit and began digging. It was almost done by dawn. One of the party came up to Yurovsky then and mentioned that, despite orders to stop anyone coming near, a man who was an acquaintance of Yermakov had appeared and had been allowed to remain at a distance.

It was obvious that they had been digging; there was clay everywhere. The plan was ruined and they decided to fill in the pit. They piled back into the cart later. The truck waited for them and naturally managed to get stuck again. They headed for the Siberian high road, crossed the railroad and, as they began transferring the corpses again, they got stuck again. They struggled for two hours. It was almost midnight. Yurovsky decided to bury the corpses close to where they were. No one was around now.

He sent for some railway ties or sleepers to cover the places where the bodies were to be placed. The railway sleepers were needed for a truck to pass over. It was a perfect hiding place as everyone would assume the ties were placed to get the truck over the ground, not that it was where the bodies were hidden. A fire was made to destroy a couple of the bodies which proved later to be Alexei and Anastasia.

The pit was dug close to the fire and the bones were finally buried. The land was levelled afterwards. A fire was again lit to destroy the remaining evidence. The bodies had the further indignity of having sulphuric acid thrown over them. The pit was filled and covered with the ties. Yurovsky then instructed everyone present to forget what they had seen.

The House of Special Purpose became a shrine to the loyal monarchists over the years and, in an effort to stop this, Boris Yeltsin had the house razed to the ground in 1977. The bodies were not discovered until 1979 and were eventually dug up some thirty years after. The men who found the site felt unable to go public with the information until they felt certain that it was safe to do so. The bodies were eventually given a more dignified funeral and buried in St Petersburg but the final two bodies, those of Alexei and Anastasia, were not found until some time after the initial findings. The two were originally burnt. Initially, there were disagreements over whose bodies they were until the last two were located. Marie and Anastasia despite being five feet nine and only five feet two were initially confused; some claimed the missing body was Marie and others Anastasia. A lady named Anna Anderson had claimed for many years that she was Anastasia but the DNA results showed that, eventually, all the bodies were accounted for.

The End

Appendix 1 – People and Places

AKSH – Briefly the *boyfriend* of the young Grand Duchess Olga Nicolaevna during 1913. He was Alexander Konstantinovich Shvedov. All her *boyfriends* were of course quite platonic.

Abby – The nickname of Alix's cousin Prince Albert of Schleswig-Holstein (b. 1869 – d. 1931), brother of *Thora* and Marie-Louise and son of Princess Helena.

Agayev, Vasya – A cadet and in 1916 became a friend of the Tsarevich Alexei.

Agooweeone – A nickname used by Alix for Nicholas and later for Alexei.

Ai Todor – The Crimean estate of the Tsar's sister Grand Duchess Xenia and her husband Grand Duke Alexander (*Sandro*). *Sandro's* brother George later acquired the neighbouring estate and got the architect Krasnov to build him a house. *Harax* perched on the cliffs of Cap Ai-Todor.

Alek – The nickname used by Tsar Nicholas for Prince Alexander of Oldenburg. He was the father-in-law of Olga Alexandrovna.

Alexander III, Tsar of Russia (b. 10th Mar 1845, St Petersburg – d. 2nd Nov 1894, Livadia) – Reigned 1881 – 1894 . He married Princess Marie of Denmark on the 9th Nov 1866 and was the father of Tsar Nicholas II. He was a loving father, especially to his two youngest children – Michael and Olga. He preferred the simple life unlike his more social wife – yet the two were devoted. He was said to have risen at 7, washed in cold water, wore simple peasant clothes, after his morning coffee would work then join his wife for a simple breakfast of rye bread and boiled eggs. He insisted that his children sleep on simple army cots with hard pillows, took cold baths in the morning and ate porridge for breakfast. He preferred the smaller Anichkov Palace on the Nevsky Prospect as he disliked the cold, and draft ridden Winter Palace. The family lived here during the Season New Year's Day to Lent. He was said to have been 6ft 4ins tall and his wife Marie was tiny. Like his son Nicholas he enjoyed hunting and shooting.

Alexander, Crown Prince of Serbia, future King (b. 16th Dec 1888, Cetinje – d. 1934) – The eldest son of King Peter I of Serbia and brother of Grand Duchess Olga Nicolaevna's friend Princess Elena. He was Crown Prince from 1909 and did not marry until 1922. His sister claimed that he and Olga were fond of each other.

Alexander, Grand Duke of Russia (b. 7th June 1869, St Petersburg – d. 2nd May 1870, St Petersburg) – A younger brother of Tsar Nicholas II, who died as a baby. He was the second son of Tsar Alexander III and his wife Marie.

Alexander Mikhailovich, Grand Duke of Russia (b. 1866 – d. 1933) – Known as *Sandro* the Grand Duke was married to Grand Duchess Xenia, the Tsar's sister. He was the son of Field Marshall Grand Duke Michael Nicolaevich and a Grandson of Nicholas I. During the Great War he commanded the air force on the Southern front and then became Supreme Commander of the Russian Air Force. He was a close friend of Nicholas II at one time.

Alexander Palace – The main home of the Tsar Nicholas II from 1895–1917. It was the birthplace of their first child Grand Duchess Olga in 1895. On the 17th Sept 1941 the furniture and other treasures were removed by the Germans. Luckily Anatoly Kuchumov, the Curator had removed as many of the important pieces as possible to safety.

Alexandra Feodorovna, Tsarina of Russia (b. 6th June 1872, Darmstadt, Germany – d. 16th/17th July 1918, Ekaterinburg, Russia) – Formerly the Princess Alix Victoria Helena Louise Beatrice of Hesse and by the Rhine and was the fourth daughter and fifth child of Queen Victoria's daughter Princess Alice Maud Mary of Great Britain and Ireland (b. 1843 – d. 1878) and Ludwig IV, Grand Duke of Hesse. She disliked high society, much as her Grandmother Queen Victoria had, and was misunderstood and disliked by them in return. She had been brought up simply by her nanny Mary Ann Orchard and ate baked apples and rice puddings. Her timetable was strictly adhered to and mornings and afternoons were divided into rigid patterns. Her spare time was spent playing in the courtyard, trying to catch goldfish from the fountain; driving in her own pony cart and wearing her mother's cast off clothes pretending to be a lady.

Alexei Nicolaevich, Tsarevich (b. 12th Aug 1904, Peterhof, Russia – d. 16th/17th July 1918) – The fifth child and only son of His Imperial Majesty Tsar Nicholas II of Russia (b. 1868 – d. 1918) and his wife the former Princess Alix of Hesse and by the Rhine (b. 1872 – d. 1918)

Alexi – Prince and Count Alexander of Erbach-Schonberg (b. 1872 – d. 1944)

Alexeiev, General Michael Vasilievich (b. 1857 – d. 1918) – Chief of Staff to Nicholas II 1915–17. Nicholas one referred to this gentleman as his crossed eyed friend. He was an extremely hard worker and greatly admired by Nicholas.

Alexeev, Eugeny Ivanovich (b. 1843 – d. 1918) – An Admiral Adjutant-General and member of the Council of State.

Alice Maud Mary, Princess of Great Britain and Ireland and Grand Duchess of Hesse (b. 25th Apr 1843 – d. 14th Dec 1878) – The second daughter of Queen Victoria and Prince Albert. She had eight brothers and sisters including the future King Edward VII of Great Britain. She married Prince Ludwig of Hessen-Darmstadt on the 1st July 1862. They had 7 children; Victoria; Elisabeth; Irene; Ernst-Ludwig, Friedrich-Wilhelm; Alix (the future Tsarina of Russia) and May. Her interests included nursing, education, employment and the health of women. She established the Frauenvereins or Women's Societies. She helped to organize and train women to perform relief work, especially nursing during wartime. She was a gifted nurse and had been taught by Florence Nightingale. She was a talented pianist and was fascinated in philosophy. Her son Ernie clearly remembered her sense of humour yet she always appeared serious in photographs. She educated her own children, as Alexandra was forced to do after the revolution. During the Austro-Prussian war she was on a different side to her older sister Victoria of Prussia. Prussia faced Austria and the smaller German states including Hesse.

Alice, Princess of Greece and Denmark (b. 25th Feb 1885 – d. 5th Dec 1969) – The daughter of Princess Victoria and the niece of Alix. Alice married Nicholas's cousin Prince Andrea of Greece and Denmark. Alice and Andrew had five children Margarita; Theodora; Cecile; Sophie and Philip. Her son was the consort of Queen Elizabeth II.

All-Night Vigil – A service that combines vespers and matins. It takes place on the eve of a holiday in the Russian Orthodox Church.

Alma-Tadema, Sir Lawrence (b. 1836 – d. 1912) – The naturalized British painter whose work Nicholas was particularly fond. He owned paintings by the artist. His paintings were basically idealized impressions of ancient Greece or Rome.

Anastasia Nicolaevna, Grand Duchess of Russia (b. 18th June 1901, Peterhof, Russia – d. 16th/17th July 1918, Ekaterinburg) – The fourth daughter and fourth child of His Imperial Majesty Tsar Nicholas II of Russia (b. 1868 – d. 1918) and his wife the former Princess Alix of Hesse and by the Rhine (b. 1872 – d. 1918).

Anastasia Nicolaevna, Grand Duchess of Russia (b. 1868 – d. 1935) – Known as *Stana* she was one of the Godparents of Grand Duchess Anastasia (1901 – 1918). She was the wife of Grand Duke Nicholas Nicolaevich.

Andrea, Prince of Greece (b. 2nd Feb 1882 – d. 3rd Dec 1944) – A cousin of Nicholas and the fourth son of King Georg I and Queen Olga of Greece. He married Alexandra's niece Princess Alice of Greece and Denmark.

Andrei Alexandrovich, Prince of Russia (b. 1897 – d. 1981) – He was the oldest son of Grand Duchess Xenia and therefore a nephew of the Tsar and was known as *Andrusha*.

Andrei, Grand Duke of Russia (b. 1879 – d. 1956) – The younger brother of Grand Duke Kyrill and Boris and a Major-General in the Russian Army. Andrei married the Tsar's former mistress Mathilde Kschessinskaya in 1921. She had a son Vladimir in 1902.

Anichkov Palace – The childhood home of the future Tsar Nicholas II, his mother the Dowager Empress continued to live here until she left permanently for Kiev during the war. The newly married Nicholas and Alix lived in a small suite of rooms at the Anichkov Palace after their wedding. They later moved into the Alexander Palace at Tsarskoe Selo.

Anthony, The Metropolitan (b.1846 – d. 1912) – He had been born as Alexander Vasilievich Vadkovsky.

Aprak – A nickname used by the Tsar for Princess AA Obolenskaya, a lady-in-waiting to his mother, Empress Marie.

Apraxin, Count Peter Nicolaevich – The Tsarina's Secretary and Grand Master of the Court. He was also Secretary of the department of Her Imperial Majesty's Charity and Military Hospitals. He worked closely with the Tsarina's private secretary Count Ivan Rostovtsov. He was in Petrograd at the start of the Revolution and was asked to return to the Alexander Palace by Count Benckendorff. He went out to see the troops within the Alexander Palace with the former Tsarina and her daughter Marie in the spring of 1917.

Arsenic – Olga Nicolaevna was injected with arsenic on many occasions from the fall of 1915 after she developed a type of depression. She was permitted to visit her former workplace at the Infirmary for merely thirty minutes a day from Oct 1915. She later returned to work at the same place but in an administrative position. She made up injections, gave out prescriptions etc.

Avdeev, Alexander Dmitrievich – The Commissar at the Zlokazovsky factory who became the Commandant of the Ipatiev House where the Imperial family were imprisoned in 1918. He was later dismissed and sent to the front. Avdeev was replaced on July the 4th 1918 by the Chekist, Jacob Yurovsky. He was tall, with a thin moustache and a heavy drinker. He referred to the mind mannered former Tsar in his presence as *Nicholas the Blood Drinker* and to Alexandra as *The German Bitch*. If anyone asked a favour of him at Ipatiev House he was alleged to always give the same reply; *Let them go to hell.*

458

Averchenko, Arkady – Nicholas read Averchenko's book, *The Blue and Gold* to his family when they imprisoned at Ekaterinburg.

Baby – The Tsarina's nickname for her son the Tsarevich Alexei.

Baby, Aunt – Alexandra called herself *Aunt Baby* to her friend Lili Dehn's young son. The name was previously used by the young Kaiser when he referred to his aunt Beatrice.

Badmaiev, DR PA (b. 1851 – d. 1920) – A doctor who treated Nicholas and was rumoured to use illegal drugs on him. Nicholas by his own admission took cocaine on occasions but only as a medicine.

Bagration-Mukhransky, Prince. Konstantin Alexandrovich (b. 1889 – d. 1915) – One of the Tsar's aide-de-camps and the son-in-law of his friend Grand Duke Konstantin. His wife Tatiana was a close friend of the Tsar's daughters Olga and Tatiana and they often saw her during the war, especially after the death of her husband. She had two children. He died in Galitzia.

Balcony – The Tsarina Alexandra lived to spent time on her balcony at the Alexander Palace even in winter. The floor was covered with carpets and in cold weather she sat in her fur coat. In Siberia Alix also spent much time on the balcony at Tobolsk and Ekaterinburg. She rarely went into the garden.

Barclay, Florence Louisa (b. 1862 – d. 1921) – The daughter of the Reverend Samuel Charlesworth and the wife of the Reverend Charles W Barclay. Florence was a well-known British author. He most famous and well-loved work was *The Rosary*. Her books were loved by Tatiana and Marie and even bizarrely Nicholas II. The author spent her honeymoon in the Holy Land and her works were of a deeply religious tone. She had eight children and according to one of her daughters she was able to communicate with animals including birds and fish.

Bariatinskaya, Princess Maria Victorovna (b. 28th Dec 1858 – d. unknown) – A close friend of the Tsarina Alexandra. She was one of Tsarina Alexandra's first ladies-in-waiting and worked from 1896–8. She fell out with the Tsarina for a while. Maria was the eldest child of Prince Victor Ivanovich Bariatinsky and his wife Maria Apollinarievna Budberg, Countess Pahlen. Her younger sister Princess Olga Victorovna was also a maid-of-honour. The Princess assisted the Mistress of the Robes, Narychkina at the coronation in 1896. She was replaced by Princess Sophia Ivanovna Djambakourian-Orbeliani (known as *Sonia*). She went to Rome for several years but returned to Russia before the war.

Bariatinskaya, Princess Olga (b. unknown – d. 1932, Rome) – She was a younger sister of Princess Maria and maid of honour to the Tsarina Alexandra.

Bark, Peter L (b. 1869 – d. 1936) – He was Minister of Finance 1914 – 17.

Bath – Nicholas II had a huge sunken bath installed in his rooms at the Alexander Palace during the renovations of 1894/5. Later his children loved to swim in it.

Bathroom, Grand Duchesses – At the Alexander Palace the four Grand Duchesses shared a bathroom. It was half-filled with wardrobes and there was a silver bath behind a curtain. It was an antique bath and had the names of each of the family babies names engraved on it. In later years there was a bar fitted over the door for exercising. Nicholas had a similar one in his bathroom, on the train and in Siberia.

Bazaars – The Tsarina attended charity bazaars near Livadia in 1911, 1912, 1913 and 1914 where she and her daughters sold items they had sewed or embroidered.

Beatty, Admiral David (b. 1871 – d. 1936) – The Admiral of the British Fleet.

Becker, Madame – Alix mentioned the mysterious Madame Becker in her letters to Nicholas. It was a code she used when she or her daughters were having a monthly period. It probably relates to Toni Becker's mother Mathilde (b. 1835 – d. 1916) who would have been who she turned to for advice on such subjects as she had no mother of her own and Alix's sisters married before she was sixteen.

Becker, Toni (b. 1868 – d. 1965) – She was a childhood friend of Alix. Toni's father Dr Ernst Becker had been private secretary of the late Princess Alice and Toni continued to visit the palace most days. Her son was Alexandra's godson.

Bedrooms, Olga and Tatiana – Olga and Tatiana shared a bedroom at the Alexander Palace which was painted pink with a stencilled Art Nouveau frieze of flowered vines and bronze coloured dragonflies. The design echoed the chintz material used to cover a large screen which partitioned Tatiana's section of the room. The soft covered armchairs were covered in the same material and several stripped green silk covered chairs completed the room. The girls hung their own pictures and icons around their beds and had silk covers sewn with their own monograms. The room also contained a fireplace surrounded by German tiles and each daughter had her own dressing-table covered in photographs and other treasures.

Bedrooms, Marie and Anastasia – Marie and Anastasia shared a room at the Alexander Palace, adjoining their older sisters. It was different from the other room only in that the frieze was decorated with butterflies instead of dragonflies.

Bedrooms, Nicholas and Alix and Nicholas – Nicholas and Alix's bedroom at the Alexander Palace was created by Roman Melzer in 1894. He thoroughly changed the original room by covering the walls with a lively cotton chintz material, covered with green wreaths laced with pink ribbons. The original furniture was lightened on the orders of Alix by painting it ivory. A curtained arcade was also painted the same colour and was divided into from the sleeping alcove from a cosy sitting area in front. Two gilt bronze beds were pushed together to make a double bed and were covered with silk covers, topped by piles of down-filled pillows. To the right of the bed was an enclosed toilet and to the left a tiny chapel. The back wall was filled with icons and two hanging rose oil lamps were constantly lit in front of the icons. Alix slept on the left and Nicholas on the right. They were awakened each morning by a servant at the door of the mauve room, who would pound three times on the door with a silver mallet.

Beds – The children of Nicholas II all slept on camp-beds and these nickel-plated beds were taken into exile with them. It was a tradition that a daughter of a Tsar was only supposed to sleep in a real bed after she married. Marie may have slept in one in 1917 when she was seriously ill. The beds were taken from palace to palace.

Beliaev, Archpriest Afansy Ivanovich – He was the senior Priest at Feodorovsky Russian Orthodox Cathedral at Tsarskoe Selo from Mar – July 1917. He replaced Father Alexei Vasiliev who was ill. The Cathedral was built in 1912.

Beloborodov, Alexander (b. 1891 – d. 1939) – Chairman of the Ural regional Soviet from Jan 1918. He was alleged to be one of those who organised the murder of Nicholas and his family.

Bibi – Varvara Afanassievna Vilchikovsky, a nurse who worked with Olga and Tatiana at the palace hospital.

Bitner, Klaudia Mikhailovna (b. 1878 – d. unknown) – The former Director of the Marinsky women's gymnasium (secondary school) at Tsarskoe Selo who tutored the Tsar's children at Tobolsk. She later married Colonel Eugene Koblinsky. She was fond of Olga, less so of the others. She thought Anastasia had too strong hold on Marie and that Tatiana was not open enough for her taste.

Benkendorf, Count Paul Konstantovich (b. 1853 – d. 1921) – The Grand Marshall of the Imperial Court 1904 – 1917. He was loyal to the Tsar and a friend of Dr. Botkin. He was the father-in-law or step-father of Prince Vassili Dolgoruky. He did not accompany the Tsar to Tobolsk because his wife had acute bronchitis and he could not leave her behind. He was replaced by Tatishchev. He had formerly been a General in the Imperial Cavalry.

Benkendorf, von Countess Marie – She was one of the Dowager Empress's maids of honour.

Bielovejie – The name of the Tsar's hunting lodge near Spala, in Poland. It was usually only visited for a week or two each year.

Bobrinksy, Alexander – He was Palace Steward under Nicholas II.

Bobrinksy, Count Alexei (b. 1852 – d. 1927) – A member of the Tsar's suite. He was a Master of the Court. He was Chairman of United Nobility and Minister of Agriculture briefly in 1916. He was a Cornet in the Pskov Dragoons Regiment and Steward at the Imperial Court. His daughter was a lady-in-waiting to Alexandra and married Count Dmitry Alexandrovich Sheremetev in 1908.

Bobrinskaya, Countess DA – She was a Lady-in-waiting to the Tsarina. She was the daughter of A.A. Bobrinsky and the wife of Count Dmitry Sheremetev.

Books – Nicholas II was extremely fond of reading as was his daughter Olga. They took many books with them into exile and on an evening Nicholas frequently read aloud after dinner. On occasions later Tatiana took over the reading, mainly to her brother after he was separated from Pierre Gilliard. Nicholas used to have a pile of books delivered each month at the Alexander Palace for him but he often failed to get through them due to over-work. Alexandra also had a selection given to her each month. On one occasion she found Olga reading one of the books and the Grand Duchess was said to have said that she was checking to see if it were suitable for her mother to read.

Boris Vladimirovich, Grand Duke of Russia (b. 1877 – d. 1943) – A cousin of the Tsar and a brother of Grand Dukes Kyrill and Andrei. He proposed to the Tsar's daughter Grand Duchess Olga (via her parents) but she refused him. He was a Major-General of the Suite.

Botkin, Dmitri (b. unknown – d. Dec 1914) – One of the eldest sons of the Tsarina's personal physician Dr. Botkin and his wife Olga. Dmitri was a Lieutenant in a Cossack regiment and died in 1914 in the eastern front. His early death greatly affected his father.

Botkin, Eugene Sergeevich (b. 1865 – d. 1918) – The son of Professor Serge Botkin

(1832 – 1889). He was one who remained at the Alexander Palace at the start of the Revolution. Botkin was the Imperial families' personal doctor and remained with the family voluntarily in Tobolsk and Ekaterinburg. He had been appointed as the Tsar's personal physician in the spring of 1908. Botkin's wife Olga ran off with her children's German tutor Friedrich Lichinger and later married him. Botkin brought up their four children Dmitri, Yuri, Tatiana and Gleb. He had two brothers Alexander and Peter. Peter Botkin was Russian Minister Plenpotentiary in Lisbon. The Tsar's daughter Grand Duchess Olga called Dr Botkin, *a deep well of profound ideas* and addressed him in all her letters as, *Dear Well*. He was tall and stout and generally wore blue suits and a gold watch chain across his stomach. He smelt of strong French perfume and the young Grand Duchesses liked to track him down from room to room by his scent. He was murdered along with the former Tsar and his family in July 1918. He became a close friend of Tsar Nicholas II and later spoke on his behalf at Tobolsk and Ipatiev House. He spoke German and was often used as an intermediary in the later years with the guards. Nicholas later referred to Botkin as his best friend.

Botkin, George (b. unknown – d. 1940s) – One of the elder sons of Dr Botkin. He died in the Second World War whilst serving as a soldier.

Botkin, Gleb (b. 1900 – d. 1969) – The youngest son of Dr Botkin and a childhood friend of Grand Duchess Marie and Grand Duchess Anastasia. In Nov 1920 he married Madame Nadine Mandragy, the widow of Lieutenant Mandragy of the Imperial Body-Guard who had been killed on the German front in 1915. She had a daughter called Kyra. He had five children including Eugene and Marina. He last saw the Imperial family in 1918.

Botkin, Tatiana (b. 1898 – d. 1986, Paris) – The only daughter of Dr Botkin and a friend of the Imperial children, especially Grand Duchess Anastasia. She first met the Imperial children in 1911, on the yacht the, *Standart* when her father was ill. She was the sister of Dimitri and Gleb Botkin. In 1918 she married Konstantin Melnik, an officer in the Ukrainian rifles. They were later divorced. Tatiana had been a nurse at the Catherine Palace. Her daughter Marina was born in Brooklyn, New York and grew up on Long Island, she later married Richard Schweitzer, an American lawyer. Her son Konstantin attended the funeral of Tsar Nicholas in St Petersburg.

Brahms, Johannes (b. 1833 – d. 1897) – The famous composer who was a friend and played piano duets with the Tsarina's mother Princess Alice.

Bratiano, M – The Rumanian Prime Minister.

Bruce-Lockhart, Robert H – The British Consul in Moscow.

Bublikov, Alexander Alexandrovich – Commissar of the Provisional Government in Russia 1917.

Buchanan, Sir Andrew (b. 1807 – d. 1882) – The British Ambassador at Berlin 1862–1864 and father of Sir George.

Buchanan, Sir George William (b. 1854 – d. 1924) – Buchanan had been born at the Legation at Copenhagen where his father was the Minister. He had a posting in Coburg as Minister at Darmstadt. He had to keep Queen Victoria informed of the state of the marriage of the young Grand Duke Ernst and his 1st wife Victoria-Melita.

Between 1904 and 1909 he was an Agent and Consul-General at Sofia. He had been appointed as the British Ambassador to the Court of St Petersburg in Nov 1910. He had succeeded Sir Arthur Nicolson to the post. He had known Alix as a child before her marriage. He later wrote, *My Mission to Russia and other Diplomatic Memories.* He married Lady Georgina Bathhurst and they had a daughter named Meriel who was a teenager at the time of his appointment. She was a playmate of Princess Alice of Battenberg. She fell in love with the Duke of Leuchtenberg, Alexander but they did not marry. She later wrote, *An Ambassador's Daughter, The Dissolution of an Empire and Queen Victoria's Relations.*

Bukhara, Emir of (b. 1859 – d. 1910) – The Emir was Abd-ul Ahad Bakhadur-Khan. He and his son Sayed Mir-Alim (the last Emir of Bukhara) were friends of both Emperor Alexander III of Russia and his son Nicholas. The Emir spent more than half the year in Russia and owned homes in the Caucasus and the Crimea. Alexander had personally supervised the education of the son. The Emir and his son were extremely wealthy and gave the Romanovs costly presents of jewels and carpets.

Butakov, Lieutenant Alexander Ivanovich (b. 1881 – d. 1914) – The Tsar's favourite and usual tennis partner who died at the front in the Great War. He went to the front with the Guarde Equipage and was killed in 1914. He was also a friend of Olga and Tatiana. He left a Swedish born widow (Aina Ottovna Lindgolm) and a young son Nikita. Nicholas II attended his funeral as did Olga and Tatiana. It was a real sign of their affection.

Butzova, Olga E – One of the Tsarina's ladies-in-waiting until her retirement in the summer of 1915. She was often used as a chaperone for Olga and Tatiana when they visited their aunt and grandmother in town.

Buxhoeveden, Sophia Karlovna (b. 1884 – d. 1956) – She was a Personal Lady-in-Waiting to the Tsarina Alexandra from 1913 onwards and was known as Isa. She was tall, with dark hair and a chain smoker in private. She was not attractive but was very friendly and a great favourite and close friend of the Tsarina. *Isa* often accompanied the Grand Duchesses as their chaperone. She had no time for Rasputin, kept her opinions to herself on the subject and the Tsarina knew that Isa did not like Rasputin. She was close friend of Countess Anastasia Hendrikova, the sisters other regular chaperone. She followed the family to Siberia but was released by the guards. She lived in a rented house in Tobolsk for a while. She was not allowed into the Governor's House. She had to borrow money from Sidney Gibbes to allow her to escape from Russia. She left for England via China. She later wrote, *The Life and Tragedy of Alexandra Feodorovna –Empress of Russa.* The Baroness visited the Tsarina's sister Princess Irene of Prussia at Hemmelmark later. She died in England in grace and favour rooms given by the Queen. She had a younger brother named Peter –who died in 1909 and she had been briefly engaged in 1914 but never married.

Carlyle, Thomas (b. 1795 – d. 1881) – One of the many friends of the Tsarina's later mother, Princess Alice. He was the author of *History of the French Revolution.*

Carol, Prince later Crown Prince and eventually King of Rumania (b. 1893 – d. 1953) – The eldest son of the Tsarina's cousin Queen Marie of Rumania. He visited Russia in the winter of 1913 and again in Nov 1916. He was seen as a potential husband for the Tsar's daughter Grand Duchess Olga in 1914 but showed more of an interest in her younger sister Grand Duchess Marie in 1916. The Imperial Family visited the Rumanian Royal Family in 1914.

Catherine Palace – The larger palace at Tsarskoe Selo which despite its obvious beauty was rarely used by Nicholas II. It was used for official ceremonies and later as a military hospital during the war. Military reviews were held in front of the Catherine Palace and larger reviews were held on the Field of Mars in St. Petersburg.

Cats – The Tsar's children owned several cats including Vaska who was owned by Olga.

Chaillu De, Paul (b. 1835 – d. 1903) – An American writer and explorer who wrote books about his travels in Africa. Tatiana was a great fan of his work and took three of his books with her to Siberia. The author actually died in Russia in 1903 and had been there for a couple of years. It is possible that the Tsar met the writer at some time during his stay in Russia.

Chaguin, Captain – The captain of the Imperial yacht *Standart* and a friend of the Tsar. He committed suicide in 1912 after his alleged seduction of a young girl threatened a scandal. He was replaced by Captain Rostislav Zelentsky.

Chaperone – The Tsar's daughters the Grand Duchesses Olga, Tatiana, Marie and Anastasia were chaperoned by Marie Nikolaevna, the Duchess of Leuchtenberg when they visited their Grandmother the Dowager Empress Marie of Russia or their aunt the Grand Duchess Olga. Marie was the sister of Count Grabbe. She had six children; Alexandra, Nikolai, Nadejda, Maximilian, Sergei and Maria. The oldest was the same age as Grand Duchess Olga. They were later chaperoned by Olga Butzova, Countess Anastasia Hendrikova and Baroness Sophie Buxhoeveden.

Chebotarievna, Valentina Ivanovna (b. circa 1879 – d. 6th May 1919) – The senior nurse at the Infirmary at Tsarskoe Selo. She was the daughter of Ivan Stepanovich Doubiagsky and his wife Olga Sergeyevna. She married Porphyry Grigorievich Chebotariev and had two children Gregory and Valentina. She volunteered as a nurse during the 1904 – 1905 war and was later asked to join a select group of women who nursed soldiers alongside the Tsarina and her daughters. She came from an ordinary background but became firm friends with the Grand Duchesses especially Tatiana. The former Tsarina, Olga and Tatiana kept in contact with her and wrote whilst in Tobolsk. Alix, however, felt hurt that Chebotarieva and her fellow nurses did not right to her directly and only her daughters. Chebotarieva could not take it upon herself to write to the former Tsarina, because she blamed Alix for the problems faced in Russia

Chemodurov, Terenty Ivanovich (b. 1849 – d. 1919) – Chemodurov replaced Raziesh as the Tsar's valet. He followed his Imperial master into exile in Tobolsk and Ekaterinburg. He left Ipatiev House in May 1918 due to illness and was in the local prison hospital. He was later freed by the White army when they arrived. He was replaced by Alexei Trupp.

Cheremetevskaya, Nathalie (b. 1880 – d. 1952) – The wife of Grand Duke Michael of Russia. She was a daughter of a Moscow lawyer. She had been married twice before. She had a daughter Tatiana and she and Michael had one son George. She was known as the Countess Brassova.

Christenson, H – Dancing Master to the Imperial children.

Christian IX, King of Denmark (b. 8th Apr 1818 – d. 29th Jan 1906 Amalienborg) – The Grandfather of Tsar Nicholas II of Russia. He married Louise of Hesse-Cassel and his children included Princess Alexandra, the wife of King Edward VII of Great Britain and the Tsar's mother Marie.

Christopher, Prince of Greece (b. 10th Aug 1888 – d. 21st Jan 1940) – A cousin of Nicholas and the youngest son of King Georg I and Queen Olga of Greece. He once proposed to the young Grand Duchess Olga (via Nicholas) and was refused.

Christmas Tree – There was a Christmas tree placed in the playroom and another downstairs for the staff and ladies-in-waiting at Christmas. The children loved the tree so much that they often slept around it. They would drag their beds into the playroom. It was lit by candles but in later years electricity was used. The family had a balsam fir at Tobolsk in 1917. The Holy Synod had intended to ban them in 1914 but Alexandra objected. It was seen as a German tradition, and they were seen as the enemy. Alix's late grandfather Prince Albert of Saxe-Coburg-Gotha had originally introduced them into Britain and as a child she always had a tree and saw no reason for denying other children the same.

Churches – In 1914 in Russia there were said to be 55,173 churches, 29,593 chapels, 112,629 priests and deacons, 500 monasteries, 475 convents and 95,259 monks and nuns.

Cigarettes – All the young Grand Duchesses occasionally smoked cigarettes and these were given to them by their father Tsar Nicholas, who smoked heavily.

Code Book – Alexandra had a code-book. It was the key to her early letters to Nicholas. She took it with her to Ekaterinburg.

Conrad – He was the Music teacher to the Imperial children. His wife appears to have taught them French.

Constantine, King of Greece (b. 2nd Aug 1868, Athens – d. 11th Jan 1923) – A cousin and friend of the young Tsar Nicholas II of Russia. He married Princess Sophie of Prussia on the 27th Oct 1889. They had six children; George; Alexander: Helen; Paul: Irene and Katherine. Sophie was a first cousin of Alix and a younger sister of Kaiser Wilhelm II of Germany.

Colorito – This was a card game which the Tsarina played, usually with her daughter Grand Duchess Marie.

Cottage – The *Cottage* was one of the small homes used by the Imperial Family at Alexandria, Peterhof. It was completed in 1829 and was the home of Emperor Nicholas I, his wife Alexandra, their children and two servants. It was enlarged in 1842 when the dining room was extended and a terrace added. The Attic had a study with views of the sea. Nicholas I observed naval manoeuvres from there.

Kotka and Zubrovska owned by Alexei and possibly a Siamese cat owned by Marie.

Cubat, JP – The Imperial families French chef who had a thankless task as neither the Tsar or his wife cared about food. The chef was a Frenchman, Cubat, a very great man in his profession. Sometimes, when an especially splendid dish had been prepared, Cubat stood in the doorway, clad in immaculate white linen, until the dish was served. Cubat allegedly became very wealthy in the Tsar's service.

Dassel, Captain Felix – A Captain in the Grand Duchess Marie's 9th Kazan Dragoons.

Dehn, Alexander Leonide (b. 1908, Peterhof – d. unknown) – The first child and only son of the Tsarina's close friend Lili Dehn, He was Alexandra's godson. He was also a playmate of Alexei. See Titi.

Dehn, Captain Charles or Karl – He was the husband of the Tsarina's close friend Lili Dehn. He was well-liked by the Tsar's children and they nicknamed him Pekin *Dehn*. He had taken part in the Boxer rebellion and the siege of Peking. He was the first officer to scale the walls of the Forbidden City in defence of the embassies. He was awarded the Order of St George. He was a Captain on the cruiser Variag.

Dehn, Yulia Alexandrovna nee Smolsky (b. 1880 – d. 1963, Rome) – A very close friend of the Tsarina and of Anna Vyrubova. She helped to organise communications between the exiled Imperial family in Tobolsk and friends and sympathisers in Petrograd. Lili was the wife of the 1st officer on the Imperial yacht, Standart and had a son called Alexander who was born in 1908. Alexandra continued to correspond with Lili for the rest of her life. She later had two daughters Catherine (b. 1919 – d. 1937) and Maria Olga (b. 1923 – d. 2007).

Delacroix – The coiffeur used occasionally by the Imperial children. They had their hair curled on special occasions.

Demenkov, Nicholas Dimtrievich – An officer of the Guards crew and said to be the, *boyfriend* of Grand Duchess Marie of Russia. He never married but survived the revolution. His nickname was *Kolya*. He was tall and well built.

Demidova, Anna Stepanova (b. 1878 – d. 1918) – The Tsarina's personal maid who followed the Imperial family into exile She worked for the Imperial family from 1905 until her death in 1918. She was murdered along with the Imperial family in July 1918. She was at one time engaged to Nicholas Ersberg, the brother of Liza, and an official for the State Railway Board. She was later enamoured with Sydney Gibbes, who was almost certainly gay.

Derevenko, Andrei – One of the two sailor nannies who were assigned to the Tsarevich Alexei. After the Russian Revolution he turned on his former charge according to Anya Vyrubova, although this was later discounted as a lie. He had two young sons who were Alexei's friends.

Derevenko, Nicholas Vladimirovich (b. 1906 – d. 1999) – The son of the Court Surgeon Vladimir Nikolaevich Derevenko. He was known as *Kolya* and was a close friend of the Tsarevich Alexei.

Derevenko, Vladimir Nicolaevich (b. 1879 – d. 1936) – The Distinguished court surgeon who treated the Tsarevich Alexei from 1912 until 1918. He was at the Alexander Palace at the start of the Revolution. He followed the Imperial family into exile and was the only person who was authorised to enter and leave Ipatiev House. He was the father of Kolya, the Tsarevich's friend. He lived at Popov House, close to Ipatiev House in 1918.

Diaries of the Grand Duchesses – It was established in the early 2000s that there were no remaining diaries belonging to the Grand Duchess Anastasia, but there were three belonging to the Grand Duchess Marie (1912, 1913 and 1916), plus nine of the Grand Duchess Tatiana's diaries (1907–16 but 1911 was missing) and twelve diaries belonging to the Grand Duchess Olga (1905–1917 but 1910 was missing) in the archives in Russia.

Marie and Anastasia were known to have destroyed theirs after the revolution.

Didkovsky, Boris (b. 1883 – d. 1938) – He was Alexander Beloborodov's deputy in the Ural regional Soviet.

Dimitri, Grand Duke of Russia (b. 18th Sept 1891 – d. 5th Mar 1942, Switzerland) – The son of The Tsar's uncle Paul who was brought up Grand Duchess Elisabeth, the Tsarina's sister until 1905 and then by the Tsar himself. Dimitri's mother had died shortly after his birth and he had a sister called Grand Duchess Marie who was a year older than him. Dimitri had wanted to marry the Tsar's niece Princess Irina at one time but he was later implicated in the murder of Gregory Rasputin. He participated in the Olympic Games in Stockholm in 1912. He eventually married Audrey Emery in 1926 but the marriage did not last.

Dimitri Konstantinovich, Grand Duke of Russia (b. 1860 – d. 1919) – Known as *Mitya* he was the brother of Grand Duke Konstantin and an uncle of the Tsar. He died unmarried.

Diptheria – The illness that claimed the lives of the future Tsarina Alexandra's mother Princess Alice and her younger daughter Princess Marie in 1878.

Dnieper – The River situated close to Mogilev where the Tsar spent much of his spare time boating during the war. His children also accompanied him when they were staying with their father.

Dolgoriukaya, Catherine (b. 1847 – d. 1922) – The second wife of the Emperor Alexander II of Russia. She was one of the six children of Prince Michael. M. Dolgoruky who were taken *under Royal guardianship* after his death. Catherine had four children by Alexander before she eventually married him they were George, Olga; Boris who died as a baby and Catherine.

Dolgorukov, Prince Vasily Alexandrovich (b. 1868 – d. 1918) – A Marshal of the Imperial Court and followed the Tsar to Tobolsk. He was later accused of plotting an escape and imprisoned, along with Gnereal Tatishchev. They were both executed on the 10th July 1918. He was known as *Valia.*

Don – The family nickname for the Tsarina's nephew Prince George Donatus of Hesse and by the Rhine, her brother's son.

Douvan, Simon – The former Mayor of Eupatoria, Crimea who met the Imperial family in 1916.

Drenteln, Colonel – The Tsar's favourite aide-de-camp. He was a Colonel in the Preobrajensky Regiment of the Guard.

Eagar, Miss Margaretta Alexandra (b. 12 Aug 1868 – d. 1936, near Bristol) – Appointed as Nanny to the Imperial children in late 1898. Miss Eagar began work in Feb 1899 but was dismissed shortly after Alexei was born in 1904. She was born in Tralee, County Kerry, Ireland but was sometimes described as Scottish. Her parents were Maurice Eagar and his wife Ellen Leahy. Margaretta had a younger sibling Maurice who was born in 1878 amongst many others.

Elephant – The Tsarevich Alexei had an elephant. It had been sent as a gift to him from King Chulalonkorn of Siam.

Elchaninov, Major-General Andrei – Authorised by Tsar Nicholas II in 1913 to write an authorised biography of Nicholas to mark the Tercentenary of the Romanov Dynasty entitled – *The Reign of the Sovereign Emperor Nicholas Alexandrovich* by Major-General Andrei Elchaninov, a member of the Imperial Entourage. The book was presented as how Nicholas saw himself, he not only read the manuscript but made personal alterations in his own hand. Editions were later printed in English and French in 1914.

Elisabeth Alexandra Louise Alice, Princess of Hesse and by the Rhine, later Grand Duchess Elisabeth Feodorovna of Russia (b. 1 Nov 1864, Bessungen – Murdered 18 July 1918, Alapaievsk) – *Ella* was an older sister of the Tsarina Alexandra and the second daughter of the Grand Duke Ludwig IV of Hesse and his wife Princess Alice. She married Grand Duke Sergei of Russia on the 15th June 1884 at St Petersburg. They had no children. She was the godmother of the Tsarina's daughter Grand Duchess Marie. After her husband was murdered she founded a religious order. Elisabeth was murdered shortly after her sister Alix. She died at Alapaievsk in Russia along with several of her late husband's family.

Elisabeth Marie Alice Victoria, Princess of Hesse and by the Rhine (b. 11 Mar 1895, Darmstadt – d. 6 Nov 1903, Skierniewice) – The daughter of Grand Duke Ernst-Ludwig and his first wife Victoria-Melita. She was a niece of the Tsarina Alexandra and died of typhoid. She was a very close friend of Olga and Tatiana. Her death had a terrible effect on the children, as they had been so close to their cousin. They were in the next room when she died. She may have seen an image of Christ on her death-bed as an icon owned by Olga indicates this. The case for her canonisation should be considered.

Elena Petrovna, Princess of Russia (b. 4th Nov 1884 – d. 16th Oct 1962) – The daughter of King Peter I of Yugoslavia. She married Prince Ioann Konstantinovich on the 3rd Sept 1911 at Peterhof. Elena and her brother Alexander were friends of the Tsar's daughter, Grand Duchess Olga Nicolaevna. Elena and Ioann had two children; Vsevolode (b. 20th Jan 1914, Pavlovsk– and Nathalia (b. 25th July 1915, Pavlovsk– d. unknown).

Eristov, Prince George – The aide-de-camp to Grand Duke George of Russia.

Ersberg, Elisabeth Nicolaevna (b. 18th Sept 1882 – d. 12th Mar 1942) – Chosen by the Empress Marie as a parlour maid and worked for the Imperial family from 1898 until May 1918. She was usually known as *Liza* and helped clean the rooms of the Imperial children. She also put together their wardrobes and taught the Grand Duchesses handwork. Later Liza taught them to look after the sick. She went with the family to Tobolsk. Her father Nikolai Ersberg who died in 1889 had been a Palace stoker, under Alexander III and had worked at the Anichkov and Gatchina Palaces. Liza had a brother who was also called Nicholas.

Ernst-Ludwig Karl Albrecht Wilhelm, Grand Duke of Hesse and by Rhine (b. 25 Nov 1868, Darmstadt – d. 9 Oct 1937, Schloss Wolfsgarten) – An older brother of the Tsarina and the first son of the Grand Duke Ludwig IV of Hesse and his wife Princess Alice. He married twice. His first wife was Princess Victoria-Melita of Edinburgh and Saxe-Coburg-Gotha (married 19th Apr 1894 divorced) and the second wife was Princess Eleonore of Solms – Hohensolms-Lich (married 2nd Feb 1905). He had a daughter Elisabeth, who died, possibly of typhoid and two sons, Georg-Donatus and Ludwig. His widow Eleanore; his son Prince Georg-Donatus; his pregnant daughter-in-law Cecilie and their two young sons Ludwig and Alexander all died in a 'plane crash over Belgium on the 16th Nov 1937. They had been on the way to attend the wedding of Georg-Donatus' younger brother Ludwig to Margaret Geddes. After the wedding the young couple adopted the only survivor of the tragedy one year-old Princess Johanna. The little girl died of meningitis on the 14th June 1939 and the couple had no children of their own. The fourth child of Cecile appears to have been born minutes before her mother's death. The family did seem to have the most terrible luck.

Epps, John B M (b. 1848, Scotland – d. 1935) – The Scottish born tutor to the Tsar's four daughters from 1905–1908. He was replaced by Gibbes after it became apparent that he was giving the Imperial daughters a broad Scottish accent. Unfortunately his memoirs were burnt after his death.

Eupatoria –The Tsar and his family had their last holiday here. They spent a total of one day here by the sea in the Crimea. They visited a small dacha that had been rented by Anya Vyrubova. The children enjoyed playing on the beach, sadly a public one which meant they had little real privacy. They were joined by Olga's tall friend Rita. There are quite a few photographs taken during the visit in May 1916 and film on the internet Youtube site.

Evreinov, Nicholas – Head of the Ceremonial Department. He was also the Commander of the Main Imperial Department.

Exercise Bar – A horizontal chinning bar was installed in the Tsar's bathroom at the Alexander Palace in 1916. The Grand Duchesses also had one. The former Tsar had a similar bar installed when they were exiled in Siberia.

Faberge, Karl Peter (b. 1846 – d. 1920) – The maker of the famous Faberge Easter eggs and jewels. He was the son of Gustav Faberge (b. 1814 – d. 1893).

Fabrice, Margarete Olga known as Gretchen von (b. 26th June 1862 – d. 1922) – Gretchen was previously the governess to Princess Helena's daughters Thora and Louise. She was appointed as Lady-in-Waiting to Alix in 1888. She later acted as a chaperone to the engaged Alix and her fiancée Nicholas. Gretchen attended Alix's wedding in 1894 and the coronation in 1896. She had been born at Grimma, Saxony in 1862 and was the daughter of Berhard von Fabrice, Captain in the Royal Saxony Cavalry Regiment (who died 1866) and his wife the Countess Ida von Schonburg-Glauchau und Waldenburg (b. 1829 – d. 1902). Her aunt Olga was married to Prince Wilhelm von Lowenstein, an old friend of the Prince Consort. She had a sister called Luise (b. 1859 – d. 1927) who married Wilhelm, Prince zu Lowenstein-Wertheim-Freudenburg on 26 Nov 1887. Gretchen married Franz Friedrich von Pfuhlstein on the 15th Mar 1898 and they had three children: Alexander, a Godson of the Tsarina (b. 17 Dec 1899 – d. unknown) and Marie-Louise (b. 1901 – d. unknown) and Friedrich (b. 1902 – d. unknown).

Farm – The *Farm* was one of the cottages on the estate of Alexandria at Peterhof. The gothic inspired cottage was situated close to a smaller of the Imperial Families houses, known as the *Cottage*. It was initially used as school-rooms for the Imperial children and had a private chapel dedicated to Saint Alexander Nevsky. At the time of Emperor Alexander III it was mainly used for guests and for receptions. The Farm was later used by Tsar Nicholas and his wife. Their second daughter Grand Duchess Tatiana was born here. They were only temporary residents however, as they were waiting for the New Palace to be built nearby. It had verandas along two sides, supported by metal columns, disguised as birch trees. Most of the upstairs rooms had balconies and it also benefited from striped awnings on one side to keep out the sun. It had a large entrance hall and a simple curved staircase inside. The outside walls were painted pale yellow.

Fedorov, Dr Serge Petrovich (b. 1869 – d. 1936) – He was the Royal surgeon who treated Alexei for many years.

Fersen, Countess Olga – One of the playmates of the young Tsarevich Alexei. She was still living in the 1990s. Countess Sophie Fersen was one of those who came to express her sympathy to the former Empress just after the abdication.

Film Projector – There had been a *Pathe* film projector installed in Alexei's rooms in 1913.

Flotov, Madame – A lady-in-waiting to the Dowager Empress. She was officially responsible for the wardrobe and jewels of her mistress but according to AA Mossolov she knew all about the Sovereign's decisions often even before him – and he was the Head of the Court Chancellery!

Flowers – Alexandra dearly loved flowers and had many vases filled with them all over the palaces. She especially loved lilies, violets, lily-of-the-valley, hyacinth, roses, orchids and lilac of course. She had tall Chinese vases, silver bowls, rare lacquered pots and glass vases from Yalta all filled with flowers. Her daughters often picked lily-of-the-valley from the park for their mother. After the revolution she was not permitted to have flowers as they were deemed a *luxury*. Olga also appeared to be very fond of flowers and liked to spend time in the greenhouse at Tobolsk.

Floors – In the USA the ground floor is known as the 1st floor. The Tsarina used the British expression so I have done the same.

Food – The last Tsar of Russia's family were said to have simple tastes. Nicholas liked simple *borsch* (cabbage soup), *kasha* (buckwheat), boiled fish and fruit, pork etc. Alix disliked food and ate mainly pasta. Alexei had a taste for old dried bread crusts and Anastasia ate mainly fruit but Marie had a taste for pastries and sweets. At Ipatiev House in 1918 meals included black bread and tea for breakfast and re-warmed soup and cutlets at 2pm. They were sent from the Soviet Public Dining Room. The cook had special supplies of macaroni for the Tsarina and the Grand Duchesses were taught how to make bread. Luckily later he had the chance of doing the cooking and miraculously the meals all suddenly arrived on time.

Forgiveness Sunday – The day when Russian Orthodox believers ask for one another's forgiveness for past sins.

Fredericks, Count Vladimir Borisovich (b. 1838 – d. 1922) – A minister of the Imperial Court and domains from 1896 until 1917. He was a close friend of both Alix and Nicholas. Fredericks according to Mossolov was subject to effusions of blood on the brain which led to loss of memory. He remained for a while in Petrograd after the 1917 Revolution and finally left for his native Finland in 1921. He was a nobleman of Swedish ancestry. His daughters Eugenia (Nini) and Emma were also close friends of the Tsarina and her elder daughters.

Fredericks, Countess Emma Vladimirovna (b. 1869 – d. 1945) – The daughter of Count Fredericks and a lady-in-waiting to the Tsarina of the Highest Rank. Alexandra frequently wrote to her friend the Countess from Siberia. Her sister Eugenia (b. 1867 – d. 1950) known as *Nini*, another of Alix's ladies, was married to Major General Vladimir Voyeikov (b. 1868 – d. 1947).

Frederick-Wilhelm August Victor Leopold, Prince of Hesse and by the Rhine (b. 7 Oct 1870, Darmstadt – d. 29 May 1873, Darmstadt) – An older brother of the Tsarina Alexandra who had died when she was a baby. *Frittie* as he was called died as a result of a fall from a window, like his Uncle Leopold and his future nephew Alexei he had haemophilia. He was playing with his brother Ernie in their mother's room. They were waving at each other from facing windows, which were at an angle on the same floor at the Palace at Darmstadt. *Frittie* fell from his chair and toppled onto the balcony below. He died later the same day despite appearing all right initially.

Franklin, Mrs Elizabeth (b. 1834 – d. 1913) – The nanny assigned to Grand Duchess Olga Alexandrovna. Empress Marie became extremely jealous of her place in her daughter's affections and called her t*hat odious woman*. She was generally called *Nanna* by Olga and like most nannies unmarried despite being called Mrs.

French – The Tsar's children were all taught French by Pierre Gilliard yet the Grand Duchesses never managed to speak fluent French unlike their brother the Tsarevich who was in constant contact with Gilliard.

Gatchina – One of the homes of the Emperor Alexander III of Russia where his son Nicholas grew up. It was some 25 miles south west of St. Petersburg and had some 900 rooms.

Gavril Konstantinovich, Prince of Russia (b. 1887 – d. 1939) – The second son of Grand Duke Konstantin of Russia. He married Antonia Nesterovsky in 1917 and after her death remarried.

Gedroits, Princess Vera Ignatievna – The Princess was a Doctor of medicine and Head Physician at the Tsarskoe Selo hospital where the Tsarina and her daughters Olga and Tatiana worked during the Great war from 1914 – 1916. She was Russia's first female doctor. Other members of staff included Doctor Nedelin and a nurse called Chebotarieva.

Gega – Tsar Nicholas called his uncle and brother-in-law Grand Duke Serge Alexandrovich, the Governor-General of Moscow, Uncle Gega.

Galitzin, Prince Dmitry – He was the Director of the Empress's Relief Services during the war. He claimed to have seen the Tsarina's brother Grand Duke Ernst of Hesse at the Alexander Palace in 1916.

Gendrikova, Anastasia see Hendrikova

George, Count Brassov (b. 6 Aug 1910, Moscow – d. 22 July 1931, Auxerre) – The only son of the Grand Duke Michael and his later wife Nathalie. He never met Tsar Nicholas II and his family. He had an older half-sister Tatiana. He was said to have met his grandmother however after the revolution.

George Donatus Wilhelm Nicholas Eduard Heinrich Karl, Prince of Hesse and by Rhine (b. 8 Nov 1906, Darmstadt – d. 16 Nov 1937, Steene, near Ostende, Belgium) – The first son of the Tsarina's brother Grand Duke Ernst–Ludwig of Hesse and his second wife Eleanore. He married Princess Cecile of Greece and Denmark on the 23rd Jan 1931. They both died in a plane crash along with their two sons.

George, Grand Duke of Russia (b. 1863 – d. 1919) – Brother of Grand Duke Alexander (*Sandro*) who married Xenia, the Tsar's sister. He was a close friend of Nicholas II and was the Head of the Alexander III Museum of Russian Art. He married Princess Marie of Greece, a sister of Alexandra, the first wife of Grand Duke Paul. George and Marie had two daughters Nina and Xenia.

George, Grand Duke of Russia (b. 9 May 1871, Tsarskoe-Selo – d. 9 Aug 1899, Abbas Touman, Transcaucasia) – A younger brother of Tsar Nicholas II and the third son of Tsar Alexander III and his wife Marie. He died of tuberculosis and was his body was dug up in the 1990s in order to prove that the bones found in Ekaterinburg were indeed those of the late Tsar Nicholas II, George's brother. He was reburied. Had he lived he would have been a great help to Nicholas as the two were very close and he was very intelligent.

George Konstantinovich (b. 6th June 1903 – d. 8th Nov 1938) – The 6th son of Grand Duke Konstantin. He never married. His older brother Oleg died during the Great War and his brothers Ioann, Konstantin and Igor were murdered in 1918. He was a friend of the young Tsarevich Alexei.

George, Prince of Greece (b. 24th June 1869 – d. 25th Nov 1957) – A cousin of Nicholas and the second son of King Georg I and Queen Olga of Greece. He was at one time a close friend of Nicholas and it was George who saved the life of the future Tsar, when he was attacked in Japan. On the 21st Nov 1907 he married Marie Bonaparte. They had two children Peter (b. 3rd Dec 1908–) and Eugenie (b. 10th Feb 1910 – d. unknown).

German Measles – The Tsar's children all caught German measles in 1918, they had measles the previous year. It is also known as rubella.

Gheringer, Madame – A Russian lady who was a member of the Tsarina's staff, who ordered gowns, did shopping, paid bills and generally attended to business for Alexandra according to Madame Vyrubova. She later rescued the children's cats at the Alexander Palace.

Gibbes, (Charles) Sydney (b. 1876 – d. 24th Mar 1963) – The Tsarevich's English tutor who had been born in Rotherham, Yorkshire on the 19th Jan 1876 He was the ninth child of John Gibbes, a Bank Manager and his wife, the former Mary Anne Elizabeth Fisher. He had been educated in Broadstairs in Kent and at Hornsea on the East coast of Yorkshire. He later attended University College at Aberystwyth and St. John's College, Cambridge. He also took theological courses in Cambridge and Salisbury. He was originally training for the church but changed his mind to the disgust of his father. Many years later he joined the Russian Orthodox Church, but in the meantime he had become a successful tutor in Russia. According to a later passport he was 5 feet 10 inches tall; had light brown hair; a small mouth; a rounded chin and a high forehead. He had previously taught the Grand Duchesses Olga, Tatiana, Marie and Anastasia. He remained with the Imperial family at Tobolsk but like many others became separated from them before they were sent to Ekaterinburg. He kept drawings done by Alexei including one of an Indian canoe. He later escaped to England where he took monastic vows in 1934 and became a Russian Orthodox Priest called Father Nicholas. He founded the Orthodox Church in Oxford. He died at St Pancras Hospital in London and was buried at Headington Cemetery, Oxford. He never married but did adopt a son named George, a Russian boy.

Gilliard, Pierre (b. 1879 – d. 1962) – The Tsarevich's French tutor and known as *Gilik* or *Zhilik*. He had previously taught the Grand Duchesses Olga, Tatiana, Marie and Anastasia between Sept 1905 and 1912. He went with the Imperial family to Tobolsk but became separated from them before they were taken to Ekaterinburg. He married Grand Duchess Anastasia's nurse Alexandra Tegleva, also known as *Shura* in 1922. He escaped to the Switzerland via Japan and the United States and became a noted Professor of the French language at the University of Lausanne. Anya Vyrubova spoke highly of him as did the Tsar and Tsarina.

Glinka, Michael Ivanovich (b. 1804 – d. 1857) – The Russian composer of one of Tsar Nicholas's favourite works, *A Life for the Tsar*.

Gogol, Nicholas Vasilevich (b. 1809 – d. 1852) – Said to be the favourite writer of Tsar Nicholas II.

Golenistchev-Koutouzova, Countesses Algaida and Matie – Ladies-in-waiting to the Dowager Empress.

Golitsyn, Prince Alexander – Chancellery of the Confidential Adviser for Matters under the Court's Authority.

Golitsyn, Prince Dmitri, Major-General – Assistant Master of the Court and Master of the Imperial Hunt and Master of the Horse. He was also Head of the Imperial Hermitage Museum. He arranged the purchase of Leonardo da Vinci's *Madonna of the Rocks* from Maria Benois in 1914.

Golitsyn, Prince Nicholas D (b. 1850 – d. 1925) – The Russian Prime Minister briefly during 1916 – 1917. He was the last Imperial Prime Minister.

Goloshchekin Philip (b. 1876 – d. 1941) – A Military Commissar of the Ural Region.

Golovina, Maria known as Munya – She was Rasputin's secretary and a niece of Alya Pistolkors. *Munya* was said to be in love with Felix Yussopov and it was she who fatally introduced Rasputin to Felix.

Goremykin, Ivan L (b. 1839 – d. 1917) – The Russian Prime Minister briefly in 1906, then again from 1914 – 1916 and later in 1917. He had also been Minister of Internal Affairs 1895 – 1899. He was caught by the Petrograd mob and strangled on the spot.

Goly – This was the nickname given by the Tsarevich Alexei to his mathematics tutor, General Voyeikov. The word means naked and Alexei used it became the man was actually bald.

Grabovi, David – An officer of the 14th Georgian Regiment who died on the 2nd/15th Mar 1915 at the Tsarskoe Selo infirmary. Alix must have extremely been fond of him as she later remembered the anniversary of his death whilst in Siberia.

Grabbe, Count Nicholas Pavlovich (b. 1864 – d. 1947) – The Palace Commandant and Commander of the Convoy. He was married to the Countess Alexandra Feodovna Orloff – Denisoff and was the father of Count Alexander and Countess Maria. His daughter married Prince Nikolai of Leuchtenberg in 1894. His Grand-daughters had attended parties with the Tsar's daughters.

Grancy, Baroness Wilhelmine von Senarclens (b. 1837 – d. Nov 1912) – Lady-in-waiting to the daughters of the Duke of Hesse, including Princess Alix. Her sister Constance (b. 1852 – d. 1933) was the wife of Carl Friedrich von Oertzen (b. 1844 – d. 1914)

Grey, Lady Sybil (b. 1882 – d. 1966) – She worked for the British Red Cross in Russia and was wounded in the face by shell-fire at the front. She was the daughter of the 4th Earl Grey and descended from Prince Albert's secretary General Sir Charles Grey. She married Lambert William Middleton in 1922 and had two children – Henry and Mary. She met the Tsarina and her daughters during the war.

Grey, Sir Edward (b. 1862 – d. 1933) – He was British Foreign Secretary at the outbreak of the Great War.

Gromova, Tatiana – A hospital sister who used to visit the Alexander Palace to massage the Grand Duchess Anastasia. She was thought to have a weak spine. Anastasia used to hide from the nurse as she did not like the fuss this caused. She later worked as a nurse during the war.

Grosspapa – The name Alexandra used to refer to her paternal Grandfather Prince Karl Wilhelm Ludwig of Hesse. He was born on the 23rd Apr 1809 and died on the 20th Mar 1877, when Alix was 5 years old. His son Grand Duke Ludwig of Hesse was Alix's father. Prince Karl also had other children; Heinrich (b. 1838 – d. 1900), Wilhelm (b. 1845 – d. 1900) and Anna (b. 1843 – d. 1865).

Grossmama – The name Alexandra used for her paternal Grandmother, Princess Elisabeth of Hesse. She was the daughter of Prince Wilhelm of Prussia. Elisabeth was born on the 18th June 1815 and died on the 21st Mar 1885, when Alix was 12 years old. She married Prince Karl Wilhelm Ludwig of Hesse and had four children, including Alix' s father Ludwig.

Groten, Colonel Paul Pavlovich – He was and aide-de-camp and a Major-General in the Imperial Suite and Commander of the Life Guards Horse Grenadiers regiment. He had been brought temporarily to Tsarskoe Selo 1916 – 1917 to serve as Palace Commander.

Guchkov, Alexander Ivanovich (b. 1862 – d. 1936) – Member of the Third State Duma (of the Provisional Government from Mar – Apr 1917). He was the Octobrist leader. He was one of the two men who came to Nicholas' train to inform him of the need to abdicate in 1917. The other was Vasily Shulgin.

Gumilev, Nicholas (b. 1886 – d. 1921) – The poet who was brought up at Tsarskoe Selo and presented Anastasia with a signed poem dedicated to her on Anastasia's 15th birthday in 1916. His first book of poetry called, *The Path of the Conquistadors* had been published in 1905, he served in the Uhlan Regiment from 1914 and had married fellow poet Anna Akhmatova (1889 – 1966) (real name Anna Andreevna Gorenko) in 1910. She had also grown up at Tsarskoe Selo and her poems included, *Rosary* in 1914.

Harax – The Crimean palace owned by Grand Duke and Duchess George of Russia. It had been designed by Krasnov (who later built the White Palace nearby for the Tsar) and built in 1907. It was later used as a hospital. Harax was visited often by the Tsar during 1913 – 14 often with Alexandra or more usually with his elder daughters Olga and Tatiana. It was mistakenly called Karacks in Olga's printed diary.

Hardinge, Honourable Emily Caroline (b. unknown – d. 1876) – Lady-in-waiting to Princess Alice of Hesse.

Heath, Charles (b. 1826 – d. 1900) – English tutor to the Tsarevich Nicholas and his younger brother Grand Duke George. His daughter married one of Nicholas II's ADC's – Mordvinov. It was Mr Heath who gave Nicholas a love of hunting, fishing and a desire for order in his life.

Heinrich Ludwig Wilhelm Adalbert Waldemar Alexander of Hess (b. 28th Nov 1838 – d. 16th Sept 1900) – Uncle of Alexandra. Heinrich was a brother of Grand Duke Ludwig of Hesse. Heinrich married twice. His first wife was Caroline Therese Mathilde von Pollnitz (b. 1848 – d. 1879) and his second wife was Emilie Mathilde Hedwig von Bassus (b. 1868 – d. unknown). Heinrich had a son by each of his wives; Karl, Count von Nidda (b. 1879 – d. 1920) and Elimar, Baron von Dornberg (b. 1893 – d. 1917).

Heiligenberg – The home of Prince Louis of Battenberg, husband of Alix's sister Victoria. He inherited the house after the death of his father Alexander in Dec 1888. It was the birthplace of their second daughter Louise in 1889. There was a serious fire at the house at the end of July 1892.

Helene, Grand Duchess of Russia (b. 1882 – d. 1938) – The only sister of the Grand Dukes Kyrill, Boris and Andrei. Helene married Prince Nicholas of Greece and Denmark. She was the mother of three daughters including Princess Marina, Duchess of Kent. She is also known as Elena.

Helen's Babies – A favourite children's book of fictional stories by John Habberton that was often read to Alexei by Gibbes and the Tsarina. It was a great favourite of the child. The books full title was the rather bizarre – Helen's babies with some account of their ways innocent, crafty, angelic, impish, witching, and repulsive' and had been originally published in about the 1870s.

Hendrikova, Anastasia Vasilyevna (b. circa 1887 – d. 1918, Perm) – She was the daughter of Count Vassilli Alexandrovich Hendrikov, who was the Grand Master of Ceremonies at the Imperial Court of Russia. She was a descendant of a sister of Peter the Great's wife Catherine I. She was a Personal Lady-in-waiting to the Tsarina and had been appointed to the position in 1910. She did not believe in Rasputin, although the Tsarina tried to convince her of his merits (she did not do this with Buxhoeveden) at first but later stopped talking about the subject, when she realised that Anastasia disliked him. She followed the family to exile in Tobolsk and was separated from the family before they went to Ekaterinburg. She was murdered in a forest near Perm, along with Catherine Schneider. She is sometimes called Gendrikova.

Hendrikov, Count Vassili Alexandrovich – He was Grand Master of Ceremonies under Nicholas II until 1911. He was replaced by Count Alexei Ignatiev.

Henry or Heinrich, Prince of Prussia (b. 1900 – d. 26th Feb 1904, Kiel) – He was the third and youngest son of the Tsarina Alexandra's sister Irene. He was, like his older brother Waldemar and cousin Alexei, a haemophiliac.

Hercules, Jim – He was one of the Tsar's servants and one of four bodyguards whose only duty was to quietly open and close doors. He took holidays in America and brought back the Imperial children jars of guava jelly.

Hermogen, Bishop b. Georgy Yefremovich Dolganov (b. 1858 – d. 1918) – The Bishop of Tobolsk and Siberia, who ministered to the Romanovs at Tobolsk. He was later murdered by being drowned in the Tura River.

Hesse, Maria – She was the widow of the Commandant of Tsarskoe Selo garrison and the mother of Darya, a friend of the Grand Duchess Olga, daughter of Tsar Nicholas II.

Hirsch, Dr – He was the Tsar's personal physician until his death in 1907. He was replaced in the Spring of 1908 with Dr Botkin. His niece was Catherine Schneider.

Horse Riding – The Tsar and his four daughters all often rode horses, the daughters *side-saddle*. They rode for enjoyment and appeared on horseback at ceremonial occasions. The Tsarina rarely rode but went for carriage rides. Alexei did not ride due to ill health but he had a donkey *Vanka* who pulled a sledge for him.

Icons – The Tsarina wore icons of St Feodor's mother of God and St. Serafim of Sarov. The Grand Duchesses wore icons of St. Nicholas from 1907 until they died. Alexei had the icon of *Faith, Hope and Love* in his bedroom. They were the daughters of Saint Sophia. All the girls were murdered like the Grand Duchesses by a remarkable coincidence.

Igor Konstantinovich, Prince of Russia (b. 1894 – d. 1918) – He was one of the sons of Grand Duke Konstantin who was murdered in 1918. He was unmarried. Nicholas once noted how fond he appeared to be of his daughters.

Ignatiev, Count Alexei – He was the Grand Master of Ceremonies from 1911 – 1917.

Ioann Konstantinovich, Prince of Russia (b. 1886 – d. 1918) – He the 1st son of Grand Duke Konstantin. He had married Princess Elena of Serbia in 1913 and was murdered in 1918. Ioann was a Staff Captain of Horse in the Russian Army and later became a sub-deacon in the Russian Orthodox Church. He left two small children; Vsevolode aged four and Nathalia aged three when he was murdered in 1918.

Ioann of Kronstadt or John – A Priest who was at one time a great influence on the Tsar and Tsarina. He died in 1909.

Ilin, Alexei – He was President of the Red Cross society.

Illinskoe – The estate, near Moscow owned by Grand Duke Serge and Grand Duchess Elisabeth of Russia. It was later gifted by Ella to her nephew Grand Duke Dmitri.

Irina Princess (b. 21st Dec 1903 – d. 15 Nov 1990) – A daughter of Grand Duke Paul and his second wife Princess Paley.

Irene Luise Marie Anna, Princess of Hesse and by the Rhine (b. 11th July 1866, Darmstadt – d. 11th Nov1953, Schloss Hemmelmark, near Eckernforde, Scheswig) – An elder sister of the Tsarina Alexandra and the 3rd daughter of the late Grand Duke Ludwig IV of Hesse and his wife the late Princess Alice. Her brother and sisters named her Aunt Fuss. She was always a busy child and tried to see the positive side. She was anxious that not only she but also her brother and sisters do the right thing. Princess Irene had married Prince Heinrich of Prussia on the 24th May 1888, the younger brother of the Kaiser Wilhelm II. They had three sons, Waldemar, Sigismund and Henry. She was one of the Godmothers of the Tsar's daughter, Grand Duchess Anastasia.

Ipatiev House – The last home of the former Tsar of Russia and his family. It was perched on a hill and overlooked a lake and the forest beyond. The house faced onto Voznessensky Square with the Cathedral of the Ascension and dusty unpaved streets. It had been the home of Nicholas Ipatiev until the Ural Regional Soviet ordered him to pack and move out as it was needed for *reason of state*. The ex-Tsar, Tsarina and their five children lived a few rooms. Nicholas, Alexandra and their son shared a bedroom, the four Grand Duchesses shared another and they had access to the Dining Room and a large double Drawing Room. The former Imperial family were all murdered here in July 1918. It was later demolished. It had been owned by Nicholas Nicolaevich Ipatiev, a local bureaucrat. The number was 49. Nicholas Ipatiev died in Prague in 1938 and the house was demolished in July 1977.

Ivanov, General II – He arrived at the Alexander Palace from General headquarters soon after the beginning of the 1917 Revolution and was sent in Command of troops who hoped would be able to put down the trouble in the capital. Ivanov left his men at Vyritza and asked Alexandra to give him authority to use the Palace guards to protect his rear. She refused and said that she could not give military orders. He returned to his troops, the St George's battalion at Vyritza and later returned to Mogilev on orders. There were false reports in 1918 that he had been murdered.

Izvolsky, Alexander P (b. 1865 – d. 1923) – He was Russian Ambassador to France at the outbreak of the Great War. He was Minister of Foreign Affairs 1906–1910 and Ambassador in Paris 1910–1917.

Jackson, Margaret Hardcastle (b. 1835, Burton Leonard, Yorkshire – d. 28 Jan 1918, London) – The former Governess of Princess Alix, she was known as *Madgie*. She was the daughter of William and Mary Jackson, but lived as a young girl on the farm belonging to her uncle Mr William Hardcastle. She lived at a retirement home for Governesses at Regents Park, London in her later years. The Tsarina had attempted to use her as a contact after the revolution with her British relatives but the lady was close to death at the time and no one ever realised. She left £3641 in her will to Emily Jackson.

Jemmy – The Grand Duchess Anastasia's Cavalier King Charles Spaniel who died at Ipatiev House along with the Imperial family in July 1918. It was said to be black and ginger in colouring and extremely small. The autopsy proved it was a female not a male as often believed. The name could have been a derivative of Jemima.

Jerusalem – The Tsarina's sister Grand Duchess Elisabeth was eventually buried in Jerusalem after her murder in Russia in 1918.

St Job – Nicholas II of Russia was born on the day set aside by the Russian Orthodox calendar for Saint Job the Martyr. It was known to be an unlucky date.

Joy – The Tsarevich's pet standard spaniel who survived the murder of the Imperial family and was rescued half-starved after their murder and eventually taken to England. He was buried in the grounds of Windsor Castle. He was described as being liver coloured and may have been a springer or cocker spaniel. He became blind after Alexei's murder.

Kalinin – A nickname for Protopopov used originally by Rasputin.

Kanin, Prince – The Japanese Prince who visited the Tsar in 1900 and again during the war, in Sept 1916.

Karangozov, Nicholas Konstantinovich – A wounded soldier of His Majesty's

Life-Guards Cuirassier regiment who became a friend of the Grand Duchess Olga Nicolaevna in 1915. He may have been an Armenian aristocrat. He appeared frequently in the photographs taken at Olga and Tatiana's infirmary and he was rather fond of Olga.

Kardovsky, Dmitry Nicolaevich (b. 1866 – d. 1943) – The Grand Duchesses art teacher. He was Professor of the Academy of Arts and a prolific artist who illustrated books.

Kasyanov – One of the wounded treated by Olga and Tatiana. He played the violin and by late 1916 Olga appeared to be increasingly fond of him.

Kerr, Mark (b. 1864 – d. 1944) – The brother of Nona Kerr. He eventually rose to the position of Rear Admiral in the British Army and was later a writer. He was also a friend of Princess Victoria and her family. He married Rose Margaret Gough on the 10th of July 1906. They had two children who were named Alix and Louise. The first daughter was almost certainly named after the Tsarina of Russia and the younger after Princess Louise of Battenberg.

Kerr, Nona – Close friend and lady-in-waiting of Princess Victoria of Battenberg. She married Colonel Richard Edward Crichton on the 24th of Jan 1915. She was the sister of Mark Kerr. Her father was Admiral Lord Frederick Kerr and her mother the former Emily Sophia Maitland.

Kharitonov, Ivan Mikhailovich (b. 1870 – d. 1918) – The cook to the Imperial family who went into exile with them in 1917 who was executed along with the Imperial family in July 1918.

Kerensky, Alexander Feodorovich (b. 1881 – d. 1970) – A former lawyer who became the leader of the worker's faction of the Fourth State Duma. He was the leader of Russia's first Provisional Government 1917–1918. He was Minister of Justice and later Army and Navy Minister. His government was overthrown by the Bolsheviks. Nicholas and Alexandra both came to like and trust him but he was prone to bad health.

Khitrovo, Lyubov (b. 1902 – d. unknown) – The sister of Rita and friend of the Grand Duchess Anastasia. She wrote to her during and after the revolution. She later married an officer in Anastasia's former regiment, Lev Alexander Grekov (b. 1902 – d. 1952).

Khitrovo, Alexander (b. 1894 – d. 1951) – The third brother of Rita who was a Colonel in an artillery regiment and married Lydia Nikolaevna Rozenbach, nee Viddinova.

Khitrovo, Konstantin (b. 1890 – d. 1919) – The eldest brother of Rita who was an Artillery officer.

Khitrovo, Margarita Sergeevna (b. 1895 – d. USA, 1952) – Known as *Rita*, the maid-of-honour to the Tsarina and the Grand Duchesses. *Rita* was the daughter of Serge Konstantinovich Khitrovo (b. 1865 – d. 1931) and his wife the former Lyubov Vladimirovna Molostovova (b. 1865 – d. 1923). Serge was at one time a gentleman-in-attendance. She was also a close friend of the Grand Duchess Olga and Countess Hendrikova. She arrived at Tobolsk to be with the exiled Imperial family but was accused of plotting a monarchist coup. She was later released due to lack of evidence. She and her family proved to be loyal friends of the Tsar's daughters during and after the revolution. She later married Vladimir Georgevich Erdeli (b. 1883 – d. 1959), his first wife had been Elisabeth Nikolaevna Stroganova. *Rita* had a step-son.

Khitrovo, Maria (b. 1899 – d. after 1921) – A sister of Rita. Married Konstantin Nikolaevich Bogdanovich and had four children including Nikolai (1914) and Vera (1916).

Khitrovo, Michael (b. 1898 – d. unknown) – The fifth brother of Rita.

Khitrovo, Sergei (b. 1896 – d. 1920) – The fourth brother of Rita Khitrovo, an officer in a grenadier regiment who married Alexandra Grigorevna Strizhevskaya.

Khitrovo, Vladimir (b. 1891 – d. 1968) – The second brother of Rita Khitrovo. He married Olga Alexandra Shepeleva-Voronovich.

Khitrovo, Xenia (b. 1907 – d. 1967) – Sister of Rita.

Khokhriakov, Paul Danilovich (b. 1893 – d. 1918) – Chairman of the Tobolsk Soviet who was responsible for transferring the Grand Duchesses Olga, Tatiana and Anastasia and the Tsarevich to Ekaterinburg in 1918.

Khlynov, Father Vladimir – Replaced Father Alexei Vasiliev at the end of 1917.

Khvostov Alexei, N. (b. 1872 – d. 1918) – The Minister of Internal Affairs 1915–16.

Kichkine – The Crimean home of the Grand Duke Dmitri Pavlovich.

Kiknadze, Vladimir Ivanovich – Handsome dark haired boyfriend (platonic) of the Grand Duchess Tatiana 1915 – 1916. He was known as *Volodia*. He was a soldier and later briefly an orderly at their infirmary. He was a Sub-Poruchik (lieutenant) in the 3rd HIM Guard's Rifles regiment of the Russian army and was awarded the St George sabre for an act of bravery. During the battle of Meyshagola, on 30th Aug 1915, whilst temporarily in charge of his company and being surrounded by superior enemy forces and suffering great losses from enemy fire, he fought his way with bayonets, threw back the enemy and took up a position at the rear, ensuring the with-drawl of Russian batteries. He was severely wounded. He was not given the award until 18th July 1916.

Kleikenburg – German teacher of the Imperial children. The Grand Duchesses had eighteen classes a month between them in 1910; at this time they had eleven Russian and eleven French.

Kleinmichel, Olga (b. 1893 – d. 1982) – A niece of the well-known Society hostess Countess Marie Kleinmichel who married Paul Voronov in 1914. Olga was the daughter of Catherine Nicolaevna Bogdanova and her first husband Konstantin Kleinmichel. She had older siblings named Cleopatra (*Clair*); Vladimir (*Dima*); Nathalie (*Tata*) and Helen (*Ella*). Olga was in a difficult situation as she was clearly a friend of the Grand Duchess Tatiana and at the time of her marriage the Grand Duchess Olga was obviously in love with Paul Voronov. The marriage appears to have been arranged to keep the young Grand Duchess away from Paul. Olga Kleinmichel and her sister Nathalie (*Tata*) first met the Grand Duchesses Olga and Tatiana in 1911 at Livadia.

Klemenz, Vera von – A piano teacher who sometimes played for the Tsarina and her daughters.

Kochubey, Prince Victor (Adjutant-General) – Head of the Imperial Appendages Department first under Tsar Nicholas II.

Kochubey, Prince Peter – Master of Ceremonies.

Kochubey, Countess Elena – Mistress of the Robes to the Dowager Empress Marie of Russia.

Kochubey, Princess Elisabeth – One of the Tsarina's ladies-in-waiting.

Koblinksy, Eugene Stepanovich (b. 1879 – d. 1927) – Commander of the special purpose detachment who guarded the former Imperial family from Aug 1917 until 2nd May 1918. He later joined the White Army and married Klaudia Bitner. They had a son Innokenty. Kobylinsky was formerly of the Life Guards Keksgolmsky Regiment and he had been treated at the hospital in the grounds of the Palace by the Tsarina and her daughters in Sept 1916. They had been photographed together.

Kokovtsov, Count Vladimir Nicolaevich (b. 1853 – d. 1943) – The Russian Prime Minister between 1911 and 1914. Also Minister of Finance and Chairman of the Council of Ministers.

Kokovstov, Vladimir N (b. 1853 – d. 1943) – The Minister of Finance 1904–1905 and 1906–1914 and Russian Prime Minister 1911–1914.

Kolia – The nickname of the Tsarevich Alexei's best friend Nicholas Vladimirovich Derevenko. His father was the court surgeon Vladimir Nicolaevich Derevenko.

Kondratiev, Vladimir Alexandrovich – Gentleman-in-waiting to the Imperial Court. He died in early 1918, Alexandra referred to him as *my old Kondratiev.*

Konstantin Konstantinovich, Grand Duke of Russia (b. 1858 – d. 1915) – The second son of Grand Duke Konstantin Nicolaevich and a Grandson of Tsar Nicholas I. Known as *Kostia* or K.R he was an uncle of Tsar Nicholas II. The Grand Duke was the Commander-in-Chief of the 15th Tiflis Grenadiers Regiment from birth and he later enlisted in the Life-Guard Izmailovsky Regiment with whom he saw active service. His funeral was attended by the Tsar's three eldest daughters the Grand Duchesses Olga, Tatiana and Marie. The Grand Duke had six sons – Ioann, Gavril, Konstantin, Oleg, Igor and George. One son died in the Great War and three died at the hands of the Bolsheviks.

Konstantin Konstantinovich, Prince of Russia (b. 1st Jan 1891 – d. 16th/17th July 1918) – One of the sons of the Grand Duke Konstantin who was murdered in 1918. He was unmarried and confusingly was also nicknamed Kostia.

Korf, Baron Paul Pavlovich – Master of Ceremonies at the Imperial Court.

Kornilov, General Lavr Georgevich – Infantry General and Supreme Commander-in-Chief July–Aug 1917. He had once been a prisoner of war in Austria. It fell to him to arrest the former Tsarina.

Korovichenko, Colonel – The Commandant of the Alexander Palace from early 1917. He was quickly replaced by Kobylinsky.

Kostritsky, Dr Serge S – He was a dentist who treated the Imperial family. He went all the way from the Crimea to treat the former Imperial family at Tobolsk.

Kozhevnikov, LM – He was amongst the close circle of male friends of the Grand Duchess Olga Nicolaevna and often attended parties when she was there.

Kozlianinova, Catherine Miss Kitty – Lady-in-waiting to the Grand Duchess Elisabeth of Russia.

Krasnoe Selo – Summer camp for all the regiments where the Tsar and his children often visited.

Kshessinskaya, Mathilde Felixovna (b. 1872 – d. 1971) – The famous Russian ballerina, the Prima ballerina of the Marinsky Theatre. She was the lover of Nicholas between 1891–1893. She later lived with Grand Duke Serge Mikhailovich and in 1921 married Grand Duke Andrei Vladimirovich.

Kulikovsky, Captain Nicholas Alexandrovich (b. 1858 – d. 1958) – The second husband of the Grand Duchess Olga, the Tsar's younger sister. He had been her first husband's aide-de-camp. He was a Captain of the Life Guards Cuirassier Regiment. They had two sons Tikhon and Guri.

Kulikovsky, Tikhon Nicolaevich (b. 1917 – d. 1993) – The eldest son of the Tsar's sister Grand Duchess Olga. He married three times. His first wife was Agnete Pederson, his second wife was Livia Sebesteyn and his third wife was Olga Pupinin.

Kuzmina – She was a former wet nurse to the Imperial children.

Kulomzin, Anatol. N (b. 1838 – d. 1921) – The Secretary to the Committee of Ministers 1883–1902 and President of the State Council 1915.

Kyrill Vladimirovich, Grand Duke of Russia (b. 1876 – d. 1938) – The brother of the Grand Dukes Boris and Andrei. He married Alexandra's former sister-in-law Victoria-Melita, known as *Ducky*.

Ladies-in-waiting – The Tsarina's ladies–in–waiting included – Princess Marie Bariatinsky; Olga Butzova: Princess Elisabeth Cantacuzene: Princess Elisabeth Kochubey; Princess Elisabeth Obolenskaya: Princess Olga Orlov; Princess Marie Vasilchikova; Countess Catherine Adlerberg; Countess Marie Lambsdorff and Countess DA Bobrinksaya.

Lamsdorff, Countess Marie – A lady-in-waiting to the Tsarina.

Languages – The Grand Duchesses were taught English, French and Russian. The daughters later learnt German from Mlle Schneider but the first three at least had lessons before 1917. The Tsar and Tsarina spoke English to each other and the children spoke Russian amongst themselves. The Tsar also spoke Danish.

Lavrova, Catherine – A music teacher from St Petersburg who often gave concerts for the Tsarina and her daughters at Tsarskoe Selo.

Lectrice – The Court Lectrice or reader to the Tsarina was Mlle Catherine Schneider.

Leikin, Nicholas Alexandrovich – The author of *Where the Oranges Ripen*. Alix read this story to her son Alexei in Siberia.

Lennart, Prince of Sweden (b. 1909 – d. Dec 2004) – The first son of Grand Duchess Marie Pavlovna by her first husband. He was brought up in Sweden after his parents divorced. He did, however, visit Russia on occasions and the Grand Duchesses found it quite adorable as they did all babies.

Leo – Servant of the Tsarina who died during the early days of the Russian Revolution.

Leskov, Nicholas – The Tsar enjoyed reading the works of Leskov and read *Cathedral Folk* aloud to his family at Tobolsk.

Letyomin – One of the guards at Ipatiev House. He *acquired* Alexei's spaniel Joy and the child's diary for Mar to Nov 1917. He also allegedly *acquired* holy relics from the boy's bed and an icon which he usually carried.

Leuchtenberg, Duchess Marie nee Countess Grabbe (b. 23rd Nov 1869 – d. 24th Oct 1948) – Chaperone for the four Grand Duchesses when they visited their aunt Grand Duchess Olga Alexandrovna at her home on Sunday afternoons. She also took her own daughters. She was the daughter of Count Nikolai Pavlovich Grabbe. Their daughters were friends of the Tsar's four daughters – Alexandra (b. 13th Mar 1895 – d. 1960); Nadejda (b. 2nd Aug 1898 – d. 1954) and Maria (b. 3rd June 1907– d. unknown). They had brothers Nikolai (b. 10th Aug 1896 – d. 5th May 1937); Maximilian (b. 8th Apr 1900 – d. 10th Jan 1906); Sergei (b. 7th July 1903 – d. 27th June 1966) and Mikhail (b. 2nd Mar 1905 – d. 9th Feb 1928)

Leuchtenberg, Duke George – He married Princess Anastasia of Montenegro but later left his wife and lived openly with his mistress in Biarritz, leaving Anastasia and his two children Serge and Elena. The Tsarina Alexandra felt sorry for Anastasia and with the help of Nicholas, obtained a divorce. She later married Grand Duke Nicholas Nicolaevich of Russia in 1907. Her sister Militiza was married to Grand Duke Peter, brother of Nicholas Nicolaevich.

Leuchtenberg, Duke of Prince Nicholas (b. 17th Oct 1868 – d. 2nd Mar 1928) – One of the Tsar's Aide-de-Camps and the son-in-law of Count Grabbe.

Leyden, Professor Ernest von (b. 1832 – d. 1910) – The surgeon to Emperor Alexander III of Russia.

Lift – Alexandra had a lift installed in 1899 to connect her rooms with the children's rooms on the floor above. The lift broke down in 1917 when the electricity was cut off.

Lili – Lili Dehn, a close friend of the Tsarina Alexandra, see Dehn.

Lili – Princess Elisabeth Nicolaevna Obolenskaia. She was a lady-in-waiting to the Tsarina and occasional chaperone of the Grand Duchesses.

Linevich, Colonel Alexander N – The Tsar's aide-de-camp. He returned to the Alexander Palace soon after the start of the Revolution to assist the Tsarina.

Livadia – The Imperial palace in the Crimea which was later used after World War II for a summit by Joseph Stalin. It was built on the site of an earlier Palace and had been designed by the architect Nicholas Krasnov. The Tsar and his family tried to visit Livadia in the Spring (Mar to May) and again in Sept until Nov. The Imperial family travelled to the Crimea in the Imperial train. The palace was made of white limestone and was built in the Italian style, with balconies and courtyards. It was perched on the edge of a cliff and had magnificent views of both the mountains and the sea. The rooms upstairs were furnished in pink chintz with mauve flowers. The new palace was generally known as the White Palace.

Liza – One of the Grand Duchesses nursemaids. Elizabeth (Liza) Ersberg outlived her charges by many years. See Ersberg.

Loman, Dmitri Nicolaevich – A Church Warden at the Feodorovsky Cathedral.

Lou – The nickname often used for second son of the Grand Duke of Hesse, Prince Louis. He was a nephew of the Tsarina Alexandra.

Louis, Prince later Earl Mountbatten (b. 1900 – d. 1979) – The youngest son of the Tsarina's eldest sister Princess Victoria and her husband Prince Louis of Battenberg. The family name was changed to the English sounding Mountbatten in 1917. The young Prince known as Dickie later admitted that as a child he fell madly in love with his young cousin Grand Duchess Marie Nicolaevna. (After Marie's death he married Edwina Ashley).

Louise, Queen of Denmark (b. 7 Sept 1817 – d. 17th/29th Sept 1898, Bernstorff) – The maternal Grandmother of Nicholas II.

Lower Dacha – The building used by the Tsar and his family for summer holidays at Peterhof between 1895 and 1914. The architect was Adjunct-Professor Anthony Tomishko (1851 – 1900). There was also a small New Palace of four storeys with a tower of six floors.

Ludwig Hermann Alexander Chlodwig, Prince of Hesse and by Rhine (b. 20 Nov 1908, Darmstadt – d. 30th May 1968, Frankfurt-am-Main) – Nephew of the Tsarina Alexandra and the second son of her older brother Grand Duke Ernst-Ludwig of Hesse, by his second wife Eleonore. Ludwig married the Hon. Margaret Geddes in London on the 17th Nov 1937.

Ludwig or Louis IV, Grand Duke of Hesse (b. 1837 – d. Mar 1892) – Husband of Princess Alice and the father of Victoria, Elisabeth, Irene, Ernst-Ludwig, Frederick-William, Alix and May. His mother-in-law Queen Victoria supervised the upbringing of his children after the death of her daughter Princess Alice in Dec 1878. He was briefly married to Alexandrine von Kolemine in 1884 but the marriage was annulled on the orders of Queen Victoria.

Lukoyanov, Feodor Nicolaevich (b. 1894 – d. 1947) – A guard at Ipatiev House.

Lvov, Prince George E (b. 1861 – d. 1925) – Prime Minister of the First Provisional Government of Russia and was a liberal. He was chairman of the Zemstvo Red Cross and was briefly in prison, sharing a cell with the Tsarevich's servant Nagorny, yet unlike Nagorny the Prince survived the Revolution.

Lyukhanov, Sergei – One of the guards at Ipatiev House. He was the driver of the house car and also the brother-in-law of Alexander Avdeev.

Maeterlinck, Maurice – The author of *La Sagesse et la Destinee* or Wisdom and Destiny. The book was one of those read by Nicholas in Siberia.

Madsen, Professor – The Professor from Copenhagen Serum Institute who was received by the Tsarina in Mar 1917 despite reports of street riots in Petrograd.

Maids – At the Alexander Palace, Tsarskoe Selo the main residence of Nicholas and Alexandra their maids had their own rooms. The maids included Madeleine Zanotti; Liza Ersberg; Anna Utkina; Alexandra Tegleva; Elizabeth Eltser and Marie Tutelberg. They had their own bathroom. Pierre Gilliard had his own suite of rooms including a bedroom, study, bathroom and his servants' room. They all had rooms on the second floor near to the children's rooms.

Maids-of-honour – The Tsarina's maids of honour included – Princess Olga Bariatinsky; Mlle A Olenina; Mlle Margarita Khitrovo; Countess Elisabeth Kelepovskaya and Madame Anya Vyrubova. The position is junior to lady-in-waiting.

Maklakov, Nicholas N (b. 1871 – d. 1918) – The Minister of Internal Affairs 1912 – 1915.

Maly Palace – One of three palaces at Livadia owned by the Tsar. It had been built in 1866 – 1868 for the then Tsarevich Alexander (later Alexander III) and his family.

Makarov, Zhenya – He was a cadet who became a friend of the Tsarevich Alexei in 1916.

Malama, Dimitri (b. 1891, Kuban – d. Aug 1919) – An Officer of the Life-Guards Uhlan (or Lancers) Regiment and a close friend of the Grand Duchess Tatiana. He was a wounded officer at their hospital at Tsarskoe Selo. It was Malama who gave Tatiana her pet dog Ortino. His sister Vera married Prince Eristov, another soldier. There is a photograph of Olga, Tatiana and Anya Vyrubova taken with Dimitri at the hospital along with other patients and members of staff. Although he may have been in love with Tatiana, she was not in love with him.

Maple Room – This was a sitting room in the Alexander Palace used by the Tsarina Alexandra. It was re-decorated in 1902. The walls were painted a warm dusty pink and all around the room was an overhanging curved cornice containing concealed electric lights. A great maple wood balcony was constructed across the length of the room and a staircase led from the right corner to the top of the balcony which led to a mezzanine level over a corridor connecting it to the Tsar's New Study. Beneath the balcony were two cosy sitting areas separated by a fireplace and bear-skin rugs were placed across the grey-green carpet. One wall contained Kaulbach paintings of the four young Grand Duchesses and an earlier painting of Nicholas. The room also contained many sculptures including ones of Alexei; the Grand Duke Ernst of Hesse and a life-sized marble sculpture of the Grand Duchess Tatiana. One door led to the Tsarina's outside balcony where meals were often served.

Maquay, George – A friend of Alix and her brother Ernie who they first met in Florence in Apr 1893.

Marie Alexandrovna, Grand Duchess of Russia and Duchess of Edinburgh and Saxe-Coburg and Gotha (b. 1853 – d. 1920) – Sister of the late Emperor Alexander III of Russia and the wife of Prince Alfred, the Tsarina's uncle. She was therefore the aunt of both the Tsar and the Tsarina.

Marie Feodorovna, The Dowager Empress of Russia, formerly Princess Marie Sophie Frederikke Dagmar of Denmark (b. 26th Nov 1847, Copenhagen – d. 13th Oct 1928, near Copenhagen) – Daughter of King Christian IX and Queen Louise of Denmark, sister of King Christian X of Denmark, Queen Alexandra of Great Britain etc. She married the future Emperor Alexander III of Russia on the 9th Nov 1866. She had six children; Nicholas II of Russia (b. 1868 – d. 1918); Alexander (b. 1869 – d. 1870); George (b. 1871 – d. 1899); Xenia (b. 1875 – d. 1960); Michael (b. 1878 – d. 1918) and Olga (b. 1882 – d. 1960). She was closest to her older children George, then Nicky and Xenia and distant to her two youngest Michael and Olga. She was extremely social and a popular Empress unlike her daughter-in-law. In 1918 she lost her two remaining sons Nicholas II and Michael; her daughter-in-law Alexandra and five Grandchildren; Olga, Tatiana, Marie, Anastasia and Alexei. In Apr 1919 the Dowager Empress left Yalta on-board HMS Marlborough and spent the rest of her life in Denmark.

Marie Nicolaevna, Grand Duchess of Russia (b. 26th June 1899, Peterhof, Russia – d. 16/17th July 1918, Ekaterinburg, Russia) – The third daughter and third child of His Imperial Majesty Tsar Nicholas II of Russia (b. 1868 – d. 1918) and his wife the former Princess Alix of Hesse and by the Rhine (b. 1872 – d. 1918)

Marie Pavlovna the younger, Grand Duchess (b. 18th Apr 1890, St Petersburg

– d. 13th Dec 1958) – The daughter of the Tsar's uncle Grand Duke Paul and elder sister of Grand Duke Dimitri. She and her brother were brought up after their mother's death in 1891 by the Tsarita's sister Grand Duchess Elisabeth until 1905. After Serge died Marie and Dmitri were brought up by the Tsar. Maria married Prince Vilhelm of Sweden on the 3rd May 1908 and after divorcing him in 1914, she married Prince Serge Mikailovich Poutiatine in 1917. She had one son Lennart in 1909 and another son after her second marriage named Roman but he died young.

Marie Pavlovna senior, Grand Duchess of Russia (b. 1854 – d. 1920) – Wife of the Tsar's uncle Vladimir of Russia. Marie had four children; Kyrill, Boris, Andrei and Helene. She was the Head of the Imperial Academy of Fine Arts.

Markov, Sergei Vladimirovich – A Cornet in Alexandra's Crimean Cavalry Regiment who had been decorated for bravery. He was sent to Tobolsk in the autumn of 1917 by the Petrograd monarchists and Anya Vyrubova to organize the escape of the Imperial family. He was arrested at one point but later sought aid from the Germans.

Marie, Princess of Greece (b. 3rd Mar 1876 – d. 14th Dec 1940) – A cousin of Nicholas and the second daughter of King Georg I and Queen Olga of Greece. She was known as *Minnie*. On the 12th May 1900 she married Grand Duke George of Russia. They had two daughters Nina (b. 20th June 1901 – d. unknown) and Xenia (b. 22nd Aug 1903 – d. unknown). The girls were somewhat reluctant playmates of the Tsar's youngest daughter, Grand Duchess Anastasia. They found her rather rough and bossy.

Mary – The name of a Governess to the Imperial children.

Massandra – An Imperial property in the Crimea. A military hospital was based here during the Great War. It had been bought by Emperor Alexander III and is now a museum.

Mather, Miss Annie D – Friend of the late mother of Sophie Buxhoeveden. This Scottish lady rented a house with Sophie at Tobolsk.

Mauve Boudoir – The Tsarina's favourite room was decorated in mauve and white, and was situated on the ground floor of the Alexander Palace. In the corner of the room was a basket of toys for her children.

Mavra – The nickname used by the Imperial family for Elisabeth Mavrikevna, the wife of Grand Duke Konstantin.

Maximimich, Konstantin – Assistant to the Commander of the Main Imperial Apartment.

Measles – All the Tsar's children were suffering from measles at the beginning of the Russian Revolution. The young Tsarevich Alexei caught it from one of his friends and passed it firstly to his older sisters Grand Duchesses Olga and Tatiana, then to the Grand Duchess Anastasia and finally to their sister the Grand Duchess Marie who also caught pneumonia and was very seriously ill. Another victim of the illness was the Tsarina's friend Anna Vyrubova.

Medicine Phials – Alexandra managed to take her medicine phials as far as Ipatiev House. They contained iodine, arsenic and morphine.

Medvedev, Paul S – The Commander of the Guard at Ipatiev House.

Mengden, Countess Zenaide (b. 1878 – d. unknown) – Maid of honour to the Dowager Empress. Her father was General-Major of the suite of Emperor Alexander

II. She grew up in the Tauride Palace in St Petersburg and in 1912 was engaged as lady-in-waiting to the Dowager Empress.

Mekk, Vladimir von – Head of the Russian Red Cross during the war. He claimed to have seen the Tsarina's beloved brother Grand Duke Ernst of Hesse in 1916 in Russia.

Metropolitan Vladimir – The Bishop of the Metropolitan of Kiev and Galicia. He was murdered in early 1918.

Michael Alexandrovich, Grand Duke of Russia (b. 4 Dec 1878, St Petersburg – Murdered July 1918, Perm) – The younger brother of Tsar Nicholas II of Russia and was heir to the throne from late Mar 1917 until his death. He married on the 15th Oct 1911 in Vienna, Austria Nathalie (Natasha) Mamontov-Wulfert, a divorcee. They had a son called George who had been born in 1910 and she also had a daughter from her first marriage named Tata, born 2 June 1903. He served in the Guards regiment from 1898 to 1911. During the Great War he led the Indigenous Cossack Mounted Division and later was in charge of the Second Cavalry Corps. He was especially close to his sister Olga. According to his father Alexander III, Michael believed without hesitancy anything and everything anyone told him. Colonel Boris Nikitine stated that Michael charmed all around him. He had at least one other vice according to his step-daughter Tatiana he tried every treatment going for baldness.

Michchenko, Adjutant General Paul Ivanovich – A Don Cossack army commander and was one of those who the former Tsarina wrote to from Tobolsk.

Militza Nicolaevna, Grand Duchess of Russia (b. 1866 – d. 1951) – She was the wife of Grand Duke Peter of Russia and the sister of Anastasia *Stana*.

Mochalov, Ippolit M – An Engine Lieutenant on the Imperial yacht *Standart* and one time close friend of the Grand Duchesses.

Mogilev – The General Headquarters where Nicholas went to during the war, between 1914 and 1917. It was situated on hills above the Dnieper River, and was some 500 miles from Petrograd. He was joined by Alexei from the autumn of 1915. The young Tsarevich was accompanied by his tutors Gilliard, Gibbes, Petrov and Voyeikov.

Moleben – This is a service of Thanksgiving and praise at a time of celebration or supplication in time of great need.

Moliere (b. 1622 – d. 1673) – The author (real name Jean-Baptiste Poquelin) who wrote *Bourgeois Gentilhomme* in 1660 in French. It was performed by Grand Duchess Marie and Grand Duchess Anastasia at Spala in 1912 while their brother Alexei was very seriously ill.

Mordvinov, Colonel Anatole (b. 1870 – d. unknown) – One of Nicholas's aides-de-camp.

Mossolov, Lieutenant-General Alexander A (b. 1854 – d. 1939) – Head of the Imperial Court Chancellery and Head of the Emperor's Secretariat for Petitions from 1900 to 1917. He was also the brother-in-law of Count Vladimir Fredericks. His assistant was Alexander Tanyeev, father of Anya Vyrubova.

Motor Cars – The Tsar owned many motor cars including a Delaunay-Belleville. He liked them driven – fast.

Murray, General Sir Archibald James – Chief of the Imperial General Staff.

Musina-Puskhkina, Countess Maria Illarionovna – A former nurse at the military hospital with whom Alix corresponded in Siberia.

Nagorny, Klementy Grigoroievich (b. 1889 – d. 1918) – The former sailor from the Tsar's yacht the, *Standart* known as *Klim* who became the personal servant of the Tsarevich Alexei in Tobolsk and Ekaterinburg. He was an assistant to Derevenko in 1910. He was taken away from Ipatiev House on the 27th May 1918 and shot the following month.

Namesdays – The names days of the Imperial children were Olga 11th July, Tatiana 12th Jan, Marie 22nd July, Anastasia 22nd Dec/4th Jan, and Alexei Oct 5th/18th, Nicholas 6th Dec, Alix 23rd Apr/6th May

Naryshkin, Kyrill – The Chief of the Tsar's private Mobile Secretariat. He was known as *Kira.*

Naryshkina, Elisabeth nee Princess Kurakin (b. 1840 – d. 1928) – The Tsarina's Grand Mistress of the Court and the highest ranked Lady-in-Waiting. She was nicknamed Zizi. She had married a gentleman-in-attendance, Anatoly Dmitrevich Naryshkin (b. 1829 – d. 1883). At the beginning of the Russian Revolution she was at Petrograd but arrived at Tsarskoe Selo soon after. She shared the Imperial families' imprisonment at the Alexander Palace, Tsarskoe Selo in 1917 and she continued to correspond with the Tsarina in Siberia. She had been appointed in 1913 and was also a close friend of the Dowager Empress. She had a son Kyril (b. 1868 – d. 1924) and daughter Vera (b. 1874 – d. 1951). Vera married Dmitri Nicolaevich Tatishchev, Governor of Yaroslav (b. 1867 – d. 1919).

Nastenka– The nickname of Anastasia Vasilevna Hendrikova Natalia, Princess of Russia (b. 23rd Mar 1905 – d. 23rd May 1905). The elder daughter of the Tsar's friend and cousin Grand Duke Konstantin.

Natalia, Princess of Russia (b. 5th Dec 1905 – d. 27 Dec 1981) – The youngest daughter of Grand Duke Paul and his second wife Princess Paley.

Nathalie –The wife of the Grand Duke Mikhail of Russia. She was never invited to meet Nicholas II or any of his family. Nathalie was known as Natasha and had two children, a daughter born in 1903 and a son in 1910. Tata was the daughter of Natasha first husband Sergei Mamontov whom she married in 1902, she had no children by her second husband Vladimir Wulfert and her son George was born two years before her marriage to his father, the Grand Duke Michael. She died on the 23rd Jan 1952. Her son George had died in an automobile accident some years earlier.

Naumov, Alexander N (b. 1868 – d. 1937) – A member of the State Council.

Needlework – The Tsarina, who was an excellent needlewoman, taught needlework to her four daughters. Her most able pupil by far was the Grand Duchess Tatiana. Tatiana made beautiful blouses, embroideries, crochets etc. The second most gifted was Marie.

Neidhard, Alexei Borrisovich – Director of Grand Duchess Tatiana's Refugee Committee.

Nephritis – Emperor Alexander III of Russia died of this kidney disease in late 1894.

Neverovsky, Captain – The captain of the Imperial yacht *Standart* until 1912 and was briefly succeeded by Captain Chaguin.

New Palace, Peterhof – There was a small new Palace with four floors, asymmetrical balconies, terraces and loggias and a six storied building standing next to it with a belvedere crowned with a spire. The tower could be seen from the seashore and the park. It was constructed of pink-red granite, the ground floor was faced with slabs of grey putilovo and the walls were yellow and terracotta decorative bricks which alternated as horizontal stripes of diverse width. It was the birthplace of Tsar Nicholas II's three youngest children Grand Duchess Marie, Grand Duchess Anastasia and the Tsarevich Alexei. It was badly damaged by the Germans in 1941 and was demolished in the 1960s.

New Study – The Tsar's *New Study* was created in 1902 in the Art Nouveau style and was connected to the Maple Room by a balcony. Nicholas rarely used this room as he didn't like its modern style. It was decorated with fabrics from Liberty in London, Tiffany wall fixtures and imported mahogany panelling on the walls and ceiling. The stencilled walls were light pine green. Roman Melzer, Alix and her brother Ernst designed the rooms but Nicholas insisted on a giant billiard table and old fashioned Chippendale furniture. He rarely used the room apart from when entertaining male guests such as Ernst and Dmitri.

Nicholas Mikhailovich, Grand Duke of Russia (b. 1856 – d. 1919) – Brother of *Sandro*.

Nicholas Nicolaevich, Grand Duke of Russia (b. 1856 – d. 1929) – Known as *Nikolasha* and married to *Stana*. Nicholas was Inspector-General of the Cavalry between 1895 and 1905. Between 1905 and 1908 he was Chairman of the Council for State Defence and Commanded the Guards and the St. Petersburg military district from 1905 to 1914. He was appointed as Commander-in-Chief of the Russian Army 1914–1915. He was the brother of Grand Duke Peter. In 1907 Nicholas married Princess Anastasia of Montenegro. They had no children.

Nicholas, Prince of Greece (b. 22nd Jan 1872 – d. 8th Feb 1938) – A cousin of Nicholas and the third son of King Georg I and Queen Olga of Greece. On the 29th Aug 1902 he married Grand Duchess Helene of Russia. They had three daughters Olga (b. 11th June 1903 – d. unknown); Elisabeth (b. 24th May 1904 – d. unknown) and Marina (b. 13th Dec 1906 – d. 1968) she married Prince George, Duke of Kent.

Nicholas II, The Tsar of Russia from 1894–1917 (b. 18th May 1868, St Petersburg, Russia – d. 16th/17th July 1918, Ekaterinburg, Russia) – The Emperor and Autocrat of all the Russia's. He was the first son of Emperor Alexander III of Russia (b. 1845 – d. 1894) and his wife the former Princess Dagmar (Marie) of Denmark (b. 1847 – d. 1928). Tsar Nicholas married Princess Alix of Hesse and by the Rhine on the 26th of Nov 1894 at St Petersburg. They had five children: Olga, Tatiana; Marie; Anastasia and Alexei. He could read equally well in Russian, English and French and could manage in German and Danish. He enjoyed the simple life much like his father and liked to go hunting, shooting and walking. He needed exercise and suffered greatly from being inside after the revolution.

Nikil – One of the French tutors to the Imperial children.

Nikolsky, Alexander V – Commissar who succeeded Kobylinsky in 1917. Nikolsky was the deputy to Vasily Pankratov. They were both Social Revolutionaries who had been exiled in Siberia. He was tall, had a broad face and thick untidy hair. Unlike Pankratov, he blamed Nicholas personally for his imprisonment in Siberia and was rude and surly towards the former Tsar and his son. He insisted that police photographs were taken of the Imperial captives. He refused to allow alcohol to be given to the Imperial family and even refused Dr Derevenko's idea of giving it to the city hospital. He had the un-opened bottles dropped into the river. He was dismissed along with Pankratov in Jan 1918 but later died fighting for the Monarch Whites against the Bolsheviks.

Nikulin, Grigory (Alias Akulov) – Alleged murderer of Prince Dolgoruky. It is also alleged that he killed Alexei.

Nilov, Admiral – The Commander of the Convoy Regiment.

Nilov, General – Ajutant Admiral Konstantin Dmitrievich (b. 1856 – d. 1919) – He was Adjutant-General and known by Nicholas as the *Little Admiral*. He was the Tsar's Flag Captain and one of the Tsar's few personal friends. He married Princess Marianna Mikhailovna Kochubey (1866–1954) in 1885 but they had no children.

Nilov, Marianne – The wife of Admiral Nilov.

Nina Georgievna, Princess of Russia (b. 1901 – d. 1974) – A childhood friend of the Grand Duchess Anastasia and the sister of Princess Xenia. She and her sister last saw the Tsar and his family in the Spring of 1914 in the Crimea. Nina married Prince Paul Chavchavadze.

Nini – The nickname of Eugenia Vladimirovna Voiekov, a lady-in-waiting to Alix and a daughter of Count Fredericks. Anna Anderson claimed that Nini was the nickname of her Aunt Irene.

Novgorod – The Tsarina visited Novgorod just before Christmas 1916 to visit wounded soldiers in hospital. She was accompanied by her children and Sophie Buxhoeveden.

Obednitsa – An abbreviated Russian Orthodox liturgy, which is usually served by a priest when the full liturgy cannot be celebrated.

Obolenskaya, Princess AA nee Countess Apraksine – A Lady-in-waiting to Empress Marie of Russia. She was known as Aprak.

Obolenskaya, Princess Elisabeth Nicolaevna formerly Princess Mengrelskaya – A lady-in-waiting to the Tsarina Alexandra who was a frequent correspondent after the revolution. She was known as Lili or Litty and was a close friend of Alix. She was the wife of Major-General AD Obolensky.

Oleg Konstantinovich, Prince of Russia (b. 27th Nov 1892 – d. 12th Oct 1914) – The fourth son of Grand Duke Konstantin of Russia and he died of wounds he received during battle in the Great War. He had been wounded in the First Army in East Prussia and died at a hospital in Vilna. His brothers Ioann, Konstantin and Igor were murdered by the Bolsheviks in 1918.

Olga Alexandrovna, Grand Duchess of Russia (b. 13th June 1882, Peterhof, Russia – d. 24th Nov 1960, Toronto, Canada) – The second daughter and youngest child of Tsar Alexander III of Russia (b. 1845 – d. 1894) and his wife the former Princess Dagmar of Denmark (b. 1847 – d. 1928). She was the younger sister of Tsar Nicholas II of Russia. The Grand Duchess married Firstly 9th Aug 1901, Gatchina, Russia, Grand Duke Peter of Oldenburg (b. 1868 – d. 1924) and Secondly 14th Nov

1916, Kiev, Russia. Captain Nicholas Alexandrovich Koulikovky (b. 1881– d. 1958). She had two sons by her second husband Yuri and Tikhon.

Olga Konstantinovna, Queen of Greece (b. 1851 – d. 1926) – Known as *Aunt Olga* to Nicholas. She was the widow of the King of Greece. The couple married in 1867 and had eight children; Constantine, George, Alexandra, Nicholas, Marie, Olga, Andrew and Christopher. Christopher had once asked Nicholas if could marry Olga. He was refused. He later married –twice. She was godmother of Nicholas II.

Olga Nicolaevna, Grand Duchess of Russia (b. 15th Nov 1895, St Petersburg, Russia – d. 16th/17th July 1918, Ekaterinburg, Russia) – The first child of His Imperial Majesty Tsar Nicholas II of Russia (b. 1868 – d. 1918) and his wife the former Princess Alix of Hesse and by the Rhine (b. 1872 – d. 1918)

Olga, Princess of Greece (b. 7th Apr 1880 – d. 2nd Nov 1880) – A cousin of Nicholas and the youngest daughter of King Georg I and Queen Olga of Greece.

Ollongren, Alexandra – The Governess of the future Tsar Nicholas II. She taught him from the age of seven until he was ten. Nicholas played with her son Vladimir.

Onegin – The Tsar's two eldest daughters were named Olga and Tatiana, after characters in Puskin's, *Onegin*.

Onor – A nickname for Eleanore, the second wife of the Tsarina's beloved brother Grand Duke Ernst of Hesse.

Orchard, Mary Ann (b. Mar 1830 – d. 8 Aug 1906) – Alix's former nursemaid. She came to Russia with the future Tsarina and was known as *Orchie*. She had her own room in the Alexander Palace. Her birthday was celebrated on the 7th/20th Mar. She was with Alix in 1900 nursing Nicholas through his grave illness but died back home in England aged 76. She was *not* nursed by Alexandra, as some assumed during her last years.

Orbeliani, Princess Sonia (b. 1875 – d. Dec 1915) – A personal lady-in-waiting to the Tsarina Alexandra. Sonia had arrived at the Imperial Court in 1898. She was from Georgia, part of the Russian Empire and was small and blonde haired. Sonia had high spirits and was both a fine musician and sportswoman. Unfortunately she became ill with a spinal condition in 1906 at Darmstadt and lingered for another nine years. The Tsarina helped her through the illness and tried to make her life easier. Sonia died in the hospital at Tsarskoe Selo where the Tsarina was treating wounded soldiers during the war. Her proper name was Princess Sophia Ivanovna Djambakourian-Orbeliani. Her brother Prince Dmitri married Vera Kleinmichel, cousin of Grand Duchess Tatiana's friend Olga Kleinmichel.

Orienda – One of the Tsar's Crimean properties. It had been built by Nicholas I as a gift for his wife Alexandra but was largely burnt down in 1881. A small wooden dacha was, however, used by the Konstantin family at the same sight.

Orlov, Prince Alexander A (b. unknown – d. 1908) – The best friend of the future Tsar Nicholas II. They had served in the Guards Hussars together. Nicholas and his wife both had great faith in Orlov and the Tsar was greatly upset at his death. Orlov had played an important role in the suppression of revolution in the Baltic provinces in 1905–1906. Anya Vyrubova was originally in love with him but Alexandra discouraged the match.

Orlov, Prince Vladimir (b. 1868 – d. unknown) – The Head of the Tsar's Mobile

Secretariat. He had a stroke at Yalta in early 1918. He was known affectionately as *Fat Orlov*. His wife was Olga. He later fell out of favour with the Tsar due to his opposition to Rasputin.

Orlov, Princess Olga – Lady-in-waiting to the Tsarina.

Ortipo – The name of Grand Duchess Tatiana's dog, French bulldog. She was a present from her friend Dmitri Malama in 1914 or 1915. She went with her to Siberia. The dog had ugly puppies, father unknown –suspect JOY. She was sometimes thought to be called Ortino. She did *not* die as often thought. Nicholas sent a message, saying that he was sorry to hear about Ortipo, why, she was pregnant. Tatiana was not impressed with the ugly puppies. The dog may have survived the murder of the family but was killed very shortly after.

Ostrogonsky, Dr Serge – Doctor who visited the Alexander Palace in order to look after the Imperial children.

Otsu – It was at Otsu in Japan that a local policeman attacked the then Tsarevich Nicholas of Russia on the head with a sabre. He suffered from headaches for the rest of his life as a result. The scar was later used after his death to identify his body.

Palaces – Tsar Nicholas owned several palaces including the Winter Palace; the Anichkov Palace at St Petersburg; the Alexander Palace, Tsarskoe Selo (his usual home); the Catherine Palace at Tsarskoe Selo; Gatchina Palace; apartments in the Kremlin in Moscow; Peterhof (on the Gulf of Finland) and Livadia in the Crimea (his favourite home).

Paleologue, Maurice (b. 1859 – d. 1944) – The French Ambassador to Russia.

Paley, Princess Olga V (b. 14th Dec 1866 – d. 2nd Nov 1929) – The second wife of Grand Duke Paul. She was the daughter of Valerian Valerianovich Karnovich and his wife Olga Meszaros. Princes Paley was previously married to Erich von Pistohlkors. She had three children by her first husband – Olga (b. circa 1880 – d. unknown), Alexander (b. 1885 – d. unknown) and Marianna (b. 1890 – d. 1976, New York).

Paley, Prince Vladimir Pavlovich (b. 9 Jan 1897 (n/s) – d. 1918) – The son of the Grand Duke Paul and Olga von Pistohlkors. He was murdered in July 1918 at Alapaievsk. He did know the Grand Duchesses but only slightly.

Paley, Princess Irina (b. 21 Dec 1903, Paris (n/s) – d. unknown) –The eldest daughter of Grand Duke Paul and his second wife Olga von Pistohlkors, later known as Princess Paley. Irina married 4 June 1923, Paris. Prince Feodor Alexandrovich of Russia. They divorced in 1936 and remarried 11th Apr 1950.

Paley, Princess Natalia (b. 5 Dec 1905, Paris – d. unknown) – The second daughter of Grand Duke Paul and his second wife. She married 10th Aug 1927. Paris. Lucien Lelong and they later divorced. She later married in 1937 to John Chapman Wilson, a theatrical producer.

Pallisander Room – This was one of the Tsarina's rooms at the Alexander Palace. It was created by Roman Meltzer between 1896–1897 and had highly polished Rosewood panelled walls and green-yellow silk wall coverings. The furniture was designed by Meltzer in the English style with inlayed Rosewood to match the panels and late Victorian style motifs. To the right corner by the doorway stood the Tsarina's personal treasure chest, containing her children's baby clothes as well as her own. She also kept her letters here. The walls contained many paintings including one of a Hessian castle Romrod, one of Alexei as an infant and an oval-framed portrait of the Tsarina's mother the late Princess Alice of Hesse. Tea was often taken in this room.

Pankratov, Vassili Semenovich (b. 1864 – d. 1925) – Appointed commissar in charge of the Imperial family in Aug 1917 but was dismissed in Jan 1918. He later served with the Red Army.

Paul Alexandrovich, Grand Duke of Russia (b. 3rd Oct 1860, Tsarskoe Selo – d. 30th Jan 1919, St Petersburg) – An uncle of the Tsar Nicholas II. He married Princess Alexandra of Greece and had two children. Alexandra died shortly after the birth of her second child. Grand Duke Paul's children Grand Duchess Maria and Grand Duke Dimitri were brought up firstly by Grand Duchess Elisabeth and secondly by Tsar Nicholas. The Grand Duke married Olga Pistohlkors at Leghorn on the 10th Oct 1902. He had three more children – Vladimir, Irina and Natalia. It was the Grand Duke who informed the Tsarina of the Tsar's abdication in 1917. He soon after offered her his home in Boulogne in case she should want it. Paul died of cancer and avoided being shot by the Bolsheviks.

Peter Alexandrovich, PRINCE of Oldenburg (b. 1868 – d. 1924) – The first husband of the Tsar's sister Grand Duchess Olga. They divorced. He was a childhood friend of Nicholas and was known to him as *Petia*.

Peterhof – The Tsar and his family spent two or three months in the summer here between 1895 and 1914, sometimes remaining until late autumn. The family lived at the Lower Dacha or Lower Palace on the seashore at Alexandria Park. The nearby Farm Palace was sometimes used by the Tsar's sister Xenia or the Tsarina's sister Elisabeth. The Tsar's mother, Dowager Empress Marie used the Cottage Palace when she stayed at Peterhof. The Lower Dacha had two floors and was built on the site of the dismantled signal telegraph. It had a small pavilion and a tall slender tower in the Italian style. It was built 1883–5 for Nicholas by his father Emperor Alexander III.

Petrov, Peter Vasilievich (b. 1858 – 1918, Peterhof) – Russian teacher to the Imperial children. He went with Alexei to Headquarters along with the other tutors Pierre Gilliard, Sydney Gibbes and Vladimir Voyeikov. He kept letters sent to him by his former pupils from Tobolsk and Ekaterinburg.

Philippe, Dr (b. unknown – d. 1905) – French friend of the Tsar and Tsarina, who claimed to be a healer of some sort but most thought a fake. He was a predecessor of Rasputin and nicknamed *Our friend* as Rasputin later was by Nicholas and Alexandra.

Photographs – All the Tsar's daughters enjoyed taking photographs and each had their own camera and albums. One of these cameras was taken to Ekaterinburg but it was confiscated. Marie was probably the most talented at taking and even developing pictures.

Piano – The Tsarina played the piano with great skill and liked to play Bach, Beethoven and Tchaikovsky. She did not like to play to an audience though. Grand Duchess Olga was also a brilliant pianist and was able to play by ear, in other words she could reproduce tunes she had just heard without needing to see the music score.

Pistohlkors von, Alexander (b. 1885 – d. unknown) – Son of Princess Paley by her first husband Major General Eric von Pistohlkors of the Chevalier Guards Regiment.

He married Alexandra (Alya) Vyruvova, the sister of the Tsarina's close friend Anya Vyrubova.

Pistohlkors von, Alexandra (b. 1914 – d. unknown) – The third daughter of Alexander and Alya von Pistohlkors and the niece of Anya Vyrubova.

Pistohlkors von, Alexandra (Alya) (b. 1888 – d. 1968) – Sister of Anya Vyrubova and wife of Alexander Erikovich von Pistohlkors. She had three daughters Tatiana, Olga and Alexandra. Her children were played with by the Tsar's daughters.

Pistohlkors von, Olga (b. 1912 – d. unknown) – The second daughter of Alexander and Alya von Pistohlkors and the niece of Anya Vyrubova. She was the godchild of Grand Duchess Olga Nicolaevna of Russia. She married Hans Ramel in 1959.

Pistohlkors von, Tatiana (b. 1910 – d. unknown) – The elder daughter of Alexander and Alya von Pistohlkors, the niece of Anya Vyrubova and the godchild of the Grand Duchess Tatiana Nicolaevna of Russia.

Pitkopas, near Biorke – This was a favourite place of anchorage for the Tsar and his family on the Imperial yacht *Standart*. It had the typical Finnish scenery; rocky islands and forests of tall pine trees.

Pobedonostsev, Konstantin P (b. 1827 – d. 1907) – Chief Procurator of the Holy Synod 1880–1905. He thought Alix believed that she was more intelligent than she actually was. He was formerly the tutor to the children of Emperor Alexander III. He was a nationalist and regarded the Constitution as a fundamental evil and the free press an instrument of mass corruption. He also believed that universal suffrage was a fatal error. He hated parliaments and proved to be a dangerous influence on the future Nicholas II, strongly influencing his future political acts. He was anti-Jewish and disliked both Catholics and Poles. The future Tsar was greatly influenced by these extreme views and yet the young Princess Alix had been taught politics by her tutor Miss Jackson and was greatly interested in the subject and held more liberal views.

Poincare, Raymond (b. 1860 – d. 1934) – The French Foreign Minister during Tsar Nicholas' reign. He visited St Petersburg in early July 1914.

Polar Star – The Imperial yacht which was used by the Tsar's mother the Dowager Empress Marie.

Polovanov, Alexei A (b. 1855 – d. 1922) – Minister of War 1915 – 1916.

Proskuryakov – One of the guards at Ipatiev House.

Prokudin Gorskii, Sergei – Nicholas II commissioned him to take early colour photographs of the Russian Empire. He travelled for six years across Russia, taking pictures of rivers, lakes, forests etc. He also took pictures of Ekaterinburg and allegedly of the Tsar's family which were owned by the Dowager Empress.

Protocols of the Freemasons – A book which was forged by the Tsarist Secret Police and claimed that these were the protocols of a Zionist organization bent on destroying civilization and creating a worldwide Jewish state. Nicholas read this in the Spring of 1918 and believed that it was genuine. The book was later found at Ipatiev House.

Protopopov, Alexei Dimtrievich (b. 1852 – d. 1918) – The Minister of Internal Affairs in the Russian government 1916 – 1917 and Vice-President of the Duma. He was sometimes known as *Kalinin*. Protopopov was a member of the moderately liberal

Octist party. He was the son of a nobleman and landowner who had gone to cadet cavalry school and had studied law. After the Russian Revolution he was shot by the Bolsheviks.

Purishkevich, Vladimir M (b. 1870 – d. 1920) – Alleged to be one of Rasputin's murderers.

Radishes – The former Tsarevich Alexei was said to have smuggled out a note from Siberia in a bunch of radishes to his friend via Nagorny.

Rasputin, Grigory Efimovich (b. 1869, Pokrovskoye, Tyumen district, Tobolsk province – d. 1916) – Rasputin was actually called Grigory Efimovich Novyhk and married Proskovia Feodorovna Dubrovina and they had three children; Dmitri (b. 1897 – d. 1937), Maria (Matriona) (b. 1898 – d. 1977) and Varvava (b. 1909 – d. unknown). He was the Russian peasant who had an influence over the Tsarina after it appeared to her that he helped to save the life of her sick son Alexei on many occasions. He may have used hypnotism but his soothing presence to the Tsarina, may have simply helped calm the sick child, while the doctors carried on treating him. Many in Russia believed that he was the lover of both Alexandra and her friend Anya Vyrubova but he was not. He influenced her choice of ministers after the Tsar left Alexandra in charge of the government during the Great War. He knew nothing of politics, often he merely opposed those who disliked him and encouraged those who appeared to like him. His influence was a disaster, as would be expected, and resulted in many comings and goings in the Russian government until his death in late 1916. He was allegedly murdered by members of the Tsar's family. Anya medically proved that she could never have been Rasputin's lover (or anyone else's) but many still believe that he was the lover of the Tsarina. Her maids and children, however, did not believe it. Nor do I.

Regiments – The Tsar's children were Colonel-in-Chief of the following regiments – Olga 3rd Yelisavetgrad Hussars, Tatiana 8th Uhlan Voznesensky, Marie 9th Kazan Dragoon and Anastasia 148th Caspian Infantry

Rehbinder, Count – The Commander of the Palace Guards in 1917.

Rehbinder, Countess, nee Moewesz – Friend of the Tsarina.

Rein, Professor George – One of the Imperial doctors.

Reports – The Tsar attended to his daily reports from 6pm to 8pm each day. They were the latest reports into various matters including politics.

Ressin, Major General Alexei A – Military Secretariat General of Constant Duty. He was at the Alexander Palace at the start of the Revolution. He had been in Command of the regiment who mounted guard inside the Alexander Palace. He reported to Sophie Buxhoeveden that morale was low in early 1917.

Richter, General Otto – Head of the Court Chancellery and Director of the Emperor's Secretariat for Petitions from 1894–1900. He was replaced by General Mossolov.

Ridiger, Marie Belaeva – Alexandra wrote to Marie from Siberia. She was the wife of Major-General A.A. Ridiger-Beliaev, formerly an officer in the Life Guards Dragoons.

Rimsky, Nicholas Korsakov (b. 1844 – d. 1908) – The composer of Tsar Sultan. It was during a performance of this piece that Peter Stolypin was shot in front of Tsar Nicholas and his daughters Grand Duchess Olga and Grand Duchess Tatiana in Kiev in 1911.

Rodionov (b. 1885 – d. 1976) – One of the Commissars in charge of the former Imperial family. He replaced Colonel Koblinsky in May 1918. He was a Latvian and was later known as Commissar Yan Svikke. He died in Riga.

Rodionov Nicholas N Lieutenant (b. 1886 – d. USA 1962) – A close friend of the Grand Duchesses, especially Tatiana. He was a senior Lieutenant of the Guards Equipage. He was Tatiana's frequent tennis partner and was one of those loyal to the Tsarina during the revolution. It was later alleged that he was in love with Tatiana. He is in no connected to the other man of the same surname.

Rodzianko, Michael Vladimirovich (b. 1859 – d. 1924) – The Chairman of the Duma 1911–1917. He left Russia after the Revolution through the Crimea and died in Belgrade. His son Georgy a Captain in the Preobrazhensky Regiment was shot on the 18th/26th Feb 1918.

Roller Skating – The Tsar's daughters enjoyed roller skating on-board the Imperial yacht on occasions and they are filmed doing so possibly in 1910.

Rosenhohe (Rosenau) – The park where the members of the Hesse family were buried. Nicholas and Alix visited this place several times soon after their engagement.

Rostovtzev, Count Ivan – The Head of the Tsarina's Chancellery. He was also her private secretary and Steward in the Affairs of the Imperial Children.

Rotherham – The Yorkshire town where the Tsarevich's English tutor, Charles Sydney Gibbes, was born. He lived with his parents at 3 High Street, Rotherham in 1881; his father John was a bank manager. His passport later mistakenly said Rotterdam.

Ropsha – One of the Imperial residences. It was rarely used by the family because of its connection with the murder of Emperor Peter III by the Orlov brothers in 1762. It was surrounded by a park with huge trees, lawns and lakes.

Rumania – The Tsar, his wife and five children visited Rumania shortly before the outbreak of the Great War. There was much talk at the time that Grand Duchess Olga would become engaged to Prince Carole of Rumania. The Imperial family travelled to Rumania on board the Imperial yacht, *Standart*.

Rus – The name of the steamboat on which the former Imperial family left for Tobolsk in 1917 and departed from Tobolsk in 1918 for Ekaterinburg.

Rusin, Admiral Alexander Ivanovich (b. 1861 – d. Morocco 1956) – The Head of Naval General Staff from 1914. In 1916 he was promoted to Head of Naval Staff.

Ruskin, John (b. 1809 – d. 1900) – A friend of the Tsarina's mother Princess Alice. He was the author of *Magazine of Natural History* and *The Poetry of Architecture*. He regularly contributed articles to *Friendship's Offering*. He spent part of his later life at Brantwood in the Lake District in England.

Ruzsky, General Nicholas Vladimirovich (b. 1854 – d. 1918) – Commander-in-Chief of the North Western and Northern Fronts 1916. He had previously been a Professor at the military academy.

S.S. Simeon and Anna – The Russian Orthodox Church commemorated Saint Simeon the God-Receiver and Anna the Prophetess on the same day.

Sablin, Admiral Nicholas Pavlovich (b. 1880 – d. 1937) – He was the Tsar's ADC in the Marine Guards and was a great favourite of the Tsar and Tsarina. He was one of the Tsar's occasional tennis partners. He was also the Commander of the Guards Equipage Naval Battalion and later Captain of the Imperial yacht *Standart*.

Samarin – The Procurator of the Holy Synod, Minister of Religion until early Oct 1915.

Samov – An officer in the Hussars who was a friend of Anya Vyrubova.

Sandro – The nickname of Grand Duke Alexander Mikhailovich (1866 – 1933). He was the son of Field Marshall Grand Duke Michael Nicolaevich and a Grandson of Nicholas I. The brother-in-law of Nicholas II yet also his uncle. He married the Tsar's oldest sister, Grand Duchess Xenia.

Saxony, King Friedrich August III (b. 25th May 1865 – d. 18th Feb 1932) – The King visited Tsar Nicholas in June 1914.

Sazonov, Madame – The sister of Senator Neidhardt. She was contacted on behalf of the Tsarina by Baroness Buxhoeveden at the beginning of the Revolution and it was her brother who informed the Baroness of the events in the capital.

Sazonov, Sergei D (b. 1860 – d. 1927) – Minister of Foreign Affairs 1910 – 1916.

Scavenius, Harold de – The Danish Minister to Russia in early 1917.

Schneider, Catherine Adolphovna Trina (b. 1856 – d. 1918, Perm) – Mlle Schneider was the Court Lectrice or reader to the Tsarina. She was a niece of the Court surgeon Dr Hirsch. She taught the future Tsarina Russian whilst she was still living in Germany before her marriage. She was of Baltic German ancestry and like the Tsarina changed her religion from Lutheran to Russian Orthodox. She was extremely devoted to the Imperial family and was like a mother to the Tsarina. She watched over the family without meddling and kept much to herself. She had her own apartment within the Alexander Palace. She did the shopping for the Tsarina and accompanied the Imperial children where-ever they went. She was said to be sweet tempered and good hearted but the children took advantage of her by not paying the slightest attention to anything she said. Like Hendrikova she remained with the Imperial family at Tobolsk but was separated from them before they went to Ekaterinburg. She was murdered along with Hendrikova in a forest outside Perm in 1918. She had a young maid called Katya who the Grand Duchesses Olga and Anastasia bullied and teased.

Sednyov, Ivan Dmitrievich (b. 1886 – d. 1918) – The former crew member of the Imperial yacht the, *Standart* and was a footman to the Tsar's four daughters. He volunteered to remain with the Imperial family in Tobolsk and Ekaterinburg. Sednyov was arrested on the 27th of May 1918 and executed with Nagorny in June 1918. He was the uncle of Leonid.

Sednyov, Leonid Ivanovich (b. 1904 – d. 1927) – The nephew of Ivan Sednyov and an apprentice cook who worked for the former Imperial family at Tobolsk and Ekaterinburg. He was sent out of the house not long before the execution of the Tsar. He may have been sent to relatives in Kuluga Province. He was a friend of Alexei Nicolaevich in later years and was described later as being tall for his age and thin with a pale face and jet black hair. He was mature for his age.

Seraphim of Sarov Saint (b. 1759 – d. 1833) formerly PS Moshnin – The former monk of Sarov monastery who was canonised by order of Nicholas II. Seraphim was a hermit and kept a vow of silence for many years.

Serge Alexandrovich, Grand Duke of Russia (b. 11th May 1857 – Murdered 17th Feb 1905, Moscow) – An uncle of Tsar Nicholas II, who married the future Tsarina's sister Princess Elisabeth on the 15th June 1884 in St Petersburg. It was the day the future Tsar and Tsarina met. The Grand Duke was Governor of Moscow and was murdered outside his home there. Two years earlier an aged nun had predicted that he would have his head blown off and he did. He and Elisabeth had no children but brought up his niece and nephew, Marie and Dimitri the children of Serge's brother Paul.

Sergei Alexandrovich, Grand Duke of Russia (b. 1869 – d. 1918) – Brother of Grand Duke Alexander *Sandro*.

Shakh-Bagov, Dmitri Artemievich (b. 9 Feb 1893 – d. after 1917) – A platonic *boyfriend* of the young Grand Duchess Olga. He was a wounded soldier at the hospital where she worked and known as *Mitya*. He was a Caucasian probably from Georgia and was a warrant officer of the Erivan's Regiment. He arrived at the Grand Duchesses hospital in the spring of 1915. He was wounded in the battle of Zagrody in May 1915 and again in July or Aug. He took part in a battle close to the village of Ghenrikuvka-Berestie in July 1915 as head of the scouts' detachment. He left the regiment in 1917 but had been one of those who attempted to put down the revolt in the capital in Feb 1917. Two companies had been sent by train to suppress the disorders but Nicholas ordered them back.

Shalferov – A valet to Tsar Nicholas II and his father before him.

Shavelsy, George I (b. 1871 – d. 1951) – Archpriest of the Russian Army and Fleet.

Shcherbatov, Prince Nicholas B (b. 1868 – d. 1943) – The Minister of Internal Affairs during 1915.

Shilka – Female dog who belonged to Tsar Nicholas II. In 1897 she had two puppies by the Tsar's favourite dog Iman.

Shot – The name of the Tsar or Tsarevich's dog. It may have been a poodle.

Shulgin, Vasily Vitalyevich (b. 1878 – d. 1976) – Member of the Interim Committee of the State Duma. It was Shulgin who along with Alexander Guchkov went to the Tsar's train in 1917 in order to ask him to abdicate.

Shura – The Imperial children's favourite nursemaid. Alexandra Shura Tegleva later married Pierre Gilliard.

Shvybz – A nickname of the young Grand Duchess Anastasia.

Shvybzik – Grand Duchess Anastasia's small dog, who died in 1915.

Sigismund, Prince of Prussia (b. 27th Nov 1896 – 14th Nov 1978, Costa Rica) – Nephew of both the Tsarina and the Kaiser. His mother was the Tsarina's sister Princess Irene. Sigismund was a haemophiliac and died in Costa Rica, after failing to receive the blood transfusion he needed to save his life.

Silaiev, Colonel IZ – Colonel in the 13th Grenadier Regiment and was attached to the Imperial Suite during the war. He was a friend of the Tsar's children. His wife's son was Boris Ravtopolo a close friend of the Grand Duchesses and Silaiev was the superior officer to Olga's friend Mitya.

Skernevitsi – One of the Tsar's Polish hunting lodges. It was normally only visited for a day or two each year.

Slower-you-ride-the-farther-you-go – The name of the card game played by

Alexei. He kept the cards in a sweet box when the family were exiled in Siberia.

Solbolev M – Arithmetic teacher to the Imperial children.

Soloviev, Boris (b. unknown – d. 1926) – He married Rasputin's daughter Maria in Sept 1917. He later visited Siberia and claimed that he was trying to arrange the rescue of the former Imperial family. The former Tsarina believed his claims and smuggled some of her jewels out of Tobolsk with the help of a maid, in order to raise funds for the rescue.

Solovyov, Vsevolod – His books were read by Nicholas in Siberia.

Sonia – The name generally used by the Tsarina's friend Princess Sophia Ivanovna Djambakourian-Orbeliani.

Spala – A Polish hunting lodge, near to Warsaw. It was at one time owned by the Tsar. Spala was usually only visited for a week or two each year. It was at Spala in 1912 where the Tsarevich became very seriously and almost died. Nicholas also had hunting lodges at Bielovezh and Skernevitsi.

Spiridovich, Major-General Alexander Ivanovich (b. 1873 – d. unknown) – Spirodovich was Chief of the Personal Secret Guard of the Emperor from 1906 to 1917. He was responsible for the safety of the Tsar and the Imperial family. He was liked by Nicholas but greatly disliked by Alexandra who felt that he gave her no privacy. In Aug 1916 he was named as the new prefect and Commandant of the Yalta garrison and became in personal charge of the Imperial properties in the area including Livadia.

Spiritual Readings – This was the complete yearly cycle of Brief Homilies for each day of the year by Grigory Diachenko. It was read aloud daily in Siberia usually by one of the Grand Duchesses.

Standart – The Tsar's yacht, built in Denmark and launched in 1895. It was 420 feet long and its engines could turn out 11,5000 horsepower – almost 22 knots. She had staterooms decorated in flowered chintz. There were rooms for the Imperial family, suite, servants, crew and a chapel. A platoon of the Guarde Equipage were also housed on-board and even a brass band and balalaika orchestra. The Tsar's study was furnished in dark leather and simple wood furniture with an electric fan placed on a dresser. He also had his own bedroom and bathroom. The Tsarina's boudoir included chintz covered desk and chairs and family photographs on the walls. There was a large Imperial dining room to seat up to 80 people and a large reception room. It had 8 main lifeboats and 3 principal decks plus 2 lower decks for service. It almost sank in 1907 off Finland.

Starkenburg, Baroness – The alias used by Alix when she stayed in Harrogate, North Yorkshire in 1894. Alix was staying there with Catherine Schneider. They left during June 1894 after the press had discovered her real identity. The interest in the future bride of the heir to the Russian throne was great. Starkenburg was one of the three provinces in the Grand Duchy of Hesse, the others were Upper Hesse and Rhine Hesse.

Stolypin, Peter Arkadevich (b. 1862 – d. 1911) – The Russian Prime Minister 1906 – 1911. Stolypin was from an old noble family and his ancestors included the poet Lermontov and his parents' friends included NV Gogol and IN Tolstoy. He was assassinated in front of the Tsar and his two eldest daughters, Grand Duchess Olga and Grand Duchess Tatiana at a performance of the opera, *Tsar Sultan* at the Kiev Opera House. Stolypin did not die immediately he survived for a few days. The assassin was

Mordka Borgrov who was both a revolutionary and a police informer. Stolypin had been the target of a bomb attack soon after he had taken office. Thirty-two people were killed and his two children had been injured.

Storozhev, Father Ioann Vladimirovich – The Protopriest of St Catherine's Cathedral at Ekaterinburg who twice served and *Obednitsa* for the Romanovs at Ipatiev House in 1918.

Strauss, David (b. 1808 – d. 1874) – A friend of the Tsarina's mother Princess Alice. He was a German biblical critic and the author of *The Life of Jesus*. He had studied theology at Tubingen.

Struskov, General – One of the Tsar's aide-de-camps. It was he who once slid down a sandy slope beside the Imperial train as the Imperial children slid past him on silver trays, after he had challenged them to a race.

Sturmer, Boris (b. unknown – d. 1918) – The Russian Prime Minister briefly between Feb and Nov 1916. He was shot by the Bolsheviks.

Sukholmlinov, General VA – A Minister of Court. Minister of War from 1909. The previous year he ran off with married Catherine Boutovich and then married her in 1909. He had an ability of telling stories in an amusing way and knowing how interested Nicholas was in the military he always praised the army and declared it as *ready to fight*.

Swastika – Alix drew this symbol of faith in the houses where the family were imprisoned in Siberia. It means *well-being* in Sanskrit and was only later adopted by the Nazi's in Germany and given a quite different meaning.

Syroboirskaia, Maria Martianovna – A friend of the former Tsarina Alexandra, with whom she continued to correspond after the Revolution. Maria was the wife of Artillery Colonel Vladimir Syroioarsky and the mother of Colonel Alexander Syroboiarsky (1888– 1946).

Taneev, Alexander S (b. 1850 – d. 1919) – The father of Anya Vyrubova. He was said to be a Master of the Court and Chief Steward to His Majesty's Chancellery. His Grandfather and Great Grandfather had held the same position under previous Emperor of Russia. Another Great Great Grandfather was the Conqueror of Napoleon-Bonaparte Field Marshall Kutuzov. He was probably also descended from Emperor Paul of Russia.

Taneev, Serge (b. 1886 – d. 1975) – The brother of Anya Vyrubova. After the Revolution he lived in New York. He married in 1915. He married Princess Tina Dzhordzhadze.

Taneeva, Madame Nadezhda (b. 1860 – d. 1937) – The mother of Anya Vyrubova. Alix kept in touch with her by letter from Tobolsk. She was a member of the Tolstoy family, but not of the writer. She had four children, Anna, Sergei, Alexandra and Eugene who died as a baby.

Tarabar – The secret language invented by the Tsarevich and his sister Anastasia.

Tatiana Konstantinovna, Grand Duchess of Russia (b. 23rd Jan 1890 – d. 1970) – The eldest daughter of Grand Duke Konstantin. She married Prince Konstantin Alexandrovich Bagration-Mukhransky on the 6th Sept 1911. They had two children Teymuraz (b. 21st Aug 1912 – d. unknown) and Natalia (b. 19th Apr 1914 – d. 1984). Konstantin died in June 1915 and Tatiana later remarried. She was a friend of the Grand Duchesses Olga and Tatiana.

Tatiana Nicolaevna, Grand Duchess of Russia (b. 10th June 1897, Peterhof – d. 16th/17th July 1918, Ekaterinburg, Russia) – The second daughter and second child of His Imperial Majesty Tsar Nicholas II of Russia (b. 1868 – d. 1918) and his wife the former Princess Alix of Hess and by the Rhine (b. 1872 – d. 1918).

Tatischev, General Count Ilya Leonidovich (b. 1859 – d. 1918) – The Tsar's Aide-de-Camp who was sent to prison along with Countess Hendrikova and Mlle Schneider in 1918. All three were executed. He had previously been attached to the Russian Embassy in Berlin 1905 – 1914.

Tattoo – Nicholas II had a large tattoo on one of his inner arms, which he had done in Japan. It was usually hidden by his shirt sleeves. It was probably a dragon.

Taube, Baron – A Lieutenant on the Imperial Yacht Standart. He was later treated at Olga and Tatiana's infirmary and later married one of the nurses.

Telephones – Telephones had been installed in the Alexander Palace but they were cut off during 1917. There had been a line installed from the Pallisander Room in 1914 direct to the Winter Palace.

Tennis – The Tsar and his four daughters enjoyed playing tennis but neither Alix nor Alexei played. Alix had, however, in her younger days.

Tennyson, Alfred Lord (b. 1809 – d. 1892) – The world famous poet. He was one of the friends of the Tsarina's later mother Princess Alice. He also visited Osborne House when summoned by Queen Victoria. His works included *The Princess, The Holy Grail and other poems, Idylls of the King and Morte d'Arthur.*

Titi – The nickname used by Alexandra for her Godson, Alexander Dehn. He was the son of her close friend Lili Dehn.

Tiutcheva, Sophie Ivanovna – Governess and lady-in-waiting to the Imperial children from about 1905 until 1910. Tiutcheva was removed from Court in 1912. She was the niece of the Great Russian poet, Fiodor Tiutchev and came from Moscow. The girls called her *Sovanna* and the four sisters sometimes visited her when they went to Moscow.

Tobolsk – This was the town in Siberia where the Tsar and his family were taken in 1917 and they lived in the Governor's House until the following year. Afterwards the former Imperial family were taken to Ekaterinburg. Nicholas had visited the town once before on the 10th July 1891.

Toddie – The nickname given to Alexandra's nephew Prince Waldemar of Prussia (1889–1945). The son of Princess Irene and Prince Heinrich of Prussia.

Tolstoy, Count Leo – The former Imperial family read Tolstoy's most famous novels *War and Peace and Anna Karenina* after the revolution.

Tolstoy, Zinaide Sergeievna nee Bekhteff – Lady-in-waiting and a close friend of the Tsarina. Alexandra continued to correspond with Zinaide after the Revolution. She was the wife of Colonel Peter Sergeevich Tolstoy, of the Guards Cavalry. Her daughters may have been Irina and Nathalie (*Daly*). She was known as *Zina* or *Zinochka*.

Train – The Tsar of Russia had his own personal train. It had one car dedicated to dining with a kitchen, dining room and anteroom. It also had a lounge car, generally used as a meeting place for members of the suite. Each member of the suite had their own compartment. The children had their own car and Nicholas and Alexandra had a car of their own, containing a bedroom (the size of 3 normal-sized compartments); a mauve and grey sitting room for Alexandra, a study with green leather chairs for Nicholas and a white tiled bathroom.

Trepov, Alexander F (b. 1862 – d. 1926) – The Russian Prime Minister from Nov 1916 to Jan 1917. He was also Minister of Communications 1915 – 1917. He was the brother of Vladimir and Dmitri Trepov.

Trepov, Vladimir F (b. 1860 – d. 1918) – A member of the State Council.

Trubetskoi, Prince VS – An officer in His Majesty's Life-Guard Cuirassier Regiment.

Trupp, Alexei –The footman to the Imperial family who was executed with them in July 1918. He replaced Chemodurov at Ipatiev House.

Turgenev – One of the favourite authors of Tsar Nicholas. He read *Spring Torrents* to his family when they were in Siberia.

Tutelberg, Marie Gustavovna (b. 1863 – d. unknown) – Known as *Toodles*, she was the second maid to the Tsarina. She was slow and quiet. She came from the Baltic region and was the mortal enemy of Zanotti and like her refused to wear a uniform. They wore simple black gowns and had ribbon bows in their hair. There were three under maids all Russian girls who wore the usual uniform of caps and white aprons.

Ulyanov, Vladimir (b. 1870 – d. 1924) – Known as Lenin. The younger son of Ilya Ulyanov (died 1886) and his wife Maria Blank. Ilya was Director of Schools for the Province of Simbirsk. In the spring of 1887 Vladimir's older brother Alexander was arrested in St. Petersburg along with four other university students and charged with attempting to assassinate Emperor Alexander III of Russia with a bomb. Alexander was hanged for the crime in May 1887. Vladimir was later arrested and exiled to Siberia for three years, after his arrest and a year in a St. Petersburg jail. He married Nadezhda Krupskaya in 1898 and they moved to London in 1902. The two resided at 30 Holford Square where Vladimir lived under the alias of Jacob Richter. In 1917 Vladimir was sent to Russia by the German Emperor in a so-called *sealed train* to cause chaos in Russia!

Utkina, Anna – Maid to the Imperial children.

Vanka – A former circus donkey owned by Alexis. He had gone to the palace stables straight from Cinizelli's circus when he became too old for regular work. The donkey, however, was capable of many tricks and charmed both children and adults alike.

Vashka– This was the name of a cat which belonged to the young Grand Duchess Olga. She was presented with it by her brother.

Vasilchikova, Princess Marie – Lady-in-waiting to the Tsarina.

Vasiliev, Archpriest Alexander – Teacher of religion to the Imperial children and the Tsar's confessor. He was senior Priest at Feodorvsky Russian orthodox Cathedral until he was succeeded by Archpriest Beliaev in Mar 1917 due to ill health. He was murdered by the Bolsheviks in 1918.

Vera, Princess of Russia (b. 24th Apr 1906 – d. unknown) – The youngest daughter of Grand Duke Konstantin of Russia (1858 – 1915) and his wife the former Elizabeth of Os-Altenburg who was a childhood friend of Alexei. Her Godmother was the Tsarina Alexandra. She never married. One of her brothers died in the Great War and another three were murdered in 1918.

Veronal – The Tsarina used this drug a great deal during the early part of the Great War. It was to assist with her heart palpitations.

Versts – A unit of measurment. One verst was equal to 500 sazhen and 3500 feet.

Vicky of Sweden – A nickname used by Nicholas and Alexandra for the Queen of Sweden. Alix sent letters to her German relatives via the Queen of Sweden. She was the daughter of one of the late Princess Alice's closest friends and known to the future Tsarina since childhood.

Victoria Alberta Elisabeth Mathilde Marie, Princess of Hesse and by Rhine (b. 5 Apr 1863, Windsor Castle – d. 24 Sept 1950, Kensington Palace, London) – The eldest sister of the Tsarina Alexandra and the first daughter of Grand Duke Ludwig IV of Hesse and his wife the former Princess Alice of Great Britain. She married Prince Louis of Battenberg on the 30th Apr 1884. She had four children including Lord Mountbatten and her Grandson was Prince Philip, who married Queen Elizabeth II of Great Britain.

Victoria-Melita, Grand Duchess of Russia (b. 1876 – d. 1936) – She had a very complicated personal relationship with the future Tsarina Alexandra. Victoria-Melita was a younger cousin of Alix, later sister-in-law when she married the Grand Duke Ernst in 1894 but she later divorced 'Ernie' and remarried to a Grand Duke Kyrill of Russia, a cousin of Alix's husband Nicholas II of Russia. She had a daughter Elisabeth (1895–1903) who was a very close friend of the Tsarina's daughters Olga and Tatiana. She later had three other children but they were not close to the Tsarina's family due to estrangement after she remarried. She was also the sister of Queen Marie of Rumania. She was known as *Ducky*.

Victoria, Queen of Great Britain and Ireland (b. 24th May 1819 – d. 22nd Jan 1901) – The mother of nine children including the future King Edward VII and Princess Alice, the mother of Alix. The young Princess Alix lost her mother when she was 6 years old and was very close to her Grandmother.

Villikins and his Dinah by John Parry – An old English song that Margaretta Eagar had sung to young Tatiana as a child when she was ill. The story of a young 14 girl who poisoned herself rather than marry a rich suitor seemed to have a great effect on Tatiana. She was very against marriage for a long time.

Vinaza, Second Count of: Cipriano Munoz y Manzano (b. 1862 – d. 1933) –The Spanish Ambassador to Russia in 1916.

Vishniakova, Maria Ivanovna – Entered the Royal household just before the birth of Grand Duchess Tatiana and in turn nursed all of the Imperial children. All the Imperial children loved her. She fell out of favour with the Empress in 1910 when she claimed that Rasputin had assaulted her. Her duties continued until 1912 or 1913 but she still remained afterwards living in the palace.

Vladimir Alexandrovich, Grand Duke of Russia (b. 1847 – d. 1909) – Tsar's uncle.

Voeikov, Vladimir Major General of the Suite, the Palace Superintendent (b. 1868 – d. unknown) – The son-in-law of Count Fredericks who was Palace Commandant. He was the Tsarevich's history tutor. He was at General headquarters at the outbreak of the Revolution. After the Russian Revolution he was held in prison for some time but eventually escaped to Finland where he went into the lumber business.

Voikov – A member of the Ural Soviet who was alleged to be one of those responsible for the murder of the Tsar.

Volkov, Alexei Alexandrovich (b. 1859 – d. unknown) – Tsarina's valet who was exiled with the Imperial family in Siberia but later escaped murder. He had been originally from the Pavlovsky Life Guards Regiment then batsman to the Grand Duke Paul, until his re-marriage.

Voronzov, Countess Elizabeth – A lady-in-waiting to the Dowager Empress Marie. She had eight children but she still had plenty of time to attend Marie. She was disliked by Marie's daughter Olga but Elizabeth's daughter Sandra became as close friend of Olga Alexandovna despite this.

Vorontzov-Dashkov, Count Alexander – *Sasha* – Favourite tennis partner of the Grand Duchess Tatiana. He is photographed with Tatiana and Sablin in *Nicholas II, the Last Tsar* by Marvin Lyons.

Vorontsov-Dashkov, Count Hiliarian (b. 1837 – d. 1916) – A former Commander of the Hussar Life Guards and Imperial Cavalry who was a Minister of the Imperial Court under Nicholas II. He resigned in 1896 after he opposed Grand Duke Serge's handing of the coronation disaster. He was replaced by Baron Vladimir Fredericks.

Voronov, Paul Alexeievich (b. 1888, Kostroma – d. 1964, Jordanville, USA) – The young Grand Duchess Olga Nicolaevna fell in love with Paul in the autumn of 1913 but the following spring he married Olga Konstantinova Kleinmichel. He was one of the six main deck officers on the Imperial yacht *Standart* in 1913. Paul's wife would remain a close friend of the Grand Duchess Tatiana. They later had a daughter named Tatiana. The family later lived in the United States of America.

Vladimir, Prince of Russia (b. 9th Jan 1897 – d. 1918) – Son of Grand Duke Paul and his second wife Princess Paley. He was a talented poet and despite assertions otherwise was known to the Tsar's daughters.

Vyrubova, Anna or Anya (b. 16th July 1884, Moscow – d. 20th July 1964 Helsinki, Finland) – The closest friend (and a maid-of-honour) of the Tsarina Alexandra who was her almost constant companion for many years. They met when the Tsarina visited her in hospital in 1901. She lived at No 2 Church Street, Tsarskoe Selo, half a mile from the Alexander Palace. The Imperial family met Rasputin at Anya's small stone house. She had been born Anna Taneeva, the daughter of the Director of the Court Chancellery, Alexander Taneev and his wife Nadezhda Tolstoy. Anya was briefly married to Lieutenant Boris Vyrubov, a naval officer and a shell – shocked survivor of the Battle of Tsushima. The Tsarina had encouraged the ill – fated marriage and felt guilty afterwards. She and the Tsar had been witnesses at the ceremony. Even Rasputin had stated that the marriage was a bad choice. She spent a great deal of time with the Tsarina and her children. She was seriously injured on the 15th Jan 1915, when a heavy iron girder fell on her on her head, in a railway accident. Anna was separated from the Imperial family before they went to Tobolsk and spent five months imprisoned in the Fortress of Peter and Paul. She was later imprisoned and released several times. Anna had been accused of being the lover of both Rasputin and the Tsar but she later proved her innocence. The Tsarina continued to write to Anna from Siberia. In 1920 she went to live in Finland. Anya had a sister Alya and a brother Serge. Alya had three daughters Tatiana, Olga and Alexandra). Anna was seen by most as being a fairly simple soul, who saw people as either good or bad, friends or enemies. Her former husband remarried and had two children.

Vyrubov, Lieutenant Boris – The former husband of the Tsarina's close friend Anna Vyrubova. Her former husband remarried and had two children it is believed.

Wagner, Richard (b. 1813 – d. 1883) – Nicholas and more especially Alexandra were both very fond of Wagner's epic *Ring Cycle* especially *Gotterdammerung* and *Siegfried*. They also loved *Tristan and Isolde*.

Week of Cheesefare – A week of pre-Lent celebration where meat is forbidden but dairy products such as eggs are still permitted.

Week of Meatfare – The last week before the Great Fast in which meat could be eaten.

Wheelchair – The Tsarina often used a wheelchair, especially after the revolution. Alexei also often used one and on occasions Marie and Tatiana also used one.

Wilhelm Ludwig Friedrich Georg Emil Philipp Gustav Ferdinand of Hesse (b. 16th Nov 1845 – d. 24th May 1900) – He was an uncle of Alexandra. Wilhelm was a younger brother of Alix's father Grand Duke Ludwig of Hesse. Wilhelm married Josephine Bender (1857 – 1942). They had a son Gottfried von Lichtenberg (1877 – 1914).

Williams, Major General Sir John Hanbury (b. 1859 – d. 1946) – Chief of the British Mission in Russia 1914 – 1917. He had two sons in the First World War. His son John Coldbrook Hanbury-Williams was born at Henley on Thames in 1892 and died in 1965.

Winterhalter, Franz Xavier (b. 1805 – d. 1873) – The German born painter who did several portraits of the British and German royal families.

Witte, Count Sergius (b. 1849 – d. 1915) – The Russian Prime Minister 1905 – 1906.

Wolfsgarten – A large country house close to Frankfurt. It was a red low storeyed building flanked by a wide courtyard –situated in the middle of beautiful wooded area. It was the home of Alix's brother Grand Duke Ernst of Hesse and had been one of the childhood homes of Alix. Ernst filled the house with objects d'art as well as paintings by the Masters and family portraits. In the summer of 1901 Ernst had it decorated with leather wallpaper. Alix, along with her father and her siblings had visited the house each summer after the death of her mother Alice. During these summer holidays the family were generally visited by Alice's sister Helena and her family. Helena's daughter Helena-Victoria (Thora) and Marie-Louise were particularly close to Alix.

Xenia Alexandrovna, Grand Duchess of Russia (b. 1875 – d. 1960) – A sister of Tsar Nicholas II of Russia. She married Grand Duke Alexander Mikhailovich of Russia in 1894 and they had seven children– Princess Irina (1895 – 1970), Prince Andrei (1897 – 1981), Prince Feodor (1898 – 1968), Prince Nikita (1900 – 1974), Prince Dimitri (1901 – 1980), Prince Rostislav (1902 – 1978) and Prince Vassily (1907 – 1989). The children occasionally played with the Tsar's children.

Xenia Georgievna, Princess of Russia (b. 1903 – d. 1965) – A distant relative and childhood friend of the Grand Duchess Anastasia and sister of Princess Nina. She was a Godchild of the Tsarina Alexandra. Xenia married William B. Leeds and had a daughter Nancy in 1925. Xenia last saw the Tsar and his family in the spring of 1914 in the Crimea.

Yakimov, Anatoly – He was one of the guards at Ipatiev House.

Yakovlev, Vasili Vasilevich – A Soviet Commissar. His real name was Konstantin Alexeyvich Myachin.

Yanushkevich, Genereal Nicholas (b. 1868 – d. 1919) – He was Chief of the General Staff 1914 and Chief of Staff to Grand Duke Nikolai 1914–15.

Yanyshev, Father Ioann – Archpriest of the Court Cathedrals and confessor to Nicholas II. He died in 1910.

Yermakov – One of the alleged murderers of the Tsar's family.

Yorkshire – England's largest county. It was to Harrogate in North Yorkshire where the future Tsarina stayed in the early summer of 1894 and Rotherham in Yorkshire where her son's English tutor, Charles Sydney Gibbes was brought up. It is known as *God's own county* or in the south in some cases *The People's Republic of South Yorkshire*. It was also the birthplace of Miss Margaret Jackson, the Tsarina's former governess.

Yurovsky, Jacob Mikhailovich (b. 1878 – 1938) – He was one of ten children born to a poor Jewish family at Klinsk, in Tomsk province. His father was a glazier and his mother a seamstress. In 1912 he opened a photographic studio. After the Revolution of he became a member of Ekaterinburg Regional Executive Committee. He was the final Commandant of Ipatiev House and was responsible for the fate of the Imperial family in July 1918. He died in a Kremlin hospital in 1938 apparently as a result of an ulcer.

Yussopov, Felix Felixovich Prince (b. 1887 – d. 1967) **and Count Sumarokov-Elston** – Younger son of Princess Zenaide Yussopov and her husband Count Felix Sumarakov-Elston, an officer in the Chevalier Guards. His elder brother Prince Nicholas had died as a result of a duel in 1908. He married Princess Irina of Russia and one of the alleged murderers of Grigory Rasputin. He was sent abroad after the murder. They had one daughter Irina born in 1915.

Zakouski – The Russian form of the French Hors d'oeuvre. It was a small meal served before the main courses at dinner and could include caviar, smoked salmon, smoked ham, pickled herring, cheeses, vodka, wines etc on a sideboard.

Zamoyski, Count Adam – One of the Tsar's aide-de-camps. When he heard that the Tsarina and her children were in danger he went to Alexander Palace, despite great personal danger. He had previously worked for the Grand Duke Nicholas at headquarters.

Zanotti, Madeleine (b. 14 Oct 1869, Darmstadt – d. 16 Feb 1941) – Chief maid to the Tsarina Alexandra. She was, according to Anya Vyrubova, very clever and inclined to be tyrannical. The second maid was Tutelberg who was her mortal enemy yet both refused to wear uniforms. She went voluntarily into exile with the Imperial family at Tobolsk. After the deaths of her employers Madeleine worked for the late Tsarina's brother Ernie, the Grand Duke of Hesse. She was the daughter of Francesco Zanotti, a former servant of Prince Alexander of Hesse and the English lady Emma Piper. Miss Zanotti was briefly married to Henry Delacroix in 1920 but quickly divorced him. She was buried at Waldfriedhof, Darmstadt.

Zborovsky, Victor Erastovich Lieutenant (b. 1889 – d. 1944) – He was a close friend of the Grand Duchesses Olga and Tatiana and one of those who remained loyal to the Tsarina after the revolution. He was a Cossack Sotnik of Her Majesty's Escort and had a sister named Catherine. Anastasia appeared to be very fond of him later. He died in Austria.

Zeime – Lady-of-the Bedchamber to the Imperial children.

Zeime, Major-General Edvard – He was an Assistant at the St. Petersburg Palace Department.

Zelentsky, Captain Rostislav (b. 1865 – d. unknown) – Captain of the Imperial yacht *Standart*. He had succeeded after the suicide of the previous captain in 1912. He was assisted by Nicholas Sablin, a close friend of the Tsar.

Zhilik – The nickname used by the Imperial family for Pierre Gilliard.

Zhuk – The medical orderly at Tsarskoe Selo infirmary during the war.

Zhuzhgov – Alleged to be one of the murderers of the Tsar's family.

Zina – Zinaide Sergievna Tolstoy, a close friend of the Tsarina and lived at Tsarskoe Selo.

Zlebov, Serge V – One of a number of male friends of the Grand Duchess Olga Nicolaevna and often attended parties with other young men when she was there.

Zoubrouka – This was a kitten belonging to Tsarevich Alexei. It was found at Mogilev.

Zwilling – He was Mr Hugo Erskine-Wemyss (b. 1861 – d. 1933), a close friend of the Grand Duke Ernst of Hesse.

Sources

A Lifelong Passion. Nicholas and Alexandra. Their Own Story by Andrei Mayuunas and Sergei Mironenko

A Romanov Diary by Grand Duchess George of Russia

An Ambassador's memoirs by Maurice Paleologue

At the Court of the last Tsar by Alexander Mossolov

Before the storm by Baroness Sophie Buxhoeveden

Empress Alexandra by Greg King

Last days at Tsarskoe Selo by Count Paul von Benckendorf

Memories of the Russian court by Anya Vyrubova

Memories of Russia 1916–1919 by Princess Olga Paley

Nicholas II by Marvin Lyons

Nicholas and Alexandra by Robert. K. Massie 1967

Nicholas and Alexandra. The Family Albums

Sisters of Mercy Valentina Chebotorieva

Six years at the Russian Court by Margaretta Eager

The Emperor Nicholas II as I knew him by Major-General Sir John Hanbury-Williams

The Fall of the Romanovs by Mark D Steinberg and Vladimir M Khrustalev

The Last Diary of Tsarita Alexandra

The last Grand Duchess by Ian Vorres

The Last Tsar. The Life and Death of Nicholas II by Edward Radzinsky

The Last Tsar and Tsarita by Virginia Cowles

The Life and Tragedy of Alexandra Feodorovna, Empress of Russia by Baroness

The letters of Tsar Nicholas II and Empress Marie edited by Edward J Bing

The letters of the Tsarina to the Tsar published 1914–17

The letters of the Tsar to the Tsarina published 1914–17

The Private world of the last Tsar by Paul and Beatrice Grabbe

The Real Romanovs *by Gleb Botkin 1931*

The Real Tsarita by Lili Dehn 1922

The Romanovs. Love Power and Tragedy Leppi Publications. By Alexander Bokhanov, Dr Manfred Knodt, Vladimir Oustimenko, Zinaida Peregudova, Lyubov Tyutyunnik and Lyudmila Xenofontova.

Thirteen Years at the Russian Court by Pierre Gilliard 1921

Tutor to the Tsarevich by J.C Trewin

Upheaval by Olga Voronov

As well as various contemporary newspapers

FAMILY TREES

Queen Victoria of Great Britain and Ireland (1819–1901) married 1840 Prince Albert of Saxe-Coburg and Gotha (1819–1861)

1) Victoria, Princess Royal (1840–1901) married Emperor Frederick III of Prussia (1831–1888)

2) Edward VII (1841–1910) married Princess Alexandra of Denmark (1844–1925)

3) ALICE (1843–78) married Grand Duke Louis IV of Hesse (1837–1892)

4) Alfred, Duke of Edinburgh and later Duke of Saxe-Coburg-Gotha (1844–1900) married Grand Duchess Marie of Russia

5) Helena (1846–1923) married Prince Christian of Schleswig-Holstein

6) Louise (1848–1939) married John Campbell, ninth Duke of Argyll

7) Arthur, Duke of Connaught (1850–1942) married Princess Louise–Margaret of Prussia

8) Leopold, Duke of Albany (1853–1884)★ married Princess Helen of Waldeck–Pyrmont

9) Beatrice (1857–1944) married Prince Henry of Battenberg

Son of Victoria and Frederick of Prussia, son of Edward VII and Alexandra

Emperor William II of Prussia (1858–1941), the Kaiser, King George V of Great Britain

Children of Alice and Louis IV of Hesse

1) Victoria (1863–1950) married Prince Louis of Battenberg

2) Elisabeth (1864–1918) married Grand Duke Serge of Russia

3) Irene (1866–1953) married Prince Henry of Prussia (brother of the Kaiser)

4) Ernst–Ludwig, Grand Duke of Hesse (1868–1937) married a) Princess Victoria–Melita of Edinburgh and Saxe-Coburg-Gotha b) Princess Eleanore of Lich

Frederick-William (1870–1873) ★

5) ALIX (Tsarina Alexandra of Russia) (1872–1918) married Tsar Nicholas II of Russia

6) Marie (1874–1878)

Children of Victoria and Louis of Battenberg

1) Alice (1885–1969) married Prince Andrea of Greece (parents of Prince Philip of Greece who married Queen Elizabeth II of Great Britain and Northern Ireland)

2) Louise (1889–1965)

3) George (1892–1938)

4) Louis, Lord Mountbatten (1900–1979)

Children of Irene and Henry of Prussia

1) Waldemar (1889–1845)★

2) Sigismund (1896–1978)

3) Henry (1900–1904)★

Children of Ernst–Ludwig by his two wives

1) Elisabeth (1895–1903)

2) George Donatus (1906–1937)

3) Louis (1906–1968)

Emperor Nicholas I of Russia (1796–1855) married Princess Charlotte of Prussia, known later as Empress Alexandra Feodorovna

Children of Nicholas I of Russia and Empress Alexandra Feodorovna
1) Emperor Alexander II of Russia (1818–1881) married Princess Marie of Hesse and by the Rhine
2) Maria (1819–1876) married King Ludwig I of Bavaria
3) Olga (1822–1892) married King Charles I of Wurttemberg
4) Alexandra (1825–1844) married Prince Frederick-William of Hesse-Cassel
5) Elisabeth (1826–1829)
6) Konstantin (1827–1892) married Princess Alexandra of Saxe-Altenburg
7) Nicholas (1831–1891) married Princess Alexandra of Oldenburg
8) Michael (1832–1909) married Princess Cecilie of Baden

Children of Konstantin and Alexandra of Russia
1) Nicholas (1850–1918)
2) Olga (1851–1926) married King George I of Greece
3) Vera (1854–1912) married Duke Eugen of Wurttemberg
4) Konstantin (1858–1915) married Princess Elisabeth of Saxe-Altenburg
5) Dmitri (1860–1919)
6) Vyacheslav (1862–79)

Children of Nicholas (1831–1891) and Alexandra of Russia
1) Nicholas (1856–1929) married Princess Anastasia (Stana) of Montenegro
2) Peter (1864–1931) married Princess Militza of Montenegro

Children of Michael and Cecilie of Russia
1) Nicholas (1859–1919)
2) Anastasia (1860–1922)
3) Michael (1861–1929)
4) George (1863–1919) married Princess Marie of Greece
5) Alexander (1866–1933) married Grand Duchess Xenia of Russia (sister of Nicholas II)
6) Serge (1869–1918)
7) Alexei (1875–1895)

Children of Emperor Alexander II and Marie of Russia
1) Alexandra (1842–1849)
2) Nicholas (1843–1865) engaged to Princess Dagmar of Denmark
3) ALEXANDER III of Russia (1845–1894) married Princess Dagmar of Denmark, later known as the Empress Marie Feodorovna
4) Vladimir (1847–1909) married Princess Marie of Mecklenburg-Schwerin
5) Alexei (1850–1908)
6) Maria (1853–1920) married Prince Alfred, Duke of Edinburg, Saxe-Coburg and Gotha
7) Serge (1857–1905) married Princess Elisabeth of Hesse by the Rhine (1864–1918)
8) Paul (1860–1919) married a) Princess Alexandra of Greece and Denmark b) Olga Karnovich

Children of Vladimir and Marie of Russia
1) Kyrill (1876–1938) married Princess Victoria-Melita, Grand Duchess of Hesse and by the Rhine
2) Boris (1877–1943) proposed to Grand Duchess Olga Nicolaevna
3) Andrei (1879–1956)
4) Helene (1882–1957) married Prince Nicholas of Greece

Children of Paul and his first wife Alexandra
1) Marie (1890–1958) married Prince Wilhelm of Sweden
2) Dmitri (1891–1942)

Children of George and Marie of Russia
4) Nina (1901–1974)
5) Xenia (1903–1975)

Children of Emperor Alexander III and Marie of Russia
1) Tsar NICHOLAS II of Russia (1868–1918) married Princess Alix of Hesse and by the Rhine (1872–1918), later known as the Tsarina Alexandra Feodorovna
2) Alexander (1869–1870)
3) George (1871–1899)
4) Xenia (1875–1960) married Grand Duke Alexander of Russia (*Sandro*)
5) Michael (1878–1918) married Natalia Mamantov-Wulffert
6) Olga (1882–1960) married a) Duke Peter of Oldenburg b) Captain Nicholas Koulikovsky

Children of the Tsar Nicholas II and the Tsarina Alexandra of Russia
1) Grand Duchess OLGA NICOLAEVNA (1895–1918)
2) Grand Duchess TATIANA NICOLAEVNA (1897–1918)
3) Grand Duchess MARIE NICOLAEVNA (1899–1918)
4) Grand Duchess ANASTASIA NICOLAEVNA (1901–1918)
5) Tsarevich ALEXEI NICOLAEVICH (1904–1918)★

Children of Xenia and Alexander of Russia
1) Irina (1895–1970)
2) Andrei (1897–1903)
3) Feodor (1898–1968)
4) Nikita (1900–1974)
5) Dmitri (1901–1980)
6) Rostislav (1902–1978)
7) Vassili (1907–1989)

★ haemophiliac

A special thanks goes to *The Doctor* for time travelling back to September 1942 in order to obtain the photographs of Livadia.